Linux for Windows Administrators

Linux for Windows®
Administrators

Mark Minasi
Dan York

San Francisco   London

SYBEX

Associate Publisher: Neil Edde

Acquisitions and Developmental Editor: Chris Denny

Editor: Anamary Ehlen

Production Editor: Liz Burke

Technical Editor: Paul Stauffer

Graphic Illustrator: Tony Jonick

Electronic Publishing Specialist: Maureen Forys, Happenstance Type-O-Rama

Proofreaders: Nancy Riddiough, Emily Hsuan, Yariv Rabinovitch, Amey Garber

Indexer: Ted Laux

Book Designer: Bill Gibson

Cover Designer: Ingalls & Associates

Cover Illustrator: Ingalls & Asscociates

Library of Congress Card Number: 2002113840

ISBN: 0-7821-4119-6

To my wife Darcee, for the last seven years' good luck

Acknowledgments

There is so much to know about Linux that I suspect that any one person trying to enter the world of Linux and to understand it in a short time, as I did, would be doomed to failure without a lot of help. I want here to thank as many of the guides that I had on my journey that I can remember.

My coauthors of the previous edition, first Craig Hunt and then Dan York, are the people who took what could have been a five-year process of digging and collapsed it into just nine months. Craig sat down with me for three straight days and filled my head with basic Linux argot and, more importantly, point of view. There are philosophies that run deeply through Linux, a blend of older tool-making, reusability, and quality paradigms inherited from its Unix roots, plus newer, near-religious fervor from the sizable number of Linux developers who are motivated *both* by the desire to create great programs *and* by the possibility that they are building a revolution that could, in their eyes, topple the existing order of Microsoft, Novell, Unix, and mainframe software. Unless you understand those philosophies, much of Linux is incomprehensible, but Craig helped me "get it."

When other commitments called Craig away partway through the book, Dan York kindly agreed to join the book and save my bacon. Dan took the process of understanding how to do the tougher things in Linux—such as, for instance, to set up web, DNS, mail, DHCP, and other kinds of servers; to recompile the kernel; or to create the Linux version of a domain—and collapsed what would have been a multimonth learning curve into just a few days. Dan wrote several parts of Chapter 5 (printing, tape backups, kernel, and application recompiles), the last third of Chapter 6 (the section on NIS and NFS), and the entirety of Chapter 8. I took his text and added a few newbie notes, recast the examples to flow together a bit better, and reworked the voice to make the whole book sound consistent, but that was the extent of my work on those sections. What's more, Dan turned all of that out in almost no time at all; it was probably the easiest job of coauthoring that I've ever done.

But Dan's contributions didn't stop there. He also went through Chapters 5 to 9—the ones that involved the most nuts and bolts—with a fine-tooth comb and both pointed out my factual errors and made helpful suggestions about commands or approaches that I hadn't figured out. Could I have gotten the book done without Dan? Oh, yeah, sure, so long as you wouldn't have minded waiting until 2004 to read the previous edition… I can't thank Dan enough.

Dan also returned for this edition, and as before his contributions have been invaluable.

Several others kindly read early drafts of this book and greatly assisted both in proofreading and, more importantly, in pointing out where I was either wrong or unclear.

Many thanks to Christa Anderson, Dub Dublin, Tim Warner, Robert Eggleston, Wayne Adams, and John McGlinchey. I must also thank the legion of volunteers who worked so hard on all of the online documentation for Linux: the man pages, the FAQs, the HOWTO and mini-HOWTO files. And of course, I wouldn't have anything to write about if that *other* legion of volunteers, the Linux programming crowd, hadn't created such a strong product; many thanks to them!

Despite the legendary helpfulness of Linux newsgroup denizens, I must regretfully say that I didn't experience any of that helpfulness, save for a fellow named Heiko Teichmann. Heiko helped me figure out how to make a Linux-based DNS server serve a Windows 2000 Active Directory domain. Many thanks for the kind assist, Heiko; I wish other Linuxers would have been as forthcoming with hints and tips.

Once the book gets written, then much of the author's work is done, but there's plenty of work left to do, as editors and production people take the author's rough-hewn manuscript and convert it into the book that you hold in your hands today. I never know how long a book's going to take me to write, which makes life hard for editing and production people who need to make and keep schedules in order to accomplish the not-inconsiderable project of getting a book to market. Despite my being the bane of many an editor's existence, however, they've all maintained a sunny disposition throughout the book's development, and I thank them (and thank them and thank them…) for that. Ellen Dendy saw to it that all of the book's pieces fit together properly, and she took the cattle prod to me when we needed a schedule. Pete Gaughan did the manuscript editing on the first edition and did a great job—either he's the manuscript editor with whom I have most completely seen eye-to-eye, or he's just an extremely easy guy to get along with. Liz Burke served as production editor and shepherded the book through the process of moving from pixels to pulp; again, many thanks.

Finally, I want to thank the people whose encouragement and patience are responsible for this book: Gary Masters and Roger Stewart were the pair of people who thought this book was a good idea from the beginning. Jordan Gold, Chris Denny, and Neil Edde believed in it enough to give the go-ahead for a second edition.

I'm sure there are many others who I've forgotten and I apologize to them—remind me and I'll get you into the third edition!

Contents at a Glance

Introduction . . . . *xxi*

Chapter 1   Why Learn About Linux? What's in It for Me?. 1

Chapter 2   What Do People Do with Linux? 11

Chapter 3   How the Linux World Operates 23

Chapter 4   Getting Red Hat 7.3 on Your System. 39

Chapter 5   Linux Hands-On: Doing Basic Things with Linux. 79

Chapter 6   User Accounts and File Permissions. 189

Chapter 7   Desktop Linux: Handling Graphics and GUI Applications 233

Chapter 8   Setting Up Linux's Server Services 287

Chapter 9   Linux/Microsoft OS Interoperability 413

Chapter 10   Conclusions: Linux versus Microsoft, Linux *and* Microsoft 473

Appendix A   Additional Reading and Resources 493

Index *497*

Contents

Introduction. . . . . *xxi*

Chapter 1   **Why Learn About Linux? What's in It for Me?** 1

Linux Can Be a Powerful Server Alternative
(or Complement) 2

Linux Software Licenses Are Very Cheap 2

NT/2000/XP/.NET Administrators Need Linux
Interoperability Facts 3

Linux Is a Cheap Way to Learn Programming,
Web Administration, and Unix 4

Linux Employs a Nontraditional Software
Business Model 5

You Can Use Linux to Create Finely Tuned
Operating Systems 5

You Can Find Uses for Older Hardware 6

Demand for Linux Administrators Is Growing 7

It'll Help You Use Your Macintosh. 8

Chapter 2   **What Do People Do with Linux?** 11

File Server 11

Print Server 12

Web Server 13

DNS Server 14

Mail Server 15

IP Routing and Firewall 16

Education and Development 16

Database Server. 17

Utilize Non-Intel Hardware 18

Linux on the Desktop 19

Chapter 3   **How the Linux World Operates.** 23

The Birth and Evolution of Linux 23

AT&T Stops Giving Away Unix 24

Linus Plus Minix Equals Linux 24

Understanding Open Source: Linux's "Price" 25

Linux, the Prequel: GPL and GNU 26

The Other Free Unix: BSD 27

Why Open Source Is So Important 29

How Linux Evolves 30

Commercial Linux: Understanding Linux Distributions 34

Red Hat 35

Other Distributions 36

Which Linux Should I Get? 38

Chapter 4   Getting Red Hat 7.3 on Your System 39

What to Expect 39

The Good News 39

The Bad News 40

Your Toughest Linux Install Tasks 41

Preparing for the Install 42

Making Space for Linux 42

Video Hardware Strategies 44

Starting the Install 46

Creating Setup Boot Floppies 47

Starting Setup 47

Language, Keyboard, Mouse Selection,
and Installation Type 48

Drive Partitioning 48

Configuring a Bootloader 53

Network and Firewall Configuration 53

Root Password and Other Accounts 53

Authentication Configuration 54

Selecting Packages 54

Video Adapter Detection 54

Linux Boot Disk Creation 55

GUI Setup 55

Logging In the First Time 55

    Shutting Down Linux: *shutdown* 57

    Dual-Booting Linux 58

Post-Setup: Check the NIC and Video 58

    Testing the NIC 59

    Waking Up the NIC: Wake It Up with *dhcpcd* 60

    Setting a Static IP for a NIC 60

    Making the NIC Wake Up Automatically 61

    Under the Hood: What *netconfig* Does 61

    Telling the NIC How to Route 64

    Setting the Host Name 65

    Setting Up a Wireless NIC: The Lucent Orinoco Gold . . . 66

Post-Setup: Dealing with X 69

    Testing X 70

    X Settings Are in *XF86Config-4* 70

    Running Xconfigurator 72

Trying to Make Sound Work 74

Getting Rid of Linux 74

Chapter 5   **Linux Hands-On: Doing Basic Things with Linux** **79**

Understanding Linux's Disk Structure 80

    Starting with the Hard Disk 81

    Adding a Floppy 81

    Mounting a CD-ROM 85

    Using Automounter 86

    Mounting a FAT/FAT32 Drive 86

    Mounting NTFS Drives: The Bad News 88

    Some Standard Directories in Linux 88

Basic Disk and File Commands 91

    Determining Free Disk Space: *df* 92

    Finding *Used* Disk Space: *du* 92

    Navigating the Disk Structure: *cd* 92

    Viewing a Directory: *ls* 92

Controlling Output: *less* 96

Finding Files: *find* 97

Fast Finding: *locate* 98

Finding Out Where a Program Lives: *which* 98

Creating a Directory: *mkdir* 99

Copying a File: *cp* 100

Moving or Renaming a File: *mv* 101

Displaying a File: *cat* 102

Erasing a File: *rm* 103

Creating a Symbolic Link—a "Shortcut:" *ln* 104

Searching: *grep* 104

Creating and Destroying Hard Disk Partitions 112

Formatting a New Hard Disk Partition 116

Formatting a Floppy Disk 117

Burning CD-R Discs 118

Running Setup without a CD-ROM 119

Create ISOs of the Three Red Hat Installation CDs 120

Collect the ISOs on a FAT Drive 120

Create a Linux Boot Floppy 121

Boot from the Floppy and Select Hard Disk Install 121

Point Setup to the ISOs and Let It Run 121

Printing with Linux 121

How Linux Prints Simple Text 121

Printing More Complex Content 122

How Linux Printer Drivers Work 124

Linux Printing Commands 124

Manipulating the Print Queue 126

Configuring Printers 128

Getting Help: Using the Online Documentation. 132

Using *man* 132

Another Source: *info* 134

How to use HOWTOs 134

Performing Common Linux Tasks 135

Dealing with Compressed Files: Understanding
.tar, *.gz*, and *.bz* files 135

Backing Up to Tape 138

Backing Up a Linux Configuration Isn't
Completely Possible 144

Combining Commands into a Batch ("Script") File . . . 145

Using Telnet to Control a Remote System 149

ssh: A Better Telnet 152

Stopping a Runaway or "Locked" Program 153

Finding Out How Much Memory Your System Uses . . . 155

Installing a New Application with RPM 156

Unzipping, Compiling, and Installing an Application . . . 162

Recompiling the Linux Kernel 166

Controlling Linux "Services" 176

Changing Your Computer's Hardware Date and Time . . . 186

Miscellaneous Linux Tidbits 187

Viewing System Messages: *dmesg* 187

Assuming Other Identities: *su* 187

Producing Calendars: *cal* 188

Counting Words and Characters: *wc* 188

Guessing a File's Type: *file* 188

Who's Using a File: *fuser* 188

Put Your Computer in "Suspend" Mode 188

Chapter 6   **User Accounts and File Permissions** **189**

Working with Linux User Accounts 190

Creating Users 190

Adding Users to Groups 192

Controlling Home Directories, Comments,
and Shells with *useradd* 193

Expiring an Account 194

Setting the User ID Number 194

Changing User Account Defaults 195

Setting User Passwords 196

Deleting User Accounts 196

Disabling User Accounts. 196

Seeing Who's on the System 197

Creating and Modifying Groups 197

Creating New Groups. 197

Modifying Groups 197

Adding or Subtracting a User to/from a Group 198

Finding Out What Groups a User Belongs To 198

Controlling Group Management 198

Deleting Groups 198

Joining a Group 198

Missing User and Group Management Commands 199

Under the Hood: Where User Accounts Are Stored 199

The */etc/passwd* File 200

The */etc/shadow* File 201

The */etc/group* File. 202

The */etc/gshadow* File 202

Linux File Permissions 203

Three Permission Types: Read, Write, and Execute 203

Permissions for Specific Functions 205

You Can Only Set Permissions for One User, the Owner . . 207

You Can Only Set Permissions for One Group for Each File. . 208

The Third Permission Group: The World 209

Reading File Permissions 209

Setting File and Directory Permissions 210

Centralizing User Accounts 213

Network Information Service (NIS) 213

Setting Up an NIS Server 215

Setting Up an NIS Client. 219

Updating Account Information on the NIS Server 223

Changing Passwords on NIS Servers 224

Summary: NIS Setup 224

Sharing Files with NFS 225

Setting Up an NFS Server 226

Putting Our Example All Together 230

Chapter 7   **Desktop Linux: Handling Graphics and GUI Applications** . . . **233**

X History 235

X Basics: Exploring X 235

Pure X 235

Basic Useful X: Introducing *xinit* and *xterm* 236

Adding a Second Application 237

Introducing Window Managers 238

What Do Window Managers Do? 239

Running More Than One Program: The Ampersand 239

Controlling Your Desktop with *twm* 240

"Raising" Windows 241

Bringing Windows into Focus: The Focus Policy 241

Creating a *twm* Menu 242

A Step Up: *fvwm2* 245

Adding Color to Your "X" Life 247

Beyond Colors: X Resources 249

Window Position and Size: *-geometry* 249

Fonts in X Window 250

Installing TrueType Fonts 251

Storing X Resource Information 253

X Freebies: X Apps You'll Usually Find 254

X across the Net: Understanding Clients and Servers 255

Setting the Scene: X's Early Days 255

Defining X Clients and X Servers 257

X Clients and Servers in a Linux World:
    A Hands-On Example 258

Avoiding the *-display* Option: *export DISPLAY* 260

X on Your PC: Making NT an X Window
Terminal / X Server 260

Another Approach: The Linux "Mainframe" 261

Keystrokes for Multiple X Sessions: A Side Note. 263

Other Window Managers 264

The Desktop Environment. 264

YARW: KDE versus GNOME 266

Getting around in KDE and GNOME 271

KDE Basics 271

A Complete Remote Desktop 275

GNOME Basics 277

Assembling the GUI: Starting Everything. 279

startx Configures *xinit* 279

xinit's Job Revisited: Reexamining X "Servers"
and "Clients" 280

startx Summarized 282

Unfreezing a GUI. 283

Finding Linux Applications 284

Run Them on Linux with Wine... Someday 284

Run VMware 284

Applications Built for Linux 285

Chapter   8   Setting Up Linux's Server Services. 287

Chapter Goals: What We'll Build 287

Server Types 287

Defining the Prototype Network 288

Cautions about Following These Examples 288

Working with Services: A Review 290

Domain Name Service (DNS). 291

Configuring the DNS on the Client Side:
The Resolver. 292

Configuring DNS Servers 296

Checking the Server Installation 297

Changing the Configuration Files 299

The Zone Files 308

The Reverse Zone File 314

Cookbook Summary: DNS 315

Going Further: Dynamic DNS 321

Linux As a DHCP Server 323

Controlling the DHCP Client, *dhcpcd* 324

Checking the Server Installation 326

Configuring the DHCP Server 327

DHCP Reservations 330

Starting and Stopping the DHCP Server 332

Cookbook Summary: DHCP Server 332

Linux As a Web Server: Apache 335

Checking the Server Installation 335

Configuring Apache 336

Virtual Hosts 344

Cookbook Summary: Web Server with Two Sites 346

Linux As a Mail Server: Sendmail 348

What Sendmail Does 348

What Sendmail *Doesn't* Do 349

Verifying Sendmail Installation 350

Installing Sendmail 350

Verifying That POP3 Is Installed 350

Starting and Stopping Sendmail 351

Setting Up MX Records 351

Configuring Sendmail 352

Tell the Server Who May Use It to Send Mail 357

Testing Your Sendmail Configuration 359

Cookbook Summary: Sendmail 363

Linux As an FTP Server 364

Checking the Server Installation 365

Configuring the FTP Server 367

Configuring Anonymous FTP Access 371

Cookbook: FTP 374

Creating a Larger Network 374

Multiple NICs and Routing 375

Installing the Second NIC 376

Assigning IP Information to the Second NIC 379

Routing between the Networks 380

Connecting to the Internet. 381

Installing a Modem 381

Dialing Out to an ISP 385

Using Cable Modems and DSL 391

Sharing the Internet: IP Masquerading 392

Configuring the Internal Network 393

Configuring the External Network 394

Configuring the Server 394

Creating a Dial-In Server 397

Checking the Installation. 398

Configuring *mgetty* 398

Configuring PPP Clients 401

Basic Server Security 401

Passwords 401

Disable Unneeded Services. 402

Disabling Unneeded Apache Modules 403

Disabling Unneeded CGI Scripts 404

Using TCP Wrappers 404

Examine Your NFS Exports 406

Modifying */etc/issue* 407

Firewalling with *ipchains* 407

Chapter   9   Linux/Microsoft OS Interoperability **413**

Converting Microsoft Text Files to Linux Text Files 414

Controlling Dual Boots: LILO 415

A Typical *lilo.conf* 415

Choosing a Default Image 417
Controlling Timeouts 417
Offering Boot Messages 418
Making *lilo.conf* Changes Take Effect 418
Run Your Windows Programs with Wine 418
Getting Your System Ready for Wine 419
Finding Out If Wine Runs 422
Finding Out If Wine Runs Your App 423
Handling a Wine Crash 423
Use VMware 423
What about DOS Apps? 424
Linux As Print Server for Windows, NT, and 2000 424
Samba: Microsoft Networking for Linux 425
SMB Clients 427
Configuring an SMB Server 436
Authenticating Linux Users with an NT/2000
Domain: *winbind* 458
Set up *smb.conf* 458
Make Samba Start Automatically 461
Create *unexpected.tdb* 461
Start Samba 461
Check NetBIOS Name Resolution 461
Join the Linux PC to the Domain 462
Edit *nsswitch.conf* 462
Make *winbind* Start Automatically 463
Lend *winbind* a Domain Account 463
Start winbind 464
Test the Domain Connectivity 464
Create the Home Directory 464
Modify the PAM Configuration 464
Setting Up Linux to Authenticate from a Domain:
An Example 467

Chapter 10   **Conclusions: Linux versus Microsoft, Linux *and* Microsoft** . . . 473

Linux's Strengths Relative to NT/2000/XP/.NET 473

Linux's Greatest Strength Is Open Source 473

Linux Is Inherently Multi-Vendor 474

Linux Benefits from Tons of Free Software 476

Linux Licensing Is Free...and Thus Simpler 477

Linux Provides Remote Control 478

Linux Is Robust 478

Linux Admin Tasks Can Be Scripted 479

LILO and/or GRUB Greatly Simplifies Dual-Booting 480

NT/2000 Strengths Relative to Linux 480

Linux Installation Routines Are Better But Still
Troublesome 480

Getting and Installing Applications Is Cumbersome 482

Basic Setup Help Is Lacking 483

Linux GUIs Lack "Fit and Finish" 484

NT/2000/.NET's File Permissions Model Is
More Powerful 485

Linux's NIS Domain Model Is Insecure 485

It's Easier to Learn Basic NT/2000 Administration 486

NT/2000 Has Better Hardware Support 486

Linux Doesn't Support All Microsoft Proprietary
Protocols and Interfaces 487

Summing Up the Differences 488

Using Linux in a Microsoft Environment: Some Ideas 489

Set Up a Mail Server 489

Use a Linux DNS Server 489

Create Web Terminals 490

Build Cheap Firewalls and Routers 490

Add an Inexpensive File Server or Web Server
with Samba or Apache 490

Appendix A   **Additional Reading and Resources** **493**

Linux Distributions. 493

Linux Information Web Sites 494

Sources of Linux Software 495

Newsgroups 495

Organizations Offering For-Pay Support. 495

Index *497*

Introduction

Ever thought any of these things?

> "What's this Linux thing all about, anyway?"

> "Does it really work? Can it really do the kinds of things that NT, 2000, XP, or .NET can do?"

> "Can it do those things better, worse, or about the same as NT?"

> "Is Linux something I need to learn to stay current in my present job, or might it open doors for better (or at least better-*paying*) jobs?"

> "Even if it's any good, who's going to support an operating system that I got for *free*?"

> "Is all of this Linux hype for real, or do some people just hate Microsoft so much that they'd embrace *any* alternative? Or... could Linux perhaps be clearly superior to NT?"

> "What does an NT or Win2000 administrator need to know about Linux?"

I wondered about all of those things. As someone who learned NT back in the early beta days of 1992, before the first version of NT, 3.1, was released, I clearly remember what it was like to climb NT's steep learning curve, and everything I'd ever heard about Linux suggested that ascending *its* learning curve would be every bit as arduous. When I went to university back in the late Mesozoic (okay, so I exaggerated a bit—the Paleocene is, technically, a Cenozoic time period), we didn't use Unix, so I didn't have the advantage of already knowing what `grep`, `chmod`, and `cat` did.

I didn't want to know *everything* about Linux, I just wanted to know what it was and wasn't good for, why so many people were interested in it, and how it compares to NT and 2000. (And, to tell the truth, I wanted to know the correct way to *pronounce* the silly thing, having heard about four variations). I say that last part—"compares to NT"—not in a competitive sense of casting the discussion in the "NT and Windoze suck, Linux rocks!" or "Linux is a toy operating system, NT rules!" tone that 99 percent of the online discussions that I found on the subject took. Instead, I wanted a book that would explain Linux to me *in an NT/XP/2000/.NET context*. For example, I don't need the whole idea of logons, usernames, passwords, and file permissions explained to me—I've already had to *take* the time to learn that in the process of learning NT. I imagined that Linux's file permission system was only about 10 percent to 15 percent different than the NT file permission system—so just teach me the 10-to-15 percent difference, saving me time and effort! In other words, don't make me relearn a bunch of stuff; instead, please effectively reuse the knowledge that I've already worked so hard to accumulate. And keep the book *short*, something I could maybe read on a flight from the East Coast to the West.

Well, that sounded like the answer for me. There was just one little problem: no one had written that book. That's where my coauthor Craig Hunt came in. I suggested the idea about the book to Gary Masters, my associate publisher at the time at Sybex. He liked the idea, but clearly we'd need a Linux expert to be my partner in putting this book together. He suggested Craig, and I immediately loved the idea.

You see, almost 10 years ago, I set out to learn TCP/IP networking with OS/2 and Windows for Workgroups. Of course, there were no OS/2 or Windows-centric TCP/IP books in those days. There were some very nice, big, fat books that explained the TCP/IP protocols in detail, but no practical ones, or so it seemed—until I found a book called *TCP/IP Network Administration*, by Craig Hunt. It was an O'Reilly book with a blue spine and a crab on the cover, and if you've been in networking for more than seven years, I'll bet that you've got a copy of the book on your shelf, even if you *didn't* recognize Craig's name when I first mentioned it. Craig's was an excellent book that told me just what I needed to know, was very practical, and had clearly been written by someone who knew what he was doing. Put briefly, when it comes to Internet software on Unix, Craig is Da Man.

We worked on the book together for a while, but Craig found himself increasingly pulled away by the needs of a series of Linux books he's doing for Sybex, so I needed another Linux expert. (Look for Craig's books if you need more detail than this book can provide; he's got a fair number of books in the Craig Hunt Linux Library done, all available from Sybex. The ones that I've read are quite good.)

I met Dan York through Karen Hyder of Influent Technology. Karen asked me to do a presentation to several dozen technical instructors on the pros and cons of Linux from the point of view of NT users. But then she told me that I'd have company—a guy from Linuxcare.

"Oh, no," I thought, "I have to debate with a Linux bigot!" But upon meeting Dan, I found that he was the perfect guy to help with this book. In addition to his day job (at the time) at Linuxcare, Dan's a big wheel at the Linux Professional Institute and was working hard at the time to create a Linux certification program that wasn't tied to any one Linux vendor. That's important, in *my* opinion, because I've never been comfortable with certification programs tied to a vendor; Cisco controlling the requirements for CCNAs, Microsoft controlling the requirements for MCSEs, and Novell controlling the requirements for CNEs all trouble me. (As does Red Hat's Red Hat–centric certification program.) Despite an extremely busy travel schedule, Dan agreed to take on the task of writing the stuff that was too technical for me, as well as reading the text and pointing out where he felt I'd missed a point or was just downright wrong.

This book is the result of Dan's, Craig's, and my collaboration. The main voice that you'll "hear" is mine—Mark's—but the facts, the lore, and the wisdom come from Craig and Dan. If you see something wrong in here, the fault is probably mine, not Dan's or Craig's. Sometimes Craig or Dan will disagree with my analysis of the Linux world, so they'll step up to center stage then to offer their perspectives, but otherwise "I" refers to Mark's point of view.

And, in case you're still wondering how to pronounce "Linux" correctly, I promise to reveal The Correct Pronunciation in Chapter 3.

What to Expect from This Book

Back in 2000, we got the first edition out, and it sold fairly well. I felt that it achieved its stated aims, to be a basic introduction and overview of Linux for people who knew Windows pretty well but didn't know jack about Linux. Furthermore, the vast majority of those who read it liked it extremely well, as evidenced by the large amount of positive reviews and e-mail. (The unhappy ones were Linux experts who felt that I hadn't answered every single question about Linux, and again I say that this book isn't *intended* to do that—it's just an introduction. You'd need a bookshelf full of books to know how to do *everything* in Linux.)

But three things made me want to come out with a second edition: Linux changed technologically, the Linux market changed, and many of you asked me to focus the book on just one distribution: Red Hat.

First, as you may know, the Linux folks got kernel 2.4 out, addressing some serious architectural problems in Linux; I wanted to cover that. Second, as you probably know, tech stocks crashed and dot-com money dried up. That affected Linux in that a number of Linux-oriented organizations either got a lot smaller or disappeared altogether. Finally, I got a lot of feedback from all of you, my readers, telling me that in the corporate environment people have standardized, like it or not, on Red Hat, and that you'd wished that I'd focused the book on just one distribution rather than trying to take on a *lot* of distros. (And if you don't know what a "distro" is, I'll explain it in Chapter 2.) Fourth, all of the programs surrounding Linux have been upgraded a bit, and so the book started looking dated. Additionally, Sybex launched a Windows 2000/.NET-oriented series of books under my name, and we thought it'd be nice to include the revised Linux book in that series.

So this edition gave me a chance to update the information that needed updating, and to change the text to focus on Red Hat 7.3. This focus will, I think, make the book more useful as a how-do-I-get-this-done book. Instead of having to say things like, "Well, you'd kinda do it this way in Mandrake, Red Hat might do this, and Slackware would do this," I can restrict my examples and command help to Red Hat 7.3's particular release.

I hope you find this edition useful; I look forward to your feedback!

Is This Book Right for Me?

Who's this book for? People who already know NT, 2000, XP, or .NET Server and who need to know the basics of Linux quickly, folks who need enough information to get started with Linux or just hold their own at a cocktail party on the subject. (Well, for a few minutes, anyway. Go investigate the hors d'oeuvres on the other side of the room quickly, before someone asks you when you last compiled your kernel. But, come to think of it, you'll learn how to compile a kernel in Chapter 5. And, most importantly, why you'd care.)

As I suggested above, we're not going to spend a lot of time explaining things that you already know. But what did we assume when we put the book together? If you've done NT or 2000 networking for a while—at least six months—then you probably have the background to benefit from this book.

This book is probably right for you if you have ever created a user account, set a file permission on NTFS or a file share, installed a program on an NT or 2000 computer, and set up an IP address on an NT or 2000 machine. You'll get even more out of the book if you've got a small amount of more technical experience, such as if you'd set up a domain controller at some point, perhaps a few basic network infrastructure services—DNS, e-mail, a web server, DHCP, WINS. That's not to say that the book will be of no value if you *haven't* done those things, but assuming a bit of Microsoft network administration experience is what enabled us to keep the book short.

The Book's Approach

We put the book together with a few basic goals. We felt that the explanations should be NT-centric so as to exploit your existing knowledge as much as is possible; we kept a weather eye to any interoperability hints we could pass along; and we tried to save you time by anticipating the "Is this possible at all, and if so, how do I basically approach it?"–type questions.

Microsoft Networking–Centric Explanations

Experience with NT or Windows 2000 leads me to approach a problem in a particular way; in consultant lingo, you could say that we NT/2000 types think in particular *paradigms*. For example, if I'm going to set up a bunch of NT computers that are supposed to talk to one another, then I'll immediately ask, "Is there an existing NT domain, or will we be creating one?" as building a network with a lot of NT systems and no domain often means a lot of duplicated work. The value of a domain is that instead of having to rebuild user accounts on every single NT system, you just have one central repository of accounts on a machine called a *domain controller*, and all of the NT machines look to that machine for authentication. (That's a simplified explanation.) When I look to understanding Linux, then, I'm likely to ask things like:

- How would a bunch of Linux boxes centralize user accounts in an NT or Active Directory domain-like fashion?
- Can the Linux boxes *use* an NT domain? In other words, if I had a mixed NT/Linux network, could I use just one user account and password to log on to both the Linux and NT boxes, or must I keep two separate accounts? How about an Active Directory—can a Linux box log on to an AD?
- If Linux can't use an NT or 2000 domain's accounts, is there some way that my NT and 2000 boxes can use whatever kind of accounts *Linux* creates?

That's the mindset that we used when writing this book: "Here on planet NT, we've got blue skies, the stars are visible at night, water is usually in a liquid state, and we've got this much gravity… what's it like on planet Linux?"

Interoperability Hints

You probably noticed with my NT domain/Linux accounts example another thing that kept cropping up, over and over: interoperability. Much as it troubles Bill Gates, it's a fact that most of us don't have networks made solely out of Microsoft products, nor do we want to.

Years ago, I "simplified" my network, eliminating the Novell and OS/2 components and deciding to run Windows or NT on the desktops and NT on the network servers. As my firm is a Microsoft Solution Provider, I get copies of Microsoft Office as part of my annual fees, so we even adopted the Office desktop tools. With the exception of Palm Pilot software, we became a nearly 100-percent "Microsoft shop." I reasoned that if I used everything from just one vendor, I'd have a more reliable network, right? Sadly, I was wrong; NT still crashes for random reasons, and my firm soon joined the ranks of those who religiously rebooted our servers weekly to reduce the random failures. (2000 is much better, thankfully.) I couldn't afford the $30,000-plus for Premier Support, so I wasn't any better off than I'd been in my previous heterogeneous environment. Although Microsoft products are quite good, going "all Microsoft" didn't magically give us 99.9 percent uptime.

That means that I think we'll see more and more networks that try to use Microsoft software in the places that it's most effective, Linux in the places that *it* shines, and others as well. But how do we make Microsoft operating systems and Linux "play nice?" That's a theme you'll see recur throughout this book.

Guideposts to the Possible and the Impossible

I find when I'm starting to learn things in a completely new body of knowledge that I have two different kinds of questions: "Is such-and-such possible?" and if the answer to that question is "Yes," then I ask, "How do I do such-and-such?" The first question is often the more important one, as there's no point in wasting hours or days trying to figure out how to do something that may not be possible at all. Furthermore, if the answer to the first question is "No," then your firm may decide to skip the product altogether. Unfortunately, the "Is this possible?" questions are sometimes very hard to get answers to, as product documentation tends to talk about what a product *can do* and remain steadfastly silent about what it *can't*.

For example, many NT administrators over the years have asked, "How do I set up a user's account so that she can only log on to one machine at a time? How do I keep Sue from being simultaneously logged in at three different machines, forcing her to log off one before logging on to another?" The answer to the question is that you *can't*—there's no way to forbid simultaneous logins in NT. (Or in Windows 2000, for that matter.) But try to find that simple answer—"Don't try to limit simultaneous logins, we don't support it."—in the NT or Windows 2000 help files, and you'll be disappointed.

In fairness to Microsoft, I should point out that eventually many of the "Can this product do such-and-such?" questions often get answered in Microsoft's Knowledge Base. But it takes a *while* for those questions to make it to the KB. Or, in another example, I'm often asked, "I've set up my NT server as a server in a workgroup; what command do I run to make it a primary domain controller?" As you probably know, the answer is, "Run Setup all over again and rebuild your server from scratch." Again, a common question that exposes a weakness in NT software, but the Help files are silent about it.

It's easy to understand why Microsoft wouldn't highlight NT's deficiencies or why a Linux vendor (or advocate) similarly wouldn't highlight Linux's weaknesses. But neither Dan, Craig, nor I have an advocacy role for either product, so one of the things you'll see in this book is an explanation of what the products *can't* do, in addition to the expected descriptions of what they *can* do.

What about the second set of questions, the ones that ask, "Now that I know this is possible, how do I do it?" Well, *sometimes* we'll offer step-by-step explanations of syntax and procedures, but again we're trying to keep this book a brief introduction. Sometimes we'll get down to the nuts and bolts, but other times we'll give you the outline of how to go about getting something done and point you at a reference for the ugly details.

Keep the Discussion Religion-Free

Let me underscore a point that I just made. We're not here to sell you either Linux *or* NT. As far as I'm concerned, Windows *9x*, NT, 2000, and Linux have all dealt me far too many troubles of various types at various times for me to get all dewy-eyed about any one of them. They're all decent tools, but imperfect ones, for their own reasons. And I've been around computers long enough to have seen plenty of save-the-world operating systems: Does anyone out there remember TopView, Desq, Memory Shift, Windows/386, Multilink, OS-9, OASIS, or Xenix?

Ultimately we won't have to *worry* about setting up networks or keeping them working. Some network software that doesn't exist yet will some day make computers all around the world able to share databases and processing power in a seamless, invisible, hassle-free manner. *That* will be great—that will be an operating system worth getting excited about. One that finally empowers users without requiring them to become junior rocket scientists in order to make it work. But that operating system isn't here now.

Put simply, one of the things that we want to do in this book is to avoid the religion and downright laughably pious attitude that many people adopt when talking about their favorite operating system, no matter what that is. There are too many of them on both the NT/2000/XP/.NET and Linux sides, the zealots in each camp unable to see the good in the other side's product and the bad in their own. And while Craig and Dan's initial leanings are towards the Unix/Linux world and mine is toward NT—they're the operating systems that we know best—we've also been in computing long enough to have been disappointed in Linux or NT, so we don't have any particular need to *get* religious in the book.

That doesn't mean that I'm suggesting I don't have biases; I'm like anyone else, and so I tend to be more comfortable with what I know. But no matter whether you hate Linux, Bill Gates, Microsoft, NT, or whatever, no one can deny that Linux and NT are the two largest players in the server operating system world. Depending on whom you believe, both Microsoft-based and Linux-based operating systems run on about 40 percent of the servers in the world. It would be hard to believe that either the Linux or Microsoft marketing people are good enough at mass hypnosis to have fooled that large a market segment. To dismiss either OS would be a serious mistake.

How This Book Is Organized

In the first chapter, we'll look at perhaps the most important question that *any* book can answer—namely, "What's in it for *me*?" NT admins are busy enough keeping up with the latest NT stuff *and* migrating (or deciding whether or not to migrate) to Windows 2000, wait for .NET, or whatever, so why busy themselves with another operating system? In Chapter 1, we offer a brief overview of what knowing Linux can do for you.

In Chapter 2, I asked Craig and Dan the question, "What can Linux do as a server, and *how* does the Linux world most commonly use Linux as a server—what are its most commonly-used functions?" As with Microsoft operating systems, Linux can potentially do a *lot* of things, but it is really only popular for a smaller set of functions—and you'll learn which ones in Chapter 2.

In Chapter 3, we zoom out a bit and look at Linux in a broader context, at the Linux world as a whole. Where did Linux come from? How can a complex OS that's basically tended by volunteer programmers function? How can companies like Red Hat possibly hope to make money and produce high-quality software when the software's basically *free*? The answers may surprise you.

If you're still with us by Chapter 4, you'll probably be itching to try Linux out by then, so we go from the general conceptual tone of the first three chapters to a practical discussion of how to get Red Hat 7.3 installed and working on your system. Linux is a lot of fun to work and experiment with once you get it up and running, but unfortunately you'll see that setup programs are not Linux's strongest aspect. Chapter 4 aims to save you the time that I spent trying to figure out how to get Red Hat set up as well as to make the two most challenging peripherals—video and network cards—work. (You'll also learn what peripherals *won't* work, like most wireless Ethernet cards and FireWire stuff. But you'll learn how I got at least *one* set of wireless cards—the Orinocos—to run.)

It's downright frustrating to move from an operating system that you know pretty intimately to another where everything you know is wrong—you can't figure out how to list a directory's contents or even how to shut it down! You'll feel that way the first time you face the Linux command prompt, but Chapter 5 (it's a *big* chapter) will take you through doing most of the day-to-day tasks that Linux (or any other operating system) requires.

In Chapter 6, you'll learn about Linux's version of NT's and 2000's domains and permission structure. You'll see how to create user accounts, set file permissions, and then centralize those user accounts on a Network Information Service (NIS) domain controller.

Chapter 7 leaves behind the up-to-then server-centric nature of the discussion and looks at the workstation side of Linux—its GUIs (yes, that's "GUIs," plural!) and how it runs as a desktop productivity operating system. You'll see how to assemble a Linux productivity desktop to your liking.

While this is not intended to teach you everything that you could possibly need to know about running Linux—that would be a somewhat larger volume—I wanted you to be able to use Linux to set up some basic and functionally useful servers. So Dan put together Chapter 8; it's a set of very brief overviews and "cookbooks" on how to set up Linux as a web server, DNS server, e-mail server, proxy server, DHCP server, FTP server, IP router, and more.

If you're getting interested in Linux by this point, then you might start wondering how hard it's going to be to get NT or 2000 and Linux to work together on your network. Chapter 9 looks at that with an explanation of how some Linux (and, surprisingly, NT and 2000) tools help the two OSs interact.

Finally, in Chapter 10, I sum up with a quick (and admittedly very subjective) review— if you're currently a Windows 2000 or NT administrator, what will you see as the relative strengths and weaknesses of Linux? Additionally, where best could you fit a few Linux machines into your network?

Let's Just Call It All "NT"

Microsoft seems to be determined to drive us all crazy with the way they name versions of NT. Back in the Old Days (1996), we just had NT 3.1/3.5/3.51/4.0. Since the year 2000, Microsoft has come out or is working on three different versions of NT, and they've named them everything *but* "NT." Windows 2000 is really NT 5.0, XP is really NT Workstation 5.1, and .NET Server (which is still in beta as I write this) is really NT 5.2. But it gets *really* tiring writing "NT/Windows 2000/XP/.NET Server," so let me adopt this convention:

> **NOTE**   Unless otherwise specified, any and all references in this book to "NT" mean "NT, Windows 2000, Windows XP, and Windows .NET Server." Basically, I had them all in mind as I wrote. (And, in many cases, DOS and Windows 9x as well, at least when comparing workstation environments.)

A Note to Linux Experts Reading This Book

While this book is, as I've said, aimed at Microsoft OS experts who are Linux novices (or innocents), some of the folks leafing through this might be Linux experts. Although the book's not aimed at you, welcome anyway! I wanted to include this note to forestall some of what I've found are common objections to some of my observations.

In the process of researching Linux for this book, I came across some interesting ideas that I then developed in several columns for *Windows NT Magazine* (now *Windows and .NET Magazine*, but it's really the same publication). In the first column, I discussed Linux's strengths; the column only generated a couple of letters. In the second column, however, I expressed my feeling that Linux's greatest weakness may be its installation programs. (Happily I can now say that this is not nearly as true as it was when I wrote the previous edition of this book. Linux setup programs are, in my opinion, still inferior to Microsoft's setup programs, particularly in the area of hardware setup, but they are miles better than they were before, and I expect that the time will come soon when getting Linux to understand a laptop's NIC and sound card will no longer be a matter to even think of.) This is not a fatal weakness by any means, but instead a symptom of the way the Linux world works—the people using Linux *initially* spent their time making the system rock-solid and spent very little effort on making it easy to install. Only in the past couple of years has the Linux community started to focus on user-friendly, graphical installation programs like the ones so familiar to Windows and NT users. As a result, the install programs are a bit rough-edged, something that I have no doubt will be fixed in time—but that can trip up a new Linux explorer today.

That column drew a lot of letters, most of which were extremely negative, from Linux experts. The gist of their letters was, "When you've worked with Linux for a few years, you'll understand how to install Linux properly and you won't experience these problems—so don't write about Linux until then, okay?" What they didn't understand was *why* I tackled this job. The Linux experts aren't the *only* members of the Linux community any more; now there are big Linux companies seeking to create market share and profits. They've hired marketers, and those folks have been telling the CIOs of big NT/2000 shops that Linux is not only reliable but a real piece of cake to install. The CIO then drops a Linux CD on the desk of some poor overworked NT or 2000 administrator and says, "Hey, get this up and running and stick a couple of our intranet websites on this by next Friday, okay?" The poor boob then tries to get Linux working and soon finds that it's *not* quite as easy to make Linux useful as the marketers claim. Part of the point of this book is to smooth the path for the newly drafted Linux administrator.

So Linux techies, let me just ask: remember that this is intended to be an introduction, not "Linux A to Z," and please read *all* of the book before you send me the flame mail. *And* remember who the book is intended for. Or come join our forum and educate us Windows dopes about Linux at `www.minasi.com/forum`!

Feedback

It was an interesting challenge putting this book together, and we'd like to hear what you think. (And we've found that most people *definitely* have thoughts about Linux, NT, 2000, XP, and .NET—and sometimes on Linux *versus* those operating systems.) Drop us a line and share your ideas; we'd also appreciate any factual errors or typos that you run across. I'm at `www.minasi.com/gethelp`, and Dan is at `dyork@Lodestar2.com`.

I'm also running a forum at my website at `www.minasi.com/forum`, which of course mainly deals with Windows things, but we've also got a Linux forum, and there might be someone who can help with a Linux problem there. I also encourage you to sign up for my free Windows 2000/XP/.NET newsletter (which occasionally includes Linux information) at `www.minasi.com`.

And I truly regret to have to say this, but we simply *can't* offer support to people with Linux problems. I would not, by any stretch of the imagination, call myself a Linux expert, and so I'm really not the place to go to ask really technical Linux questions. Just a short trip to any of the Linux newsgroups shows that the need for Linux help and support is like a deluge; if Dan, Craig, and I were to try to help just *one percent* of the people looking for Linux help, we still wouldn't have time left over to sleep, eat, or earn livings.

Thanks for reading, and we hope you find this book to be the shortest and most entertaining path to Linux familiarity!

—Mark Minasi

1

Why Learn About Linux?
What's in It for Me?

"**I**'ve already got Windows 2000 and XP running and mostly stable—and *they* were no picnic—why should I care about Linux?"

There are several reasons. For one, Linux can do many things that your network needs and, furthermore, it may be able to do at least a few of them better than any Microsoft OS can. Second, even if it's just a toss-up between NT and Linux in functionality, you can get as many copies of Linux as you want, free.

And don't forget that there's a decent chance that at some point the boss is going to come ask you about "this Linux thing"—a couple of his golf buddies claim to be using it to good effect, so he's giving you the hairy eyeball and asking why *we're* not using this modern software miracle? Knowing about Linux may either equip you to tell him why it's not the answer for you, or enable you to explain that yes, Linux would be useful, here's how, and here's what you'll need in the way of resources to make it happen. And if he takes you up on the request for more resources, then it'd be nice to know how to make NT and Linux interoperate!

Also, Linux is a cheap way to learn many skills that are not extremely operating system–specific but that are marketable: for less than 20 bucks, you have a tool that will let you learn C, Perl, or Python programming, webmaster skills, or basic e-mail server administration, to name a few things. Those skills might be of dollars-and-cents value to you personally, as demand for Linux administrators is growing rapidly. And, finally, whether it succeeds or not, Linux offers an alternative model for software development and marketing, and that different way of thinking cannot help but affect how more traditional software firms like Microsoft sell their wares.

Linux Can Be a Powerful Server Alternative (or Complement)

As you'll read in the next chapter, people who use Linux tend to use it for a particular set of tasks, a set that's a bit different from what people use NT or 2000 for. By knowing what Linux is good for (and what it's not so good for), you can intelligently plan where to use it and where to use NT instead.

For example, if you need a file server that Windows boxes can talk to and you've already got NT running, then you're probably best off leaving that unchanged. But if you're thinking of setting up a DNS server, then you might want to slap Linux on a box and run DNS on the Linux box instead of an NT box. First, every copy of Linux includes, free of charge, a piece of DNS server software called BIND, which is the most well-known, tested, robust piece of DNS server software that you can get your hands on. Second, as you'll read in the next section (and as you probably know), Linux is basically free software. Third, you can get DNS running well on PC hardware as modest as a 100MHz Pentium with 32MB of RAM, or perhaps less. Fourth, you might just want to run Linux as a DNS server *even if* you're running an NT or 2000 DNS server, because you might need a second DNS server (as you do if you're hosting your own DNS server on an Internet domain) and don't have an extra NT license for that second one.

Linux Software Licenses Are Very Cheap

Notice I *didn't* say "free."

Yes, if you have the bandwidth and/or the patience, you can surely download an entire Linux distribution and not pay anyone a dime for it. When Craig Hunt and I worked on the first version of this book, we thought it'd be interesting to try to download Red Hat Linux from Red Hat's site with my 56K modem. Windows 2000 Professional started downloading the Red Hat files, reporting that the estimated remaining time was "13 days, 6 hours, and 13 minutes." Needless to say, we terminated the download and decided that it'd be quicker to run up to Best Buy and get the CD-ROM.

But is Linux *really* free? Absolutely not. Suppose I gave you, free of charge, all of the NT Server licenses that you could ever want. Would NT then be free? Well, the software might be, but NT doesn't run itself. You need administrators and consultants to keep NT running, and those administrators and consultants aren't cheap. (And speaking as a consultant, let me say, "Thank *heavens* that we're not cheap!")

It's the same story with Linux. Sure, Linux is powerful, but it's not simple. Despite the efforts of large Linux vendors to make GUI front-ends for Linux almost mandatory, the fact remains that any Linux administrator worth his or her salt is comfortable working with cryptic-looking configuration files. One doesn't learn to be a Linux guru overnight any more than one can become an NT, 2000, XP, or .NET guru overnight. So let me be clear about the fact that if you choose to incorporate Linux in your network, then you should expect either to incur some training costs or be prepared to pay for someone who's already taken the time to develop a Linux expertise.

On the other hand, I should add a positive note here: while Linux techies may not be plentiful, Unix techies *are* a bit more common, and Linux's similarity to Unix means that it's moderately simple for someone who already knows Unix to "cross over" to Linux expertise.

The fact that Linux software licenses are free, though, *can* save you money. Yes, Linux-savvy administrators cost money, but just one administrator can watch over several servers. Going from one Linux box to two, then, entails very little marginal cost. Even better, you can often put Linux on lower-power hardware than you'd normally choose for NT, so you can save money on the hardware as well. In the case of my network, I found that moving from Windows NT to Windows 2000 Server forced me to retire my old primary domain controller, a Pentium Pro 200MHz system; I replaced it with a Pentium III 600MHz server. That Pro 200 would have done a terrible job of running Windows 2000, but now that it's freed up, it's a terrific Linux server.

On the one hand, then, introducing Linux into your network can cost you in terms of personnel. But on the other hand, Linux can save you money on software licenses and on hardware.

NT/2000/XP/.NET Administrators Need Linux Interoperability Facts

Microsoft never lets a year or two go by without a major change in NT, which typically means that just when you've got "Windows ZZ.DOT" mostly figured out, then you've got to dope out "Windows US.XXX," so it's not like you've got a pile of free time. (Don't worry, those aren't real versions of Windows, just names I made up. Remember you heard them here first.) But, as I've already said, that doesn't stop the boss from asking you, "Hey, how come we're not using Linux like all my golf buddies … errr, I mean, other CIOs in town?" So now you have to figure out Linux, and more important, you may have to figure out how to make Linux fit into your existing network, whether Linux is right for your organization or not.

Why? Well, of course, some of you need to know how to integrate Linux into your Microsoft-based network just because Linux makes *sense* in your organization. Some will just have to do it because Linux is the "flavor of the month," a new thing to try for the early accepters in the management suite. No matter what the reason, it's a fact that many Windows administrators will benefit from knowing at least enough Linux to know what they can do to integrate it with their system.

And there are a *lot* of things that you can do to make Linux and Windows networks work well together, as you'll see. They can easily share files and printers, work together in sup- plying e-mail, web, and other Internet infrastructure services.

As an NT/2000/XP/.NET administrator, your boss and/or clients are very likely to look to you for advice about Linux—should they include it in their existing Microsoft-based networks? Can it replace or complement some or all of their existing network infrastruc- ture, or is it a waste of time to even consider that? Knowing at least a bit about Linux will help you answer those questions.

Linux Is a Cheap Way to Learn Programming, Web Administration, and Unix

If you have an interest in learning the Perl, Python, or C languages, then Linux is a great and nearly free platform—free, that is, excluding the time to learn a new environment. In some ways, education was Linux's first task, as it started out as a learning tool for Linus Torvalds. To this day, students at hundreds of universities use Linux to learn not only programming, but also how operating systems work. If you want to learn programming using the Microsoft tools, you have to buy a lot of stuff—the operating system, the C compiler, the development environment. But every version of Linux that I've ever seen ships with all the tools you need to create and test programs of all kinds, whether they're graphical games, hardware device drivers, network services, or even basic internal oper- ating system functions like memory managers. And all at that attractive Linux price!

But Linux isn't just for learning to program. It's also a good way to learn and practice many administration tasks. Experience with Linux's Apache web server, its Sendmail mail server, or its BIND DNS server would all translate to good knowledge of how these work on a Unix system, which might pave the way for more job opportunities. Even *if* Linux doesn't succeed, it can't hurt to know how to run Unix networks, and Linux expertise takes you an awfully long way toward being a Unix expert.

Linux Employs a Nontraditional Software Business Model

The Microsoft Way to make money in the software business is to build software and sell it, and not to let the buyer see the "source code"—the blueprints for the software. Many other firms, like Novell, Lotus, Symantec, Corel, and Intuit, have prospered using that same model of software manufacture and sales. But that's not the only way, as firms like MandrakeSoft and Red Hat Software have demonstrated; *their* model is to build it, then give it away. Clearly *someone's* making money doing software a different way. Here's an easy way to learn more about it.

> **NOTE**   You can learn more about this innovative approach to software marketing in Chapter 3.

You Can Use Linux to Create Finely Tuned Operating Systems

While this isn't something *everyone* is going to do, many people have exploited the fact that Linux ships with its complete source code to do something pretty neat: they simply cull from the operating system anything that they'll never use.

Suppose you knew that you were going to roll out 200 machines that would be e-commerce web servers, and that your firm had decided to use Linux and its included web server, Apache. Two hundred machines are a *lot* of machines; buying them represents a fair amount of money that your firm is laying out. How, you are asked, can we get the maximum performance from these systems?

Well, if these were NT or 2000 servers, you'd study up to find the right Registry entries that would tweak more throughput out of your machines—that's about the most that you could do. But these are *Linux* boxes. So you go hire a C-and-Linux expert. She then modifies the Linux code, throwing out the pieces that you will never use: the servers will never have FAT or NTFS partitions, throw that code out … no need for Samba, or NFS… power management's unnecessary…and in no time she has pared the base Linux operating system down to half its size.

NOTE Don't believe me? There are several groups that have boiled down Linux to *one single floppy disk* so that you can use an old machine without a hard disk as an IP router! One example is at www.linuxrouter.org. And Dan tells me, "The list of distributions at Linux Weekly News now lists 19 distributions that can run off a floppy! See the list at http://lwn.net/Distributions/. Floppy 'distros' start down around 148 with Brutalware." And if that's not enough, I've seen business-card-sized CD-ROMs with bootable copies of Linux.

But she doesn't stop there. All of that free space lets her expand some of Linux's memory buffers, allowing Linux to keep more of its essential data in RAM rather than having to constantly run out to the far-slower disk drive for that data. Result: a special-purpose version of Linux that runs like the wind on fairly modest hardware.

So perhaps you only need *one* hundred of those machines. Hey, who knows, you might even get a bonus for saving the company a couple of bucks! (No, huh? Yeah, I think I used to work for that company, too.)

You Can Find Uses for Older Hardware

Part of the Linux Legend is that you can get fantastic performance out of ancient hardware—that all of those moldy old 486s can run Linux and outperform NT or 2000 on Pentium IIIs. My personal experience leads me to say that much of that is merely hype, as a Red Hat 6.1 system running the GNOME graphical interface needs (in my opinion) 64MB of RAM, as well as at least a 1024 × 768 graphic mode and a Pentium II to offer decent performance.

But if you can live without that graphical user interface stuff, and if you have a distribution of Linux that doesn't *require* you to load graphics, then yes, some of the legends of still-useful 486s aren't completely absurd—although for fairness' sake, you might consider putting Linux on a senescent 100MHz Pentium rather than the *extremely* senescent 486.

What would you expect to get done with a 100MHz Pentium with 32MB of RAM and a 2GB hard disk? Very little, with NT Server or 2000. But such a system could work admirably as a DNS server or a web server, provided again that you don't throw away most of the CPU's power on an unnecessary GUI. Or, you might well decide that you'd *like* to throw away some of the CPU's power on a GUI, but only occasionally—that's the beauty of Linux. Depending on the version of Linux that you use, you'll probably be able to set the system to come up in text mode with only a text shell and no graphics, but then to start up the GUI when you need to do administration, if you prefer to use graphical administration tools. (You needn't—every administration task that I've come across can be done from the text shell, and I will try very hard throughout this book to show you how to do everything from the command shell. Furthermore, I live that reality—as my e-mail server is a Linux box running on an Alpha chip, I can't get the GUI to work at all, so I *have* to do all of my administration from the command line.)

Demand for Linux Administrators Is Growing

What better reason is there ever for learning things than filthy lucre? For many NT administrators, NT administration is their first IT-related job, and they made the choice to go get some NT training specifically so that they could move from a non-IT job to one that paid more money. NT jobs pay well because of the demand for NT administrators, a demand that grew out of companies adopting NT in great numbers. While it's still true that more and more firms are adopting NT and 2000, and so that demand will continue for the near future, it's every bit as true that many of those same firms and others besides are incorporating Linux in their networks. So it's reasonable to guess that there will be a demand for Linux administrators as well.

But is that guess valid: is there really a great unfulfilled demand for Linux administrators? Believe it or not, that's a somewhat tough question to answer. I attended the 1999 Fall Comdex in Las Vegas because I was invited by the Comdex folks to give a couple of talks about the then-upcoming Windows 2000. While I was there, I noticed that Comdex offered talks on Linux as well—in fact, an entire other track. I sat in one panel discussion where the participants talked about whether or not there was a growing market for Linux administrators. Each of the panel members had one of two different points of view. The first point of view was, "Yes, it's hard to find Linux administrators. It's *always* been tough to find good Unix administrators, why would Linux be any different?" The other point of view was, "Look, almost anyone graduating with a computer science degree since 1995 has been using Linux at his or her college/university classes—just hire a youngster right out of school."

In his Comdex talk, Craig—who was one of the invited Comdex speakers, although on Linux, not 2000—observed that a recent salary survey showed that Linux system administrators were being paid more than NT administrators. (There were no 2000 administrators at the time, recall.) He had an interesting perspective on what causes that. In Craig's view, NT administrators are suffering salary-wise "because your managers *don't respect you*!" He says that with tongue partly in cheek and goes on to explain that what he means is that NT *looks* like Windows, and managers use Windows, so they reason to themselves, "Hey, *I* can use Windows, so how hard could it be to run a network based on this Windows-like thing?" In contrast, Linux carries with it the complexity of Unix, which "everyone knows" is an operating system that requires at least minor genius to keep working—so *of course* we have to pay those Linux guys a lot!

Craig got the salary figures from the *1999 SANS System, Network and Security Administration Salary Survey* from the SANS Institute. The majority of the administrators in the survey, 63.5 percent, are NT administrators, and the next largest group, 30.5 percent, are Unix/Linux administrators. Page 9 of the survey states that the "average NT salary was $53,598/year" with the "average Unix salary at $62,907/year." A difference of almost $10,000! Despite the fact that the demand for NT administrators is so high that more than twice as many respondents use NT than Unix, the value assigned to the Unix positions is $10,000 greater than the NT positions. Clearly having some Unix/Linux skills can be good for your wallet. (The SANS Institute is an organization of system administrators focused on system and network security. You can find them at `www.sans.org`, and no, I've not been able to find a more up-to-date survey, but I still believe that Linux/Unix knowledge is a useful asset for an IT administrator.)

It'll Help You Use Your Macintosh

Believe it or not, this is utterly true.

I bought a couple of Macs back in 1993 so that I could learn how to network them to NT for the first version of my NT book. (A IIci and a LCii if I recall right.) Playing with them was fun but ultimately caused me to write off the Mac as religion and hype.

Why do I say that? Because of the basic architectural weakness of its underlying operating system. First, the Mac had a basically nonexistent memory management system: you, the user, had to hand-allocate more or less memory to every application. Second, the multitasking system was a very weak "cooperative" multitasking system, meaning that once a given application got control of the computer, there was nothing that anyone could do to wrest control back from that application. Thus, every application was on the "honor system" not to hog the computer.

In short, the Mac OS was, in my opinion, as architecturally bankrupt as Windows 3.0. That didn't bother many users, as Macs benefit from the fact that 99 percent of the hardware in a Mac is hardware all designed by the same people who built the operating system, and because the smaller nature of the Mac market means that there are fewer applications and therefore the average bear ends up trying to make a smaller number of apps work together. As a result, purist geeks like me were right in turning up our noses at the Mac on theoretical grounds… but Mac lovers were right in a practical sense that their Macs did what they wanted them to do. Then came Mac OS/X.

Apple did an incredibly smart thing with OS/X: they blew up the Mac OS and started over. And, as you may know, here's what else they did: they started from a variant of Unix called BSD (which stands for Berkeley Software Distribution, not that that tells you anything), a rock-solid OS. Then they put a GUI atop it that was as beautiful as you'd expect from the Guys From Cupertino. The result is one nifty-looking OS that answers all of my objections: BSD does quite well in the memory management and multitasking areas, thank you very much.

Now inasmuch as BSD and Linux are both just variations on Unix, much of the stuff that you'll learn here can be immediately converted into useful Mac geek knowledge. (A side benefit, yes, but perhaps a useful one.)

Because it has clearly passed the "laugh test," and because it's an arguable good value for many businesses, Linux is an opportunity for the IT world in general. But that also means that it's an opportunity for your professional growth. *That's* probably the best reason to find out about Linux.

2

What Do People Do with Linux?

People buy NT and 2000 to solve particular problems. But we know that NT and 2000 can't solve just any old problem; rather, they are better at solving some problems than others. In other words, NT can *potentially* do many things, but in *reality* the business world uses it to solve a particular set of problems. For example, when a firm needs a database server, NT springs to mind quickly as a good platform. But when a firm needs a micro-to-mainframe gateway, NT *doesn't* usually spring to mind, even though Microsoft has a tool (SNA Server) that can act in that role.

What, then, do people do with Linux? In this chapter, we'll quickly review that. This chapter's approach is very broad-brush by intention—I'm not going to go into great detail, as that's the job of later chapters, but I hope that by the end of this chapter you'll have a quick-and-dirty overview of what people use Linux for in the real world.

File Server

Linux can act as a file server, just as NT does. Furthermore, Linux can act as a file server in more environments than NT does. However, as you'll learn later in the discussion of file permissions in Linux, Linux doesn't offer as flexible a permissions model.

Linux comes with three different pieces of file server software:

- *Samba* lets you use a Linux box to emulate a Microsoft file server. Once you have Samba configured, it will show up on Network Neighborhood or My Network Places in the same way that any system running Windows 2000, NT, Windows 9*x*, or Windows for Workgroups would, assuming that the system has file sharing enabled. Nor is this a minimalist emulation, either—by some benchmarks, Samba actually outperforms NT and 2000 as a file server!

- *NFS*, the Network File System, is the preferred file server software in the Unix world. Linux includes software to be able to act as an NFS file server.

- In addition, a specialized file server software called *Coda* is designed to allow high-speed file server service between Linux boxes—but, again, it mainly only works Linux-to-Linux.

- Linux has also had support for acting as a Novell NetWare fileserver, since the days of the 2.0.x kernel. The mars_nwe (Martin Stover's NetWare Emulator) project can be found at `http://systemhaus.gkdmedien.de/mars_new/` (in German).

- As of Linux kernel version 2.4.15, there is also support for acting as a server for the InterMezzo network filesystem. See `http://www.inter-mezzo.org/` for more details.

- There are also a number of AFS (Andrews Filesystem) server projects for Linux that are in wide use, including OpenAFS (`http://www.openafs.org/`), Arla (`http://www.stacken.kth.se/project/arla/`), and a commercial one from Transarc/IBM. AFS is heavily used in academic and research environments, and allows for a single transparent distributed filesystem shared amongst hundreds of different universities and other organizations.

- Linux also includes *netatalk*, which lets it talk to networked Apple computers. (I'm not going to cover it in this book, but it's worth mentioning.)

Linux also includes client-side software for each of these network file sharing systems. It's fairly simple for a Linux box to attach to an NT or 2000 file server, as you'll see in Chapter 9.

Print Server

Linux can act as a print server and, as with file serving, there is a "Microsoft way" and a "Unix way" to share printers. Linux supports them both.

- In the Unix world, two programs, lpd and lpr, provide print sharing services. Unix print servers run a server-side program called lpd (line printer daemon). Client machines run lpr, the corresponding client-side tool. Linux includes both lpd and lpr. Interestingly enough, NT has for years included lpr, the client-side tool. You could, therefore, set up a Linux system as a Unix-style print server and still exploit it from an NT system.

- For the largely Microsoft-centric shops, that may not be a great answer. But that's no problem, as once again the Samba program allows a Linux system to share a printer in such a way that the other machines on the network think that the printer is being shared by a Microsoft server, perhaps an NT or 2000 server.

As with file services, Linux contains client software as well. A Linux box can use either a printer shared by a Microsoft-type server or a Unix box.

Web Server

Here we arrive at one of Linux's great strengths. Linux ships with a free web server designed and developed jointly by several people and companies. The web server program is called Apache because in its very early stages it was bug-ridden (as is all early software, of course) and its designers banished the bugs with host of fixes or "patches," leading one developer to call it "a patchy server"—"Apache server," get it? (If not, take a look at the sidebar titled "Naming Unix and Linux Programs.")

Dumb name aside, Apache is a *major* force in the World Wide Web. Take a peek at www.netcraft.com to see why. Netcraft keeps a census of all web servers running on the Internet, and they publish monthly statistics about who's using what. For as long as I can remember, the single most-used piece of web server software in the world has been Apache. Now, understand, that's not all Apache on *Linux*—I'd guess that most of the big commercial sites were running Apache atop some commercial version of Unix—but there is no small number of people using Apache on Linux. NT's Internet Information Server accounts for a pretty good percentage of servers on the Web, but Apache beats it, six ways to Sunday. And it comes free with Linux.

That said, however, I don't run Apache on my website, and I'm not likely to in the near future. Why? Well, the macro language that I've become most comfortable with over the years is VBScript, and Apache doesn't support that. I run Internet Information Server on an NT box because my website needs a bit of light-duty programming, and I didn't want to hire a consultant or learn some new language, so I chose Active Server Pages (ASPs). I just love the power of ASPs with VBScript, and as IIS is the only web server supporting them, I'll probably stay with it.

(Dan disagreed with me on this point, as there are add-ons for Apache that support Active Server Pages—www.apache-asp.org and www.chilisoft.com are links for them, in case

Naming Unix and Linux Programs: PUN = "PUN Until Nauseated"

When I said elsewhere "'Apache server,' get it?" I was actually trying to prepare you for an inescapable truth about the names of Linux programs. Basically, if you didn't get it, then you'd better have a stiff drink or two before learning much more about how Unix and Linux programs get their names.

It seems that a necessary rite of passage for every major piece of Unix/Linux software is to name the software with either a pun or a recursive acronym. Apache is an example of a pun. A recursive acronym is an acronym that includes the acronym in its name. (See, I warned you to go grab a couple of fingers of Macallans.) I know that's confusing-sounding, but it gets clearer with a few examples. For example, an early Unix e-mail client program was named elm, short for "electronic mail." A successor program was recursively named pine, which stands for "Pine Is Not Elm."

That kind of recursion appears in a more recent piece of software, one that runs on Linux and lets you run many Windows programs, sort of a Windows "emulator." Its name is Wine, which, according to a Wine speaker at Comdex Fall 99, is an acronym for "Wine Is Not an Emulator," although I'm not sure why they don't want you to think that it emulates Windows. (He might have been joking about that, as the Wine website, www.winehq.com, doesn't mention in its FAQ what Wine actually stands for.)

you're interested—and he's right that these support ASP-*type* pages. What they *don't* support, however, is VBScript. You write your ASP pages with either PHP or Perl. Understand that I have no problem with Perl at all … it's just that I don't know it. Many, many, *many* people do web (and other) programming with Perl, and it looks like a powerful language. It's just not one I've had time to pick up, and I think I speak for the majority of people who hack together ASP pages in saying that most of us use VBScript.) But my preferences probably don't match those of the general population, given Apache's large market share. Many websites are built around the Perl, Python, and PHP programming languages. And by now, it should come as no surprise when I tell you that development environments for Perl, Python, and PHP ship free of charge with Linux.

DNS Server

If you're going to be part of the Internet (or even part of an intranet), then you must have a way of keeping track of the names of your computers. The system used since 1987 in the Internet world has, of course, been the Domain Name System or DNS. Running a DNS server requires some server software, and the vast majority of the thousands of DNS servers in the world run a Unix program called BIND, which stands for Berkeley Internet Name Domain. Put simply, BIND isn't simply compatible—it *is* the standard. And (I know it's getting monotonous by now, but I include this for the sake of completeness) BIND comes free with Linux.

In comparison with NT and 2000's DNS servers, however, BIND is a mite sparse in the user interface department. (I'll ask your forbearance in advance here, but trust me, this will *also* be a theme that you'll hear over and over again when it comes to basic Linux services.) It doesn't come with a well-designed GUI like NT and 2000, but that's not a crippling defect, and you'll learn how to set up a basic DNS server with Linux in Chapter 8.

Mail Server

The original Internet mail servers were Unix boxes, so it's no surprise that Linux machines can make great mail servers. The basic piece of software that runs most Internet mail servers to this day is a program called Sendmail. There is a Sendmail implementation as part of Linux. But, as Craig observes, it's not just an implementation; "it's the original code, written by the original designer of the protocol." And, you know, it just doesn't get more compatible than that!

Well, that was the good news. Now for the bad news.

Years ago, I wanted to learn Sendmail, so I bought the seminal book on the topic, written in part by the guy who *designed* Sendmail. I *still* haven't finished it. I'm not exaggerating when I say that there are more ways to configure Sendmail than there are stars visible in the sky. It is possible to make it work, and we'll show you how to do that in Chapter 8, but it's not easy.

There is more good news. Several other mail servers are available for Linux that are simpler and easier to use and are becoming increasingly popular. Two of the more common are qmail and Postfix. I am going to focus on Sendmail as it is the "standard," but you should know that you have more choices.

Furthermore, many of you are probably running Microsoft Exchange. I am not an Exchange fan, so you won't hear me singing its praises, but many people who I know and respect tell me that they like its public folders and other features that you won't find in a vanilla Internet mail server. So what does Linux offer you? Well, Microsoft probably won't ever implement Exchange on a Linux box, so you can't expect to use Linux as an Exchange server.

IP Routing and Firewall

Part of the job of setting up an Internet involves the very basic, low-level "plumbing" of making all the computers in your network able to talk with one another—in other words, routing. Another part of the job is building basic precautions to disallow some computers *outside* of your network from talking to your computers—in other words, security and firewalls.

Linux boxes can act as quite powerful and fast IP routers. They support virtually any routing protocol in general use. And, as you read in the previous chapter, there are even implementations of Linux that will run from a floppy disk and that contain Linux's routing software. You can therefore take something as slow as a 486-based computer with 16MB of RAM and make it into a pretty good-performing IP router, using only Linux.

Linux can also make a pretty good basic firewall. It ships with a program called `ipchains` (in the 2.2 kernel) or `iptables` (in the newer 2.4 kernel) that can do not only firewall functions—packet filtering and the like—but also can act as a proxy server.

One of the neat features of Windows 2000 (and Windows 98, Second Edition) is something called Internet Connection Sharing. In case you don't know ICS, it lets you share a high-speed Internet connection with other local machines. So suppose you've shelled out some bucks for a fast DSL connection to the Internet. It's nice, but it only serves one computer. And, if you're like me, you have a couple dozen computers in your house, all hooked up with a network and ... well, okay, even if you're *not* like me, you might have a couple of little ones with computers of their own who want to hog—sorry, I meant *share*—that amazingly fast connection. But how to set things up so that two or more computers can share a single cable modem, DSL, or other Internet connection? Well, ICS is one way.

But in the Linux world, `ipchains` and `iptables` can accomplish the same thing. The whole idea of several systems sharing a single Internet connection gets a different name—*IP masquerading* is the Linux term, you may know it as Network Address Translation or NAT—but in the end analysis it all gets the same thing done.

Education and Development

As you read in the previous chapter, Linux was first developed as a free Unix clone. It includes all of the program development tools you'd find in a commercial Unix system, making Linux a perfect platform for students to learn C, try out operating system enhancements, and the like. Furthermore, Linux's strong closeness to Unix means that Linux is a great low-cost platform for developing Unix programs.

This is a seriously significant part of the answer to the question, "How do people use Linux?" When I asked Craig to enumerate the main uses of Linux, this was the first thing that he listed.

In the long run, this may be the greatest strength of Linux. Suppose that 20 years from now, the majority of the IT professionals learned about operating systems by playing with Linux. Wouldn't that strongly affect their choice of operating systems?

Years ago, Digital Equipment Corporation used to basically give away their computers to educational institutions, reasoning that the computers people learn on are the ones that they'll buy once they get into a decision-making position. It worked moderately well for them; perhaps it'll work for Linux.

Database Server

Many NT shops adopted NT not as a networking platform, but as a database platform. They put NT on their servers and then spent even more money on SQL Server or Oracle. As a result, a lot of database work is being done on NT.

In the first edition of this book, I commented that while there were databases on Linux, none of them had really taken off; in fact, I didn't think there'd ever be a serious market for Linux-based databases. Well, so much for my crystal ball.

There's a free database built on Linux called MySQL that appears to have garnered a *lot* of interest. I know this because I've recently become immersed in the database world as a result of having built my own e-commerce site. I needed to understand how to use web-based scripts to work with SQL databases. Now, of course I was doing my work with VBScript-based ASP pages, as you'd guess from what I wrote a few pages back. But while browsing newsgroups for help with Microsoft SQL Server 2000 programming, I noticed that at least as many people were asking about MySQL as were asking about Access/SQL Server/Microsoft Database Engine. The fact is that there are a *lot* of MySQL-based databases out there. (And in case I've piqued your interest, there is a version of MySQL that runs atop Microsoft operating systems—visit www.mysql.com to find out more.)

Dan furthermore reminds me that Oracle is now selling its database on Linux, and IBM has been pushing Linux on their larger systems in combination with DB2. So clearly Linux as a database engine is not to be sneezed at. And while I am not an expert database programmer by any means, it appears to me that it would be quite possible to build and run an IIS-based web application running on a Microsoft OS, but whose database needs were met by a database server running on a separate Linux box.

Nowadays we have dedicated web terminals, e-mail servers, DNS servers, and the like. Many of them run Linux, but you don't know that because their designers shield you from their Linux underpinnings with a web or other similarly simple interface. Such a computer is often called an "appliance" or a "toaster" because in theory you just buy it, plug it in, and get it to do your bidding with a relatively small amount of fiddling—thus, you hear of "server appliances" or "e-mail toasters" built atop Linux. Perhaps in the near future we'll see "SQL database toasters" running Linux.

Utilize Non-Intel Hardware

The Intel CPUs that most of our PCs are built around, the so-called "$x86$" processors, are wonderful in that there are so many of them around. The years from the 8086's introduction in the late '70s through the present-day Itanium have probably seen Intel ship more than a billion processor chips. That many chips means lots of available programs. And Intel doesn't let any moss grow under its feet as it constantly releases newer and faster versions of its chips, leading to the common lament of PC buyers that "as soon as I buy a computer, it's obsolete."

But Intel is very constrained as to what it can do with each new generation of processor chip; each new chip must not only run faster than the previous ones, it also must *be compatible* with them. That constraint keeps Intel from building the fastest chips possible.

For a while, that seemed a way for Intel's competitors to muscle in on some market share. In the latter part of the '90s, Digital Equipment Corporation (now a part of Hewlett-Packard) built a CPU that ran considerably faster than any Intel offerings at the time. At the same time, IBM and Motorola turned out the PowerPC chip, a CPU that's best known these days for powering Apple Macintoshes but was the first CPU to attain the magic 1GHz processing speed, beating Intel's $x86$ line by over a year. As I write this, AMD is working on a completely new 64-bit chip called the Hammer that might end up faster and more attractive than Intel's own Itanium.

One the one hand, it was neat to know that if you needed *real* power out of a PC-sized computer, you could always switch processors. The only trouble with this thought was that you were a mite limited as to what *software* ran on those unusual but fast processors.

For a few years, Microsoft fed our need for speed by offering versions of NT that ran on the PowerPC and the Alpha, but those versions never succeeded very well, and, in the end, Microsoft abandoned the non-Intel versions, unfortunately. One of the biggest problems with the non-Intel versions of NT was a scarcity of applications. A program built to run under NT on an Intel box would not run on an Alpha box under NT; instead, the application's developer would have to create and sell two versions of the code, one compiled for the Intel *x*86 systems and one compiled for the Alpha systems. (And the PowerPC as well.)

Linux has been implemented on several processors, including the Alpha and the PowerPC. That's nice, you might say, but won't it run into the same problems that NT experienced, the problem of commercial software compiled and available for Linux on an Intel box, but no software compiled and available for Linux on a PowerPC or Alpha? Partially yes, but not to as great an extent as for NT.

You see, in the NT world, 99.9 percent of the applications are distributed in binary form—EXE files rather than C code. And, as I've already observed, EXE files must be compiled to run either on the Alpha or the Intel chips. But that's not the only way to release a program. The alternative method, and one which is fairly widespread in the *Linux* world, is to ship not a binary EXE, but instead the C code, the "source code."

Shipping source code to a customer means that the customer must do a little more work— compile the application—and, of course, shipping the source means that anyone can peek into your code and see how you made the program work. That's the main reason that you don't see too many people shipping source code in the NT world.

But now consider what happens if the application's developer ships the source code rather than binaries: you can run the application on virtually any processor that runs your operating system! For example, I recently went to the Web to get the latest version of Samba. I downloaded the source code, not a binary, and that source code compiled with no trouble on both my Intel boxes and my Alpha computer. Of course, not every application developer in the Linux world ships source code—I don't think you'll see Applixware, Oracle, or Corel shipping source code—but enough do to ensure that anyone running Linux on a non-Intel system will have a good selection of applications to choose from. And that's probably why Linux is still going strong on non-Intel platforms, while Microsoft has ceded the field.

And in case you think I'm just *talking* about non-Intel architectures and Linux, you shouldn't. If you ever send me e-mail, you'll be sending it to an Alpha box running Red Hat Linux and Sendmail.

Linux on the Desktop

Thus far, the examples that I've offered are all about Linux as a server or basic network appliance, such as a router or firewall. But what about Linux on the desktop?

Some people certainly use Linux on the desktop as a replacement for Windows. There are applications, a growing number, that run atop Linux and provide word processing, e-mail, web browsing, spreadsheets, and the like. But on the whole, most people do *not* use Linux on the desktop.

As far as I can see, there are several reasons Linux isn't used much as a desktop workstation:

- Inertia. Most people know Windows or the Mac, consider them "good enough," and aren't thrilled at the idea of learning a new operating system, particularly when it's not clear that switching to Linux will yield compelling benefits.

- Fewer applications. Yes, there are apps for Linux, but the number of those apps is tiny compared to what's available for Windows.

- Linux is more difficult to configure than Windows. Linux enthusiasts claim many benefits for Linux, but the fact remains that getting Linux configured in the first place is tougher than Windows. Tough enough to discourage most desktop users. This improved a bit since my first look at Linux, particularly in the area of GUI tools, although not as much as would have been hoped. Linux's GUIs (tools called GNOME and KDE) have gotten better in that they're nicer-looking and they produce nice visual effects, but they're no easier to try to figure out how to control. An out-of-the-box configuration of KDE 3.0, for example, offers no help for doing tasks as simple as changing display resolution or configuring a NIC.

- Reliability may be critical for a server, but it is not the driving force behind selecting a desktop. Craig claims that Linux is more reliable than Windows and crashes less often than Windows does. That *may* be true—while I have seen that Linux's old-style Unix command-line server code is indeed solid, it hasn't been my experience that Linux *GUI* programs are any less prone to crashing than Windows GUI programs are—but it doesn't matter as much as you might believe. Many users still turn their desktop systems on every morning and off every night. They aren't looking for 24-by-7 reliability. They're looking for applications and ease of use.

- File format incompatibility. While I've spent years working with Word—I'm writing this book in it, for example—I've never liked it. But I use it for a simple reason: the companies that publish my books and magazine articles require my writing submissions in Word format. I spent a lot of time 10 years ago writing things with a different Windows word processor (Ami Pro, a great tool but one that's no longer available), and the time required to convert my writing from Ami to Word introduced far too much expense into the writing process. People expect spreadsheets in XLS format, documents in Word's DOC format, and presentations in PowerPoint's PPT format. I should comment, however, that this has gotten easier since I first looked at Linux. But, understand, that's easier, not easy—moving Office XP documents around between Linux and Windows is still not transparent.

I expect that these things will change with time, but for now I think most people will adopt a "wait and see" approach to putting Linux on their users' desktops. Even Craig, who's an unabashed Linux fan, argues against putting Linux on the desktop *at this time*, reasoning that because Linux is still a bit complex to configure, if you push it on users now you'll see a backlash against Linux—which isn't a positive outcome for anyone who believes in Linux.

There *is*, of course, one group of people who might quite intelligently decide to adopt Linux on the desktop and probably have quite a good experience. Firms that are already using some version of Unix on the desktop wouldn't have very much of a learning curve to overcome and, of course, they'd benefit from Linux's low cost.

In this chapter, I gave you a quick overview of where Linux is (and to an extent, *isn't*) used in the computing world. The overall point? There are many things that Linux can do and do well, and that it's making some inroads into. But there *are* some significant areas of the IT world—mainframe gateways, directory servers —that for some reason Linux has not conquered.

Or, at least, hasn't conquered *yet*.

3

How the Linux
World Operates

Most of the other operating systems you've ever worked with were probably the brainchild of someone or some group of people, all working for the same company. Those people all sought on behalf of that company to create a piece of software that was a commercial product. Building operating systems is time-consuming—forget "man-hours," operating systems consume person-*millennia* in their birth struggles. All of that time is expensive, which is one reason why big commercial concerns are the only entities that can afford to build a new OS.

Well, *usually* the only entities. With Linux, we have a huge operating system basically built as a volunteer effort. How did this happen? How is ongoing Linux development managed? Who "owns" Linux? And just how do all of these Linux proponents expect to make a living *giving away* software? In this chapter, we'll look at those questions.

The Birth and Evolution of Linux

What inspired Linus Torvalds to create Linux in the first place? As so often the case in hobbyist computer projects, he started out to put together a small project...and it just grew.

AT&T Stops Giving Away Unix

The story starts in the late '60s. In 1969, a computer programmer named Ken Thompson at AT&T's Bell Labs (with Dennis Ritchie and many others) developed what eventually became Unix. AT&T was regulated and could not sell software at the time, so they basically gave away copies of Unix, source code and all, to whomever wanted it. In the early 1980s, the U.S. government broke up AT&T's monopoly and AT&T itself, leaving the remaining part of AT&T (which included Bell Labs) able to sell software. As Unix was pretty popular by then, AT&T management figured they'd cash in on Unix's popularity, charging thousands of dollars for what was once free in their 1983 edition of Unix, Unix System V.

In addition to charging for the system, AT&T also forbade universities and colleges from using Unix source code as an example in operating systems classes. This was a devastating event, as many such classes depended on Unix. So a fellow named Andrew Tanenbaum decided to create a substitute. In 1987, Tanenbaum wrote an excellent text, called *Operating Systems,* about how OSs work. He wanted instructors to be able to use it as a teaching text, and he knew it would be helpful if students could experiment with some basic operating systems notions, but again, AT&T forbade doing that with Unix source. So Tanenbaum wrote a "teaching" OS, a simple Unix-like OS built from scratch—no AT&T code. As PCs are cheap, he built this teaching OS on a PC. Tanenbaum called his operating system Minix (pronounced "minn-icks") in recognition of its minimal nature.

Linus Plus Minix Equals Linux

In 1991, a Finnish student named Linus Torvalds was studying operating systems and working with Minix. He decided to learn more about OSs by building his *own* version of Minix from scratch and then to add functionality to it, eventually enhancing it to the point where his expanded Minix would be a useful PC operating system. Partway through the process, he decided that what he wanted to do with Minix would involve so much revamping of Minix that he would do just as well to start from scratch and build a whole new operating system from the ground up. As his name was Linus, he decided to name the new OS Linux. Even though his name is pronounced "lee-nus," he decided to rhyme with Minix—so Linux is pronounced "linn-icks," as I learned while listening to him speak at a Comdex a few years ago. Linus released his OS to the world on October 5, 1991, as a kind of "better Minix." (You can read his initial Internet posting, and the reaction from Minix's author, at http://groups.google.com/groups?selm=1991Oct5.054106.4647%40klaava.Helsinki.FI. It's history in the making; you don't want to miss it.)

But no new operating system is of value unless it has applications. As a techie, Linus knew Unix, and he also knew that there were many, many applications—*free* applications—that ran under Unix. So he decided to build Linux with an identical programming interface to Unix. That meant that Linux would, once finished, let him download source code for any number of Unix programs, compile those programs, and run them on Linux, often with no changes at all to those programs, even though Linux wasn't Unix—so long as the programming interface that the applications rest upon is the same, then the applications have no idea that they're not running Unix. The name of this programming interface, by the way, is POSIX, and in fact NT is equipped with a POSIX interface, albeit not a complete one, which means that you could sometimes even get some of those free "Unix" programs to run on NT!

Once Linus got Linux up and running, he saw that he had done a pretty cool thing, a from-the-ground-up clone of Unix. It lacked some major pieces, including networking and graphics, but it was a basically sound, PC-based operating system that could exploit all of the memory on a 386-based system and that could multitask programs in a pretty stable fashion. But even *that* wasn't the most impressive part of what Linus did.

Understanding Open Source: Linux's "Price"

Here's the impressive part of what Torvalds did: he decided to basically give Linux away, but with a few very significant strings attached. He decided not to charge people to use it, and to let them copy it to their heart's content. But he *didn't* put it in the public domain. Instead, he retained the ownership of Linux so that he could control *how* people copied Linux. Linus lets you use Linux only subject to a *license* that basically says this:

- You are free to copy Linux as much as you want.
- You are free to sell copies of Linux.
- You are free to modify Linux and redistribute it.
- You *may not*, however, restrict the abilities of *others* to copy, modify, or distribute your modified Linux. In other words, if you come up with some terrific "fix" to Linux that makes it run 100 times faster, then you're welcome to sell this amazingly fast Linux, but you cannot forbid your customers from copying and giving away your amazingly fast Linux.
- When you distribute a copy of Linux, modified or not, then you must make the source code available. So once you come up with that amazingly fast Linux code, you can't just compile your Linux and give that away, retaining the secrets of how you made Linux faster. You must offer the source code as well—you must share your secrets.

This license is a modification of the standard copyright provisions, so Linuxers, inveterate punsters that they are, often refer to this license as a "copyleft." (Get it? copy*right*...copy-*left*? Bet these guys are a laff riot at parties.)

Notice that this license applies to the operating system only, not to applications. Just because the Linux OS operates in what is called an "open source" fashion—"open source" meaning "you must make the source code available"—doesn't mean that applications for Linux must be open source. There's nothing stopping someone from offering a video driver for Linux without having to release the source code for the driver. There's nothing stopping Corel from creating a version of WordPerfect that runs on Linux, selling that version of WordPerfect, and not releasing the source code. Furthermore, many of the hundreds of free programs that come with Linux do not have a copyleft license. Some *are* public domain.

Linux, the Prequel: GPL and GNU

The particularly interesting thing about the modified copyright that Torvalds holds for Linux is what has been called the copyleft's "viral" nature. Sure, you can use Linux as a base for some other project. And the fact that it is an already-functioning operating system, that you can obtain its source code for no charge and use it as a launching pad for another OS product, are all very attractive points. But once you incorporate *any* Linux code (licensed under the GPL mentioned below) into your product —one measly line of code—then you are bound by the copyleft to leave the source code of *your* resulting product open and accessible to the users of your product. In other words, make free use of this open source code—but if you do, you must open the source of whatever you made with it.

But Linus Torvalds didn't invent the terms of his Linux copyright, nor was he the first person to use those terms. The copyright terms that you've just read about are generally known as the GNU Public License or GPL.

For GPL's story, let's return to the mid '80s, when the government deregulated AT&T and AT&T started charging for Unix. Having to pay for Unix irritated a lot of hackers, as they'd become somewhat dependent on Unix. They viewed dimly the prospect of suddenly having to spend tons of money on Unix licenses, and then being restricted on what they could do with the source code to that Unix … *if* they got any source at all.

Nor was their annoyance merely born of a habit of openness. Unix gurus built hundreds of programs for Unix and then gave them away to the Unix community. Many of the best features of Unix didn't originate in AT&T; they originated in some of the very shops that AT&T now wanted to charge a king's ransom for Unix.

One longtime Unix user, Richard Stallman of MIT, responded by gathering together volunteer programmers to build a completely new Unix, free of any vendors who would hide the source code. He called the effort to build this open-source Unix the "GNU" project. (It's pronounced "g-new;" the "g" is not silent.) GNU is a recursive acronym standing for "GNU's Not Unix." He also formulated the GPL that Linus Torvalds used for Linux and that many others have employed for tens of thousands of open source programs. (By the way, please note that the history of Unix, and of the open source movement, could go on for volumes and volumes; what you just read is the briefest summary.)

Although the fantastic success of Linux has attracted a lot more attention to Linus Torvalds and his operating system than Richard Stallman has enjoyed with GNU, it's only fair to point out that many, many of the utilities and programs shipped with Linux were developed by the GNU volunteers. Remember, that's one of the reasons that Torvalds put a Unix programming interface on Linux: so that he could exploit all of the free Unix-compatible software out there; much of that is GNU software. Without GNU, there wouldn't have been a Linux. In fact, according to Stallman, Linux *is* the completed version of GPL Unix, and he refers to Linux as "GNU Linux."

The Other Free Unix: BSD

Linux users have yet another source of free Unix software that you'll hear mentioned: the Berkeley Software Distribution, or BSD. As you've already read, one of the reasons that Unix is so powerful is because many individuals and groups contributed programs and bug fixes to it, and one of the most significant contributors since as far back as 1975 was the University of California, Berkeley.

Origin of BSD

In early 1978, several Berkeleyites released a set of useful utilities for Unix that they called the Berkeley Software Distribution. Over the years, BSD grew to more than just utilities. For example, 3BSD, the third edition, was a full-featured version of Unix that incorporated virtual memory. Sun Microsystems' Unix, Solaris, was originally based on BSD. BSD's Version 4.0 was a fully 32-bit version of Unix, available before AT&T had even released a 32-bit version! With government funding, Berkeley created version 4.1, the first version of Unix to incorporate TCP/IP. The release of 4.1BSD in 1982 both created the foundation of what is now the Internet, and cemented Unix's place in that Internet.

But BSD Unix *did* partially incorporate AT&T's source code, and so anyone wanting to "stay legal" needed to pay AT&T some money when using BSD. So yet *another* group of volunteer programmers labored away at creating yet *another* AT&T-free version of Unix and, on November 1, 1988, the first no-license version appeared, named BSD Networking Release 1.

The Linux before Linux

Here, then, was a full-featured, cost-free implementation of Unix, available in 1988. In some senses, BSD was the Linux *before* Linux. If it hadn't been for a bit of bad luck for BSD, then this might have been a book about BSD, and you'd never have heard about Linux.

Come to think of it, if there had been a reliable, inexpensive, 32-bit version of Unix without any fear of lawsuits in 1988, you might have never even heard of *NT*. But that didn't happen.

AT&T Releases the Hounds

While AT&T hadn't objected to people like Andrew Tanenbaum cloning Unix in his Minix, AT&T saw BSD as a real threat and unleashed the legal beagles on the BSD folks, alleging that they'd infringed upon AT&T's license. The suit wasn't settled until 1994 and left BSD free to distribute as it pleased. But the suit had robbed the BSD-ers of six years of potential market growth.

While the lawsuit was going on, the existence of that suit made people reluctant to get too attached to BSD, even *if* it was a high-quality implementation. Many programmers who might have helped expand BSD were probably attracted to Linux partly because of BSD's legal troubles, but that wasn't the only reason; much of Linux's success is often attributed to Linus Torvald's easygoing and engaging personality.

BSD Today: More Free Software for Linux Users

But BSD isn't dead, not by any means. Nor is it off the Unix radar screen—Yahoo, UUNet, MindSpring, and CompuServe use BSD, and Macintosh OS/X from Apple is based on BSD.

There is also a free version of BSD around for Intel processor systems, called FreeBSD. The utilities associated with FreeBSD are a very big source of free Unix—which means *Linux*—programs. In fact, some Linux distributions seem to favor the BSD versions of some basic utility programs over the GNU versions.

> **NOTE** Again, I am simplifying for the sake of space. Dan points out that there are three BSDs around and refers me (and anyone else who's interested) to a lecture about the BSDs; find it at www.freebsddiary.org/talks/oclug/.

There is, however, a small but significant difference between the license used by the BSD folks versus the GPL. You may, as you've just read, use any code from a GPL-licensed program in an application of your own, but if you do, then you must make the source code generally available. The BSD license differs because it lets you do *anything* with BSD code. That means that you could take a nice-but-unpolished piece of code licensed under BSD, clean it up, and offer it as a commercial program that you sell—and you needn't offer the source code.

Why Open Source Is So Important

Before going on, I want to take a moment to return to the issue of open source. In my opinion, the single most significant fact about Linux is its open source license. While I wouldn't argue that commercial software firms should just give away their products for no charge, I think there are some extremely powerful benefits that both buyers and sellers of software would gain if every copy of NT or 2000 contained that source code.

Users Can Fix Bugs Themselves

If every owner of a copy of an operating system has a copy of the source code, they can approach bugs differently. Right now, if I stumble over what looks like a bug in NT, I must *first* prove that it is indeed a bug. How do I do this? By putting NT on a variety of machines and trying to reproduce the bug on those machines. Once I have a fairly repeatable set of undesirable outcomes to a given set of inputs, I feel confident enough to get on the phone and pay Microsoft $245 for a "per-incident" service call. The result that I usually get is confirmation of the bug and a suggestion that perhaps the next Service Pack will fix it.

But if I had the NT source code, a bit more money, and the will, I could hire a programming expert. She could find the bug, isolate it, and prove beyond a shadow of a doubt that there is, indeed, a defect in NT. But then she could take things a bit further and fix the bug. I could then, if I wanted to, share the bug and its patch with Microsoft—I'm assuming here a license that only lets me see the source and modify it for my own uses, not a full-blown GPL go-ahead-and-distribute-your-own-fixed-version license—and then hope that Microsoft would share them with the world.

Users Can Add Features

For years, people wanted a disk defragmentation program for NT, but Microsoft didn't include one. So Executive Software spent a lot of time reverse-engineering NTFS's drive organization structure. Had they had the source, however, they could have gotten their Diskeeper product to market much more quickly and would probably have ended up with an even more reliable product.

Keeping the source a secret is very much like selling cars with the hoods welded shut. Hey, I own the silly car, I want to decide what I do with it! Users with the source could build terrific utilities—which in turn would strengthen NT in the marketplace (to use NT as an example).

Third Parties Can Offer "White Box" Support

When you hire an NT consultant like me to do some job, you're not hiring me for my inner, source-code knowledge of NT; I don't have that. I've never seen the source, nor am

I likely ever to. What you're paying for is my empirical experience with the "black box" behavior of NT: push *this* button, and *that* light flashes. You're likely to pay for my time because my suggestions based on my experience will save you far more time.

But imagine how much better a job I could do as a support person if I had access to the source code. *Anyone* could do a top-drawer job of supporting NT, if she wanted to badly enough. Of course, the software's designer—Microsoft—would always have the edge, as the program's developers are right there and would be very facile in their ability to recognize and resolve problems.

This Isn't a New Idea

The final reason why open source is a good idea in my mind is that, simply put, *this isn't a new idea*. Back in the early '70s, I started working with computers in my last year of high school and then at university. At my university, they ran Digital PDP computers, an IBM 360, and later a Univac mainframe. Each of these computers came with operating systems, and each of those operating systems came with the source code. People wouldn't even *dream* of buying a mainframe's OS without the source.

IBM's mainframe operating system MVS is considered pretty solid, as is Digital's (now Compaq's) VMS. But these products started life as wobbly, unreliable, buggy pieces of code, often shipped late. What happened between their release and now? Why is it that you can run an IBM mainframe for months or perhaps years between reboots? A lot of the reason is the users: over the years, users have fixed IBM and Digital's bugs *for* them. Any vendor who revealed its source could benefit in this way. To paraphrase Linus Torvalds, no bug is hard to find when millions of eyeballs are looking for it.

But wouldn't any open source vendor open itself to theft by competitors by revealing its source code? Couldn't another vendor just steal a large chunk of code and insert it in their product? That is certainly a risk, but then if *that* vendor were open source as well, then the theft would be easily detected. And if you had a choice between two roughly equivalent products, but one was open source, which would you buy? The open source product, I'd guess, so the sneak thief wouldn't benefit anyway.

I don't know whether or not Linux will be the most-used operating system in the world in 10 years. But I believe that if Linux accomplishes nothing else, then having brought open source *back* to the computer business earns it a place in Operating System Heaven.

How Linux Evolves

All right, so let's say we buy this open source stuff. As you've already read, Linus Torvald's original Linux offering was pretty minimal. But Linux nowadays is a completely full-featured system, and Linus didn't have to do all of that coding. The majority of the

Linux code was written by others, volunteer programmers who just want to see Linux become more powerful. But how is it organized? Five gazillion people all come up with their ideas for a wonderful new operating system and send their patches to … who? Linus? Red Hat? Someone else? Is Linus Torvalds some kind of benevolent dictator? If someone writes a neat new hack for Linux, who says whether or not it goes into the "official" version of Linux? And suppose Linux needed to change in some fundamental way, perhaps by moving from a 32-bit architecture to a 64-bit one; how would that happen? And isn't that a weakness of Linux over NT, as Bill Gates can simply observe a flaw in NT and *direct* his programmers to do something about it?

Linus Only Controls the Kernel

When you get a copy of Linux from a Linux vendor like Red Hat Software, you get a lot of code that Linus has nothing to do with. You might get some application software, like the StarOffice suite of desktop applications. You almost certainly get the BIND DNS program, the Apache web server, and the Sendmail mail server. You get a graphical user interface like KDE and/or GNOME. None of those are Linus's concern, officially. Those are all just other programs that either someone else has written, that work on Linux, and that the commercial Linux vendor has included for your convenience. Most of the programs are open source code that the authors do not charge fees for, but some might be commercial software, and you might not get the source code for them.

The part that is the heart of Linux, however, is a piece called the *kernel*. Every operating system has a kernel. The kernel does things like memory management (keeping track of what application owns each part of memory so that two apps don't accidentally damage each other's data), multitasking, communications between different processes in a computer, handling multiple processors on systems that have more than one CPU, and similar tasks. *That's* what Linus (and some close lieutenants) "controls."

Suppose I get a great idea to modify the memory management part of Linux, something that will run more quickly and use less space. So I work feverishly to implement my changes and build my own modified Linux. I test it and am eventually satisfied that it works well. How do I get my changes into the "official" Linux kernel?

Anyone can send a suggested patch to Linus. He, or someone from a group of other volunteers who help him oversee kernel developments, review the change and either bless it or reject it.

Why Doesn't Linux Splinter into Hundreds of Versions?

Let's take that example a bit further. Suppose Torvalds & Co. reject my changes. Embittered, I slink back to my lonely developer's garret, lick my wounds, and plot revenge.

Rereading the GPL, I realize that there is nothing keeping me from putting my Linux with the modified memory management module on the Internet for anyone to download. So I do it. Now there are two Linuxes out there: Linus's version and mine. Won't this introduce confusion into the Linux world?

Well, it could, but it probably won't. First of all, let's define a term: *forking*. By releasing a modification of Linux that is different from the official Linux kernel, I have created a "code fork." (Actually, there's another meaning of "fork" in the Unix/Linux world. When one program starts up another program, Unixers wouldn't say that the first program had "started" the second program; they'd say that it "forked" the second program.) One could imagine dozens, hundreds, or thousands of forks appearing in a short time, leaving Linux a morass of mildly incompatible versions. It tends not to happen for several reasons.

First, there is a lot of peer pressure in the Linux universe not to fork. Unix forked years ago, splitting between the BSD and the AT&T releases, and the infighting that resulted hurt Unix's overall acceptance and growth, in the opinion of many Unix users. Basically, about a dozen Unix vendors have been waging religious wars against each other for the past 10 or so years, fighting to divide up Unix's small share of the market, leaving Microsoft to flourish. As Linux is more than just a product for many Linux users, there's a real fervor to avoid anything that could slow Linux's market acceptance, and forking would be a market disaster.

Second, the scenario that I play out probably wouldn't happen, because Linus is no dummy; he wants Linux to be good more than I likely would.

Third, forking would deprive me of Linux's benefits. When the next official Linux was released, it would no doubt contain a ton of bug fixes and performance improvements. But my forked Linux wouldn't have that stuff, unless I went to all of the trouble to go reimplement my memory management changes on the *new* version of Linux. And, of course, I'd have to do that *every single time a new Linux kernel appeared*. That would get old quickly.

I should mention that there *is*, however, one place where a kind of low-level forking goes on all of the time: in research and educational institutions. As you've already read, it's wonderful for teachers to have a full working operating system complete with all of the source code to let students use to experiment with OSs. And some firms with specialized needs might decide that they could meet those needs by creating a specialized kernel just for themselves. Sure, there would be the trouble required to reimplement their changes with every new version of Linux, but they might decide not to upgrade constantly, and that trouble might still be far cheaper than finding a commercial OS that solves their problem. One interesting case is NASA, which created a specialized version of Linux that lets many Linux boxes work together over a network to solve large computing problems. Doing this, NASA was able to replace some supercomputers costing tens of millions with less than a quarter million dollars' worth of PCs running this Linux modified to allow clustering. And as the Linux community is never slow to incorporate a new idea, these clustering concepts are finding their way into the standard Linux kernel.

How Linux Grows

But suppose that sometime soon the computing world all decides that 64-bit processing is the only way to go. Once Intel's Itanium processor has been on the market for a year or so, its price drops to just a few dollars and, in no time at all, virtually every new PC has a 64-bit processor—and we want to start exploiting that power. But Linux is a 32-bit operating system, right? So how does Linus nudge his volunteer programmers to rework the entirety of Linux to run in 64-bit mode?

In any number of ways. First, as you've probably guessed, there is no shortage of people ready, willing, and able to help out. Second, remember all of those research projects? The chances are good that there would already be someone with an experimental version of Linux running in 64-bit—and, in fact, there is. There has been a 64-bit version of Linux running on the Alpha processor for a couple of years now. One could imagine a firm like Red Hat developing a major improvement. (IBM throws a lot of money at Linux development.) Of course, their work would then be open-sourced, so their competition would benefit from the work as well. But that's the price to pay for the benefits of open source.

Ultimately, much of what drives the Linux programming hordes is a desire for their OS to remain one of the best—simple pride of workmanship. For example, when I first looked at Linux in late 1999/early 2000, a company named Mindcraft put the Linux world into a stir. They'd just published a series of benchmarks that demonstrated that Linux ran terribly on multiprocessor systems.

The original response of the Linux community was to call for Mindcraft's collective head for having the temerity to shine a light on a Linux weakness. People were even more irate when it turned out that Microsoft had hired Mindcraft to run and publicize the benchmarks. "Aha!" they said, "Numbers tainted by the attar of Redmond bias!" But just about anyone could reproduce the numbers, so while Microsoft's surreptitious funding of the benchmarks was a bit sleazy, the numbers told an important tale.

Ultimately, the Linux community's answer was to buckle down and redesign the kernel to make Linux run better on multiprocessor systems. It took about 15 months longer than anyone expected, but the 2.4 version of the Linux kernel arrived in January 2001.

It'd be one thing to hear that NT had a multiprocessing bug of some kind and that Microsoft sent their army of coders into a room and didn't let them out until they solved the problem—coding NT is their *day job*. But to tell an army of volunteers that their built-in-their-spare-time operating system was seriously flawed and needed a major piece rebuilt from the ground up might discourage many people. The fact that they got it done in about the same time frame that Microsoft might have fixed a similar NT kernel bug is impressive as well.

And here's an interesting thought: as time goes on, some of Windows development looks more and more like Linux. Linus Torvalds is fond of enumerating several reasons to use Linux, one of which is that with Linux, "The bug report comes with the fix included." That's a bit of an exaggeration, but *just* a bit—big nasty bugs get stomped when discovered. Whether because of the greater incidence of worms and viruses on the Internet or due to a bit of "Linux envy," it's certainly a fact that more and more Microsoft bug reports *also* come with a bug fix.

Commercial Linux: Understanding Linux Distributions

So we've seen that Linux is available free and, while I haven't mentioned it yet, it is the case that you can download a copy of Linux from any number of websites for free. But a casual perusal of the Linux world shows that despite the fact that Linux is free, *several* companies are *selling* Linux. How can this be?

Well, first of all, you'd buy Linux on a CD-ROM for the convenience. Downloading several hundreds of megabytes of Linux files off the Internet with a 56K modem just isn't a realistic possibility and, in that light, sending Red Hat 60 bucks so that they'll put the seven CDs' worth of files onto CDs for me doesn't sound like a bad idea. (Or you can go to www.cheapbytes.com and pay them about 10 bucks for the CDs.)

Second, recall that there are a whole lot of programs out there that aren't "officially" part of Linux proper, but which are pretty useful to have around—utilities, editors, games, server software, and the like. You *could* download a Linux kernel from one place and then go find the GNU and BSD files in another place and so on, but again it's a fair amount of work and download time. Additionally, you typically don't download ready-to-run copies of these free programs; instead, you download their *source code*, and then you have to compile these programs before you can use them.

Third, setting up Linux by hand—copying files onto a hard disk, making the hard disk bootable by Linux, and the like—is no fun, and unless someone adds a "Setup" program to your Linux files, then that's what you'll have to do: set it up by hand. We in the Windows world are used to having nice, pretty, graphically based installation programs that ask us a few questions and then let us just go away for a while as the Setup program installs our operating system. But in the Linux world, such a convenience is an add-on.

Several vendors make it easier to get Linux by putting together what is called a "Linux distribution," "distribution," or, as the Linux insiders say it, "distro." Distribution vendors gather the basic Linux files, get the additional free programs and compile them, collect whatever documentation is available, and put it all on a CD. They then typically sell that CD for under $50, a fairly reasonable deal.

Other vendors sweeten the pot further with extra programs that they've created themselves. Or they include commercial programs, such as perhaps an office suite like Star-Office or Applixware. And the most important thing that a Linux distribution can offer to many people is support.

Red Hat

Perhaps the best-known distribution is Red Hat. They offer high-quality support and do more than just redistribute free programs—for example, they created the Red Hat Package Manager, a system that aims to make installing commercial applications on Linux as easy as it is in the Windows world. Red Hat is also the Linux chosen by most corporations, which is why I focused the revised version of this book on Red Hat instead of Mandrake (which I based most of the first edition's examples on.)

Red Hat packages Linux in several ways, from Red Hat 7.3 Personal ($60) to Red Hat Professional ($200) to Red Hat Linux Advanced Server (they're not advertising the price on Advanced, so you know it's expensive). Interestingly enough, the first two are basically the same product except for service—buyers of Professional get 60 days of telephone support, and in my experience it is pretty good support. That might be a bit confusing for the first-time buyer, as the Red Hat web pages pretty strongly hint that Personal is a "workstation" operating system while Professional is a "server" operating system. That's not true at all, of course—Linus and the boys don't artificially separate desktop from server OSs, and in fact it's as easy to install (for example) Sendmail atop 7.3 Personal as it is 7.3 Professional.

Don't be scared away by that cost, however. If you have decent bandwidth, then it's still possible to download the Red Hat operating system and its manuals for free from Red Hat's website, `www.redhat.com`.

You can, alternatively, spend $1500 per year for Red Hat's Advanced Server support. For $1500 per year, they'll help you with just about anything Linux-related, including the "add-ons" like the web, DNS, Samba, and similar servers. Sounds like a lot of money? Ask Microsoft six questions a year and you've run up that large a tab—by the seventh question every year, Red Hat Advanced Server starts to look like a good deal.

Red Hat includes all of the usual suspects: the web, mail, database, and DNS servers, as well as a web browser (Netscape) and a copy of StarOffice. Red Hat offers both popular Linux GUIs, GNOME and KDE, offering GNOME by default. (Setting up KDE is simple, however, in contrast to Red Hat 6's Setup routines.) Advanced Server includes clustering and higher-level support.

One of the things that I like best about Red Hat, however, is that it allows you to forgo a GUI altogether during the initial setup—I prefer to do it later. (One of the great strengths of Linux, in my opinion, is the optional nature of the GUI. GUIs burn up RAM and CPU horribly; I wish I could run my Windows 2000/.NET Servers without a GUI. Linux lets me fire it up only when I need it to do some GUI-based administrative task, and, of course, in Linux it's often not necessary at all to go to the GUI.) Additionally, the Red Hat Setup is far better than it was in the 6.*x* days.

In general, Red Hat's pretty good but suffers in a few areas—areas that just about every Linux distribution suffers in—getting various kinds of hardware to work. I'll cover these in the next chapter, but in brief you'll find that getting all of the hardware in your computer to work under Red Hat is a bit more challenging then it is under Windows. But it's getting better; Red Hat's Setup routine has matured tremendously.

Other Distributions

Red Hat isn't the only distribution around; a look at www.linux.org/dist/list.html showed 164 distros in total. A few stand out:

Caldera Systems   Offers a Linux distribution under the trade name OpenLinux. They sell it in both a desktop-oriented version (OpenLinux Workstation) and a server version (OpenLinux Server). Caldera's focus once seemed to be getting Linux on the desktop rather than on the server, but nowadays their website seems more oriented to just selling *something*. I saw a lot of that when revising the book, as I wrote the first version back in 2000, when people were throwing dot-com money at any Linux shop that would stand still. 2002 entrepreneurs are clearly a bit more flinty-eyed, so Linux purveyors are forced to spread their nets a bit wider. Caldera has an attractive GUI-based setup program that you can even start from inside Windows. Furthermore, they have solved the problem of setting up your graphics board, monitor, and X Windows with a routine that is far and away the best graphics setup program I've seen on Linux. Caldera also includes all of the usual server and network appliance programs. They ask $100 for the workstation version, $249 for the server.

Debian   An organization that seeks to both develop Linux and keep it commercial-free. To that end, they do not sell any Linuxes, although they have no problem with *others* selling their Linux. The name suggests that the people who put Debian together live somewhere in the constellation Cygnus, but the name is just a combination of the names of the couple who founded Debian, Deb and Ian Murdock. Like Red Hat, Debian is developing essential add-ons for the Linux world, including an application installer ("package manager" in Linux-speak) that is somewhat incompatible with Red Hat's. In my experience, Debian had the most cryptic setup program. I wouldn't recommend it to a Linux novice.

Slackware   One of the old-time original Linux distributions and one of my favorites. They were shipping version 8.1 as I wrote this. Slackware has an older-style, non-GUI "feel" to its setup program that at first might seem off-putting to a non-techie. But once you get past caring whether you're using a GUI—and as I've already explained, I'm really not much of a GUI fan, and *extremely* dislike the fact that NT, 2000, and several Linux distributions require you to get the GUI up and running before you can get anything done—you find that the help files are quite well done. They read like text that has been written not only by a seasoned veteran but by someone who has helped a lot of newbies get past understanding the basics and has incorporated that experience into the help files. Slackware's CD price is $40. Even better, they haven't fallen into the "let's call it a Server distro and charge them $10,000 for it" mode that some of the others have. And of course like other distros, Slackware includes all the standard useful Linux programs to make your system a DNS server, mail server, web server, or the like.

Slackware does not try to force you into using a GUI, but that doesn't mean that it lacks for tools to assist you in setting up your system. For example, many Linux distributions require a fair amount of knowledge to get an Ethernet card up and configured properly with a host name, DNS server, IP address, gateway, and subnet mask. Slackware, in contrast, just asks that you type `netconfig`, and you're led through the process. And it's a small item, but Slackware also lets you try out several dozen screen fonts, something I've not seen any other Linux distribution do.

SuSE   A Linux distribution based out of Germany. One of its great strengths is that it isn't just an English-language version of Linux that you can, with enough knowledge and sweat, work in a language other than English.

SuSE is also reputed to be a "techie's" implementation of Linux, and my experience with it would seem to agree with that. For example, I never *did* get my Ethernet card to work on it, despite grabbing a copy of the latest SuSE now and then. Many Linux aficionados swear by it, however, so it may just be something that I'm missing.

UnitedLinux   Not really a distribution, but, as it has gotten a bunch of press recently, let me explain what it is, and you can figure out whether or not you care.

The realization in the past two years that (1) Linux isn't just a hacker/hobbyist operating system, but that (2) businesses have absolutely zero interest in the politics or religion of how one "should" use Linux, led Red Hat to offer its Advanced Server.

Other distros, realizing that (1) the dot-com money is gone forever, and (2) businesses are where the money is, started to say, "Hmmm ... what do we do?" So four big distros—SuSE, Caldera, Conectiva (a Brazilian distro), and TurboLinux (a distro that in theory is intended to aim at high-end computing and reliability but that I found to be hampered by a bunch of terrible setup programs)—have banded together to mount some competition to Red Hat and make a few bucks (hmmm, given that SuSE and Conectiva are one half of the deal, I guess I should add "euros and reals" to that sentence) in the process.

They plan to release some kind of unified product in late 2002.

Which Linux Should I Get?

But these aren't your only options for Linux distributions. There are other Linux distributions as well that I haven't covered only because I didn't have the time to try them out. The important point to get out of this is that your idea of the best Linux and mine may well differ, and an equally important point is that Linux allows the flexibility for more than one Linux distro to exist—one of Linux's neatest features.

There's no "best" Linux implementation. Corporations seem to have settled on Red Hat because it has managed to do the best job of conveying the appearance of a "real" company, with a decent support infrastructure, certification program, and so on. Their Setup program is still, in my opinion, inferior to some of the other distros—Caldera's is pretty nifty in comparison —but Red Hat is the market leader at the moment. Slackware intends to be a good techie's implementation, built for someone who wants to create a Linux-based server environment but doesn't want to spend a lot of time messing with the GUI and with making hardware work. Caldera wants to appeal to the vast number of people born and bred, so to speak, on reliable GUI setup routines, and I think they still have the easiest "just ask me questions and let me click the answers" kind of setup. But other big distros are creeping up on them: Red Hat's graphical Setup program, which was horrible in version 6.*x*, is merely annoying in 7.*x*, and I'm sure will be considerably more polished in its next incarnation.

So, again, what's the best distro for you? I dunno. But here's my suggestion. Go to www.cheapbytes.com; they're an outfit that collects distributions, burns them onto CDs, and sells them for really cheap—typically under 10 bucks. Get a bunch of them and try them out ... you'll probably find one or two that you like better.

On the other hand, for the rest of *this* book you'll mainly hear of Red Hat 7.3. No matter *which* distribution you get, however, I hope that by now Craig, Dan, and I have excited you enough about the possibilities of Linux that you'll get *someone's* Linux. That would mean that your next job would be getting to work on your PC—and you'll see in the next chapter how to do that.

4

Getting Red Hat 7.3 on Your System

By now, I hope I've interested you enough in Linux that you're feeling a little itchy to try it out. In this chapter, I'll give you some overview advice on installing Linux on your system. As I've already said, this edition of the book focuses on Red Hat Linux, specifically the 7.3 Personal edition, so if you want to follow along exactly, then you might want to buy or download a copy.

What to Expect

Before I get into the nitty-gritty of the chapter, I should in good conscience warn you that Linux setup routines—and every distribution's installation program is different—are pretty rough-edged, compared to what you're used to if you've been installing Windows, NT, 2000, or XP systems. Red Hat is, unfortunately, no exception to that.

The Good News

But I don't want to sound negative here. Let me make very clear that two things *have* improved when it comes to setting up Red Hat since the book's first version: the Setup program and the documentation for setting up your Red Hat system. Two years ago, the Red Hat 6.0 Setup program ran terribly in graphical mode—*wouldn't* run in graphical mode on most systems—and the text mode Setup program would crash over things as silly as the type of your mouse. In contrast, the 7.3 Setup program runs equally well in GUI or text mode, and I have been completely unable to find a single computer that Red Hat's graphical Setup fails on. (That doesn't mean that I haven't found a computer that Red Hat's *GUI* won't run on. For reasons I'll discuss later, it turns out that on some computers, Red Hat's Setup cannot figure out how to run day-to-day in GUI mode even though the Setup program itself runs fine in GUI mode!)

Red Hat's Setup manual, a small, 140-page printed book that Red Hat includes with the Personal edition (it's also online at `http://www.redhat.com/docs/manuals/linux/RHL-7.3-Manual/install-guide/` or downloadable in HTML or PDF format at `http://www.redhat.com/docs/manuals/linux`) is a very nice treatment of how to do different kinds of setups and how to troubleshoot a fair amount of problems. I *strongly* recommend that you give it a read if Setup is giving you heartburn over something.

Furthermore, you might consider buying the so-called Professional edition of Red Hat 7.3. It's $200 instead of $60, and as far as I can see you don't get any more files or programs, but for that extra $140 you get 60 days of help from Red Hat's tech support folks in getting your systems up and running. Imagine that… for $245 Microsoft will answer *one* question. For $140, Red Hat will answer as many as you can ask, either through the Web or over the phone. I gave this a shot while working on this book because I was curious to see how good the support is… and it's quite good. If you have never installed a Linux system and really need to be assured that someone will hold your hand when you run up against one of Linux's many brick walls, then you should seriously consider buying Professional. (On the other hand, I *really* hope that this book will answer all of your questions!)

The Bad News

Where Microsoft systems are pretty good at detecting hardware, choosing and loading the correct drivers, and then activating the systems that utilize that hardware, Linux isn't always good at that. That's where Setup will drive you crazy. Linux setup programs (including Red Hat) *are* good at detecting and handling standard mice, keyboards, floppy drives, EIDE hard disks, SCSI hard disks, CD-ROMs, DVD-ROMs, USB devices, and parallel and serial ports (COMs 1–4, at least). Linux setup programs will give you varying degrees of trouble, however, with:

- PCMCIA network cards
- Sound boards
- Video capture boards
- Wireless network cards
- FireWire devices
- Video boards and graphics in general

In some cases (video, sound, and PCMCIA NICs), the problem lies in automatic detection. In other cases (FireWire and 802.11b wireless networks), Red Hat says that the hardware simply isn't supported in this release. (I'll show you how to make at least one wireless NIC—the Orinoco—work, however.) Some things that you might expect to cause trouble, however, might offer no trouble at all; here I'm thinking of EIDE CD burners.

> **NOTE**   But lest I scare you away, let me reiterate an important point: yes, Red Hat's Setup routine is less polished than Microsoft setup routines, and you will have some trouble with some kinds of hardware, *but* you can get around most of the hardware issues with a minimum amount of work, *and* Red Hat's Setup routine is much, much improved over the vintage that I last wrote up back in 1999 and 2000.

Your Toughest Linux Install Tasks

More specifically, there are in my experience four things that will give you the most trouble in getting Linux on your system:

Partitioning Your Disk for Linux   You'll need to partition your drive to install Linux, as Linux doesn't usually install on FAT or NTFS partitions; rather, it uses a file system type called EXT3. If you want to keep your existing Microsoft OS on your system and dual-boot Linux, then you'll see that Linux has a couple of nice utilities that allow multibooting. They are called LILO (LInux LOader) and GRUB (GRand Unified Bootloader), and Red Hat can install them quite competently—but you still need enough space on your hard disk for Linux's partitions.

Starting the Installation   In the perfect world, you'd just pop Installation CD 1 into your CD drive and reboot the system, it'd boot from the CD, and all would be well. Some systems, however, don't seem to recognize that the Red Hat CDs are bootable. The answer is to create Linux boot floppies; you'll see how to do that later in this chapter.

NIC Configuration   While PCMCIA NICs are the most troublesome, you'll find that some distributions have trouble making even common, big-name NICs like 3Com's PCI-bus 10/100 Ethernet card (3C905B-TX) function. In other cases, I've run into Linux distributions that can activate the NIC and even obtain an IP address from a DHCP server, but not *all* of the information from the DHCP server. You'll learn in this chapter how to do just a tiny bit of scripting to wake up your NICs and get them working for you. NIC configuration under Linux is much better than it was in 2000, however.

X Window Configuration   This is essential if you're going to run any Linux graphical tools, but frankly there are no trouble-free X configuration tools. I must say that I'm pretty surprised that this is still the case. I honestly thought that by 2002, Linux setup programs would have figured out how to detect video cards and install the proper graphical systems for them... but Red Hat's Setup program still guesses wrong about a quarter of the time, and when it guesses wrong, it can't get the GUI to work without some help from you. Again, let me be clear: this is still much better than what I saw two years ago!

You'll see more about all of these issues in the rest of the chapter. But before getting into the meat of the chapter, let me suggest one more thing to be aware of: Red Hat's installation program takes *forever* to run. I'm not kidding—if you try to install the entire Red Hat 7.3 OS and all of its attendant programs, it can take three hours to feed CDs to the computer (there are three of them) and wait for files to copy.

Preparing for the Install

Before you even pull out your Linux distribution CD, you need to do two things. First, you have to do a bit of hardware inventory on your computer system and, second, you have to create some free, unpartitioned space on your hard disk for Linux's use.

Making Space for Linux

You can convince Windows, NT, 2000, and even OS/2 to coexist on a single FAT drive, but most Linux distros won't join the party. It can certainly read and write FAT drives (and NTFS and FAT32 drives), but it prefers to be installed on a drive partitioned in its own format, called the EXT3 format. (Again, a few distros will live on a FAT drive, but as far as I know none of the big ones will—Red Hat included.)

The easiest way to make room for Linux is to just let it take your whole hard disk, but of course that has the possibly undesirable side effect of destroying any data on that hard disk. If you have a machine that you keep around for testing things, then go ahead, turn the whole drive over to Linux. But if not, you'll need to make space.

TIP   But how *much* space? I strongly recommend clearing out about 4 to 5 gigabytes, with a minimum of about 2 GB. Choosing 4 or 5 gigs will allow you to choose the "install everything" option on Red Hat, which will take about 3.6GB. Having everything on the hard disk will make experimenting with Linux easier, as everything's then at your fingertips.

Option 1: Re-create Partitions

Most people know that you cannot resize an existing disk partition with the tools supplied with Windows in its various incarnations, but in case there's someone that doesn't, it's true: you can't use FDISK, Disk Administrator, or Disk Manager to resize an existing FAT, FAT32, or NTFS partition without destroying the data on that partition. (Although you *can*, of course, enlarge an NT volume set without destroying data.)

One way to create space for Linux, then, is to just back up your existing data, repartition so that you leave 4GB of unpartitioned space, reinstall Windows (or NT or 2000 or whatever operating system you were running), and restore your data. First install the Microsoft OSs, *then* install Linux, so that Linux can then install either LILO or GRUB.

Option 2: *fips*

But what if you don't feel like all that backing up, repartitioning, reinstalling, and restoring? Well, if you are (to refer to the infamous Dirty Harry quote) feeling lucky today, you might even try downloading the *free* Linux utility called `fips`, which will resize partitions on your disk without damaging the data. Personally, the idea of a program that resizes partitions but comes with no warranty scares the bejabbers out of me, but if you're brave, you might surf over to `metalab.unc.edu/pub/linux/system/install` and download `fips-2.0.zip` and give it a whirl. Or look on Red Hat 7.3 Installation CD 1 in the `/dosutils` directory, and you'll find `fips` in there.

According to the documentation, if you do a defrag beforehand, then `fips` *ought* to work. Here's Craig's take on it:

"First boot the system under Windows, scan the disk for errors, and defragment the disk. Reboot the system to MS-DOS mode and run `fips`. (`fips` is a DOS program and must be run under DOS.) After a few preliminary questions, `fips` displays the proposed size for an 'old' and a 'new' partition. The old partition is your current Windows partition. Use the arrow keys to adjust the size of the partitions so that you have enough space for Windows and enough room to install Linux. (You'll install Linux in the space made available by the new partition.) When you're ready, write the new partition table. `fips` comes without any warranty and with no real documentation. But beware—it's for the adventurous."

Option 3: PowerQuest's Partition Magic

Craig agreed with me that the better way, however, is probably to get a commercial program that can resize partitions without destroying data, can handle partitions of various types, and comes with some documentation. You can't go wrong with Partition Magic from PowerQuest, and it's reasonably priced. An essential part of my Linux install toolkit is a bootable DOS disk with Partition Magic on it.

WARNING   If you intend to resize a partition on a system with Windows 2000, XP, or .NET, however, take a couple of extra minutes and be 100-percent sure that your repartition tool understands post–NT 4.0 NTFS volumes. Older repartition routines will not work on NTFS for Windows 2000, XP, or .NET. Check that you have the latest version of Partition Magic if you're working on a Windows 2000, XP, or .NET system. Unless that data on the disk isn't that important…

Video Hardware Strategies

A couple of years ago, I found that I couldn't even get *started* installing Linux without first doing some serious spelunking in my system to find out what kind of video, NIC, and mouse I had. Again, there's good news here: nowadays it seems that of those three, you only need to get information on your video board, and truthfully this is only an issue about one time out of four. Nevertheless, it's worth getting the information ready.

Almost anyone who wants to put Linux on a system will probably want to get the X Window GUI running. To do that, you'll have to know a few things about your video system:

- The video chip that the video board uses, manufacturer, and model number (Linux can usually figure this out automatically now.)
- The amount of video memory on the video board (Red Hat's video configuration routine usually cannot figure this out.)
- The range of horizontal frequencies that your monitor can accept (a value in kHz)
- The range of vertical frequencies that your monitor can accept (a value in Hz; Red Hat's Setup still can't figure this one out by default on any of my systems.)

You don't have to do that when installing Windows 9x or 2000, because the Windows Setup program has a set of finely honed programs that do a top-notch job of detecting your system's video board. Then Windows Setup can either detect the video monitor directly (if the monitor is a Plug and Play monitor), or it makes a conservative guess and offers you the chance to tell it what kind of monitor you've got.

Unfortunately, the video hardware detection routines for most Linux distributions aren't as sophisticated as the ones in Windows Setup. Sometimes a Linux setup program will *tell* you that it's figured out what video board you have, but in reality it has guessed wrong. That's not the end of the world, *unless* you have told your copy of Linux that you want it to boot straight to the GUI.

You can, in fact, avoid graphics altogether when installing Red Hat 7.3; you might consider doing that the first few times, so that you can avoid dealing with the hassles of video drivers while you figure out how to make the rest of the operating system work. Whether now or later, however, you may find yourself needing to know the intimate details of your video hardware; here are two approaches to getting that info.

Examine the Board and Monitor

If you don't mind popping the top on your system, you can (if you're handy that way) open your computer, remove the video board, and read the video board manufacturer name and model number right off the board. Then get on the Web and look up the board on the vendor's site. It is *very important* to get an exact chip designation, as "almost" usually doesn't count. I have seen many video vendors change chip makers from one model to another, meaning that it's quite common to see a vendor who used a Chips & Technologies video chip on their Graphics Wizard board change to a Cirrus Technology chip when they release their new-and-improved Graphics Wizard Plus. Chip model numbers are important as well; things that run on a Chips & Technologies 65554 chip won't always run on a C&T 65555 chip.

Monitors are easy to get information on. You don't have to take anything apart, just look at the back of the monitor for the model number and manufacturer. Then, again, get on the Web and find out the range of horizontal and vertical frequencies for the monitor. Or you could simply "cheat," as I do, and go look it up in the documentation that came with your monitor. After you've bought a few computers, you'll probably just surrender (as I did a long time ago) and write this kind of hardware information onto labels and then stick them on your computer. As a matter of fact...

> **TIP** If you're going to do a lot of Linux, buy some computer-printable mailing labels and stick them on the outside of your computer, then write on the labels what's inside the computer—video information, NIC information, the amount of memory, hard drive type, that sort of thing. This also gives you a place to write IP addresses for systems that you've assigned particular addresses.

Open the 2000 or 9*x* Device Manager

If you already have Windows, NT, or 2000 on your system, then you're in luck; you've probably got all of the data that you need. The Device Manager (or, for NT 4 users, Windows NT Diagnostics) is a great source of information about your system's hardware, as you probably already know.

No, let me take that back—if you're a seasoned NT user, then you don't *probably* know that, you *certainly* know that. I didn't mean to insult your intelligence in that last paragraph. But I pointed it out for a simple reason. In my experience, when I get excited about a new project, I tend sometimes to rush things, costing me time later. It's easy to just shove some Linux CD-ROM into the drive and start its setup routine running without proper preparation beforehand. But when you're partway through installing Linux, it's too late to fire up the Device Manager or NT Diagnostics—so save yourself a whole mountain of trouble and just gather the video info under your *existing* operating system, if there is one, before starting a Linux install.

In any case, you can see a sample Device Manager screen (this one's from Windows 98, but they're all similar) in Figure 4.1. I got this by right-clicking the background, choosing Advanced, and then choosing the Adapter tab.

Figure 4.1   Sample advanced video information from Windows 98

If There's No Driver...

If you have a board that's new or obscure, then Linux simply might not have a driver for your hardware. But don't despair, there's a sort of "video driver of last resort" called the framebuffer driver. I'll show you, at the end of the chapter, how to set it up.

Starting the Install

Armed with 4 gigabytes of unpartitioned space and a bit of information about your hardware, you're ready to start installing. Every Linux distribution I've come across is available in a CD-ROM format, and the CD-ROMs are bootable. If your system allows you to boot from CD, then all you need do is insert the CD and reboot your system. Most of the time, that'll work, but when it doesn't, then it's time to tackle our next setup dragon...

Creating Setup Boot Floppies

If you have an older system that doesn't allow for CD-based boots, then most Linux CDs either ship with a boot floppy that'll kick off the setup process or contain a Windows-compatible program that will let you create such a floppy.

I don't know why this happens, but I've seen a number of systems that won't boot from the Red Hat Installation CD 1 of 3. This is puzzling because those same systems boot from bootable Windows CDs with no trouble. I've even wiped their hard disks clean, master boot record and all... and the systems refuse to boot from the Red Hat CD. In this case, it's time for a boot floppy.

Fortunately, that very CD has a `dosutils` directory containing a program called `rawrite.exe` that will create the boot floppy. Create a Red Hat Setup boot floppy by following these steps:

1. Find a computer with both a CD-ROM drive and a floppy disk drive. Also, make sure you have a blank, formatted floppy diskette handy. For this example, I'll assume that your CD-ROM drive is drive letter E; if yours is different, then substitute that drive letter in these instructions.

2. Put the Red Hat CD 1 into the computer's CD-ROM drive.

3. Open a command prompt.

4. Change to the CD drive by typing `E:` (or whatever the CD's drive letter is) and pressing Enter.

5. Type `cd dosutils` and press Enter.

6. Start up the utility by typing `rawrite` and pressing Enter. It will respond `Enter disk image source file name:`

7. Type `..\images\boot.img` and press Enter. It will respond `Enter target diskette drive:`

8. Type `a:` and press Enter.

`rawrite` will create the bootable floppy; now just pop CD 1 into the system that you want to install Red Hat on, put the floppy that you just created into that system's A drive, and reboot—resetting the system's configuration, if necessary, to tell it to boot from A.

Starting Setup

Red Hat's Setup program will run either in graphical or text mode, as I've already mentioned. It starts up with a text screen with some explanatory text and the word "boot:"—just press Enter, and it'll kick off the graphical setup. In a minute or two, you'll see the Welcome to Red Hat Linux screen pop up.

If, on the other hand, you've discovered a system that Red Hat's Setup program *can't* run on graphically, then just reboot. When the text screen says, "boot:," just type text and press Enter. The text version of Red Hat's Setup is almost identical to the graphical one, so you won't miss anything in this explanation.

From the Welcome to Red Hat Linux screen, click the Next button.

Language, Keyboard, Mouse Selection, and Installation Type

The next four screens let you choose the language that you want Red Hat to work in, what kind of keyboard and mouse you have, and what type of Linux installation you want. Although I use a Microsoft Natural keyboard, Red Hat Setup usually just detects a standard 101-key keyboard. I've installed Red Hat both as 101-key and Microsoft Natural; both seem to do about the same thing.

Linux's GUIs make use of three mouse buttons, so if you have a two-button mouse, pay close attention to the mouse screen. In the case of a two-button mouse, you can tell Linux to "Emulate 3 Buttons," which means that when the GUI needs the third button, you just press *both* mouse buttons.

But the chances are that you have a third mouse button, whether you realize it or not—your scroll wheel. I have not seen Linux GUIs use the scroll wheel to scroll, but I *have* seen them use the scroll wheel, which you can click like a mouse, as the third button.

Then Red Hat 7.3 Setup will ask you what kind of installation to do, offering as choices Workstation, Server, Laptop, or Custom. I usually choose Custom because I want to install everything—but even in the cases where I *don't* want to install everything, I still choose Custom, as it gives me the most flexibility.

Drive Partitioning

Next, you'll need to partition your drives. Red Hat Setup offers you three choices for drive partitioning: a command-line tool called fdisk (Linux's version, not the Microsoft one that you already know), a GUI tool called Disk Druid, or automatic partitioning of your system by the installer. But let me digress for a minute about the kind of partitions that Linux needs.

The Swap Partition: What Is It, and How Large Should It Be?

Linux systems prefer to work with at least two partitions (though tt can run just fine on one partition). One is called a *Linux swap partition*. It serves a role somewhat like the pagefile under Windows 9*x*, 2000, or NT. Why doesn't Linux just store its swap space on the same partition as the operating system, as Microsoft OSs do? The idea, Dan tells me, is performance. That's not surprising, as you probably know that NT/2000/XP/.NET perform better if you have as many pagefiles as you can stand, all spread across different drives. But you may also know that this only makes sense if the different drives are different *physical* drives. Taking a big hard disk and partitioning it into several different drive letters, then putting pagefiles on the separate drive letters, does not help performance at all. So I'm still wondering about whether Linux's performance is really improved with a different swap partition. Perhaps having a separate partition dedicated solely to swap data makes it easier to keep the swap data defragmented. In any case, Linux prefers a separate swap partition. (When I say "prefers," what I mean is that you can tell Linux to install on a computer with just one big partition, and it'll work... but the Red Hat Setup program will squawk about the lack of a swap partition several times during the partitioning process, and you'll have to answer a few "Are you sure?" questions before Red Hat will install on a "swapless" system.)

Now, the logical question to ask at this point is, "How large should I make my swap partition?" As near as I can tell, the answer is, "Nobody knows."

There is a document called a "mini-HOWTO" (we'll talk about these files in the next chapter) that addresses this, and it provides some good background information. Unfortunately, there are a ton of other web pages offering just as intelligent information. And none of them agree.

Swap partitions were once essential in that Linux took about 16MB of memory to run, but a lot of folks only had 12MB of RAM. A swap partition of 4MB, then, would supply Linux the 16MB that it needed to run without requiring the user to go buy another 4 megs of RAM. (Actually, you'd certainly size the swap area larger to leave yourself a bit of elbow room.) Swap partitions are, then, essential in systems where you're running a lot more programs than you've got the RAM to support.

The fact is, however, that nowadays many of us have considerably more RAM on our systems than Linux needs. For example, I've got a system in front of me with 512MB of RAM that I loaded all of Red Hat 7.3 onto, and it's not using more than 100MB. Do I need any swap area at all?

In theory, I shouldn't, and in fact I've set up systems without swap partitions, and they've run all right. But some discussions on the Web, including one contributed by Linus Torvalds himself, indicate that the new kernel 2.4's memory manager really prefers to have a lot of elbow room. (See `http://kt.zork.net/kernel-traffic/kt20010126_104.html#2` for more details.) Several of Linus's comments pretty strongly state that a no-swap-partition machine or a machine with a minimum amount of swap space would see some performance degradation, and that Linux's memory manager would be happiest with a swap partition whose size doubled the size of your RAM. (Yikes, a gig for swap space!) And while it doesn't make all that much sense to me, I'm not the guy who designed Linux... Linus and company are. So create a swap partition whose size is equal to twice your RAM. (If you let Red Hat's automatic partition routine chop up your drive, then it will create a twice-RAM-size swap partition all by itself.)

Linux System Partition

The second—and main—Linux partition is called the *system partition*, the place where all of Linux's files go. The Linux setup routine calls it a *Linux native* partition. Again, if you intend to devote a computer's hard disk solely to Linux, then you needn't read any more about partitioning—just let Red Hat Setup do the partitioning automatically and take the defaults. But here's a few other details.

As with any other operating system, a default Linux install creates a number of subdirectories on your hard disk. But, as you'll learn in the next chapter, Linux is pretty flexible in the way that it handles disk space, which means that those directories do not all have to be sitting on the same physical hard disk—they can be easily spread across many physical hard disks or even, in some cases, network file shares. Thus, for example, Linux installs create a directory called /usr. That's normally on the same partition as all of your other Linux files, but, if you wanted to, you could create a separate partition on your disk and store /usr there. (I'm not sure *why* you'd want to, except if your system were growing out of its hard disk, I suppose—but it *is* possible to do this, and more simply than it would be in 2000 to move, for example, Documents and Settings to another drive.)

Naming Linux Partitions: / and */boot*

If you let Red Hat's Setup routine automatically partition your drive, then it will take advantage of Linux's ability to spread directories across different partitions, as it will create not two but *three* partitions: the swap partition, the main system partition, and a partition named /boot. That's an interesting thing about Linux: it names partitions, and the names are important.

In the world of Microsoft operating systems, we're familiar with the idea of naming partitions, but we usually don't bother, as it doesn't matter. But Linux needs that information. What I've been calling the main Linux system partition, *Linux* calls / —that's a forward slash all by itself, although you or I wouldn't call it "the forward slash partition;" instead, we'd say "root" aloud when referring to this partition. Creating a Linux system partition, then, requires allocating space for the partition *and* naming the partition.

As I mentioned earlier, letting Red Hat Setup automatically partition your drive will result in you getting a swap partition, a root partition, and a /boot partition. As with the swap partition, the boot partition is not necessary—if you were to override the partitioning routine in Setup and create only the swap and the root, then Linux would install without a hitch. So why would the Setup routine bother with a /boot partition? To make sure that old systems with big hard drives work properly.

This isn't, let me stress, a Linux limitation; it's a limitation of the BIOSs on older systems. Recall that the software that starts up your system's boot process is the BIOS; the BIOS locates the partition on your first physical hard disk that is marked "active" and loads that partition, then starts executing the code in that active partition.

Older (before roughly 1998/1999) BIOSs could not understand logical drives larger than about 8 gigabytes. Don't misunderstand—that didn't limit modern operating systems like Windows 2000 from using more than 8 gigabytes, as Win2K didn't use the BIOS at all, it used its own atapi.sys device driver, and atapi.sys is smart enough to understand drives considerably larger than 8 gigs. But, again, we needed the BIOS to get the PC going, which meant that the original boot code for the operating system—*any* operating system—had to live in the first 8 gigs of the first physical hard disk, or the BIOS couldn't load it, and the OS couldn't start.

Imagine, then, that you have a computer with an old BIOS and a 30GB hard disk. You want to set it up to dual-boot Windows 2000 and Linux. How to partition the hard disk? Windows 2000 starts off the boot process with a file named NTLDR, which usually lives as a hidden file in the root of C. C, therefore, must exist in the first 8 gigabytes of the computer's hard disk. But Win2K works fine if you put the rest of the operating system—\winnt, \Documents and Settings, \Program Files and the like—on the D drive. So you set up a partition for C that is large enough to store NTLDR—a few tens of megabytes is sufficient—and you position that partition somewhere in the first 8 gigabytes of the hard disk. D goes on a different partition, and you don't care where it lives on the hard disk.

You might have guessed by now that in this situation, the /boot partition does for Linux what the C drive does for Windows 2000: it starts off the party, containing just enough files to activate *Linux's* disk drivers, and of course those disk drivers also understand drives larger than 8 gigs. You would find about 60MB of unpartitioned space in the first 8 gigs of your hard disk and use that space to create a new partition of type "Linux native" and call it /boot. You'd then allocate whatever other space you wanted to yet another Linux native partition and call that / for the root. (And in case you're wondering how I'd put five partitions—C, D, Linux swap, /, and /boot—on a hard disk, then D and / can coexist nicely on an extended partition, just as you could have logical drives D, E, F, and so on all on the same extended partition.)

I should mention also that if you read older Linux documentation, you might read that your /boot partition must be in the first 1024 cylinders of your hard disk (which works out to 8 gigs on a particular common class of hard disks) because of a limitation in the LILO boot loader. That's no longer an issue with the current version of LILO. To the best of my knowledge, GRUB doesn't have any issues requiring you to put your /boot partition in any particular part of a hard disk.

If this is getting complex-sounding, let me remind you of a couple of things: first, the Red Hat Setup program's automatic partition option will handle it all automatically, and second, the all-boot-code-must-be-in-the-first-8-gigs restriction isn't a concern for most of the computers that you'd be installing Red Hat on nowadays.

Running Red Hat Setup's Automatic Partition Option

Even if you *do* tell Red Hat Setup to automatically partition your drive, it still asks a few questions. Choose the option "Have the installer automatically partition for you" and click Next, and Setup will ask you how much of your disk's space to let the automatic partitioner work with. Your options are these:

Remove all Linux partitions on this system.   This tells the partition routine that it can first delete all Linux partitions—old swap, /boot, /, or whatever—from previous Linux installations, and that it can then use that space to create its three partitions (again, Red Hat Setup likes to hedge its bets by creating a small, separate /boot partition). This is useful if you have a computer that's already set up to dual-boot a Microsoft OS and Linux. This way, the partitioner leaves the existing Microsoft OS alone.

Remove all partitions on this system.   Wipes the disk clean and builds a 52MB / boot partition, the main / Linux partition, and finally a swap partition. On my computer, it automatically sized the swap partition at about twice the size of my system's RAM. Useful if you're blasting all existing partitions and rebuilding from scratch.

Keep all partitions and use existing free space.   Just what it says. Clearly you need to have either a clean disk here or one that's already been formatted in a Red Hat–friendly way.

There is also a Review check box. Unless you need to check what Setup's partitioning routine has done, just uncheck the box. Assuming that you're working with a new system or one that you're just going to wipe and rebuild, take the second option, "Remove all partitions on this system," and click Next. If you've already got an operating system on the computer, want to keep it installed, and have enough unallocated space on the hard disk for Linux, then choose "Remove all Linux partitions on this system." You'll get a dialog box reminding you that you're going to destroy data on the hard disk, and do you truly want to? Click Yes, and Setup will delete the Linux partitions and then re-partition the space newly-freed on the drive. If you chose to review Setup's work, then you'll see that it has created a / partition, a /boot partition, and a swap partition that is, again, about twice the size of your RAM.

Configuring a Bootloader

Next, Setup will ask which bootloader, if any, you want to run: GRUB, LILO, or neither? I use LILO because I know it, but GRUB seems to work well also. You can either place the bootloader in your system's master boot record or in the /boot partition; either works as well, although I typically just use the MBR option.

If you've already got a bootable operating system on your hard disk, Red Hat Setup will detect it and add it to the list of OSs that LILO or GRUB will offer, adding your new Red Hat install as an option as well. So, for example, if you have Windows 2000 already on your system, Setup will show that as a GRUB/LILO boot option, as well as a new Red Hat Linux option. You can also tell GRUB/LILO which OS to boot by default. Then click Next.

Network and Firewall Configuration

Assuming that Setup was smart enough to find your Ethernet card—laptops with PCMCIA Ethernet cards may not be so fortunate—you'll get a screen offering to configure that NIC.

Linux does not turn on every device automatically at start time. You need to select a check box that tells Linux whether or not to start up the Ethernet card automatically on startup. You can also either configure the card with a static IP address or tell it to find a DHCP server.

The next page configures Linux's firewall. I disable it here in Setup, choosing the No Firewall option. Once your system is set up, you can add the firewall later or reconfigure an existing firewall by typing setup from a command line and following the menus. (It's a text program, so you don't even need a functioning GUI.) I should stress that this is a matter of taste, and some folks might want to *start* their systems with everything locked down and loosen up the controls as needed later. However, to ensure that the examples in this book work, I recommend turning off the firewall initially.

The next two screens let you tell Red Hat to run in languages other than English and set your computer's time zone. Unfortunately, Setup doesn't configure a Simple Network Time Protocol (SNTP) client and allow you to point your system to a time server as Windows 2000 and XP do.

Root Password and Other Accounts

After that, Setup will tell you to choose a password for a user account called *root*. What we call in NT or 2000 the "default administrator" account is an account named "root" in Linux. (This is a different root from /, the name of the Linux native partition that you just read about.) This is a very important account, so whatever password you choose, remember it!

> **NOTE**   Don't even think about leaving the root password blank or setting it to "password." There are lots of jerks out there who'd love to be able to take control of your machine.

You can also create other user accounts at this time. You needn't do that, however, as you'll see in Chapter 6 how to do that later.

Authentication Configuration

The following screen lets you tell Linux how sophisticated you want its local account administration to be (that is, how heavily encrypted the passwords should be), as well as whether or not to load logon clients for several network authentication systems—NIS (an old Unix system we'll discuss in Chapter 6 that lets groups of Linux boxes share user accounts sort of like an NT 4 domain), Kerberos, LDAP, and even an "SMB Authentication" that lets you use any NT system—workstation, member server, or domain controller's SAM to authenticate users. (Not that I've ever been able to make it work.)

You can easily change any of these options once your system is installed; just go to a command prompt and type setup. You'll see an "authentication configuration" option there.

Selecting Packages

The next-to-last step before you get to spend three hours feeding Red Hat Setup CDs is to choose the packages you want to install. Pick particular programs if you like, but again at this stage I recommend that you install everything ("everything" is one of Setup's options at this point) so that you've got it all available to play with. Once you know Linux better, *then* you'll probably want to build systems with smaller, more specific sets of packages. For example, "everything" requires about 3.6GB; if you just want to create a DNS server, you clearly don't need that much stuff!

Video Adapter Detection

Red Hat Linux wants to install and configure Linux's graphical subsystem (something called the "X Window system") and Linux's two GUIs, but to do that, Setup must know what kind of video board and monitor you have. It'll ask you about the monitor later, but just for now it wants to know what kind of video board you have and how much video RAM it contains. Setup has tried to autodetect your hardware and will show you what it *thinks* you have; check it and either change the values, accept what it's offered, or choose to configure video later by checking the Skip X Configuration box. After clicking Next, you'll get a last chance to bail out and not go ahead with the Setup. Click Next, and away we go…

Linux Boot Disk Creation

After you've inserted CDs 1, 2, and 3 into your system as instructed by Setup, your system is almost ready… but it's got to ask you for just a bit more guidance. Once it's copied all of the files to your system, Red Hat Setup asks if you want to create a boot floppy. You can either do it now or, as you'll see in the next chapter, at any time you like with the mkbootdisk command.

GUI Setup

The last thing that you'll have to respond to Setup about is graphical configuration. Recall that before you started shoving CDs into the system, Setup asked about what kind of video card you had, but it didn't ask about the monitor type. For some reason, Setup waits until now to ask. It either will have detected the monitor type, or you can tell it what brand your monitor is, choose a generic monitor type, or, if you've gathered the horizontal and vertical frequency information I suggested you get earlier, you can punch those values in as a custom monitor type.

The next Customize Graphics Configuration screen is important. Using the information about your video card and monitor, Red Hat Setup offers a suggested video resolution and color depth and lets you test the setting. (This is a *great* improvement over earlier Red Hat Setups!) Oddly enough, however, if you choose a resolution that Setup thinks your board can't handle, it just tests a lower resolution—"Setup knows best," is, I guess, the message here.

Once you've got a resolution you like, you can choose the GUI you'll use when in GUI mode. There are two, one named KDE and another named GNOME. My preference is for KDE, but either choice works; it's simple to change your mind later—you'll see how in Chapter 7.

Finally, Setup asks if you want to boot directly to text or graphical mode. Choose Text— it's not the default, so check that you've got it selected—and if you decide that you'd like to boot to graphical mode later, I'll show you how to make a graphical mode your default startup. Click Next and Enter, and Setup's done.

Logging In the First Time

If all went well, then once Red Hat boots, you will get a text screen that looks something like this:

```
Red Hat Linux release 7.3 (Valhalla)
Kernel 2.4.18-3 on an i686
localhost login:
```

We'll be messing with the system, so log on as the all-powerful "root" user: type in the word root. The password is what you set back when the Setup routine was running. As with NT and 2000, case matters; opensesame is not the same password as OPENSESAME.

You'll get a text prompt that looks like this:

```
[root@localhost root]#
```

It's showing three things: root@localhost shows that you are logged in as the account named "root" and that you're logged into a computer named "localhost." The root to the right of root@localhost means that your current directory is named "root." That's because by default Linux's shell puts a user into his or her home directory and the root account's home directory is named /root.

NOTE   Notice that the end of the Linux prompt is an octothorp, the # symbol. That's a reminder that I'm logged in as root. If I were logged in using a nonroot account—as a mere mortal, you might say—then the last character in the prompt would be a dollar sign rather than an octothorp.

Want to try something to see if your system's working? Then let's do the Linux version of a dir command. Type:

```
ls -1 /
```

That's all lowercase. ls is the command that says, "Show me the files and directories in a particular directory." The option -1--that's a lowercase *l*, not a numeral one—says to show the long listing. And the / says, "Show me the top-level directory." You'll probably see a listing that goes on for a while, but looks something like Figure 4.2.

Figure 4.2   Sample ls output

Notice that I did just an `ls -l` rather than `ls -l /`, because I didn't want lots and lots of lines in the listing on my screen shot. (Notice also that I'm running my commands in a window, where you're probably running a completely text window. `ls` will behave the same way in either case; the only reason that I ran my command-line session in a window is that it makes getting screen shots easier.) Here's what `ls` is telling you:

- The strings of characters and dashes, like `drwx------`, that you're seeing to the left do two things. The leftmost character tells whether you're looking at a directory entry or a file: d means directory entry, - means file. Thus, as you see in Figure 4.2, mbox is a file; the other entries are directories. That leftmost character can also be l, which means "link." Links in Linux are sort of like shortcuts in Windows, NT, and 2000, and I'll show you how to create links in Chapter 5. The rest of the characters define the file and directory permissions, which we'll describe in detail in Chapter 6.

- The number in the second column defines how many links exist to this file (so mbox has one link).

- The next two names define who owns the file—yes, Linux has the notion of file ownership, just like NT and 2000—as well as the name of the *group* who owns the file. Now, that *is* a new notion, but I'll have to put off explaining its significance until Chapter 6. In the case of mbox, root and the root group own the file.

- The number to the right of the group name is the file size in bytes. Directories get allocated space in increments of 4096 bytes by default, so they'll always be a multiple of 4K. (mbox is 6398 bytes—not a multiple of 4K—because I'm using a screen shot from an earlier Linux that is otherwise identical).

- After that is the date that the file or directory was last modified. Notice that two of the dates are "Feb 7 2000," and the other two dates are "Feb 6 10:27" and "Jan 29 13:26." When `ls` shows you a date, it always shows the month and day. If the file modification date was in the last six months, then `ls` also shows you the time. But if the file was last modified more than six months ago, *or* if the file modification date is in the future, then `ls` skips the time and instead shows you the year.

- Finally, you see the file or directory name—`Desktop`, `GNUStep`, `mbox`, or `nsmail`.

Good work—you've executed your first Linux command! But before we get too involved in how to *start* using Linux, let's go see how to *stop* using Linux.

Shutting Down Linux: *shutdown*

For some of you, your Linux setup program rebooted before giving you the option to log in, but for others, you got to log in right after setup. Either way, let's shut down and reboot the system before going any further. That way, I can show you how to shut down a system and then how to dual-boot from Linux. Even if your Linux *did* reboot, go ahead and use this process to reboot anyway; I know from experience that the first command *I* want to learn on a system is usually how to turn it off, anyway!

If you've booted to a GUI, then get yourself a console (text command prompt) session. If you didn't boot to a GUI, then you've already got a command prompt, so you are ready to shut down the system. Shut down the system with this command:

```
shutdown -r now
```

The -r option says to reboot; there is also a command reboot that does the same thing. Alternatively, shutdown -h now or the halt command. now means, well, to shut down the system, rather than reboot it, and to do it immediately. The "now" refers to the fact that you don't want a delay, you just want it shut down or rebooted *now*, rather than after a delay. You'd use a delay like shutdown -r 8 to give users attached to a Linux box 8 minutes (the unit that shutdown understands) to stop whatever they were doing in time for a shutdown. If you do not specify a time (or now), then Linux won't accept the shutdown command.

Dual-Booting Linux

When the system reboots, it'll probably start with a low-resolution graphics screen that shows the Red Hat logo and says "Red Hat Linux" and "Press Ctrl-X for text mode." It'll also have a box listing the operating systems that will run on this system—possibly only Linux if you installed Red Hat after wiping the hard disk clean, or possibly also naming whatever other operating systems you have on your system. How would Linux know about the non-Linux partitions? Well, recall that Red Hat's Setup program senses them and asks you about them during Setup. That information is stored in an information file called /etc/lilo.conf, which tells the Linux boot program LILO about the non-Linux partitions. Or, if you like, you can do a bit of fiddling with lilo.conf yourself, as you'll read in Chapter 9.

As before, please log in using the root user account. We're still fiddling with the system, and you need root-level powers to do that most easily.

Post-Setup: Check the NIC and Video

By now, you probably have a basic Linux running, or you've decided that it's impossible to get your Linux on your machine and so are simply reading to pass the time while you wait for FedEx to deliver a different Linux distribution. Before you really have a system that's useful, however, you need both the network card and X Window working.

Testing the NIC

Maybe the NIC is working fine, and you have nothing more to worry about; it could happen. Try it out with a ping to some distant location. From a Linux command prompt, type:

```
ping 206.246.253.1
```

That's my network's gateway, and you should get a positive response. If so, you're in business; skip to the next section. If not, either the NIC isn't configured right, or the floodwaters from Back Bay have risen over my local telephone switch—which *does* happen a couple of times a year. The next thing to try is to type ifconfig and press Enter. You *should* see something like Figure 4.3.

Figure 4.3   Sample **ifconfig** output

This command is the rough equivalent of a combination of the Windows/2000/NT ipconfig command and the Device Manager. You use it to configure a NIC (which you *shouldn't* have to do, usually; the NIC should configure automatically) and optionally (if DHCP's not working) give the NIC its IP address, or to query the status of the IP software on an already-configured-and-running NIC. So before you look at the seeming complexity of that figure and run in panic, let me make a very important point: **If your system's ifconfig output looks something like Figure 4.3, then relax—your NIC is functioning, and IP is running on it.** In fact, you can safely skip down to the section "Setting the Host Name," and if you can, then do so—this manual setting-up of Ethernet NICs isn't any fun, and I hope you can avoid it.

In your output, what you're looking for more specifically is an eth0 section. To see what I mean, look more closely at my ifconfig output; notice that it has two sections—one called eth0 and one called lo. lo stands for loopback, and every system has one; if you see a section for lo, then you don't necessarily have your NIC working yet. If you have an eth0 section, you know that your NIC is working.

Waking Up the NIC: Wake It Up with *dhcpcd*

My experience with Red Hat 7.3 differs from my experience with earlier Linuxes in that Red Hat seems to be able to detect and activate all kinds of Ethernet cards—PCI cards, mini-PCI NICs built into modern laptops, and PCMCIA NICs. What's odd and annoying about Red Hat 7.3, however, is that it sometimes *detects* NICs and can even *activate* them… it just chooses not to. Don't ask me why—but here's how to look a bit further to see if your system can be convinced to use your NIC.

At the command prompt again, type:

    dhcpcd -d -B -D

and press Enter. dhcpcd is the name of the Red Hat DHCP client. It seems, however, to have a nice side effect: it forces the system to go have another look to see if there's an Ethernet card or two out there that haven't been properly awakened. (For example, when I work with a system whose Ethernet card has an "awake" LED, I'll see the LED wink out and then come back on while dhcpcding.) *Now* try an ifconfig; I'll bet the NIC is present and accounted for.

Setting a Static IP for a NIC

What I just said is true, of course, unless you don't *have* a DHCP server around and need instead to assign a static IP address to your NIC. In that case, you'll use the ifconfig command in a couple of new ways. First, ensure that the NIC is disabled before you configure it with this command:

    ifconfig eth0 down

(If you got the dhcpcd to work a few paragraphs back but want to try this out, then type dhcpcd -d -k eth0, the "release DHCP lease" command.) Now use ifconfig to both enable the NIC and assign it a static IP address like so:

    ifconfig eth0 ipaddress netmask subnetmask

For example, to assign IP address 192.168.0.111 with subnet mask 255.255.255.0 to your Ethernet card, type:

    ifconfig eth0 192.168.0.111 netmask 255.255.255.0

Now try the ifconfig all by itself, and your NIC is probably set up. (If this doesn't do it, then I'm at a loss... by this time I've gotten every NIC to work under Red Hat 7.3.)

Making the NIC Wake Up Automatically

So we've probably established by now that you can use either dhcpd to wake up your NIC and make it go get an address from DHCP, or you can use ifconfig to give the NIC a static IP address. But you don't want to have to type that stuff every time you boot. Here's how to avoid it. From a command prompt, type:

```
netconfig
```

That's a Red Hat text-mode routine that both configures your NIC to use either DHCP or some static address and also sets up your system so that it wakes up the NIC automatically. Again, in my experience, this will make every NIC work for Red Hat 7.3, a great relief after the Byzantine procedures that Red Hat 6.*x* required.

Under the Hood: What *netconfig* Does

In case you're interested, you could have done what netconfig did. As it turns out, netconfig just creates a file in a directory that Red Hat looks in when booting. Files in that directory tell Red Hat to start up networking devices. netconfig just created a file telling Red Hat to wake up an Ethernet card address, and also set up your system so that it wakes the NIC up automatically.

Located in a directory /etc/sysconfig/network-scripts is a file named ifcfg-eth0. For a NIC configured with DHCP, it's just three lines:

```
DEVICE=eth0
ONBOOT=yes
BOOTPROTO=dhcp
```

You can see the contents of your ifcfg-eth0 file by typing:

```
cat /etc/sysconfig/network-scripts/ifcfg-eth0
```

For a system with a static IP address, it's a bit more complex, looking something like this:

```
DEVICE=eth0
ONBOOT=yes
BOOTPROTO=static
IPADDR=192.168.1.16
NETMASK=255.255.255.0
GATEWAY=192.168.1.1
```

You can even make these changes yourself, as these files are simple ASCII text files. But how do you edit text files in Linux? With a venerable old text editor called vi—see the following sidebar on how to use vi for your editor.

Using *vi* to Edit Files in Linux

Experience with Linux will show you that fixing or configuring a lot of things requires the ability to edit simple ASCII files. If you have the GUI up, then this is relatively easy to do: just poke around the menus and you'll find a wealth of simple Notepad-type editors. I needn't tell you how to run them—it's the same old GUI paradigm of menus and icons and dialog boxes.

If, however, you're working from the command line as I've suggested, then you'll need at least a basic ability to edit files with a text editor. As is always the case with Linux, you have plenty of choices when it comes to editors. I believe that novices should avoid at all costs the emacs editor. It's a powerful tool in the hands of the experienced, but bewildering to those just starting out.

Linux offers another editor, an old standby called vi. vi is by no means user-friendly, but you'll only need to know a few basic commands in order to edit text files.

You should *not* be in a GUI to do this. As with NT, 2000, and Windows, Linux will provide you a "console"—a window that contains a text command prompt that *looks* just like the Linux text screen—but programs don't work exactly the same inside a console window as they do in a purely text screen.

Let me show you how to use vi with a few examples. We'll create a brand new file, add some text to it, save it, then reload it and edit it some more. Start vi by typing:

```
vi sample.txt
```

Your screen will clear and you'll see a column of tildes on the screen, with a message like "sample.txt [new file]" at the bottom of the screen. Press i to put vi in "insert" mode. If you ever want to add new text to a file, you have to put the file in insert mode, and you do it with the i key. You exit insert mode with the Escape key. Type these three lines:

```
A is for apple.
B is for banana.
C is for cantaloupe.
```

If you make a mistake, just use the Delete, Backspace, and arrow keys, just as you'd expect that you could do. When you're finished, exit the insert mode by pressing Escape.

Now save the file. You can do that by typing :x (that's a colon followed by a lowercase *x*). The vi screen will disappear, and you'll be back to the Linux command prompt.

Start vi again with the vi sample.txt command. Now let's delete the middle line, "B is for banana." Position the cursor anywhere on that line and type dd; the line will disappear. Notice that the "dd" did not appear on the screen; instead, vi took it to be a command. How did it know that "dd" was a command and not some text that you wanted to enter? Simple—you weren't in insert mode. The editor always starts in edit mode, and almost every keystroke has a meaning, which can be pretty confusing if you try to type a sentence while in edit mode! Just about the only keys that do the same things in both modes are the Delete and arrow keys.

Let's next quit out of this file and not save changes. Type :q! (a colon, the lowercase *q*, and an exclamation point). Once back at the Linux prompt, return to vi by typing yet again vi sample.txt, or just press the up arrow and then Enter.

For our last example, let's find the line that contains the word "banana" and change "banana" to "betel nut." Again, type vi sample.txt and press Enter, or just the up arrow and Enter.

Of course, this is a tiny file, and anyone can see that "banana" is on the second line. But if it were huge, then finding the line containing "banana" would be nontrivial, which is why vi has a "find" capability. Just type /banana and then press Enter, and vi will position your cursor at the beginning of the "banana" string. Press the i key— or the Insert key—and type betel nut, then use the Delete key to eliminate the banana. (Or, alternatively, you could hit the Insert key twice to enter "replace" mode.)

If you want to delete a whole *bunch* of lines, you can start highlighting the lines by pressing V (a capital *v*) while in edit mode. Move the cursor down as far as you like to highlight the stuff that's got to go. Then just press d once, and it's deleted.

In summary, the basic vi commands that you need are these:

- Pressing i or Insert puts you in "insert" mode, essential for entering new text.
- The Escape key gets you out of insert mode and into "edit" mode, where pressing a key doesn't enter that key's character, it issues some command.
- When in edit mode, you can exit and save your changes by typing :wx and Enter.
- When in edit mode, you can exit and abandon your changes by typing :q! and Enter.
- When in edit mode, you can delete an entire line by typing dd—no Enter required.
- When in edit mode, you can search for a string by typing /*string* and Enter.

- You can tell vi to do a search and replace from edit mode by typing :s/ *oldpattern*/*newpattern*/ and vi will replace the first occurrence of *oldpattern* on the current line.

- You can tell vi to do a *global* search and replace from edit mode by prefixing the s with a percent sign and adding a g to the end of the command:

  :%s/*oldpattern*/*newpattern*/g

  and if you'd like to be asked to confirm every change, add a c to the end:

  :%s/*oldpattern*/*newpattern*/gc

- Highlight a block line by line: press V (Shift+V) and move the cursor. Press d to delete the block.

- Highlight a block character by character: press v (lowercase in this instance) and move the cursor.

- Copy a block: press y.

- Paste a block: press p.

Telling the NIC How to Route

You probably won't need this, but as long as I'm talking about bending a NIC and an OS to your will, let me mention how to handle static routing with Linux. Once the eth0 device is working, you *might* find that you can't yet ping. That's because you might have to feed the NIC some routing information. You do this with a route add command, which should look familiar to anyone who's worked with this under Windows, NT, or 2000. (Again, if you don't know about IP routing, you might take a look at Chapter 14 of *Mastering Windows NT Server* or Chapter 6 of *Mastering Windows 2000 Server*, both from Sybex. I'm not trying to duck explaining the issue, but it is a nearly identical issue on both NT/2000 and Linux, and replicating the IP routing explanation would increase the size of this book by 40 percent just for that one issue.)

First, you have to tell the board how to find its own subnet. You do that with this command:

```
route add -net network_number netmask subnet_mask dev eth0
```

For example, for a system on a C network, with an IP address of 206.246.253.56, I'd type:

```
route add -net 206.246.253.0 netmask 255.255.255.0 dev eth0
```

And any system connected to the outside world needs to be able to find its default gateway, the router that connects it to the Internet, or perhaps to all of your firm's intranet. You do that with this command:

```
route add default gw routeraddress
```

If a machine's default gateway had an IP address of 206.246.253.1, you could configure the machine to use that default gateway with this command:

```
route add default gw 206.246.253.1
```

You can tell Linux to display the current routing table by just typing route.

Setting the Host Name

Now that you have the IP stack functioning, you'll want to set the host name and DNS domain name. But how to do that? Well, this is another one of those things where Linux vendors seem unable to agree.

You can *always* change a system's host name on the fly with the hostname command. For example, I have a system that I want to name cclinux.minasi.com. I can do that like so:

```
hostname cclinux.minasi.com
```

This change will not, however, survive a reboot; here's how to change the host name and make it stick.

Creating a HOSTS Entry

You may know of the HOSTS file in the NT world—it's either stored in C:\Windows for Windows 9x machines or C:\WINNT\SYSTEM32\DRIVERS\ETC on NT and 2000 boxes—as a kind of "backup" to DNS. It's a simple ASCII file that contains IP addresses and DNS names. In any case, we really don't use it much in the Windows world.

Linux, in contrast, makes use of the HOSTS file. Apparently, Linux boxes need to be able to look *themselves* up in their HOSTS file, which is stored in /etc/hosts. Add a line to your system's /etc/hosts file with the system's IP address, followed by at least one space, followed by the full name of the machine. For example, to configure a system named cclinux.minasi.com at IP address 200.100.100.5, add this line to /etc/hosts:

```
200.100.100.5    cclinux.minasi.com cclinux
```

TIP   Look back to the earlier sidebar "Using vi to Edit Files in Linux" if you need instruction on editing /etc/hosts.

Causing a Host Name to Survive a Reboot

But you're not done yet; you've also got to set the host name in another place—which varies—to make the name "stick."

Red Hat and Mandrake Linux use a file called /etc/sysconfig/network, although they use them differently. In Red Hat, you include a line in that /etc/sysconfig/network file like so:

```
HOSTNAME="cclinux.minasi.com"
```

Of course, replace the name I've got in there with the host and domain name of the machine you're working on.

Identifying DNS Servers

Finish setting up your NIC and TCP/IP stack by telling your system where to find a DNS server. In the /etc directory you'll find a file (ASCII, of course) called resolv.conf. Tell your machine to use a particular DNS server by adding a line to resolv.conf with the parameter nameserver *ipaddress*, where *ipaddress* is the IP address of a DNS server. For example, if you had one DNS server at 10.10.10.3, you'd add a line to resolv.conf like the following:

```
nameserver 10.10.10.3
```

You should now be ready to use the Internet. If you're actually connected to the Net, ping something far away to check that your connection's working—try Craig's website www.wrotethebook.com, Dan's www.danyork.com, or mine, www.minasi.com.

Summarizing, then, to get your NIC working:

- Run an ifconfig to see if the NIC is already up and running. If not, run netconfig or directly create a script named ifcfg-eth0 in /etc/sysconfig/networking-scripts.
- Set a hostname by editing /etc/sysconfig/network.
- Configure the system to use a particular DNS server by editing /etc/resolv.conf.

Setting Up a Wireless NIC: The Lucent Orinoco Gold

As I've already said, the official position of Red Hat's support team is that Red Hat 7.3 does not support wireless NICs. If you ask about setting them up, they say that they can't help you. But I have a few Orinocos (Gold and Silver) and really wanted them to work under Linux, so I did some poking around the Internet. I can't offer any help on any cards but these, but I *can* detail what I did to make the Orinocos work on my laptops.

We're going to be doing a fair amount of noodling with our system here, using commands that will not look familiar. You'll learn these commands, however, in the next chapter. You do not need to understand the material in the next chapter to type these commands—but if you'd prefer to have a better understanding of what you're doing, then you might want to skip this section and do it after you've gotten through Chapter 5. (But I *did* try to make this as "cookbook" a section as possible.)

Step One: Disable Your Wired NIC

If you have a built-in Ethernet card, as I do in my ThinkPad T21, then disable it before going any further:

```
ifconfig eth0 down
```

If you don't have a wired Ethernet card, then don't worry about this.

Step Two: Make Sure You've Got the PCMCIA Service

If you installed "with everything," then you should have a Linux service called "pcmcia" that, not surprisingly, supports PCMCIA and Cardbus cards. Or, if you did a limited install, then choosing Laptop Support would have gotten the pcmcia service. To ensure that you've got the pcmcia service running, try this from a command line:

```
/etc/rc.d/init.d/pcmcia status
```

You should get a response like this:

```
cardmgr (pid 785) is running…
```

or:

```
cardmgr is stopped
```

If you got "cardmgr is stopped," then type:

```
/etc/rc.d/init.d/pcmcia start
```

Step Three: Insert the Wireless NIC

Next, put the Orinoco card into a PCMCIA slot. If you have sound set up, you'll hear two beeps. Type the command lsmod and press Enter. In the resulting module listing ("modules" are somewhat like drivers in Linux), you should see lines referring to modules named orinoco_cs, orinoco, and hermes. If you don't, then there's either something wrong with your wireless card, or your laptop's PCMCIA hardware isn't fully supported by Red Hat 7.3.

Step Four: Disable Your Wired Ethernet Card at Startup

Your network can get confused if you have both a wired Ethernet card and a wireless card on the same subnet, so let's tell the system to not automatically start up your wired Ethernet card. Obviously, you'll only do this if you have a wired Ethernet card on your system.

- If your system uses a wired *PCMCIA* Ethernet card, then just physically remove the wired Ethernet card from the system. In this case, your wireless Ethernet card will be eth0, and there's nothing more to do in this step.

- If your system has a built-in Ethernet card, then that card will be eth0, and your wireless card will be eth1.

In the second case—where your laptop has a built-in Ethernet card—you'll do some work with network startup scripts. First, create a startup file for your wireless card, which will be eth1:

```
cp /etc/sysconfig/network-scripts/ifcfg-eth0 /etc/sysconfig/network-
    scripts/ifcfg-eth1
```

That's all one big line, don't press Enter until you've typed it all.

Next, edit the file /etc/sysconfig/network-scripts/ifcfg-eth0, the startup file for your built-in wired Ethernet card. Change the line ONBOOT=yes to ONBOOT=no and save the file. Finally, edit /etc/sysconfig/network-scripts-ifcfg-eth1 and change the line DEVICE=eth0 to DEVICE=eth1.

Again, if you have a laptop whose wired Ethernet card is a PCMCIA card and you've removed it and replaced it with your wireless card, then you needn't do anything in this step—that ifcfg-eth0 is going to do double duty for your wired and wireless card, so long as you never have them both inserted at the same time.

Step Five: Configure *wireless.opts*

Red Hat's wireless networking subsystem uses a setup file called /etc/pcmcia/wireless.opts, which is based on an older set of wireless drivers than is shipped with Red Hat. We do *not* want Red Hat using that setup file, so let's rename it:

```
mv /etc/pcmcia/wireless.opts /etc/pcmcia/wireless.opts-old
```

Then use vi to create a new /etc/pcmcia/wireless.opts file. It should contain just a few lines:

```
INFO="Orinoco gold card"
ESSID="wirelessnet"
MODE="Managed"
KEY="no"
NICKNAME="Thinkpad"
```

That's my file—yours will look different. The INFO and NICKNAME sections are just labels and are unimportant, but you'll want to change ESSID, MODE, and KEY:

- ESSID is the SSID for your wireless network.

- MODE should be either "Managed" or "Adhoc." *Ad hoc* means that you do not have a wireless access point. *Managed* means that you use a wireless access point. Many PC wireless setup routines call this setting "infrastructure."

- KEY is either the word "no," which means that you are not using the Wireless Encryption Protocol (WEP), or it is a string representing your WEP key. My house is apparently built of neutronium, as I have a hard time getting a signal three rooms away from the WAP, much less worrying about my neighbors hitchhiking on my wireless network. If you use WEP keys, then you'd enter the keys in a number of ways:

  - If you use an ASCII key, then enter it like KEY="s:<your key> [1]"

  - If you use four ASCII keys (128 bits), then enter them like KEY="s:<key1> [1] key s:<key2> [2] key s:<key3> [3] key s:<key4> [4]key [1]".

  - If you use four hexadecimal keys then enter them like KEY="hhhh-hhhh…"

Save /etc/pcmcia/wireless.opts. Restart the PCMCIA subsystem: /etc/rc.d/init.d/pcmcia restart. The Orinoco has two green LEDs; the one closest to the "L" in the "Lucent Technologies" label will be solid green, and the other will be off. You can find information about your link with a new command, iwconfig. (You may have to type iwconfig eth1 if you've got a built-in wired Ethernet adapter.) An ifconfig should show that your wireless NIC now has an IP address; if not, then type:

    dhcpcd eth*n*

where *n* is either 0 or 1, as necessary. Try a reboot… the card should come up automatically this time.

You should be able to ping a particular IP address and, with hope, a DNS name. Now take a break before you tackle the next challenge: X.

Post-Setup: Dealing with X

We're almost done with the Linux setup, but there is probably one more thing left to do: make Linux's graphical user interface run satisfactorily.

Linux's GUI is different from Windows's GUI in that it's a separate and essentially optional module, so you don't *really* need to get the GUI running. But most desktop productivity tools—word processors, web browsers, spreadsheets, and the like—need a GUI to run. Additionally, some Linux distributions absolutely refuse to run without the GUI, which in my opinion is a mistake on the distributors' parts but is a reality nonetheless.

The stumbling block to getting Linux's GUI to run is usually the foundation piece of that GUI, a tool called X Window System or, often, simply "X." As you'll learn in Chapter 7, Linux GUIs consist of at least three pieces:

- X, which provides the graphical underpinnings and a font model
- A window manager, which lets you run more than one graphical program at a time without having them interfere with one another's position on the screen
- An "environment," like the two you'll meet, KDE and GNOME (which basically provide a "desktop" paradigm like the ones that we're used to in Windows)

Window managers and environments typically run fine, so long as X works—it's X that causes the trouble when Linux is having difficulty supporting a GUI. That's because X is the piece that talks to your particular mouse, keyboard, video adapter, and monitor. So getting X comfy with your hardware is essential. Unfortunately, the X setup routines out there are a bit rough-edged.

Testing X

The quickest and easiest way to see if X is configured right is to go to a command prompt and type X just a capital X. Your screen should clear and shift from text mode to graphics mode, presenting a mottled gray background and a mouse cursor shaped like a large X. If you get that, then congratulations, you can skip the rest of this chapter! But if not...

NOTE You can exit X and get back to your command prompt by pressing Ctrl+Alt+Backspace.

I assume that you took my advice and told Red Hat's Setup program to boot your system into text rather than GUI mode, so we'll be starting X configuration programs from the command line.

X Settings Are in *XF86Config-4*

Let's see how to make life easier for the first two groups. The trick to controlling X is through its configuration file. The file's name is XF86Config-4.

Linux does not, as Craig likes to remind me with an annoying chuckle—"annoying" because he's *right*, dagnabbit—store its configuration information in a cryptic binary format, tucked away in a hard-to-edit Registry. Instead, Linux's configuration data is all sitting in text files that could be edited with Notepad. (Oops, I meant vi.)

A strategy that I've found works well when faced with a badly configured X Window System, then, is to just let the setup routines run and create their own XF86Config-4. Then I open up a command window or boot to a command prompt (again, assuming that's possible; this doesn't work for every distribution) and directly edit the XF86Config-4.

> **WARNING** And remember that in the Linux world, upper- and lowercase *matter* when it comes to filenames—trying to find xf86config will either meet with failure or will find a *different* file. In this instance, xf86config in lowercase is the name of an X configuration *program*, not an X data file.

There are, unfortunately, several programs around that will in theory help you create a working XF86Config-4 file. Every Linux I've ever seen includes xf86config, a text-oriented program that asks you lots of questions, most of which you wouldn't have a prayer of answering. Some Linux distributions include a nice graphical program called XF86Setup, but for some reason Red Hat doesn't include it. Instead, Red Hat includes a fairly lame video configuration program called Xconfigurator.

Xconfigurator tries to probe your hardware and make some educated guesses about your video; it does a so-so job at that. Before even trying to run Xconfigurator, you absolutely must know a few things, as its probing abilities aren't of much help:

- Your monitor type, and you'd better pray that it's a type that Xconfigurator knows. If not, then you'd better know your monitor's range of vertical and horizontal frequencies.

- How much RAM your video card has; Xconfigurator seems unable to probe this also.

The shame of it all is that most Linux distributions that I know of used to include a program called SuperProbe that could at least tell you how much video RAM you had in most cases. Red Hat's documentation even refers to SuperProbe in several cases. But SuperProbe doesn't ship with Red Hat 7.3.

Oddly enough, the video detection and configuration routine in Red Hat 7.3's graphical Setup routine is much, much better than Xconfigurator. It's a shame that you can't run it separately outside of Red Hat Setup, but you can't. One very good thing about Xconfigurator, however, is that it will automatically employ a sort of one-size-fits-all video driver called the "framebuffer" driver, so even though Xconfigurator's not too bright, it can usually get your graphics running. And it's fortunate for me, as I don't have to take 12 pages to tell you how to set it up, as I did in the first edition—so perhaps I'm being too hard on Xconfigurator. But I really *did* like XF86Setup better…

Running Xconfigurator

Xconfigurator is a text-mode program. Start it from a command prompt by typing:

```
Xconfigurator
```

And remember, capitalization counts! In theory you can run Xconfigurator, tell it to just probe as well as it can, and then set up your system automatically by typing:

```
Xconfigurator --kickstart
```

Assuming that you run Xconfigurator in its nonkickstart or "interactive" mode, it starts up with a Welcome screen; choose OK to continue.

Xconfigurator then pauses a moment to probe your video adapter, reporting on what sort of video chip it thinks that it found. If you *don't* get a screen with a report—its title is "PCI Probe"—then Xconfigurator hasn't a clue about what kind of video chip you have. If that's the case, then you'd better be ready with your video board's chip type, or choose OK, then Back, then Cancel.

Note on that screen that Xconfigurator says, "X Server: XF86_Mach64," or something similar. That refers to the fact that X doesn't really have graphics drivers. The X world doesn't start from a basic XFree86 graphics engine and then add drivers to support various video boards. Instead, X programmers build entire graphics subsystems with the hardware support *inside* the XFree86 program itself! There *isn't* a VGA driver for X. Instead, there is a version of the X graphics subsystem that is a complete, stand-alone program named XF86_VGA16. Most of the time, your system will use an X system called XF86_SVGA, or perhaps XF86_FBDev. No matter which system you use, understand that it's a complete, stand-alone package. There actually *is* no program called "X;" instead, video configuration helps your system figure out which X system—XF86_VGA16, XF86_SVGA, XF86_FBDev, or whatever—is right for your system, and then it just basically renames that particular system "X."

Assuming that Xconfigurator came up with a plausible description of your video chip type—ATI, Voodoo, or whatever—then click OK and tell Xconfigurator about your monitor. It has the descriptions for a number of monitors prebuilt into it, so take a minute and see if it's got yours. If you're using a laptop, press G and scroll down a page or two; you'll see "Generic laptop panel" in various resolutions, meaning that in this case laptops are the *simplest* systems to configure for Linux—at least as far as their monitor goes. (This is a nice change from earlier versions of XFree86.) If your monitor doesn't appear on the list, then choose Custom. It'll present you with another Welcome screen—click OK—and will then offer you a bunch of nice generic monitor types, like "Monitor that can do 1024 × 768 at 70Hz." This isn't bad, and if you haven't that much information about your monitor, you can run Xconfigurator a few times and just try different generic monitor types. Or you can do it the other way: get on the Web, visit your monitor vendor's website, find the horizontal and vertical frequency ranges, and then punch them in. To do that, choose the Custom option, which is *inside* the Custom menu. When finished, click OK to continue.

In the next screen of the Custom Monitor Configuration, Xconfigurator asks for the horizontal frequency range, and it *always* asks that, although I don't know why—if I chose "Monitor that can do 1024 × 768 at 70Hz," didn't I just *say* that its horizontal frequency was 70Hz? In any case, either punch in the actual range if you have it, or select one of the offered values that fits with your previous selection. For example, if I'd picked "Monitor that can do 1024 × 768 at 90Hz" and then said that the horizontal range was 50–70Hz, that wouldn't work so well. Click OK to continue.

Next, tell Xconfigurator how much video RAM your system has. If your system can do 1024 × 768 resolution, the chances are very good that you have at least 2MB of RAM. If it can do 1280 × 1024 resolution, the chances are that you have 4MB of RAM (although it's not necessarily so).

Click OK at the next screen, as it asks about something called a *clock chip* (not the sort that keeps the time and date, but a different sort specific to older video boards). As all modern video boards do not have clock chips, the default option of "No clock chip setting" is correct.

The next screen, Select Video Modes, lets you tell the X server which resolutions you wish to use. X's configuration file XF86Config-4 can, in theory, describe a number of video resolutions that the video board will support, so you could tell X that your board works fine at 1024 × 768 in 16-bit color *or* 1280 × 1024 in 8-bit color. Using the Tab key, you navigate the page and press the spacebar to enable any given resolution/color depth combination.

You *could* do this. But in actual practice, you probably only want to choose one resolution/color depth combination. X is pretty flexible when it comes to multiple resolutions, but the KDE and GNOME desktop environments work best when given a particular resolution — shift the resolution around and parts of the desktop disappear, in my experience. But if you *do* want to use this screen to set your X server up for multiple resolutions, then remember this:

> **NOTE**   You cycle between the screen resolutions that you've given X by pressing Ctrl+Alt+Plus or Ctrl+Alt+Minus. And, as I've mentioned before, ctrl-alt-backspace terminates X, no matter how many graphical programs you're running at the moment.

Once you click OK, Xconfigurator asks you to click OK again so that it can test your settings. Don't be surprised if it takes a minute or two for X to start up. And if you can't see the screen, then just wait a few seconds, as Xconfigurator puts up a dialog box on the graphical test screen that asks if you can see the screen and gives you 10 seconds to respond. If you don't, Xconfigurator assumes that the resolution didn't work.

Now is the time that you can use Ctrl+Alt+Plus to try out several resolutions to see which, if any, you like. Xconfigurator also asks if you want it to set you up so that you boot directly to the GUI—again, I recommend that you not do that.

Once you've responded to the GUI dialog box, Xconfigurator exits, writing out your new /etc/X11/XF86Config-4 file. At this point, you've got a completely running version of Linux... whew! Congrats.

Trying to Make Sound Work

No promises here, but...

Until Red Hat 7.3, I'd about gotten to the point where I didn't even bother trying to make sound work on Linux. But, as with many other things, Linux in the twenty-first century is better than it was back in the bad old twentieth century.

Now, as far as I'm concerned, making sound work on Linux is black magic, so we're going to try one thing, and if it works, great; if not, I have no further suggestions. From a command prompt, type:

```
setup
```

This will offer a menu of things that you can do. One of the options is Sound Card Configuration. Turn your speakers up a bit, select Sound Card Configuration, follow the prompts, and cross your fingers... best of luck!

Getting Rid of Linux

Before I leave the topic of Linux installation, let me cover one more point... Linux *de*installation. At some point, you may want or need to delete all of the partitions off of your drive so as to start over. Unfortunately, that may prove more of a challenge than you were expecting. You see, if you try to use a bootable DOS/Windows floppy and Microsoft's FDISK program to delete an EXT3 or swap partition created by Linux, you'll be told that FDISK is unable to delete "non-DOS" partitions. In other words, Microsoft's FDISK won't delete Linux partitions. (Some versions of FDISK, that is; others are able to do it.)

You *can* use Linux's FDISK to delete partitions, as it is quite capable of deleting either EXT3, FAT, FAT32, NTFS, Linux swap, or just about any other kind of partition. Typing m and pressing Enter will display the Linux FDISK commands, but the ones you'll need are d, which deletes a partition; p, which displays the partitions on the disk; and w to write your changes. Linux's menu-driven CFDISK program works well also.

The trouble with using Linux's FDISK is that it may not be around when you need it. (That's not true, of course, if you created a Linux boot floppy when your Setup program offered it.) For those needing a quick "partition zapper," I've written a very small program that can delete all of the partitions on a hard disk; it's less than 1K in size and so fits nicely on any floppy disk. I call it mbrwipe.com.

WARNING   Now, there's one thing that you've *got* to understand about mbrwipe: it doesn't warn you that it's going to zap all of the partitions on your disk, it just does it. Any NT partitions disappear, any DOS, Windows, OS/2, Linux, you name it—all of the disk's partitions are history. There's no "are you sure?" prompts or the like. So don't use it unless you really mean to destroy all of a disk's partitions!

You can create mbrwipe yourself in just a few minutes, using the DEBUG program that comes with DOS, Windows, NT, and 2000. Following are the instructions. Be sure to follow them *exactly* or your program won't work—and you could damage partitions on the computer that you're using to build mbrwipe!

In the following description, you'll see the exact things that you're supposed to type in the monospaced, typewriter-like font. I've put underscores where spaces should be. Following the command, you can read in the more normal typeface exactly what each line is doing. Again, let's stress that with a warning:

WARNING   Only type the items in the monospaced (typewriter-like) font. Where you see an underscore, don't actually type an underscore; instead, press the spacebar. Press Enter at the end of each command.

I should explain also that you do not at all need to read the comments that I've added to each command; they're just there for the curious.

Start out by putting a formatted floppy disk with at least 768 free bytes of space in drive A.

debug_a:mbrwipe.com   This starts the Debug program and tells it that, when you will later tell it to write out a file, the file's name should be mbrwipe.com. It will complain that it can't find any file named mbrwipe.com, but don't worry about it, that's normal.

f_200_1_200_0   This prepares a section of memory by filling it with zeroes. We'll tell the program to write the data in that memory to the first sector of the hard disk, which will have the effect of deleting all of the disk's partitions. The command is f, which means "fill," and the 200 1 200 0—that's the letter *l*, not a one—says to fill the space that starts at address 200 and goes on for a length of 200 more bytes with the value 0.

a   Next, we're going to enter an assembly language program. a tells Debug that from now on, anything we type is a line in an assembly program, until we press Enter on a blank line.

mov_bx,200   The next few lines load values into memory areas inside your system's CPU called *registers*, areas named AX, BX, CX, and DX. BX gets 200 because it points to that block of zeroes that we just created in memory.

mov_cx,0001   Register CX gets 0001 because we want the computer to write to cylinder number 00 and the sector numbered 01 on that track. (The partition information is located on cylinder number 00, head number 00, and sector 01.)

mov_dx,0080   Register DX gets 0080 because we want the data written to head number 00 on the first hard disk—what the system calls "drive 80." The second hard disk would be "drive 81," by the way.

mov_ax,0301   Register AX gets 0301 because 03 is the command to write data—there are commands to read data, get status information, and other things—and to only write one sector.

int_13   The int 13 command tells the computer to run its built-in routines to control the disk drives.

int_20   This command tells the computer that your program is done, and to return to the command prompt.

<enter>   Don't type <enter>, just press the Enter key. It gets Debug out of "I'm entering assembly language code" mode.

r_cx   The program's written; now we have to write it out. Typing R CX and pressing Enter, then 300 and pressing Enter puts the value 300 into the CX register. Debug needs that because when we tell it to write out the file mbrwipe.com, we must tell Debug how many bytes to write out for the file.

w   Things are set up; this says to just write the file.

q   This quits Debug.

Now, just boot the machine whose partition you want to wipe with a DOS or Windows boot floppy and—*remembering that this will delete the partitions on that computer's hard disk without a single "Are you sure?"*—type mbrwipe. In an instant, you'll get your C:\> prompt back, and the partitions are gone from the first hard disk.

The chances are decent that you'll never have to do that, but I get a few letters on the question of removing all traces of Linux from a disk every month, so I offer mbrwipe.com. But, one more time, I remind you: there is no turning back once you've run this tool. Run it on a hard disk, and your disk will lose any existing partitions.

Still with me? Good—then you're probably wondering how to get some basic tasks done in Linux, assuming that you didn't accidentally zap your drive with mbrwipe. Now that you've got a Linux screen staring you in the face, what can you do with it? That's the next chapter's topic.

5

Linux Hands-On:
Doing Basic Things
with Linux

It wasn't too long ago that I first faced a Linux prompt:

```
[calinux@minasi.com /root]#
```

It was pretty humbling. I'm an old DOS, OS/2, Windows, and NT veteran, and pretty much nothing that I tried worked. dir and cd worked, sure, but copy, rename, move, edit, debug, basic, basica, and md just earned me a response like:

```
bash: debug: command not found
```

Well, I thought, at least I recognize that response—that must be Linux's version of DOS's old file not found error message. Yes, Linux offers the same kind of tools for controlling a computer's information as DOS, Windows, OS/2, and NT do—but the tools are just a bit different. In this chapter, I'll briefly introduce you to these tools.

One thing about Linux that is different from DOS et al., however, is the breadth that its tools often possess. Thirty-plus years of use—and user access to its source code—has left Unix (and therefore Linux) commands with a wealth of options. For example, the command most like the dir command, ls, has 48 options. This chapter is intended, therefore, to only introduce you to the most-used commands, and only the most-used options in those commands. There are some very good books out there that do a pretty complete job of showing you how to operate a Unix-based computer, and they're considerably fatter than Craig, Dan, and I intended this book to be. In this chapter, you'll learn the basics of getting around in Linux. That includes:

- Disk structure: There are no drive letters in Linux. There are subdirectories—that'll look familiar—but Linux glues all storage devices together so that they look like one big drive.

- Basic disk and file manipulation commands: How to view a directory, list a file, copy, move or rename a file, erase a file, and the like.

- Getting help: Understanding how to use the several online help facilities in Linux.

- Doing common tasks: You've probably never had to download the source code for an application, then compile and install while working with NT. But you'll do that in Linux. You'll also need to know how to do several other basic tasks, which we'll cover later in this chapter.

WARNING   I want to stress that our goal for this chapter is *not* to be a complete Linux command-line reference: Craig tells me that the first set of Unix documentation came with *seven manuals*—and that was before Berkeley added TCP/IP to Unix! Many Unix commands have dozens of options; all I want to accomplish in this chapter is to show you a few particular command/option combinations so that you have the basic tools you'll need to work in a Linux environment. As you'll read later in this chapter, Linux comes with online documentation that will then allow you to explore further.

Understanding Linux's Disk Structure

In the Windows world, we're used to the idea of drive letters and of logical and physical drives. Despite the fact that floppy disks, hard disks, and CD-ROMs are very different devices, software engineers at Microsoft and other places have managed to provide a nearly identical "look and feel" for these storage devices, and Microsoft's network software even extends that look and feel in that you can connect to a storage device attached to a different computer and still see the same idea of a drive letter containing subdirectories, which in turn contain files.

Linux arranges directories and files in a very similar fashion, except for a few important things. First, as you've already read, where Microsoft operating systems use backslashes to separate the parts of a file's full specification, Linux uses forward slashes—a minor cosmetic item, granted, but one you'll have to get used to. Second, there are no drive letters. Instead, every hard disk partition, every floppy drive, CD-ROM, Zip, etc. all appear to be directories inside a single disk structure. I'll demonstrate that by building a simple example PC.

Starting with the Hard Disk

Thus, for example, suppose you have a PC with a large hard disk partition where Linux, the programs, and your data reside. Suppose also (for the sake of simplicity) that the hard disk contains only a few directories named /etc, /bin, /usr, and /sbin. We might diagram that directory structure as in Figure 5.1.

Figure 5.1   Simple disk directory structure

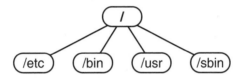

Notice that the top of the structure is simply a directory named / or, to pronounce it, "root." As with root directories in Microsoft operating systems, you can place both files and directories in the root. If we were to peer into one of the subdirectories, we'd find that, as with Microsoft operating systems, we can nest subdirectories inside subdirectories, to whatever level of complexity that you'd like. The Linux command to view a directory, as you learned in the previous chapter, is ls. You can, then, view the contents of the root directory by typing ls /.

Adding a Floppy

But now suppose that our example computer has a floppy disk drive. How would you go about ls-ing that? Well, believe it or not, there are three steps to accessing a floppy. First, you need a subdirectory on the existing root that you don't mind wasting, as you'll connect the floppy drive to that subdirectory (I'll expand on this in a moment). Second, you issue a command to "mount" the floppy. Mounting a floppy introduces the floppy hardware to Linux, but with an odd twist. A mount command says to Linux, "I'm bringing this piece of hardware—this floppy drive—to your attention. Notice also that there's this subdirectory that I'm not using. Until I tell you otherwise, whenever I ask to see the contents of that subdirectory, don't look in that subdirectory; instead, look in this floppy drive that I just told you about." Finally, you need only ls that subdirectory to see the floppy's contents.

Step by step, it looks like this. First, we'll need a directory on root to "glue" the floppy onto. What's a good name for this? Hmmm… "myfloppy" or "floppy" works well, but it could be anything—"adrive," "Calvin," "144drive" all work as well. You create a sub-directory with the `mkdir` command:

```
mkdir /myfloppy
```

You'll only have to do that once, of course—the next time that you need to mount the floppy, you'll already have a directory ready: /myfloppy. Next, tell Linux to notice the floppy drive and glue it to the /myfloppy drive:

```
mount -t vfat /dev/fd0 /myfloppy
```

There are three things that this command communicates to Linux:

- What to expect in the way that the data is laid out on the disk. The `-t vfat` tells Linux that the floppy is formatted in the post–Windows 95 version of the FAT file system. (VFAT covers both FAT32 and FAT16 with long filenames.) And yes, in case you're wondering, it is entirely possible to format a floppy in ext2 format with Linux—not all floppies are FAT!

- The particular piece of hardware you're telling Linux to recognize. You may recall that in Microsoft operating systems, there are some "magic names" that refer to pieces of hardware. For example, if you were to copy a simple text file to a file named LPT1, then you wouldn't get a file by that name—instead, you'd get a printout of that file. Other DOS, Windows, and NT device names include COM1, COM2, AUX, C:, and CON, the keyboard. Linux uses a far larger group of these "device names," and they all look like names of directories or files—for example, /dev/psaux is the device name for the mouse input device, and /dev/tty is the name for the key-board. The /dev/fd0 device describes the first floppy drive. See the sidebar "How Linux Names Devices" for the names of drive partitions.

- The subdirectory to associate the device with. Before you issue this command, `ls /myfloppy` will show you what's in the directory on the root partition named myfloppy. After the command, an `ls` will ignore that directory altogether and instead read the floppy disk.

TIP You may also see reference to floppy mounts that use `-t msdos` instead of `-t vfat`. The difference is that `vfat` supports long filenames. `-t msdos` is older, so if for some reason you can't get `-t vfat` to work, try `-t msdos`.

WARNING Sometimes when you try to mount the floppy disk, you get an error message like "/dev/fd0 is already mounted" or "/myfloppy busy." That might be because you've already mounted it and forgot that you did (just type mount all by itself to see what's mounted), or it might be that the system has automatically mounted the floppy. For example, the KDE and GNOME GUIs for Linux feature an icon on their desktops that, if clicked, will show you the floppy's contents. Clearly something has to mount the floppy before that will work. In general, Linux distributions tend to use the /mnt directory as a catch-all location for their automatically mounted volumes—/mnt/floppy, in this case.

How Linux Names Devices

Way back a long time ago, someone decided to make everything in Unix look like a file. Files are, of course, files, so that was pretty easy to accomplish. But directories look a lot like files as well, when you take a peek inside them, and as you'll see in the next chapter, you set security on both files and directories in a very similar manner—which should seem familiar to anyone well-versed in NT, as NT just borrowed the idea from Unix. But Unix even makes pieces of hardware look like files, and I guess it makes sense sometimes, but it still seems kind of odd to me. I suppose the Unix guys were trying to establish the "unified file theory" or the like. (Sorry, hanging around these Linux characters is bringing out the punster in me.)

Device names all look like files that live in a directory named /dev. You can sometimes use the fact that devices have bogus filenames to perform useful tricks. For example, here's a quick way to create a short text file. Use the cp, or copy, command, to create a file by copying the /dev/tty "file"—that is, anything from the keyboard—to some file. That has the effect of taking anything that you type and copying it into the file. You press Ctrl+D to tell Linux that the "file"—that is, your keyboard input—is terminated. So, for example, to create a file named sample.txt, just type cp /dev/tty sample.txt and press Enter. Type a few lines, and press Ctrl+D. You'll get the Linux prompt back. You can see that you created an actual file by typing cat sample.txt.

You can see some common Linux device names in Table 5.1.

Table 5.1   Common Linux Device Names

Device	Linux Name
A: floppy	/dev/fd0 or /dev/floppy
B: floppy	/dev/fd1
Keyboard	/dev/tty
Master drive on primary IDE channel	/dev/hda
First partition on master drive on primary IDE channel	/dev/hda1
Third partition on master drive on primary IDE channel	/dev/hda3
Slave drive on primary IDE channel	/dev/hdb
Master drive on secondary IDE channel	/dev/hdc
Slave drive on secondary IDE channel	/dev/hdd
SCSI target ID 0	/dev/sd0 or /dev/sda
SCSI target ID 1	/dev/sd1 or /dev/sdb
Second partition on the hard disk at SCSI target ID 0	/dev/sda2
CD-ROM	either /dev/cdrom or IDE/SCSI designation (/dev/hdb, /dev/scd5, etc.)
Keyboard	/dev/tty
Modem	/dev/modem
Sound system	/dev/sound

From this point, an `ls /myfloppy` will display the contents of the floppy in the A drive. But Linux assumes that drives, once mounted, don't change. So if you want to swap floppies, be sure to unmount the drive, like so:

`umount /myfloppy`

Swap the diskette, then remount the drive.

> ***TIP*** You don't have to do all that just to work with DOS/Windows floppies on most Linux distributions. Most Linuxes contain a set of programs called the mtools programs: `mdir`, `mcopy`, `mdel`, `mdeltree`, `mformat`, `mmove`, `mren`, and `mtype` are programs that take the same syntax as their DOS equivalents. For example, to copy a file named `/myfiles/diary` to the floppy in the A drive, you'd type `mcopy /myfiles/diary a:`. You could view the directory of a floppy with `mdir a:`. You needn't mount or unmount to do these operations—the mtools are terrific. mtools is a separate package, though, so there's the possibility that your Linux distribution doesn't include it. Note, however, that mtools only work with FAT-formatted floppies; they won't work with floppies formatted in the Linux ext2/3 format. (For that, you do the mount/umount stuff that you just read.) You might get an error like "Can't open /dev/fdo0: Device or resource busy" from Red Hat; that's because Red Hat has already mounted the floppy as /mnt/floppy. In that case, you can do a `umount /mnt/floppy`, then the mtools will work.

Mounting a CD-ROM

Next, let's add a CD-ROM to the system. As with the floppy, you'll mount the CD-ROM to access it. But CD-ROMs are a bit easier, as you needn't tell Linux what kind of file system is on the CD-ROM—there's basically only one kind, ISO 9660, or CDFS in NT lingo. As before, create a directory to glue the CD-ROM to, then mount the CD-ROM. You can probably use the /dev/cdrom device name, but if all else fails, describe it by its IDE name /dev/hda, /hdb, etc., or its SCSI name /dev/scd0, /dev/scd1, etc. If I'd never attached my CD-ROM to my Linux system, I'd have to first create a directory and then mount the CD-ROM like so:

```
mkdir /mycd
mount /dev/cdrom /mycd
```

You'll find that you can now read the CD-ROM with an `ls /mycd`, but that the eject button doesn't work on that CD-ROM drive. Again, this makes sense, as Linux assumes that once you introduce it to a drive, then Linux has complete control over it. (Try ejecting the CD partway through a Linux installation to see another example of this—you won't be able to.) To change CDs, you must unmount with the `umount` command. (There is also an `eject` command—Linux seems to have a command for everything—that will both unmount and eject a CD.)

Just as DOS won't let you delete a directory if you're currently in that directory, Linux won't let you `umount` a device if it is your current default directory or if some other process or application is currently using it. So if you get a "device busy" or similar message, then you should check to see if you're currently in the directory that you're trying to unmount!

Using Automounter

If all of that sounds like an excessive amount of work just to get to a floppy or CD-ROM, then I've got to agree. That's why it's nice that Linux has a service called the "automounter." Some distributions turn it on automatically, but Red Hat 7.3 doesn't. It's a simple matter, however, to get it working, as I'll show you.

You've already read that you have to mount a device to read it, and then unmount it to stop using it; for example, if you read five CD-ROMs over the course of the day, you'd have to issue a mount command to read the first one, then you'd have to unmount (or eject) to release that CD-ROM, then do it again for the second, and so on. I find this a bit annoying; I'm used to just pressing the eject button to get a CD-ROM drive to cough up my CD disc. Automounter works around this.

The idea behind the automounter is this. You define commonly mounted things like floppies and CD-ROMs. They then get "magic names" that you can use to refer to them. (In the case of Red Hat, it's "/misc/cd" and "/misc/floppy.") Whenever you refer to one of those magic names, automounter wakes up and mounts the device automatically. Automounter also watches how you access the device; if you leave it alone for 60 seconds, then automounter automatically unmounts it. Thus, when you press the eject button on the CD-ROM, you get your disc without any backtalk from Linux because the chances are good that you haven't touched the CD in the past 60 seconds—and therefore automounter has already unmounted the drive. (If you need the disc *now,* then typing the eject command works as before.)

Automounter is, as I suggested, about 98 percent configured in Red Hat. Here's what you have to do to finish the job.

1. Edit the file /etc/auto.misc. It will contain a line that says something like #floppy -fstype=auto…; delete the # at the beginning of the line, save the file, and exit the editor.

2. Edit the file /etc/auto.master. It will contain a line that says something like #/misc /etc/auto.misc --timeout=60; remove the # from the beginning of the line, save the file and exit the editor.

3. Finally, restart a service called autofs, which is the automounter:

   ```
   /etc/rc.d/init.d/autofs restart
   ```

Now you can refer to the CD-ROM as /misc/cd and the floppy as /misc/floppy.

Mounting a FAT/FAT32 Drive

Now Linux can read the floppy and the CD-ROM, but suppose this system has one more drive to read—the FAT or FAT32 drive that Windows, NT, or 2000 sit on, assuming that this is a dual-boot system. Let's assume for this example that you have only one hard disk, an EIDE drive. As is usually the case, that drive is set up as the master device on the primary EIDE channel. (If you don't know how your EIDE hard disk is set up, reboot your computer and watch the messages from the BIOS; many BIOSs report what drives they find, as they find them.) Suppose the computer has only one hard disk, which you have partitioned like so:

- First partition: FAT32, contains Windows 98
- Second partition: Linux swap partition
- Third partition: Linux ext2 partition

We need to tell Linux, then, to mount a drive that's on device /dev/hda, and the first partition on that device.

First, create a directory to mount this drive to:

```
mkdir /cdrive
```

As before, you can use any directory name that you like; "cdrive" was completely arbitrary. Mount the drive with this command:

```
mount -t vfat /dev/hda1 /cdrive
```

The vfat type tells Linux to support a FAT32 drive, or a drive with long filenames. You may find that you don't need to bother with -t vfat, as Linux usually seems to figure out when drives are FAT or FAT32 drives. You may, however, see this message when you try to mount the Windows, NT, or 2000 partition:

```
mount: /dev/hd1 already mounted or /cdrive busy
```

```
mount: according to mtab, /dev/hda1 is mounted on /disks/c
```

Again, here's evidence that you've either already mounted this before or your system is running automounter. Remember that if you're ever confused about what's mounted, you can always just type mount all by itself, without any options. I got output like this:

```
/dev/hda1 as /disks/c vfat rw
```

This shows that the first partition on the master hard disk on the primary EIDE interface is mounted as /disks/c. With this information, you're equipped to give Linux access to any of your storage devices.

At this point, I have four different storage devices (the ext2 partition, the C: FAT32 partition, the CD-ROM, and the A: floppy disk) under the same / root directory, just as if they were all one big hard disk under a Microsoft OS.

Enhancing my earlier example, then, Figure 5.1 can be redrawn to look like Figure 5.2.

Figure 5.2   A Linux disk hierarchy

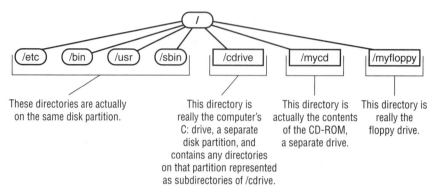

Mounting NTFS Drives: The Bad News

So is there an NTFS file system for Linux? Yes, but it has three limitations:

- First, every document about it warns in big scary letters that the NTFS file system driver is experimental and that no one will help you if you lose data from it. (Yeah, right like someone's going to help you if *anything* blows up in Linux.)

- Second, it's a read-only driver. You can enable read/write functionality on it, but every document says in even bigger and scarier letters that it is a Truly Bad Idea to try to write data to an NTFS drive under Linux.

- Third—and here's the incredibly frustrating part—Red Hat has decided for some reason to *leave NTFS support out of their distribution*. This stunned me—when I worked with Mandrake Linux earlier, they included NTFS automatically. Not Red Hat. To get NTFS support, you need to recompile the kernel. That's right, you've got to rebuild the whole system. It's not pretty, but I'll show you how to do it toward the end of the chapter, and I'll walk you step by step through the process of making Red Hat 7.3 support NTFS.

Once you have NTFS support installed, you seem not to have to tell Red Hat about what kind of file system it is, but if you like, you can use the –t nfts option, as in:

```
mount -t nfts /dev/hda1 /myntfsdrive
```

Some Standard Directories in Linux

Once you have Linux set up, you'll find that there are a whole bunch of directories. What do they all do? Here's a brief rundown on the directories that you'll probably see on your disk. Remember, however, that your distribution just might do something different. There is a recommended standard for Linux directory hierarchies (and actually for Unix disk hierarchies in general) at `www.pathname.com/fhs`; the standard is called the File Hierarchy System (FHS).

/bin   The Unix world tends to store binary files (programs, mostly) in directories named bin, and Linux is no exception. This directory contains programs, but in particular it contains the programs that Linux uses in its maintenance or single-user mode. (It's kind of like Windows' Safe Mode.) The programs in this directory are usually accessible to users as well as administrators. Compare this to the `/sbin` directory, which should in general only contain programs that administrators use. According to the FHS, if it's not completely essential for single-user mode, then put it in `/usr/bin`.

/boot   As this directory's name suggests, it contains many of the files that Linux uses to boot (except for the textual configuration) and the LILO Linux Loader. According to some documents, the intent of this directory is to contain anything that Linux uses before the Linux kernel starts up. It's also segregated into a different directory, because older Linux distributions typically needed this information in the first 1024 cylinders of the disk drive, so some older Linux systems have an entirely separate partition for the `/boot` information. You'll recall that Red Hat's "autopartition" module in their Setup program still creates a separate `/boot` partition.

/dev   You've already met this directory. Linux treats every input/output device as a file. The `/dev` directory contains the bogus "files" that actually point to those pieces of hardware.

/etc   The files in `/etc` are basically the configuration information for Linux. It's not far off to say that you could back up a Linux configuration by backing up /etc. The configuration files are either simple text files required for particular applications or scripts to start up system services. You won't usually find any binaries in `/etc`.

/home   As you'll learn in Chapter 6, this is where the home directories go in Linux. And that's important, as home directories are more important in Linux than in NT/2000. In general, a user named Wally will have a home directory named `/home/wally`. (That's assuming that his Linux username is "wally" with a lowercase, as is the custom for usernames. Unlike NT, Linux is case-sensitive about usernames, so you could have one user named "wally" and another named "Wally.")

/lib   This is where Linux stores the libraries, which are the Linux equivalent of Windows NT or 2000 DLLs.

/lost+found   Remember lost clusters? They're parts of the disk that a Microsoft operating system discovers to contain a file, but that the OS can't figure out what file to associate with. Linux can sometimes run into the same problem, but instead of creating files with names like `file0000.chk`, it stuffs the file fragments into the `/lost+found` directory.

/mnt or /misc This seems to vary quite a bit from distribution to distribution, but the basic idea with /mnt is that it's the top level for a set of subdirectories that get mounted to devices on your system. (RedHat seems to use /misc also; its auto-mounter uses /misc, but another part of the OS -- fstab -- uses /mnt, so you might see both.) (Dan tells me that "most distros [that's the in-crowd shorthand for 'dis-tributions'] use this as the temporary mounting point for things like the floppy and CD-ROM.")

/opt This where commercial or "add-on" applications should go. This comes out of Unix, where it is a common practice. Often when you add things like Applixware or StarOffice, they will go in /opt (think "optional"—stuff that you don't need for the system). KDE also typically gets installed in /opt.

/proc This is a directory that seems to act something like /dev, but instead of using bogus filenames to stand in for hardware devices, this seems to create bogus filenames that stand in for processes. For example, one file, /proc/kcore, isn't really a file at all—it's a bogus file that contains the entire current contents of your computer's RAM! Dan also observes that "/proc/interrupts shows you the list of IRQs being used by different devices."

/root This is the home directory for the root user. Why not just give her a home directory named /home/root? Here's how Dan explains it:

"Say you have a system with the following partitions:

- /
- /usr
- /home

And let's say that some clueless user now goes and copies something large into their /home/joe directory and winds up filling up /home. You want to log in as root to go make some changes and delete files... if you were to log in, and your directory was /home/root, you might get a 'no space left on device' error and not be able to do any-thing... well... actually... here's a better example:

Same scenario, but say that /home is really a mount point for an NFS-mounted vol-ume (NFS is a tool that lets you network users' home directories, as you'll see later in the book) coming from some central Linux/UNIX server. All of your users now have their home directories stored on a central server. Say there's a hardware error, and you need to reboot the system into single-user mode so you can do some main-tenance. You reboot, it comes up in single-user mode (no networking yet), and root suddenly has no home directory (because /home isn't yet mounted, so /home/root isn't available). Leaving it at /root solves this. "

/sbin You'll notice this directory has that magic "bin" in its name; sbin seems to be short for system binaries. The directory contains programs and other binaries. As noted in the explanation of /bin, programs in /sbin should be only intended for administrators. According to the FHS, if it's a tool that normal, nonadministrator users would use, then it goes into /bin, /usr/bin, or /usr/local/bin. If it's a tool that only administrators would use, then it goes into /sbin, /usr/sbin, or /usr/local/sbin.

/tmp As you'd expect, it's for temporary files.

/usr This houses data that should be available to anyone, users and administrators. No one should write to this directory, and the data in the directory should not be machine-specific. For example, the Linux documentation goes in /usr. For some reason, Linux distributions usually include a /usr/bin and a /usr/sbin–more directories for programs. Dan tells me that "/usr/sbin is typically for nonessential system admin commands."

TIP Some Linux distributions seem to put programs into /usr/sbin or /usr/bin but then don't include those directories in the system's PATH. (Clearly, however, if you log on as a user and not an administrator, then /usr/sbin shouldn't be on your PATH in any case.) If you're trying to run a command and Linux tells you that the program isn't found, then take a look in /usr/bin and /usr/sbin.

/var This directory stores system logs, spool files, security logs, and the like. Taken together, the files in /var/log are the Linux equivalent of the NT or 2000 Event Viewer. The directory's name comes from the fact that the data in it is "variable." /var/log contains several interesting files including dmesg, the set of messages emitted by the system as it boots up. There is also /var/log/messages, which is a central log file used by many programs. It is sort of similar to the System log in the Event Viewer. Dan tells me that /var/log/messages is probably the single most useful file for troubleshooting.

Basic Disk and File Commands

Now that you have a feel for how drives and directories fit together, let's see how to view and modify files and directories.

WARNING Uppercase and lowercase count! Unix and Linux commands are case-sensitive: ls -l shows you a long listing of the current directory; LS -l or ls -L or LS -L will not. When using Linux commands, adhere to the upper- and lowercase as you see in the examples. Most commands and options are lowercase, but you'll sometimes see uppercase.

Determining Free Disk Space: *df*

A lot of things that would *normally* work don't, if you don't have enough (or any) free disk space! Find out how much free space you've got on your disk with the df command.

Left to itself, however, df will report free and used space on every single disk that you're attached to, including network drives, so you may want to add the –l option (that's a lowercase "L").

Finding *Used* Disk Space: *du*

Ever wonder how much space a directory and the directories inside it are taking up in Windows? Of course you can find out—right-click the directory and look at Properties. Or do a dir /s and wait for the display to flash by. Linux has du, "disk space used." Find out with du; use the –h option to have it report information in "human readable form"— that is, kilobytes—instead of numbers of disk blocks. The –s option says to summarize the results, shortening the output. The –S option says *not* to look in subdirectories; a recursive search through a directory's subdirectories is the default. So, for example, to see in summary form how much disk space is used in the directory /home/lou (Lou's home directory), including any directories inside Lou's home directory, type du -hs /home/lou.

Navigating the Disk Structure: *cd*

As I said before, this is an easy one, as it works just as it does in Microsoft operating systems—just cd directory and you're there. As in Microsoft operating systems, following cd with a period— cd . —doesn't do anything (because . is shorthand for "the current directory") and following it with two periods— cd .. —backs you up a level: if you're in /usr/share and type cd .., you end up in /usr.

One thing about cd works differently than you're used to, however. Merely typing cd all by itself in Microsoft operating systems reports what directory you are currently in. In Linux, however, cd all by itself takes you back to your home directory. To see the full pathname of your current directory, type pwd, "print working directory."

Viewing a Directory: *ls*

The first thing you'll usually want to do once you've navigated to a directory is to look around that directory. You'll do that with ls. It's the Linux version of the dir command, but it does lots more. It has several dozen options, but I'll show you the basic ones.

Red Hat 7.3 and many other distros color their ls output by default. Directories are blue; executable files are green. Normal text files are standard gray/white text. Symbolic links (explained later) are cyan. Devices are an orange-yellow. Archive files (also explained

later) are red, and graphical files are purple. If the colors annoy you, you can add
--color=none to the ls statement.

Long Listings: -l

You can get a long listing, with more information, by typing ls -l, as you learned in the
last chapter. And, as with the dir command, you can give ls patterns to match and it will
restrict its output using those patterns; ls c* will only show files and directories whose
names start with *c*.

Suppressing Directory Contents: -d

But doing an ls -l c* will probably give you a result that you weren't expecting, because
ls will then not only show you every file whose name starts with *c*, it will then show you
the contents of every directory whose name starts with *c*! To Linux, then, "long listing"
means really long—include-the-names-of-the-files-in-the-directory long. You can defeat
that behavior by adding the d option, as in ls -ld. Here, I've combined the -l (long listing)
and -d option; -d means, "Only show the directory names, not the directory contents."

Notice that in Linux you use more than one option by typing a single dash followed by
options' letters: it's ls -ld, not ls -l -d. You actually *could* put the options separately, but
you will find that most Linux people (and instructions about Linux) combine the options
together. Usually the order of the options doesn't matter, although sometimes it may.

In each of these examples, ls has started working from the current directory, whatever
that is. You can tell it to start from somewhere else by adding directory names and, if you
like, filename patterns to the right of the options. For example:

```
ls -l /
```

says to do a long listing starting at /, the root. To see all of the files in a directory named
/mystuff whose names start with the letter *x*, type:

```
ls /mystuff/x*
```

Handling Filenames That Include Blanks

Sooner or later, every Windows or NT power user gets around to having to do some
command-line work on their system, and at some point, she'll have to issue a dir command on a directory whose name contains a space or two—for example, whenever she
wants to look in the Program Files directory. In Microsoft operating systems, you keep
from confusing the command shell by enclosing names that includes spaces in double
quotes, like this:

```
dir "c:\program files"
```

You may run across Linux directories that contain embedded blanks as well—particularly when you've mounted a FAT, FAT32, or NTFS volume used to dual-boot a Microsoft operating system. But how do you tell ls to show you a directory whose name contains blanks? Linux offers you two ways. First, you can prefix every blank with a backslash, like so:

```
ls /cdrive/program\ files
```

Or you can instead use double quotes, as in this:

```
ls "/cdrive/Program Files"
```

Exploring Subdirectories: -R

It's often useful to use the Windows dir command to view not only a directory but that directory's subdirectories. Microsoft's dir /s command does that, visiting a directory's subdirectories, and those subdirectory's subdirectories, and so on. Linux calls that recursion, and you can trigger recursion with the -R (notice that it's uppercase) option. To see what's in /mystuff and all of the directories inside /mystuff and all of the directories inside the directories in /mystuff, and so on, type:

```
ls -R /mystuff
```

Seeing "Hidden" Files: -a

Linux doesn't really have a "hidden file" attribute, but it uses something kind of like that. Many low-level configuration files' names start off with a period, files with names such as .forward or the like. By default, ls doesn't display those files. But you can tell ls to display these "hidden" files with the -a option. To see a long listing of all of the files in the root directory, including those whose names start with a period, type:

```
ls -al /
```

Notice again that the options come first, then the directory name and possibly a filename pattern.

Sorting Output

Finally, it's often useful to be able to sort the directory output—biggest files first, smallest files first, most recently created files first, that sort of thing. ls will do that as well:

- The -S option (uppercase, note) sorts by size, largest first.
- The -r option reverses any sort command, so, for example, to see a directory's files listed with the smallest files first, use ls -rS.
- The -t option sorts by modification time, most recently modified first.
- The -u option also sorts by time, but it sorts by access time—the time the file was most recently examined.
- The -X option sorts by file extension, clearly a sop to us DOS/Windows/NT users, as Linux doesn't really rely on file extensions the way we do.

More Advanced Pattern Searches

Earlier, I noted that a command like `ls c*` would show all files and directories that matched the pattern c*; as in DOS, the * (asterisk) is a wildcard that, in this example, enables `ls` to match any file or directory name that starts with *c*. That basic search capability has existed in DOS/NT/Windows/2000 since 1981. But Linux offers a few file and directory search patterns that Microsoft's operating systems never had.

The simplest regular expression—that's the term in many programming languages for this kind of search-pattern syntax—is just a string of characters, one that only produces a match to something identical to that string of characters. Regular expressions are built from a set of flexible patterns that Linux utilities can use to search for files, text, directories, or whatever. I'll discuss them in detail later, but for now just understand that regular expressions are like the asterisk, but on steroids—they're incredibly powerful, as you'll see. For example:

```
ls markfile
```

would only match a file or directory named `markfile`; things named `markfile2`, `markfile.txt`, or `xxmarkfile` wouldn't match. This shouldn't be a surprise, as our familiar NT/DOS/Windows/2000 operating systems work like this. And although I've been saying "file or directory," Linux has many more uses for searches—for example, you can use Linux regular expressions in the `vi` editor to find strings.

It also shouldn't be surprising that you can put an asterisk at the end of a string of characters that tells Linux to match anything to that asterisk, so:

```
ls markfile*
```

would match `markfile`, `markfile2`, `markfile.txt`, or the like. So far, no surprises.

But it gets better. Clearly, I could ask to see everything that begins with *s* using the s* regular expression (`ls -d s*`), or I could ask to see everything that ends with *s* using the *s regular expression. But how would I ask to only see those items that both begin and end with *s*?

Quite easily, as Linux's * pattern is very flexible; Linux lets you use it in the middle of your search string. For example, a command like:

```
ls -d /etc/s*m*b*
```

would turn up files named `smb.conf`, `smbusers`, and `samba`.

Better Than 2000: Multiple Choice Searches

This is all very nice, you may be thinking, but also quite possible with Windows, DOS, and the like. What can Linux offer in searching for files that DOS & Company can't?

As you know, you could find everything that started with a *c* by searching with the regular expression c*–but what if you wanted to find everything that started with either *c, k,* or *p*? DOS & Company can't help out there, but Linux can. You can tell Linux to search for several possible characters by putting those characters inside brackets, like this:

```
ls [ckp]*
```

Try out an `ls -d [ckp]*` in your /etc directory, and you'll get all of the file and directory names that start with *c, k,* and *p*—although there aren't any that start with *k* on most systems, you'll get some *c*'s and *p*'s. (I included the -d option, and recommend that you do if you're trying this out; otherwise recall that `ls` will helpfully show you not only the directory names, but the contents as well!)

You can indicate a range of characters with a dash; the command:

```
ls [b-g]*
```

would show all files and directories that start with *b, c, d, e, f,* or *g*. Remember case counts, so *B, C, D, E, F,* and *G* wouldn't match—but you could include B-G on the same line by just including it after b-g, to construct a command to show any files that start with *b, c, d, e, f, g, B, C, D, E, F,* or *G*:

```
ls [b-gB-G]*
```

To construct that pattern, I just combined the regular expression's feature that lets you just specify a list in brackets, like [ckp], with its ability to read ranges, like [b-g].

You can also use the curly braces {} to provide a number of options to a command.For example, say you want to list every file that ends in .aux, .log, or .dat. You can do this simply by typing:

```
ls *.{aux,log,dat}
```

Notice that the options inside the braces are separated by commas.

What's that you say? You need even more search power? Well, you can get it from Linux, by coupling the `ls` command with a Linux command dedicated entirely to searching, a command called grep. But stay tuned for that—let's get a few more basic commands out of the way first.

Controlling Output: *less*

You probably notice if you did any test `ls` commands that `ls` output can quickly scroll off the screen. You probably already know the DOS command more, which will take the output of any command and display that output one screen at a time. You tell a program to send its output to more rather than the screen by adding the | or "pipe" symbol—for example:

```
dir|more
```

This would execute a standard DOS/NT/Windows "list a directory" command, but wouldn't let the output scroll off the screen. You then press a key to see the next screen, and so on.

While Linux has a more command that you can use, it also has a somewhat more powerful command, less. You pipe output to less and, like more, it pauses at the first screenful. But less then lets you use the PageUp and PageDown keys to scroll back and forth in the output. You can press the q key to stop less and return to the command prompt. For example, you could view every single file on your Linux disk hierarchy by typing:

```
ls -R / |less
```

That would run a simple ls, but with the -R recursive option, which examines all directories below ls's starting point. Because I designated / as the starting point, that shows all files. Then the output goes to less, and I can scroll up and down the output to my heart's content.

Finding Files: *find*

"Hmmm… let's see, where did I put that file containing those notes from my meeting with George; I called it georgenote.txt or something like that…" The bad part about having lots of hard disk space is trying to find things in it. Under DOS/NT/Windows, you can use the dir command to find files. But ls doesn't do that job for you—a different command, find, does. In its simplest form, find looks like:

```
find startingdirectory -name searchpattern
```

find works recursively, so you point it at some directory (*startingdirectory*) and it searches not only that directory but all directories underneath it, looking for files that match *searchpattern*. That pattern can be as simple as a filename, or it can include wildcards. For example, if all I can remember about my file is that its name starts with *george*, then I'd type:

```
find / -name "george*"
```

As in DOS/NT/Windows, the asterisk matches anything, so find would report any filenames starting with *george*. Notice that I put the search pattern in quotes. Sometimes search patterns, like *, confuse Linux, and the operating system tries to do the searching itself before passing that information on to find, with the result that the find fails. But if you put the search pattern in quotes, then the operating system leaves the pattern untouched and hands it directly to find. Then it'll work fine, as in the previous example.

But remember that Linux is case-sensitive about filenames; if I'd named my file Georgenotes.txt, then find wouldn't find that file. You can alternatively tell find to be case-insensitive with the -iname option:

```
find / -iname "george*"
```

Bracketed lists work for search pattern also. To find all files starting with *j* through *l* and those starting with *q*, type:

```
find / -name "[j-lq]*"
```

find will also report files that have been modified within a particular time period. As with ls, find has more options than I'm going to cover in this text, but here are two useful examples. The -mtime option reports any files modified in some specified number of days; to show any files modified in the past 20 days, type:

```
find / -mtime -20
```

To find any files modified in the past 20 minutes, use -mmin:

```
find / -mmin -20
```

Fast Finding: *locate*

Because find has to poke around your hard disk, it can take quite a while. Another command, locate, does a similar job. But it's a lot faster, because it answers your question based on an indexed database of all files on a disk, a database automatically rebuilt every night. Its syntax looks like:

```
locate [-i] filename
```

The –i says to do a case-insensitive search. But locate can sometimes tell you a bit more than you bargained for, as it finds any file with *filename* in its name. For example:

```
locate auto
```

would find every single file on the disk with *auto* in its name. So sometimes it's a bit more chatty than you'd like... but it's always fast!

Finding Out Where a Program Lives: *which*

Suppose you know a program's name, but don't know where it is? You type abcd and something happens (that's not a real Linux command as far as I know), but you're pretty sure that you've got more than one abcd on your system—which one ran? The which command looks on your path and tells you which file actually ran.

For example, I recently tried to set up a mail server on a Linux box. The SMTP portion worked fine, but I couldn't retrieve mail. Looking further into the problem, I found that the POP3 service wasn't running.

The next logical thing to do was to find out the name of the actual program that implements the POP3 protocol. I looked in a file named inetd.conf and found this line describing POP3:

```
pop-3 stream tcp nowait root /usr/sbin/tcpd ipop3d
```

I don't know or care what most of that says, but I know (because Dan told me) that the last item is the name of the program: ipop3d. Next order of business, then, was to check to see if I had a program named ipop3d on my system. I did that with the command `which ipop3d`, which returned a message telling me that there was no ipop3d detectable on my path. That turned out to be the problem: I'd chosen the "server" configuration when installing the mail server, and apparently Red Hat's "server" configuration includes Sendmail (the SMTP component) but not ipop3d (the POP3 component). (Or it might have meant that ipop3d wasn't on my path, but inasmuch as I was logged in as root, that'd be the same as saying that the operating system itself couldn't find it. This command is, then, most useful for this kind of troubleshooting if you're logged in as `root`.)

Another use for `which` is to help you figure out which copy of a program is working. I installed a newer version of Samba on a system that was already running an existing version, and while Samba ran, all right, I wasn't sure which Samba was running. Typing `which smbd` (smbd is one of the basic Samba programs) showed me which version was active—the old one, as it turned out.

Creating a Directory: *mkdir*

This command should be familiar. To create a new directory under a Microsoft operating system, you use the `md` command, and that works in some flavors of Linux but not all; the `mkdir` command is the reliable command if you want to make a new directory. To create a new directory named `pictures` in my home directory (which is named `/home/mark`), I'd type:

```
mkdir /home/mark/pictures
```

Or, if my current directory were already `/home/mark`, then simply:

```
mkdir pictures
```

As with Microsoft operating systems, the difference between the first `mkdir` and the second was that I fed the first `mkdir` the entire directory path, starting with /; in the second case, I did not precede `pictures` with a slash, so Linux knew that I meant, "Create this directory inside the directory that I'm currently sitting in."

TIP Note that if you wanted to make the directory /home/mark/pictures/ vacation, and the directory /home/mark/pictures did not yet exist, you could use the -p option to create the entire 'path' you are requesting. So the command would be mkdir -p /home/mark/pictures/vacation.

Copying a File: *cp*

Linux's file copy command works almost the same as the copy command in Microsoft operating systems:

```
cp [options] file_to_copy place_to_copy
```

For example, to copy a file named smb.conf in the /etc directory to the /home/mark directory, I'd type:

```
cp /etc/smb.conf /home/mark
```

As with the copy command, you can specify a name for the newly created file. To copy /etc/smb.conf to a file named example.conf in /home/mark, I'd type:

```
cp /etc/smb.conf /home/mark/example.conf
```

As with the Microsoft xcopy command, you can use cp to copy entire directory trees; the -r (recursion) option accomplishes that. To copy every file and directory in the /home directory to another directory named /backups, for example, I'd type:

```
cp -r /home /backups
```

This command will behave in one of two ways, depending on whether your disk already contains a directory named /backups:

- If your disk does not currently contain a directory named /backups, then cp creates a new directory named /backups, which contains copies of all of home's subdirectories: /home/mark is copied to a new directory named /backups/mark, /home/jerry is copied to a new directory named /backups/jerry, and so on.

- If your disk already has a directory on it named /backups, then cp creates a directory under /backups named /backups/home, and then re-creates all of /home's directories under that. If /home contained a directory named /home/mark, then /backups would now contain /backups/home/mark.

This leads to the following odd circumstance: if your disk doesn't currently contain a directory named /backups and you execute cp -r /home /backups twice in succession, then you will not get a message asking you if you're sure, because it's not overwriting any files. The first time you execute the cp command, cp creates /backup with all of the /home directories; the second, it creates /backup/home and then creates the /home subdirectories below that. The third time, however, cp will try to re-create /backup/home, and at that point it'll start overwriting things—which will lead to the "Are you sure?" type of message.

You can make things a bit clearer by adding a file wildcard character to the source directory:

```
cp -r /home/* /backup
```

This is an unambiguous command that says to re-create the directory structure currently inside the /home directory inside the /backup directory—/home/mark is copied to /backup/mark, and the like. But the command will fail if you don't already have a /backup directory created and waiting.

If executing a cp command will overwrite an existing file, cp will stop and ask if you really want to do it. The -f or "force" option tells it to just shut up and do what you told it to do:

    cp -f /etc/smb.conf /home/mark

Remember that you can combine Linux options with a single dash; to use both the -r and -f options, you'd type cp -rf or cp -fr rather than cp -r -f.

cp will also let you copy with an "only overwrite older files" option. For example, suppose I take the directory that contains this book on the road with me, on my laptop. I modify a few files while traveling and then want to save my changes back to the master directory on my server. There's no point in recopying the megabytes and megabytes of files in the book's directory over the network to the server, as the vast majority of those files haven't changed while I've been gone. I can tell Linux to only copy the files that have changed with the -u (update) option. If my book is sitting on my laptop in /home/mark/linuxbook, and I save the book on the server in /ntserver/books/ linuxbook–and yes, that's a share on the network, even though it looks like a local directory; remember that Linux makes all data look like it's attached to a single drive— then I'd do this command:

    cp -ruf /home/mark/linuxbook/* /ntserver/books/linuxbook

The -r option lets me copy all of the directories in /linuxbook; the -u option says to only copy the ones that are newer on the laptop than on the server; and the -f option says don't ask me if I really want to do it, just do it.

Moving or Renaming a File: *mv*

In Linux, one command both renames and moves files: mv. In its simplest form, it looks like:

    mv *oldfilename newfilename*

For example, then, typing:

    mv preliminary-report final-report

would rename a file named preliminary-report to final-report. Notice that there wasn't any directory information—no slashes—so clearly preliminary-report existed in my current directory. But both the old filename and the new filename can include full or partial directory paths.

For example, suppose my current directory is /home/mark. Suppose also that there are two directories under /home/mark, /home/mark/dir1 and /home/mark/dir2. In /home/mark/dir1 is a file named file.txt. Typing:

```
mv dir1/file.txt dir2/file.txt
```

would move file.txt to dir2. Typing:

```
mv dir2/file.txt file.txt
```

would have the effect of renaming dir2/file.txt to simply file.txt. What's the difference? Well, what directory would file.txt now be in? The current or default directory, of course—so mv dir2/file.txt file.txt had the effect of moving file.txt from /home/mark/dir2 to /home/mark.

In the process of renaming a file from one name to another, mv might have to overwrite an existing file. For example, if I have a file named file1 and another named file2, and I typed mv file1 file2, then Linux will be happy to rename file1–but as there's already a file named file2, renaming file1 to file2 will have the side effect of deleting the original file2. mv offers two options for that: -b, which backs up the old file2 to its old name with a tilde attached (file2~), and -f, which tells mv not to ask you if you really want to do it.

Dan adds that mv left to itself will *not* in fact plague you with the "Are you sure?" messages; as it turns out, you must invoke mv with the -i for "interactive" option to get it to do that. Why then, you ask, does mv act as if you invoked it with the -i option if you never typed -i? There is a file called .bashrc that configures the command-line behavior of your Linux machine—it's in your home directory, we'll talk about them in Chapter 6—that contains this line:

```
alias mv='mv -i'
```

Sneaky, eh? mv comes with airbags, but leaves them turned off. Red Hat and other distributions, however, turn the bags on! If you really hate that the "interactive" mode is turned on, then you could modify your .bashrc file. It's in your home directory, which is named /home/*username*, where *username* is, as you'd guess, your logon name. The exception is the root account; its home directory is not in /home; instead, it's called /root.

Displaying a File: *cat*

Microsoft operating systems have a command, type, that will display a file on the screen: type c:\config.sys will dump the contents of config.sys (which won't be very large on an NT system) to the screen. Linux also has a command like this: cat. To see a file, just type cat followed by the file's name:

```
cat /etc/smb.conf
```

As is the case with Windows' `type`, `cat` output can cause scrolling, so it's often a better idea to pipe `cat`'s output to the `less` filter:

```
cat /etc/smb.conf|less
```

Now, if we were talking about the Microsoft `type` command, we'd be done. But Linux and Unix commands tend to have a "Swiss army knife" aspect to them—they can do a lot of useful things. `cat` will list a file and include line numbers for each line if you like; just include the -n option. If you for some reason want to list a file that isn't all text data, then `cat` will represent the nonprintable characters as control characters if you use the -v option—for example, a "null" character, a binary zero, will show up as ^@ with this option.

Perhaps most interesting is where `cat` gets its name from. Its actual job is to concatenate or join files. You feed `cat` a list of files, and it glues them all together and then writes them to the "standard output" file—which you and I know as the display. You can redirect standard output to another file, which would then let `cat` do its intended job:

```
cat file1 file2 > sumfile
```

That line would let `cat` glue together a file named `file1` and another named `file2` and then write the combined file to a file named `sumfile`. So how does `cat` normally work as a `type`-like command to display files? Well, if you type `cat myfile` and press Enter, then Linux gives `cat` the file named `myfile` and no others. `cat` sees that its job is to collect together only one file—easy enough—and then write it out to standard output, as always. As you haven't redirected standard output, it goes to the screen, with the result that you've displayed `myfile`.

You could, if you wanted, tell cat to display more than one file with `cat file1 file2 file3...`, or you could even type `cat *`, which would display all files in the current directory. As with other Linux commands, you could even give it more complex commands like `cat [qx]*`, which would tell `cat` to display any file whose name starts with a lowercase *q* or *x*.

Erasing a File: *rm*

Linux's file erase command is `rm`, which I suppose is short for "remove." You invoke it as usual, the command followed by a filename:

```
rm myfile.txt
```

It wants to confirm every single erasure with you, but you can tell it to suppress the confirmations with the -f (force) option, as with `cp` and `mv`. `rm` will take wildcards—rm *, rm [qx]*, and the like—and you can even tell `rm` to delete entire directory trees with its recursion (-R) option. For example, the command:

```
rm -Rf /home/mark
```

would delete /home/mark as well as any directories inside /home/mark, any directories inside them, and so on. You would then delete the top-level directory with the rmdir command.

Creating a Symbolic Link—a "Shortcut:" *ln*

Linux incorporates the idea of a "symbolic link." In some ways, it is like a Windows shortcut. Shortcuts are, as you know, icons that look like files but that aren't—they're nothing more than pointers. Despite that, if you double-click a shortcut's icon, then you get basically the same result as if you double-click a regular file's icon: Windows opens a document or starts a program.

Symbolic links are things that look like files but are simply pointers to files. Doing something to a symbolic link usually does it instead to the file that the link points to. For example, if I had a program named do-something in a directory named /mystuff that, well, did something, then I could of course start it up by typing /mystuff/do-something. But if I didn't feel like typing the whole name, then I could create a symbolic link with a shorter name, like ds, and whenever I typed ds, then Linux would figure out that I really wanted to run the do-something program.

Here's another example. Linux's GUI, the X Window System, relies on an important configuration file called XF86Config, which usually lives either in /etc or in /etc/X11. I might want to have several of these configuration files, however, to let me run X under different conditions. I could, then, have any number of XF86Config files located around my hard disk, and when I wanted to use any one of them, I could just create a symbolic link in /etc or /etc/X11 named XF86Config, linked to the particular XF86Config that I wanted at that moment.

You create symbolic links with the ln -s command, like so:

```
ln -s name_of_actual_file name_of_link
```

So, for example, if I have an X configuration file named xfile sitting in /home/mark, I could fool my system into thinking that it's sitting in /etc with this command:

```
ln -s /home/mark/xfile /etc/XF86Config
```

TIP   In general, you should create symbolic links rather than their alternative, "hard" links.

Searching: *grep*

Unix (and therefore Linux) has a long tradition of searching and pattern-matching tools. The basic one is a tool called grep, for "global regular expression print." If the name sounds cryptic, then all I can say is, "Get used to it," as using it is no less so. But it's worth learning grep, because it's staggeringly powerful.

grep = "global regular expression print"

The name "global regular expression print" breaks down to mean this:

- It's a command that searches an entire file to find something—for example, grep could find all of the lines in a file that contain the word *Microsoft*. As grep searches the *entire* file, it is (in the eyes of its original developer) **global**.

- It can match a wide variety—I wasn't exaggerating when I used the word "staggering" a paragraph or two back—of different patterns. Want to find every line that has the word *the* in it three times, regardless of how those words are arranged in the line? Or how about lines that contain a three-letter acronym—that is, lines that contain a word that is exactly three characters long but is only composed of capital letters? grep can do that without even breathing hard. You just describe to grep what you want to see, using grep's built-in "language" for searching. Where you or I might call instructions for searching a "pattern" or a "search pattern" or perhaps a "search template," Linux calls such a pattern a *regular expression*. I don't know where they got that phrase from, but it's an important one in Linux, as commands besides grep need to be able to search things, and so you'll find that other Linux commands can also accept some kind of pattern-matching instructions via **regular expression**s.

- Finally, once grep finds the pattern you've asked it for, it "**print**s" it on the screen.

Hence grep: global regular expression print.

Basic grep

The idea with grep is that you feed it a file and the thing to search for, or it can act as a filter like less, accepting input from standard input; it then emits any lines that match the pattern on standard output, which can either display on the screen by default or be redirected to a file.

If I had a file named myfile, and I wanted to find all of the lines that included the word *system* in it, I'd type

```
grep system myfile
```

I would then see every line that contains the word *system*. I might just want to count the number of lines that contained *system*; I could then use the -c option:

```
grep -c system myfile
```

This would not report the number of occurrences of *system*—I don't think grep can do that—but instead reports the number of lines where *system* appears, so a line with two *systems* would only count once. (For a tool that can count all the occurrences, skip to the end of the chapter and read about the wc command.) Or you could use grep to find out whether or not there's an account on this system named mark:

```
grep mark/etc/password
```

I'll explain the /etc/password file in the next chapter.

grep As a Filter

You can, as I've already said, use grep as a filter. For example, a very useful program named dmesg stores and then displays messages from the system, mostly messages that popped up during boot time. Suppose I want to see what it reported about my Ethernet card? Typing dmesg produces a result that quickly scrolls off the screen. I could type:

```
dmesg|less
```

That would at least capture the information, but then I'd have to scroll up and down looking for the line or lines describing my NIC. But if I recall that Linux calls my first Ethernet card (which is the *only* Ethernet card in most cases) "eth0," I can use grep to my advantage here:

```
dmesg|grep eth0
```

The result will be that instead of getting all of dmesg's information, I'll just get the one or two lines that contain eth0, which will report my NIC's MAC address, board type, and IRQ.

Telling *grep* to Search with Regular Expressions

To get the most out of grep, though, you don't just have it look for simple strings like system or eth0. Instead, you give it powerful search commands using the search language called *regular expressions*.

It's easiest learning about regular expressions if you have a file to try them out on. Many Linux distributions, including Red Hat, come with a file named /usr/share/dict/ words, which is a list of tens of thousands of English words. I'll use that in my examples; I'll assume that your Linux has the "words" file and that you've cd-ed over to /usr/ share/dict.

Simple Strings   You've already met some of what regular expressions can do. The command:

```
grep baste words
```

returns *alabaster, baste, basted,* and *bastes*. grep will match a string whether it's in the middle of a line or not, hence both *baste* and *alabaster*.

Lists of Possible Matches   As with other Linux commands, you can use a list of possible matching values in brackets. We can see if there are any words that contain capital letters with the [A-Z] pattern. But before we can hand a pattern of any complexity at all to grep, we have to enclose it in quotes:

```
grep '[A-Z]' words
```

And, judging by the minor blizzard of lines that flew by, it's safe to say that yes, the "words" file *does* contain capital letters.

Digression: *grep* and *egrep*   Before I show you any more regular expressions, however, let me make an important point. I've already said that Linux commands other than grep can support regular expressions. The collection of patterns that those commands can *use* varies a bit from program to program; for example, as you've seen, ls takes *some* regular expressions, but not very many of them. grep can handle a somewhat wider set of regular expressions than ls can, but not *all* regular expressions, at least not in its basic form.

"Basic form?" Yes.

Apparently the original version of grep was only designed to handle a limited amount of regular expression (i.e., pattern search) types. A later tool, egrep–"enhanced" grep– could do more flexible kinds of searches than grep could, so modern greps have an option -E that let them do egrep-type searches. There's two points that I want you to understand here. First, you shouldn't take what I'm showing you as something nice and uniform that'll work across all Linux commands; and second, you will often find that, if grep can't use a regular expression, you should use it with the -E option (yes, it's case-sensitive like all Linux options; you need a capital *E*).

The Basic Metacharacters: . ^ $ Suppose you want to find any word that starts with *rest*; what would that expression look like? Well, if you try:

```
grep rest words
```

then you'll not only get r*est*, *restaurant*, and the like, you'll also get words that contain that string, as in *Everest*. How to tell grep that you only want words that start with *rest*? With a *metacharacter*. Doing *any* kind of snazzy search requires knowing metacharacters.

A metacharacters is a character that has a special meaning. For example, you've already met two of them: [and]. You told grep to look for [A-Z], and it was somehow smart enough to know that you didn't really want to find a line that started with a left bracket, a capital *A*, a dash, a capital *Z*, and a right bracket. Rather, you wanted anything that matched any capital letter. grep knows that a left bracket means "a list of possible desired characters is beginning." The circumflex, ^, is another metacharacter that means "start of line." This command would tell grep to only show those lines that not only include *rest*, but specifically start with *rest*:

```
grep -E '^rest' words
```

Sometimes you might want to match the *end* of the line rather than the beginning. There's a metacharacter to do that, too: the dollar sign, $. To find only those words that *end* with *rest*, try this grep:

```
grep -E 'rest$' words
```

And there are no shortage of *those* words. You can combine both ^ and $ like so:

```
grep -E '^rest$' words
```

This is a very specific query: it looks for a beginning of a line, the string *rest*, and the end of a line. In other words, we've described this line exactly.

TIP   And if you've been trying all of these commands, I hope you've discovered the "history" function of the bash shell that lets you press the up arrow to retrieve the last command. You can then edit the command and resubmit it.

A third very basic and useful metacharacter is the period (.). It matches any single character. Perhaps you want to find all references to defense in a document but are not sure if it was written using American English or British English—was it spelled *defense* or *defence*? You can match either one like so:

```
grep -E 'defen.e' words
```

Of course, I could have used a list as well:

```
grep -E 'defen[cs]e' words
```

Or how about this query: how many 20-character words are in the "words" file? Well, let's see—we need to build a regular expression that asks for 20 characters and 20 characters *only*. That might look like:

```
grep -E '^...................$'
```

Repeating Search Patterns   But that's a bit sloppy, actually. Putting the ^ at the beginning and the $ at the end with 20 periods really only tells grep to find us lines that only include 20 *characters*. *Words*, in contrast, consist only of letters, *a–z* and *A–Z*. So the better way to build the regular expression would probably be to build it out of 20 lists: [A-Za-z][A-Za-z][A-Za-z][A-Za-z]...

Well, that would work, but it'd be a pain to type. Fortunately, there's a way to save typing there: you can indicate a number of times that a pattern must repeat by following the pattern with a number in braces:

```
grep -E '^[A-Za-z]{20}$' words
```

You can specify a possible number of repetitions by offering a range—just enter two numbers separated by a comma. For example, to display all 18-character through 23-character words in the "words" file, use this command:

```
grep -E '^[A-Za-z]{18,23}$' words
```

Finally, you can specify that you don't care how many times the pattern repeats by forgoing the braces and just putting an asterisk in. For example, how many words start off with *ab* and end with *a*, like abracadabra? The regular expression to search for that would be:

- Find a word that starts with *ab*,

- Then we don't care how many other letters appear,

- And finally the word should end with *a*.

The expression for a word that starts with *ab* is ^ab–don't forget the circumflex to establish that the line *starts* with *ab*! The pattern for "any letter" is, again, [A-Za-z], and the metacharacter for "we don't care how many" is *. To force a line that ends with *a*, use a$ for the following command:

```
grep -E '^ab[A-Za-z]*a$' words
```

Cryptic? You bet—it's the Unix way. But also compact and powerful; that's also the Unix way. Here's another example. How many words have the letter *t* in their tenth position? Well, we're going to count, so don't forget the -c option for grep. How to check if there's a *t* in the *tenth* character position? Simple: look for a line with nine "don't care" characters, followed by a *t* or *T*:

```
grep -Ec '^.{9}[tT]' words
```

My "words" file comes up with 984 of them!

Excluding Lists: Double Duty for the Circumflex   We've searched for things that are present, but how can we search for things that *aren't* present? For example, you probably know that the letter *e* is the most common letter in the English language. How can we list all of the words in the "words" file that do not contain any *e*'s?

Recall that you can specify a list in brackets: [ab] would match either *a* or *b*. You could, if you wanted to, create a list with just one item, as in [e], and of course, normally you wouldn't. But you can include a list in a regular expression that is not a list of things to *match*, but rather to *not match*, provided that you start the list with a circumflex. *As long as it is the first character in a list*, then the circumflex means "don't match" rather than the job it usually takes on, which is to match the beginning of a line. (Why didn't they just use a tilde or an octothorp or some other oddball character? I have no idea.) So, for example, suppose I wanted to see every three-letter word composed of *n*, another character, and a *t*, but I *didn't* want to get the word *net*? The regular expression would look like this:

```
grep -E '^n[^e]t$' words
```

The first circumflex ^ says to match the beginning of the line; the n says to match the letter *n*; the [^e] says, "Match this with *anything* but *e*!"; and the t$ says to match to the letter *t* and the end of the line.

Now let's assemble the "Find the words with no *e*" regular expression. My first guess would have been something like this:

```
grep -E '[^e]*' words
```

My reasoning was that this matched an unlimited string of "not *e*'s." Which is what I'm looking for—almost. The problem is that it doesn't *force* every character to be "not *e*." Thus a word like *everything* certainly contains a string of characters that are not *e*—two, in fact: *v* and *rything*. How to dictate that every single character not be *e*? By using ^ and $:

```
grep -E '^[^e]*$' words
```

This is a great example, because it shows the circumflex in *both* of its roles—the first time to match the beginning of a line, the second to negate the contents of a list.

Escaping Metacharacter Status   Sometimes you want to search in a file for a character, but realize that the character *is* a metacharacter! For example, suppose I wanted to search a file for every decimal numeric value, every time that something like "3.1416" or "6.02" appeared. The pattern seems easy to write, looking something like [0-9].[0-9], but that won't work, as . doesn't just match "period," it matches *anything*. How do we tell grep to just look for a match to a period? For that matter, how would we search for a bracket, a brace, an asterisk, a circumflex, or a dollar sign? By preceding the character with the escape character, the backslash (\), so that the pattern looks like this:

```
grep -E '[0-9]\.[0-9]' words
```

(Actually, as "words" is just a list of English words, you won't come up with any matches on that file.) How do you search for a backslash? By using *two* backslashes in your regular expression.

Finding Types of Characters   I've already offered examples where I'd want to search for classes of characters—lowercase letters, uppercase letters, and numbers. But I needn't use [A-Z] to match all uppercase letters, as regular expressions include some "prebuilt" classes of characters. Instead of A-Z, I can alternatively use [:upper:]; instead of a-z, I can use [:lower:]; and instead of 0-9, I can use [:digit:]. I can specify uppercase *and* lowercase letters with [:alpha:]. Prebuilt patterns like these bracketed options are called character classes.

Recall that a page or two back, I wrote a grep command to find all of the 20-character words in the "words" file. It looked like:

```
grep -E '^[A-Za-z]{20}$' words
```

I could recast that with character classes like so:

```
grep -E '^[[:alpha:]]{20}$' words
```

Notice the extra brackets. The "match all letters" pattern itself is written [:alpha:]; if you want to make it a member of a list of things that you search, however, then you have to enclose it in *another* set of brackets, as you always must with a list. For example, if I wanted to find all words in the "words" file whose first character was *either* a digit or a lowercase letter and whose second character was an uppercase letter (don't ask me why I'd want to do this, I'm just looking for a simple example), I'd use this grep command:

```
grep -E '^[[:lowercase:][:digit:]][[:upper:]]' words
```

The expression starts with a circumflex to say, "Start at the beginning of the line in matching," then the [[:lowercase:][:digit:]] is a list that will match *either* a lowercase or numeric value—note that both character classes are enclosed in the same set of brackets—and finally another, simpler list [[:upper:]] just says to match an uppercase letter.

There are 12 character classes, as you see in Table 5.2.

Table 5.2   Predefined grep Character Classes

Character Class	Description: What Does It Match?
[:print:]	Letters, digits, punctuation, and space
[:graph:]	Letters, digits, and punctuation
[:alnum:]	Letters and digits
[:alpha:]	Letters (uppercase A–Z and lowercase a–z)
[:digit:]	Digits, 0 through 9
[:upper:]	Uppercase letters (A–Z)

Table 5.2 Predefined grep Character Classes *(continued)*

Character Class	Description: What Does It Match?
[:lower:]	Lowercase letters (a–z)
[:punct:]	Punctuation
[:blank:]	A space character or a tab character
[:space:]	"Whitespace" characters: space, tab, carriage return, or line feed
[:cntrl:]	Control characters (ASCII 0 through 31)
[:xdigit:]	Hex digits: 0–9, a–f, and A–F

One could write an entire book on regular expressions—in fact, a few people *have*—but those are the basics.

Other *grep* Notes

grep can accept a pattern for its input files; for example, I could search for the word *aardvark* in my current directory by typing:

```
grep aardvark *
```

grep also allows a recursive option, -r, that lets you search throughout the entire drive. So, for example, you could search all of my drives for all files that contain "aardvark" like so:

```
grep -r aardvark *
```

But that may lock up once grep starts looking in the file-like things that aren't really files, like the /dev directory. So Dan recommends a way to get grep to search an entire directory tree:

```
find / -type f -exec grep -H aardvark {} \;
```

I gather that the find command first finds only the "true" files—that's the -type f option—and then passes those to grep.

Creating and Destroying Hard Disk Partitions

Suppose you add a new hard disk to your system. Or perhaps you've decided to remove Windows from one of your system's partitions and dedicate the partition in the service of Linux. You're familiar with the process under Microsoft operating systems: First you create partitions on the hard disk, using either FDISK under DOS or Windows 9*x*, Disk Administrator under NT, or Disk Manager under Windows 2000. Then you high-level format the partition, either using the format command or some other tool (Disk Administrator, Disk Manager, and Windows 9*x*'s My Computer can do high-level formats as well). But how is all that accomplished in Linux? With another set of tools, but they're not bad. In fact, the program that Linux uses to create and destroy partitions is called fdisk, although it doesn't do as much hand-holding as DOS's FDISK.

Once upon a time, Red Hat included a disk partitioning program called cfdisk that was a nice, easy-to-use, menu-driven program... but not anymore; according to Red Hat support, "cfdisk is no longer utilized." Oh well... I guess too many of those Windows GUI addicts were getting comfortable with Linux, so now we're forced to use Linux's fdisk. (Hey, if they really wanted things to be cryptic, they could make us create partitions with an editor that only speaks hex; there's an idea.) I'm sure that an Internet search would yield not only information on putting cfdisk on your system, but also the source code, notes from the author, and so on... but I'm trying to keep this Red Hat 7.3-centric, so we'll surrender and show you how to partition disks with Linux's fdisk.

You start fdisk with one parameter: the name of the device that you want to partition. For example, if your computer has just one EIDE hard disk, then you'd start fdisk like so:

```
fdisk /dev/hda
```

Once started, you control fdisk with single-letter menu options. As you probably don't want to have to fuss with help files, online or otherwise, when doing disk partitioning, I've summarized the subset of commands that you'll probably use in Table 5.3.

Table 5.3 Common *fdisk* Commands

Letter	Result
a	Toggle a partition as bootable or not
d	Delete a partition
l	List the partition types that fdisk knows how to set (essential for creating new partitions)
m	Display help information
n	Create a new partition
p	Display the current partition table

Table 5.3 Common *fdisk* Commands *(continued)*

Letter	Result
q	Quit without saving any changes to the disk
t	Change a partition's system ID
u	Toggle whether fdisk displays space in terms of cylinders or sectors
v	Verify the partition table is internally consistent
w	Write the partition table to disk and exit

You'd probably start off by typing p to see the current state of the partition table for whatever drive you're working on. If you want to wipe a disk clean and repartition, then just use d to delete the partitions one by one.

No matter how large your disk, you can only partition it into four partitions. The partitions on a physical disk are described in a table on that disk's first sector in an area called the *partition table*. The table's pretty simple: it records the first and last cylinder of each partition, what kind of partition that is—FAT, NTFS, NetWare, or whatever—and whether the partition is bootable or not.

To create a partition, then, you press n and Enter, and you'll be prompted for a first cylinder. fdisk offers the first cylinder available, so you can usually just press Enter when asked where to start the partition. When it comes to sizing the partition, though, that can be a pain if you have to sit there and figure out "Ummm, I want a 200MB partition, and it starts on cylinder 1300... let's see, how many megabytes on a cylinder so that I can figure the last cylinder number..." So fdisk makes your life easier by letting you either punch in the last cylinder number, like 1462; or you can just prefix the answer with a plus sign followed by the size that you want the partition to end up in kilobytes, like +200000; or you can prefix the answer with a plus sign and suffix it with an *M* to specify the size in megabytes, as in +200M. "G" works for "gigabytes" as well.

By default, Linux's fdisk sets the partition type of any partition that you create to "Linux," which seems reasonable. On the off-chance that you decide to partition your system from the ground up with fdisk, however (Red Hat's Setup gives you that option), here are the numerical values for the various types of partitions that Linux uses:

- Linux: 83
- Linux extended partition: 85
- Linux swap: 82

If you're setting up a new system, then you'd use a standard Linux (type 83) partition for both the /boot and / (root) partitions, and a Linux swap (type 82) partition for, not surprisingly, your swap partition.

Creating a new Linux swap partition of 50 megabytes on a second EIDE hard disk, then, might look something like this:

```
[root@mypc root]# fdisk /dev/hdb
Command (m for help): n
Command action
   e   extended
   p   primary partition (1-4)
partition number (1-4): 1
First cylinder (0-1023, default 0):
Using default value 0
Last cylinder or +size or +sizeM or +sizeK (0-1023, default 1023): +50M

Command (m for help): t
partition number (1-4): 1
Hex code (type L to list codes): 82
Changed system type of partition 1 to 82 (Linux swap)

Command (m for help): w
The partition table has been re-written!…[output shortened]
[root@mypc root]#
```

If for some reason you are seized with the desire to use fdisk in the middle of RedHat's Setup program instead of using autoconfiguration, then you'll need three partitions:

- A partition of type "Linux" (value 83) of about 55MB for the /boot partition. You never get to tell fdisk that this is the /boot partition. But you *do* use fdisk to make this partition actually bootable—from fdisk, press a, and when you're prompted, type in the partition number of the 55MB partition that you just created.

- A partition of type "Linux swap" (value 82) of whatever size you want. In kernel 2.4, Linus and the boys strongly recommend setting this to twice your RAM size, as you read in the previous chapter.

- A partition of type "Linux" (value 83) that holds the bulk of the Linux install.

TIP   If you need to find out about the hardware characteristics of your hard disk, many distributions have an hdparm command: hdparm -i devicename gives some great information. For example, to find out about the first IDE hard disk on my system, I type hdparm -i /dev/hda.

Formatting a New Hard Disk Partition

Linux uses the same program to do high-level formats of hard disk partitions as it does to do high-level floppy formats—variations of the mkfs (make file system) command. You can format hard disk partitions to the FAT or FAT32 file systems with the command mkfs.msdos and partition disks to the ext2 format with mkfs.ext2.

The tricky part about both commands is that they require you to name the exact partition of the exact physical hard disk. I talked earlier in the chapter about how Linux names hard disk partitions, but basically if you're working with an IDE drive, you have partitions on devices /dev/hda, /dev/hdb, /dev/hdc, and /dev/hdd–the a, b, c, or d indicate whether the physical drive is on the primary or secondary IDE channel and whether it's the master or slave on that channel. You then add a digit to the hda, hdb, hdc, or hdd to indicate partition number, and you always count from one, not zero—so the first partition on the first physical hard disk is /dev/hda1.

To create a FAT or FAT32, partition, you'd use the mkfs.msdos command like so:

```
mkfs.msdos [-F 32] [-v] devicename
```

That's a lot to swallow, so let's take it in pieces: mkfs.msdos is the command; -F 32 is an optional parameter that you use to create a FAT32 disk drive. -v is another optional parameter that means "verbose"—in other words, "Linux, tell me what you're doing!" devicename is as I've previously described. So, for example, to format the first partition of the first disk to FAT32, you'd type:

```
mkfs.msdos -F 32 /dev/hda1
```

On the other hand, to create a more Linux-friendly ext2 partition, use mkfs.ext2:

```
mkfs.ext2 /dev/hda1
```

WARNING   Be sure that the partition identifier—the "type" that you designated in fdisk–matches the type that you format your disk as. At least in the case of most Microsoft operating systems, you won't be able to recognize even FAT drives— unless the type value is correct. What I mean is this: you can use mkfs.msdos until the cows come home, but DOS/Windows 9x/NT/Windows 2000 will not recognize the resulting disk unless its partition ID matches that of a partition that they know, like FAT or FAT32.

> **NOTE** Wondering how to create an NTFS partition with Linux? Me too. Apparently it's impossible.

Formatting a Floppy Disk

From the Linux perspective, preparing a floppy disk is pretty much the same as preparing a hard disk, with the one exception that you needn't partition it. (Although I'm sure there's some Linux hacker somewhere who has, just for the fun of it, figured out how to partition a floppy into FAT, FAT32, and ext2 partitions.)

Low-Level Formatting a Floppy Diskette

You low-level format a floppy diskette using the `fdformat` command:

```
fdformat /dev/fd0H1440
```

That assumes that you're formatting a 1.44MB diskette in the A drive; the device parameter would be `/dev/fd1H1440` if you were doing it in the B drive. The `H1440` means you're formatting a 1.44MB floppy—`H720` handles 720K diskettes, `d360` handles 5.25-inch 360K floppies, `h1200` handles 5.25-inch 1.2MB floppies.

In my experience, this just doesn't work on some laptops. If that's the case, I wouldn't worry about it. Most floppy diskettes come low-level formatted from the factory. If you can't get Linux to low-level format, just skip the step and go straight to high-level format.

High-Level Formatting a DOS Floppy

You probably won't have to low-level format floppies all that often; instead, do what the Microsoft operating systems call a "quick format" and just create a blank file system, which has the net effect of wiping the data off the floppy disk. (Note that if you're concerned with security, then this procedure does *not* delete data, just the "table of contents" that points to the data. A skilled disk mechanic—or someone who'd read my *Complete PC Upgrade and Maintenance Guide*—could reconstruct much of the data if all you did was a high-level format.)

You high-level format a DOS floppy with the `mkfs.msdos` command:

A drive `mkfs.msdos /dev/fd0`

B drive `mkfs.msdos /dev/fd1`

Or you could use mtools with `mformat b:`. Note that `mformat` will *only* do a high-level format, so if you want to create a floppy formatted for DOS *and* create a fresh set of format information, then you must first do an `fdformat`, then an `mformat`.

Creating a Bootable Floppy

Linux will create a floppy with just enough code to boot from with the mkbootdisk command. It only needs one argument: the kernel version. You can find that out by doing:

```
ls /lib/modules
```

You'll then see a directory name like 2.4.18-3 or something similar. Whatever the name, just type its exact value as a parameter to mkbootdisk, as in:

```
mkbootdisk 2.4.18-3
```

Linux will prompt you to insert a floppy, and away it goes. Add the -v option for a bit more verbosity.

Burning CD-R Discs

Formatting floppies is useful, but more and more systems don't come with floppy drives of any kind. For many computers, the only way to create transportable media is through a CD burner. Fortunately, burning CDs is pretty easy with Linux. It's a two-step job:

- First, you tell Red Hat to collect together all of the files that you want to burn to the CD in a file called an "ISO" because of its file format.
- Then you tell Red Hat to burn that ISO file to the CD burner.

The command to make the ISO is mkisofs, and, simplified, it looks like this:

```
mkisofs -o isofile directory-to-copy
```

To create an ISO of a directory named /archive, then, I'd type:

```
mkisofs -o saveit.iso /archive
```

That would create an ISO file named saveit.iso. You'd then burn it to a writeable CD with the cdrecord command... but first you've got to find out a "device ID" for your burner. You do that with the cdrecord -scanbus command:

```
cdrecord -scanbus
```

After some lengthy output, you'll see a line that describes your burner, like:

```
1,0,0  100) 'PHILIPS'  'CDRW...'
```

You now know that your burner is device "1,0,0." Now burn the ISO with this command:

```
cdrecord -eject dev=1,0,0 saveit.iso
```

You can add options like –v to add verbosity, or –speed=n (cdrecord –speed=2 for 2x writes, etc.) to control write speed. There are many more options on cdrecord and mkisofs, of course, but those are the basics. Try this... I've found that mkisofs and cdrecord can burn CDs very quickly!

> **TIP** Sometimes on systems with EIDE burners, cdrecord will report that there are no available burner devices. In that case, try typing modprobe ide-scsi sg. Then try cdrecord -scanbus again.

Running Setup without a CD-ROM

I'd have liked to put this section in the previous chapter, but it required too much knowledge of getting around files and partitions in Linux. But I think you'll find that the wait was worthwhile.

Did you find having to wait around for Red Hat Setup to prompt you to insert CDs irritating? I did. In the process of writing this book, I had to reinstall Linux a *lot*, and I came to dread playing "CD autoloader."

I wanted a way to just start Setup, answer its initial questions, and then leave it for an hour or two. I wondered if there was a way to do something like an NT I386 install, where you copy the installation files over and start the install from them instead of a CD-ROM. It *is* possible to get the CD files over to a hard disk on the PC and then start off a Red Hat Setup from the files on the hard disk, but as far as I can see you need to be able to boot from a floppy disk. If that's not a deal-breaker, then here's how to do it:

1. For each of the three Setup CDs, create a single file that describes that CD, in ISO format. (If you're a veteran CD creator, this term will be familiar.) Or, if you have a broadband connection, you can just download them from ftp:// ftp.redhat.com/pub/redhat/linux/7.3/en/iso/i386/.

2. Create a FAT partition on the target PC—the one that you want to put Red Hat on— of about 1.9GB.

3. Copy the three ISO files (one for each CD) to the FAT partition.

4. Create a Linux boot floppy using the boot.img image file.

5. Boot from the boot floppy and start Setup.

6. When asked if you want to set up from hard disk or CD, tell Setup that you want to start from hard disk.

7. Setup will ask the device name of the FAT partition and offer you the names of the devices that it knows. Choose the one with a name like "/dev/hdsomething." From that point, Setup will run as before.

Here are the details.

Create ISOs of the Three Red Hat Installation CDs

An *ISO* is a geek term for a single file that contains everything on a CD. It comes from the original way to burn CDs—the data had to be formatted in an ISO format, so Step 1 to burning CDs was (and still is, usually) to assemble the image for the prospective CD onto the hard disk of the computer that will burn the CD.

Here, we want to do the opposite: rather than collect a bunch of files into a single ISO file so that we can burn a CD, we want to examine an already-burned CD and suck its data off onto a hard disk, assembled as a single ISO file. The easiest ways that I've found to convert a CD disc into an ISO is either the dd command in Linux or just about any CD copier program under Windows. I use Ahead Software's Nero Burning ROM to create ISOs, and it works great.

From Linux, put a CD disc into the CD drive *but do not mount the CD drive*—if using an automounter then use umount to unmount it. Then create the ISO by typing:

```
dd if=source device of=output file name
```

For instance, if my CD-ROM were /dev/hdb, then I could convert the disc in it to a file named cd1.iso by typing:

```
dd if=/dev/hdb of=cd1.iso
```

If you're using Nero under Windows, just choose Recorder/Save Track. It's intended to only grab one track of a music CD, but if you put a data CD into the drive, then it'll convert the whole CD into an ISO.

Collect the ISOs on a FAT Drive

On the PC that you want to install Linux on, create a FAT drive large enough to hold all three ISOs—about 1.9GB in size. Copy the ISOs to that directory.

> **NOTE** I spent a good amount of time trying to figure out what I was supposed to *call* the ISOs. It turns out that any name works, so I just go with cd1.iso, cd2.iso, and cd3.iso.

Why a FAT partition rather than, say, an EXT3 partition? Two reasons. First, a number of people on newsgroups have reported that for some reason, Red Hat Setup recognizes ISOs on a FAT partition more easily than an EXT3 partition. Second, remember that, at least in my case, I reinstall Linux a lot, as I'm experimenting with it. I like having the ISOs on a FAT drive so that I can tell the autopartitioning routine in Setup, "Delete all *Linux* partitions"—and that way I don't have to worry that the partition with the ISOs somehow gets deleted.

Create a Linux Boot Floppy

Using the rawrite utility in the `dosutils` directory of Red Hat's Installation CD 1, create a floppy using the image on that CD in `/images/boot.img`. A regular Linux boot floppy will not work!

Boot from the Floppy and Select Hard Disk Install

Now you've got the images on a FAT partition on the computer and a floppy that will start off the boot process. When you get the "boot:" prompt, just press Enter. Red Hat's Setup will start in text mode, asking what kind of keyboard and mouse you have. Then it will ask where to do the install from—CD-ROM drive or hard disk? Choose hard disk.

Point Setup to the ISOs and Let It Run

Once you've told Red Hat Setup to run from the hard disk, Setup looks around at your disk partitions and asks where to find the ISOs. It lists all of your storage devices—`/dev/hda1`, `/dev/hda2`, and so on. Choose the one with the FAT drive (in case you've forgotten the device name by then, it reminds you how the device is formatted), and you're off.

From this point on, it's a standard Red Hat Setup… but only in text mode. For some reason a hard disk–based Setup will only run in text mode. You will be amazed how much faster this is. (I wonder if I can burn those three CDs to a DVD-ROM and end up with an all-in-one install disc? Hmmm…)

Printing with Linux

Next, let's see how to print from Linux. Essentially, Linux uses a printing system that originated years ago with Berkeley Unix. That system was suited only to simple text-only printers, but the system has been adapted to support modern printing needs, as you'll see.

How Linux Prints Simple Text

Two programs accomplish most of Linux printing: `lpr` and `lpd`. `lpd` stands for "line printer daemon." When you tell Linux to print something, `lpd` takes the destined-for-the-printer output and sends it to the printer. That doesn't sound very complex, and it isn't, *except* when more than one print job is waiting to print; then `lpd` must manage the queue. `lpr` *feeds* the queue; when a Linux application needs to print some output, it sends that output to `lpr`. In a client-server sense, `lpr` is both client and server—server to an application, client to `lpd`. `lpr` is the "front man," so to speak, in the Linux printing subsystem.

NOTE   Even if you *think* you've never worked with 1pr or 1pd before, the chances are good that you *have*. Ever installed Microsoft TCP/IP Printing on Windows NT? It's an NT implementation of 1pd/1pr. We'll use that information later in Chapter 9 to let Windows, NT, and 2000 machines use Linux printers over a network.

In their basic form, 1pr and 1pd don't really *do* all that much. If you were the only person who used your system, and if you didn't mind sending a document to the printer and then waiting for it to finish before sending the next document, then you wouldn't actually *need* 1pr or 1pd; instead, you could just copy a text file to the printer in the same way that you'd copy it to, say, a floppy drive, or another directory on the hard disk. Actually, though, you'd have to be logged in as root to copy something directly to the printer, which is one of 1pr's values: anyone can tell 1pr to print something. In its earliest form, 1pd's main job was to just manage the queue. That way, you could tell 1pr to print as many files as you liked all at once, without having to wait for the printer to finish one print job before you gave it the next one.

Printing More Complex Content

In their original state, 1pr and 1pd didn't have a clue about the fact that different printers needed different printer escape codes, as printers *didn't* need different codes: all printers just printed simple old text in a fixed-space font, with no graphics, no selectable fonts, no italics, nothing like that. But modern printing needs more than that—we *want* fonts, graphics, and the like. So how did the Linux/Unix community solve the problem? Well, they *could* have thrown away 1pr/1pd, but they didn't; instead, they built upon them.

Here's the problem that any OS faces if it wants to support many applications and wants those applications to be able to talk to many different printers. I know about this because I lived through MS-DOS, which *had* that problem and solved it in exactly the worst way.

The Hard Way to Control Printers

Suppose I want to write a word processor that does fonts, text formatting, and the like. When I get around to writing the "print document" part of the program—a fairly important part of a word processing program—then I need to write some code that tells the printer to italicize a word when the user wants that word italicized. Sounds simple enough, *except* for the fact that there's more than one way to italicize a word. Hewlett-Packard laser printers do it one way, Epson ink-jet printers do it with a different set of commands, and you tell PostScript printers to italicize in a completely different manner—and that's just three printer types. As you know, there are many more types. So what do I do with my word processing program? I guess I could just sit down with the programming manuals for every printer and create a "printer driver" file for each one of those printers. Then, when my word processing program needs to italicize a word, it just looks up in its configuration file to find out what kind of printer the user owns, and *then* looks in that particular printer's printer driver file to find the instructions that the printing program needs to use to get that word italicized. In other words, if there are 200 printers on the market, then I have to write 200 printer driver files.

But now let's say that someone else writes a different program, perhaps a spreadsheet program with some reporting capabilities—in other words, one that needs to be able to do a bit of text formatting also. The spreadsheet creator has the same problem that I just had: his program needs to be able to tell a printer how to italicize a word. So he goes through the same process that I did, building 200 printer driver files. *Now* suppose that there are 100 applications on the market for our operating system that do some kind of printing—100 different companies had to reinvent the same wheel 100 times, each creating 200 printer driver files. If some poor fool were to buy all 100 programs, she'd end up with 20,000 printer driver files on her hard disk!

A Better Way to Control Printers

Clearly there must be a better way, and there is: unified drivers. In the Windows, OS/2, NT, Macintosh, and 2000 world (as well as other operating systems), you get one printer driver for your printer. That printer driver then serves any program that you buy. But there's a cost to this also: in order for one printer driver to be of value to both the word processor's creator, the spreadsheet's creator, and all of the other developers, then the operating system vendor must create a whole new programming language.

The idea with the Windows printer drivers, for example, is that Microsoft created an *imaginary* printer called a "GDI printer." This imaginary printer accepts a set of commands to do text formatting—italics, font selection, and the like—as well as commands to print graphical images. Programmers wanting to build Windows programs just learn how this imaginary printer works and then build their programs to control it. The programs then print by sending a series of commands in the imaginary GDI printer language, and Windows collects all of those commands into a file. Windows, meanwhile, has a set of printer drivers for each of those 200 real-world printers. Once Windows receives the sequence of printing commands for the imaginary GDI printer, it runs those commands through the driver for the user's actual printer, translating the GDI commands to actual printer commands. (You may know that some printers now actually *use* GDI as their native language, but that's not really relevant to this example.)

The beauty of a system like this is that application programmers must only write code to command one kind of printer, the imaginary GDI printer, and also that we only need one printer driver for each kind of printer. Before, 100 applications and 200 kinds of printers led to 20,000 printer drivers; after, each of the 100 applications programmers must only write one set of code, and the operating-system programmers need only build 200 files.

How Linux Printer Drivers Work

MS-DOS used the first printer programming model; Windows uses the second. Which does Linux use? Something in between the two, but closer to the GDI approach. I'm simplifying here, but many Linux programs write their output in PostScript. PostScript is a nice, powerful, flexible printer control language, and it's natively supported for many printers. But how to convert PostScript to the language of your particular printer? With gs, or GhostScript. gs is not GPLed, but it's close: the people who make GhostScript give away an *old* version of GhostScript and sell the latest version to commercial users. Private users can download the current version and use it, but as it's not a GPL license, commercial distributions can't include it in their CDs. If you want the latest GhostScript (again, it's free for personal use), you can find it at www.cs.wisc.edu/~ghost.

So, in theory, all a Linux application need do in order to accomplish all of the fancy printing that it could want is to write its output as PostScript. GhostScript then grabs that PostScript and converts it to whatever language your printer uses. Good so far, but that's not the whole story—remember, not *every* application writes PostScript. Some just emit standard ASCII text. Others produce files in text formats used before PostScript came around: for example, Unix has had a text-formatting language called nroff, usable for producing nice-looking output on simple line printers, and troff, which was similar but suitable for more complex output devices like typesetters. Since then, an even more powerful formatter called TeX (pronounced "tek") appeared; none of these programs produce PostScript. As a result, Linux includes a set of "filter" programs that will convert something like TeX output into PostScript. To print a TeX file, then, your system would first get the TeX output from the TeX formatter program, then it would convert the TeX output to PostScript, then it would hand the PostScript to GhostScript to convert into printer-specific codes.

Linux, then, has an intermediate step between program output and PostScript—a set of filters. These filters are smart enough to sense what kind of file they're dealing with, so they know what kind of filtering to do. Actually, the filters do several things: they filter the print stream into PostScript, then they activate GhostScript, and GhostScript then converts the GhostScript codes into printer-specific codes. The resulting data then sits in the printer queue waiting for lpd to send it to the printer. But enough theory, let's do some commands.

Linux Printing Commands

The basic Linux print queue control commands are lpr and lpd, which you've already met, and three others:

- lpq lets you examine a print queue.
- lpc lets you shuffle jobs around in the queue.
- lprm lets you delete things from the queue.

In the simplest example, where you want to print a file (let's say /etc/hosts) to your default printer (more on that later), the command is:

```
lpr /etc/hosts
```

When you execute that command, lpr copies this file to a spool directory specified by a printer configuration file called printcap. (We'll see more about the printcap file in a minute.) Then lpd takes over and queues the file to go to the printer. If you want to send the file to a particular printer, you add a -P (yes, that's a capital) option and the name of the printer, as in this example:

```
lpr -Phplj4 /etc/hosts
```

Notice that I typed the printer name hplj4 right up against the -P. My understanding is that historically that was how the command was used, although with modern implementations you can put a space between the -P and the printer name. (I did it without the space so as to better fit in with the Unix guys—"when in Rome" and all that.)

Another interesting point is that if you don't type a filename for lpr to print, then lpr will look in the "standard input" device for that filename (or filenames). Recall that, by default, standard input is the keyboard, but you can alternatively pipe in output from another program. For example, if I wanted to print a list of all of the files in a directory, then I could tell lpr to print those files like so:

```
ls | lpr -P myprinter
```

Here, I've just taken the output from ls (the Linux version of the dir command, recall) and piped it to lpr. Dan observes that this allows you to do interesting command combinations, offering this as another example. Say you want a printout of the names of all the files in /home that have been modified in the last two days, and you want it to go to the printer called dj600. Here's the command string to do it:

```
find /home -mtime -2 | lpr -P dj600
```

There are all sorts of other possibilities that you can do and, of course, lpr has a ton of other command-line options.

Now behind lpr, the workhorse of this all is the lpd daemon. It just sits there waiting for requests and will spawn additional copies of itself if necessary to handle the volume of requests. You can verify it is running by using a command such as:

```
$ ps aux | grep lpd
```

which will generate output something like:

```
root 227 0.0 0.3 1116 496 ? S Jun18 0:00 lpd
```

If it is not running, you'll also know when you try to print:

```
$ lpr /etc/hosts

lpr: connect: Connection refused

jobs queued, but cannot start daemon.
```

To fix this, you'll need to restart lpd using its system initialization script (usually found in /etc/rc.d or /etc/rc.d/init.d). On a Red Hat system, the command would be:

```
# /etc/rc.d/init.d/lpd start
```

Or restart if it looks like it is running, but you are still getting error messages. Beyond that, there's not a whole lot we'll do directly with lpd. Instead, we'll use commands mentioned below to work with the print queues.

Manipulating the Print Queue

As you work with printers, you'll no doubt at some point want to see what is queued up to print, or to cancel a print job. The basic command to view a queue is lpq, and with no options it displays the default printer's queue:

```
$ lpq

Rank  Owner   Job Files      Total Size

1st   root    838 /etc/hosts  395 bytes
```

If you want to see the queue of a different printer, you simply append the -P as with lpr:

```
lpq -Phplj4
```

The job number becomes important if you want to remove that print job from the queue using the lprm command, as in:

```
# lprm 838

dfA838AUpjSJw dequeued

cfA838AUpjSJw dequeued
```

Similar to NT, a user can remove their own jobs from the print queue, but they cannot remove the jobs owned by another user. Unless, of course, they are root, who can do pretty much anything. Note that if you want to modify the print queue on another printer, the job number alone will not do it; you still need to use the -P option:

```
# lprm -Phplj4 235

dfA235AxW1TGL dequeued

cfA235AxW1TGL dequeued
```

> ***TIP***   If you want to cancel *all* print jobs you own, simply issue the command
> `lprm -` or `lprm -Pprinter -`. All of your entries in that queue will be removed.

Another command that you can use as root to control the print queues is `lpc` (think
of "line printer control"). `lpc` allows you to control whether a print queue is available
and to take printers offline. From the command line, you can see the status of your
printers with:

```
# lpc status
lp:
    queuing is enabled
    printing is enabled
    no entries
    no daemon present
lj4:
    queuing is enabled
    printing is enabled
    no entries
    no daemon present
```

Don't panic when you see "no daemon present." All this means is that `lpd` is currently not
printing to that printer. The major commands for `lpc` are down and up, which either disable or enable both printing and queuing:

```
# lpc down lj4
lj4:
    printer and queuing disabled
#
# lpc up lj4
lj4:
    printing enabled
    daemon started
#
```

If you want to let the printer keep printing whatever is in the queue, but not have it accept new entries into the queue, you can use the `disable` option:

```
# lpc disable lj4
lj4:
        queuing disabled
#
```

The opposite of `disable`, as you might guess, is `enable`.

If you think the `lpd` daemon for a printer is stuck and not responding for some reason (it does happen once in a while), you can issue a `restart` command:

```
lpc restart lj4
```

Finally, just a note that if you want to perform several of these commands in a row, `lpc` has an "interactive mode" where you can execute all the commands mentioned above:

```
# lpc
lpc> status lp
lp:
        queuing is enabled
        printing is enabled
        no entries
        no daemon present
lpc> down lp
lp:
        printer and queuing disabled
lpc>
```

To leave, type q for quit.

TIP If you want to stop the print queues for all the printers connected to your system, there is a special keyword `all` that can be used with `lpc` commands, as in `lpc down all`.

Configuring Printers

Thus far, my examples will work on just about any printer, as we've only printed simple text. How do you tell Linux that you've just attached a printer to your computer? In the

Windows world, of course, we open up Control Panel or Settings and run a wizard. In the Linux world, well, it depends. There really isn't a single uniform way to add a printer under all distributions. Red Hat and Mandrake have a pretty nice tool called printtool, SuSE uses something called YaST, Caldera has a program called coas. So how do you know how to install a printer on your distribution? You can try several things:

- Much as I hate it for its cumbersome interface, there's a program called linuxconf that attempts to unify all of your system's administration tools—the doodads that install network cards, video, and printers; set up TCP; and the like. Not every distribution comes with a linuxconf, but you might try typing the command linuxconf to see what comes up. There might be a printer install tool in it.

- Most distributions have a whole bunch of available documentation on their website and on the distribution CD. If you bought the $30+ version of the software, then you probably got a printed installation guide as well. Look in this documentation for hints (or even occasionally extremely clear explanations) on how to install a printer. But be prepared to do a bit of looking. Most distributions include lots of generic Linux help text files as a matter of course, but they won't help you—you're looking for the particular install guide for your particular distribution.

NOTE I'm really sorry to have to give such vague direction, but unfortunately this is one of those dusty and unlit areas of Linux. *Additionally*, let me point out that you typically will not be able to download new Linux print drivers from printer vendors' websites (for example, a quick check in mid-2002 of the HP, Lexmark, and Epson driver sites yielded no Linux printer drivers), so check a distribution's list of supported printers before you try to install that distribution and get your printer working. And remember, if you're looking for the name of the tool that'll install a printer in Red Hat, then you needn't search for that information—it's called printtool. It *is* a GUI tool, so hang on until we get to the GUI chapter before you can run it.

Printer "installation" really consists of telling lpd that you have a printer and which filter to use for it. lpd finds out about your printers by looking in a file called /etc/printcap (for "printer capabilities"). Here's a sample from a Red Hat system:

```
##PRINTTOOL3## LOCAL ljet4 300x300 letter
lj4|lp1|Laser Jet 4:\
    :sd=/var/spool/lpd/lj4:\
    :mx#0:\
    :sh:\
```

```
    :lp=/dev/lp0:\
    :if=/var/spool/lpd/lj4/filter:
##PRINTTOOL3## SMB ljet5 600x600 letter
lp|lj5|Laser Jet 5:\
    :sd=/var/spool/lpd/lp:\
    :mx#0:\
    :sh:\
    :lp=/dev/null:\
    :if=/var/spool/lpd/lp/filter:
##PRINTTOOL3## REMOTE POSTSCRIPT 300x300 letter
lp0:\
    :sd=/var/spool/lpd/lp0:\
    :mx#0:\
    :sh:\
    :rm=10.1.0.6:\
    :rp=:\
    :if=/var/spool/lpd/lp0/filter:
```

This sample provides three different types of printers. The first is local to the system, the second remote via SMB (using Samba), and the third a remote lpd system (typically another Linux/Unix box, although it could be an NT box running the TCP/IP Print Server). The lines are essentially one long line of fields separated by colons. (The \ character continues a command line onto the next line.)

So let's just take a real quick look at what we see here in the first printer description in the sample above:

```
lj4|lp1|Laser Jet 4:\
    :sd=/var/spool/lpd/lj4:\
    :mx#0:\
    :sh:\
    :lp=/dev/lp0:\
    :if=/var/spool/lpd/lj4/filter:
```

The first line of the entry is the names by which the printer can be called, separated by the pipe symbol; you can, then, refer to this printer as either lj4, lp1, or Laser Jet 4. The first entry, lj4, is the name you will see in lpc status reports. Using -P and one of these names with any of the lp commands will connect you to that printer.

The second line with sd is for the location of the spool directory. mx#0 says that there are no restrictions on the file size sent to the printer; a number other than 0 would be the max file size. sh suppresses headers so you don't get a "header page" printing out before your document. The lp line specifies which local printer you will be using. (In NT terms, think of this as the print device.) Your first parallel port will be /dev/lp0, your second /dev/lp1, etc.

And then there is this line for if or "input filter." (This is the "filter," the "print driver," so to speak.) And this is the reason why you can't really configure /etc/printcap by hand anymore. This filter program varies from distribution to distribution, but essentially it is a black box that takes in your file, whatever format it is in, and spits it out in the format appropriate to the target printer. You want to print a text file? PDF file? PostScript file? Graphic? And you want the output to be PCL? PostScript? Some other printer language? Need to go to a remote printer? An SMB printer? A NetWare printer? No problem.

Oh, you can look in the spool directory and view the filter script and the other configuration files there. You *could*. And with great effort you could probably figure out how to configure it all yourself. But the reality is that with all the different types of printers available, your best bet is probably to use one of the administration tools provided that create the printcap file for you.

So what should you care about here? For one thing, the printer names. Whichever printer has the name lp somewhere in its list of names is your default printer. You can change the names around here at any time, although just as an FYI you'll need to restart lpd if you do.

Another reason to look here is for the location of the spool directories. If something is stuck or if you are concerned about disk space as you go to print a huge file, a look here can tell you where the spool directory for a printer is located. Sometimes, printers will be configured with a log file (option is lf), which may be useful for you to find.

Finally, if you are printing to a remote lpd printer, you can see (and change) the IP address of the printer here if you are having problems communicating with the printer. (That's the rm line in the third printer.)

Beyond that, there's probably not a whole lot you'll do here. If you look at the man page for printcap, you'll see a zillion cryptic lines that can be included, many dating from the early days of computing.

As far as configuring printers, what I said above is true: the Linux print system can be configured to print to Windows printers using SMB or to NetWare printers. Like NT, you can configure different "printers" that go to the same print device but have different options like paper size and such. Unlike NT, you don't have all the permissions and scheduling options you may be used to. Generally, though, the new tools make it almost trivial to set up new printers.

NOTE   Some commercial applications for Linux may require additional configuration to use your printers. For instance, with WordPerfect 8.0 you need to set up printers, as it has its own print drivers.

Getting Help: Using the Online Documentation

As I've already said, I'm just skimming the surface of what Linux and Linux commands can do. You'll want to find out more about how to do things in Linux, and while there are many books out there on Linux, you'll soon find that many of them are little more than reworked versions of the free documentation that *comes* with Linux. So it's worthwhile to get to know the *free* documentation that you've already got on your Linux system.

As Linux grew out of Unix, and Unix is more than 30 years old, Linux inherited a large amount of documentation—which explains why you'll sometimes find two or three separate pieces of documentation on a particular command! The basic types of documentation that you'll find on your system include:

- built-in help: you can run most Linux commands with the --help option—that's *two* dashes—to get a synopsis of the command's possible options. Some commands use -h instead of --help, so if one doesn't work, try the other.
- man pages: the original online Unix documentation.
- info: a later text-based documentation.
- HOWTOs: a series of documents that don't typically document a single command, but instead tell you how to do some task or discuss issues in trying to get a particular thing done.

Using *man*

Unix has had an online help system called man–short for *manual*—for as long as I can remember. It grew out of an online version of a set of manuals that Unix came with. As the online version had the same information as the manual, people often use the phrase *man pages* when they're talking about the information that man offers. Basically, you look up the manual pages for a command by typing man followed by the command's name:

```
man grep
```

man Strengths and Weaknesses

The man pages can be useful in that they document all of the myriad options for a given command. Where they fall down, I believe, is that in general they don't really explain basic concepts very well; it's quite normal for a man page to refer to a "regular expression" as if everyone knew that "regular expression" is the Unix term for "pattern to match in a search operation." Additionally, they almost always lack examples, something that always drives me crazy in any text claiming to inform or document. I often walk away from man pages thinking that their goal seemed to be to remind someone who *already knows* a program how to use the program, rather than instructing someone new to a program.

"Worse yet," Craig told me when I asked him about it, "many of those man pages are sorely outdated, based on some old version of the program." Too true, I soon found out: I've run across cases where the man page for a command says that it can do one thing, but trying it out shows that the command can't. If you come across a case where man says something should work but it doesn't, try getting help from the command itself with the --help option—again, that's two dashes. For example, to find out what grep can do, type

```
grep --help
```

and you'll get a list of legal options. It's often a good idea to follow that with the |less pipe, as the list of options on the average Linux command can easily fill a screen! But remember: the man pages are sometimes out of date, so don't be afraid to experiment a bit.

man and Those Numbers in Parentheses

Something drives me crazy as I read Unix reference materials, including man pages. There's a tendency for those texts to follow certain keywords with a number in parentheses. For example, if you use man to look up man, you get a line toward the end of the man pages telling you to see also "apropos(1), whatis(1), less(1), groff(1)." What are those numbers doing there?

According to Craig, the original Unix manual arrived in seven books. The idea of putting the numbers after keywords was to make your life easier when trying to find something. You can still force man to look in just one "book" with the -S option. For example, you could say to search for information on mv only in the third and fourth books with this command:

```
man -S3:4 mv
```

Dan adds this comment:

> *Sometimes you need to use the number of the section. For instance, when you want to know about the crontab file, if you just do:*
>
> ```
> man crontab
> ```

you get the page about crontab(1) that is the standard user command that accesses the crontab file. However, if you want to read about the format of the file itself, that is stored in crontab(5), and you would need to use:

```
man 5 crontab
```

Notice that that is without the -S option—it works, too, but why type -S when you can just type the number alone?

Perhaps more useful is the -k or "keyword" search. If you can't find a man page on something just by typing man subject, then try:

```
man -k subject
```

Dan says, however, that this may not work on a new system until the user sets up a database used by man -k, that you may have to type:

```
makewhatis
```

before this works. In my experience, I've never done a makewhatis and man -k has worked, but it can't hurt to give this a whirl.

Another Source: *info*

After man came a different help routine called info. It's from the GNU folks, and Dan tells me that it hasn't caught on in the entire Linux community, so I don't want you to get the impression that info has replaced man, just supplemented it. Some commands are better documented in info–just type info followed by the command name, as in:

```
info ls
```

The result of this command, by the way, is a far better discussion of ls's options than man offers. info has articles on many but not all of Linux's commands. info documents include a kind of hyperlinking: they offer you subheadings in the document that you can position your text cursor over, then press Enter to jump to that document. You then use n to move to the next topic, p to return to the previous topic, and q to exit info. There are other commands, but these basic ones will do most of what you'll need. To do a keyword search, press s and enter the keyword.

How to use HOWTOs

Assuming that you installed your Linux with "the works"—everything—then you probably have a directory on your system named /usr/share/doc. Take a look in it, and you'll see several dozen directories. /usr/share/doc is where you're supposed to store documentation for Linux programs. In addition, you'll see a directory in /usr/share/doc named /HOWTO.

Unless, of course, you're running Red Hat 7.3. (Grumble grumble grumble…) Other distros include it, but Red Hat doesn't for some reason. (You'd think on those 451 CDs that the thing ships with that the HOWTOs would be there *somewhere*.) Never fear, however, you can find them all on the Web at `tldp.org`, home of the Linux Documentation Project. They even sell every byte of text from the website on a CD for under $20, and given the speed of their website, you might consider it a good investment.

HOWTOs are more than 100 large text files that describe how to do any number of things, from making Linux use Chinese characters to getting started in networking. If you happen to have a distribution that included a HOWTO directory, then inside that directory is yet another directory named `/mini`, which contains the "mini-HOWTOs"—which, as you'd expect, are just short HOWTOs on a variety of topics, including how to get your Linux computer to control a coffee machine. The mini-HOWTOs are on the `tldp.org` site and their CD as well.

> **NOTE** Most Linux systems used to put all the documentation in `/usr/doc` and some still do. However, the File Hierarchy System (FHS) specifies the use of `/usr/share/doc`, and most Linux distributions have now moved to be FHS-compliant.

If you're stuck doing something in Linux, then take a moment and visit `tldp.org`. There might be a brand-new HOWTO on how to solve your problem, or the HOWTO might have been revised—some HOWTOs are constantly being improved.

Performing Common Linux Tasks

Learning to do everything in Linux would take quite a while—but here are a few of the common tasks and how to do them.

Dealing with Compressed Files: Understanding *.tar*, *.gz*, and *.bz* files

Many times I'll need to send some information to someone over the Net, but that information appears in the form of several files, rather than just one file. I can certainly send those files one at a time, but sometimes I'd just prefer to collect them all together into one big file and send *that* file. Of course, I'm not the only person who's ever wanted to do that, so it's common in the Windows world to collect files into a single file with the extension `.zip` and send that file. Alternatively, as you surely know, many documents and programs are stored on FTP and websites in ZIP format. Furthermore, as you probably also know, zipping a set of files does two things: first, as I've already said, it collects them into one file; and second, it often compresses those files so that they take up fewer bytes. (I say "often" because some files, like JPEG image files, are already about as compressed as they're going to get, and so zipping a bunch of them only offers the first benefit, "collect the files into one place.")

The Linux world works much the same way, but you don't see as many files with the extension .zip; instead, there are .tar, .gz, .tgz (a combination of .tar and .gz), and .bz. Here's what they do and how to extract them. (Dan notes that he's seeing more and more ZIP files in the Linux world, no doubt due to the slow incursion of us Windows dweebs.)

Zip-Like Functions: Extract *.gz* and *.bz* with *gunzip* and *bzip2*

The Unix world has a ZIP utility that is (naturally) free, gunzip, created under the GNU license—hence the *g* at the beginning of the name. Any file with the extension .gz is a file that can be extracted with gunzip like so:

```
gunzip filename
```

gunzip leaves the unzipped file behind, deleting the original .gz file. But more recent compression algorithms have enabled techies to crunch data down about another 20 percent smaller using the "Burrows-Wheel block sorting text compression algorithm," so Linux users have yet another compression and decompression tool, bzip2. bzip2 will both compress and decompress (and if you ever want to create a "gzipped" file with Linux, there's a gzip program that'll do that), but when invoked without any options it extracts files. When bzipped, files normally get the .bz extension, so if you come across a file with that extension, just extract it like so:

```
bunzip2 filename
```

Like gunzip, bzip2 deletes the zipped file after it has successfully extracted its contents.

> **NOTE** Note that gzip will only compress a *single* file into a gzipped file ending in .gz. If you do gzip -r *directoryname*, you would probably expect it to wrap up all of the files into a single gzipped file. In reality, it will descend into that directory and gzip each individual file into its own compressed file. If you want to zip up a collection of files, you should either use the zip command, or the tar command described below.

tar Combines and Compresses Files

You may know that the whole notion of ZIP files first appeared in the PC world in the mid-1980s. By then, Unix was a teenager, though, and it had already figured out how to collect files together—with a program called tar. The name stands for "tape archive," and its original job was to collect up a bunch of files and, optionally, even an entire directory structure into a single file that could then be written out to tape. But `tar`'s combined file needn't be written to tape, hence its value as a ZIP-like utility in the Linux world. `tar` will also compress files by running them through `gzip`.

> **NOTE** These conglomerated files created by `tar` originally bore the extension
> `.tar`, which is why they came to be known as "tarballs." Nowadays, they're
> called tarballs if they've been created by `tar`, even if they don't have the exten-
> sion `.tar`.

You can identify tarballs by any of the following file extensions:

- `.tar` usually means that the file is not compressed.
- Either `.tar.gz` or `.tgz` usually means that the file was first combined into a `tar` file, then compressed into a gzipped format. Similarly, `.tar.bz` means that the file was tarred, then the resulting `.tar` file was compressed with `bzip2`.

Extracting Files from *.tar* Format

You can extract a file from a simple uncompressed .tar file by invoking `tar` with the xvf options, like so:

```
tar xvf tarfilename
```

where *tarfilename* is the name of the file that you want to break apart (e.g., `mystuff.tar`). In my experience, some distributions' version of `tar` won't work if you put a dash before the options, and others want the dash, like:

```
tar -xvf tarfilename
```

But what about uncompressing those files, unzipping them? You have two options. First, you could simply unzip the file with `gunzip`, which you've just met and would produce an uncompressed-but-still-combined `tar` file. You'd then run the `tar` file through `tar` xvf. You run `gunzip` with no options. For example, suppose you found the source code for an application called CoolApp, version 1.02, somewhere on the Net and downloaded it. It came as a file named `coolapp-1.02.tar.gz`. You could unzip it like so:

```
gunzip coolapp-1.02.tar.gz
```

That would leave a file named `coolapp-1.02.tar`. You'd then break that apart with `tar`:

```
tar xvf coolapp-1.02.tar
```

That usually creates a whole bunch of directories, extracts the files in the tarball, and puts them into the proper directories. In the case of source code, you typically then look in the directory structure that untarring the files created for a directory named source, do a `cd` over to that, and type `./configure` or the like, then make, and then `make install`, as you'll see later in this chapter.

Alternatively, most Linux implementations of tar know how to both unzip and untar with the xvzf options:

```
tar xvzf coolapp-1.02.tar.gz
```

Again, you may alternatively see the extension `.tgz` instead of `.tar.gz`.

Backing Up to Tape

Now at some point here, you are probably going to wonder about backing up the data on your system. As in the world of NT, there are numerous commercial backup programs available for Linux. Many distributions come with a free version of BRU, a backup program available for many versions of UNIX and Linux. Many others can be found on the Web.

But also as with NT, there are some basic tools included with the system. In fact, you just met one of them: tar. I just showed you how to extract files from a tar archive, but now all we need to do is *create* an archive. The syntax is quite similar:

```
tar -cvf filename files-to-add
```

So, for instance, if we just wanted to create a quick backup of all the files within the /home directory, we would just do:

```
tar -cvf home-backup.tar /home
```

Because we've used the v option for "verbose," we'll see a long list of all the files as they are added to the archive file. Now, if we had wanted to use compression while doing this, we could simply do:

```
tar -cvzf home-backup.tgz /home
```

Note that Linux doesn't really care at all what you name the file, but it's the convention to use `.tgz` or `.tar.gz` after compressed tar files.

So what does all this directly have to do with backing files up to tape? Well, remember that Linux has this wacky idea of treating devices as if they were simply files? Given that, using tar to back up to a tape device is purely an exercise of figuring out what your tape device is called and substituting that device name in place of the filename above. For instance, if you have a SCSI tape drive connected to your system, it is almost always called /dev/st0 (if you had a second one, it would be /dev/st1). So a backup might look like:

```
tar -cvf /dev/st0 /home /etc /var/spool/mail
```

> **WARNING**   You'll note that I didn't use the z flag for compression. This is one of those issues that Unix/Linux people can get religious about, but generally it seems people avoid using compression with tar on tapes because there is the potential that if some part of the tape itself were to fail, you could lose the entire archive, whereas without compression you could probably recover much of the data even with failures on the tape media.

That's the basics of it. Note that because we're using /dev/st0, when the tape reaches the end, it will automatically rewind. If you wanted the tape to not rewind so that you could put additional backup sets on the tape, you would use /dev/nst0.

If you look at the manual page for tar, you'll find that, like most Linux commands, it has a zillion options that allow you to do almost anything short of slicing bread. One option I should mention here is the M (yes, that's a capital M), which allows your archive to go across multiple tapes:

```
tar -cvMf /dev/st0 /home /etc
```

With that, you're pretty much ready to go. Note that we used /dev/st0 to write to a SCSI tape drive, but tar will also work with other devices, such as floppy drives and ZIP disks. (Dan tells me a colleague of his backs up his home directory to a writable CD and carries that with him when traveling.)

For floppy disks, simply use /dev/fd0 to write to what you would think of as your A drive in Windows. Be warned that when you do this, Linux is writing to the disk drive as a character block device, meaning that the floppy is now formatted as a tar file. If it was an DOS FAT floppy before, it's not anymore. Oh, and by the way, in typical Linux/Unix fashion, tar assumes you know what you are doing and it won't warn you before overwriting the disk. Oops.

Zip drives are a bit different, so I'll discuss them more below. Also realize that with tar, you can easily back up to another filesystem across the network. We'll talk about mounting a remote filesystem later in the book, but once mounted, it is just another directory in the overall Linux directory tree. So if you have a huge drive on another server, you can back up data to it. More on that later.

> **TIP**   Although I'm talking about using tar, there are, of course, other ways to do this in Linux; and, of course, these things tend to be religious issues if you get talking to people. There are two other commands, cpio and afio, that are similar to tar but provide compression and other benefits according to their fans. There is also an age-old Unix command called dump (with its companion restore) that works on backing up complete filesystems, sort of like Ghost or Drive Image.

Verifying an Archive

As seasoned network veterans of all operating systems know, tape drives are Out To Get Us. So how can you find out whether the thing worked—how can you verify an archive? The way to test is to use the -d option (think of "diff," as in difference):

```
tar -df /dev/st0
```

This will show me any files that are different in the archive from their originals on the disk. If this is done immediately after a backup, you should just be given the prompt back with no output. Had I included the usual -v, it would have listed every file on the tape as it examined it and printed any errors after the end of the filename. This could be useful, but if I'm just trying to see what's different, I probably don't want the entire list.

Note that you could do this some time after the backup and -d would tell you what has changed on your system since the time of the backup.

Seeing What Is on an Archive

But now suppose that some time has gone by and you haven't got a clue what's on the tape. How do you find out? The answer is to use the -t option (think of it as seeing the "table" of what's on the tape):

```
tar -tvf /dev/st0
```

With the -v option, you will see the owners and permissions, whereas without it you will just see the list of files.

Note that using -tvf is also a very useful way to see what is inside a tarball before you go and extract it onto your system. If you want to view the contents of a gzipped tarball, you can, of course, throw in the z option, as in:

```
tar tvzf coolapp-1.02.tar.gz
```

Restoring an Archive

So here you are, working with your system, and you accidentally blow away a directory and need to restore it from your backups. With tar, you just extract the files like we mentioned before. If you wanted to restore the entire archive, just do:

```
tar -xvpf /dev/st0
```

You'll notice I added a -p here. This will preserve the permissions of the files as they were stored on the tape. Now this will bring back everything, but what if you just wanted one directory, say /home/mark? All you need to do is add the name after the extract command:

```
tar -xvpf /dev/st0 /home/mark
```

If you listed several directories or files, only those names would be retrieved from the archive.

The Care and Feeding of Tapes

If you used Windows NT Backup with magnetic tapes, you're probably wondering how you perform actions on tapes like retensioning, rewinding, or erasing. The answer in Linux is yet another command called mt. (mt equals "magnetic tape," in case you're wondering.) The structure is quite easy:

```
mt -f /dev/st0 rewind

mt -f /dev/st0 retension

mt -f /dev/st0 erase
```

There are, of course, more options. (It's a Linux application, there are *always* more options.) See the man page for details, but these are the basic ones.

Doing Incremental or Differential Backups Isn't Easy

This is great for a full backup, but what about an incremental or differential? Actually, there isn't a straightforward way to do incrementals or differentials with tar.

If you really want to use incremental backups, your best bet is either to look at commercial products that are out there or to use the dump and restore commands. The only issue with dump and restore is that they only work on complete filesystems (think "partitions"). This may be exactly what you want if you have set your system up with several different partitions for directories like /home and /usr/local. With a simple dump command, you can easily back up the entire /home partition. However, if you wanted to just back up part of a partition (say just the /etc directory in the root partition), dump won't let you do this. You have to back up the entire partition. Still, you may find this an easy way to do large backups to tape.

Automating the Backup

Of course, once you have a backup technique worked out, you might want to automate the process so that every night at, say, midnight, the backup automatically runs. To do this, you need to use the cron command, which is similar to the NT Scheduler, but like most things in Linux, requires you to edit a configuration file, referred to as a crontab file ("cron table," get it?). As there is a separate crontab file for each user, you would probably want to be root when you edit the file in order for the backup to run as root.

If you want all of the details to crontab, issue the command man 5 crontab. But here's a basic example. Suppose you want to run this tar backup command:

```
tar -cf /dev/st0 /home /etc/ /usr/local
```

As with the Scheduler service in NT and 2000, you have to associate some user account with the scheduled program; again, that's why you're editing root's crontab. This file should, then, be in /root—its full file specification should be /var/spool/cron/root. While logged in as root, type crontab -e and enter in the line:

```
0 0 * * *  tar -cf /dev/st0 /home /etc /usr/local
```

This will execute this command at 0 minutes after the 0 hour of each day. (You needn't run tar, by the way. You could alternatively create a script and name the script rather than typing the whole tar command.)

Backing Up to a Zip Drive

Many of you probably have Zip drives around, and you'll be pleased to know that these work just fine with Linux, although your system won't just detect and automagically make them available like it does in Windows. Instead, like the floppy drives and CD-ROM drives we discussed earlier, you have to mount a Zip drive onto a directory. So the first step is to make the mount point:

```
mkdir /mnt/zip
```

Next, you'd expect to run a mount command—but first, you'll have to get Linux to recognize the Zip hardware. As you may know, there are several options for Zip drives—SCSI, EIDE, parallel, and USB Zip drives. In theory, Linux supports them all, although USB support is newer with kernel 2.4… and that's worth a digression.

When working on the first version of this book, 2.4 was only out in very late beta. But I downloaded and installed it, and got some USB Zip-100 drives to work.

For a while.

After about three reboots, however, the Zip drive stopped working. For good. It no longer worked on any computer under any operating system. Thinking that I'd just coincidentally stumbled upon a bad drive, I tried my other Zip-100 USB drive. And got the same result: Linux toasted two Zip-100 drives.

So you won't be surprised when I say that I approached testing Red Hat 7.3's USB support with some trepidation. Thankfully, though, Linux seems to have gotten through its USB support infancy. (That's USB 1.*x*; I don't have any USB 2.0 stuff around to try out.)

If you have a SCSI drive, it should have been detected when you booted the system and should be available to you as a SCSI device (exactly what device may vary depending upon what else you have on the SCSI chain). It will, then, have a device name like /dev/sda, /dev/sda1, or the like. If you have an EIDE Zip, then it also should have been detected on boot, and it'll have an EIDE name like /dev/hdc, /dev/hdc1, or the like.

If you have a *parallel port* version of the Zip, then you'll have to do a bit more work to make Linux be able to see the drive—you'll have to load the module into the kernel that supports the Zip drive. What's a "module?" I'll explain modules in a bit more detail later in this chapter. But briefly: When you are configuring the Linux kernel, you can choose to have support for various services/protocols/devices/etc. either built directly into the kernel or available as a "loadable module." For whatever reason, modern Linuxes include support for things like parallel ports and Zip drives as a module, and we have to load it before it can be used.

You need to load one of two possible modules, depending on the kind of Zip drive you have. The older parallel-port drives use a module called ppa, while the newer drives, especially the "Plus" models, use a module called imm. Load the proper module with the modprobe command: modprobe ppa or modprobe imm. If this command works, you should just get a prompt back. If not, you'll know, as you'll get a bunch of error messages.

> **WARNING**   You have to be running as root to run modprobe!

Okay, so after all of this, the Zip drive should now be available. Up until now, it hasn't mattered whether there is a Zip disk in the drive or not. But at this point, you need to have a disk in the drive, because the next step is to mount it onto the directory we created earlier:

```
mount -t vfat /dev/sda4 /mnt/zip
```

I'm using vfat to get long filenames, and /dev/sda4 just because that seems to be how it works for most Zip drives. Why sda4? The HOWTO on Zips suggests using sda4 and claims that this was somehow Iomega's issue, and Dan says that he had to use /dev/sda1 to mount one of his Zip drives. I cheated by plugging in my USB Zip drive and rebooting the system, then I peeked into the file /etc/fstab, where I found a line that looked like:

```
/dev/sda4 /mnt/zip250.0…
```

Which seemed like a good enough hint, so I mounted it as /dev/sda4. And while I have never tried out an EIDE Zip drive, I'd guess that you'll have to use a device name like /dev/hdb4, /dev/hdc4, or /dev/hdd4. And, by the way, the Zip automounts just fine; I just added this line to my /etc/auto.misc file:

```
zip -fstype=auto :/dev/sda4
```

I can then refer to my Zip drive as /misc/zip. But to return to the matter of backing up, now just use the tar command to create an archive file in /mnt/zip:

```
tar -cvzf /mnt/zip/homebkp.tgz /home
```

And there you have it. Note that at this point your Zip drive is just another directory, and you can use any of the standard Linux commands to work on files there. If you want to eject the disk, you will first have to unmount it:

```
umount /mnt/zip
```

Those are the basics for a Zip drive, but again there's a HOWTO on Zips—give it a look if you're having trouble.

Backing Up a Linux Configuration Isn't Completely Possible

After you've been using your system for a while, you no doubt have it tuned just the way you like. How do you back up that "customized" part of Linux so that you can quickly restore all of your customizations on a fresh Linux box?

Well, the good or bad news, depending upon your perspective, is that unlike Windows, there is no central "Registry" of all information. So if you're looking for something like `regedt32.exe`, don't bother. Think back to the DOS/Win3.1 days when there were .`ini` files scattered all over the place. That's more of how it is in Linux. The good news, however, is that most of the configuration files are all located in the /`etc` directory, so if you back up that directory using one of the previously mentioned methods, you should get most of your system configuration files.

But wait, you say, what do you mean by "most"? Well, it is the convention to put configuration files in /`etc`, but that doesn't mean that some of the programs you may have installed have to conform to that convention. Certain programs may put their config files in the installation directory, somewhere in /`usr/local`, or pretty much anywhere. For instance, the KDE desktop stores most of its configuration data in subdirectories underneath /`opt/kde`. As you install new programs, you need to watch carefully to see where in fact the important configuration files are going—that is, if you can figure out how. Searching around for files with recent dates is one clumsy but effective way.

Linux programs may store other configuration information as "hidden" files in your home directory. Recall that in Linux, a file is hidden if its name is prefixed by a period or, as some say, a "dot," leading to hidden files' other name—"dot-files." Dan tells me that there are kernel configuration files found in /`boot`, /`usr/src`, and /`lib/modules`, which we'll discuss in more detail later when I show you how to recompile your kernel.

In short, there *isn't* any complete and reliable way to back up a Linux configuration, sadly. You can get a lot of it by backing up /`etc` and your home directory. Dan notes further that "if you've explored the Linux filesystem, you've probably found the /`proc` directory and seen all the information there. You might be tempted to back this up to save all your configuration information, but this is a really *bad* idea. Consider, for instance, that

/proc/kcore is actually a view of everything stored in your system's RAM at that point in time. Do you really want to back that up? No!"

Combining Commands into a Batch ("Script") File

Many of you with NT or 2000 administration experience have run into situations where you need to run more than one command in order to get something done—or perhaps you need to run just one command, but it's a long one. In both cases, you can make life easier by packaging the command or commands into a single file and then telling NT/2000 to execute the commands in the file; as you know, we call that file a batch file.

Introducing Linux Script Files

Linux uses batch files as well, but calls them scripts rather than *batch* files. There are just three steps to creating a script: design the script, type it into a text file, and set the file's attribute to tell Linux that it's a script file. For example, here's an extremely simple script that just echoes back to you whatever you type in, called `sayit`:

```
echo $1
```

It's not very exciting, but it'll do for a basic script example. Supposing that I've written this script and placed it in /home/mark, I can invoke it like so:

```
[mark@linuxbox]# /home/mark/sayit Howdy!
Howdy!
```

I typed /home/mark/sayit Howdy! and it responded, "Howdy!" Here's what I did to make that happen.

Making a File Executable

First, I created a text file named `sayit`. I didn't give it an extension like `.cmd` or `.bat`, as you'll see. I then used a text editor like `vi` to type the one line `echo $1` into the file, then saved it.

Next, if I were to try typing /home/mark/sayit Howdy! I'd get an error message, *because Linux doesn't recognize sayit as a program*! In the Microsoft world, we're used to designating a batch file as a batch file by giving it the extension `.bat` or `.cmd`. In Linux, however, you modify a file attribute, sort of like the notion in Microsoft operating systems of read-only, archive, or system—but not exactly like that. I'll explain file attributes in the next chapter, and they're not anything that I can explain quickly, so please forgive me, but I'm going to give you only a sketchy explanation right now. For now, I'll just say that the following command will make Linux see your `sayit` file as a script file:

```
chmod a+x sayit
```

Once you do that, typing /home/mark/sayit Howdy! will get a response other than an error message.

Pitfall: Linux Doesn't Run Programs in the Current Directory

But you *might* run into one problem running this script, if you assume that Linux executes things the same way that Microsoft operating systems do. You probably know that in general operating systems rely upon a "path," which is a list of directories that contain programs.

When you type a program's name, the operating system tries to find that program by looking in that list of directories; that's true even for non-Microsoft OSs, like OS/2. But Microsoft operating systems don't look for programs on the path until after they look in the current directory.

Thus, if you're working at an NT machine and your current directory is C:\HOME\MARK, and that directory contains a batch file named SAYIT.BAT, and you type SAYIT Howdy!, then NT tries to figure out where there's a batch file named SAYIT by first looking in your current directory for SAYIT.BAT. *Then* it searches the directories in the PATH environment variable. This means that if you've just written a batch file on an NT system and you want to try it out, you can try it out by typing its name, even *if* the file isn't sitting in a directory in your path.

Linux, however, doesn't work that way. Even if you're sitting in a directory and you type the name of an executable file in that directory, Linux will not "see" the file and will complain that it can't find the program. There are two ways to get around this problem.

First, you could just surrender and specify the entire path to the program. Even though I'm sitting in /home/mark while I'm doing this exercise with the script named sayit, simply typing sayit Howdy! won't work, so instead I type /home/mark/sayit Howdy! and that works fine. You can *always* get Linux to run a program if you tell Linux the fully specified filename—directories and all.

Alternatively, here's a shorter way of specifying a full path. You may know that there's a magic directory named . (yes, that's a period) that always means "the current directory." You could, then, specify the script as ./scriptname; for example, I could type:

```
./sayit Howdy!
```

Now the script file will run just fine.

There is the third option, of course, to change the path to include the current directory, and I'll deal with that in just a little bit.

This seems to me to be something of an irritation, as I'm used to operating systems that look in the current directory by default, but Dan tells me that there's good reason... security. "Say that I convince you to save a file called 1s to your home dir. You then type it there.... and get the version in your home dir instead of the 'real' one. Maybe I have set this to override some system settings and do something else (mail me your ssh key?). You have now been compromised. So the idea was to prevent people from inadvertently executing a local copy instead of the 'real' system copy." Oh great. Next thing you know, Microsoft will change Windows so that the path doesn't include the current directory as part of its new awareness of security.

More on Variables: *echo*, *export*, and the Environment

Anyone who's ever hacked around with DOS, Windows, NT, or 2000 batch files knows that the operating system stores some facts about its current session in areas in memory called its *environment variables*. For example, if you're running NT and are suddenly stricken with amnesia, you can find out your username by typing echo %username%. That tells the operating system to display (the echo command displays) the contents of an environment variable username.

Linux uses much of the same kind of syntax and maintains several dozen environment variables. You can see all of your Linux system's environment variables by typing:

```
set | less
```

Of course, you don't have to use the less, but the output will exceed the number of lines on most screens. You'll notice that Linux has an environment variable named USERNAME, just as NT and 2000 do. (Notice that all of the environment variables seem to have uppercase names for some reason, although I don't know why.) If you wanted to display the current value of the USERNAME variable, then you could just type set | less again and scroll through the results, but you can ask specifically for just one variable with the echo command:

```
echo $USERNAME
```

It's worth pointing out the differences between NT's echo %username% and Linux's echo $USERNAME commands. NT and 2000 are, as you know, mainly case-insensitive, so you could type username with either upper- or lowercase letters and get the same result. Linux, on the other hand, is case-sensitive. You could have an environmental variable named username that was separate and distinct from an environmental variable named USERNAME.

Additionally, the way that you get NT and 2000's echo commands to reveal a variable's values is to surround the variable's name with percent signs. Linux, in contrast, just needs you to prefix a variable with a dollar sign.

That explains why the main line of the sayit script file said echo $1. You see, whenever you execute a script file in Linux, you can pass that script file parameters separated by a blank. Linux (or, actually, the bash shell) stores each of these parameters in its own variable. It names the first parameter 1, the second 2, and so on. The command echo $1 tells Linux to display on the screen the value of the variable named 1, which, again, contains the value of the first parameter passed to the script.

But how could I modify an environment variable? What if I wanted to write a script file that could modify my PATH variable, or perhaps my USERNAME value? The exact way varies from Linux shell type to Linux shell type, but the bash shell (which you'll most probably be using) uses the export command. For example, there's a built-in environment variable that you'll use in Chapter 7 to do some intermachine graphics control. As you'll read then, Linux lets you run graphical programs like NT and 2000 do, but it goes them one better by letting you run the programs on one machine and then *display the output* on a different machine. Part of how you do that involves modifying an environment variable called DISPLAY. For example, if I wanted my system to display its graphical commands on a machine named terminalpc.acme.com, I'd want to set the value of DISPLAY to that name, like this:

```
export DISPLAY=terminalpc.acme.com
```

As with echo, notice that the case of the environment variable must be correct. Notice also that you do not prefix DISPLAY with a dollar sign.

Now what if I want to append or prepend something onto an environment variable, but not affect the other contents? For example, what if I want to add my current directory (.) to my PATH variable, but keep the rest of the path intact. It turns out to be quite easy:

```
export PATH=$PATH:.
```

Now, I happen to know (from doing echo $PATH) that the PATH variable is a set of paths separated by colons. So to add my current directory to my path, I just assign the current contents *plus* the . symbol to my PATH variable. From this point forward, when I type a command, it will check the rest of my path first, then check my current directory. I could have reversed the order so that it would check the current directory first, but this is a bit safer from a security point of view. (I won't inadvertently run a modified command from my home directory when I meant to run one from a system path.)

Summarizing, then, you can see all of your environment variables with set | less, you can see a particular environment variable with echo $variablename, and you can either create a new environment variable or modify an existing environment variable with the command export variablename=value.

A Bit of Scripting Help: *script*

You may be familiar with macro recorders, programs that let you build macros in programs like Word by watching you perform some operation. The recorder makes note of every command that you execute and puts them into a ready-built macro program. It's a nice, simple automatic-learning approach to writing simple macros. Linux has a tool like that too, called `script`.

Just type `script` *filename* and Linux will begin recording your command-line session to a text file named *filename*. It records not only what you typed but what the system responded, so it can be a great way to remember what the heck you did! You can, if you like, edit the file to remove the system responses, and you're then on your way to building a useful script.

Oh, and one more thing: you tell `script` to *stop* recording by typing Ctrl+D. You can then edit out everything but the commands, and you've got a script.

Using Telnet to Control a Remote System

NT has always had a problem with remote control; not all of the administration tools worked remotely, and when they did, they behaved differently when controlling a remote system than when controlling the local system. Windows 2000 has greatly improved that situation, as every W2K server comes with Terminal Services, a tool that lets you create a "remote desktop" on another computer.

Linux, in contrast, has never had a problem with remote control, because Unix always *had* to support the idea of a remote user controlling a Unix box. The reason for that is simple: 30 years ago, almost *nobody* ever got to actually sit at a computer and control it locally—they were too expensive. Decades ago, many computers lacked any local kind of keyboard or display, so *anyone* interacting with a computer did it via a remote terminal. You'd use the same kinds of cables and terminals to connect to a Unix box six feet away as you would to connect to that Unix box from half a world away. (Although you were probably connected at higher speed when only six feet away.)

Telnet and Linux

Again revealing its Unix roots, Linux is also very easy to control remotely and, in fact, every Linux includes a Telnet server (oops, I meant "Telnet daemon"). You can sit on one machine, open up a Telnet client, point it at your Linux box, log in, and it's just like you're sitting at the Linux box. From any Microsoft Windows 9x, 2000, or NT box, or any Linux box, you'd connect to a machine named `mylinux.acme.com` by typing:

```
telnet mylinux.acme.com
```

Well, actually as of Red Hat 7.3, that won't work; Red Hat disables Telnet by default. You can change that with the following steps:

1. Edit a file named `/etc/xinetd.d/telnet`.

2. Find the line that says `disable=yes`.

3. Change the `yes` to `no`.

4. Save the file.

5. Make the changes take effect by typing `/etc/rc.d/init.d/xinetd restart`.

Telnet will now work. Try to telnet to your Red Hat box from a remote system, and you'll see the usual Linux login screen. Type in a password, and you're in!

But root Can't Directly Log In

Well, that is, you're in, *provided* that you didn't try to log in as root. By default, Linux doesn't let the root log in over Telnet for security reasons. There are two ways to get around this.

First, you could tell Linux to stop worrying and just let the root log on remotely. The way that Linux knows not to let the root log in is via a file called `/etc/securetty`. It contains a list of the remote terminals that the root is allowed to log in at. If you take a look at it, you'll see `tty0` through `tty8` on most Linux distributions. That's Linux's way of saying "local logins."

NOTE   Remember you can log on to a Linux box locally multiple times: press Alt+F2 to see your second screen (`tty1`), Alt+F3 to see the third (`tty2`), and so on. As far as Linux is concerned, your local keyboard and display card are basically just a very fast remote terminal.

On some Linuxes, you can allow logins from Telnet. Linux allows many simultaneous logins over Telnet. It then gives "tty"-type names to each of these sessions, names like `/dev/pts/0` for the first, `/dev/pts/1` for the second, and so on. The *p* in `/dev/pts/0` stands for "pseudo"—it's a pseudo-session in some designer's eyes. (People connecting to a Linux box over dial-up have sessions with names like `ttyS0`, `ttyS1`, and so on—the *S* stands for "serial port," which modems are attached to.) So you might try just adding a line like `/dev/pts/0` to `/etc/securetty`. You can find out what session someone's logged in as with the `finger` command; if I were logged in to a Linux box as "mark," then I could find the name of my connection by typing:

```
finger mark
```

and I'd see that among other things I'm connected on `tty0`, as I'm sitting at the Linux box. (Dan adds that the w command does everything that `finger` does, and more.)

WARNING But loosening up `/etc/securetty` is not the best idea. Linux doesn't have the most secure security in the first place, and if your system's connected to the Internet, well, there are always dirtbags looking to exploit your machine. There's no sense in making life any easier for them.

The other way to get root access to a machine remotely is a two-step process. First log on with any old account, so long as it's not the root. Then use the su ("substitute user" in recent Unix docs, "super user" in really old Unix references) program to "change identities" and become the root. It's simple: just type su and press Enter; you'll be prompted for the root password. Fill that in and you'll assume the godlike powers of root.

"Hey, PgUp and PgDn don't work!"

Once you've seen the inherent power of remote control afforded by Telnet, you may end up stumbling on one of those annoying little Linux/Microsoft incompatibilities. You will no doubt one day need to make some change to a Linux box, but find that you are nowhere near the Linux box. You get up to walk down two flights of stairs to where the Linux box is located, when you get The Epiphany:

"Hey, it's Linux! I don't have to be sitting at the computer to control it! I'll just telnet over to it from my Windows computer."

So you use the built-in Telnet client that Windows for Workgroups, Windows 9*x*, NT, and 2000 include. You log in, and it appears that all is well... until you need a cursor key. The up and down arrows work fine, and you can recall your old commands without a hitch. But when you're in vi, or when you're examining a file with cat *filename*|less, and you need to press PgUp or PgDn, nothing happens.

Oddly enough, if you telnet to the Linux box from another Linux box, then all of the cursor keys work. Why don't they work from Windows? Because the Telnet client software shipped with Microsoft operating systems is very minimal and doesn't send cursor movement commands the way that Telnet expects them. But there's a partial work-around: Ctrl+F generally moves you forward a page (PgDn), and Ctrl+B generally moves you backward one page (PgUp). So when working from a PC, remember:

NOTE Ctrl+F = PgDn; Ctrl+B = PgUp.

You can improve upon the standard Telnet client just a bit by downloading an upgrade to the standard Hyperterminal that comes with Windows 9*x*, NT, and 2000. You may not have ever noticed, but Hyperterminal is a Telnet client: you can choose to connect with COM1, COM2, or "winsock"—winsock means "Telnet." Hilgraeve offers a somewhat improved version of Hyperterminal (for private use only, so commercial users would have to shell out a few bucks) at `ftp://ftp.hilgraeve.com/htpe/htpe5.exe`. PageUp and PageDown still don't work, but many of the funky escape sequences that appear on the screen when you use the built-in Telnet client don't show up with the upgraded Hilgraeve software. Another nice free Telnet client is Tera Term Pro, which you can find at `http://hp.vector.co.jp/authors/VA002416/teraterm.html`; you can do scripting and `ssh`, and there's even a CE version.

Running a Remote Graphical Session

That's all nice, you may be thinking, but I want to do more than just get a command prompt from a remote system. I want to run an entire graphical desktop at my computer, but all of the computing should be taking place on a remote system. Windows 2000 can do it with Terminal Services—can Linux?

Yes, Linux can do that, and it's a logical question at this point in the book. But I'm afraid I've got to ask you to be just a *bit* more patient, as I haven't covered Linux's GUI yet. In Chapter 7, I'll not only discuss the Linux GUI, I'll also show you how to run a complete remote desktop.

ssh: A Better Telnet

While Telnet has been used since the dawn of network communication, it has one fundamental security flaw: *it transmits passwords in the clear!* (This is not true for the Telnet system built into Windows 2000, XP, and .NET, which use a modified Telnet subsystem that does NT 4–type encrypted authentications.) So yes, if you telnet into a system as root, you are transmitting your root password as clear ASCII text in a packet that someone between you and your server can easily intercept.

For this reason, pretty much most of the Linux in-crowd won't touch Telnet with a 10-foot pole. Instead, they use `ssh`, or "Secure Shell." From a user perspective, it is not a whole lot different from Telnet. Just type:

```
ssh servername
```

and , after you provide your password, you are looking at the same Linux prompt that you would with a Telnet client.

What is different is that `ssh` uses public-key encryption to have a secure channel of communication between the client and the server. In fact, the first time you connect to a server via ssh, you will be asked to verify the authenticity of the public key of the server that you are connecting to. You will be shown a "fingerprint," and the truly paranoid can match what they see to the fingerprint that they know the server should have (and that, presumably, someone e-mailed or faxed them).

One thing you will note is that you were not asked by ssh for your username. There was no login prompt or anything like that. This is because ssh just assumes that you want to log in to the remote machine with the same username as you are using on the current system. So it just presents its login name as the one you are using on your client. If you want to use a different login name, you can use either the -1 option or put the username in front of the server name, similar to how an e-mail address would look. Either of these examples will log me in as mark:

```
ssh -1 mark mylinux.acme.com
ssh mark@mylinux.acme.com
```

> **NOTE** While pretty much every version of Linux and UNIX now includes an ssh client and server, Microsoft has yet to see the light on this and does not include an ssh client in Windows. You can, however, find free versions out there for download. Two of the most popular are PuTTY and TTSSH (the latter is an extension to the free Tera Term Pro). More details can be found at www.openssh.com, www.freessh.org, and www.ssh.com.

Now, on the server side, a service is running called sshd. You should see it running. Configuration occurs through the /etc/ssh/sshd_config file.

Stopping a Runaway or "Locked" Program

Sometimes a program will stop responding and just "lock up." (Yes, it happens under Linux as well, no matter what the zealots tell you.) If this happened under NT, you'd just press Ctrl+Alt+Delete, bringing up the Task Manager, and kill the application. You do something very much like that in Linux as well, although you'll usually do it from the command line. Two programs help out here: ps and kill.

The way that you stop a program dead in its tracks is simple; just type:

```
kill -9 processID
```

What's a "process ID?" A number that identifies a program to the operating system. Windows, NT, and 2000 all do the same thing—ask developers what a "pid" is, and they'll tell you that it's short for "process ID," no matter what OS they work on. That's why zapping a program is a two-step process: first find its pid, then use kill -9 on its pid.

> **NOTE** In theory, I could just type kill processid without the -9, and that should instruct the program to stop. But if it is completely locked, it probably won't just stop because I told it to. You know how Windows gives you the error dialog box that says, "This program is not responding…," when you try to end the task? Well, kill -9 is basically like clicking End Task on that dialog box. I am telling it to die *now*!

But how to get a pid? With ps, or "process status." Type ps -A (that's a capital *A*) and you'll see a screenful or two of output like this:

```
 896 tty1    00:00:00 krootwm
 897 tty1    00:00:00 kbgndwm
1625 ?       00:00:00 pickup
1626 tty1    00:00:00 konsole
1627 pts/0   00:00:00 bash
1713 ?       00:00:00 in.telnetd
1714 pts/1   00:00:00 login
1715 pts/1   00:00:00 bash
1728 pts/1   00:00:00 su
1729 pts/1   00:00:00 bash
1743 pts/1   00:00:00 vi
1776 ?       00:00:00 in.telnetd
1777 pts/2   00:00:00 login
1778 pts/2   00:00:00 bash
```

The first column shows the pid, then there's a label identifying which "terminal" is running the process—tty usually means one of the local sessions on the machine, pts means someone's telnetting in from the outside. The time values are a measure of CPU time, and finally there's the name of the process. But you needn't do all that scrolling to find a particular process's ID—let grep do some of the work. To find all of the vi sessions running, I'd just type:

```
ps -A|grep vi
```

kill -1, also known as kill -HUP, is used to tell a process to reread its config files and restart. So, for instance, you can change the config file of something called xinetd (which we'll cover in a bit), and then do a kill -1 *xinetdpid* to have it reread its config file. It hasn't always worked for me, but it's worth trying.

Linux offers a fair amount of information about the currently running processes; for a bit more info on what's running than ps -A offers, try ps x.

Linux includes another nice utility to monitor processes that's a bit fancier than ps, called top. Just type top, and it'll fill your screen with as many processes as it can fit, one to a line. It works sort of like the Task Manager in NT and 2000, but it takes one-character commands to control it. You cannot scroll up and down—however many processes fit on your screen, you see that many. But which do you see? Why, the top ones, of course—the top CPU users, top RAM users, or the like. You control which to see with top's sorting commands. Some of the ones you'll probably use most often are described in Table 5.4. Finally, for those using a GUI, there's a nice graphical version of top called gtop.

Table 5.4   Sorting Options for *top*

Option	Action
-h	Gets help
-k	Prompts you to let you kill a process
-n	Lets you specify how many processes you'll see, instead of just filling the screen
-N	Sorts by PID numerically
-A	Sorts by age, longest-running processes last
-P	Sorts by percent of CPU usage
-T	Sorts by total cumulative CPU time used
-M	Sorts by memory use
-u	Tells top to only show the processes associated with a particular user

Finding Out How Much Memory Your System Uses

Once you've got a system installed, how do you know if it's comfortably sitting in memory or bursting at the seams? With the free command, or just look in a "fake" file called /proc/meminfo. (Type cat /proc/meminfo, and you get some up-to-date statistics on memory use.)

free takes a number of arguments, but you'll probably want to use –m, which says to report the totals in megabytes. –o simplifies the report a bit. For example, on my e-mail server, I get this free result:

```
[root@mailguy /root]# free -mo
          total   used   free  shared  buffers  cached
Mem:        123    109     14       9       74       7
Swap:       133      3    129
```

The command reports physical memory (Mem:) and virtual memory (Swap:). Note that for some reason it always underreports physical memory: for example, this server has 128MB of RAM but free shows 123. On another system, I've got 196MB of RAM but free reports 186MB, and on yet another there's 64MB of RAM but free reports 60MB, so clearly there's some basic OS overhead that free isn't reporting. I find the Swap: line interesting: on modern systems with 256MB or more of RAM, I often see the amount of memory used is zero… so I could choose to run without a swap area.

Installing a New Application with RPM

Eventually, it'll be time to branch out beyond the wealth of free stuff that came in your Linux distribution and start adding even more power with commercial applications, new free stuff, or perhaps just updated versions of programs that you've already got.

That means it's time to talk about installing new applications under Linux. There are basically three kinds of installs that you'll do:

- In the simplest case, someone has conveniently compiled the application, set it up to work with your particular distribution, and stored all of the application's files, settings, and setup information in a file called a package; in that case, you install it with a tool called RPM, the Red Hat Package Manager.

- You won't always find nicely prebuilt RPM packages. In that case, you just have to put the knife between your teeth and dive on into compiling applications from source code.

- Sometimes you'll need a fundamental change in Linux's capabilities, or you'll need to incorporate some very recent improvement in Linux. In that case, you'll need to learn how to recompile the Linux kernel itself.

Let's first take up the idea of packages. Decades ago, compiling a program generally produced just one file, a big program file. We called files like that load modules on the IBM mainframe system at the university where I first hacked around with computers, Microsoft operating system veterans would call them *EXE files*, and Unix and Linux people tend to call them *binaries*. Installing the program file was really easy—you didn't *have* to. You just told the operating system, "Hey, there's a program file sitting over in such-and-such directory, you wanna run it for me?"

Simple as that approach was, it's not practical for larger programs, as they'll inevitably need more than one file. Some of those files might be multiple versions of some piece of data; for example, if I were writing an outer-space type video game, I might set it against a bitmap that showed a field of stars on a black background, with a planet or two visible. But I might want to use different versions of that bitmap depending on what resolution the game ran in, so part of the entire collection of files that compose the game might include several variations on that bitmap. More commonly, modern programs use files called *libraries* that contain part of the code the program relies on. Whatever the reason, installing a modern application requires copying more than one file to your computer's hard disk. Furthermore, those files don't all go in the same place; several may go into one directory, others into a different one, and so on.

That's where a *package manager* comes in. The idea is that when someone wants to distribute a program in a precompiled form, she compiles the program and collects all of its files together into a single file, a package. The package contains not only the files, but the instructions about where the files go, what version of the program is associated with the files, and other application-specific pieces of information. (If you're familiar with Windows 2000 MSI files, which the Windows Installer reads, then this will be a familiar notion—it's basically the same idea.)

The Red Hat Package Manager (RPM)

There isn't any *one* standard for packages in the Linux world, but there are two major ones—Red Hat has a package format and Debian does. It seems that Red Hat's is the most widely used.

Red Hat offers as open source a program to install and manage Red Hat packages; the program is called RPM, the Red Hat Package Manager. But you won't just find it in the Red Hat distribution; every other Linux distribution that I've seen comes with it.

> **WARNING**   RPM is an exception to the usual style of writing about Linux. Both the program and its file type are referred to by the acronym RPM (all caps), but using the program is invoked at the command line as rpm (lowercase).

RPM has a few basic goals and abilities:

- First, as you've already seen, it simplifies installing applications.
- Second, it's a *generic* installer technology. Not only can developers of *applications* use it to simplify installation for users, developers of *operating systems* can also use

it. What that means is that major subsystems of Linux—such as, for example, the GUI—can be upgraded without having to completely reinstall the operating system.

- RPM keeps a database of all of the files that it has installed and which applications need those files.

- RPM lets you not only install but also uninstall applications.

- RPM will "audit" your applications to ensure that all of your installed applications have all of the files that they need—a handy way to find out if you just accidentally erased something important!

Installing and Uninstalling with RPM: An Example

Let's work through using an RPM package to show you how to install and then uninstall an application with RPM.

A bit of web searching shows me that there's a nicely preRPMed version of the old text-only Adventure game floating around under the name adventure-2.5-1.i386.rpm. Struck by nostalgia, I download it, and it goes into /root/adventure-2.5-1.i386.rpm. It's a relatively small file, about 77K. Notice that most Intel RPMs have filenames that end with i386.rpm. That doesn't mean that you need a 386 to run it, any more than the fact that NT and 2000 store their installation code in a folder named I386 means that you could—or would want to—install NT or 2000 on a 386. Instead, "386" means "runs on an Intel processor with 386 or better capabilities." Now, you might see a few files out there that end in i586.rpm or i686.rpm. This just means that the developers of the program chose to compile it on those processors, and therefore it should be optimized for those chips and might not run on older chips. Most of the time, though, you'll see files ending in i386.rpm.

Installing an RPM Package   So I go to install Adventure:

```
rpm -ivh /root/adventure-2.5-1.i386.rpm
```

But I get an error message:

```
failed dependencies:

libc.so.5 is needed by adventure-2.5-1.
```

Yes, error messages are a pain, but at least this one's useful. It's telling me that when someone put together the RPM package for Adventure, he assumed that my system already had a library of programs called libc.so.5. In other words, Adventure's not running on my system until I get a copy of libc.so.5! But where to find such a thing? Well, some kind souls at the World Wide Web Consortium and MIT keep a machine around that's a kind of archive of RPMs at http://rpmfind.net. I download the file—a much larger one, at 2 megabytes—and install it with rpm:

```
rpm -ivh libc-4.3.33-1glibc.i386.rpm
```

It installs fine, and so I try the `rpm -ivh` command to install Adventure once more, and this time, I'm successful. RPM doesn't offer much in the way of commentary as it installs the app, however; its output looks like this:

```
Preparing... ############################# [100%]
1. advent   ############################# [100%]
```

But Where *Is* It? What RPM *Doesn't* Do   Well, as there were no error messages, clearly it installed. But where? How do I start up Adventure? As near as I can tell, RPM doesn't really cough up that information very readily; there's no option that makes it say, "To run the application you've just installed, just type /usr/games/adventure." Of course, you could return to wherever on the Web you found the program, hope there's a file named README or something like that, download the file, and hope that you'll get a clue there.

But you can make a decent guess at what RPM did when it installed an app by querying the package to find out what files it installs, and where it installs them, with -qpl (that's a lowercase *l*, not a one), like so:

```
rpm -ql adventure
/usr/games/adventure
/usr/lib/games/adventure.data
```

It seems a good bet, then, that typing /usr/games/adventure and pressing Enter will fire the thing up. While I'm on the topic, you can get some other very nice query information with the -qi option; it dumps about a screenful of information about who wrote the package and what the program in it does.

> **TIP**   If you would like information about the RPM *before* you install it, add the p option to the commands above and supply the full name of the RPM file, for example, rpm -qlp adventure-2.5-1.i386.rpm (assuming you are in the same directory as the RPM file). You can also do -qip with the RPM filename; alternatively, you can just type rpm -ql adventure or rpm -qi adventure; in those cases, you don't need the full filename of the package, just the program name, but only if you've already installed it.

While I'm discussing the fact that RPM doesn't help you figure out how to install an application, I should mention another fact about RPM. If you install a graphical application via RPM, you'd kind of expect RPM to add your shiny new app to your GUI's menu, perhaps create what we'd call in the Microsoft world a "program group," maybe an icon on the desktop somewhere, wouldn't you? Unfortunately, RPM doesn't—and can't. The obstacle, as you'll learn in Chapter 7, stems from the fact that there is no standard in the Linux world about which GUI to use, and lots of GUIs are available. RPM would have to be aware of all of those GUIs and how to add things to their menus.

Uninstalling a Package   Once I'm tired of Adventure, I can get rid of it with the -e option:

```
rpm -e adventure
```

Notice, however, that I don't type the name of the package, I type the name of the application to remove the package.

Other RPM Features

But suppose I don't uninstall Adventure. A few months down the road, I erase a few files accidentally. Did I goof up and erase something important? To find out, I type:

```
rpm -Va
```

This command is a "No news is good news" command—if it doesn't print out any response, then all of your packages are fine. But what packages do I have installed? RPM can tell you that, also:

```
rpm -qa
```

That will dump out the names and version numbers of all installed RPM packages. Note that not everything installed on your system was installed by RPM.If you've just installed a brand-new system, don't be surprised if you type rpm -qa and get no response.

Or suppose you're about to delete a file but wonder if any of your RPM-installed applications depend upon it. Use the --whatrequires and -q options to find that out, like so:

```
rpm -q --whatrequires /bin/mylib
```

Once, I needed to know what package a particular program came from. As I mentioned earlier in this chapter, I set up a mail server but it seemed to lack the POP3 program ipop3d. Another Red Hat system, however, clearly had the ipop3d file, as its POP3 server was working fine. Once I realized that the first mail server's problem was only a lack of ipop3d program, I saw that the way to fix it would be simple: just install the RPM package that contains ipop3d. But which package?

To find out, I went to the system with the working copy of ipop3d and typed:

```
rpm -qf ipop3d
```

RPM then told me that the package I was looking for was named imap-4.5-4.rpm; I looked on the Red Hat distribution CD, found it, and installed the package to the POPless server... problem solved. (Not that I could have figured most of that out without Dan.)

Getting Red Hat Packages

You can actually make your own RPM packages, but that's a discussion for a more in-depth book. Most of us will just use RPM packages supplied by vendors or available right on the Web. Many of the same organizations that offer software in source code format will also have precompiled RPMs on their sites.

WARNING   Unlike source code, RPMs are architecture-dependent! If you wanted, for example, to put Samba on your Compaq Alpha–based computer, you could configure, make, and install it from the Samba source code in the same way that you'd do it on an Intel-based system, and starting from the same source code files. But if you wanted a precompiled RPM package, then look closely to ensure that you're getting an RPM built for an Alpha—Intel RPMs will not work on an Alpha! Packages also sometimes seem to be distribution-specific, unfortunately, so a package that works on Red Hat might not work on Slackware. It doesn't hurt when looking over RPMs to choose the ones built for Red Hat and in particular Red Hat 7.3.

RPM Command Summary

I'll finish up this section with a quick reminder (Table 5.5) of the RPM options that I've shown you, for convenient reference later.

Table 5.5   Essential Commands for RPM

What You Want to Do	RPM Options
Install a package	`rpm -ivh packagename`
Uninstall a package	`rpm -e applicationname`
List all installed packages	`rpm -qa`
Check that all packages are installed correctly	`rpm -Va`
See the names of files installed by the RPM	`rpm -ql applicationname`
Get general information about a package	`rpm -qi applicationname`
See the names of files contained in an (uninstalled) RPM	`rpm -qlp packagename`

Table 5.5 Essential Commands for RPM *(continued)*

What You Want to Do	RPM Options
Get general information about a (uninstalled) package	`rpm -qip packagename`
Find out which packages rely upon a file	`rpm -q --whatrequires filename`

Unzipping, Compiling, and Installing an Application

Packages are great, but sometimes you are going to find a program out on the Internet that you want to install and, surprise, there's no RPM file! Instead all you see is a `.tgz` file (a tarball, recall) and some vague instructions about how to install the program "from source." I guess the correct phrase at this point is, "Welcome to the next level of Linux administration." Dan tells me that many old-time Linux users and zealots believe that the only "real" way to install is directly from source, instead of those wimpy old RPMs. (Or it might just be that some of those folks have *way* too much free time on their hands.)

Uncompressing the Source

So where do you begin? Perhaps you find a great new application on some web page and you download it; perhaps it's a file called `foo-1.0.tgz` from somewhere on the Web. Well, the first thing to do is to unpack the file into a directory. If the person who made the tarball was good, they tarred the files up in their own subdirectory. That's been my experience with every tarball that I've downloaded, but if they *didn't* create a subdirectory, then when you extract the files, they will be extracted into the directory where you currently are, which might be a bit of a mess if other files are in that directory. My approach is just to always create a new directory for tarballs while I'm getting them compiled. Dan's is to use the `-t` option to `tar` to check first:

```
tar -tvzf foo-1.0.tgz
```

You should see that the files are all in their own subdirectory. If not, then that's your clue that untarring the file would make a big mess, and so you'll want to create a subdirectory, `cd` into it, and then extract the files into that directory:

```
tar -xvzf foo-1.0.tgz
```

Read the Documentation

Once you've extracted the files, you'll want to `cd` into that directory (if you aren't already there) and look for a `README` file. By convention, most authors create this file and include information there about how to install the software. Sometimes you might find an additional file called something like INSTALLING, but the README file will usually tell you about this.

Sometimes it's not a compiled program at all; sometimes it's just a program written in a scripting language such as Perl or Python. In that case, there's no compiling to do; usually, you just have to copy the main program to some directory in your path. Linux convention says to put programs that you install after setting up your system into /usr/local/bin, but it's just a convention. Sometimes you might have to edit the actual Perl or Python files to change environment variables or command paths, but this is something you do with a text editor like vi and a lot of help from the READMEs, one hopes! Or, if you're impatient, you could of course just execute the program out of the current directory, too. But remember Linux's peculiarity about its path—your local directory isn't usually on the path, so instead of running a Python file in your current directory named foo.py by just typing foo.py, you'd have to type ./foo.py instead.

Compiling the Software

Now if the program was written with C, C++, or another language that needs a compiler, you're going to typically run three commands: configure, make, and make install.

> **WARNING** But not always. Simpler systems may require nothing more than simply make. (That's why reading the README is so important.)

Compiling really simple programs involves two steps: compiling and "linking" the programs. Compiling takes the English-like commands in a programming language like C, C++, COBOL, or Java (which are understandable to human programmers) and converts them into bunches of hexadecimal codes (which are understandable to your CPU). Linking then finds and connects the new program to system services; for example, the average program knows that it can put a line of text on the screen with the help of *another* program that is part of the operating system, but that average program has no idea *where* that helpful part of the operating system is. Linking resolves that.

What compiling and linking actually do isn't that important here, however; what is important is that over time, programmers developed a tool called make, which is kind of a super-batch file. It can do things far beyond simple compiles and links, and that turns out to be necessary for converting modern source code into usable software. So, for a while in the mid-'80s I recall getting OS/2 source code that consisted of a whole *bunch* of files, none of which I wanted to have to figure out, and one file called make. I'd just run make and everything would be *handled*. Sure, I was compiling, but not in a way that involved me having to really *know* anything.

But, as time went on, things got even more complex. Now we need programs to make the make files, so that the make files can do the compiling, the linking, and the like. That's where a program called configure comes in. You usually start the compile-link-and-install process by typing ./configure.

NOTE Some applications are still simple enough that they only require a make. For example, I recently found the Adventure game that I referred to earlier, in its original source code rather than an RPM file. I downloaded and untarred it. No README. No file named configure. *But* there was a file named makefile, so I just typed make. It compiled and linked in seconds, leaving me with a binary file named advent. I typed ./advent and returned to Colossal Cave. The moral of the story is: if you can't find a README, a readme.txt, or a configure, but you *can* find a file named makefile, then just type make. (While Adventure's file was makefile, Dan notes that most apps use a capital *M*, Makefile.)

Also, make has grown to the point where it can not only prepare a program, it'll install it as well, with an option install. In the simplest (!) case, then, many compiles boil down to three commands:

```
./configure
make
make install
```

Run ./configure and you'll see all sorts of lines scrolling by your screen as the configure program determines what commands are available on your system and where they are installed. configure's job is to figure out what special tweaks the program will need in order to run on your system—if it's a Linux system instead of a Solaris system, then perhaps a function call or two has to be changed, for example. Sometimes you'll need to use some specific options on configure; they're usually preceded by two dashes:

```
./configure --for-Linux --include-FAT-support
```

That's just an imaginary example, but that's what a configure with options typically looks like. Assuming everything goes okay and there are no errors, then configure creates a file called Makefile; make will use that in the next step. The preliminaries are over; time to start compiling. All you do to start the compiling is type make.

Depending on the size of the program and the speed of your computer, you may now have time to go get a cup of coffee while the compiler chugs away building all the component modules and then linking them all together into a binary executable. When it is finally done, you'll get a prompt back, and if you look at the directory contents, you should see other files now in the directory. Note that unlike Windows, Linux binary executable files do not end in `.exe` and, in fact, usually do not have any extension. Odds are in our example above the executable is simply named `foo`.

Now let's get all of the files where they're supposed to be. Many programs' Makefiles will do that for you if you type:

```
make install
```

It could be that you're now done. But not everyone provides a nice `make install`. In that case, there's more work to do. (Read the README to find out.)

Normally, you should see the output of the commands scrolling by on the screen as files get moved to their new positions. If `make install` does not work, you will need to move the executable file to a directory in your path, or execute it out of the current directory.

Assuming it did work, the README file (or other documentation, including a new man page that might be installed) really dictates what you have to do next. Sometimes you might have to edit a configuration file. Other times, you may be able to simply execute the command, as in our example:

```
foo
```

If a man page was installed, we can now do:

```
man foo
```

That's really about it. The program should now be installed and functioning for us.

There is one more thing, though. Remember back when we did the initial `make`, I mentioned it was compiling all the modules and linking them together? Well, all those compiled modules are still there in the source directory and are taking up disk space. Once the program is installed and it's working for you, you can get rid of all those compiled files (typically ending in `.o`). Most Makefiles are already set up for this. All you have to do is `cd` into the source directory and type:

```
make clean
```

and all the unnecessary files created in the process are deleted. Essentially, this is resetting it back to the way it was when you first extracted it.

WARNING Be careful with `make clean`. If you couldn't use `configure` and had to hand-edit the Makefile or make any other manual changes, a `make clean` may destroy all those changes.

If you find that make clean doesn't work in your source directory, try:

```
make mrproper
```

According to Dan, this is a convention that started with the Linux kernel and "Mr. Proper" is a cleaning solution in some European TV commercial.

Recompiling the Linux Kernel

One of the big things Linux zealots brag about is that you can build your own kernel. Citing the fact that every copy of Linux comes with the complete source code, Linuxers like to answer queries and "I wish Linux would…" complaints with, "Use the Source, Luke!" which means, "Hey, friend, you can answer your own question or solve your own problem—just sit down and read the C code that is the Linux blueprint." Yup, I'll be doing that just about as soon as I learn to draw the blueprints for my house. Sigh. But for some Linuxers, it's a rite of passage for you to "roll your own kernel," and they would never even dream of using a "stock" kernel that comes with a distribution.

Interestingly enough, though, the "You're not a real Linux user until you've rolled your own kernel" folks are sort of right for us Windows users. As I noted earlier, NTFS drives are unreadable by a Red Hat 7.3 box… so we need to do a recompile.

Reasons to Recompile a Kernel

But for us Linux newbies—we poor benighted fools who care not a whit how the code works, who are just trying to get our hands on a reliable and working operating system—the question is, "Why bother?" If you install Linux and it does everything you need it to you do, why do you care about recompiling the kernel? Why do you need to do this? Well, the short answer is that today you probably *don't*. Most Linux users can probably work perfectly fine with the standard kernels provided.

So why should you care? Well, there *are* a couple of situations where you might need or want to recompile the kernel. One would be that you might want to optimize the kernel to run as fast as possible on your machine. Until recently, most distributions came with a kernel that was compiled to run on, believe it or not, a 386 processor. The idea was that it would then work with any Intel box from a 386 on up. But if you have a Pentium II processor and you're running a 386 kernel, you're *not* getting the optimal performance from your machine. Dan tells me that when the Mandrake distribution first came out, it was essentially a literal copy of the Red Hat distribution (which is perfectly legal under the GPL, recall) with a kernel that was optimized for the Pentium. Today, many of the distributions have installation routines that determine what processor you have and drop in the appropriate kernel, but you still might want to tweak it yourself.

On the same topic, you might want to optimize the kernel by removing services, devices, network protocols, etc., that you don't need in order to increase speed. For instance, if your machine had no SCSI devices, you could rebuild the kernel without SCSI support. You'd get a smaller kernel and fewer moving parts to break. Another reason you might build your own kernel is if you need to install additional software to fix hardware problems. Dan said that when he first installed Linux on a particular laptop, he couldn't get PCMCIA services to work. He had to download the latest version of the PCMCIA services, run a script that patched the kernel, and then rebuild the kernel. After which, his laptop *did* work properly.

A final reason may be if you just want to stay up on the latest developments with the Linux kernel. Typically, by the time a CD is pressed for a distribution and it reaches you, several newer kernel releases have already either fixed problems or added enhancements. So you might want to get the newest kernel to make use of new features; see the section below on downloading a new kernel.

Our goal in compiling a kernel is simple: we want to be able to read NTFS volumes from Linux.

Understanding How the Kernel Is Stored

Before we start compiling a kernel, let's take just a minute and get a bit more specific about what we exactly *mean* when we say "create a kernel." Where is the kernel? Is it one file, many files? Where are they stored? What are their names, or what is its name?

Most of the kernel, the "heart" of Linux, lives in a single file stored in /boot, called vmlinuz. It's called vmlinuz rather than "linux" or "linuxkernel" because it was a big deal years ago when Linux got a virtual memory subsystem—a necessity for big-time operating systems—and so any kernel with that capability added *vm* to distinguish itself. The name ends in *z* rather than *x* to reflect the fact that the file is compressed. Reboot your system, and one of the first things that you'll see on the screen is:

```
Uncompressing Linux...
```

That's just the process of basically unzipping the kernel. I'm not sure why the Linux world keeps its kernel compressed; you'd think that storing it uncompressed would save a bit of time on boot, and hard disks are cheap nowadays. But remember that Linux grew up as the "runs on low-power hardware" operating system, so perhaps that's where the desire for compression arose.

You can see your current kernel by looking in the /boot directory. In mine, I see a file named vmlinuz, as expected, *but* it's not really a file. It's just a symbolic link to a file named vmlinuz-2.4.18-3. The "2.4.18" tells me that this was built from the source code for the Linux kernel version 2.4.18.

Red Hat, Mandrake, and some other distros put their kernels in /boot and use a symbolic link from vmlinuz to the kernal file, but not everyone does it that way—other distros use other approaches, but we're working with Red Hat, so we'll stick with their approach. To find out where Linux expects to find your kernel, look in /etc/lilo.conf or /etc/grub.conf for something like this:

```
image = /boot/vmlinuz
  label = linux
  root = /dev/hda5
```

The image= line tells me where Linux looks for the kernel, in /boot/vmlinuz; in other words, Linux expects to find the kernel in the /boot directory in a file (or a symbolic link pointing to a file) named vmlinuz.

That one file contains almost all of the basic "engine" that is the Linux operating system. If you have a SCSI host adapter, then there's probably no separate file that is a device driver for that adapter; instead, the program that supports the SCSI host adapter—we Microsoft OS types would call it a driver—is embedded right inside the kernel file and, in fact, the kernel *probably* contains the drivers for many SCSI host adapters. The kernel contains within itself the drivers for many network cards; again, you won't usually see a separate NIC driver file. Doesn't that sound terribly wasteful of space, housing drivers that you'll never use? There are two parts to that answer. The first answer is "Yes," and *that's* one reason why people build their own kernels, to pare down the size of the kernel by discarding pieces that they don't need.

Understanding External Kernel Pieces: Modules

The second answer is that I haven't told you the whole story yet. Not *every* part of the Linux kernel lives inside the vmlinuz file. Linux supports the idea of storing chunks of the operating system in separate files called *modules*. They're in /lib/modules, where you'll see yet another directory reflecting your kernel's version number. (For example, I have a directory named /lib/modules/2.4.18-3 that contains my modules.) Modules are binary files whose extensions are .o. Linux can load and unload modules dynamically, no reboots required.

One of the choices that you get when you set up a new kernel is whether to incorporate a piece of code directly into the kernel, keep it separate but available for loading, or skip it altogether. Linux gives you four commands for working with modules:

- lsmod lists the modules that you've currently got loaded.
- insmod *module-name* tells Linux to load a particular module.

- modprobe *module-name* is a somewhat smarter version of insmod. It not only loads a module, but also checks to see whether that module needs *another* module in order to function. If the first module needs another module, then modprobe loads that other module (or modules, actually) as well.

- rmmod *module-name* unloads a module.

The process of creating a kernel, then, boils down to just a few steps. First, you tell Linux which pieces you want in the kernel, which to skip altogether, and which to keep around but only as optional modules. Then you tell Linux to create the big, all-inclusive kernel file. After that, you tell Linux to create the separate module files and put them in /lib/modules. You then copy your new big kernel file into /boot, and tell LILO or GRUB to boot from it rather than any existing kernel file. Along the way, of course, it might not be a bad idea to back up the old modules and kernel, just in case the new kernel doesn't work so well and you need to revert to the kernel of yore. Those steps are what we're about to embark upon.

Finding the Source Code and Cleaning Up the Area with Mr. Proper

Let's get started, then, on creating our Linux kernel that can read NTFS volumes. You start out by going to where the kernel source code is installed on your system. Typically the source code is in /usr/src/linux, although linux in /usr/src might be a symbolic link to a directory called 2.4.18 or whatever version of the kernel you have on your system. For example, Red Hat 7.3 keeps its source code in a directory named /usr/src/linux-2.4.18-3, but there's a symbolic from the simpler directory name "/usr/src/linux-2.4" to /usr/src/linux-2.4.18-3. To actually make changes here, you will need to be the root user.

WARNING   If you've made configuration changes to your kernel in the past and don't want to lose those changes, then copy the file /usr/src/linux-2.4.18-3/.config to somewhere else. Once mrproper has run, copy the file back to /usr/src/linux-2.4.18-3/.config. If you have never messed with your kernel before or you've done some kernel work before but don't particularly care about keeping those changes, then don't worry about this warning and go ahead and run make mrproper as you'll see below.

Once inside the /usr/src/linux-2.4.18-3 directory, you issue the command:

```
make mrproper
```

which will clean the kernel source tree of any previously compiled modules and configuration files.

Choosing Kernel Features ("Configure")

You *don't* directly build a configuration file from a text editor specifically because the Linux kernel has so many options that you'd never get them all straight; in fact, the standard `configure` that you just learned about just isn't sufficient. Instead, Linux offers you three configuration tools, all with the same job: to create your `makefile`.

You have a choice of using one of three commands:

```
make xconfig
make menuconfig
make config
```

`make config` is the Spartan approach; it just asks a lot of questions and you'd better have the answers ready, because there's no way to go back and change a previous answer. (Well, of course there *is* always another way: you could Ctrl+C out of the program and start over.)

`make menuconfig` is a text-based configuration program that lets you wander around all of your kernel options; it'll create the `makefile` when you tell it that you're ready. I've used it and find it useful, and we'll use it in this NTFS-enabling example.

`make xconfig` is a GUI version of `make menuconfig`. It has lots of buttons for choosing from the zillions of kernel configuration options. Even better, it has a pretty good help system that does a decent job of explaining the options and recommending which options to take if you're clueless about them.

> **TIP** If you are logged in as a regular user with a GUI and have used su to change to root in a terminal window, you may need to issue the command export DISPLAY=:0 in order to use make xconfig. You may also have to run "xhost local-host" as the logged-in user, to allow other users (ie, root) to run GUI programs on your display.

Whichever tool you choose, your task now is to go through the different options and decide whether or not you want to include a particular item in the kernel you are building. Your choices are usually Yes, No, or as a module. As I explained earlier, "Yes" means to not only use the code, but to house it inside `vmlinuz`, the big kernel file. "No" means you'll never need it. "Module" means to compile it into a program file with a `.o` extension, store it in `/lib/modules`, and let Linux load or unload it as needed.

Put it in the kernel or in a module? It's a trade-off. The more that you say Yes to, the larger the kernel will be and the more memory it will take. There are limits to how large the kernel can be, so you don't want to include too much. On the other hand, including something directly into the kernel means it will always be available and thus may execute faster. You'll notice that the defaults for many options are to load it as a module.

TIP If you are on a system with only SCSI disks, make sure to answer Yes to built-in support for SCSI drives and also for your specific SCSI controller. If you fail to do so, you may not be able to boot the system properly and load the modules. (There is a way around this using a RAM disk, but let's leave that detail for now.) I would include SCSI support in general, because Linux uses SCSI as a way to describe "oddball" devices to its storage system. For example, once they get USB Zip drives working (which could well be by the time you read this), those drives will look like SCSI drives—you might address a USB Zip drive as /dev/sda.

No matter which of the three tools that you use, remember that they've all got the same goal: to produce the file /usr/src/linux-2.4.18-3/.config. Let's see how to that with make menuconfig.

First, type make menuconfig.

After a bunch of file copying whizzes by, you'll see a menu-driven text mode program. Next, choose NTFS support. Scroll down to "File systems --->" and press Enter. Then scroll down to "NTFS file system support (read only)" and press the spacebar twice. To the left of "NTFS file..." you will see "<*>," which indicates that you've told menuconfig to include NTFS rather than make it a module (which would look like "<M>") or skip it altogether (which would look like "< >").

Press Tab to highlight Exit to return to the main menu, then highlight Exit again and press Enter. When menuconfig asks, "Do you wish to save your new kernel configuration?" choose Yes.

You should still be in the /usr/src/linux-2.4.18-3 directory. You can verify that your NTFS choices made it into the configuration by typing:

```
cat .config | grep NTFS
```

You will see a result like this:

```
CONFIG_NTFS FS=y
# CONFIG_NTFS_RW is not set
```

Compiling and Linking the Kernel

After you have gone through and made all your choices and let the configuration program (whichever one you used) create the Makefile, the next part of the process is very similar to the make process described earlier. The first step is:

```
make dep
```

This will check all the dependencies of the configuration you have now chosen. If you told Linux to include piece A but not piece B, and Linux discovers that A needs B, then it'll squawk; `make dep` discovers these potential dependency problems. Then run:

```
make clean
```

And we're almost ready to create a new kernel… but first, let's name it. You've probably noticed that Red Hat 7.3's kernel calls itself version 2.4.18-3—what's that "-3"? Just a Red Hat-ism. I want to be able to remember that I built this kernel with NTFS support, so I want my kernel to call itself "2.4.18-NTFS." To do that, type:

```
vi Makefile
```

and look down about four lines for the line EXTRAVERSION =. It'll probably say this:

```
EXTRAVERSION = CUSTOM
```

Change CUSTOM to "-NTFS, so that the line looks like EXTRAVERSION, a space, the equals symbol, another space, and -NTFS. Save the file. *Now* we're ready to make the actual kernel image:

```
make bzImage
```

Note the capital *I*. This part of the process will probably take some time—about 10 minutes on my system—as the system builds the new kernel and creates that new kernel file.

Once it's finished, look in your /usr/src/linux-2.4.18-3/ directory; there should be a directory named /arch inside it, one named /i386 inside that, and one named /boot inside *that*. Inside that directory will be a big file named bzImage–that should be your new kernel! If you're still in that /usr/src/linux-2.4.18-3 directory, type `ls -l arch/ i386/boot` and you'll see it in the directory listing.

Compiling and Linking the Modules

Once that is done, you need to build all the modules for the kernel, based on all the choices where you said something should be loaded as a module:

```
make modules
```

This *is* the time to go get a snack, start that laundry, catch up on the stuff that Tivo's recorded for you, whatever will pass the time, because it's going to be a while—on my 800MHz laptop, it took about 40 minutes make the modules.

Once that's done, you'll use `make` to copy those modules over to a directory in /lib/ modules; in particular, you may recall that the directory name is usually /lib/modules/ *kernelversion*. Copy them by typing:

```
make modules_install
```

It should go relatively quickly, as it's just copying files. You will now have a bunch of new modules in /lib/modules/2.4.18-NTFS.

Create an *initrd* Image

Because of the way that Red Hat sets up its standard configuration, whenever you create a new kernel, you must also create something called a *RAM disk image* for that kernel. You do that with the program mkinitrd:

```
mkinitrd /boot/initrd-2.4.18-NTFS.img 2.4.18-NTFS
```

Then type:

```
make install
```

That'll take just a moment, while it copies the new kernel image to /boot.

Set Up Your New Kernel As a Boot Option

Because you named your new kernel by a different name from the old one—you suffixed it –NTFS instead of –3–you didn't overwrite your original kernel. (This is a particularly good thing, as it's easy to create a useless kernel, and if it's the only one on the disk at the moment, then you'd better get your installation CDs out, if you know what I mean.) Let's add this new kernel as a boot option in LILO, the LInux LOader. LILO is configured with a file /etc/lilo.conf. Inside this file, you should see a group of lines called an *image section* because they start with the line image = that look like this:

```
image=/boot/vmlinuz-2.4.18-3
    label=linux
    initrd=/boot/initrd-2.4.18-3.img
    read-only
    root=/dev/hda8
```

They may be slightly different on your distribution and may or may not have indenting, but the key things you need to do are:

- Copy the lines in the image section to create a new image section for LILO.
- Make sure that the image= statement points to your new kernel.
- Modify the new label to give it a new name, something like "Linux-NTFS."

For example, your new file might look like:

```
image=/boot/vmlinuz-2.4.18-3
    label=linux
    initrd=/boot/initrd-2.4.18-3.img
```

```
        read-only
        root=/dev/hda8
    image=/boot/vmlinuz-2.4.18-NTFS
        label=linux-ntfs
        initrd=/boot/initrd-2.4.18-NTFS.img
        read-only
        root=/dev/hda8
```

The `label` is something you'll see at the boot prompt you receive when you restart your system. The `root` line is the disk partition that contains your root file system.

Okay, the final command we need, and the one that so many people forget to do, is just simply this:

```
    lilo
```

Essentially, this reads the /etc/lilo.conf file and configures the boot loader to boot the appropriate images.

WARNING   You *must* execute this command every time you copy a new boot image into /boot. Even if later on you go back and modify your kernel again and simply copy it over the existing kernel in /boot (perhaps because the earlier kernel you made didn't work), you still must run the lilo command.

After all of this, you're ready to reboot. As root, execute either of the following commands:

```
    reboot
    shutdown -r now
```

When the system comes back up, you will get a `boot:` prompt. If you hit the Tab key, you should see the labels that appeared in /etc/lilo.conf. If you just hit the Enter key, you will get the first one listed (by convention, it is usually called `linux`). If everything works right, your system should just boot normally and you can log in as usual and just start using the system.

If it doesn't boot properly, you can just reboot and choose the original "linux" option. If there was some problem with your new kernel, you probably have to go back and start again with make xconfig or make menuconfig. The good news is that you'll still have the configuration from before, so you can just undo whatever choices you made that caused your problem.

Let's summarize the steps to making a Red Hat 7.3 kernel that supports NTFS and is Pentium II-optimized.

1. Type cd /usr/src/linux-2.4.18-3 to move to the source code.

2. If you want to start from a previous configuration, copy /usr/src/linux-2.4.18-3/.config to somewhere else.

3. Type make mrproper.

4. If you just copied a .config file from a previous kernel make, then copy it back now.

5. Type make menuconfig.

6. In menuconfig's main menu, choose File Systems --->.

7. Find "NTFS file system support (read only)" and press the spacebar twice so that <*> appears.

8. Choose Exit twice, and when prompted with, "Do you wish to save the new kernel configuration?" choose Yes.

9. Type make dep.

10. Type make clean.

11. Edit Makefile, find EXTRAVERSION =, and delete anything after the equals sign. Then, to the right of the equals sign, press the spacebar once and type -NTFS. Save the file.

12. Type make bzImage.

13. Type make modules–this will take a long time.

14. Type make modules_install.

15. Type mkinitrd /boot/initrd-2.4.18-NTFS.img 2.4.18-NTFS.

16. Type make install.

17. Edit LILO to add the option to boot from the new kernel.

18. Type cd /boot.

19. Type lilo when done.

20. Reboot and choose the new kernel.

And when this is all done, congratulations, you've now built your own kernel! You should be feeling quite macho or macha now; I know I had to go eat a raw steak after compiling *my* first one...

Downloading a New Kernel

Now that we've talked about recompiling the kernel, you might be tempted to get a new kernel and try it out. Here's how the kernel distribution works. The central download point is at www.kernel.org, with mirror sites available off of there. The kernel is ultimately still controlled by Linus Torvalds, with Alan Cox serving as his second-in-command.

It is important to understand how versions of the kernel are numbered. Right now, the first number is always 2, but the second number is the important one. If it is an even number (such as 2.0 and 2.2), it is a *stable* kernel. If it is an odd number (such as 2.1 or 2.3), it is a *development* kernel. Unless you really feel like being on the bleeding edge, you probably want to stay away from the development kernels. They are works in progress and can easily break your machine. Things may appear and disappear out of the development kernels, too, while they are being worked on.

Within both the stable and development tracks, the third number denotes the version within that track. This number may change quite often. For example, back when I was working on the first version of this book in June 2000, the 2.2 kernel was up to version 2.2.16. Meanwhile the development kernel has reached 2.3.99-pre9. In that case, there was also a brand-new "test" version of the 2.4 kernel, 2.4.0-test2. Think of this like Microsoft's Release Candidate 2.

Once you decide which version of the kernel you want to download, you simply download the tarball, extract it, and follow the directions mentioned above to recompile the kernel.

> **NOTE**   A final note about numbering. What typically happens now is that when a stable release has been made, Linus Torvalds then goes off to work on the new development kernels and hands off maintenance of the stable release to Marcelo Tosatti. Linus still signs off on a new stable version, but Marcelo does most of the maintenance. However, there are times when Linus is not available and, perhaps because of a security fix, Marcelo needs to put out a new version, which he typically calls 2.4.19-pre for example. The "-pre" simply means it's a prepatch that Linus hasn't yet signed off on.

Controlling Linux "Services"

Much of NT and 2000 administration involves starting and stopping programs and services—Exchange, IIS, and DHCP are three significant examples of NT/2000 services. Linux has a class of programs that are essentially what NT-ers would think of as services, but they're called *daemons*. As a Linux admin, you'll need to understand how Linux handles those daemons, if for no other reason than you'll probably need to be able to start or stop a particular daemon.

Here's a major difference between the way that NT and 2000 load services and the way that Linux loads daemons: Linux's boot process is a lot different from NT's and 2000's because much of Linux gets its instructions about *how* to boot from ASCII scripts, rather than opaque compiled programs. That means that you have a lot of flexibility in setting up how your system works and—you guessed it—that means that different Linux distributions build their startup scripts differently. I'll focus on how Red Hat does it here.

Linux starts up with three high-level scripts, each of which start other scripts:

- The sysinit script (`/etc/rc.d/rc.sysinit` on Red Hat 7.3)
- The runlevel script (`/etc/rc.d/rc` on Red Hat 7.3)
- The rc.local script (`/etc/rc.d/rc.local` on Red Hat 7.3)

Running the sysinit Script

Early on in the boot process, a Linux program called `init` starts. `init`'s job is basically to start all other processes, and it finds out which processes to start by looking in a file named `/etc/inittab`. `init` needs /etc/inittab to tell it where to find two scripts: a script called the sysinit script, and one called the runlevel script.

NOTE Take a look at a `ps -A` output and you'll see that `init` has a pid of 1, making it The First Process. (A geek detail for sure, but interesting nonetheless.)

Look in the `/etc/inittab` and search for sysinit, or si, or even better, don't look for it, let Linux do the work. Type:

```
cat /etc/inittab|grep si
```

or, as Dan reminds me:

```
grep si /etc/inittab
```

On Red Hat, you'll get this one line of response:

```
si::sysinit:/etc/rc.d/rc.sysinit
```

The last piece, the part to the right of the last colon, is the location and name of the sysinit script: `/etc/rc.d/rc.sysinit`.

Finding and Running the Runlevel Script

After the sysinit script runs, `init` runs a script to activate a Linux *runlevel*. Linux runlevels are different configurations, different modes for using Linux. They are sort of like NT or Windows startup modes. For example, by default Windows *9x* starts up by booting into the GUI with all drivers and services running, but you can choose to run in Safe Mode, a graphic mode with just the VGA driver and no network services, or Safe Mode

Command Prompt, a mode with neither graphics nor networking, for system maintenance functions.

Most Linux implementations, including Red Hat, define six runlevels.

> **NOTE** Note that I said "most Linux implementations." There's nothing sacred or standard about how to set up Linux runlevels, just some industry tendencies, so if you find that your Linux works a bit differently, don't be surprised.

Runlevel 0 is the "system halted" runlevel. *You* wouldn't ever set up Linux to boot to runlevel 0, but the system sets itself to runlevel 0 in order to shut down. Runlevel 1 is a single-user maintenance mode. You'll probably never use runlevel 2, which is multiuser but without networking.

Runlevel 3 is the basic, default startup mode for most Linuxes, including Red Hat. You'll see variation in runlevel 3, however, as different Linux distributions seek to serve different market segments. For some systems, runlevel 3 boots you to a simple command prompt, without a GUI. That's probably the best choice for a server system, as there's no point in burning up CPU power on a GUI when the computer's just going to be tucked in a corner somewhere servicing network requests. Other Linux implementations, however, seek to serve the workstation, Windows-using market, so they define *their* runlevel 3 to boot you into a GUI environment. (Either way, remember that you can redefine exactly what runlevel 3 does.) You probably won't use runlevel 4, as it isn't defined on most distributions. Runlevel 5 starts Linux as an X Window terminal—in other words, in GUI mode. Some Linux vendors who want to start Linux in GUI mode don't redefine runlevel 3; instead, they make runlevel 5 the default startup runlevel. Runlevel 6 reboots the system.

There are scripts for each runlevel in inittab, but it's not always easy to figure out which one goes with runlevel 3, which is probably your default runlevel. Your best bet is to look for lines that have /etc/rc.d in them *and* have a 3 between their first and second colon. In Red Hat's case, the line looks like:

```
l3:3:wait:/etc/rc.d/rc 3
```

That line has a label l3. The :3 that comes after it (the 3 that I told you to look for) says, "This refers to runlevel 3." We can ignore the wait: parameter, and the /etc/rc.d/rc 3 says to run a script file named rc in the /etc/rc.d directory and to pass it the parameter 3.

The rc script tells Red Hat to look in the /etc/rc.d/rc*n*.d directory, where *n* is the value of the runlevel, and to run all of the scripts in that directory. For example, when entering runlevel 3, the rc script will run *all* of the scripts that it can find in the directory /etc/rc.d/rc3.d. Thus, if you take a look in /etc/rc.d/rc.3 on your Red Hat 7.3 system, you'll see a list of files with names like K05innd, K35smb, K35dhcpd, S10network, S80sendmail, and so on... all scripts whose names start with a capital *K* or a capital *S*. You'll see why they all start with *K* or *S* in a minute.

Runlevel Scripts Start Your Services—But in Several Ways

You may never mess with your sysinit script, but you'll care about what your runlevel scripts do, because they do the Linux equivalent of something that you almost certainly have to worry about on your NT servers: they control which services start up on your server.

As I mentioned a page or two back, they're not called services but daemons (pronounced "demon," recall), the term that Unix people use for programs that run constantly, awaiting the chance to perform some service. The Apache web server software (a file named httpd), the Samba file server (smb), and the BIND DNS server (a file called named) are three examples of programs that are built as daemons to perform some service.

If all we're doing is starting up some programs, what's the big deal? Using the three example services that I just mentioned, why not have a simple script file that just looks like:

```
httpd
smbd
nmbd
named
```

In other words, why not start those programs? Several reasons. First, some of the programs need a bit more setup than to just start them up. Others need particular options; for example, to start up smbd and nmbd as daemons, you must use their -D options:

```
smbd -D
nmbd -D
```

Also, whatever we *start*, we'll need to stop sometime. A graceful shutdown usually requires specific instructions to each daemon; you can't just use the kill command to shut every daemon down. For example, you may be familiar with the idea of dependencies in NT services—if you shut down the "server" service in NT, then you've also got to shut down the "computer browser" service. Simply shooting "server" in the head will leave "computer browser" running, and that wouldn't be good.

Now, because NT has the notion of dependencies, then it's simple to shut down a service gracefully—tell NT/2000/XP/.NET to stop a service, and the operating system automatically figures out which services are dependent on the soon-to-be-dead service and shuts them down. Red Hat, however, doesn't have anything that powerful. So it provides a workaround using yet another set of scripts.

For each daemon process, someone writes a script that generally takes one of four options: start, stop, restart, and status. Some have five options—the first four and reload–and some have only stop, start, and restart, but the idea's the same no matter what. Red Hat puts those scripts into /etc/rc.d/init.d. So, for example, there's a /etc/rc.d/init.d/ network script that controls the TCP/IP networking code, and I could type:

```
/etc/rc.d/init.d/network restart
```

to restart the network code; there's a Samba script /etc/rc.d/init.d/smb that I could use to restart Samba by typing /etc/rc.d/init.d/smb restart; and so on.

NOTE There doesn't seem to be the notion of "pausing" a daemon in Linux in the same way that NT and 2000 let you pause some services.

Associating Particular Daemons with Particular Runlevels Thus far, you've seen that Linux has daemons—what we'd think of as services. And, as with NT, you don't want to run every single service whenever you start the operating system, so instead of "normal," "safe mode," "safe mode with networking," and other boot-up options, Linux offers run-levels—runlevel 2 runs some set of daemons and not others; runlevel 5 runs a different set; and so on.

How do we draw the lines between each runlevel and the daemons that they should run? You've already seen a bit of it, but let's look at it in greater detail.

Linux uses scripts to control what does and doesn't start in each runlevel; how those scripts work are important to any would-be Linux administrator, so let me zoom in on that a bit. These start/stop/restart scripts turn out be extremely important, because the only real difference between one runlevel and another is which services the runlevel uses. You'd think that it wouldn't be that hard to set these scripts up; recall that every daemon has a script that will accept the commands "start," "stop," and "restart" at minimum.

In my simple-minded view, here's a very simple example of how a Linux runlevel script might work. Suppose the difference between runlevel 2 and runlevel 3 is that runlevel 2 runs the web server, but runlevel 3 runs the web server and the DNS server. If that were true—it's not, Linux needs a lot more stuff to be useful—then I could have a runlevel 2 script that looked like:

```
httpd start
```

and a runlevel 3 script that looked like:

```
httpd start
bind start
```

And in fact one group of Linux distributions builds their runlevel scripts this way; apparently this is the BSD way of doing things. Simple? To some, yes, but to others the idea of having to hack a script file to disable a service at startup lacks elegance. So there's another approach, the System V approach. It's the one that Red Hat and most other Linux distros employ. (Apparently AT&T's System V Unix did something like this, hence the name.) Remember that /etc/rc.d/rc.3 directory with the scripts whose names started with *K* and *S*? Now I can explain what's going on there.

I know there are a lot of goofy-looking files, directories, and scripts to remember, so let me review a few points:

- /etc/rc.d/init.d contains the scripts for starting each daemon. (Go ahead and take a look —they're all there, and they're basically understandable.)
- /etc/rc.d contains a script named rc, the runlevel script. It (basically) works by looking in one of seven directories in /etc/rc.d (rc0.d, rc1.d, rc2.d, rc3.d, rc4.d, rc5.d, and rc6.d) and running all of the scripts in that directory. If you choose runlevel 3, then you are essentially telling Linux to run the scripts in /etc/rc.d/rc3.d.
- The scripts in /etc/rc.d/rc*whatever*.d all have names that start with *S* and a number (e.g., S85httpd) or *K* and a number (e.g., K35smb).

And here's a new piece of information: the scripts in the various rc*number*.d directories are nothing more than links to the scripts in /etc/rc.d/init.d, *renamed*! Now we've got all the pieces in place; let's see more specifically what those runlevel scripts do.

Those scripts in rc*number*.d have names like S85httpd, S50inet, and K35smb to represent three things. The first letter indicates that the script either kills a process (*K*) or starts a process (*S*). Then two digits tell Linux what order to run these in—S50inet runs before S85httpd. The remaining part of the name indicates what it does: K35smb kills the Samba processes, S50named starts up the DNS server, and S85httpd starts the Apache web server.

The rc script—the guy who does the runlevel setup work—basically just looks in the appropriate directory for a given runlevel, /etc/rc.d/rc*n*.d. It then executes each of the scripts whose names start with *K*, in numerical order. Why is the runlevel script so interested in killing processes? Because Linux uses a change in runlevel to shut itself down. The next time you initiate a shutdown, notice the message:

```
INIT: switching to runlevel 6
```

Take a peek in /etc/rc.d/rc6.d and you'll notice that almost all of the scripts start with *K*, because that's shutdown's job—to kill everything! Other runlevel changes won't be as drastic, but if you switch from runlevel *x* to runlevel *,* and runlevel *y* doesn't want the web server running, then it'll want to kill the httpd service whether it's running or not, just to be sure.

Once the *K* scripts finish running, the rc script runs the scripts whose names start with *S*, again in numerical order. These scripts *start* processes. Now you can see in detail what the rc runlevel script does:

- Using the runlevel that you direct it to use, it chooses a directory in /etc/rc.d: /etc/rc.d/rc1.d, /etc/rc.d/rc2.d, or whatever.

- The script then looks at all of the files in that directory. (Recall that they're not really files, they're just links.)

- The fact that we've named the "kill" scripts starting with a *K* and the "startup" scripts with an *S* means that if the rc script just picks up the files in alphabetical order, then it will naturally perform the "kills" before the "starts." Including the numbers after the *K* or *S* means that, again, if the script examines the files in alphabetical order (yes, I know, it's technically "lexical order" or "collation sequence," but how many normal humans do you know that use those phrases?), then it'll end up seeing the scripts in a particular order—it will see S10network before S80sendmail, and so will start up the network before trying to run the e-mail server. Thus, the numbers let us tell Linux what order in which to start (or stop) the services, so that we can ensure that a given script or daemon doesn't run until the things that it relies upon are available. It's not as powerful as NT's dependency system, but it's a pretty darn good workaround.

- The rc script knows the location of the actual start/stop/restart script, as the filenames that it's looking at are just links to those scripts. But recall that each script needs a stop or start parameter. Which should the rc script send: start or stop? Simple: if the file's name starts with *K*, then send the stop parameter. If the file's name starts with *S*, then send the start parameter.

All in all, a pretty neat hack—just creating a bunch of links to scripts, and prefixing the names of those links with a letter and a number, and then relying on the directory's normal sort order to control the order of stopping and starting services allows a simple script to offer a fair amount of power.

With that explained, I can more easily show why the System V approach has its adherents. Suppose I *don't* want the web service (httpd) running at runlevel 3. How do I make sure that runlevel 3 doesn't include httpd? By putting a symbolic link in /etc/rc.d/rc3.d to the httpd script, but giving the link a name that starts with *K*. Looking in /etc/rc.d/init.d, I notice a script file named httpd, so it's a good bet that's the script for controlling the httpd daemon.

I don't want to start the web server, but I'd like to get rid of it, so I'll put a link in /etc/rc.d/rc3.d whose name starts with a *K*, followed by some number from 00 to 99. The order won't matter unless another program depends on httpd, in which case you should shut that one down too before shutting down httpd. No one's using number 51, so we can set up a link using that number:

```
ln -s /etc/rc.d/init.d/httpd /etc/rc.d/rc3.d/K51httpd
```

Does this sound like a lot of organizational work? It might be, so there are a few GUI tools around to let you control what gets stopped/started at the various runlevels. (Although your Linux-using friends *will* call you a wimp for using a GUI tool when there's a perfectly good command-line way, as you've just seen.) KDE comes with a program called ksysv and Red Hat has a program named tksysv; both let you choose which scripts start or stop at each run level.

The Third Way to Start a Service: *xinetd*   Almost every Linux distribution that I've seen uses a System V–like approach, and the rest use a BSD-like approach. But BSD and System V approaches don't affect all of the Linux daemons/services. Instead, some subset of network daemons on each system is started by a daemon itself—the xinetd daemon. (If you've worked with earlier Red Hats, it was called just inetd then; apparently this is the "xtra special" inetd.) You control it with three things:

- a file named /etc/xinetd.conf
- a file named /etc/services
- a directory named /etc/xinetd.d

Here's how it works.

When Red Hat starts up, it kicks off daemon called xinetd. xinetd, the Internet daemon or "Internet super-server," listens at TCP and UDP ports, waiting for activity. Remember that a TCP or UDP port is just the way that an Internet service like a web server or mail server differentiates itself from the other programs running on that system. For example, suppose I had a PC at IP address 100.100.100.100, which was running both web server and mail server software. When a communication comes in, how will the PC know whether it's a browser requesting to see our web pages (meaning that the incoming communication should be directed to the web server), or another mail server trying to send my mail server a message (meaning that the incoming communication should be directed to the mail server)? Both communications go to 100.100.100.100, so how would the TCP/IP software on the PC know what to do?

The answer is, "Using the port of the incoming data." Think of every piece of Internet software on a given PC as living in an "apartment" in that PC. You can't just address a letter to someone in an apartment building by street address—you need the street address and room number. The port number is that room number. The mail server is always in room 25 (port 25), and the web server is always in room 80. (You can change them, but then they wouldn't be standard and you'd have trouble communicating with others.)

That's the first important part—xinetd services are identified first by their numeric port number; remember that.

The xinetd daemon listens for communication, and when it "hears" TCP/IP packets, it looks at the port that the packets are destined for. It has in it one of the files that I mentioned earlier, /etc/services. That table tells xinetd which port goes with what program.

That's the *second* important part: given a port number, xinetd uses the file /etc/services (it's an ASCII file; you can open it up and look in it) to associate a program with that port. For example, while mail servers receive mail on port 25, a separate module called a POP3 (Post Office Protocol) server delivers the mail, using port 110. So when someone tries to talk to the local mail server with the intention of getting her mail, xinetd sees that packet going to port 110 and looks up "110" in /etc/services. According to /etc/services, port 110 is associated with the "pop3" service in /etc/services.

Finally, xinetd looks in /etc/xinetd and finds a file there called ipop3, which looks like this:

```
# default: off
# description: The POP3 service allows remote
➥ users to access their mail \
#               using an POP3 client like Netscape Communicator.
service ipop3
{
        socket_type             = stream
        wait                    = no
        user                    = root
        server                  = /usr/sbin/ipop3d
        log_on_success  += HOST DURATION
        log_on_failure  += HOST
        disable                 = yes
}
```

Notice the disable=yes; in this case, it means that Red Hat has disabled the POP3 server by default. (I'm not sure why.)

If you make a change to /etc/xinetd.conf or /etc/services, then you have to restart xinetd before it'll recognize your changes with the /etc/rc.d/init.d/xinetd script.

Notice one final thing about services started with xinetd: there's no way to restrict them to particular runlevels. Once you start xinetd in given runlevel, then any or all of the xinetd-activated services could start. Dan notes that there *is* one drawback to starting daemons with xinetd: the daemon has to be spawned each time there are inbound packets. While this may be fine in most circumstances, if you wanted extremely high performance out of a service, you might start it directly instead of having it handled by xinetd.

/etc/rc.d/rc.local

Finally, after the runlevel script runs, a script named rc.local residing in /etc/rc.d runs. (It is *normally* in /etc/rc.d, but you might have to search for it.)

rc.local is the "autoexec.bat" of Linux scripts, the last startup script. As it's the last startup script, it's also the one that you'd be most likely to want to put any of your own customizing scripts into, as commands that run later will generally override earlier commands. For example, remember in the last chapter that I showed you how different distributions use different methods to accomplish the simple task of setting their hostname? You could decide to do away with all of that nonsense, using rc.local. If you wanted your computer's hostname to be linuxbox.acme.com, you could just put this command at the end of rc.local:

```
hostname linuxbox.acme.com
```

That would supersede any previous hostname-setting routines.

There may be a distribution or two that don't put rc.local in /etc/rc.d, but *most* of them seem to put it in /etc/rc.d.

Startup Script Summary

Reviewing, then: several files control Linux's startup, and you can modify these as they are just ASCII text files. In order of execution, they are:

- /etc/lilo.conf, loaded by the boot loader.
- /etc/inittab, read late in the startup process.
- The sysinit script, which can appear in any number of places—but you can look in inittab to find it.
- The runlevel scripts, which again you have to find in inittab.
- The runlevel scripts find and run all scripts in /etc/rc.d/rcn.d, where *n* is the runlevel—and recall that the file locations or names there can easily change, as they're embedded in inittab and so a different Linux distribution may use different names.
- The /etc/rc.d/rc.local script, the last one to run.

Knowing these things can make tracking down a startup problem a lot less mysterious.

Starting and Stopping Services

Now you've seen how to set up particular runlevels to start or stop particular services. But how can you start or stop a service on the fly? By now, you actually know the answer, if you think about it: the start/stop/restart scripts sitting in some directory on your system. On Red Hat and Mandrake, it's the `/etc/rc.d/init.d` directory, on Slackware it's the `/etc/rc.d` directory, but it'll be somewhere near there. Once you've found the script, just invoke it with `stop`, `start`, or `restart` like so:

```
/etc/rc.d/init.d/fooservice restart
```

Changing Your Computer's Hardware Date and Time

While writing this book, I ran into a problem that reminded me of how many basic maintenance tasks I do all of the time, and how helpless it makes me feel to move to a new operating system and be unable to figure out how to *do* those tasks.

PCs have a hardware chip that keeps track of (or *tries* to keep track of) date and time, called the real time clock (RTC). Unfortunately, that clock chip isn't exactly an atomic clock when it comes to accuracy, so you'll probably have to reset it at some time. While working on this book, I noticed that a few of my computers (some of which were running Linux) got their calendars set a day ahead. It turned out that for whatever reason, their hardware clocks were confused about the day. I needed to move the calendar back one day—but how to do it? Of course, I could always just reboot the system, enter the CMOS, and reset it that way—but that's so inelegant, and would require that you *reboot your Linux box*, which all good Linuxers know is a terrible sin. How, then, can you control the clock/calendar under Linux?

Well, actually, Linux keeps two clock/calendars: in addition to the RTC's date and time information, Linux keeps its own time as well in what it calls the *system clock*. When you boot your system up, Linux reads the RTC and uses that information to set the system clock and does not check with the RTC again until you tell it to, or until you reboot. As it has two clocks, then, Linux has two clock-setting commands:

- `hwclock` lets you set the hardware, RTC clock.
- `date` lets you set the system clock.

Set the system date by typing `date mmddhhmmyyyy`, where *mm* is the number of the month, *dd* the day of the month, *hh* the hour in military format—1 P.M. should be expressed as 13—*mm* the minutes, and *yyyy* as the year. So, for example, to set your system date to March 1, 2001, at 1:20 P.M., type:

```
date 030113202001
```

You then control the RTC with `hwclock`. Simply typing `hwclock` all by itself and pressing Enter displays the current time. Adding the option `--systohc` (that's two dashes, directly followed by `systohc`) sets the hardware clock to the current system date—"system clock to hardware clock." The option `--hctosys` (again, two dashes followed by `hctosys`) sets the system clock to whatever date is stored in the RTC.

To summarize, then: you change the date (or time) in the hardware clock in two steps. First, change the system date with the `date` command. Then transfer that date information to the hardware clock with the command `hwclock --systohc`.

Dan adds this extra advice: "There is also an `rdate` command. I routinely execute the command `rdate -s clock.sgi.com`, which sets my system time to that of `clock.sgi.com`. I would then need to use `hwclock --systohc` to make that time go into the hardware clock."

Miscellaneous Linux Tidbits

Over the years, Unix has accumulated an impressive list of simple utilities. I haven't got space (or time) to cover them all, but here are a few interesting or odd ones that I came across.

Viewing System Messages: *dmesg*

I've mentioned this in passing, but let me highlight it. Several screenfuls of specific and useful information show up when you boot your system, and it'd often be nice to see what all of those messages were.

You can replay those messages with the `dmesg` command. As you'll get a lot of output, either use `less` or `grep` as a filter to control `dmesg`'s output.

Assuming Other Identities: *su*

There's another command I've mentioned in passing that I want to highlight. Sometimes you're logged in as one user but need to temporarily have the system see you as another user—perhaps to test some security item or, more commonly, to increase your abilities to root level. You do that with the "substitute user" or `su` command. It looks like:

```
su username
```

The username is optional—if you don't type in a username, it just assumes that you want to be the root. The system then prompts you for the other user account's password. Assuming you've typed in the right one, you become that account, until you type `exit`.

Simply running `su` all by itself gets you to the root account, but it doesn't execute the root's login script, so you won't have the root's PATH values—so many commands won't work unless you specify their full directory and command name instead of just the command name. You can fix that by running `su -`; that's `su` followed by a space and single dash.

Producing Calendars: *cal*

It's a little goofy, but I've liked this since I ran across it. From a command prompt, type cal 9 2000 and you'll get a calendar for September 2000. In general, cal *monthnumber year* produces a text calendar—useful for quickly finding out what day of the week October 14, 2007 will fall on.

Counting Words and Characters: *wc*

As a writer I am no doubt biased about this, but I've always liked little tools that count words in files. (All magazine and newspaper writing depends on articles of a particular word count.) So it's nice that Linux includes one: wc. Just type wc followed by a file's name, and you'll get a count of the lines in the file, the words in the file, and the total number of bytes in the file. For example, wc /etc/profile on my system yields the response:

```
34 84 537 /etc/profile
```

Guessing a File's Type: *file*

You see that a file is executable. But is it a binary file or a script? You could cat it, but binary files make such a mess of your screen when catted. Find out by typing:

```
file filename
```

file looks inside the file and announces whether it seems to be a script file, an executable, a regular old text file, or other type.

Who's Using a File: *fuser*

Sometimes you'll want to delete or move a file, but Linux tells you that the file is in use. But by whom? The fuser command can tell you. It looks like:

```
fuser filename
```

Put Your Computer in "Suspend" Mode

Suppose you have a laptop that supports Standby mode under Windows, putting the laptop in a kind of "light sleep"—it still uses power, but a lot less, and you can take it out of Standby mode quickly. Can Linux do that? Probably. A daemon process called apmd lets you put to sleep a computer that is capable of Standby mode with this command:

```
apm --suspend
```

As I've said, although this chapter showed you how to move around inside Linux, it only scratches the surface; it's truly amazing how many commands Linux includes. But now that you can work your way around in Linux, let's take a look at the basics of securing your system, with next chapter's discussion of user accounts and permissions.

6

User Accounts and
File Permissions

By now, you have some distribution of Linux running and you have the basics of controlling it down. But at this point, you can't make the system available to others unless you tell every one of them the password to the root account, and believe me, giving users the root password is not exactly the smartest thing you could do.

The next order of business, then, is to start creating some user accounts. And once you have some user accounts, you'll want to extend different access powers to different users. In this chapter, you'll see how to create local user accounts and groups, set file and directory permissions, and then centralize user accounts using Network Information System (NIS) so that you needn't re-create them on every machine in your network.

I think you'll find this chapter interesting for several reasons. First, of course, being able to manipulate user accounts and file and directory permissions is valuable. In addition to that, however, I think you'll find that user accounts and permissions are one part of Linux that is *very* different from NT/2000/XP/.NET. In fact, it's one of the places where I'd have to say that NT has Linux beat—but read on and decide for yourself.

Working with Linux User Accounts

In my experience, the best user management tools in Linux are command-line tools, so even the text-phobic really need to learn how to use a few command-line tools to create, maintain, and delete user accounts and groups. Fortunately, it's pretty easy. Here are the commands:

- `useradd`, `usermod`, and `userdel` create, maintain, and delete user accounts.
- `groupadd`, `groupmod`, `gpasswd`, and `groupdel` create, maintain, and delete user groups.
- `users` tells you what users are currently logged onto the computer.
- `groups` tells you what groups a user belongs to.

Creating Users

Without getting into too much detail, here's what prompted the need for the three-user management tools `useradd`, `usermod`, and `userdel`. Unlike Microsoft network operating systems, Linux stores user information in ASCII text files. Until the mid-90's, all Linux systems (and some other Unix variants) stored their entire database of users in a file called `/etc/passwd`.

There wasn't really anything wrong with that except for the fact that not only did `/etc/passwd` contain all of the user information, it also contained the user's passwords. Not in plain text, mind you—the passwords were encrypted. But the method of encryption was extremely vulnerable to attack. The passwords could be cracked pretty easily using something called a "dictionary hack"—you just use the password encryption algorithm to encrypt every word in the dictionary, then compare the resulting encrypted words to the encrypted passwords in `/etc/passwd`.

In response, most Linux distributions now give you the opportunity to install an improved user account storage system called the *shadow password* program. It doesn't encrypt any differently, but it does make one very important change: only the root user can access the file that replaces `/etc/passwd`, a file named `/etc/shadow`. Thus, only root could run a dictionary hack—and if your root user is a bad guy, then there's not much you can do in any case.

You'll see the option for shadow passwords when you install Linux—take it. With this new account storage system came tools to manipulate those accounts: `useradd`, `usermod`, and `userdel`. `useradd` creates a new user account, `usermod` modifies an existing user account, and `userdel` deletes a user account.

To create a user account, you need to know these things:

Username   It can be up to eight characters long. Upper- and lowercase are okay, but they count—wally is a different username (and account) than Wally.

Password   There are no rules here, but clearly longer is better.

Home directory   In Linux, we usually give users a home directory in /home/ *username*. Home directories are *important* in Linux, much more so than in NT. That's because by default, Linux users can generally only write into one directory on the disk—their home directory. The other directories tend to allow users to look around and execute commands in them, but not to create or modify files. As a result, Linux user data tends to sit in just one place—the home directories. That sounds like a godsend to anyone who's ever tried to find and back up all of a user's files on a workstation. The answer to the question, "Which directories on the computer contain user data files?" could be more easily answered if the question were, "Which directories *don't* contain any user data files?"

NOTE   It's part of the Unix/Linux culture that in general users can't—or shouldn't be able to, in any case—modify any directories except their home directory, although there may be a /home/public that *everyone* can write to. And there's the /tmp directory, a place for temporary files; everyone can write to that also.

User description   This is an optional label that tells us more about the user, perhaps a full name, a phone number, or the like. We might, for example, want to know that a person with the user account name "paul" is "Paul Smith, manager of the Baltimore office."

Default shell   The *shell* is the program that lets the user type things into the command line and get a response. In the DOS and Windows world, what we'd call COMMAND.COM or CMD.EXE, Linuxers would call a shell. There are a handful of available shells, but the one that most Linux users employ and that you'll probably find most useful is in /bin/bash. A modified version of an older shell named the Bourne shell (after its inventor), the common Linux shell is named bash, which is short for the "Bourne Again shell."

Group memberships   A user can be a member of any number of groups. When she creates a file, however, that file gets associated with one of her groups. (You'll read more about that in the upcoming discussion of file and directory permissions.) *One* of the user's groups, therefore, has this mildly special characteristic— it gets "attached" to any files that she creates. But which group should it be? That's answered by the administrator, who designates one group as her *initial* group. The others are said to be *supplementary* groups.

You can use useradd without any options at all and you'll get a basically useful result. For example, if you just type:

```
useradd joe
```

and useradd will create a user account named joe. He will be assigned a home directory named /home/joe, and he'll get the bash command shell.

Adding Users to Groups

So far, this sounds reasonable, and it is, except for the groups. If you don't specify a group then, believe it or not, in Red Hat Linux, useradd thinks it's just a great idea to create a completely new group named joe and makes that Joe's initial group. So, while it seems that we can let the shell and home directory run on autopilot, clearly we need to know about setting groups. Dan points out that some distributions, in contrast, just put every new user into the users group, which makes more sense to me.

Assigning Membership with *useradd*

You use the -g option to assign a user to his initial group. You use the -G option to set a user's supplementary groups. So if we instead want to create a user named joe whose initial group is users and who is *also* a member of groups named managers, sales, and engineering, we type:

```
useradd -g users -G managers,sales,engineering joe
```

Notice that there are no spaces in that list of associated groups. And any time that you want to find out what groups a given user is a member of, just type groups *username*; or, alternatively, you can just type groups and Linux will tell you what groups the currently logged-in account is a member of.

Changing Membership with *usermod*

As time goes on, Joe's role might change, and so he might have to move into and out of any given group. You have two tools to let you do that: usermod and gpasswd.

usermod takes the same options as useradd and doesn't affect anything you don't state. So, if I needed to add Joe to a group called employees, I'd type:

```
usermod -G managers,sales,engineering,employees joe
```

leaving his initial group (users) unchanged. Notice that in order to add Joe to just one group, I had to retype *all* of his associated groups. Had I just typed usermod -G employees joe, I would certainly have added him to the employees group, but I also would have *removed* him from managers, sales, and engineering.

Changing Membership with *gpasswd*

usermod is useful, but it's cumbersome to have to not only type in all of the groups that you want to add Joe to, but also to have to remember what groups he's already in. Another command, gpasswd, offers us a bit more flexibility. It looks like:

```
gpasswd -a username groupname
```

So in Joe's case, just typing gpasswd -a joe employees would have the same effect as the usermod command above. You can remove (delete) users from a group with the -d option, as in gpasswd -d joe employees. gpasswd -M lets you specify the group's entire membership, removing any previous members:

```
gpasswd -M user1, user2, user3 groupname
```

This puts user1, user2, and user3 in the group *groupname* and removes any previous members of that group.

Modifying /etc/group

Dan suggests a third option. If you have to make multiple changes at once, just directly edit the /etc/group file. Inside the file are several lines like:

```
sales:x:501:joe,fred,sally,jose
```

```
management:x:510:mark,katrina,chinqui,joe
```

Adding someone to a group is just a matter of adding their user ID to the end of the comma-separated list (or after the colon if there is no list yet).

Controlling Home Directories, Comments, and Shells with *useradd*

But suppose you want to use something other than the defaults for home directories and shells, and you want to add descriptive information; for that, there are, of course, options.

As is usually the case in Unix and Linux tools, uppercase and lowercase are important. The -m option directs useradd to create a new home directory for the new user. The -M option is the opposite, telling useradd *not* to create a new home directory. The -s option lets you specify the path to a shell program (/bin/bash is the path for the Bourne Again shell, but again it's the default, so you may never have to worry about this). The -d option lets you designate a home directory. The -c option lets you add a description—the *c* stands for "comment."

So, for example, if bash were sitting in a different directory, like /shells/bash, and you want Joe to have a home directory named /joesdir, want useradd to create that directory, and want to label Joe as "Joe Jones, extension 2345," type:

```
useradd -g users -G managers,sales,engineering -m -d /joesdir -s /
shells/bash joe -c "Joe Jones, extension 2345"
```

Expiring an Account

Occasionally in the NT world, we want to create an account that automatically self-destructs at some point. Linux can do that also, by adding the -e option to useradd. The -e option takes a date in the form of *yyyy-mm-dd*. For example, if I want to create an account that will expire on March 15, 2004, I include the option -e 2004-03-15 to my useradd command.

Setting the User ID Number

This next option is going to seem completely strange for NT veterans. You may know that every user account in an NT or 2000 network is distinguished by a unique security ID, or SID. The number is more than 128 bits long, and NT types don't usually even think about SIDs, as they can't do anything with them.

With *Linux*, in contrast, every user account still has a distinguishing ID, but the value can only range from 0 to about four billion (a new kernel 2.4 feature -- it was about 32,000 before), and the first 500 values are typically reserved by convention for the system's use. This user ID number is called the *uid,* and you can, if you like, control it with the -u option; a command like:

```
useradd -g users -G managers -u 610 paul
```

would create a user account named paul, whose initial group was users and who had a supplemental group membership in managers, with user ID of 610.

But the big question is, when would you *use* this feature? Well, suppose you had a small network of Linux boxes, and you wanted Paul to be able to access data on all of those machines. You could do that by creating a user account for Paul on each of the machines. (NT workgroups must do this, as they don't have a central domain controller to hold usernames. It's a pain, but some networks just can't have a domain controller for one reason or another.) With Linux, however, it's not enough to have the same user *name*—you must have the same user ID on all systems.

You're probably wondering if there is a way to avoid all of this work and just centralize the user accounts on a central machine, as we do in NT. There is indeed a way to do this, with Network Information System (NIS). You create an NIS server and then log on using your NIS account rather than a local account; you'll read how to set that up later in this chapter.

NIS can be a real network security headache, however, as it actually passes passwords across the network in *plain text*! That's why Sun Microsystems, which invented NIS, has since replaced it with NIS+ ("NIS plus") and shipped Solaris 8 with an even more secure shared-account system. Unfortunately, however, NIS+ is not shipped with Linux distributions.

Table 6.1 summarizes the options for the useradd command. You can always grab summaries like this with useradd --help, and it's a good idea to do so because some options with the same letter serve different purposes depending on context.

Table 6.1   Basic Options for **useradd**

Option	Action
-m	Creates a new home directory for the new user
-M	Tells useradd *not* to create a new home directory
-s	Defines path to user's default shell
-d	Defines path to user's home directory
-c	Attaches comment text to user
-e	Defines date the account expires
-u	Sets user ID

Changing User Account Defaults

But perhaps you're homesick for the NT/2000 way of doing things, and so you want all of your home directories in a directory named /users rather than /home. Or perhaps you've created a new shell, located in /bin/nshell, instead of bash. You could certainly retype the -s and -h options every time, but that's a pain.

useradd has an option –D, which will change its defaults. It looks like:

```
useradd -D -b top_of_home_dirs -e days -f disable_days
➥ -g group -s shell
```

The -D option must *precede* other options to produce its global effects. Some of this is pretty self-explanatory because the -g and -s options work identically, as you've already read.

The -e option lets you set how often users must set new passwords. The -f option lets you disable an account if a user neglects, after some number of days past the -e option, to change his password; setting it to zero means that accounts do not expire. (Instead, users would be forced to change their passwords before the system would log them on.)

The -b option is new, corresponding to the -h [AU: -d] option for setting home directories. Where the -d option lets you specify a particular user's home directory (as in -d /home/pete), the -D options refer to defaults for *all* new user accounts, not particular accounts. You don't want to set everyone's home directory to /home/pete; you want to be able to say that by default all home directories go in /home, or /users, or whatever. -b, then, lets you define the *top-level* directory (or, I suppose, you could consider it the "base" level, hence b) for home directories.

So, for example, let's say that we want everyone to have their initial group set to users, to use shell /bin/nshell, and have their home directories in /users/*username*. Let's also make them change their passwords every 120 days, and let's not disable the account if users don't change their passwords—instead, we'll just refuse to log them on until the password is changed, and offer the option to change it right then and there. We'd then type:

```
useradd -D -b /users -g users -s /bin/nshell -e 120 -f 0
```

These defaults are stored in /etc/default/useradd. By the way, this command works as advertised on Red Hat, Mandrake, and Slackware, but not Caldera, so do a useradd --help before assuming that this will work.

Setting User Passwords

But you're not done yet. There's one more thing to do: you have to set the password for the new joe account. The passwd command lets you do that. Operating as root, you type passwd joe, and Linux will then prompt you to type in a new password for Joe.

Deleting User Accounts

You've seen that you can create user accounts with useradd and modify them with usermod, but what about deleting accounts when they're no longer needed? For that, you use userdel *username*.

TIP This does *not*, however, delete the user's home directory. You could delete the home directory either directly, or with userdel -r joe.

Should you ever want to delete Joe's account, use userdel like so:

```
userdel joe
```

Disabling User Accounts

You know how in NT User Manager you have the ability to check off a box for Account Disabled, so that someone can't log in? usermod provides the same functionality in Linux with -L (capital *L*), the lock option:

```
usermod -L joe
```

Just like NT, if the user is currently logged in, he or she will not be logged out, but will be unable to log in when they next attempt to do so. To unlock a disabled account, the command is simply:

```
usermod -U joe
```

Seeing Who's on the System

Once you've created all of those user accounts, you might want to know who's logged on to the system. There are a few commands to help there:

- `finger`
- `who`
- `w`
- `users`

They offer the same basic kinds of info: how long the users have been on, how they're connected, and so on. `w` gives a bit more info than the others.

Creating and Modifying Groups

As with NT, Linux uses groups to simplify an administrator's life. You can have groups with names like sales, engineers, and managers, and create files and directories that can only be accessed by the sales group, or the engineers group, or the managers group, as in NT. *Unlike* NT, however, Linux's file permissions system is not nearly as flexible, but you'll learn more about that later. All of the group information is stored in the file /etc/group.

Creating New Groups

You can create and modify groups with two simple commands, `groupadd` and `groupmod`. (There's a `groupdel` command to delete groups as well, of course.) Simplified, `groupadd` looks like:

```
groupadd [-g groupID] groupname
```

Recall that users have an ID number like the NT SIDs; groups have them as well. You probably won't often need to preset the group ID number when you create a new group, so creating a group named managers would only require this command:

```
groupadd managers
```

Modifying Groups

And if you need to rename a group, use `groupmod -n` *newname* *oldname*; to rename the managers group to the bosses group, do this:

```
groupmod -n bosses managers
```

Adding or Subtracting a User to/from a Group

Recall that to add or remove a user to or from a group, use the usermod command with the -g or -G options:

```
usermod -g primarygroupname -G list_of_associated_groups username
```

You can also, recall, use the gpasswd command to add a user to a group without having to remember what other groups that user is a member of:

```
gpasswd -a username groupname
```

Just as the -a option adds, the -d option removes; gpasswd -d arnold users would remove Arnold from the users group.

Finding Out What Groups a User Belongs To

You can easily find out the names of the groups that a particular user is a member of with the groups command. Simply typing groups shows what groups *you* are a member of. Typing groups *username* shows which groups the user named *username* belongs to.

Controlling Group Management

Not just anyone can add people to a group or delete them from a group; only group administrators can do that. You define group administrators with the -A option. So, to make Joe a group administrator of the bosses group, you'd type:

```
gpasswd -A joe bosses
```

Deleting Groups

As you've probably guessed, there is also a program for deleting groups: groupdel. You'd delete the bosses (and yes, there's a joke lurking in there begging to get out, but I'll avoid it) with the following command:

```
groupdel bosses
```

Joining a Group

If you're not already a member of a group, you can enter that group with the newgrp command. You just need to know the group's password assuming it has one. If it doesn't (the default), then you can't join it. If my system included a group named netgeeks and I needed to work in it, I could type:

```
newgrp netgeeks
```

Linux would prompt me for a password and, if I knew the netgeeks password, I'd be admitted. The important effect of newgrp is this: from this point on, any files that I create will be associated with netgeeks. In fact, it becomes your new "initial" group. It sort of highlights a misnomer, which is why a lot of Unix folks use the term "default group" instead of "initial group."

Missing User and Group Management Commands

While all of these commands are collectively a pretty complete suite, there are a few things that, as far as I can see, you can't accomplish from the command line.

- There doesn't seem to be a way to list all of the user accounts in the system. As you will see, there's a kind of roundabout way of accomplishing that, by just looking in a file named /etc/passwd, but that's a bit ugly. Additionally, the linuxconf GUI tool can list user accounts, but it's a GUI tool and I'd like a command-line tool. There's users, but that only lists the names of the users who are currently logged on to the system. But Dan points out that you *could* use Linux's power to extract just the usernames like so:

    ```
    cut -f1 -d: /etc/passwd |sort
    ```

- Similarly, there doesn't seem to be a way to list the names of the user groups on the system. There's a groups command, but that just lists the groups that a particular user is a member of. As with my previous point, there's a roundabout way to list groups, by examining a file named /etc/groups, but you get a lot of other junk in addition to the groups, so it's not very convenient.

- Finally, while the groups command shows the groups that a user is a member of, there doesn't seem to be a command to list the converse—that is, given a group's name, there doesn't seem to be an easy way to find out what users are a member of that group. Dan points out, however, that you can just type:

    ```
    grep groupname /etc/group
    ```

    to get the same effect. That leads me to comment that there *are* ways to answer these questions if you're willing to get your hands dirty, so to speak—to poke around the files where the system stores user and group account data. So let's digress a bit and do some file spelunking.

Under the Hood: Where User Accounts Are Stored

NT experts know that user accounts are stored in an encrypted file named SAM on NT 3.*x* and 4.*x* systems, as well as member servers and workstations under Windows 2000, and that user accounts are stored in a file named ntds.dit on Active Directory servers. Those files are encrypted and binary under NT, and so we would not in general think about trying to find out user account information by directly examining these files. But it's a different story with Linux: user and group account information is stored in four files:

- /etc/passwd
- /etc/shadow
- /etc/group
- /etc/gshadow

Interestingly enough, these files are *not* encrypted (unlike NT), so we can peek inside them to see how Linux stores user and group information.

The */etc/passwd* File

Take a look inside the /etc/passwd file, and you'll see seven items separated by colons:

```
User_account_name:x:userID:groupID:comment:home_directory:shell
```

The x is in the second part because it's where Linux *used* to save the passwords before shadow passwords came around. Now the x just means "Go look in the /etc/shadow file for this user's password."

Suppose we have Jane Smith whose username is jane; her entry in /etc/passwd might look like this:

```
jane:x:1122:100:Jane Smith:/home/jane:/bin/bash
```

I chose 1122 as her user ID arbitrarily. I set her group ID to 100 because that is the group ID of the users group.

This is what I meant when I suggested a while back that you could always find the names of the user accounts on a system by looking in the file /etc/password. But a look inside *your* /etc/password will show that every system comes preconfigured with a fair number of accounts that you never created; adm, sync, halt, and news are four accounts that I find on my system. Your Linux's setup program created those accounts because some Linux server programs require special user accounts to get their jobs done.

> **NOTE** Furthermore, note that there is *no way* for anyone to log in to any of these special accounts. If you look in /etc/shadow (or /etc/passwd if not using shadow passwords), you'll see a * in the password field, which means that this account can never log in to the server.

The */etc/shadow* File

Now let's peek into the /etc/shadow file to see Jane's password. Lines in /etc/shadow look like /etc/passwd: a series of eight data fields and a reserved field about the user account, separated by colons. (Only the root account can read /etc/shadow, so log on with that account if you'd like to poke around yours as you're reading.) Those data fields are:

Username   The account username, the name that was used to log on.

Password   Yes, the password's here where you can see it—but what you're seeing is the *encoded* password.

Last change   The date that the password was last changed.

May change   The number of days before the password may be changed again. As is the case with NT, you can forbid users to change their passwords too often.

Must change   The number of days before the user *must* change her password.

Warning days   If the user will have to change her password sometime soon, we can warn her some number of days beforehand.

Disable days   If the user does not change her password by the required day, we'll give her a few grace days to change it. (When she tries to log on, we'll force her to change her password before allowing the logon.) But if she doesn't change her password after some number of days, we'll just disable the account altogether.

Expire date   Date to expire the account.

Each line of /etc/shadow looks, then, like this:

```
username:passwd:last_change:may_change:must_change:warn_days:
➥  disable_days:expire_date:reserved
```

Dates in Linux are expressed as integers: the number of days after January 1, 1970. (This means that Linux never had a "Year 2000" problem, but it *will* have a "Year 2038" problem if something isn't done before 2038.) So suppose we have a user whose account name is jsmith. We created his account on January 26, 2000 (10982 in Linux-ese). We'll make him keep a password for 4 days before he can change it, force him to change his password every 120 days, warn him 10 days before that, disable his account if he doesn't change the password 15 days after deadline (the 135th day), and disable his account on December 31, 2010 (represented as 14974). His shadow entry would look like this:

```
jsmith:encrypted_password:10982:4:120:10:15:14974:134550556
```

Of course, in most cases you won't set all of those values. In that case, leaving a field empty disables it. Most shadow entries look more like this:

```
gary:encrypted_password:10982:0:99999:7:::134549420
```

That tells us that the gary account was created on Linux day 10982, that he can change his password immediately, and that he need never change his password (99999). For some reason, Linux always includes the next field—number of days in advance that we must warn Gary before forcing him to change his password—and sets it to 7, so clearly Linux requires us to warn a user one week before "never" to change his password. The other fields are blank save for the reserved field, so the account never expires or is disabled.

The */etc/group* File

Before the advent of shadow passwords, all group information sat in a file called /etc/ group. Like the /etc/passwd and /etc/shadow files, group is an ASCII file that contains lines with four fields separated by colons: the group's name, an x, the group's ID number, and a list of its associated members. So, for example, if we had a group named managers whose members had user accounts named larry, pointy, and jsmith, then the entry in /etc/group for managers would look like:

```
managers:x:500:larry,pointy,jsmith
```

As I said earlier, you *could* peek into this file to see the list of user groups on your system. But, as with user accounts, you'll probably also be surprised at the sheer number of groups that you never created: wheel, mail, popusers, and news are a few of the ones that I find on my system. (Dan tells me that in the Old Days, you had to be in the wheel group or you couldn't use su to become the root. Linux doesn't have this restriction, however, so apparently wheel is a useless group now.)

Recall that Linux's improved security via shadow passwords means that in addition to the /etc/passwd file, you now have a /etc/shadow file. Groups need a shadow password file as well, named /etc/gshadow.

The */etc/gshadow* File

Entries in the /etc/gshadow file look pretty much the same as entries in the /etc/group file, except that the x is replaced with an encrypted password and there's an extra field for group administrators. This field comes *before* the list of associated members. The managers record in gshadow, then, might look like:

```
managers:65egro/17:500:wally,sue:larry,pointy,jsmith
```

The only difference between the contents of the /etc/groups file and the /etc/gshadow file (besides the encrypted password) is that users named sue and wally are designated the group administrators for the managers group. As with /etc/shadow, you must be root to read the /etc/gshadow file.

Now you've seen how to manage users and groups; let's put them to work by using them to control file and directory access.

Linux File Permissions

For the NT user learning Linux, many things will seem familiar. That's because Linux is, of course, based on Unix, and Unix concepts are so basic to modern computing that it's almost impossible to find an operating system that *hasn't* stol—oops, I mean *borrowed* an idea or two from Unix. When you whisk away the partisan nonsense, NT and Linux often seem to be cousins.

But that's not *always* true. One place where NT and Linux part company is in the matter of file and directory permissions.

In the NT/2000 world, we're used to having a fairly flexible set of options in the file and directory permissions department. We can create a wealth of user groups and then say that a particular file or directory can be read by the managers group, read and written by the engineers group, and completely controlled by the administrators group. In Linux, in contrast, it just wouldn't be possible to describe permissions for three separate groups. As a matter of fact, it wouldn't be possible to describe permissions for *two* separate groups. Here's how permissions work in the Linux world.

Three Permission Types: Read, Write, and Execute

Linux describes what you can and can't do with a directory or a file with three permissions: read, write, and execute. Actually, you should probably think of them as *six* permissions—read directory, read file, write directory, write file, execute directory (which would be better described as "traverse directory"), and execute file. In general, the read and write permissions work much as you expect them to, but, as with NT file and directory permissions, the execute permission is a bit nonintuitive.

Read Permission

On a file, read permission lets you read the file. You also need read permission on a script file in order to be able to run that file (in addition to execute permission, as you'll see later). Other than that, a file-read permission doesn't really do much; for example, you can examine a file's permissions even if you don't have the ability to read, write, *or* execute the file.

Read permission on a directory, in combination with execute permission on that directory, lets you see the contents of the directory. As with read permission on a file, the directory-read permission is kind of weak all by itself and tends to become relevant only in combination with other permissions.

Write Permission

Just as Linux's read permissions aren't exactly the same as NT's read permissions, it's also the case that Linux's write permissions aren't exactly what your NT experience will lead you to expect. Write permission on a file lets you modify a file. It does *not*, however, let you delete the file.

Write permission on a directory lets you create new files or directories inside the directory. You also need write permission on a directory to delete a file in that directory.

Counterintuitive as it may sound, you do not need any permissions on a *file* at all to delete the file. By eliminating its directory entry, you effectively erase the file—so you must have write permission on the *directory* that the file is in. (As you may know, NT has a similar characteristic: if you give someone Full Control to a directory, then that person can delete files in the directory even if he's been assigned No Access to the file. The NT folks did it to maintain POSIX compliance, actually.)

Execute Permission

In some ways, the execute permission is the *über*-permission. You'll see that you can do very little without it.

Execute permission on a file marks a file as executable. It signals Linux that the file is executable in some way, either as a binary file (like an EXE file in the NT world) or as a script file (like a BAT or CMD file in NT).

In the NT world, we sometimes need to execute the same sequence of commands over and over again. It's a pain to have to remember those commands and their sequence, so we can just type the commands *once* into an ASCII text file, creating a batch file. NT will then execute the commands in that text file, as long as NT *knows* that it's a batch file. You communicate the fact that a text file is a batch file by giving it a file extension of either .bat or .cmd. In Linux, you can also put a bunch of commands into a file and then tell Linux to execute the commands in that file, although Linux doesn't call it a batch file; Linux calls it a script file. But how would Linux know that a file contains commands that it can execute? You signal Linux that a file is a script not by adding a file extension but by changing the file's execute permission.

> **NOTE**   You need both read and execute permissions to run a script, but you only need execute permission to run a binary program file.

Execute permission on a *directory* doesn't have much to do with executing, but for NT experts it'll actually be quite familiar, as NT uses the same notion. In addition to wanting to read or modify the contents of a directory, you might sometimes need to "traverse" the directory—to "move through" it on the way to another directory. It's simpler to explain traversal rights with an example. Suppose we have a directory structure on a disk with a top-level directory called /top, a directory below it named /middle, one below *that* named /bottom, and yet another below that named /subbasement. The full path to that lowest-level directory, then, would be /top/middle/bottom/subbasement.

Now suppose that I have full read, write, and execute permission to the /subbasement directory, but no permissions at all to /top, /top/middle, or /top/middle/bottom. Here's the question: "How do I get to /top/middle/bottom/subbasement in the first place?" If I try to do a cd /top/middle/bottom/subbasement, Linux will try to fulfill my request by working its way down from /top, but /top will deny me entrance, and the command will fail. *But* if I have execute permissions on /top, /top/middle, and /top/middle/bottom, then I'm allowed to essentially "pass through" those directories on my way down to the directory where I'm the master of all I survey: /top/middle/bottom/subbasement.

The bottom line, then, about the execute directory permission is that you cannot do *anything* with a file unless you have execute permission on its directory, and the directory that the file's directory lives in, and so on—you need execute permission on every directory back up to the root, or Linux will deny any attempts to manipulate a file (or directory) in any way. So, in the previous example, I'd need execute permission on the /top directory, the /top/middle directory, the /top/middle/bottom directory, and the /top/middle/bottom/subbasement directory.

And in case you're wondering, read/write/execute is all that Linux has for permissions. NT's notion of a Set Permissions or Take Ownership permission doesn't exist, as Linux is much simpler in the way that it handles those matters: only the root can assign ownership, and only a file's owner (or the root) can change a file's permissions.

Permissions for Specific Functions

Let me try to solidify this discussion of permissions with some specific examples.

Permissions to Execute a Program

To execute a program in a directory, you must have execute access to the program's directory and all of its parent directories. Again, that's simply because you need traversal rights to get to the program's directory itself.

You'll *then* need execute rights on the program file itself. If it's a script, then you'll also need read rights on the program file.

Permissions to List a Directory

Listing a directory simply means to read it, so you'll of course need the read permission for the directory. But you have to get to the directory in order to do anything with it, so you'll need directory-execute permissions for the directory and its parent directories.

Permissions to List a File

Suppose you wanted to see all of the information about a file—in particular, its date and time, or perhaps its permissions. What file and directory permissions would you need? Well, to my way of thinking, listing file information means getting that information from the file's directory, so I'd *guess* that I'd need read permission on the directory (and directory-execute permissions, as usual). Oddly enough, though, that's not true—all you need are the directory-execute permissions; you don't need any directory permissions at all, nor do you need any file permissions. You can type `ls -l /apps/secret/somefile.txt` and have it work even if the only permissions that you have are traversal permissions—that is, directory-execute permissions for `/apps` and `/apps/secret`.

Permissions to Change (*cd*) to a Directory

By now, you won't be surprised to hear that you can't change to a directory unless you have the traversal permissions to that directory. But that's all you need. In the previous example, I could `cd /apps/secret` if all I had was directory-execute permissions for `/apps` and `/apps/secret`. Once there, however, I wouldn't be able to do much—a simple `ls` would be rebuffed by Linux, as I wouldn't have the permission to read the directory.

Permissions to Make a New Directory

Same as changing to a directory, but with the write permission added to the container directory. For example, if I wanted to create a directory named `/apps/secret/bin`, then I'd need directory-execute permissions for `/apps` and `/apps/secret` in order to get started, but then I'd need directory-write permission to `/apps/secret` in order to create `/bin` with the command `mkdir /apps/secret/bin`. I *wouldn't* need directory-write permission on `/apps`.

Permissions to Read a File

This should *mostly* make sense. As always, you need those directory-execute permissions to get to the file's directory. But do you need directory-read permissions? No, not at all, not unless you want to do an `ls` to find the file in the first place. But you *do* need *file*-read permissions.

Permissions to Modify a File

To change a file's contents, you first need to be able to read it, so you'll need directory-execute permissions and file-read permission. To be able to go further and *change* the file, however, you'll need another permission, the file-write permission.

Permissions to Delete a File

As noted earlier, Linux sees file deletion as a directory operation rather than a file operation. That means that in order to delete a file, you needn't have any file permissions at all on that file. You need only have the usual directory-execute permissions for the file's directory and its parents, but you *also* need write permission *on the directory*. Then you can delete a file.

I summarize this permission information in Table 6.2, where (in Linux style) r means read permission, w means write, and x means execute.

Table 6.2   File and Directory Permissions

Operation	Required Directory Permissions	Required File Permissions
Create new file	-wx	none
Execute a program	--x	--x
List a directory	r-x	none
Change to a directory	--x	none
Create a directory	-wx	none
List a file's permissions and attributes	--x	none
Display a file	--x	r--
Modify a file	--x	rw-
Delete a file	-wx	none
Change a file's owner (only root can do this)	none	none
Change file permissions (only root or the file's owner can do this)	--x	none

Now let's look at how you can *set* these permissions in more detail.

You Can Only Set Permissions for One User, the Owner

In Linux, every file has an owner, as in the NT world. But we usually don't worry too much about ownership in NT because of the flexibility of file and directory permissions in NT. In Linux, however, it's very important who owns a file or a directory, as you can explicitly describe the permissions that the file or directory's owner has. In fact, that is the *only* case where you can specify permissions for a particular user account!

As long as I'm on the topic of file owners, by the way, here's another thing that's different between Linux and NT. In the NT world, you cannot *give* ownership of a file—you can only be given the permission to *take* ownership. So, suppose under NT that I wanted to snoop in your file and I didn't have any permissions to the file. As an administrator, I have the right to seize ownership of the file and once I have that, I can grant myself permission to access the file. But once I've done that, there's no way to cover my tracks. When you return to your desk and try to access your file, you can see that someone—me—has seized ownership, and the jig is up; I'm caught with my hand in the cookie jar.

In the Linux world, you get ownership when someone *gives* it to you. Only the root user can give ownership away. Root can give ownership away with the chown, "change ownership," command. It looks like this:

```
chown account_name file_or_directory_name
```

Thus, for example, I could (assuming I'd grabbed root powers) give a user named jane ownership of a directory named /janestuff with this command:

```
chown jane /janestuff
```

Again, you can do that with either files or directories; chown jane /janestuff/ journal.txt would give jane ownership of the file journal.txt in the directory /janestuff.

The owner of a file or a directory can be granted any combination of the three permissions read, write, or execute. And if you want to give away ownership of an entire directory tree, the -R makes chown recursive.

You Can Only Set Permissions for One Group for Each File

Here's another idea that will be completely different for NT experts. In the Linux world, every file is associated with a particular *group*. I know, you're saying, "Huh? What's the point of *that*?" Well, the idea is that you can set read/write/execute permissions for a particular user—the owner, recall—and you can also set read/write/execute permissions for a particular *group*. So, for example, if I'm the author of a document that I want my coworkers to be able to examine and comment on, I could be the owner of that document, with full permissions to the document, and I could then give read permissions to a group called, say, coworkers. They'd then have the ability to read the document, and they could either comment via e-mail or by creating files of their own.

The logical question at this point is, "How do I assign different permissions for different groups?" How would I say that everyone in the Managers group can read and write a file, but the people in the Marketing group can only read the file? The answer is, you can't, as least not as far as I can see.

When I was trying to understand this and I needed to make sure that I'd gotten it right, I literally asked five different Unix/Linux experts the above question and, every time, I got the same answer: "Well, NT does role-based permissions, right, that's what you're talking about, isn't it?" So I guess the idea that a lot of different groups can have different permissions on a given file or directory is called *role-based permissions*. In any case, Linux *doesn't* have role-based permissions.

Recall that in Linux a user can be a member of more than one group. If you are associated with a given file's group, then Linux will grant you the group permissions on that file. Thus, if Jill is a member of the engineers group, the users group, and the managers group, and a file named `raises.txt` is associated with the managers group, and that group can read and write the `raises.txt` group, then Jill will be able to read and write that file.

You can change which group a file is associated with, with the `chgrp` command. It looks like:

```
chgrp groupname file_or_directoryname
```

Thus, to assign a file named `report.txt` to the group coworkers, you'd type

```
chgrp coworkers report.txt
```

The Third Permission Group: The World

What if you want to access a file or directory and you're not the owner or a member of the file's group? In that case, Linux extends to you the third set of permissions on every file—the "rest of the world" or, in Linux-speak, *world* permissions. As with owner and group permissions, there are three world permissions: read, write, and execute.

Reading File Permissions

You can find out what the permissions are on a file with the `ls -l` command. A typical output might look like:

```
drwxr----- 1 mark users 21003 January 20 11:54 markstuff
-rwx------ 1 mark users 4523 December 31 13:20 mark.scrt
```

Even if you've never used Linux, this may look familiar—ever done a `dir` command in an FTP site and seen something like this? What you're seeing is an indication whether it is a directory (if so, there's a `d` in the leftmost character), a nine-character description of file or directory permissions, the number of hard links to the file or directory, the name of the file or directory's owner, the name of the file or directory's group, the file's size in bytes, the date last modified, and, finally, the name of the file. Looking at the above example, I see a `d` starting off the first line, so it's a directory, and a dash on the second, so it's not a directory and therefore a file. In other words, `markstuff` is a directory and `mark.scrt` is a file. In both cases, mark is the owner and users is the name of the group that the file or directory belongs to.

The string of drwxr----- or -rwx------ is a shorthand way of describing permissions. There are 10 positions in the string if we include the directory character. The leftmost position is always a dash or d and, as you've already read, designates whether you're looking at a file or a directory. Moving right, the first three characters indicate the permissions for the owner, the next three for the group, and the last three for the world. Each three-character group represents read (r), write (w), and execute (x) permission, in that order. A dash in a position indicates that permission hasn't been granted. Thus, to dissect drwxr-----:

- d means it's a directory.
- rwx means that the owner can read, write, and execute the directory.
- r-- means that the group can read the directory, but can't write or execute it.
- --- means that the world—anyone who's not the owner and who isn't a member of the users group—cannot read, write, or execute the directory.

Take the -rwx------ string on the mark.scrt file as another example. Break it up into pieces:

```
-              rwx        ---          ---
file/directory  owner perms  group perms  world perms
```

So it's a file, not a directory; the owner can read, write, and execute it; the group (users) cannot read, write, or execute it; and the world cannot read, write, or execute it.

Setting File and Directory Permissions

Now that you can read file permissions, you might want to take them in hand and change them. Only the file's owner or the root account can change permissions, and sometimes even the *owner* can't change those permissions.

TIP The owner must have execute permissions on a file's directory, or else they cannot change the file's permissions, because they can't traverse the directory tree to get to the file in the first place. Of course, the root can do anything it wants.

In NT, we change file and directory permissions either graphically with the Explorer/ My Computer, or, less often, from the command line, using either the CACLS or XCACLS command. Linux has a command-line command, as you'd expect: chmod. It looks like:

    chmod permissions file_or_directory

Simple, eh? Well, it looks that way, until I explain to you how you designate those permissions. One might imagine that chmod would require a simple nine-character string of permissions like the ones that `ls` displays—that `chmod rwxrw-r-- report.txt` would set full access permissions on a file named `report.txt` for the owner, read and write for the group, and read-only for the world at large (assuming the directory character wouldn't be needed). But that's not how it works. Instead, `chmod 764 report.txt` would do the trick. 764? Wheretheheck did *that* come from? As is the case with so many things Linux (or Unix, for that matter), it's simplicity itself, *once* someone explains it.

The `chmod` permissions are described as three digits. The leftmost digit describes the permissions for the owner, the middle the group permissions, and the rightmost the world permissions. Each digit is computed in the following way:

- If the entity being described (owner, group, world) can *read* the file or directory, add a 4.
- If the entity being described can *write* the file or directory, add a 2.
- If the entity being described can *execute* the file or directory, add a 1.

For example, suppose we want to set permissions on a file named `speech.txt` so that the owner has full (read, write, and execute) permissions, the group has read and write permissions, and the world has only read permission. (I'm not certain when this would happen, but I needed a bit of variety for the example.) We'd compute `chmod` values like so:

- The owner can read (which adds 4 to his `chmod` value), write (add 2), and execute (add 1 more), so his `chmod` permission value is 4 + 2 + 1 or 7.
- The group can read (4) and write (2), so its `chmod` value is 4 + 2 or 6.
- The world can only read, so its value is 4.

Result: to set these permissions, just type `chmod 764 speech.txt`. You can see all possible `chmod` values in Table 6.3.

Table 6.3   Values of chmod for Permissions

chmod **Value**	**Meaning**
7	Read, write, execute
6	Read, write
5	Read, execute
4	Read
3	Write, execute
2	Write

Table 6.3 Values of chmod for Permissions *(continued)*

chmod **Value**	**Meaning**
1	Execute
0	No access

To set what we'd call in the NT world the Everyone/Full Control permission for speech.txt, you'd type chmod 777 speech.txt.

Alternatively, chmod offers a slightly friendlier option than having to figure numbers: you can change only one permission for only one entity without disturbing the others, using an alternate syntax. Suppose I want to change speech.txt's world permission from 7 (read, write, and execute) to just 4 (read). In building the chmod command, I'd know already that I wanted the command to look like chmod ??4 speech.txt, where I don't know initially what goes in the places that currently have question marks. (You can't actually type the command chmod ??4 speech.txt, that won't work. I've put the question marks in there to illustrate the fact that, as I build the command in my mind prior to actually entering it, I've already got one of the numbers figured out but need now to figure out the other two digits.)

As I've already noted, you can't simply do an ls with some option and get it to spit out the current three-digit permission level, so I'd then have to do an ls -l to get the permissions in -rwxrwxrxw format, then I'd get to compute the digits that correspond with the current permissions, and I'd finally figure out that I could type chmod 774 speech.txt.

It would be far easier, however, if I could simply tell chmod to change the world permissions and leave the owner and group permissions alone. I can do that with this command:

    chmod o=r speech.txt

The o=r means, "Set only read permissions for the world." Here's how you decode that. The o refers to the world—o seems to stand for "other," as in "owner, group, and 'other'," I guess. The plus sign says to add the read permission, and r refers to the read permission. Instead of the plus sign, you could use the equals or minus sign:

- o+r means "add the read permission to the 'world' group and leave any other permissions unchanged."
- o=r means "delete any permissions that the 'world' group had and set the permissions to only read."
- o-r means "remove the read permission from the 'world' group and leave the other permissions unchanged."

Including o, chmod recognizes four possible entities for setting permissions:

- u says to set the permission for the owner ("user").
- g says to set the permission for the group.
- o says to set the permission for the world.
- a says to set the permission for the owner, group, and world—it's the "all people" permission.

The values for permissions are, as you've probably guessed, r, w, and x for read, write, and execute, respectively. So, for example, g-w would take the write permission from the file or directory's group, a+x would grant everyone the permission to execute the file or directory, or u+r would grant the owner read permission. You can combine these together into a single command. For example:

```
chmod g-w,a+x speech.txt
```

will remove the group write permission and set the execute bit for everyone. Note that the options are separated by a comma, but there are *no* spaces between the options. And, finally, you can specify multiple values in both the u/g/o and r/w/x fields, so "chmod ug+x foo.txt" grants execute permission to both user and group, and "chmod g+rwx foo.txt" grants full permissions to group.

Centralizing User Accounts

In a network of NT systems, we might want user susan to be able to access data on all of those systems, but we don't want to have to go around building susan user accounts on every system. Instead, NT lets us centralize our user accounts by putting them on a central system called a domain controller, and all NT systems then use that central system to do logins.

Similarly, a network of Linux systems wouldn't want to have to rebuild duplicate accounts on every system, so Linux offers something sort of like a domain controller, called Network Information Server, or NIS. But it needs a file server to work with, as home directories are so important in Linux, so that users can easily get to their home directories no matter where those users log in. That's why we'll *also* cover NFS, one of Linux's file server systems.

Network Information Service (NIS)

NIS (pronounced either as an acronym or by some people as "niss") is not a creation of Linux at all. In fact, it originated with Sun Microsystems in the mid-1980s as a way to share configuration information between SunOS (Unix) systems. Originally, it was called Yellow Pages, but that term is trademarked in the United Kingdom by British Telecom, and BT would not allow Sun to use the name. So the name changed to NIS but, as you'll see, all the commands begin with yp.

NIS works like this. All participating computers are members of an NIS *domain*. A *master* NIS server keeps the original set of NIS *maps*. Typically, these maps are your lists of users, groups, hosts, and other information you wish to share. There may be one or more *slave* NIS servers that periodically receive updated copies of the NIS maps from the master NIS server. When a user goes to log in to an NIS *client* computer, the system first checks its local user database and then attempts to authenticate the user through one of the NIS servers.

Hmmm... is any of this sounding familiar?

master NIS server	=	primary domain controller
slave NIS server	=	backup domain controller
NIS domain	=	NT domain
map	=	SAM file

Well, no one ever claimed that Microsoft's PDC/BDC domain structure was an original idea! The truth is that the two systems *are* similar in concept, but the implementation is quite different.

For instance, NIS passes information across the network in clear text, including password information. (Okay, the password is still encrypted with the normal password encryption, but that's well known and easy to break with a brute-force attack.) NIS master servers also transfer the *entire* map to slave servers when there is a change, so if you have large lists of users or groups, all of that is consuming network bandwidth. And the NIS namespace is flat, so there are obvious naming issues that can come into play.

Remember those shadow passwords we talked about earlier as being much more secure? Unfortunately, NIS removes that security, and you're basically back at the pre–shadow password security level.

WARNING   Before early 1999, Linux client workstations couldn't use shadow passwords *at all* if they were acting as NIS clients. That's not a problem for any modern version of a distribution—Red Hat 7.2 or later, for example—but just be aware that if you're using a distribution created before early 1999, you might not be able to connect to an NIS domain if you've installed your system to use shadow passwords. You can always fix this by either reinstalling your old distribution without shadow passwords, *or* you could just get a newer version of the distribution (which I recommend). There is nothing to worry about if you're using Red Hat 7.3; it lets shadow passwords coexist with NIS client software without any trouble. But remember that, unfortunately, adding NIS to shadow passwords makes those passwords easier to get to than they would be otherwise.

Well, the folks at Sun Microsystems aren't dumb, and so in the mid-1990s as part of their new version of Unix, called Solaris 2.0, they rolled out a new version of NIS called NIS+. NIS+ uses encryption for communication between clients and servers, performs incremental transfers between the master and slave servers, and uses a hierarchical naming system. In fact, it's, um, well, a tree, kind of like, oh, NDS and Active Directory. It just goes to show you that good ideas just keep going around and around and around...

Okay, so why isn't this section titled "NIS+"? Well, there's this minor detail that NIS+ has been quite popular within Solaris environments, but that usage doesn't seem to have migrated over to Linux yet. In fact, there are some implementations of an NIS+ *client* for Linux, but as of yet no NIS+ server. This is actually okay on one level, because in the end all of this NIS/NIS+ stuff will probably fade away to be replaced by LDAP servers. (Yes, there are LDAPs for Linux, and they work perfectly fine. Visit `www.openldap.org` if you want to see one that works.) But until that happens, NIS is the tool that we have to simplify system administration on existing Linux boxes.

NOTE   For some reason or another, there is an NIS+ *client* in Red Hat 7.3. It's just the server that's missing.

Setting Up an NIS Server

Our first task is to set up an NIS server ("primary domain controller") on our network. There's a whole lot of theory about NIS map files that we could go into here, but let's just plunge in and get the system set up, explaining along the way.

Before we get started, in order to try out NIS, we'll need a few user accounts on this NIS server that don't exist on your workstations, so use the normal `useradd` commands to create a few accounts on the NIS server.

Checking That the portmap *Service Is Running*

NIS depends on a Linux service or daemon named the *RPC portmapper*, so let's make sure it's running. This daemon, called `portmap`, translates remote procedure calls (RPCs) into the appropriate TCP/IP ports. Since NIS clients and servers use RPCs to communicate, we kind of need this service to be running. A quick way to check is to type:

```
ps aux | grep portmap
```

On my Red Hat 7.3 system, I get:

```
rpc     672    0.0  0.1  1508 544 ?   S   06:37  0:00 portmap
```

My Red Hat 7.3 system seems to load it automatically, but if yours doesn't for some reason, then use `ksysv` as described in the previous chapter to tell your Linux to load it at boot time. (Or you could run "chkconfig portmap on".) To start the `portmap` service now, find and run its start/stop script. If you don't see a result like the above, you need to start the portmap service. Typically, this is out of the directory where your init scripts are stored. In Red Hat or Mandrake, the command you would issue (as root) would be:

```
# /etc/rc.d/init.d/portmap start
```

Checking That You Have the NIS Program Files

If you installed your Linux with "everything" (which I suggest for beginners; disk space is cheap, and it's a pain searching through the RPMs to load something later), then you should have all of the NIS files on your disk—but let's just double-check. Type the following whereis commands:

```
# whereis ypserv
ypserv: /usr/sbin/ypserv /etc/ypserv.conf
# whereis ypbind
ypbind: /usr/sbin/ypbind
#
```

If you *didn't* install everything, then you can add NIS now. Pop the Red Hat 7.3 Installation CD 2 into your CD drive and, assuming that you set up automounter as we did in the last chapter, it is now mounted as /misc/cd. (If you mounted it differently, then no problem, just change /misc/cd in the next few paragraphs to wherever you mounted the CD.) Then type:

```
rpm -ivh /misc/cd/RedHat/RPMS/yp*
```

Choosing What Files to Centralize with NIS

NIS lets us centralize more than just the list of users; the next step is to select which files we want to make available through NIS. Go to the directory /var/yp and edit the file Makefile. Look for a line that looks like:

```
all: passwd group hosts rpc services netid protocols mail \
```

All of these are the files that are typically found in /etc that will be converted into *maps* and distributed by NIS. You can modify this line to include or exclude any files you wish. In most distributions, you'll find a helpful line nearby in the file that will list all the available files for you.

If you page through the file, you'll find there are any number of various options that you can set. Some of the more interesting include MERGE_PASSWD and MERGE_GROUP, which allow you to use shadow passwords on the server but distribute out a regular password file through NIS. There's also YPSRCDIR, which is the source directory, usually /etc, for all of the files to be distributed. Another is MINUID, which prevents lower-number users (such as root) from having their information distributed across the network.

After you're done editing that, check to be sure you have a /etc/ypserv.conf file. You can open it, but in a default configuration, there's honestly not much for us to do here. If you don't have it, see if there is a sample in /var/yp or check the man page to figure out what you need to have here. All you really need for a minimal ypserv.conf is this one line:

```
dns: no
```

Naming the NIS Domain and Starting the Server

Now let's actually do something. First, we need to set the NIS domain name. The name can be anything up to something like 255 characters, and people generally advise *against* using something like your DNS domain name. So, for example, I'll just make up Minasi Computing and abbreviate it as mincomp. Type this at a command prompt:

```
domainname mincomp
```

And just for now, let's call this server nis1.mincomp:

```
hostname nis1.mincomp
```

Now, we should start the ypserv daemon, from its init script. On a Red Hat or Mandrake system, this will be:

```
# /etc/rc.d/init.d/ypserv start
```

Next, we need to generate the maps that ypserv is going to use. The very first time we do this, we run the command:

```
# /usr/lib/yp/ypinit -m
```

This will take a minute or two and will issue various messages about building the maps. Then it asks what hosts will run NIS servers. It offers first the name of the machine that you're working on and then prompts next host to add. We're not going to add any more NIS servers at the moment, so just press Ctrl+D. The routine ends, saying:

```
nis1.mincomp has been set up as an NIS master server.

Now you can run ypinit -s nis1.mincomp on all slave servers.
```

Running the Client-Side Tool: *ypbind*

At this point, your NIS server should be fully functional, and clients should be able to connect to it using ypbind. (Now, that was easier than setting up an NT domain controller, wasn't it?) If you want to use some of the yp commands yourself on the server, then you, too, will need to start up ypbind so that you can connect to the server process. Before you do, though, there's one more thing you should know.

The default behavior of ypbind is to send out a broadcast on the local network looking for an NIS server. Perhaps this is okay on a small network, but on a large network there is a security issue here. Anyone with a Linux/Unix box can set up an NIS server using your domain name, and all of a sudden you could find yourself binding to someone else's machine (and getting *their* password and other files). To prevent this, before starting ypbind, edit a file called /etc/yp.conf (you might have to create it) and put in a line like:

```
domain mincomp server nisserver
```

where *mincomp* is your NIS domain name and *nisserver* is the host name of your NIS server (you could also use the IP address if you wanted to).

Okay, now let's just try this out by binding the NIS server to itself, just as a test. Run ypbind, either using the init script or launching ypbind as a separate command:

```
# /etc/rc.d/init.d/ypbind start
Binding to the NIS domain:          [ OK ]
Listening for an NIS domain server.  [ OK ]
#
```

Okay, it works, so what? Now what? Well, to verify that you are receiving the password maps, type the following:

```
# ypcat passwd
```

You should see a nice list of the user account info from /etc/password for all the user IDs transmitted through NIS. Try using ypcat to view the contents of the other maps that you set up via the Makefile back at the beginning of the process (group and hosts are easy choices).

A fun little command is ypwhich. This will tell you which NIS server you have bound to:

```
# ypwhich
nisserver
```

Another entertaining command is ypmatch. Type this:

```
# ypmatch username passwd
```

where *username* is one that you know is in the NIS-distributed passwd file. You should see the line from passwd with that user's information.

Setting Up an NIS Server to Start Automatically

Now you have the NIS server running, but if you reboot it, it won't run anymore. You'll need just a few tweaks to make the NIS server service survive reboots. An NIS server needs three things to start properly:

- The domain name must be set with the domainname command before ypserv tries to start. As you learned in Chapter 4, you can edit /etc/sysconfig/network to set domainname.

- The portmapper must start before `ypserv`.
- You have to get `ypserv` to start upon startup.

First, set up the `domainname` by editing `/etc/sysconfig/network`. You'll see `HOSTNAME=` and `NISDOMAIN=` lines; set them to match your server name and NIS domain name. In my case, I'd make them:

```
HOSTNAME=nis1.mincomp

NISDOMAIN=mincomp
```

You can (or should be able to) get `ypserv` to start at boot time via the standard System V startup script method, and on Red Hat 7.3 you'll find a script in `/etc/rc.d/init.d` named ypserv. Like other startup scripts, it takes arguments like `start`, `stop`, `restart`, and `status`. Find the `ypserv` script, as you'll need it for the next step.

Then, make sure that `ypserv` loads with the other daemons. For example, on one system, I created this symbolic link to ensure that it would start in runlevel 3 on a Red Hat 7.3 system:

```
ln -s /etc/rc.d/init.d/ypserv /etc/rc.d/rc3.d/S70ypserv
```

My main concern is that `ypserv` loads *after* the portmapper and, I suppose, after the network code; they load as S13 and S10, so any value above 13 ought to work.

Setting Up an NIS Client

Getting an NIS server to listen to itself wasn't terribly impressive, so now let's make a client join an NIS domain and get connected. Move on over to another machine and let's get started.

Setting Up the Domain Name and Checking the Portmapper

Much of client setup will resemble the server setup for NIS. As before, check that the client machine has the yp programs. Then let's set the NIS domain:

```
# domainname mincomp
```

where *mincomp* is the name of your NIS domain. Next, you need to check to see if the portmap daemon is running:

```
# ps aux | grep portmap
bin 6091 0.0 0.2 1092 320 ? S Jun23 0:00 portmap
```

If not, you'll need to start it up. Best bet is to go into your directory of init scripts and start it there, as with the server. After you're sure that it's running, check to make sure you have a directory called `/var/yp`. If not, create it:

```
# mkdir /var/yp
```

Next, let's go into /etc/yp.conf and add one line:

```
domain mincomp server nisserver
```

You would change *mincomp* to whatever your NIS domain is named, and *nisserver* to the DNS name of your NIS domain controller or, if you prefer, its IP address.

Starting the Client Program

Now you just start up ypbind, the client-side piece of NIS, either as an init script or simply by typing at the command line:

```
# ypbind
```

When started from the command line, ypbind won't offer any feedback. Now we're ready to test it out. You can use the ypwhich and ypcat commands mentioned earlier, such as:

```
# ypcat passwd
```

You should see the list of passwords coming out of the host's file on your server. If you don't, check over the previous steps and also make sure that ypserv is still running on your server. You can also check to make sure that the name you put into /etc/yp.conf will in fact resolve correctly (use ping or something like that to test).

Telling Your System to Use NIS

So now you're set up as an NIS client. You'd *think* that means that you could log on with a domain account. But it doesn't; try it, and you'll get a nastygram claiming that it nevah hoid of da guy. Here's a surprising thing about NIS: *just because you join an NIS domain does not mean your local files will use the NIS files!* Pretty weird, eh? I mean, when you join an NT domain, presto! You're authenticating against the domain controller. Not so with Linux/Unix. When you join an NIS domain, basically you're saying that your system *could* use the NIS files if so configured. (Remember, Linux is all about choice.)

Why'd they do it this way? Well, consider that your system already has a set of local user account files (/etc/passwd, /etc/group, /etc/gshadow, and /etc/shadow), and now it has the ability to use the NIS server to authenticate. It needs to know exactly how you want to do it. Would you like users to *have* to authenticate from the NIS domain controller? Or will you only accept authentication from the local files? Perhaps local files then NIS controller, or the other way around? Of course, in the NT and 2000 world, you log on by telling your system your name, password, and domain, so you *tell* it where to find your user account. But you don't do that in Linux—you'd just log on as jane with password swordfish, and then it's Linux's job to figure out where to check out that password/user account combination. You tell it how in a file called /etc/nsswitch.conf.

Open yours up with vi; you'll see a bunch of comments and then perhaps a few lines that look like this:

```
passwd:    files nisplus
group:     files nisplus
hosts:     files nisplus dns
services:  files nisplus
networks:  files
netgroup:  nisplus
automount: files nisplus
aliases:   files nisplus
...
```

What you're seeing here is a list of the files that you might centralize using NIS. The words after it—files, dns, nisplus–tell your NIS client where to look for information:

- compat is a relic from an earlier type of NIS client. If you have a modern distribution, like Red Hat 7.2, then this is irrelevant.
- files refers to the local files. passwd: files would mean, "When you need to look up a user in passwd, first look at /etc/passwd, the local file. If you can't find the user there, then don't log him/her in."
- nis says to look to the NIS server for information.
- nisplus says to look to an NIS+ server for information.
- dns says to look it up in DNS. This isn't meaningful for user accounts, but would be for host names.

You can, as you can see from the examples, specify more than one value. The files we're interested in are passwd and group; if you want to be able to log on anywhere in an NIS domain, then the clients have to look to NIS for both user accounts (passwd) and group membership (group). In the example above, I have:

```
passwd: files nisplus
```

The effect of this is that when I log in as mark with password opensesame, the login routine first looks on the local /etc/passwd file. If it finds me there, then I'm logged in. If not, it looks in the /etc/passwd file on the NIS server.

Unless you're ready to do some serious messing around with NIS, I'd really recommend that your nsswitch.conf look like this:

```
passwd: files nis
group:  files nis
```

That will require changing a number of lines because again, for some reason, the Red Hat client prefers NIS+—most lines say `files nisplus`—even though there isn't an NIS+ server shipped with Red Hat 7.3. Change the `files nisplus` references to `files nis` and resave /etc/nsswitch.conf.

After making changes to /etc/nsswitch.conf, you need to reboot your machine. Oops... just kidding, this isn't NT. Actually, you need to do... nothing. This will just work.

To see, press Alt+F2 or Alt+F3 and log on as a regular old user—anything but root. Then try to su to an account on the NIS server. Assuming that joe has an account on the NIS server but not the local /etc/passwd file:

```
$ su joe
Passwd:<type in Joe's password>
$ whoami
joe
$
```

Hey, it worked! Well, sort of. Yes, you're now logged in as user joe, but if you notice what directory you're in (pwd), it's not /home/joe. su joe just switches you to user ID joe, but doesn't go through the normal login process. However, had we done su - joe, we would have. Let's try it. Type exit to get out of the user's shell and back to your own user account. Now:

```
$ su - joe
Passwd:
su: warning: cannot change directory to /home/joe:
➥ No such file or directory
$
```

Hmmm... what happened here? Well, remember the importance of home directories? The home directory for joe is on the server, but not on the local machine. So if joe's going to be a roaming kind of guy, we'll need to put his home directory on some central location and let him get to it via the network. That's why we'll need NFS, which we'll get to in a page or two.

TIP If you did not get this warning message, odds are that you *do* have a directory for that username in /home (such as /home/joe), but it's not the one from the server.

Setting Up an NIS Client to Start Automatically

Just as with the NIS server, you've now accomplished getting an NIS client to work, but what you've done won't survive a reboot. Making an NIS client run automatically on startup is very similar to making an NIS server boot, with one difference: you don't load ypserv, you load ypbind.

Again, you need the domainname command executed before ypbind tries to do anything. So modify /etc/sysconfig/network as before.

Then put a symbolic link in the runlevel 3 directory (/etc/rc.d/rc3.d, as before) so that the ypbind script runs.

For example, on one system I created this symbolic link to ensure that it would start in runlevel 3 on a Red Hat system:

```
ln -s /etc/rc.d/init.d/ypbind /etc/rc.d/rc3.d/S98ypbind
```

Notice that I gave ypbind a pretty high number, S98. That's because I found that the Red Hat designers give it a lower number, and that makes ypbind fail on laptops. You see, on a laptop, you have to have the PCMCIA pieces loaded *before* ypbind, or ypbind can't find an NIS domain controller—after all, the computer doesn't even have a functioning NIC yet!

Updating Account Information on the NIS Server

On NT, when you add a user to the PDC, that user can essentially log in immediately anywhere within the NT domain. That's almost true here with NIS, but there's one more step.

As root, try this sequence of commands *on the NIS server*, and watch for the difference in output of the last two:

```
# useradd fred
# cat /etc/passwd
(you see the list)
# ypcat passwd
(you see the list)
#
```

What was different? You should see that user fred is in /etc/passwd, but is not yet in the NIS passwd map. Here's the deal... the NIS maps have to be updated manually. Every time you make a change to the configuration files, you need to go into the directory /var/yp and do a single make command:

```
# cd /var/yp
```

```
# make
gmake[1]: Entering directory `/var/yp/mincomp'
Updating passwd.byname...
Updating passwd.byuid...
Updating netid.byname...
gmake[1]: Leaving directory `/var/yp/mincomp'
#
```

That's it. Try the ypcat passwd now and you should see that your new user is now available. Yes, it's a pain to have to do this, but you just have to get into the routine of going there and issuing a make after editing files.

> **NOTE** To review: to create domain users, connect to the NIS server (either sit down at the server and log in or telnet over and su to root) and use the standard useradd command. Then cd to /var/yp and type make.

Changing Passwords on NIS Servers

Okay, you'll try this out, but as you use it, you suddenly think, "Hey, what if users want to change their passwords? How do they, if the system administrator has to do a make in /var/yp?"

The answer is that there is a special command called yppasswd that does this. There needs to be a service running on the master NIS server called, brilliantly, yppasswdd (yup, that's an extra *d* at the end for *daemon*). As in NT, where password changes occur on the PDC, yppasswd connects to the master NIS server and makes changes there. Just set it up as you'd set up any other service, via the System V startup script approach.

That's the basics of NIS. We haven't discussed slave servers or some of the other strange and interesting aspects of NIS, but that's as far as I wanted to get you, in this introductory book—there are sizeable books on NIS. Now, let's talk about how to get those home directories.

Summary: NIS Setup

Before moving on to NFS setup, here's a quick synopsis of the steps you follow to set up the NIS server and client.

To set up an NIS server:

1. Check that you have the yp* programs.

2. Check that the portmapper service is running.

3. Set the domain name with the domainname command and modify /etc/sysconfig/network to reflect the changes.

4. Edit /var/yp/Makefile to list the NIS files to share.

5. Check that you have an /etc/ypserv.conf file. If not, just create a one-line file that says dns: no.

6. Start the ypserv service.

7. Create maps from the existing passwd, group, etc., files:

   /usr/lib/yp/ypinit -m

Then make sure that the ypserv script starts at bootup. Do the same for yppasswdd.

To set up an NIS client:

1. Check that you have the yp* programs on the client computer.

2. Edit /etc/yp.conf to point to the domain and server with one line:

   domain *domainname* server *NIS-server-name*

3. Check that the portmapper service is running.

4. Set the domain name with the domainname command and make the change to /etc/sysconfig/network.

5. Edit /etc/nsswitch.conf to tell ypbind to look to NIS for (at least) passwd and group information. Specify files nis so that the system first looks to the local passwd and group files and then, if it can't authenticate there, it should ask NIS to authenticate. /etc/nsswitch should look like:

   passwd: files nis

   group: file nis

6. Start the ypbind service.

Then make sure that the ypbind service starts automatically upon bootup.

Sharing Files with NFS

To solve the problem of sharing files over a network, Sun Microsystems also developed the Network File System (NFS) protocol. While it originated with Sun, NFS has come to be the standard used for sharing files within the Unix and Linux worlds. As you might expect, there are two parts to NFS: servers and clients. A Linux system can be either.

Setting Up an NFS Server

Because NFS uses RPCs, we need to have the portmapper running. Since you already did that earlier to get NIS working, I'll assume you have it functioning. If in doubt, take a look at the instructions earlier in the chapter.

NOTE   Please note that, as with NIS, a full NFS discussion could take a full book. All I want to accomplish here is to show you how to be able to put everyone's home directory on a single server and then let everyone get to their home directories, no matter what computer they log on to the NIS domain from. If NFS interests you, get a book on Linux servers (like one from the Craig Hunt Linux Library published by Sybex), look at a HOWTO, or search any of the online resources about NFS.

Defining the Shares with */etc/exports*

NFS is Unix's most-used file server software. Like NT and 2000, you have to tell it which directories to share and what permissions to allow when sharing them. In NT and 2000, of course, you use the GUI and the Explorer to create file shares and set permissions on them. In Linux, it's a configuration file called /etc/exports—that's the /etc directory of the NFS *server*, not the client. The file is simple:

```
directory-to-share   client-computer-name(permissions)

directory-to-share   client-computer-name(permissions)

directory-to-share   client-computer-name(permissions)

...
```

On the left side of each line, you name a directory, then leave at least one space, then name the machine that the NFS server should accept a file server request from, followed by a set of parentheses and either rw to give read/write access or ro to give read-only access. For example, one line might look like:

```
/home/mark      markspc.minasi.com(rw)
```

As you can might guess, this allows the directory /home/mark to be exported with read/ write access to a computer named markspc.minasi.com. Note that you type the (rw) right after the machine name, no spaces in between.

Does it seem odd that this file server seems to hand out share permissions based on the machine asking for it, rather than the user? It *is* a bit different from what we expect in the NT or 2000 world, but remember also that there are file and directory permissions on /home/mark. Let's say that someone gets onto my computer and logs on as larry. Larry could connect to my home directory over on the NFS server—but he wouldn't be able to read or write it unless the Linux file and directory permissions let him. (And my tech editor adds that "the perhaps-not-immediately-obvious result of this (in)security model is that you should not export NFS filesystems to any machine you don't fully trust, since whoever has control of the client machine can always create an account with whatever UID he wants, to enable him to bypass any inconvenient filesystem permissions on the exported directory. The only time it's safe to do this is if 1) the export is read-only, and 2) privacy is not an issue; for example, if you're exporting a directory of binaries or other read-only public files or something.")

Anyway, to return to the lines in /etc/exports, I want to show you a few other examples to demonstrate the flexibility that NFS offers us. I could allow more computers access with a list of machine names:

```
/home/mark    markspc.minasi.com(rw),pc1.acme.com(ro)
```

Now this could be a bit cumbersome, so we can use wildcards and IP addresses, such as:

```
/home/mark    *.minasi.com(rw)
/home/fred    192.168.10.0/255.255.255.0(rw)
```

You probably won't be surprised to hear that there are actually a great many more options (if you're interested, look at man exports), but those are the basics. But now let's return to my original purpose: to share home directories. Suppose I had 500 users and therefore 500 home directories; I really don't want to have to type 500 lines into /etc/exports to tell NFS to share all of those home directories! There are several answers, but I'm taking the easy way out and offering the simplest one. I'll just share the top-level /home directory, and let the individual Linux file and directory permissions keep the users out of each others' directories. As long as that's acceptable, then my entire /etc/exports boils down to just one line:

```
/home    *.minasi.com(rw,root_squash)
```

Notice this option, root_squash. Essentially, this is a protection against root users on the client machines. If someone is root on a client machine, when they access files on the NFS share, the user root (user ID 0) is instead mapped to the user nobody.

Starting the NFS Server

Once the /etc/exports file is configured, we need to make sure the NFS daemons are up and running. There are two of them:

```
rpc.mountd
rpc.nfsd
```

Essentially, `rpc.mountd` accepts incoming requests from NFS clients, verifies whether that client can mount the requested filesystem (by looking in /etc/exports) and then passes the request off to `rpc.nfsd`, which handles the actual file-sharing connection.

You could launch them directly from the command line, but a better technique is to go to your /etc/rc.d/init.d directory and type:

```
# ./nfs restart
```

I say `restart` purely because if they are running, it will stop them first, and if they are not running, there will just be a momentary delay (as it tries to stop them) before they are started up.

The daemons should now be running. One way to check is with the `showmount` command (if it is installed):

```
# showmount -e
Export list for nisserver:
/home     *.minasi.com
```

If you supply a hostname after the -e, the `showmount` command will query that host and you'll see its export list.

Changing the */etc/exports* File

Before we look at the client side of things, there's one more issue. If you change the /etc/ exports file, either to change permissions or to export other filesystems, then you need to let the NFS server daemons know about the changes.

One way to do this is to restart the NFS daemons from the init directory as mentioned above. On some older Linux systems (and some Unix systems), you may need to do this. However, most Linux systems support an easier way to do this with the `exportfs` command. All you have to do is type:

```
# exportfs -r
```

with -r meaning "re-export." Your modifications should now take effect. If you simply type the `exportfs` command alone, you see the current list of which computers are connecting to which of your exported filesystems.

Setting Up the NFS Client

The client side of all of this is relatively trivial. You do *not* need to have the NFS daemons running on the client. To simply mount a filesystem, you type:

```
# mount -t nfs servername:shared-file-system mount-point
```

as in the example:

```
# mount -t nfs nisserver:/home/public /mnt/public
```

Note that on most systems, you could omit the -t nfs, and Linux would figure it out perfectly fine.

Now here's a big detail. What if the directory we mount this onto already has data in it? For instance, given our example above, what if we have directories in our local /home and then do this:

```
# mount -t nfs nisserver:/home /home
```

Well, when you look in /home, *your local directories are gone!* Okay, they're not really gone, they're just not visible right now, and, in fact, there is no way for us to access them. When we "glued" the remote filesystem onto /home, it took precedence.

Maybe this is what you want. Maybe not. On some systems Dan says he's seen, people do it the way I've described, and just pretty much from the very beginning had all users using information out of the remotely mounted directories. He also says he's seen other configurations where users who will be logging in remotely (i.e., not directly on the NFS server) have their home directories set to be /mnt/home/*user,* and the server's /home is then mounted onto the client machines in that fashion.

In any case, you should just be aware of this so that you don't become too attached to anything in the directory that will serve as your mount point. Move it out of there before you do the mount.

That mount command got us connected to the file server, but the command won't survive a reboot of the client machine. To do so, we need to add a line to /etc/fstab along the lines of:

```
nisserver:/home  /home  nfs   hard,intr 0 0
```

so now my whole /etc/fstab file might look like:

```
/dev/hda8       swap      swap    defaults 0 2
/dev/hda1       /boot     ext2    defaults 1 2
/dev/hda9       /         ext2    defaults 1 1
/dev/hda5       /usr      ext2    defaults 1 2
/dev/hda6       /home     ext2    defaults 1 2
proc            /proc     proc    defaults 0 0
/dev/cdrom      /cdrom    auto    ro,noauto,user,exec 0 0
/dev/fd0        /floppy   auto    noauto,user 0 0
nisserver:/home /home     nfs     hard,intr 0 0
```

Let's take a look at this. The first three fields are easy: the remote filesystem, the local mount point, and the mount type (nfs). Then there's this hard,intr. This has to do with NFS mounts. They can be either *soft* or *hard*. With a soft mount, if there is a server or network outage, the local NFS client will report back to programs trying to access the filesystem that there is an error. Some programs can handle this error and know what to do, but many, if not most, don't know what to do with this.

A hard mount, on the other hand, does what you expect. If there is a server or network crash, the process accessing the NFS-mounted filesystem will just hang.

The intr part says, "If the system hangs, let me interrupt the process (using something like Ctrl+C)." Without that, the process would basically hang until either the NFS server came back up or you found the process ID and killed off the process that way. When in doubt, I would strongly recommend using hard mounts.

There are lots of ways to optimize the connection and increase speed, etc., and for more information on this huge topic, I direct you to the NFS HOWTO as well as the man pages for exportfs, exports, nfsd, mountd, and fstab.

Putting Our Example All Together

Okay, so now you have NIS running, and I just explained how NFS works. Let's go back to our earlier example and make this all work. On your client machine, issue this command:

```
# mount -t nfs nisserver:/home /home
```

where nisserver is the NFS server where you want the users' home directories to come from. Yes, this will cover up whatever else is in my home directory, but that's fine for the purposes of this exercise.

Now let's do the little su fun we did before. Drop out of root or switch to another window where you are a regular user, and do the following (again using the user account from earlier):

```
$ su - joe
Passwd:
$ whoami
joe
$ pwd
/home/joe
$
```

Hey, what do you know... it worked. This time, we went right into the home directory and should have access to all the files normally stored there. If we were doing a graphical login (or were on a console and typed `startx` right now), the user would have full access to all of their normal graphical startup files and defaults.

Well, this ends our little exercise for the moment. Type `exit` to get back to your regular user ID. If you want to unmount the /home filesystem (and get back access to your regular /home), just do:

```
# umount /home
```

and you should be back in business.

As you can see, there's some planning that needs to be done here about where the user's home directories are located. Also, in our example, both the NIS and NFS servers were the same machine, but there is nothing at all that prevents those from being on two different machines.

With a little bit of planning, the combination of NIS and NFS allows users to log in to any machine on a Linux/Unix network and have full access to all their files and their windowing environment. To them, it's really transparent where their files reside. They just know that when they log in to any machine, they get all their regular information.

You've seen in this chapter that Linux faces the same issues of user accounts, passwords, and permissions that Microsoft operating systems do. Now, what would be *really* cool would be some kind of magic piece of software that would fool a Linux box into thinking that it's logging on via NIS when it's *really* logging on to an NT or 2000 domain controller—but I don't know of any software like that. But if you want to unify both your NT/2000 and Linux accounts, here's one slightly bizarre answer: run Samba on a Linux box and tell it to mimic an NT primary domain controller. *Also* make it an NIS master server. Join the NT machines to this domain, and tell the Linux boxes to log on using this NIS domain. One computer, one set of accounts, two operating systems! I'm not sure this is actually a great idea, but it's an interesting one, and I'll tell you more about Samba in Chapter 9. But first, let's switch away from using Linux as a server and consider Linux as a graphical desktop operating system, in Chapter 7.

7

Desktop Linux: Handling Graphics and GUI Applications

Up to now, most of this book has focused on doing things from a textual command line. That reflects my personal biases on two things: First, I see Linux in its current state as a far more promising server operating system than a desktop operating system. That doesn't mean that won't change, but right at the moment, if an IT director were to ask me to make a case for Linux in her organization, I'd find it much easier to argue for Linux servers than Linux desktops.

That point of view then leads to another bias: I believe that servers should be able to run without GUIs. Server software typically doesn't have to interact very much locally; most servers don't also act as personal workstations for particular individuals—or, at least, I *hope* that most servers don't! Adding a GUI—a tool that makes for better workstations rather than better servers—adds complexity, code, and drivers. PC graphics nowadays are inclined toward speed rather than stability; when a trade publication writes about a new 3D video card, it is to extol its speed rather than to laud the fact that its drivers never crash. I would, therefore, feel much more comfortable rolling out a file or web server that runs on a GUI-less operating system than an operating system that needs a GUI for its very existence, all other things being equal.

Having said that, Linux *does* have a value as a desktop OS, and modern desktop OSs need a GUI—so we'll take up Linux's GUI in this chapter. But my focus here will be different from your basic here's-how-to-click-and-drag chapter. I won't bore you with a lot of here's-how-to-use-Notepad explanation because, quite frankly, you will find the Linux GUIs *very* easy to learn to use, and for a very good reason: the two that you're most likely to use (KDE and GNOME) were developed years after Windows 95, in a worldwide computing environment that was familiar with and understood the Windows 95 user interface. Also, of course, much of that Windows 95 user interface was stol—I mean, borrowed from Apple's Macintosh. That means that, today, a sort of consensus has emerged in the desktop computing world among Apple, Microsoft, and now Linux as to what a GUI should look like—and that's why I needn't spend a lot of time telling you how a menu works. What *is* unusual from the point of a veteran Microsoft OS user, however, is the way in which Linux assembles many programs into a GUI.

There's an old joke in the computer business that you might have seen, comparing operating systems to airlines. According to the joke, Macintosh Airways features ticket agents, flight attendants, and pilots that all look the same, and whenever you ask them a question, they tell you that you don't need to know, so just sit back and have a drink. Windows 95 Airlines, in contrast, has a huge fleet of attractive-looking jets that take off in a wonderful multimedia display of sound and lights, climb above the clouds and, just as they reach 20,000 feet, explode without warning. In Unix Express (the joke predates widespread Linux acceptance), each passenger brings a piece of the airplane and a box of tools to the airport. They gather on the tarmac, arguing constantly about what kind of plane they want to build and how to put it together.

In no case is the joke more apropos than on the subject of GUIs in Linux. Unlike the Microsoft GUIs, the Linux GUIs didn't appear all at once. Instead, Linux's (and Unix's) GUIs grew one piece at a time. Despite the fact that a graphical Linux desktop looks an awful lot like a Windows or Macintosh one, there's a very important difference: you have a choice—perhaps too *many* choices—about the GUI's pieces and how they all fit together. Linux's GUIs are a "mix and match" combination of three parts.

First is the *X Window System*. X's job is to provide the foundation for graphical programming. Second is the *window manager*, which sits atop X. Basically, a window manager makes it possible for you to run more than one GUI application—without a window manager, you can't move windows around, resize them, minimize them, or the like. More recently, the Linux world (and, before it, the Unix world) has seen a third piece called a *desktop environment*. The desktop environment sits on top of X, like the window manager, but adds features to let Linux better integrate applications in the same way that COM and OLE do in the Microsoft world. Desktop environments also extend the abilities of window managers to give Linux users much of the GUI functionality that Windows and Macintosh users have come to take for granted, but that Linux users have only gained in the past few years.

In this chapter, I'll show you how a Linux GUI is assembled. That's not merely an academic exercise, as you'll find that being able to activate just a portion of a GUI will assist you in troubleshooting Linux issues and solving those annoying it-works-in-this-distribution-why-doesn't-it-work-in-*that*-distribution problems. I'll also pick apart the Linux scripts that assemble your GUI, so that you can understand them better and get some ideas about how you can customize your system to your liking.

X History

Linux and Unix's graphics are based on a tool called either *the X Window System* or, simply, *X*. (Notice that's not Windows, plural, but instead Window.) X originated at MIT in 1984 with help from DEC. Robert Schliefler headed the project, part of an MIT group called Project Athena (that also built another important Unix tool, a security system called Kerberos, which, you may know, is now an important part of Windows 2000 security). Anyway, MIT is no longer in charge of X; something called The Open Group maintains it now. There are commercial versions of X, but there are free versions as well, and most Linuxes come with a free version called XFree86.

As I've already suggested, X itself is really only one of three pieces of software that Linux needed in order to get a GUI on your system. But it's the foundation piece, so let's examine it. (Notice I did not say "X-amine" it, but let me tell you, the temptation to sink into "X" puns is X-cruciating...)

X Basics: Exploring X

X is really just a toolbox of basic graphic tools. Someone wanting to write a word processing program, for example, would need to figure out how to display text on the screen and how to display that text in different fonts and sizes. She might need to draw lines to display a table. That's where X is useful: it has built-in programming commands that can display text in a given font and commands to draw lines. So someone writing a GUI word processor for Unix or Linux would logically want to build it on top of X, as X would save development time.

Pure X

You can see X in its simplest form by just typing X. You'll get a gray mottled background and a mouse cursor shaped like an X. You can get out of it—as you can always get out of X—by pressing Ctrl+Alt+Backspace. If you didn't get a graphical screen with a gray background and an X-shaped cursor, and instead got an error message, then look back to Chapter 4 to see how to set up X.

What possible value could that command have? Well, I use it on systems that I'm configuring to ensure that X is configured correctly. Loading just plain X tells me whether X is running or, more importantly, if it's not. That's *extremely* useful, as one of the most difficult parts of getting Linux to run is just getting X to work; in some senses, a simple X command does for GUI setup and troubleshooting what ping does for network setup and troubleshooting—it's a basic "sanity test." Once *that's* configured for a system, making the window manager and desktop environment work is child's play.

> **NOTE**   If X doesn't run for you, then go back and take a look at Chapter 4 for some hints on getting X working.

Basic Useful X: Introducing *xinit* and *xterm*

Still got X on your screen? Well, you have to admit, it's a very *simple* user interface…just kidding; let's take it just a step further and see what X looks like with a program running. Type:

```
xinit
```

What you'll probably see is something like Figure 7.1. (This won't work if X isn't working.)

There's a mottled gray background with a box in the upper-left corner. If you look closely—the fonts are kind of tiny—you'll see that box is a *terminal, console,* or *command-line* session, depending on your favorite term. Whatever you call it, however, it is nothing more than the Linux GUI version of the command prompt that we've been using so far.

Figure 7.1   xterm window and basic X background

Recall that from the point of the Unix and Linux world, this is supposed to be mimicking an old-style terminal, so this kind of text command screen is sometimes called a *terminal window*. As the program that gives us this command prompt is an X Window implementation of a terminal program, it's called xterm.

That "box" is actually a window, in the most primitive X sense. (They'll get snazzier later, don't worry.) Notice, however, what that window *lacks:* no minimize, no maximize, no menu, no border; we'll return to that in a moment. Notice also that when the mouse cursor is sitting over the gray part, it looks like an *X*, but when positioned over the terminal window, it becomes an I-beam shape; controlling cursor shapes is another of X's built-in abilities. Finally, notice that there's a black rectangle in the xterm window, and that it becomes a *filled* rectangle when the X cursor is anywhere in the box. Why does it do that? Because of something called *focus*, which I'll cover soon.

Adding a Second Application

Let's try out X's multitasking abilities by running a second GUI program, a very basic program that comes with every copy of X. Type:

    xcalc

What you'll probably see is a screen like Figure 7.2.

If you're following along on a Linux machine, then you probably see the mottled gray background with your terminal-like xterm box in the upper-left corner, overlaid by a simple GUI calculator. Play around with the calculator—notice the cursor shape changes to a third shape, like a pointing hand, when you position the cursor over the calculator. You can use xcalc like other calculator programs you've worked with in the past. But, as with the xterm terminal window, notice what the calculator window *can't* do...

Figure 7.2   Adding a second program, a calculator

Introducing Window Managers

Try to click the calculator and drag it elsewhere on the screen; you won't be able to. Even though there's an xterm command-line session sitting underneath the calculator, you can't get to the command-line session because X has laid one window program on top of another program, without giving you a program to *manage* these windows. Programs that manage windows are, not surprisingly, called *window managers*. Let's run the simplest and oldest, called twm for the *tab window manager*. (The "tab" part actually came later; originally, twm stood for Tom's Window Manager after its creator, Tom LaStrange.)

Press Ctrl+C to shut down xcalc. You'll be back at the terminal window; if you type and nothing happens, make sure your mouse is positioned somewhere over the terminal window. Then start up the twm window manager by just typing:

    twm

Look at Figure 7.3 to see the result (or your screen, if you're following along).

Figure 7.3   xterm running with the twm window manager

See what happened? All of a sudden, the terminal window got a border. You can move the terminal window around to your heart's content. This is a pretty *primitive* window manager, but a little experimentation will show you that you can click the upper-left corner to minimize (oops, the twm phrase is *iconify*) the window. Click the upper-right corner and a grid appears, showing the outline of the window. Click and drag its borders to resize the window.

What Do Window Managers Do?

We'll play around a bit more with twm in a minute, but let me briefly digress and talk about what window managers do:

- They add controls to allow more than one window. As you've already seen, running more than one window under X is largely pointless, as one window stacks on top of another. Window managers add a place—usually a title bar—that you can grab to move the window around.

- They add controls to resize, minimize ("iconify"), restore ("de-iconify") and maximize windows.

- Window managers let you control the *focus policy,* which means "which window gets your keystrokes." For example, if five windows are open and you press a key, which window gets that keystroke? I'll discuss more on that in a page or two.

- If your window manager lets you overlap windows—older ones didn't, they tiled them instead—then it lets you bring one window "above" another. In other words, GUIs are in some senses three-dimensional, not two-dimensional; sure; there are height and width, but there's also the notion that one thing can lie atop another, so you might say that a window not only has an X/Y position on the screen, but an "altitude" as well.

It's easiest to explain some of these benefits with an example, so let's return to twm.

Running More Than One Program: The Ampersand

Let's start a second program—but hmmmm, it appears that the terminal window's not paying attention to us right now. That's because we started twm, and twm's still running, so Linux won't return the command prompt to us until twm has stopped, which isn't too useful. How can I start twm but then tell the terminal window to come back for more instructions? With a little Linux trick, the ampersand. Add an ampersand (&) to any Linux command, and the terminal window will start up the command, then come back for more commands. In Linux-speak, adding an ampersand runs a program "in the background."

First, stop twm by just pressing Ctrl+C. That'll wake up the terminal window, and it'll start paying attention to you again. Then type:

```
twm &
```

and you'll get twm back, but also your command prompt. Now try starting that calculator again:

```
xcalc &
```

You'll see an outline of a window appear, a three-by-three set of boxes that looks like a tic-tac-toe board with a small header rectangle. twm wants you to show it where to place the new program. As you move the cursor, the box moves also; click the left mouse button to indicate where twm should put box.

TIP   Dan points out as a "geek note" that I needn't have pressed Ctrl+C to stop the existing copy of twm. Instead, he says that you can press Ctrl+Z. You get your prompt back, and then you type bg; Linux will put the already-running twm in the background. fg *pid* will return it to the foreground.

Controlling Your Desktop with *twm*

Now let's put twm through its (limited) paces. Bring up twm's system menu by finding an empty bit of background (one that's not covered by any application windows) and left-clicking that part of the background—but when you click, click and *hold*. A menu appears, as you see in Figure 7.4.

Figure 7.4   The twm menu

Hold down the left mouse button and move to any command; let up and the cursor changes to reflect what that command does (note the skull and crossbones when you choose Kill). Then, when you click a window, twm performs that function on that window. If you like, try out Kill on the calculator. Pretty cool, eh? I mean, I've always liked the ability to zap a program from the Task Manager, but the skull-and-crossbones in Kill really adds value.

Seriously, you'll need to absorb a few new concepts in order to get the most out of twm and other Linux window managers. Specifically, two common actions operate differently than in Microsoft OSs:

- Bringing a window "up top" on a stack of windows
- Indicating which window should receive your keystrokes

"Raising" Windows

Try opening a few windows and you'll see something else that defies a Windows user's intuition. If one window overlaps another window and you click on the "lower" window—the one sitting "underneath" the upper window—then in the Windows world we expect the window underneath to jump to the top. But twm doesn't do that, unless you click somewhere on the *title bar* of the lower window. In Windows, all you need do is click *anywhere* on a window and it pops to the top; in twm, you have to click somewhere on the window's title bar. But there's another way to bring a window "up top," as well. Open the system menu (left-click and hold, in any vacant area of the background) and notice the Raise command. Choose Raise, then click a window, and it'll move to the top of the heap.

Bringing Windows into Focus: The Focus Policy

Similarly, suppose there are several windows open and you press a key. Which window gets that key—in programming terms, which window has the *focus*? Of course, in Windows, it's the top application, the one with the differently colored border. Clicking a window in Windows both raises it to the top of the desktop *and* gives it the focus. twm doesn't see it that way, however (and neither do many other X window managers), and in fact gives you a choice about focus.

Try this. Run xcalc, and then run xclock. Arrange xclock so that it covers most of xcalc, but leave part of xcalc uncovered—be sure to leave the calculator display uncovered. Move the mouse somewhere over the uncovered part of the xcalc window and press the 5 key. Despite the fact that xcalc is the lower window than xclock, a 5 appears in the calculator display—in other words, merely moving the mouse over a part of a window gives that window the focus. Even though xcalc was below xclock, I didn't have to click it to get it the keyboard focus, as we're used to in Windows.

Alternatively, try this. Open the system menu and find the Focus command. Move the cursor down to Focus and release the mouse button; the cursor becomes a small circle. Move the circle over to the xclock window and click that window. You've now told twm to connect the focus to xclock and to essentially *glue* it there. Hover the mouse over xcalc now and type—nothing happens. You can tell twm to get out of this "fixed focus" mode by opening the system menu again and choosing Unfocus.

There are three basic focus policies that I've seen in X window managers:

Click-to-type This is the only focus policy that Windows users will be familiar with. When you click anywhere in a window or on its border, two things happen: the window rises to the top of the screen or the *foreground*, and any keystrokes that you type are sent to that window—it gets the focus.

Focus follows mouse With this approach, all you need do is to simply *move* the mouse pointer over part of a window—no click necessary—and any keystrokes get sent to that window, even if the window isn't the top, foreground window. This is like twm's Unfocus option.

Fixed-focus With this approach, you use a system menu item like twm's Focus command to fix the focus on a particular window. No matter where the mouse pointer is, your keystrokes go to the window that you've fixed the focus upon.

NOTE Dan comments that some window managers even have an "autoraise" feature, sort of an extension of "focus follows mouse." If you hover the mouse cursor over a window for more than a few seconds, the window manager automatically raises the window to the top—a kind of e-levitation, I guess.

Creating a *twm* Menu

You'll notice that twm doesn't have a program menu. There's no built-in menu to fire up a calculator, text editor, or whatever. You *could* create such a menu, but it's not around by default. Once in a while, however, it might be useful.

As Linux only requires low-power hardware, I thought I'd dust off an old Pentium 133 system with 32MB of RAM and some pitifully small hard disk, just to see if I could make it a useful Linux box. I wondered if I could take a basically useless computer and make it a useful secondary DNS server. (I could.) Along the way, I tried to put a GUI on it. I certainly could run GNOME or KDE on it, if "run" is the correct verb, but such big GUIs were a pointless endeavor. Still, it would've been nice now and then to run a low-octane GUI, so I tried running just X and twm. Turned out that it ran pretty well; it's light on memory and CPU drain and, of course, light on features as well, but that's the price you pay to get value out of a six-year-old computer.

One thing troubled me about twm, however: the lack of a program menu. I just needed to add an option to start up another xterm window, but how to do it? A bit of puzzling through the man page helped me figure it out.

twm's menu information is in a file called system.twmrc. You *could*, if you wanted to, have a twmrc that is yours and only yours, but I'm the only person using my system, so I figured I'd just modify the system-wide twmrc.

TIP   If you *do* create your own personal twm configuration file, it must be named .twmrc (note the leading period), and you have to put it in your home directory.

Find system.twmrc with this command:

```
find / -name system.twmrc
```

cd over to whatever directory it lives in, do an ls -l, and you'll see that system.twmrc has read-only permissions even for the root ("WHAT???? You DARE to deny ME, the ROOT, access???? Well, we'll just fix that..."); you can change that by typing:

```
chmod u+w system.twmrc
```

Then vi the file and look for the menu section; it'll probably look something like this:

```
#
# Add a menu with the usual things
#
menu "defops"
{
"Twm"           f.title
"Iconify"       f.iconify
"Resize"        f.resize
"Move"          f.move
"Raise"         f.raise
"Lower"         f.lower
""              f.nop
"Focus"         f.focus
"Unfocus"       f.unfocus
```

```
"Show Iconmgr"   f.showiconmgr
"Hide Iconmgr"   f.hideiconmgr
" "              f.nop
"Kill"           f.destroy
"Delete"         f.delete
" "              f.nop
"Restart"        f.restart
"Exit"           f.quit
}
```

This is the file that created the menu that you saw in Figure 7.4. Adding an item to kick off another program is simple; just add a line that looks like this:

```
" label"   f.exec  " command"
```

So to start xterm, I'd add the following line:

```
"Xcalc"   f.exec  "xcalc"
```

But the first time that I tried clicking the Xcalc option, the system locked up cold—a little wristwatch icon popped up and I couldn't do *anything*. Eventually it dawned on me that I wanted twm to come back and respond to me after it started xcalc, so I needed to tell twm this:

```
"Xcalc"   f.exec  "xcalc &"
```

Without the &, you'll lock it up every time. But when I tried this new-and-improved version, twm just popped up one of those dumb tic-tac-toe boards, which required an extra click. And the window that popped up showed 25 lines and took up a lot of space when, in actuality, all I usually want to do is to type a command or two, sort of like the Windows Start/Run box. So I modified the command a bit with an option that you'll learn in a few pages, the -geometry option. The final result left the new menu item looking like this:

```
"Xcalc" f.exec  "xcalc -geometry 300x200+200+200"
```

The next time I started up twm, I had my menu item. Yup, it's limited, but what do you want—this is the Mercury spacecraft of Linux window managers! Hang on and you'll see the Starship Enterprise soon; I just want you to understand how the pieces of the GUI fit together right now, and that's most easily done with a simple example. But I want to stress that this *isn't* just a toy. Yes, twm is simple, but you can get a Mercury into orbit with just a bit of chemical fuel and liquid oxygen, where in contrast the Starship Enterprise runs on dilithium crystals—and dilithium (that is, a really fast processor) is sometimes in short supply. You wouldn't run KDE or GNOME on a system with 8MB of RAM and a

75MHz 486DX4... but you *could* run X and twm on such a system, *particularly* if you only needed the GUI now and then to accomplish some administrative task best done with a GUI tool.

Now take a closer look at some of these X apps. Notice that these windows still lack menus. xcalc's buttons are flat and simple—the curves that define the buttons are jaggy and lack color. Any designer wanting to add the familiar Windows 95/NT 4/Windows 2000 pizzazz to the user interface is going to have to do a lot of work! You *can* see an example of an application whose developer *did* that work in a program called xfm, the X file manager. (RH 7.3 doesn't include it, although other Linuxes do, so you'll have to trust me on what it does.) There's color, menus, and a more Windows-like feel to the app. But where Windows apps just come to that feel naturally—the base operating system provides those "look and feel" widgets—xfm required some real work to accomplish. As you'll see later, one of the benefits of KDE and GNOME to programmers is that those GUIs come equipped with a toolbox of such widgets, so building more professional-looking windowed apps is easier with those environments.

A Step Up: *fvwm2*

Let's look at one more window manager, then return to look a little more closely into how X gets started in the first place. Repeat what you just did, but replace twm with fvwm2.

```
xinit
xcalc &
fvwm2 &
xsetroot -solid GhostWhite
```

With a little cosmetic window arranging, your screen will look something like Figure 7.5.

I changed two things here. First, I got tired of that ugly gray mottled background, and now it's a snowstorm-y white. (Replace GhostWhite with MidnightBlue if white's too stark for you.) You didn't need to add an ampersand after the xsetroot command because it does its job and returns control to you immediately.

Second, you're now running not twm but fvwm2, the Friendly Virtual Window Manager (some claim a different meaning for the *f*), which is a bit more powerful than twm. For one thing, notice that the windows now all have system menus in their upper-left corners—click one and you get a Windows-like menu letting you minimize, maximize, close the application, or the like. As with twm, click an empty bit of the background and a menu appears—notice that it's a program menu that lists some X applications. A bit of experimentation will also show that you can resize a window just by moving your cursor to a corner, then clicking and dragging, as Windows lets you do.

Now let the cursor drift down to the bottom of the screen. In a flash, the screen will seem to clear! What's actually happened is that fvwm2 gives you a GUI desktop that is considerably larger than your actual screen, four times the size in fact. You have four *quadrants* on your screen, but you can only see one at a time. You move from one quadrant to another by moving your mouse to the edge of the screen in the direction of the quadrant that you want to visit. But the transition to the next screen isn't a smooth, scrolling change; instead, it's a jarring "jump." Notice the area labeled the Pager; it is a miniature of the overall desktop, divided into four quadrants with tiny representations of windows—you'll probably see a few small objects in the upper-left quadrant, as that's the one that you start off in by default. You can either return to that quadrant by moving your cursor up to the top of the screen, making it jump up a quadrant, or you can just click the desired quadrant in the Pager.

Figure 7.5   X with **fvwm2** window manager

WARNING   You can only run one window manager at a time. Try to run fvwm2 from inside twm, and you'll get an error.

Notice that fvwm2 has a program menu; play around with it a bit, and you'll find that some of the program entries may point to programs that don't exist. How do items get on this menu? As with twm, there's a text setup file that completely describes the program menu, system.fvwm2rc in /etc/X11/fvwm. Remember, text files are *very* Unix-y. It's nice because it means that it'd be easy to write a script to create or modify a program menu file for a user—also very nice, from an administrator's point of view (which is *also* very Unix-y).

NOTE   Don't get the impression here that window managers are a passé kind of thing. There is a www.fvwm.org site where apparently people are working day and night to improve fvwm2! That's the neat thing about the combination of the Internet and open source; if cars worked like that, you *know* there would be a bunch of guys incrementally improving the Model T: "We will have MT v10.18-A ready for release in the next month or so; major improvements include airbags and fuel injection..."

Adding Color to Your "X" Life

Wondering in the xsetroot how I knew that there was a color MidnightBlue? X has an entire database of color information, complete with a whole bunch of predefined color names. You can see them by typing:

```
showrgb
```

but I highly recommend piping the result to less, as there are *lots* of them. But what's that you say—you've got a particular color that isn't in the database? No problem; instead of using a text name like *midnightblue*, you can specify the color as a combination of red, green, and blue. For example, to get a yellow background, you'd type this command:

```
xsetroot -solid RGBi:1.0/1.0/0.0
```

You control the color with the three decimal numbers after RGBi:; each is a value from 0.0 to 1.0 inclusive. The numbers are separated by a slash and represent, in order, the intensity of red, green, and blue to describe the color. Values toward zero will produce darker colors; values toward 1.0 will produce brighter colors. If you're feeling nostalgic for that sea-foam green background that NT 4 used by default, try this:

```
xsetroot -solid RGBi:0.0/0.1/0.1
```

And to mimic Windows 2000's default background color, just use a predefined color:

```
xsetroot -solid cornflowerblue
```

You may be more familiar with specifying colors as three hexadecimal values, each ranging from 00 to FF. (That's how we usually tell a web page to use a particular color.) You can do that as well, using not RGBi but rgb, again separating the values with forward slashes and specifying first red, then green, then blue. An alternative way to get that yellow background would look like this:

```
xsetroot -solid rgb:ff/ff/00
```

You can apply colors to more than just the background. By convention, X Window programs all accept a fairly large set of uniform startup options. (It's only a convention, so don't be surprised if any given program doesn't support the options.) For example, to start up a command prompt window—xterm, recall—with a blue background and a yellow foreground, you could type the following:

```
xterm -fg blue -bg yellow
```

You can control a program's colors in four ways, as you see in Table 7.1.

Table 7.1 Standard X Window Color Options

Option	Function
-bg	Specify the window's background color
-bd	Specify the window's border color
-fg	Specify the window's foreground color
-rv	Use the default background color as the foreground color and use the default foreground color as the background color ("reverse")

xsetroot can let you specify a bitmap for a background as well:

```
xsetroot -bitmap /home/mark/m57.bmp
```

This would tile the m57.bmp bitmap; unfortunately, there's no way with simple X to just center a bitmap on the desktop.

Beyond Colors: X Resources

I want to return to the notion of window managers and then move on to desktop environments so that I can finally introduce Linux's two main GUIs, KDE and GNOME, but let me pursue an item related to color so as to introduce a phrase that you'll need to understand: the notion of X's *resources*.

It's pretty handy that X apps mostly agree to the same rules when it comes to controlling their colors, but it doesn't stop there. You'll also find that you can configure a window's location on the screen, the fonts that it uses, that it should start up iconified (X terminology for "minimized"), the title of the window that the application exists in, and other things. These window characteristics—colors, fonts, position, title, and the like—are called *resources*. Most X applications support options like the color options, as described in Table 7.2.

Table 7.2   Standard X Window Formatting Options

Option	Function	Example
-g or -geometry *widthx height+ xoffset+yoffset*	Position window on the screen	xterm -g 70x35+10+10
-iconic	Start app as an icon	xclock -iconify
-title *string*	Specify name of window	xclock -title myclock
-display *displayed*	Tell X application which computer to display on	xclock -display herbspc:0.0
-fn *fontname*	Specify font for window	xterm -fn rk24

A few of these need a bit more explanation. The -display option is pretty important, but I'm going to put off explaining it for a while; here's the background on the rest.

Window Position and Size: *-geometry*

X Window apps often support a -g or -geometry option that takes four numbers as options: the first two are the desired width and height of the window, the second two are the window's position. A geometry option could, for example, look like:

```
-geometry 80x25+50+75
```

What you specify for the width and height values varies with the application. Text-based applications, like xterm, take width and height in characters; most other X apps seem to take it in pixels. There are exceptions; xedit, a Notepad-type text editor, only works with text but takes pixel values: xedit -g 40x15 yields a *very tiny* editing screen!

The last two values specify position as an offset from the upper-left corner of the screen. Left to themselves, most programs will jam themselves up against the northwest (upper-left) corner of the screen, but you can change that. The first value is the x offset—that is, how many pixels from the left edge of the screen you would like the window to be. The second is the y offset, which is the number of pixels down from the top you would like the window to be. (These offsets define the exact location of the window's upper-left corner, by the way.)

Fonts in X Window

As with other windowing systems, X includes fonts. *Lots* of 'em, *thousands* of 'em. You can see them all with this command:

```
xlsfonts | less
```

You tell an X application to use them with the -fn option. For example, on a RedHat 7.3 system, you could type this:

```
xedit -fn - adobe-times-medium-r-normal--20-140-100-100-p-96-iso8859-1
```

and xedit wouldn't start up in its usual Courier-like font, but instead in a Times Roman font. Notice that the font's name has 13 pieces to it:

- The first field, adobe, identifies who created it.
- The second field, times, describes the font's family. Other common families include helvetica, courier, symbol, lucida, and arial, all names that should be familiar to any Microsoft operating system user.
- The third field, medium, describes the *weight* or "darkness" of the font. Other typical values are bold, book, black, light, regular, and demibold.
- The fourth field, r, describes the *slant*—whether the font is italic (i) or not (r). There's also a value o, which seems to mean italic with some extra space added between lines. Dan tells me that we can blame this on typographers; apparently some fonts do not have an italic face but an *oblique* face, hence the o.
- The fifth field, normal, describes the horizontal width of the font. Other values include narrow, condensed, semicondensed, and bold. And yes, it *is* odd for bold to be an option, as the third field ought to cover it.
- The sixth field is empty, hence the two dashes next to each other. It would be filled with a value describing any "additional" styles. It's not used on many fonts, but typical values are medium or sans.

- The seventh field, 20, describes the maximum height of the characters in pixels.
- The eighth field, 140, describes the maximum height of the characters, their *point size,* in the typographic unit *points,* which are 1/72 of an inch.
- The ninth and tenth fields, 100 and 100, describe the horizontal and vertical sizes (in dots per inch) of the printed font that this font is based on.
- The eleventh field, p, says that this is a proportional font. The alternative would be a fixed-space or *monospaced* font, indicated by an m.
- The twelfth field, 96, is the average width of the font, in tenths of a pixel.
- The final field, iso8859-1, describes the character set.

You can, if you like, replace any of those fields with an asterisk, and X will substitute any font that meets the remaining criteria. If you want to see what a font looks like, use a program called xfd with the -fn option, like this:

```
xfd -fn -adobe-times-medium-r-normal--20-140-100-100-p-96-iso8859-1
```

xfd's not the only program that can let you play with fonts; there are also xfontsel and showfont.

Together, fonts, colors, offsets, and the like are generically referred to in X as *resources.* Now that you understand what "resource" means from an X point of view, it'll be easier when, a bit later, we take up X configuration files. In the next section, I'll show you how to improve the look of your GUI programs.

TIP You may be wondering if it's possible to change an X program's resources *after* it's started. For example, how would you change the font size on the xterm window that appears with xinit, once that xterm session is running? As far as I can see, there's no way to do that easily. But more recent programs may have ways exposed through their user interface to change colors, fonts, and the like.

Installing TrueType Fonts

You may have noticed that the fonts that come with Linux are a bit more rough-edged than the TrueType fonts that you're used to. No problem—Red Hat 7.3 supports True-Type fonts. Just get ahold of some—you can find a link to several sources of free fonts at http://www.microsoft.com/typography/links/links.asp?type=free&part=1. Here's how to install them.

1. Get some TrueType fonts and copy them to /usr/X11R6/lib/X11/fonts/TTF.

2. Change to that directory:

   ```
   cd /usr/X11R6/lib/X11/fonts/TTF
   ```

3. Create a scale guide for the font system:

   ```
   ttmkfdir > fonts.scale
   ```

4. Copy that file to fonts.dir:

   ```
   cp -f fonts.scale fonts.dir
   ```

   You will probably also need to add this directory to the xfs font path before restarting it, or it won't see any TrueType fonts. In /etc/X11/XF86Config-4, add a line like the following to the Files section:

   ```
   FontPath    "/usr/X11R6/lib/X11/fonts/TTF/"
   ```

5. Restart the font system:

   ```
   /etc/rc.d/init.d/xfs restart
   ```

If you're running Linux on a computer that's also got Windows on it, and Windows is on a FAT or FAT32 drive, then it's even easier.

1. First, mount the drive so that Linux can see it. I'll assume for this example that you've mounted it as /cdrive.

2. Edit /etc/X11/XF86Config-4.

3. Look for the string FontPath.

4. Under that line, add the line Fontpath /cdrive/windows/fonts

5. Save the file.

6. Navigate over to the fonts directory: cd /cdrive/windows/fonts so that you can run two commands that will get the fonts ready for Linux.

7. Type ttmkfdir > fonts.scale and press Enter.

8. Type mkfontdir and press Enter.

9. Restart the X server, if it's already running.

Run xfontsel and choose Foundry, and you'll see that you have fonts from whoever made the fonts you downloaded. You can optimize further and edit /etc/X11/fs/config. Look for the line that starts catalogue = ...; you'll see a list of directories for the font system to look through when searching for a font. Notice that the TTF font directory is pretty far down on the list; bring it up top, and you'll get TrueType fonts more often.

Storing X Resource Information

Now suppose you have a particular group of settings that you like for a particular application. For example, suppose you long for the days of the IBM 3270 terminal, and so you want xterm to always come up with a black background and bright green letters. You could ensure that by always starting xterm with the command:

```
xterm -bg black -fg green &
```

This will work admirably, but it's a pain to have to remember to type all that. You can, alternatively, tell X to *always* start up xterm with those colors. Upon startup, X looks in your home directory for a file with named .Xresources or .Xdefaults—in Red Hat, it's .Xdefaults. Those files *do* indeed start with a period, followed by a capital X. Because their names start with a period, ls doesn't show them—again, it's Linux's way of hiding a file—so you'll have to use ls -a to see them, if they're there.

Either way, these are ASCII files that contain lines like the following:

```
xterm*cursorcolor: Orchid
```

That line and the other lines in a Linux resource file tell Linux how to run various programs. The first item, before the asterisk, is the program's name. The second is the particular attribute of the program that you want to control, and the third item, separated from the attribute name by at least one space, is the value to set the attribute to. The above example is saying, "When running the xterm program, set its cursor color equal to Orchid, a purplish color." It's a lot like a value entry in an NT/2000 Registry key or a setting in an INI file. In the NT world, for example, we might have an imaginary key named something like HKEY_CURRENT_USER\Software\Microsoft\xterm \parameters with a value entry called "cursorcolor" of type REG_SZ and a value of "Orchid."

We could make xterm behave in a 3270ish fashion by placing these three commands into the .Xdefaults or .Xresources file:

```
xterm*background: black

xterm*foreground: green

xterm*cursorcolor: green
```

X also lets you load a new set of resources at any time with the xrdb command; xrdb *filename* does the trick. If you have personal resource settings, you'd store them in .Xdefaults on most distributions.

The only unfortunate part about this is that these resource settings only work for the basic X applications. Linux GUI apps written for the more modern KDE and GNOME desktop environments will not, in contrast, look to X resources files for color or other setting information. That's not to say that KDE and GNOME apps don't allow you to configure them—they do—but rather that you'll have to configure them through their particular menus rather than with a central resources file. Applications ported over from Unix, however (such as FrameMaker, WordPerfect, and Applixware) *do* use resource information stored in Xdefaults.

X Freebies: X Apps You'll Usually Find

Before I get much further along with the discussion of running X in more complex configurations, I don't want to forget to briefly run down a panoply of useful (and sometimes fun) applications that come with X. As they are basic X apps, they'll run on pretty much any Linux GUI, whether it's twm or it's GNOME and Enlightenment with all the trimmings. And this is just a partial listing, there are tons of more X apps on most Linux distributions and out on the Net.

- xman is a graphical man page browser.
- xset lets you adjust some basic X user preferences.
- xkill lets you point to a program and terminate it.
- xload is a simple graphical CPU utilization monitor.
- xbill is a game that starts out with a bunch of happy-looking computers running either Apple, NeXT, Unix, or Linux operating systems. A guy with glasses and his clones start marching towards these computers with the intent of putting Windows on the computers. Your cursor is now shaped like a hand, and your job is to smack the little guy with glasses before he gets Windows running on every computer. (And Linux people call *Microsoft* mean-spirited! I mean, it's not like Windows comes with a "Crush the Linus Torvalds" game. On the other hand, I suppose Linux folks would describe Microsoft's OEM licensing, a marketing scheme that makes Windows cheap for hardware manufacturers—so long as they put Windows on *every single machine*—as sort of a real-world "Crush the Linus Torvalds" game.)
- xboard is a chess game, and if you poke around the KDE and GNOME menus then you'll see that there is no shortage of free X-based Linux games.
- xmag will magnify any part of the screen.
- xfontsel graphically assists you in selecting files.
- xchat is an IRC chat program.
- xemacs offers a graphic version of the emacs editor, a favorite tool among many Unix/Linux veterans. (Don't ask why or you'll start another flame war.)
- xpdf is a PDF file viewer.

- `xterm`, of course, is an X-based terminal emulator. You can start it not only with the usual X geometry, color, etc., parameters but also with the `-sb` option, which puts scroll bars on the `xterm` window.

- `xwininfo` lets you point to a window and receive a detailed list of information about that window's program and configuration. Adding the `-children` option also dumps information on any windows that the window has generated.

- `xlsclients` lists the programs (as you'll see in the next section, "clients" is X-ese for "graphical applications") running on the system and their configurations.

- `xfishtank` and `xearth` run animated background programs to either simulate an aquarium (very few "fishtanks" have the space for eagle rays and shovelnose sharks!) or display a world globe, depicting what parts are in sunlight at the moment.

- `xclock` and `xcalc` you've already met.

Some of them are bit skimpy on the documentation, but the price is right. But enough fooling around with the free software—let's get back to work and see how to extend X beyond just one computer.

X across the Net: Understanding Clients and Servers

The next X concept we'll need is the notion of *clients* and *servers*. Back when the folks at MIT first invented X, in the early '80s, graphics were somewhat unusual and expensive in micros, minis, and mainframes.

Setting the Scene: X's Early Days

Sure, graphical applications *existed*, but they were a bit unusual, sort of special-purpose things. Most people interacted with computers through simple text interfaces, and almost everyone connecting to a powerful mainframe computer did so through a text-based interface, whether that was a dumb terminal that could only display text characters and had only a keyboard with no mouse, or perhaps a PC pretending to be a dumb, text-based computer.

It would have been great to add graphics to just about any application, as we do today, but the cost was prohibitive and the benefits dubious. Consider how often you use graphics in your word processor or e-mail package—if you had to pay $10,000 more for your computer just to get graphics on e-mail and word processing, would you? Most of us wouldn't. That's not to say that graphical applications didn't exist—drafting packages, solid modeling programs, and other computer-aided manufacturing (CAM) tools were pretty important even then—but they weren't ubiquitous. Some graphical systems ran as PCs do nowadays, with both the computing power and the user interface all on the same system, but many large systems divided things up, doing the heavy-duty computing (which graphics can require) on a large mainframe or supermini system and leaving the actual image display, keyboard, and mouse or other pointing device on a separate, expensive graphics terminal.

In this environment, X's designers reasoned that a typical Unix and X user might sit down at a graphical workstation and run several programs *from different mainframes*. In other words, suppose I'm working for JPL, processing incoming images from a space probe. One of my jobs is to keep an eye on the incoming data stream so that I can alert the engineers if I see a problem, but I mostly use some high-end image processing software to clean up incoming images by hand. The data might be coming in quickly, so it might make sense to have *one* computer process and assemble the incoming data; that computer will issue me alerts if there's a problem in the data stream. Another computer then does the image processing. I want to be able to both run the program that shows me the status information on the incoming data in one window and run the image processing program in another window.

Now suppose the computer in front of me is the 133MHz Pentium that I mentioned earlier in this chapter. (Budget cuts, you know.) Clearly this box can't do *either* of those computing tasks, but it *can* put X graphics on my screen. So I've got three computers involved here: the big machine processing the incoming data, the other big machine running the graphics program that lets me manipulate the images, and my creaky old system, which is basically acting like a dumb terminal. Despite having just one screen, I want the data from the first and second big machines to show up on the same screen in a nice, integrated, uniform fashion.

X was built to accommodate that kind of work, as it lets you separate the computing from the displaying.

NOTE   Actually, after writing up that mid-'80s example of distributed graphics processing, it occurred to me that there's a more modern example that might be more familiar: web browsers. Ever had more than one web browser open at a time, perhaps surfing more than one site? Well, in X-like terminology, you were running programs on several *mainframes* (the web servers) and seeing the *sessions* (the web browser windows) on a single *graphics terminal* (your PC).

Defining X Clients and X Servers

The X designers defined X in terms of a client/server model... but I promise you, you won't be able to guess what they made the client and what they made the server! Remember, in the early '80s, hardware that could display high-quality graphics was expensive. (And don't tell me about that terrible $320 \times 240 \times 4$-color stuff we could do on PCs in the early '80s—it wasn't expensive, but it hardly high-quality.) Sure, mainframes and super-minis were expensive, but IT shops were used to buying expensive computing equipment in the back room. Putting expensive hardware on a *user's* desk was something new, and the goal of X was to display graphics.

That's why they called the device that *displayed* the graphics the *server*, because in some senses it was doing the hard work, as graphics were unusual and expensive at the time. (Strictly speaking, the *program* running on the device is called the server. The device is just a "display.") For example, suppose I'm running a CAD application on some mainframe; I tell it to load and display a picture of a part that I've designed, so it starts drawing, and let's say that the first thing that it needs to draw is a circle. It's not the *mainframe* that's computing which pixels on the screen to turn on to display the circle; nope, all it does is just tell the graphics terminal, "Draw a circle with this center, that radius, and in this color." Figuring where the pixels go and putting them on the screen is the terminal's job.

Additionally, suppose this graphics terminal is displaying different programs from different computers; whose responsibility is it to manage the windows that each of these programs run in, handling the window management concerns of overlapping windows, iconizing, focus, and the like? Not the mainframes—they're probably not even aware of each other, so they could hardly manage the relative positions of each others' windows. Clearly that has to be the job of some hardware in the graphics terminal. The terminal is *serving* the graphics display needs of the applications running on the mainframes, hence it's a server.

TIP Some people don't use the phrase X server, but instead "X Window terminal." It means the same thing but is clearer for some to understand—and certainly more intuitive for those of us used to Microsoft operating systems.

But what's the client—the mainframe, perhaps? Not exactly. The client is the *application* running on the mainframe. So, for example, suppose you're running Linux stand-alone on your computer and you have an e-mail program, a web browser, and a game running. In X terms, we'd say that your system is running an X server (the program that shows the graphics and controls the display on your monitor) and three X clients (i.e., three graphical apps built for X).

X Clients and Servers in a Linux World: A Hands-On Example

But this notion of mainframes and terminals doesn't really apply in the Linux world, does it? Well, actually, it does and, if you've got two computers around, you can do a bit of fooling around with separate X clients and servers.

Getting Started

Basically, all you need are two computers running Linux that have networking functioning. They should also have X configured, *and* you should be able to run them without X (sorry, Corel). In my case, the computers are configured like so:

- The first computer has IP address 10.10.10.10, running Mandrake 7.0.
- The second computer has IP address 10.10.10.20, running Slackware 7.0.

You don't have to run Mandrake and Slackware to follow along; I'm just doing it so that I can easily remember which machine is which, so I'll refer to the first machine as the "Mandrake" or "10.10.10.10" machine and the second as the "Slackware" or "10.10.10.20" machine.

Run xinit on both machines. By now, you should recognize the mottled gray background with the xterm window in the upper-left corner. Go over to the first machine (Mandrake, 10.10.10.10) and type xeyes. This is the X version of a program that you might have seen on Windows systems. It puts a pair of eyes on the screen that follow the mouse cursor's movement—try moving the mouse around and you'll see.

So far, which machine is running the X server and which is running the X client? Clearly the Mandrake 10.10.10.10 machine is the one that that's doing the computing, *and* it's also the one displaying the program's output, so it is acting as both X client and server, as is normally the case in the Linux world.

Eyeballing Another System

Press Ctrl+C to shut down xeyes on the first machine, the Mandrake 10.10.10.10 machine. Then try this command:

```
xeyes -display 10.10.10.20:0
```

You'll get an error message like this:

```
Xlib:  connection to "10.10.10.20:0.0" refused by server
Xlib:  Client is not authorized to connect to Server
Error: Can't open display: 192.168.0.3:0
```

You got that error because the X client (that is, the first machine, Mandrake 10.10.10.10) tried to use the second machine, 10.10.10.20, as its X server. But, for security reasons, the X server on the second machine refused the connection.

Authorizing X Clients: *xhost*

You can tell the second machine to allow clients from the first machine to use the second's X server by going to the second (Slackware, 10.10.10.20) machine and typing this:

```
xhost +10.10.10.10
```

You'll get a response like this:

```
10.10.10.10 being added to access control list
```

The xhost command tells an X server, the machine doing the graphics, whether or not to accept incoming connections from particular X clients. Notice that I used the prospective X client's IP address, but I could just as easily used a regular old DNS name. (The only reason I'm using IP addresses in this example rather than DNS name, in case you're wondering, is that IP addresses simplify the example. By sticking with IP addresses, I didn't have to make you set up a bunch of DNS records or entries in a hosts file.)

By default, any given X server on a Linux machine only accepts connections from X clients running on the same machine as itself; you add a host with the plus sign, as you saw in the example above. You can, if you like, set up an X server to accept requests from *any* client by turning off X access control with this command:

```
xhost +
```

You can then reenable X access control with the minus option, like so:

```
xhost -
```

You can see what clients are currently allowed to connect—who's on the access control list—by just typing xhost all by itself, with no parameters. xhost settings do not survive from X session to X session; if you do an xinit and use xhost *+hostname* to put a host on the server's access control list, then exit X and once again type xhost, you'll see that the host is no longer on the access control list.

Eyeball Redux: Now It'll Work

Now try this command again from the keyboard at the first machine, the Mandrake box at 10.10.10.10:

```
xeyes -display 10.10.10.20:0
```

This time, you should see xeyes appear on the second machine. Success, you've created distributed X computing right before your very eyes (or xeyes)! To review, you have an

X server running on the second machine, the Slackware box at 10.10.10.20, serving requests from an X client, xeyes, running on the first machine, the Mandrake box at 10.10.10.10.

If the person sitting at the Slackware machine wondered where those eyes came from, he could type xlsclients. That will list all of the X applications running on his desktop and where they came from.

Press Ctrl+C to stop xeyes. But which machine do you do the Ctrl+C on? The first, as it's the one that started it. Now, I'll bet you're thinking that this'll only work for a little "toy" program like xeyes, right? Well, try it out on a 17MB+ monster—run Netscape remotely with this command:

```
netscape -display 10.10.10.20:0
```

Either closing Netscape from the second machine or doing a Ctrl+C from the first will stop it.

Avoiding the *-display* Option: *export DISPLAY*

So far, so good, but you may be wondering if you have to add that extra -display 10.10.10.20:0 option every time you run a remote program? Well, you can, but there's an alternative. You can tell X to direct any output to a particular system by default with the export command:

```
export DISPLAY=10.10.10.20:0
```

You need the uppercase DISPLAY or it won't work. This command doesn't survive from one X session to another, so once you exit X and restart it, you'll have to retype your export command if you want to continue redirecting X output to another system.

X on Your PC: Making NT an X Window Terminal / X Server

Now, if you thought inflicting xeyes on a remote system was pretty cool, then how about this? Instead of using a Linux machine as the "second" machine—that is, the X Window terminal or X server—you can use your Windows, NT, or 2000 machine. All you need is a program to enable that PC to understand the X Window graphics language.

You can spend a fair amount of money on a piece of X server software for a Microsoft operating system, but if you just want to try one out, then a firm named MicroImages (www.microimages.com) has a nice, basic X server for Windows, 2000, and NT that you can download from their website and use for 15 days without paying for it. If you want to use it for longer, the cost is reasonable: $25. It's simple to use; just install it and start the program, called MI/X, and your screen will fill with a big window that is essentially the "canvas" for the X server to "paint" upon, or you might think of it as the "X Window terminal screen." Then go over to your Linux box and start up some GUI application, but add the -display option followed by the IP address or DNS name of your Windows, NT, or 2000 machine. You'll see the X app pop up on your PC screen. Notice that you don't have to do any kind of xhost command to make the X server on the PC accept the X client's request.

MI/X is a bit limited in some ways. Don't minimize its window and then try to run an X app (it'll crash); and it seems wed to running twm as a window manager—I'd have preferred the simpler xterm-only screen without a window manager. But the price is right and it's some fun to play with.

Another, more recent, free X server is an actual implementation of XFree86 for Windows called Cygwin. You can find it at http://cygwin.com. Or there are a number of other X servers for Windows:

- X-WinPro from Labtam Finland runs 30 minutes in demo mode and includes several other useful Unix/Windows integration tools; www.labf.com, $90.
- Omni-X from Xlink; http://www.microsoft.com/typography/links/links.asp?type=free&part=1, $135 for the NT version.
- Reflection X from WRQ; www.wrq.com, $360.
- PC-Xware from NCD; www.ncd.com/products/software/pcxware (no price info on the website).
- KEA! X from Attachmate; www.attachmate.com/products/profile/0,1016,3194_1,00.html (no price info on the website).
- X-Deep/32 from Pexus Systems; www.pexus.com, $56.
- Exceed from Hummingbird; www.hummingbird.com (no price info on website).

You can see, then, that there's a Windows-compatible X server for any price range.

Another Approach: The Linux "Mainframe"

The xeyes example with two Linux boxes was interesting and simple to do, but truthfully doesn't reflect all that well how you might actually *use* remote X sessions. Here's a closer representation of how you might use remote X sessions.

Suppose you have two Linux machines: a powerful four-processor Alpha with 512MB of RAM, and a Pentium 100 with 32MB of RAM. The Pentium 100 is the one on your desk. You *really* want to do some heavy-duty image manipulation of a few bitmaps using The Gimp, a powerful graphics program that comes free with Linux. It wouldn't be that terribly *hard* to take that picture of Jeri Ryan and make it look like she was having dinner with your buddy Sam the other night (Sam's birthday is coming up, and he's a Voyager fan), but your system is *just so slow* for this kind of thing and the Alpha could get done in a twinkling. Fortunately, you even have an account on the Alpha. If only you could have the Alpha do the CPU work on The Gimp, and use your puny system essentially as nothing more than a graphics terminal.

Fortunately, you *can;* here's how. Let's dispense with the IP addresses this time and use somewhat easier-to-follow DNS names; the Alpha's name is mainframe.acme.com and your computer is terminal.acme.com. Let's assume that you've already gotten the bitmaps in question over to the Alpha, with FTP or something like that. And let's review who's to be the server and who's to be the client: The Gimp, running on mainframe.acme.com (the Alpha), will be the client. Your system, terminal.acme.com, will be the server. You can run The Gimp on the Alpha but see it on your system with the following steps.

Check Two-Way Connectivity

First, double-check that each system can "see" the other system. Start out at a text screen (don't run X on your system yet). Check that your system can find the Alpha by pinging mainframe.acme.com. If that works, then telnet over to mainframe.acme.com:

```
telnet mainframe.acme.com
```

You'll be prompted for your username and password and, when you supply them, you'll be connected. Commands that you type execute on mainframe.acme.com, not the computer that you're sitting at. If this is working, then mainframe.acme.com can "see" terminal.acme.com, and you know that you've got two-way communication. Exit from the Telnet session; we'll return to the Alpha later.

Start *xinit* on Your System (the Server)

Now that you're back controlling your local (terminal.acme.com) system, you have to start X, so type xinit and you'll get the now-familiar gray screen with the xterm window in the upper-left corner. Start up a window manager as well if you like, it'll make handling The Gimp's multiple windows easier; twm works fine.

Authorize Connections from mainframe.acme.com

Next, use xhost to tell your system that it should accept X sessions from mainframe.acme.com:

```
xhost +mainframe.acme.com
```

Reconnect to mainframe.acme.com

Now that your X server's ready, reconnect to the Alpha with Telnet again:

```
telnet mainframe.acme.com
```

Log on with your account name on that system.

Redirect X Output to terminal.acme.com

Despite having seized remote control of the Alpha (mainframe.acme.com), you have to do one more thing before it'll know to use your computer as its X server—the `export` command.

```
export DISPLAY=terminal.acme.com:0
```

Of course, if you're only running *one* command remotely, then you can always just add the `-display terminal.acme.com:0` option to that one command, assuming the command in question supports that option. Setting the DISPLAY variable, however, will *always* work.

> **NOTE** Notice that you do *not* have to start X on mainframe.acme.com. The Alpha might not ever have any kind of graphics ability for all we know; it's just going to be crunching numbers and moving bytes around. The only machine that needs an `xinit` is the terminal.

Finally, Run The Gimp!

Start 'er up by just typing `gimp`. You have your mainframe! When you're done, shut down The Gimp from its menu and type `exit` to disconnect the Telnet session.

Keystrokes for Multiple X Sessions: A Side Note

One more thing about basic X before I return to my discussion of the parts of the Linux GUI: moving around the sessions. You may recall that Linux prebuilds a bunch of text-based sessions and that you can jump around from one to the other with the Alt key—Alt+F1, Alt+F2, and so on. But you may notice that when you're in X, the Alt+F1 sequence doesn't work. When you're running X, you need to know a new key sequence: Ctrl+Alt+F1. That'll bring you back to your first text session; Ctrl+Alt+F2 takes you to the second, and so on.

Ctrl+Alt+F7 takes you to the X session. You can even run more than one X session (perhaps to run several window managers at once, for demonstration purposes), and Ctrl+Alt+F8 takes you to that, Ctrl+Alt+F9 to the third X session (assuming you're running one), and so on.

If you *want* to start multiple X sessions, then try this. First do an `xinit`, as you've done before. Then, inside the `xterm` window you'll see, type:

```
xinit -- :1 &
```

At that point, you'll flash over to a second X session. Ctrl+Alt+F7 takes you back to the first session, and Ctrl+Alt+F8 to the second.

Other Window Managers

Enough X hacking for now—let's get back to the GUI pieces. A bit earlier, you saw that both twm and fvwm2 manage windows, doing some things in the same way and others differently. In both cases, you bring up the system's menu by clicking and holding any empty point on the background; that seems to be the norm for most simple window managers, although one named wmaker requires that you *right*-click the background. If you'd like to play around with a few other window managers, look around the Web for these:

- XFCE (www.xfce.org) is, Dan tells, me, a "lightweight" window manager gaining popularity among Linux techies.
- AnotherLevel looks a bit more Win95-ish (I'm not sure of a URL for it).
- Afterstep (www.afterstep.org) is built to emulate the NeXT computer's interface.
- www.icewm.org hosts the ICE Window Manager (it's "pretty cool," get it?), which looks nice and in my experience is pretty quick.
- /usr/bin/wmaker attractive and afterstep-ish (requires a right-click on the desktop to bring up the menu).
- www.enlightenment.org hosts the Enlightenment window manager, which used to be the window manager that Red Hat set up with GNOME.
- Another window manager, sawfish, ships with Red Hat and is configured as GNOME's window manager under Red Hat 7.3. Sawfish is interesting because you customize and extend it with a language closely based on Lisp (LISt Processor), an old artificial intelligence language.
- A window manager named kwin comes with the KDE environment—we'll cover KDE in a moment. I don't know that anyone uses it in a stand-alone mode, however; it's pretty much only used as part of KDE.

But those aren't the only window managers available for X; to see more of them, look at www.plig.org/xwinman/index.html. X servers running on commercial Unixes also commonly use mwm, the Motif Window Manager—it's included in Red Hat 7.3. Motif is built to look like the old OS/2 Presentation Manager—which may bring some painful memories for long-time users of Microsoft operating systems. And remember that if you get stuck, you can always press Ctrl+Alt+Backspace to shut down X altogether!

The Desktop Environment

Both Enlightenment and kwm are sort of oddball window managers, as they're not usually run all by themselves; instead, they act as window managers for a three-part, modern Linux GUI. But the third part? That's called the *desktop environment*. The two popular ones are the "K" desktop environment (KDE) and the GNU Network Object Model Environment (GNOME), which its users normally pronounce "guh-nome" or, perhaps more accurately, "g'nome," making the initial *g* more of a glottal stop than an actual syllable. (My first guess had been that I'd pronounce it as I pronounce the name of the mythical creatures by the same name: "nome.")

What's a desktop environment got that a simple window manager lacks? As far as I can see, desktop environments add:

- A more sophisticated menu system; you needn't perform different mouse clicks to bring them up.

- A suite of utilities. While the typical X distribution *does* come with a simple text editor, a calculator, and some other apps, that list can't compare to what a Windows user gets "right in the box" in terms of GUI applications. KDE and GNOME come with an impressive and ever-growing group of applications, games, and utilities.

- An underlying programming substructure called an *object model* that simplifies sharing data. Windows has had a series of such models with names like Dynamic Data Exchange (DDE), Object Linking and Embedding (OLE), and Common Object Model (COM). They're the elements that enable you to take a piece of an Excel spreadsheet and paste it into WordPerfect as a table. GNOME uses Common Object Request Broker Architecture (CORBA), a model that's been around for at least 10 years. To underscore exactly how much they want GNOME apps to be able to work together via objects, the GNOME folks have built a programming toolkit that simplifies exploiting CORBA and have named that toolkit *bonobo*, after a variety of chimpanzee-like ape that apparently is reported to have sex with other bonobos about a *dozen times* a day.

- A desktop *metaphor*. In Microsoft operating systems, we're used to the idea that we have a "desktop," a place that we can leave things. You can, for example, put a document on your Windows desktop. What that really means is that Windows (and NT and 2000) somewhere have a directory called Desktop or something similar, and any files in that directory show up as icons on the desktop. If you turn your computer off and then back on, those icons will still be there. You can't do that with a window manager; twm doesn't have the idea of a desktop.

- A strip along the bottom of the screen that holds icons for quickly starting applications and spaces that show what applications are running, like the Windows Taskbar.

Of course, desktop environments cost you in terms of CPU power and memory. For example, X and twm use 12MB on my Red Hat 7.3 system, while X, KDE, and its window manager on that same system use about 29MB. While you can get plenty done with just Linux, X, and a window manager, most modern Linux GUI users use either the KDE or GNOME desktop. But as to *which* one they use… well, there's a story there.

YARW: KDE versus GNOME

Not only are there two major desktop environments, but if you ask a Linux expert about which one is "better," then—surprise!—you'll find that there's a religious war in the Linux world over the issue. The Unix world loves acronyms that start with *ya*, which stands for "yet another;" for example, there's *yacc*, short for "yet another compiler compiler." In the spirit of that, I've labeled the debate YARW, or Yet Another Religious War.

KDE

Back in the late '80s and early '90s, several Unix vendors worked to create the Common Desktop Environment, an effort to bring the increasing popularity of a graphical desktop metaphor as seen in the Mac, OS/2, and Windows to Unix. It succeeded, and big-name Unixes like Sun Solaris use CDE as their desktop to this day.

As is the case with most things Unix, the Linux world looked at CDE and said, "Cool, let's add it to Linux." Unfortunately for Linux, however, CDE is a for-profit tool. As paying for software is anathema in the Linux world, they just did without.

Until 1996, that is. A German programmer named Matthias Ettrich announced that he was going to build a state-of-the-art desktop for Linux, hopefully with the help of the Linux programmer horde. In July 1998, KDE 1.0 arrived. It wasn't really a CDE clone but rather an amalgam of ideas from all of the various GUIs around. KDE takes its name from CDE, however, although the KDE folks say that KDE stands for the K Desktop Environment. This C-to-K translation appears in several KDE tools. For example, I gather that they were thinking of calling their CORBA (the object model, recall) implementation KORBA. But it's klear that kooler heads prevailed, and modern KDE documents call the object model CORBA. In his initial call-to-arms asking for programmer volunteer help in creating KDE, Ettrich says that KDE stands for Kool Desktop Environment but, again, I'd guess that someone said, "What if this thing is still around in 100 years? Do we *really* want people thinking we couldn't spell?"

KDE, however, *is* pretty cool. It works quickly, uses fonts well, and will run competently on resolutions as low as 640 × 480. It's a little sloppy with screen space—its taskbar is bigger than Windows' and therefore steals more screen real estate—but it probably won't take a lot of getting used to for a Windows expert, and besides, nowadays virtually every system supports 1024 × 768, which both KDE and GNOME look better in.

What *will* take some getting used to is what KDE—and GNOME, for that matter—*can't* do. We Microsoft users are accustomed to being able to adjust things like screen resolution and color depth directly from the desktop, and that's not really easy for either KDE or GNOME to accomplish, because they don't handle resolution, X does—you might say that it's "not their department."

> **NOTE** Actually, it wouldn't be *impossible* to shift X resolution from KDE or GNOME, but apparently it's not easy to do either. Corel's Linux used to do it, but they're out of the Linux business now, so clearly on-the-fly screen resolution changes weren't a Linux killer app.

KDE comes with an amazing number of applications, with more on the way. There's even a klone—sorry, couldn't resist—of Microsoft's Office apps: KWord, KSpread, KPresenter, and so on. It also has its own window manager, kwm, which is the *only* window manager intended to work with K's desktop environment.

So why doesn't everyone use KDE? Well, KDE is built on top of a set of Linux graphics programs called Qt, which was *commercial* software. Qt's license didn't match the copy-at-will freedom of the GNU Public License, restricting a distribution's ability to charge for any distribution that included KDE. Eventually, Qt's creators liberalized their license to a very GPL-like wording and called their license the QPL. Finally, in September 2000, Qt went GPL... but by then GNOME had some momentum, hence Linux's two-environment nature.

You can start a KDE session by hand on most systems with these two commands:

```
xinit
startkde&
```

You may, if you like, see how KDE starts by examining the /usr/bin/startkde file—it's just a script.

GNOME

While Qt's license was up in the air, however, a group of open source coders launched a project that intended to resolve the KDE dispute by creating an alternative desktop environment written *entirely* to the GPL license. That project got the name GNU Network Object Model Environment, or GNOME, and as you'd expect, it works in the spirit of the GNU folks. Built atop a graphics toolkit called GTK+ instead of Qt, GNOME is completely free software. Like KDE, it comes with a fairly large number of basic desktop tools.

GNOME offers much of what KDE does, but there *are* differences. It uses a bit more memory and runs more slowly than KDE. But what some people like about GNOME is that it's not closely bound to a particular window manager; there isn't a GWM or the like. That's different from KDE, which pretty much requires that you run it with its bundled KWM window manager. You'll normally see GNOME ships on RedHat 7.3 with the Sawfish window manager, but you don't *have* to use it. According to the GNOME FAQ, you can also run GNOME with Window Maker, IceWM, and another window manager named Enlightenment. The FAQ goes on to claim that fvwm, scwm, AfterStep, and qvwm either work with GNOME, or will shortly.

> **NOTE**   In the time between the first and second editions, an interesting thing happened between KDE and GNOME. In the first edition, I liked KDE better because it was faster, used less memory, and had a cleaner screen. It's still faster and uses a bit less memory—the margin is smaller now—but oddly enough GNOME's screen has gotten less cluttered and KDE's has gotten more cluttered. On a fast enough system, I might say that GNOME would be the more interesting of the two environments for Windows users... but both environments are in constant change, so keep an eye on them both.

KDE and GNOME are both programming projects initiated in Europe by people for whom English is a second language. It's interesting because international language support for large computer programs, and GUI tools in particular, has always been a bit spotty, because the major GUIs have always been built either in the U.S. or the U.K. (that's where many of the graphics programmers for IBM's OS/2 lived); non-English versions of GUI programs have often been poor stepchildren. Windows 2000's and XP's support of multiple languages in a single binary may improve that (although it hasn't so far—people tell me that the "localized" versions of Windows in their languages are so terrible that they just surrender and use the English version), but so also may having two Linux GUIs from outside of the English-speaking world.

I find the 2002 edition of GNOME more appealing than I did the 2000. I commented in 2000 that GNOME looked far too cramped and crowded, and that on a 1024×768 system, it would probably be more appealing. I still think that. Now that 1024×768 is pretty ubiquitous, GNOME looks pretty good on a number of systems. But some of my old grumbles remain. I often work using the root account, and GNOME never fails to tack an annoying message up reminding me that I'm running as root and that root has the power to accidentally destroy the world (or something like that). The Mozilla browser is painfully slow compared to Internet Explorer running under Windows on the same system. However, once you've added the TrueType fonts, as I described earlier, then for the first time a Linux browser produces text that looks as nice as what you're used to in the Windows world. GNOME includes a really nifty Outlook knockoff called Ximian Evolution (it's on KDE as well) that can even talk to Exchange servers, sync to a Pilot, and so on. As with the KOffice stuff, the fit and finish of Evolution is quite good, in Microsoft Office's league.

You can start up GNOME on most systems with these two commands:

```
xinit

gnome-session&
```

Unlike startkde, gnome-session is a compiled binary, so you can't peek to see what steps it employs to start up.

As I mentioned, GNOME has a kind of annoying quirk: if you're running as root and you start GNOME, then it stops in the initial X screen and raises an error message:

```
You have logged in as root. It's very easy to accidentally damage your
system while you are root, you should use this login session only to do
administrative tasks, and use your user account instead when possible.
```

You then have to click OK for GNOME to start. Now, this is kind of irritating if you've chosen GNOME as your standard GUI, so I looked around to find out how to keep GNOME from popping up that message. Here's what the FAQ says at `http://www.gnome.org/faqs/users-faq/using.html#AEN794`:

Q: How do I disable that annoying "Warning! You are running as root!" message?

A: Just get an up-to-date copy of the code in question, investigate what generates the message, tweak the code to remove it, recompile it, and you're done.

If that doesn't look helpful, then it's because it's not meant to be. That warning is there for a reason. Running as root should be reserved for system administration tasks only, and this does not include recataloguing your jpgs, chatting on IRC, or playing with Napster. It's a security risk, and it's very easy to have accidents as root and remove things you didn't mean to. Running as a normal user is safer and more sensible. It is assumed that people who can remove the message are the people who won't normally be running as root in the first place.

Clearly the GNOME folks have transcended that old twentieth-century notion of user-friendliness. As I write this in mid-2002, though, I see that there's a GNOME 2.0 (Red Hat 7.3 includes GNOME 1.4) on the drawing boards; with hope, it'll be a little more flexible. "Linux is about choice," right? (I suppose you could choose KDE.)

KDE or GNOME?

This was an easier section to write in the first edition...

My *a priori* bias was in favor of KDE, but as I use it more I find that I like some things about KDE less and some things about GNOME more, so I'm not sure which to recommend. I'm not being wishy-washy when I say that you will do about as well with either. Both have improved in that they both look a lot more professional and boast large arrays of programs, many very well done. When I said in the year 2000 that about the only decent desktop apps were StarOffice, I had to bite down hard a bit—StarOffice has always seemed very kludgy to me, and it still feels that way. But KOffice and Evolution to use two examples, are pretty neat programs.

KDE is still a bit faster than GNOME, but it has acquired a lot of desktop clutter. Its default web browser, Konqueror, is clearly a young browser—several websites that look fine in Internet Explorer or Mozilla look odd under Konqueror. (Including my own, admittedly.) Konqueror is also KDE's answer to Explorer, so you'll have to use it to visually browse your directory structure, and that's annoying, as it tends to get locked up—it says "stalled"—for long periods of time when showing you part of the file system. But KDE has a large and ever-growing set of programs, and probably offers the Gates-haters a good enough desktop environment. (You can easily open a command prompt and type `netscape` to start that browser under KDE.)

GNOME is, again, a bit slower and a bit more memory-hungry, but it also seems a bit cleaner and more intuitive. I suspect a lot of that comes from Red Hat's deciding to configure GNOME with Sawfish rather than Enlightenment.

Both GUIs will still, I think, annoy the veteran Windows user. In my opinion, Linux's much-touted reliability and stability is still well-deserved... *until* you start a GUI. I can, without too much trouble (far too little trouble, actually) get KDE running with a bunch of windows that are simply frozen solid: they don't respond to input, you can't close them, and even opening up a shell and using `kill -9` to get rid of them has no effect.

It's kind of unfortunate that Linux has ended up with two desktop environments, because the only real reason that GNOME came into existence in the first place was the initial KDE licensing, and that issue's been basically resolved. The GNOME folks used to explain in their FAQ why you'd use GNOME over KDE (the KDE people are silent on the subject in their FAQ):

> *There are significant design differences between KDE and GNOME. Top of the list is a difference in widget set. We find GTK+ to be nicer, more customizable, more friendly to development in various programming languages, and more flexible than Qt; others may disagree. Also near the top of the list is the fact that GNOME is not tied to any single window manager. You don't have to use Enlightenment; you can use any GNOME-compliant window manager. In all, the projects are different enough so that both should be able to coexist and even collaborate.*

In other words, the two reasons that the GNOME people offer to choose GNOME over KDE are (1) there are better GUI programming tools, and (2) you can use a window manager other than kwm. I'm not a programmer, so I don't care about the first reason; and while the second is interesting, when last I checked only a handful of window managers work with GNOME, none of which seem all that appealing to me.

On the other hand, if I'd been using Linux for years, then I might well have become extremely attached to IceWM; in that case, I'd probably choose GNOME. Also, as you'll see later, GNOME's easygoing nature vis-à-vis window managers makes it actually possible to run an entire Linux GNOME desktop on your Windows machines!

In the end analysis, I'd guess that the existence of both GUIs means that we'll either continue to have a choice of GUIs as time goes on, or perhaps they'll just steal from each others' ideas, and KDE will become indistinguishable from GNOME. Perhaps the best news, however, is that as far as I can tell from examining both KDE and GNOME's websites in 2002, the hatchet has been buried. In 2000, the GNOME website had this to say about KDE versus GNOME:

> *This matter has been hashed out time and time again on the gnome-list mailing list. Asking this question on gnome-list is discouraged behavior. If you want to go somewhere and start a flame war on this topic, then please do it somewhere far far away where we don't have to listen to you.*

Ah, that classically Linuxian tact… But in 2002, you can see an even more conciliatory tone:

> *One way of helping GNOME is to avoid getting into rows about desktop environments, licences, window managers, Linux distributions and UNIX flavours. Honestly. It's lots of fun for many people, but it puts another group of people right off. "Why my preferred choice is good" is one thing. "Why everything else is rubbish" is not helpful. Really.*

Getting around in KDE and GNOME

If you already know the Windows interface, then you can pretty much get around in KDE and GNOME without too much help. But here are a few pointers to help you get started with the Linux GUIs.

KDE Basics

Once started, a KDE session looks like Figure 7.6.

Basic Navigation

Across the bottom of the screen is a group of icons for often-launched applications, just like the Quick Launch bar in Active Desktop. Across the left part of the screen are some icons; just as with a Windows desktop, you can place icons on the desktop that activate a program. (I know the screen shot looks crowded; that's because in the publishing biz, it's hard to use screen shots larger than 800×600, so I reconfigured my X server to 800×600. Trust me, in 1024×768 it looks somewhat cleaner.)

Figure 7.6 Basic KDE desktop

If you click one of the arrows on the extreme lower-right-hand corner then a big letter "K" appears with a small up-pointing arrowhead above it. It indicates that if you click the K logo, then a program menu pops up, very much like the familiar Start/Programs menu.

In-the-Box KDE Programs

As most Linux distributions come with a large number of programs, you'll see many, many menu items:

- An applications menu usually includes a text editor or two (or three or four— remember this is Linux), a viewer for PostScript files called GhostView, a PDF file viewer like xpdf, and fax programs, among others.

- A Games menu usually contains a couple dozen games, including Tetris, PacMan, Minesweeper, Poker, and a neat little game that the Macintosh people have been keeping to themselves called Same Game.

- Graphics includes The Gimp (a full-featured graphics program), a screen-capture program, assorted simple paint programs, image viewers, drawing programs, a fractal generator, and a fax viewer.

- Internet includes a suite of Internet client tools—mail clients, routines to help you dial up the Internet, Konqueror, Netscape Navigator or Communicator, and the like.

- Multimedia has sound mixer panels, sound and video players, and CD players. There's even a CD burner program for K, although I've had better luck with the command-line tools for CD burning.

- Settings includes various programs that either let you set up parts of the system or let you view how the hardware is set up.

- Utilities has a calculator, the console (the command prompt windows), text editors, Explorer-like file managers, programs to apply and manage packages, and whatever else the distribution's creator included.

- As I've already mentioned, there is a suite of KOffice tools that look and act something like Microsoft Office.

Session-to-Session Memory

The first thing you'll notice about a KDE session is how *cluttered* the screen is. KDE opens a file manager and a bunch of other stuff, which made me wonder, "Is this going to happen every time I start KDE?" Fortunately, the answer is no. KDE notes how your desktop is set up when you exit and attempts to re-create it the next time you start it up. (Compare this to GNOME when I discuss it later.)

But where is all of your desktop information stored? In a directory in your home directory named /Desktop. For example, I'm running as root at the moment, and so my desktop directory is named /root/Desktop. My Desktop directory contains a directory named /Trash and another named /Autostart, like the Recycle Bin and Startup group in Windows 9*x*, NT 4, and Windows 2000.

> **TIP** If you have an NIS domain set up with centralized home directories, then the net effect of having all of that user-specific stuff in /Desktop is that you can log on anywhere and see your same desktop—in effect, it's "user profiles" in Linux.

The other thing that you'll see in the /Desktop directory, as well as a hidden directory in your home directory called /.kde, are a lot of files with the extension .kdelnk. These are small files that contain very little save for links to other files. They're basically similar to shortcuts in Windows, shadows in OS/2, or aliases in the Mac world. Simplified, .kdelnk files look like this:

```
[KDE Desktop Entry]
Name=Backgammon
Comment=Runs the X Backgammon Game
```

```
Exec=xgammon
Icon=gamgame.xpm
Terminal=0
Type=Application
```

This is a `.kdelnk` file that I cooked up to run the X Window Backgammon program. The sections in it are pretty self-explanatory. KDE uses `.kdelnk` files both to place the icons on your desktop *and* as the basis of its menu structure. Sure, Windows does that as well with its shortcut files, but shortcut files are binaries that you can't do much with—I find the editable, ASCII nature of `.kdelnk` files appealing. Furthermore, `.kdelnk` files contain dozens of alternative labels in different languages—as I suggested earlier, KDE's European ancestry has served it well in a multilingual world.

TIP   By the way, if your session still looks crowded, then use KDE's "window shade" feature. Double-click a window's title bar, and the window "rolls up" into the title bar. Double-click again, and it rolls back down.

KDE Tricks

I promised you in the Introduction that I wouldn't waste your time, so I'll spare you the 40 pages of how to click and drag in KDE. Both the KDE and GNOME user interfaces are very, very similar to the Windows, NT, and 2000 models, so you'll find that your skills will transfer over very quickly. But there are two things you may find useful that aren't part of the standard Windows UI features.

First is the *middle* mouse button. You may recall from Chapter 4 that Linux wants to set up a three-button mouse, and, if you only have two mouse buttons, Linux offers you the option of simulating a third mouse button by pressing both of the mouse buttons down at the same time—as we used to call it in OS/2, "chording" the mouse buttons. You may have wondered what good a third mouse button was.

In any X application, you can copy and paste information from one window to another very quickly using the middle mouse button like so:

1. Highlight the data that you want to copy by clicking and dragging across the data with the left mouse button.

2. Move the cursor to the window that you'd like to transfer the data to, and bring that window to the foreground with a left-click.

3. Position the cursor to the place where you want to paste the data and press the middle button.

The data will appear where you clicked the middle button. Very nice—just highlight, move the cursor, hit the middle button, and you're done. You can even skip the click-in-the-middle step if you have the windows arranged so that they don't overlap—so long as your first click in the target window ends up where you want it, that middle-button click can serve double duty to both shift the window focus *and* paste.

The second trick is simpler. You probably make regular use of the Windows, NT, and 2000 Start/Run box. (Click the Start button, then the Run option. You get a text field that lets you fill in the name of a program so you can directly run any program without needing a menu item for it.) KDE has something like that as well: Alt+F2. Just press Alt+F2 and a command: window appears. If you type in a command that doesn't work, however, you won't get an error of any kind—the system just won't respond.

While I'm on the subject of keystrokes: Alt+Tab moves from application to application as it does in Windows. Ctrl+Tab moves you from desktop to desktop—remember that Linux GUIs seem inextricably wed to the idea of multiple desktops. Ctrl+F1 through Ctrl+F8 moves you directly to the different desktops.

Alt+F1, *not* Ctrl+Esc, raises the program menu. Ctrl+Esc *does* have a job, though; it brings up a sort of Task Manager–like window that shows your running applications and won't let you kill those apps but lets you switch from one to the other. Alt+F4 closes windows, as in Windows et al. Alt+F3 drops down the system menu for the focus window. (The same menu that you get when you click the little icon in the upper-left corner of the title bar in Windows.)

A Complete Remote Desktop

Before I leave my look at KDE, here's a neat tip that'll create a kind of Windows Terminal Services session, a complete remote desktop. As with my earlier remote examples, one computer—the one on your desk—is acting merely as a terminal, and a distant computer is doing all of the work.

As before, let's call the computer acting as the terminal terminal.acme.com, and the system doing all the work mainframe.acme.com. Here are the steps to run a complete desktop remotely. I'll presume that you're sitting at terminal.acme.com. Basically you're going to do the same thing as before:

- Run an X session on the terminal, none needed on the mainframe.
- Tell the X server on terminal.acme.com to accept X clients (applications) running on mainframe.acme.com.

- Telnet into mainframe.acme.com from terminal.acme.com and issue the command:

  `export DISPLAY=terminal.acme.com:0.0`

- In the Telnet session, start the graphical program (which, in this case, will be KDE or GNOME.)

Here are the specific steps to take. I assume in these instructions that you're sitting at terminal.acme.com.

1. Start an X session on terminal with `xinit`. Don't start a window manager, it gets in KDE's way when it loads.

2. In the `xterm` window, authorize mainframe to send X requests to your system: `xhost +mainframe.acme.com` will do it.

3. Establish a Telnet session to mainframe (`telnet mainframe.acme.com`) and then log in with an account name that mainframe knows.

4. Just to be on the safe side, try `pinging` terminal.acme.com so you know that mainframe knows how to resolve terminal's name.

5. Tell mainframe to route its graphical requests to your computer by typing `export DISPLAY=terminal.acme.com:0.0`.

Finally, you're ready to fire up a desktop environment; type `startkde` and stand back! You'll have a familiar-looking KDE desktop in a few seconds, but, again, it's running on mainframe, not your system.

To start a GNOME session, type `gnome-session` instead of `startkde`. You can use that information to create a truly strange situation: GNOME running on Windows! I ran a Windows-based X server on a Windows 98 computer, telnetted to one of my Linux computers, exported the display to the Windows machine, and typed `gnome-session`. You can see the result in Figure 7.7. (You can look ahead a page or two to see a sample native-Linux GNOME desktop for comparison.)

No, that's not a faked screen shot. Once GNOME started running on the Windows box, it placed its *panel* (the GNOME word for what Windows users would call a Taskbar and a system tray) across the bottom of the screen. You can see the xsysinfo and gnomeRPM programs running as well, on the same screen as Word and a DOS command prompt window. I ran GNOME rather than KDE because both of the Windows-based X servers that I had came with their own hard-wired window manager, and as KDE just plain can't work with any window managers except its own, KDE wouldn't run. But GNOME, which is more flexible about which window manager it uses, started up fine. (Unfortunately, I could not make this work with the inexpensive MI/X X server; it crashed as I tried to start gnome-session.)

Figure 7.7   A GNOME session on a Windows 98 desktop

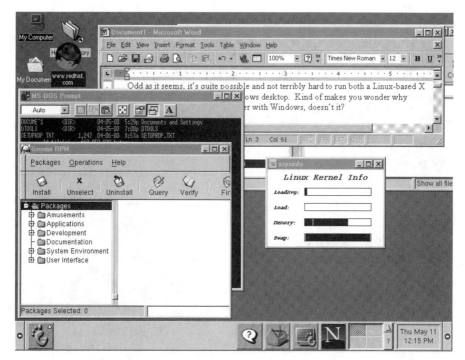

GNOME Basics

Exactly how you'll start GNOME varies from distribution to distribution, but you can always get it to start with an `xinit` followed by `gnome-session`, as you've already read. Once you start up GNOME, you'll see an initial screen that looks something like Figure 7.8.

This is one of the things that I find annoying about GNOME: its "autoclutter" feature. My desktops are usually cluttered enough; the last thing I need is my GUI helpfully worsening the matter by popping up unnecessarily large warnings that I'm running as root. And it's not like GNOME only tells you the first time, no—even on your 100th visit to GNOME-land, you get that annoying little box, sort of the GUI version of a seat-belt chime in a car. Then it pops open a File Manager–like box showing you some directory and, again, no matter how many times you clear the box, it insists on showing it to you at every startup, unlike Windows and KDE, which let you tell them to skip the clutter.

Figure 7.8   Opening GNOME screen

As you read a couple of paragraphs before, the bar at the bottom of the screen is a called the GNOME panel. It's like the Windows Quick Launch bar, Taskbar, and system tray. The part on the left, called the Quicklaunch bar, contains icons that let you start often-used programs in a manner similar to Windows' Quick Launch. The piece in the middle contains icons that indicate what's currently running; GNOME calls this area the *pager*. To the far right is where some special apps like the clock live, similar to the Windows system tray. The little arrows on the extreme right and left roll up the panel to the left or right of the screen.

WARNING   As is common in Linux X-based environments, don't be surprised if the screen seems to clear when you move your mouse to the edge of the screen. You didn't lose your apps, you just jumped from one virtual desktop to another, the *quadrants* I described earlier. Just move the mouse in the opposite direction, and your old desktop will flash back on the screen.

Another thing that takes a bit of getting used to in GNOME is that you *must* click a window to give it the focus. Here's how it'll trip you up: Suppose you want a terminal window so that you can type a command-line command or two. You click the icon in the Quicklaunch bar that looks like a terminal, starting the GNOME xterm-like program named gnome-terminal. Now, if you have experience with Windows, NT, 2000, or KDE, then you'll assume that you can start typing immediately and have the gnome-terminal window accept and act upon your keystrokes. But that won't work—you not only have to start gnome-terminal, you must then click it before it gets the keyboard focus.

If you like doodads, icons, different kinds of scroll bars (yes, there are "look and feel" issues in scroll bars, believe it or not), then you'll like GNOME. Its underlying GTK+ graphics toolkit apparently offers so many different ways to control how a GUI represents things that GNOME's developers couldn't resist passing the benefits on to their users.

You may recall that I said distributions seem to load menus with both KDE and GNOME apps no matter which desktop environment you load. As a result, you'll often find the same program in two different implementations, or two very similar implementations— for example, KDE has a Notepad-like application called kedit and GNOME has yet another called gedit. One GNOME program well worth taking a look at is gnumeric, a spreadsheet. It can't do graphics and is fairly primitive compared to commercial spreadsheets, but for basic number crunching, it seems to work fairly well. Most important, though, is the fact that the GNOME menus include the KDE menus, and just about everything that runs under KDE seems to run under GNOME.

Assembling the GUI: Starting Everything

By now, I'm guessing that you haven't decided to standardize on fvwm2 for your desktop and, even if you *did* decide that, it might be a bit of a pain to have to remember to always start it up with an xinit followed by some other commands (which need to be suffixed with an ampersand) and finally a fvwm2 command. It'd be nice if you could just type one command to kick off your entire GUI—X, window manager, and desktop environment.

startx Configures *xinit*

In general, Linux *has* such a command. It's a script called startx, usually located in a directory named /usr/X11R6/bin. And by now I'm sure it'll come as no surprise that different Linux distributions may have startx scripts written differently—as Craig says, "Linux is about choice…," although sometimes you might wish that Linux offered a few less choices! The man pages explain startx in the following way, but your distribution may vary.

No matter what the distribution, however, startx's job can be explained simply: it configures and launches xinit. startx looks around the system to find some configuration scripts (which I'll explain in a moment) and then feeds those scripts to xinit by assembling a potentially long, drawn-out xinit invocation.

xinit's Job Revisited: Reexamining X "Servers" and "Clients"

The main part to getting your GUI running, then, is to get xinit functioning properly, so let's reexamine xinit in a bit more detail. We know that simply typing xinit gets you a gray screen with an xterm session running in it. But xinit can accept a pretty rich set of parameters. Generalized a bit, an xinit invocation looks like

```
xinit X-client client-arguments -- X-server display server-arguments
```

Just so that's clear, an xinit command is followed by the name of some program that will run under X, followed by any arguments that the program might need, followed by two dashes, followed by the name of an X server program, followed by a display indicator, and finally any arguments for the X server program. (And yes, I promise I've got examples coming up.)

It's important for startx to feed xinit at least one parameter, because we already *know* what we get if we just type xinit–it just starts up the default X server on display :0 and runs xterm, and there wouldn't be much use in startx then. Let's take a minute and reexamine the X notion of "clients" and "servers" and also look at some specific examples of invoking xinit with parameters.

X Clients Reexamined

Remember that in X talk, "client" doesn't mean you or me, or some computer. Instead, it means "a graphical program that runs on top of X." So any file that tells X to load, say, a graphical calculator program—oops, I meant "an X client that happens to be a calculator"—and perhaps tells X what colors to make that calculator, would be a client configuration program. But recall that X is just the graphics foundation, and that you'll typically run a whole bunch of applications before you even start using your GUI—namely, the components of your window manager and your desktop environment. But before going any further, let's look at few examples of passing a client and client arguments to xinit. I could tell xinit to start X and just run the clock (instead of xterm) like so:

```
xinit /usr/X11R6/bin/xclock
```

Notice something unexpected about this—I had to feed xinit the entire path of the xclock command. Merely typing xinit xclock would have caused the X setup to fail because xinit is wired to assume that any client information that you send is *just an option for* xterm. But when xinit sees any client information starting with a slash or a period, it knows that you're telling it the name of a program, rather than an option to xterm. Here's another example where I use xinit to start up xedit and edit the /etc/hosts file:

```
xinit /usr/X11R6/bin/xedit /etc/hosts
```

X Servers Reexamined

Not only can you tell xinit about the X clients to start up, you can also give it instructions about the X *server* that it should start. Remember that in X talk, "server" really just means "the code that makes graphics work on this system." An X server grabs your keystrokes and mouse clicks and ships them off to your clients, who in turn send graphical information to the X server to show to you.

You feed xinit instructions about what X server to run, and how to run it, after the two dashes—recall that when simplified, xinit's syntax looks like:

```
xinit <instructions about clients> -- <instructions about servers>
```

But why on Earth would you want to tell xinit anything about your X server? Remember that you start an X server by just typing X. Well, you could tell xinit to do that, like so:

```
xinit -- /usr/X11R6/bin/X
```

Notice the syntax – xinit, followed by a space, followed by two dashes, followed by a space, followed by /usr/X11R6/bin/X. Notice also that you've got to use the full path to the command here, as you did with clients—xinit -- X would not work. Why would you want to execute that particular command? Well, you wouldn't; it's a simple example.

You *might*, however, want to start up an X server other than the one that comes with Linux. (Granted, a low-probability event, but possible.) I've seen two commercial alternatives for XFree86's X server: Metro-X at http://www.metrolink.com/products/ metrox/metrox.html and Xi Graphics at http://www.xig.com/Pages/Atop/ SummitDownloadables.html offer commercial X servers. If you had, say, Metro-X and XFree86 on the same system, you might want to switch between them. Or recall that you can run multiple X virtual terminals ("displays"); you might choose to run one X session with XFree86 and another with Metro-X. Which brings me to the next parameter: *display*. Recall that you can use :0 to refer to the first virtual terminal, :1 for the next, and so on, and that you can shift between them by pressing the Ctrl+Alt+Function key.

You could, then, tell xinit to start up an X session on a second virtual terminal like so:

```
xinit -- :1
```

xinitrc and *.xinitrc*

startx tells X (and xinit) how to start up the clients necessary to get your GUI going with a script. What's that script's name? It depends, but it's usually either xinitrc or

.xinitrc–and no, that's not a typo, the difference between the two is only a leading period. By convention in the Linux world, a well-designed startx will first look in your home directory for a file named .xinitrc (pronounced "dot X init R C"), and if you have one (you usually won't), then xinit will use your .xinitrc script to kick off applications, a window manager, desktop environment, or whatever. If startx *can't* find a .xinitrc in your home directory, then it looks for a generic script, which is usually just called xinitrc, without the leading dot. As to *where* it finds it, well, that varies quite a bit from distribution from distribution. On various distributions, I've found it at /usr/X11R6/lib/X11/xinit/xinitrc, /usr/X11R6/lib/X11/xinitrc, or /etc/X11/xinit/xinitrc, but it could be anywhere, so here's another chance to try out the find command.

Assuming that you're working from Red Hat 7.3, your xinitrc is in /etc/X11/xinit. You could, then, forgo startx altogether and start your system—desktop environment, window manager, and all—with this command:

```
xinit /etc/X11/xinit/xinitrc
```

That's why xinitrc or .xinitrc are so important: they tell X how to load your window manager and desktop environment. Without an xinitrc or .xinitrc, you're left looking at a mottled gray background.

No matter *where* it is, your system's xinitrc is a pretty powerful file, as it does most of the GUI configuration, so it's well worth finding. You'll see how in the next section, when we pick apart the startx script.

startx Summarized

I hope that by now I've given you some notion of what startx does, so I'll summarize how far we've gotten before moving to the next step: startx script dissection.

- You start a Linux GUI by typing startx to start a script by that name.
- startx's job is to assemble and run a command that invokes xinit.
- At minimum, xinit needs to know the location of a script file that tells it which clients (window manager, desktop environment, applications) to load. That script file can be a single file that anyone on the system might use, or some or all users might have their own personal client setup script files. The system-wide client setup script is named xinitrc, and there's no fixed location for it; different distributions store it in different locations. If users have their own personalized version of xinitrc, then they rename it to .xinitrc with a leading period and put it in their home directories.
- While it's not common, some installations or users might want to modify xinit's defaults for starting up an X server. They'd do that with a script containing the commands needed to start the script, and the script would be named xserverrc. If

a particular user wants to create some nondefault behavior, she should write an xserverrc file, rename it to `.xserverrc`, and place it in her home directory.

- As specific user preferences should override generic system settings, part of `startx`'s job is to look for user-specific client or server setup files, which means to look in the user's home directory for `.xinitrc` and/or `.xserverrc` files. `startx` should also look to see whether or not system-wide `xinitrc` and `xserverrc` files exist. On every system that I've ever seen, there are system-wide `xinitrc` files, but I've never seen an xserverrc file.

- Once `startx` has determined whether there is a client setup script and whether there is a server setup script, then `startx` assembles the command to execute `xinit`. Armed with this information, `startx` runs `xinit`.

Notice that X needs two scripts to start up: `startx` gets the GUI started, then `xinitrc` or `.xinitrc` feeds commands to the already-running GUI. It's a little bit like the way that many Windows systems used to use `autoexec.bat` to load the Windows GUI, then used the `load=` and `run=` commands in `WIN.INI` to load programs in the GUI.

Unfreezing a GUI

While Linux code is pretty stable, I have seen cases where KDE or GNOME simply freeze up and refuse to respond. While that means in the Windows world that you'll probably have to just turn the computer off, that's not necessary in Linux. Here's a quick way to force your GUI to shut down.

First, get to a text login screen. Assuming that you're only running one terminal session, press Ctrl+Alt+F2, Ctrl+Alt+F3, Ctrl+Alt+F4, or Ctrl+Alt+F5 to get a `login:` prompt. Log in as root. Next, find the process ID of the X server—kill that and the whole GUI goes away.

> **WARNING**   Of course, when the GUI goes away, so do your GUI apps. If the GUI's locked up and you rip it out by the roots like this (and I don't know another way), then you'll lose whatever GUI apps you're running. But at least the non-GUI apps, like the web server, mail server, Samba server, etc., won't be affected.

To get X's process ID, just type:

```
ps -A | grep X
```

The number on the extreme left is X's process ID. Put that in a `kill` statement:

```
kill -9 pid
```

The GUI is now shut down. You can restart it as you like now, and you didn't have to reboot or cycle the power switch to fix it. Dan points out that you needn't get this drastic; he uses top to get an idea of what's sucking up the CPU and kills *that* rather than all of X. This has the advantage that you don't lose all of your other GUI apps, just the one that was locking up the system.

Finding Linux Applications

Now that we've worked our way through Linux graphics from the ground up, let's ask the hard question—namely, what applications can I *run* on this GUI?

Run Them on Linux with Wine... Someday

Well, you'll probably be able one day soon to run your favorite Windows applications on Linux, courtesy of the Wine (Wine Is Not an Emulator) Project. Headquartered at www.winehq.com, the Wine folks seek to implement the APIs that are the foundation of Windows applications. You can download and install an early version of Wine—see the website for specific download URLs, though it may even be sitting on your Linux CD—but don't expect rock-solid performance.

Late in 1999, when Corel decided to get serious about Linux, they released a distribution of their own with some very cool utilities aimed specifically at the Windows-using market. Many things about Corel Linux were familiar to Windows users, and that was a clever move on Corel's part. Making a Linux that's more Windows-user-friendly could in the end sell a lot of Linux. In keeping with that, Corel threw programmer support behind the Wine Project. Unfortunately, when Corel abruptly left the Linux world in 2001, it left the Wine folks in the lurch, so it'll probably be a bit longer before you can just drop your favorite Windows programs onto a Linux desktop. Still, it's interesting to play with their interim versions. You can read more about Wine in Chapter 9, where I'll talk about the specifics of setting it up and running it.

Run VMware

A clever program called VMware allows you to run multiple operating systems on the same computer at the same time. Created by VMware, Inc. (www.vmware.com), this program is a great way to make Linux and NT or 2000 work well together.

If you haven'tworked with this tool, I strongly suggest that you give it a look. I have been able to build entire networks of computers—virtual computers—on a single machine, reducing my "test lab equipment" to one PC with a ton of RAM. For example, I needed to work on some of this book while on the road, and I use Microsoft Word for my word processor—but how to run both Red Hat 7.3 and XP on the same box? Simple: VMware.

Applications Built for Linux

Running Windows or NT applications atop Linux will *always* be a bit shaky, so in the long run anyone really wanting to get the most out of Linux should be looking for native Linux applications.

So where *are* they? Well, there are a few parts to that answer. First, there *are* applications for Linux, but not nearly as many as for Windows, NT, or 2000. But some of the players that have signed onto the Linux bandwagon are pretty impressive.

Most of the major database vendors now offer something on Linux. Oracle runs on Linux, and that's the platform that enabled SAP to put their MySAP product on Linux. Informix and Sybase have Linux versions as well. Microsoft *doesn't* offer SQL Server for Linux for some reason. You can even get the old Pick database for Linux.

That so many free applications come with Linux tends, I think, to kill some of the app categories. For example, while Apache's not the absolutely best web server in the world, it's pretty darn good, and I'd be hard-pressed to come up with a reason to replace it with a server that I had to pay money for; the same can be said for BIND or Sendmail. Enough people like Exchange that an Exchange for Linux would probably sell well, but I doubt we'll ever see it (except in the unlikely event that Exchange ever turns out to be sold by a different company than the one that sells Windows 2000).

Most Linux distributions don't come with a CAD package, however, which may be why VariCAD, LinuxCAD, and Varimetrix CAD exist for Linux. I've not used any of them, as I really don't do much CAD, but various reviews on the Web have nice things to say about the packages, even if the tone of the reviews seems to be, "It's a great start, and I'm sure it'll get better."

That seems to be a common theme in Linux applications; for example, in the office desktop applications realm, there are a couple of contenders: StarOffice and Applixware. They're both good early efforts but, again, they don't feel (in my opinion, anyway) as "finished" as commercial Windows applications. But the biggest problem that StarOffice and Applixware face is one that, I think, they can't control: file format compatibility. Like most publishers, Sybex wants its documents in Microsoft Word format. I would have liked to write this on a word processor running under Linux, but I didn't want to incur the extra work of converting a document from a Linux word processor's format to Word format. It is certainly the case that both StarOffice and Applixware claim their word processors offer Word compatibility… but I have some trouble trusting that. It's a promise I've heard in the past from other products, but Microsoft just isn't very forthcoming in explaining the bits and pieces of their file formats. As a result, third-party vendors end up having to reverse-engineer or guess exactly how some portions of the Word format work.

As I hope I've shown you in this chapter, graphics aren't a necessary part of Linux, but they can be a useful add-on, as so many applications rely upon them. Linux's built-in remote control and networking abilities mean that you can run a program as well locally as remotely. And the modular nature of Linux's GUI—or, rather *GUIs*—means that you can build a desktop to suit your needs. Once you've built that desktop, you may find that you have trouble finding a lot of applications that will work on Linux, but most Linux distributions ship with a pretty impressive set of basic applications, and, as always, the price is right.

8

Setting Up Linux's Server Services

By now, you can navigate Linux and do a bit of file editing. In this chapter, you'll get a quick explanation of how to do a basic setup on the most important server software. Before getting into the meat of the chapter, though, I need to offer a general note or two.

Chapter Goals: What We'll Build

The goal Dan and I had in putting this chapter together was to offer you a brief overview and a set of cookbook-style recipes for getting some basic but useful servers up and running. That way, you'll have something to play with and get the "feel" of the major Linux server tools.

Server Types

We'll create these types of servers in this chapter:

- A DNS server
- A DHCP server
- A web server
- A Sendmail e-mail server

- An FTP server
- An Ethernet-to-Ethernet IP router
- A proxy server that lets you share an Internet connection with just one routable IP address with as many other computers that you like
- A dial-in server

We'll also show you how to connect a Linux machine to the Internet via a dial-up modem, cable modem, or DSL connection.

This isn't a comprehensive explanation of how all of these things work—that would be an entire shelf (or perhaps wall) of books. Again, it's just a set of explained examples that intend to let you play with some working Linux tools.

Defining the Prototype Network

In the process of writing this, I've tried to assemble these "cookbooks" to be as internally consistent as possible, as if to help you build a fairly complete Internet framework for an imaginary small- to medium-sized organization. I'll assume that the organization has these characteristics:

- It uses the nonroutable C-class IP network at 192.168.0.0, which is to say that it "owns" the 256 addresses between 192.168.0.0 and 192.168.0.255, uses subnet mask 255.255.255.0, and has a broadcast address of 192.168.0.255.
- Its default gateway is 192.168.0.1.
- It uses two domains: foobirds.org and birdeaters.com.
- It intends to set a machine up at 192.168.0.10, name it wren.foobirds.org, and make it the DNS, DHCP, web, FTP, and e-mail server, all on one box. More specifically— and here's part of what makes the example interesting—wren.foobirds.org will be the DNS, DHCP, web, FTP, and e-mail server for both foobirds.org and birdeaters .com. Furthermore, the fact that foobirds.org and birdeaters.com share the same server won't be obvious; for example, pointing your browser to www.foobirds.org will show something completely different from pointing it to www.birdeaters.com.

Cautions about Following These Examples

If you're not clear on what nonroutable means, please read this; it'll save you a lot of frustration. I wanted to make this example as usable as possible for as wide a range of readers as possible, but I ran into a snag: What IP addresses to use? It would have been simplest to say something like, "I'll build this example based on the C-class network starting at 200.200.200.0/24, and you should replace the leftmost three quads (200.200.200) with whatever the leftmost three quads of your C-class network are," but, of course, most of us don't have a C-class network at our disposal. But I wanted you to be able to build a network with at least a few machines, and so opted to use a nonroutable address range. That way, you can set up as many machines as you like, and they can all communicate with one another without the need to try to get more of the routable IP addresses from your ISP.

The downside of using a network of machines with nonroutable addresses is, of course, that they can't talk to the Internet without a bit of magic. One kind of magic is a simple address-translation scheme like the one offered by Windows 98 Second Edition, Millennium, and Windows 2000, called Internet Connection Sharing (ICS), wherein you have a computer with two IP addresses—one to a routable network and the other to a nonroutable network. Anyone inside the nonroutable part of the network makes requests of the outside Internet, and ICS then pretends that it is making the request with its valid IP address. When it gets the response, it passes that back to the machine with the nonroutable address.

This is a great workaround, a terrific way to share one Internet connection with a bunch of machines. And, as you'll learn in this chapter, Linux can do that as well, with a program called `ipchains` (or `iptables` with the 2.4 kernel). But it's only good for allowing machines inside the nonroutable network to access machines on the Internet. There's no way for a machine on the routable Internet to make a request of a machine in the nonroutable network, so, for example, you couldn't have a web server sitting on one of the nonroutable addresses and still have people on the Internet get access to that web server.

You can do that with the next step up, something called Network Address Translation (NAT). With NAT, you have a router (which could be a PC running routing software or could be a dedicated router device like a Cisco box) again sitting between the Internet and the nonroutable network, and that NAT box can still do the magic to let the systems with the nonroutable addresses get access to systems on the Internet.

But NAT can go one further: if you have more routable IP addresses handy, NAT can "connect" a routable IP address to a nonroutable IP address. So with NAT, you could have a web server at the nonroutable address of 192.168.0.20, and your network might have a routable address of 185.60.53.19 available. So you tell the router to "map" 185.60.53.19 to 192.168.0.20. People on the Internet who want to access the web server would end up asking for the web server at 185.60.53.19, and the NAT router would seamlessly translate that to 192.168.0.20. The only trouble with this approach is that, again, you need a few extra IP addresses—your DSL connection already needs its one IP address for the "router" (which is probably just a PC anyway) itself, and you usually don't get a second address.

Summarizing, then: If you want to follow the examples in this chapter—and I recommend that you do so in order to get a better understanding of how all of these services work—then you'll need a working intranet that communicates amongst itself. But the outside Internet will not be able to "see" your DNS, DHCP, web, or other servers, unless you put all of those services on the in-between computer, the one attached both to your internal network and to the external Internet. That's true even if you use Internet Connection Sharing or ipchains, although any of your intranet systems could access resources on that outside Internet if you're using ICS or ipchains; it's a one-way connection only. But if you do get a second IP address and something with NAT capability, such as a Windows 2000 Server, then you can set up a PC to let your intranet connect completely with the Internet—again, only if you (1) get at least two IP addresses and (2) set up a NAT router of some kind. (You could do that with ipchains, but Dan and I had to stop somewhere.)

> **NOTE** Note that as I'm explaining the basics of how something works, and before developing the actual step-by-step cookbook, you'll often see examples of systems that are indeed attached to the Internet, and that aren't necessarily addressed in the 192.168.0.0/24 network. But in the final cookbooks, I'll work in the 192.168.0.0/24 network.

Working with Services: A Review

In the NT and 2000 world, we're used to having one nice, central location where we can turn services on or off—the Control Panel Services applet in NT, and the Services part of the Manage Computer tool in 2000. Linux doesn't have that, as you learned in Chapter 4. Instead, Linux distributions typically have a set of scripts that can tell a service to start, stop, restart, and perhaps offer status information. For example, on Red Hat 7.3, I can type any of these five commands to control my web server:

```
/etc/rc.d/init.d/httpd status
/etc/rc.d/init.d/httpd stop
/etc/rc.d/init.d/httpd reload
/etc/rc.d/init.d/httpd start
/etc/rc.d/init.d/httpd restart
```

There's a similar script to control the mail server, the DNS server, the routing and firewall tool ipchains, the Samba suite, and so on. You'll need to be able to find and use those scripts in order to get your administration done. Additionally, you typically configure these servers by typing lines into ASCII configuration files—for example, to set up a DNS server, you'll type some information into a file called `named.conf`, because DNS is the name daemon and so gets the nickname `named`. You configure the DHCP server by modifying a file named `dhcpd.conf`, you control Samba with a file called `smb.conf`, and so on: files are typically named *something*`.conf`. You need to be able to find and modify those files in order to configure your server programs.

As you learned in Chapter 5, Red Hat keeps the scripts that control services in `/etc/rc.d/init.d`. Most configuration files—the ones with names that end in `.conf`—tend to be in `/etc`.

Don't forget that the `find` command can help you locate existing `.conf` files. You can also try to `find` the scripts, but you'll see that typically the script has the same name as the program that it starts—for example, the Apache program itself is named `httpd`, and so is its script that controls the web server—so you'll have to do a bit more poking around to figure out which of the files that you see is the script. You can employ a snazzy version of the `find` command to help out, using the `-exec file {} \;` option to first find the files and then run them through the `file` command, which guesses what type of files they are. For example, to find all of the files named `httpd` and then get a comment on what type of files they are, I could enter:

```
find / -name httpd -exec file {} \;
```

On my Red Hat system, that command reports finding several directories named `httpd`, a script named `httpd` in `/etc/rc.d/init.d` (that's what I'm looking for), an empty file (the log file, probably, as I've never started Apache up on that system), and an executable (the Apache program itself). So if I didn't already know that the scripts are in `/etc/rc.d/init.d` on my Red Hat system, then that `find` command would have lit the way for me.

In sum, then, my opening advice to you for this chapter is to take a moment and find where your distribution keeps its scripts, then make a note of it to make following the chapter's contents easier.

Domain Name Service (DNS)

On all Linux systems, domain name service (DNS) is implemented with the Berkeley Internet Name Domain (BIND) software. BIND 9 is the most recent version of the software and is used by all new Linux distributions.

BIND DNS is a client/server system. The client is called the *resolver*, and it forms the queries and sends them to the name server. Under BIND, the resolver is not a distinct process. It is a library of software routines, called the *resolver code*, that is linked into any program that requires name service. Every computer on your network runs a resolver. (If you can start up a web browser on your system, tell it to go to www.birdeaters.com, and have it get there successfully, then you're running a resolver.) Many systems, such as Windows 98 desktops, only run a resolver.

The server side of BIND answers the queries that come from the resolver. The name server daemon is a distinct process called named. The configuration of named is much more complex than the configuration of the resolver, but there is no need to run named on every computer. It only runs on name servers.

Configuring the DNS on the Client Side: The Resolver

On Windows NT/2000 systems, you're used to configuring the DNS servers in the TCP/IP configuration properties—or receiving the list of DNS servers automatically from a DHCP server. While we don't think about it much, Windows systems all contain a piece of software that knows how to ask DNS servers questions and what to do with that information—a "DNS client."

In Linux, the DNS client is the resolver. It is ultimately configured by the /etc/resolv .conf file, although many distributions may now provide a GUI tool to make this configuration "easier"—a comment that I put in quotes because I don't find anything easy to do in linuxconf. Every time a process that uses the resolver starts, it reads the resolv .conf file and caches the configuration for the life of the process. Because every Linux system, both clients and servers, use the resolver, a basic resolv.conf file was probably created by the Linux installation program as described in Chapter 4. Use cat to check what's in the file the installation program created:

```
$ cat /etc/resolv.conf
search foobirds.org
nameserver 192.168.0.10
nameserver 192.168.5.100
```

Note that because Linux reads this file each time it needs to resolve an address, any changes you make to the file take effect immediately and do not require you to modify or restart any services.

NOTE   What happens if you specify a DNS server in resolv.conf, but get your IP address from DHCP? Well, on a Windows system, you know that punching in a DNS server IP address right at a workstation causes that value to override any DHCP-supplied DNS server. That's *not* the case with Linux: the DHCP client actually deletes the old resolv.conf—the one that you made the changes to—and writes a brand-new one that tells the system to use the DNS server that *it*—the DHCP server, that is—wants you to use. You can change this behavior by adding the -R option to the dhcpcd DHCP client, as you'll see in the DHCP section below.

The Resolver Configuration Commands

The sample `resolv.conf` file shown above contains three configuration commands: a `search` command and two `nameserver` entries. `resolv.conf` is a text file that can contain the following commands:

nameserver *address*   The `nameserver` command defines the IP address of a name server the resolver should use. Up to three `nameserver` commands can be included in the configuration. The servers are queried individually in the order that they appear in the file until an answer is received or the resolver times out. The additional servers act as backup servers to the first server listed. The only time the second server is queried is if the first server is down or unreachable. The third server is only queried if both the first and second servers are down or unreachable. If no `nameserver` entry is found in the `resolv.conf` file, the name server running on the local host is used as the default.

domain *domainname*   The `domain` command defines the local domain, which is used to expand the hostname in a query before it is sent to the name server. If the `domain` command is not used, the values defined in the `search` command are used. I'll explain this all a bit more in the text below.

search *searchlist*   The `search` command defines a list of domains that are used to expand a hostname before it is sent to the name server. *searchlist* contains up to six domain names separated by spaces. Each domain specified in the search list is searched in order until the query is answered. Unlike the `domain` command, which creates a default search list containing only the local domain, the `search` command creates an explicit search list containing every domain specified in *searchlist*.

options *option*   The `options` command defines processing options for the resolver. You probably won't use any of them, but I know you're curious, so here they are:

debug   Turns on debugging. When `debug` is set, the resolver prints debugging messages to standard output. This option is of marginal value; turning on debugging in the basic resolver configuration produces too much output and produces it at inappropriate times.

timeout:*n*   Sets the initial query timeout for the resolver. By default it is 5 seconds for the first query to every server. I have never had occasion to change this value, but if you knew for certain that your name server generally took longer than 5 seconds to respond, you could increase the value to reduce the number of duplicate queries.

attempts:*n*   Defines the number of times the resolver retries a query. The default value is 2, which means the resolver will retry a query twice with every server in its server list before returning an error to the application. The `attempts` value might need to be increased if you have a poor network connection that frequently loses queries, perhaps a connection to a remote office in a developing country or at the end of a narrow-band satellite link. I have never had to change this value.

rotate   Turns on round-robin selection of name servers. Normally, the resolver sends the query to the first server in the name server list and only sends the query to another server if the first server does not respond. Traditionally, the second and third name servers were defined to provide backup name service. They were not intended to provide load sharing. The **rotate** option makes it possible for you to tell the resolver to share the name server workload evenly among all of the servers. Here's how it works. Assume the **resolv.conf** file has the following **nameserver** entries:

```
nameserver 192.168.0.1

nameserver 172.16.20.5

nameserver 172.16.55.1
```

Further assume that FTP has asked the resolver for the address of **crow**, Telnet has asked for the address of **kestrel**, and Apache has asked for the address of **grackle**. Without **rotate** set, all three address queries are sent to the name server at 192.168.0.1. With **rotate** set, the resolver sends the query for **crow** to the server at 192.168.0.1, the query for **kestrel** to the server at 172.16.20.5, and the query for **grackle** to 172.16.55.1. The resolver starts at the top of the server list, sends a query to each server in the list, and then starts at the top again.

no-check-names   Disables checking of domain names for compliance with RFC 952. By default, domain names that contain an underscore (_), non-ASCII characters, or ASCII control characters are considered to be in error. If you must work with hostnames that contain an underscore, you should use this option.

TIP   If you have Windows systems on your network that use the underscore in their hostname, you *will* need to use this option in order for your Linux systems to find those Windows computers using DNS.

---

inet6   Causes the resolver to query for IPv6 addresses. The version of the Internet Protocol used in today's Internet is IPv4. IPv4 uses the 32-bit addresses we are all familiar with. IPv6 expands those to 128-bit addresses. IPv6 is a future protocol toward which networks are evolving. Only use this option if you connect to an experimental IPv6 network. You wouldn't normally use this in a business environment.

These options are all put on a single line such as:

```
options rotate no-check-names timeout:10
```

Despite this long list of configuration commands (and more that you can find in the documentation), most `resolv.conf` files contain only a list of name servers and either a `domain` command or a `search` command. Configuration files generated by the Linux installation never contain any other commands, and even those that are manually built by system administrators rarely contain any other commands. For most configurations, you only have to define the name servers and the domain search list; that's sufficient.

The Search List

Most administrators find everything about the resolver easy to understand except how the resolver expands hostnames and how it uses the search list. The search list has only one purpose: to make things easier for users by allowing them to enter short hostnames. Queries to the name server must provide fully qualified domain names (FQDNs), which are names that start with the host and list every domain up to the root. For example, crow is a partial domain name and crow.foobirds.org. is an FQDN. The resolver uses the search list to turn the short hostname entered by the user into the FQDN required by the name server.

Here's how a Linux system resolves a name like wren.foobirds.org. If the user enters a name that contains one or more dots, the name is sent to the name server as is. It is only extended with a domain from the search list if it cannot be resolved as typed by the users. Thus, wren.foobirds.org would not be extended.

If, on the other hand, the user enters a name that does not contain any dots, the resolver appends the domain name stored in the search list and then sends the result to the name server. If the name server cannot resolve the name, the resolver tries again using the next domain name in the search list and keeps on trying until the list of domain names is exhausted. If none of the domain names works, a final attempt is made by sending the name to the name server exactly as it was typed.

For example, assume your `resolv.conf` file includes a `search` command that defines a search list containing swans.foobirds.org and foobirds.org. If the user enters the name wren, the resolver extends it to `wren.swans.foobirds.org`. If the name server cannot resolve the requested name, the resolver tries again with `wren.foobirds.org`. If the name server can't resolve `wren.foobirds.org`, the resolver makes a final try by sending just wren.

To have more than one domain in the search list, you must use the `search` command. The `domain` command defines just one domain—the local domain. The local domain then becomes the only value in the search list. In general, however, that is all you need. This permits the user to access computers that are in the local domain by hostname alone, and for most users, this is sufficient.

> **NOTE**   The `domain` command and the `search` command are mutually exclusive. Whichever command appears *last* in the `resolv.conf` file is the one that defines the search list.

Configuring DNS Servers

DNS clients aren't any good without DNS servers, so now let's see how to set up a DNS server with Linux. Like Windows NT/2000, Linux supports three basic name server configurations:

- A *master* (or *primary*) server is the main server for a DNS domain. It loads the domain information directly from a local disk file maintained by the domain administrator. The master server is considered authoritative for the domain, and its answers to queries are always considered to be accurate.

- A *slave* (or *secondary*) server is also considered an authoritative server, because it has a complete and accurate domain database that it transfers from the master server at a regular interval.

- A *caching* server is a nonauthoritative server. It gets all of its answers to name server queries from other name servers. The main reason for setting up a caching server is to speed up the time it takes for local clients to receive the answers to their DNS requests.

> **NOTE**   On most Linux systems, DNS servers combine elements of more than one configuration. All DNS servers cache answers, and many primary servers are also secondary servers for some other domains. Mix and match these server configurations as needed for your network.

You should create only one master server for each DNS domain. It is the ultimate source of information about your domain. Create at least one slave server. It shares the workload and provides backup for the master server. (Many domain administrators create two official slave servers.) Use caching servers throughout your network to reduce the load on your master and secondary servers, and to reduce network traffic by placing name servers close to your users.

> **NOTE** If you're fuzzy on how DNS works, you'll find a more complete discussion in *Mastering Windows 2000 Server,* Fourth Edition (Chapter 7).

Checking the Server Installation

Before we configure our DNS server, we need to be sure that it is installed correctly. The simplest way to see if it's there is to use the `which` command when you are logged in as root:

```
# which named
/usr/sbin/named
#
```

Assuming you got back a response, you'll know that your system has a DNS server installed. If you just got a prompt back, it might not be installed. On systems with the `rpm` command, you can also try:

```
# rpm -q bind
bind-9.2.0-8
#
```

Note that you might need to do `rpm -q bind9`. If that comes back empty, you might just see if the file `/usr/sbin/named` exists. On Linux systems, `named` is almost always located in `/usr/sbin`.

Installing BIND If It's Not Already There

If you *don't* have a DNS server installed on your system already, then mount Red Hat Installation CD 2.

Loading the RPMs   Assuming you've mounted it as `/misc/cd`, you can then install it and its attendant programs:

```
cd /misc/cd/RedHat/RPMS
rpm -ivh bind-9.2.0-8.i386.rpm
```

Creating a Basic Set of Configuration Files   For some reason, `rpm` does not include two files that you absolutely need to get BIND started: a `named.conf` file and a `named.ca` file. The `named.ca` file is the file that tells your DNS server where the world-wide "root servers" are. It's also known as a hints file, and in the NT world it's in `\winnt\system32\dns\cache.dns`.

You can get a named.ca file directly from the root servers themselves:

```
cd /var/named
ftp ftp.rs.internic.net (Note: log on as anonymous.)
cd /domain
get named.ca
bye
```

Don't be surprised if you have to do it a couple of times—that server is very busy. Another approach is to copy it from an NT/2000/.NET DNS server; the file is the same. Just be sure to use mcopy on the Linux side to copy it to your Linux box so that the carriage return/line feed issue is fixed.

You'll then need a basic named.conf file. Create it with vi in the /etc directory:

```
options { directory "/var/named"; };
zone "." in {type hint; file "named.ca";};
```

You can also cheat a bit and use a prebuilt set of configuration files on that same Red Hat Installation CD 2:

```
rpm -ivh caching-nameserver-7.2-1.noarch.rpm
```

Hands-On: Trying Out the DNS Server

If you're one of the impatient types who *just wants to see it do something and do it NOW*, then let's jump ahead and just test-drive this server. This will only work if you're connected to the Internet, so make sure you have a live connection to the Net before trying this. (If you don't, then don't worry about doing this exercise.) If you're running Red Hat and have either installed with the "everything" option or installed the RPMs as described above, then you *already* have a basic DNS server running.

For some reason, even if you install the DNS server, Red Hat doesn't start it up. Check whether or not your DNS server is running by typing:

```
ps -A | grep named
```

If you get any lines with named as output—I get four lines when I run a DNS server—then the server's already running. If not, type:

```
/etc/rc.d/init.d/named start
```

Now you're ready to take it out for a spin.

1. You can test it out with a tool called nslookup, as you learned while setting up NT- or 2000-based DNS servers. Type nslookup and press Enter.

2. Type `server 127.0.0.1` to make `nslookup` use this computer as its server.

3. Now ask it for the IP address of a DNS address, any address. Try my web server— type in `www.minasi.com` and press Enter.

4. You should get the answer `206.246.253.111` (unless I've changed it by the time you read this).

5. Type `exit` and press Enter to exit `nslookup`.

That's it—your DNS server is now officially up and running. It doesn't have any zones on it, but it can resolve addresses, so long as it's connected to the Internet. Let's return to the nuts and bolts of DNS setup to see how to take this further.

Starting and Stopping the DNS Server

Once you have it installed, you start and stop the DNS server with the named script found in `/etc/rc.d/init.d`. If you want to manually issue the command, you can do something like:

```
# cd /etc/rc.d/init.d
# ./named stop
Stopping named: [ OK ]
# ./named start
Starting named:    [ OK ]
#
```

or use `./named restart` to perform both actions at once. If the `stop` command does not work, you'll need to use `ps` to identify the process ID and then kill off the process.

As I mentioned before, for some reason Red Hat setups seem *never* to create a startup link for any of the runlevels, so if you want this system to come up as a DNS server, you're gonna have to put a link like S11named or something like that in one or more of your runlevel directories. Or here's a nice Red Hat utility that'll make it a bit easier: from a command prompt, type `setup`, choose `System services`, and then check the box next to `named` to make it start automatically.

NOTE   Don't forget that setup routine—it's a nice text-mode system configuration utility that ties together a bunch of other setup routines.

Changing the Configuration Files

Now with Windows NT/2000, you're used to using a graphical tool such as the DNS Manager to configure DNS. There *are* GUI tools available for Linux, and you could configure DNS using those tools, but ultimately they all control a series of text files. For that reason, and because you might not have a server with a GUI, we're going to look directly at the files themselves.

Up to five different types of files are required for a named configuration. All configurations require these three basic files:

named **configuration file** The named.conf configuration file defines basic parameters and points to the sources of domain database information, which can be local files or remote servers. It's usually in /etc.

Hints file The hints, or cache, file provides the names and addresses of the root DNS servers that are authoritative for the top-level domains of the DNS hierarchy (like .com, .edu, .org). This is usually in the /var/named directory.

Local host file All configurations have a local zone file for resolving the loopback address to the hostname localhost. This is /var/named/named.local on RH73.

> **NOTE** If you have used other Unix systems or older Linux systems, you may be familiar with a file called named.boot. With BIND version 8, named.conf replaced the named.boot file. On many Linux systems, you'll still find a named.boot file, although it is there primarily for compatibility purposes and is no longer used. The syntax and structure of the file is completely different, so you can't just rename a named.boot file to named.conf or something.

The other two files that are used to configure named are only used on the master server. These are the two files that define the domain database:

Zone file The zone file defines most of the information. It is used to map hostnames to addresses, to identify the mail servers, and to provide a variety of other domain information. These files are usually in the /var/named directory.

Reverse zone file The reverse zone file maps IP addresses to hostnames, which is exactly the opposite of what the domain file does. These files are usually in the /var/named directory.

A domain database file is called a zone file because the piece of the domain name space over which a master server has control is called that server's *zone of authority*.

To configure DNS, you need to understand how to configure all five configuration files. We will begin with the named.conf file, as it is used on every name server and defines the basic configuration.

The *named.conf* File

There are seven valid configuration statements for the BIND named.conf file. They are listed alphabetically in Table 8.1 with a short description of each command.

Table 8.1   named.conf Configuration Statements

Command	Usage
acl	Defines an access control list of IP addresses
include	Includes another file into the configuration file
key	Defines security keys for authentication
logging	Defines what will be logged and where it will be stored
options	Defines global configuration options and defaults
server	Defines a remote server's characteristics
zone	Defines a zone

Most configurations use only two of the commands: options and zone. The next sections examine the most commonly used commands in more detail.

The *options* Statement   Most named.conf files open with an options statement that defines global parameters for BIND and sets the defaults used by other statements in the configuration file. Only one options statement is allowed. On most Linux systems, the options statement looks just like this:

```
options {
    directory "/var/named";
};
```

This statement defines the working directory for the server. The curly braces in an options statement enclose all of the options. In the example, which is the most common case, only the directory option is used. It defines the directory that named reads files from and writes files to. The directory name is also used to complete any filenames specified in the configuration file. The literal enclosed in quotes is the path name of the directory. Notice that both the directory clause and the options statement end with a semicolon.

One other option handles something that I was interested in. I wanted to make sure that I could use underscore characters (_) in hostnames. Normally, these names are rejected by BIND because they violate some rules defined in RFC 974. The check-names option specifies what the server should do if it finds invalid hostnames in the zone file. The default is for a master server to discard the offending name and display an error message. The default for a slave server is to accept the offending name and issue a warning, and the default for a server receiving a noncompliant name in a response is to accept the name and ignore the error. The check-names option lets you map the situation (master, slave, or response) to the action you want to take (fail, warn, or ignore). fail discards the name and issues an error message. warn accepts the name and displays a warning message, and ignore just ignores any errors. To load names with underscore characters into my master server, I use this options statement:

```
options {
    directory "/var/named";
    check-names master ignore;
};
```

The check-names option affects all zones for which this computer is the master server. In most cases, I prefer to set an option specifically for the zone that is being affected. The designers of BIND have set the defaults correctly for the vast majority of zones. Zones that need other values are exceptions and should be treated as such by defining the exceptional characteristics directly on the zone statement.

The *zone* Statement   The zone statements are the most important statements in the configuration file, and they constitute the bulk of the named.conf file. A zone statement performs the following critical configuration functions:

- It defines a zone that is serviced by this name server.
- It defines the type of name server that this server is for the zone. A server can be a master server or a slave server. And because this is defined on a per-zone basis, the same server can be the master for some zones while being a slave for others.
- It defines the source of domain information for a zone. The domain database can be loaded from a local disk file or transferred from the master server.
- It defines special processing options for the zone.

A sample zone statement can illustrate all of these functions:

```
zone "foobirds.org" in {
    type master;
    file "foobirds.hosts";
    check-names fail;
};
```

The statement begins with the `zone` command. The name of the zone is written as a literal enclosed in quotes. The `in` keyword means that this zone contains IP addresses and Internet domain names. This is the default, so `in` is not really required. The curly braces enclose a list of options for this zone.

The `type master;` option says that this server is the master server for the `foobirds.org` domain. Other possible values are:

`slave`   This is a slave server for the domain.

`hints`   This is the hints file that is used to initialize the name server during startup. Every server has one hints zone.

The `file "foobirds.hosts";` option points to the file that contains the domain database information. For a master server, this is the file that is created by the domain administrator.

The last option is in the example primarily to illustrate that options can be defined for individual zones. The `check-names warn;` option tells the server to accept hostnames that contain underscore characters and to give me a warning about them. In this case, there is no need to specify `master` on the `check-names` command line, because the zone type is already set to master by the `type` command.

In most `named.conf` files, the `zone` statements are no more complicated than the example shown above.

A Sample *named.conf*   So let's put this all together and show an example of `named.conf` in a typical situation with the same machine being the master server for two domain names:

```
# cat /etc/named.conf
options {
    directory "/var/named";
};
zone "foobirds.org" {
    type master;
    file "foobirds.org.zone";
    check-names ignore;
};
zone "birdeaters.com" {
    type master;
    file "birdeaters.com.zone";
};
```

> **NOTE** The actual name of the DNS zone files does not matter to the named server. In NT/2000, these files are usually called *zonename*.dns, and you can use that convention here in Linux as well. You'll find that some Linux administrators will use db.*zonename* or *zonename*.zone. It makes no difference to named.

Note that this DNS server could answer queries about foobirds.org or birdeaters.com *but nothing else*. If this were your only DNS server, it couldn't resolve other Internet addresses, such as www.microsoft.com or the like. To add the general-resolution-ability feature, we need to add a few files, the ones that a caching-only configuration uses.

A Caching-Only Configuration

The caching-only configuration is the foundation of all server configurations, because all servers cache answers. The basic caching-only configuration created by Red Hat 7.3 during the Linux installation is shown below:

```
# cat /etc/named.conf
options {
    directory "/var/named";
};
//
// a caching only nameserver config
//
zone "." {
    type hint;
    file "named.ca";
};
zone "0.0.127.in-addr.arpa" {
    type master;
    file "named.local";
};
```

The two zone statements in this caching-only configuration are found in all server configurations. The first zone statement defines the hints file that helps the name server locate the root servers during startup. The second zone statement makes the server the master for its own loopback address and points to the local host file. The hints file and the local host file, along with the named.conf file, are required for every server configuration.

The Hints File

The hints file contains the names and addresses of the root name servers. The file helps the local server locate a root server during the startup. Once a root server is located, an authoritative list of root servers is downloaded from that server. The hints are not referred to again until the local server restarts.

> **NOTE**   Note that versions of BIND prior to version 8 referred to the *hints* file as the *cache* file. You may find this still true in other DNS implementations or on older Linux/Unix systems.

The named.conf file points to the location of the hints file. The hints file can be given any filename. Commonly used names are named.ca, named.root, and root.cache. In the example above, the hints file is called named.ca and is located in the /var/named directory.

You will not ever need to create or edit this hints file, and it should be provided by the Linux installation, provided you install the RPM with the caching-only files. But even if your system doesn't provide a hints file, it is easy to get one. The official list of root servers is kept at the InterNIC. Download the file /domain/named.root from ftp.rs.internic.net via anonymous FTP. The file that is stored there is in the correct format for a Linux system, is ready to run, and can be downloaded directly to your hints file.

The Local Host File

Every name server is the master of its own loopback domain, which only makes sense. The whole point of creating the loopback interface (lo0) is to reduce network traffic. Sending domain queries about the loopback address across the network would defeat that purpose.

The loopback domain is a reverse domain. It is used to map the loopback address 127.0.0.1 back to the hostname localhost. On a Red Hat system, the zone file for this domain is called named.local, which is the most common name for the local host file. (You may also see it as 127.0.0.zone.) The Red Hat installation provides the following file:

```
# cat /var/named/named.local
@    IN    SOA    localhost. root.localhost. (
                  1997022700  ; Serial
                  28800       ; Refresh
                  14400       ; Retry
                  3600000     ; Expire
```

```
                 86400 )       ; Minimum
     IN     NS     localhost.
1    IN     PTR    localhost.
```

Every Linux system that runs named has an essentially identical local host file. This one was created automatically by the Red Hat installation; if your system doesn't create one, you can copy this one. There is really no need to edit or change this file to run it on your system. At this point, the contents of the file don't need to be discussed, because they are always the same on every system. (You will see examples of all of these database records later in the chapter.)

Acting As a Slave or Secondary Server

Okay, so we've talked about being the master server for a domain and also about the caching and localhost issues, but what about having a Linux server be a slave (or secondary) server? It turns out to be quite simple. The entry in named.conf looks almost like the master server entry:

```
zone "bluegold.com" {
    type slave;
    file "bluegold.com.zone";
    masters { 192.168.50.1; };
};
```

You'll notice that you still have a file directive, as ultimately named is going to store the information inside of a text file. However, you do not need to create this file, as named will do so automatically when it first downloads the information from the master server.

Notice that your type is now slave, and more importantly there is a masters line that identifies the master server from where your local named should download the zone information. You could put multiple IP addresses here, but in practice there is generally only one IP address.

Note that your Linux DNS server could be a slave server to another Linux server, a Unix server, or a Windows NT/2000 server.

WARNING   A Linux server can be a slave server to a Windows NT 4 DNS server provided that the NT server is not using the WINS record to provide dynamic updating of DNS through a WINS server. (I found this out the hard way when one of my NT 4 DNS servers just about blew up my poor ISP's Unix DNS servers back in 1996.) This is not supported by Linux servers. However, the newest versions of BIND *will* interoperate with Windows 2000 servers and Active Directory. The version of BIND supplied with your Linux distribution may not do this, though, and you may need to download and install a new version from www.isc.org/products/BIND.

We'll talk later about setting the length of time between downloads by the slave from the master. Suffice it to say that the interval is controlled by a record in the zone file on the *master* server and can therefore vary from zone to zone. But more on that in a few minutes.

Assembling an Example *named.conf*

First, let's take our earlier example and add the other normal entries for the hints and localhost files, as well as an entry for being a slave to another domain. This named.conf allows this server to resolve DNS names in the general Internet, to act as the primary server for forward-resolved foobirds.org and birdeaters.com zones, a primary for the reverse-resolved 192.168.0.0/24 zone, and a secondary server for bluegold.com:

```
# cat /etc/named.conf
options {
    directory "/var/named";
};
zone "." {
    type hint;
    file "named.ca";
};
zone "0.0.127.in-addr.arpa" {
    type master;
    file "named.local";
};
zone "0.168.192.in-addr.arpa" {
    type master;
    file "192.rev.zone";
};
zone "foobirds.org" {
    type master;
    file "foobirds.org.zone";
  check-names ignore;
};
zone "birdeaters.com" {
    type master;
```

```
        file "birdeaters.com.zone";
    };
    zone "bluegold.com" {
        type slave;
        file "bluegold.com.zone";
        masters { 192.168.50.1; };
    };
```

This is all the configuration you normally need to do for the named.conf file. Now let's look at the zone files.

The Zone Files

When you created a new DNS domain in Windows NT using the DNS Manager, the application created zone files for you and automatically created entries such as your SOA (start of authority) and NS (nameserver) records. You didn't have to do anything else except add new hosts. Nor did you really have to care about the actual files, although it is possible in NT to write out the DNS files and take a look at them.

Well, here in the land of Linux you have to create the files yourself. (Okay, yes, there are GUI tools that do this, too, but we're talking about the basic way you'd do this without any fancy tools. And, in my opinion, most of the Linux GUI-based admin tools are pretty wobbly, although the webmin tool of Mandrake 7.1 isn't bad.)

TIP   If your DNS server is secondary for some zone, then you needn't create a zone file for that zone—named automatically creates zone files on secondary servers. And in case it's not clear yet, a given DNS server can be both primary for some zones and secondary for others at the same time.

All the zone files have the same basic format as the example that follows. I'm going to jump right in and give you a full listing of a file that might be foobirds.org.zone.

```
    $TTL 1d
    ;
    ;   The foobirds.org domain database
    ;
    @  IN SOA    wren.foobirds.org. sara.wren.foobirds.org. (
                 2000031301 ; Serial
```

```
              21600        ; Refresh
              1800         ; Retry
              4w           ; Expire
              1h )         ; Negative cache TTL
; Define the nameservers
              IN      NS        wren.foobirds.org.
              IN      NS        falcon.foobirds.org.
              IN      NS        bear.mammals.org.
; Define the mail servers
              IN      MX        10 wren.foobirds.org.
              IN      MX        20 parrot.foobirds.org.
;
;     Define the hosts in this zone
;
wren          IN      A         192.168.0.10
parrot        IN      A         192.168.0.3
crow          IN      A         192.168.0.5
hawk          IN      A         192.168.0.4
falcon        IN      A         192.168.0.20
puffin        IN      A         192.168.0.17
              IN      MX        5 wren.foobirds.org.
robin         IN      A         192.168.0.2
              IN      MX        5 wren.foobirds.org.
;
;     Define the aliases in this zone
;
redbreast     IN      CNAME     robin.foobirds.org.
www           IN      CNAME     wren.foobirds.org.
news          IN      CNAME     parrot.foobirds.org.
```

The first things you'll probably notice are the comments. Where are the # signs? In yet another example of things being done slightly differently in Linux, the DNS zone files use the semicolon (;) for comments.

The first "real" line contains an at symbol (@), which is a variable representing the domain name this file is for. Think of it this way. In named.conf we said we were a master server for foobirds.org and that the file for that domain was foobirds.org.zone. So now @ represents "foobirds.org".

WARNING   Notice that all of the DNS names, like wren.foobirds.org. here or in the named.ca file "localhost." previously, end in a period. That's really important: if you don't end a name with a period, then BIND adds the domain name to get what *it* thinks you intended for a name. For example, if I hadn't included a period at the end of wren.foobirds.org, then BIND would think that I was directing it to a machine named wren.foobirds.org.foobirds.org.

Beyond that, you'll see many of the records you'll remember from working with Windows NT/2000. Table 8.2 summarizes the major types of records.

Table 8.2   DNS Database Record Types

Record Name	Record Type	Function
Start of authority	SOA	Marks the beginning of a zone's data and defines parameters that affect the entire zone
Nameserver	NS	Identifies a domain's name server
Address	A	Maps a hostname to an address
Pointer	PTR	Maps an address to a hostname
Mail exchanger	MX	Identifies the mail server for a domain
Canonical name	CNAME	Defines an alias for a hostname

I'm not going to go into excruciating detail on all of these, but I do want to explore the SOA and MX records.

Before that, though, what about the first line, $TTL 1d? The first line in the file is not actually a record. It is a zone file directive. It defines the default time to live (TTL) for the entire zone file. This is the time that records from this zone will be cached by other DNS servers. The default TTL is used by any resource record that does not contain an explicit TTL. The sample sets the default TTL to one day (1d), which is an average TTL. If the data in your domain is stable, you can set a high default TTL of several days and explicitly set a shorter TTL on those individual records that you expect to change.

The SOA Record

The first resource record in all zone files is an SOA record. As mentioned above, the @ in the name field of the SOA record refers to the domain name defined in the zone statement of the configuration file, which in this case is foobirds.org.

The data field of the SOA record is so long it normally spans several lines. The parentheses are continuation characters. After an opening parenthesis, all data on subsequent lines are considered part of the current record until a closing parenthesis.

The seven components of the data field in the sample SOA record contain the following values:

wren.foobirds.org   The hostname of the master server for this zone.

sara.wren.foobirds.org   The e-mail address of the person responsible for this domain. The at sign (@) that is normally used between the username (sara) and the hostname (wren.foobirds.org) is replaced with a dot (.).

WARNING   Note that the e-mail address must NOT contain the @ sign, because that is now a variable representing the domain name. When you're typing a DNS zone file by hand, it's easy to make this mistake. Don't.

2000031301   The serial number, a numeric value that tells the slave server that the zone file has been updated. If the serial number in the master server's SOA record is greater than the serial number of the slave server's copy of the zone, the slave transfers the entire zone from the master. Otherwise, the slave assumes it has a current copy of the zone and skips the zone transfer. The serial number must be increased every time the domain is updated in order to keep the slave servers synchronized with the master.

NOTE   Note that you can use any number for the serial number as long as it constantly increases. Windows NT 4 starts out using a serial number of 1 and increments it with each change. The format shown here is a common convention *yyyymmddxx*, where *xx* is a number incrementing on that day. This format serves two purposes: (1) it will always increment positively, and (2) it gives you a date stamp of when you modified this file.

21600   The length of the refresh cycle. Every refresh cycle, the slave server checks the serial number of the SOA record from the master server to determine if the zone needs to be transferred. This is how you control the time interval between when the slave server downloads a new zone file from the master.

1800   The retry cycle. The retry cycle defines the length of time that the slave server should wait before asking again when the master server fails to respond to a request for the SOA record. Don't set the value too low; an hour (3,600 seconds) or a half-hour (1,800 seconds) are good retry values.

4w   The expiration time, the length of time that the slave server should continue to respond to queries even if it cannot update the zone file. The idea is that, at some point in time, out-of-date data is worse than no data. This should be a substantial amount of time. After all, the main purpose of a slave server is to provide backup for the master server.

1h   The TTL used by remote servers to cache negative information. For example, if your server tells a remote server that the host ibis.foobirds.org does not exist, that server will remember that negative information for one hour (1h).

NOTE   There are two ways to define time limits: either as a number of seconds, as in the refresh and retry examples, or as a combination of letters and numbers, as in the $TTL, expire, and negative cache examples. The letters that can be used are: w for week, d for day, h for hour, and s for second.

All of the components of the data field of the SOA record set values that affect the entire domain. Several of these items affect remote servers. You decide how often slave servers check for updates and how long caching servers keep your data in their caches. The domain administrator is responsible for the design of the entire domain.

Defining the Mail Servers

The MX records in the sample file define the mail servers for this domain. The name field is still blank, meaning that these records pertain to the last named object, which in this case is the entire domain:

```
; Define the mail servers
        IN    MX    10 wren.foobirds.org.
        IN    MX    20 parrot.foobirds.org.
```

The first MX record says that wren is the mail server for the foobirds.org domain with a preference of 10. If mail is addressed to user@foobirds.org, the mail is directed to wren for delivery.

The second MX record identifies `parrot` as a mail server for `foobirds.org` with a preference of 20. The lower the preference number, the more preferred the server. This means that mail addressed to the `foobirds.org` domain is first sent to `wren`. Only if `wren` is unavailable is the mail sent to `parrot`, which acts as a backup for those times when `wren` is down or offline.

The MX records redirect mail addressed to the domain `foobirds.org`, but they do not redirect mail addressed to an individual host. Therefore, if mail is addressed to `jay@hawk.foobirds.org`, it is delivered directly to `hawk`; it is not sent to a mail server. This configuration permits people to use e-mail addresses of the form `user@domain` when they like, or to use direct delivery to an individual host when they want that. It is a very flexible configuration.

Some systems, however, may not be capable of handling direct delivery e-mail. An example is a Windows 98 system that doesn't run an SMTP mail server program. Mail addressed to such a system would not be successfully delivered and, worse, would probably be reported to you as a network error! To prevent this, assign an MX record to the individual host to redirect its mail to a valid mail server. There are two examples of this in the sample zone file. Look at the resource records for `puffin` and `robin`:

```
puffin      IN    A      192.168.0.17
            IN    MX     5 wren.foobirds.org.
robin       IN    A      192.168.0.2
            IN    MX     5 wren.foobirds.org.
```

The address record of each system is followed by an MX record that directs mail to `wren`. The MX records have a blank name field, but this time they don't refer to the domain. In both cases, the last value in the name field is the name from the preceding address record. It is this name that the MX record applies to. In one case it is `puffin`, and in the other it is `robin`. With these records, mail addressed to `daniel@puffin.foobirds.org` is delivered to `daniel@wren.foobirds.org`.

> **NOTE**   Actually, I only included the notion of MX records for particular computers for the sake of completeness—I've never had a real-world situation where I needed to do that, so you'll probably only need an MX record or two for your one or two mail servers.

The MX record is only the first step in creating a mail server. The MX is necessary to tell the remote computer where it should send the mail, but for the mail server to successfully deliver the mail to the intended user, it must be properly configured.

The Reverse Zone File

Okay, so that was the zone file, but what about the reverse zone file? This file maps IP addresses to hostnames. This is the reverse of what the domain database does when it maps hostnames to addresses. Think about it. There's no order to the IP addresses listed in a regular zone file. Someone wanting to find what host belonged to what IP address would have to search all the zone files on the local system and, indeed, on the Internet. It could be a nightmare. To solve this, the system of reverse zone files was put into place.

So, why do you care about this? Well, many operations on the Internet will work perfectly fine *without* a reverse zone file (sometimes called a *reverse lookup* file). But in the age of spam e-mail, some sites on the Internet will only accept e-mail from servers for which they can look up the domain name given the IP address. Likewise for security reasons, some sites (such as FTP archives) may again deny access if they cannot determine the hostname of the IP address from which you are coming. You don't have to set up reverse zones—and, in fact, your ISP may not let you—but if you can, it may help your users as they work across the Internet.

For your information, there is another reason why these files are called reverse domains: all of the IP addresses are written in reverse. For example, in the reverse domain, the address 192.168.0.2 is written as `2.0.168.192.in-addr.arpa`. The address is reversed to make it compatible with the structure of a regular DNS domain name. An IP address is written from the most general to the most specific. It starts with a network address, moves through a subnet address, and ends with a host address. The hostname is just the opposite: it starts with the host, moves through subdomain and domain, and ends with a top-level domain. To format an address like a hostname, the host part of the address is written first, and the network is written last. The network address becomes the domain name, and the host address becomes a hostname within the domain.

In our example, the network address 192.168.0.0/24 becomes the domain `0.168.192`
`.in-addr.arpa`. The zone file for this domain is shown below:

```
;     Address to hostname mappings.
;
@  IN SOA  wren.foobirds.org. sara.wren.foobirds.org. (
         1999022702  ;  Serial
         21600       ;  Refresh
         1800        ;  Retry
         604800      ;  Expire
         86400 )     ;  Minimum
```

	IN	NS	wren.foobirds.org.
	IN	NS	falcon.foobirds.org.
	IN	NS	bear.mammals.org.
10	IN	PTR	wren.foobirds.org.
2	IN	PTR	robin.foobirds.org.
3	IN	PTR	parrot.foobirds.org.
4	IN	PTR	hawk.foobirds.org.
5	IN	PTR	crow.foobirds.org.
17	IN	PTR	puffin.foobirds.org.
20	IN	PTR	falcon.foobirds.org.

Like other zone files, the reverse zone begins with an SOA record and a few NS records. They serve the same purpose and have the same fields as their counterparts in a domain database, which were explained above.

PTR records make up the bulk of the reverse domain, because they are used to translate addresses to hostnames. Look at the first PTR record. The name field contains 10. This is not a fully qualified name, so it is interpreted as relative to the current domain, giving us 10.0.168.192.in-addr.arpa as the value of the name field. The data field of a PTR record contains a hostname. The hostname in the data field is always fully qualified to prevent it from being interpreted as relative to the current domain. In the first PTR record, the data field is wren.foobirds.org. A PTR query for 10.0.168.192.in-addr.arpa (192.168.0.10) returns the value wren.foobirds.org.

The reverse zone may seem like a lot of trouble for a little gain; after all, most of the action happens in the hostname space. But keeping the reverse zone up-to-date is important. Several programs use the reverse domain to map IP addresses to names for status displays; netstat is a good example. Some remote systems use reverse lookup to check on who is using a service and, in extreme cases, won't allow you to use the service if they can't find your system in the reverse domain. Failing to keep the reverse domain updated is sure to generate complaints from your users.

And where, by the way, would BIND complain if something went wrong? Look in /var/log/messages; BIND's (and other programs') messages are there. I filter out just the BIND messages by doing cat /var/log/messages|grep named.

Cookbook Summary: DNS

Let's finish this "cookbook" by summarizing exactly what you have to do to make this basic DNS server work on your Linux system and by assembling the complete set of configuration files. This DNS server will act as a primary DNS server for foobirds.org and birdeaters.com. Additionally, foobirds.org will allow underscores in its hostnames. I'll get rid of the bluegold.com secondary role, because I'd need to set up another server as primary for bluegold.com in order to complete the example, and I'm trying to keep this a tractable example! I've also simplified the example a bit for the same reason, employing just one name server and one mail server for each domain.

This system will *also* be able to resolve DNS names in general from the Internet hierarchy of DNS servers, *if* you have Internet Connection Sharing, ipchains, or something similar to allow those one-way communications from inside your private nonroutable network. If not, then trying to resolve DNS names for the outside world will fail.

We'll end up with these files:

- /etc/named.conf, the overall named configuration file
- /var/named/foobirds.org.zone, the forward-lookup zone file for foobirds.org
- /var/named/birdeaters.com.zone, the forward-lookup zone file for birdeaters.com
- /var/named/192.rev.zone, the reverse-lookup zone file for the 192.168.0.0 C-class subnet
- /var/named/named.ca, the "hints" file of root DNS servers
- /var/named/named.local, the reverse lookup zone file for 127.0.0.1

Install the DNS Server

Locate your Red Hat 7.3 distribution CD-ROM and put it in the CD-ROM drive. Then install the server and some starter files with these commands:

```
rpm -i /misc/cdrom/RedHat/RPMS/bind
rpm -i /misc/cdrom/RedHat/RPMS/cach*
```

You should now be able to do a which named and get a response; you should have a directory named /var/named that contains a file named named.ca and another named named.local, as well as a file in /etc named named.conf.

Create the Files

You don't have to create two of the five configuration files in this example, named.ca and named.local. But in case you're trying to follow along on a non–Red Hat system, here are their contents, stripped of nonessentials, as well as the new zone files and named.conf. I have assumed that your Linux machine is at IP address 200.100.100.10, but just change that to whatever its actual address is.

Listing 8.1   /var/named/named.ca

```
. 3600000 IN NS  A.ROOT-SERVERS.NET.
A.ROOT-SERVERS.NET. 3600000 A 198.41.0.4
. 3600000 NS  B.ROOT-SERVERS.NET.
B.ROOT-SERVERS.NET. 3600000 A 128.9.0.107
. 3600000 NS  C.ROOT-SERVERS.NET.
C.ROOT-SERVERS.NET. 3600000 A 192.33.4.12
. 3600000 NS  D.ROOT-SERVERS.NET.
D.ROOT-SERVERS.NET. 3600000 A 128.8.10.90
. 3600000 NS  E.ROOT-SERVERS.NET.
E.ROOT-SERVERS.NET. 3600000 A 192.203.230.10
. 3600000 NS  F.ROOT-SERVERS.NET.
F.ROOT-SERVERS.NET. 3600000 A 192.5.5.241
. 3600000 NS  G.ROOT-SERVERS.NET.
G.ROOT-SERVERS.NET. 3600000 A 192.112.36.4
. 3600000 NS  H.ROOT-SERVERS.NET.
H.ROOT-SERVERS.NET. 3600000 A 128.63.2.53
. 3600000 NS  I.ROOT-SERVERS.NET.
I.ROOT-SERVERS.NET. 3600000 A 192.36.148.17
. 3600000 NS  J.ROOT-SERVERS.NET.
J.ROOT-SERVERS.NET. 3600000 A 198.41.0.10
. 3600000 NS  K.ROOT-SERVERS.NET.
K.ROOT-SERVERS.NET. 3600000 A 193.0.14.129
. 3600000 NS  L.ROOT-SERVERS.NET.
L.ROOT-SERVERS.NET. 3600000 A 198.32.64.12
. 3600000 NS  M.ROOT-SERVERS.NET.
M.ROOT-SERVERS.NET. 3600000 A 202.12.27.33
```

If, on the other hand, you know that your network will *never* be connected to the Internet, then just put this in your `named.ca`:

```
. 3600000 IN NS wren.foobirds.org.

wren.foobirds.org. 3600000 A 192.168.0.10
```

And in case you can't see it on the printed page, the first line of each pair consists of a period, then at least one space, then 3600000, then another space, then IN, then another space, then NS, then another space, then `wren.foobirds.org`. The following line contains `wren.foobirds.org.`, 3600000, A, and 192.168.0.10, each separated by at least one space.

Listing 8.2   /var/named/named.local

```
@ IN SOA localhost. root.localhost. (
   1997022700 ; Serial
   28800      ; Refresh
   14400      ; Retry
   3600000    ; Expire
   86400 )    ; Minimum
    IN   NS   localhost.
1 IN PTR localhost.
```

Listing 8.3   /var/named/foobirds.org.zone

```
$TTL 1d
;
;   The foobirds.org domain database
;
@   IN   SOA   wren.foobirds.org. sara.wren.foobirds.org. (
    2000031301 ; Serial
    21600      ; Refresh
    1800       ; Retry
    4w         ; Expire
    1h )       ; Negative cache TTL
;   Define the nameservers
     IN NS  wren.foobirds.org.
;   Define the mail servers
     IN  MX 10 wren.foobirds.org.
;
; Define the hosts in this zone
;
wren       IN A  200.100.100.10
parrot     IN A  192.168.0.3
crow       IN A  192.168.0.5
hawk       IN A  192.168.0.4
falcon     IN A  192.168.0.20
puffin     IN A  192.168.0.17
robin      IN A  192.168.0.2
;
; Define the aliases in this zone
;
```

```
redbreast  IN  CNAME  robin.foobirds.org.
www        IN  CNAME  wren.foobirds.org.
news       IN  CNAME  parrot.foobirds.org.
```

Listing 8.4   /var/named/birdeaters.com.zone

```
$TTL 1d
@ IN SOA  wren.foobirds.org. mark.birdeaters.com. (
    2000031301 ; Serial
    21600      ; Refresh
    1800       ; Retry
    4w         ; Expire
    1h )       ; Negative cache TTL
    IN NS  wren.foobirds.org.
    IN  MX 10 wren.foobirds.org.
www IN CNAME  wren.foobirds.com.
```

Let me add a note or two here about the `birdeaters.com.zone` file. In this example, birdeaters.com is a pretty small zone, in the sense that there are no computers that are really *in* birdeaters.com! The primary name server for birdeaters.com is the same machine as for foobirds.org: wren.foobirds.org. The mail server for birdeaters.com is *also* wren.foobirds.org. And the `CNAME` shows that there's a machine that will answer to "`www.birdeaters.com`," but it's actually, once again, wren.foobirds.org.

This is an interesting example, because it's an example of how you'd host someone else's domain name. If all they want is to receive mail and host a web server, then you could set up their domain something like this, so long as you also made arrangements for a machine like wren to receive mail and host web pages (both of which you'll see how to do later in this chapter).

Listing 8.5   /var/named/192.rev.zone

```
;     Address to hostname mappings.
;
@  IN SOA  wren.foobirds.org. sara.wren.foobirds.org. (
        1999022702  ;  Serial
        21600       ;  Refresh
        1800        ;  Retry
        604800      ;  Expire
        86400 )     ;  Minimum
        IN   NS    wren.foobirds.org.
        IN   NS    falcon.foobirds.org.
10      IN   PTR   wren.foobirds.org.
```

```
2       IN   PTR    robin.foobirds.org.
3       IN   PTR    parrot.foobirds.org.
4       IN   PTR    hawk.foobirds.org.
5       IN   PTR    crow.foobirds.org.
17      IN   PTR    puffin.foobirds.org.
20      IN   PTR    falcon.foobirds.org.
```

Listing 8.6 /etc/named.conf

```
options {
  directory "/var/named";
};
zone "." {
  type hint;
  file "named.ca";
};
zone "0.0.127.in-addr.arpa" {
  type master;
  file "named.local";
};
zone "foobirds.org" {
    type master;
    file "foobirds.org.zone";
  check-names ignore;
};
zone "0.168.192.in-addr.arpa" {
    type master;
    file "192.rev.zone";
};
zone "birdeaters.com" {
    type master;
    file "birdeaters.com.zone";
};
```

Start the DNS Server

Now start the DNS server:

```
/etc/rc.d/init.d/named start
```

Fire up nslookup and try resolving a few names in foobirds.org, or look up www
.birdeaters.com—don't forget to first point nslookup at that machine with server
127.0.0.1. Or, alternatively, modify the value in resolv.conf so that your Linux box
looks to itself for DNS name resolutions.

TIP I've often found that nslookup won't work if your DNS server cannot reverse-resolve its own name, so it's particularly important to get the reverse lookup domains working.

Set Up the DNS Server to Start Automatically

If you're happy with your foobirds.org and birdeaters.com domain, then you can make your server start up BIND automatically. On a Red Hat system, just create a few symbolic links. We'll do this just for runlevel 3 for the sake of space, but you can do the same thing for any other runlevel.

1. First, change to the runlevel's directory:

   ```
   cd /etc/rc.d/rc3.d
   ```

2. Then look to see if there's already a link telling Linux to kill named by typing ls K*named. If there's a file whose name starts with *K*, followed by a number and *named*, then delete it by typing rm K*named.

3. Now create a link to start up BIND:

   ```
   ln -s /etc/rc.d/init.d/named S11named
   ```

Your basic DNS server is now completely functional.

TIP You can also do this simply by using the setup command from the root prompt, choosing System services, and then checking the box next to named.

Going Further: Dynamic DNS

Windows 2000 has acquainted us with a new feature of DNS: Dynamic DNS, or DDNS. Can Linux do this? Sure—and the version of BIND that comes with Red Hat (9.2.0) can do it simply.

All you have to do to tell BIND to accept dynamic updates for a given zone is to add allow-update{list}; to the zone definition in named.conf, where *list* is just a list of places that BIND will accept an update from. For example, I could define birdeaters.com to accept dynamic DNS registrations from anywhere with a definition like this:

```
zone "birdeaters.com" {
    type master;
    allow-update{any};
    file "birdeaters.com.zone";
};
```

Just make that change to named.conf, save it, and restart named. Then try it out by firing up a Windows 2000 Professional or XP system and changing its name to *anything*.bird-eaters.com, and specify your BIND server as the 2000 or XP machine's DNS server. Reboot the 2000/XP machine (you have to do that when you change its domain), then try an nslookup to see if it is indeed registered with the BIND server. Or, to force your 2000/XP system to reregister with BIND, type ipconfig /registerdns.

Here are a couple of tips to make your experimentation easier. When you stop named, it writes out the zone information to the zone file that you named (such as foobirds .org.zone, for example), erasing whatever you had in there before. Take a peek in there and you'll see the dynamically registered records, which you can now delete if you like. When you restart BIND, it won't know about those records until the client reregisters. Note, however, that BIND sets that file to read-only, so you'll have to change its file permissions (chmod a+w foobirds.org.zone, for example) before you can tinker with it.

Additionally, there's an easy way to get nslookup to cough up all of the information about a zone: just type ls -d zonename (while in nslookup, recall) to see all records relevant to a zone. And remember to restart named when you make a change to named.conf! Further, you may be wondering why I keep recommending that you play around with a 2000 client rather than a Linux client in order to try out DDNS. The reason's simple: the DNS client built into Linux doesn't know how to register itself with a DDNS server.

I wouldn't recommend actually using any in the braces on the allow-update line. Much better would be a more specific definition; it can take any of the following values, separated by semicolons:

- An IP address, as in allow-update{192.168.0.1;};.
- Multiple IP addresses, as in allow-update{192.168.0.1;192.168.0.40;};.
- A subnet, as in allow-update{192.168.0/24;};.
- The keyword any, as you've already seen, which says to accept DDNS registrations from any machine.
- The keyword localnets, which says to accept DDNS registrations from any machine on any subnet that the server is directly attached to—so, for example, if your DNS server lives in an intranet of 20 subnets but the DNS server itself lives on subnet 200.100.100.0, then it'll only accept updates from machines on the 200.100.100.0 subnet if you use allow-updates{localnets;};.

> **WARNING**   Because dynamic zones get their zone files rewritten automatically by named, you need to make an extra step or two to modify information in that zone. For example, if I wanted to change the MX record of foobirds.org and if I'd made foobirds.org dynamic, then I wouldn't just modify /var/named/ foobirds.org.zone, save the file, and restart named. That's because whenever you stop or restart named, it erases the old zone file and writes out a new zone file with the latest zone information—so my MX change would be overwritten! Instead, I'd have to *first* stop named. Then, as named has made the zone file read-only, I'd have to change its file permissions so that I could edit it. Then I'd change the MX info and save the file; *then* I could restart named.

Once you have DDNS set up, you can actually use a Linux box running a recent version of BIND as the DNS server in your Windows 2000 AD domain. Just remember: before you run DCPROMO on a Windows 2000 server computer to create a Windows 2000 Active Directory domain, first tell the Windows 2000 Server machine to use the Linux box as its DNS server. Then run DCPROMO, and in no time, you'll have an Active Directory that relies on Linux and BIND for its DNS.

Linux As a DHCP Server

One of the services provided by many Windows NT/2000/.NET servers is to dynamically allocate IP addresses through the use of the Dynamic Host Configuration Protocol (DHCP). While many hosts within the Linux/Unix environment have traditionally been configured using static IP addresses, Linux distributions also come with a solid DHCP server so that they, too, can perform this role on a network. As with NT/2000, the Linux DHCP server can provide IP addresses to DHCP clients running on any platform. As you'll see below, it can even provide the Windows-specific options (such as WINS) needed by Windows 95/98/NT/2000 systems. Unfortunately, however, it can't do dynamic DNS updates on behalf of clients as Windows 2000's DHCP server can; that might cause you not to use a BIND server in an Active Directory environment—although it's not a show-stopper. In an NT 4–based environment, however, Linux's DHCP makes a perfectly good replacement. A couple of years ago, it looked as if the Linux DHCP server would get the ability to register dynamic DNS names for older clients, but I've not seen any activity, so I'm guessing that it was shelved.

The DHCP server daemon is a process called dhcpd. The configuration file is /etc/ dhcpd.conf, and current leases are stored in a file called dhcpd.leases, which is usually, but not always, also located in /etc. On Red Hat 7.3, the dhcpd.leases file can be found in the directory /var/lib/dhcp.

NOTE   If you're fuzzy on how DHCP works, you'll find a more complete discussion in either *Mastering Windows NT Server 4* (Chapter 14) or *Mastering Windows 2000 Server* (Chapter 7).

I'm going to show you how to set up Linux's DHCP server, but first let's briefly look at the DHCP client.

Controlling the DHCP Client, *dhcpcd*

The DHCP client on most Linuxes is a program named dhcpcd, the DHCP client daemon. The DHCP client under Linux is the tool that you use to obtain and discard DHCP leases in the same way that we'd use ipconfig /renew or ipconfig /release (or the GUI winipcfg) in a Microsoft operating system. But here's a cool thing about dhcpcd: you can start it up any time, meaning that if you have an Ethernet card with a static IP and you want it to take a DHCP address, then it's simple to make that happen, as I'll show you.

NOTE   Very important: note that the DHCP *server* daemon is named dhcpd (DHCP daemon), and the DHCP *client* daemon is named dhcpcd (DHCP *client* daemon). They are *very* similar-looking, and it'll drive you crazy looking for information on dhcpcd in the man pages on dhcpd.

Releasing a DHCP Lease

To release an IP address that DHCP gave one of your Ethernet cards, use this command:

```
dhcpcd -d -k ethn
```

where *n* is 0, 1, or whatever the adapter number for your Ethernet card is. The -d option, which I *strongly* recommend, writes a lot of descriptive information into a file called /var/log/messages; you can follow the entire process whereby dhcpcd tries to get a lease. The -k option is the "release" option.

Obtaining a DHCP Lease

To get a new IP address from DHCP, you use dhcpcd with different options:

```
dhcpcd -d -B -D ethn
```

This time, the -B option asks the DHCP server to broadcast its responses, which is more NT/2000-like behavior. The -D tells the Linux computer to set its domain name as DHCP tells it to; otherwise, Linux seems to ignore domain names. There's also a -H option if you need it, which tells Linux to set its hostname according the DHCP's dictates, if you use DHCP to set hostnames.

Telling DHCP Not to Overwrite *resolv.conf*

I mentioned in the earlier DNS section that the DHCP client overwrites any `resolv.conf` files that you have; you can suppress that behavior—and thereby keep your preconfigured list of DNS servers—by adding the -R option to `dhcpcd`. You would, then, obtain a DHCP lease like so:

```
dhcpcd -d -B -D -R
```

Renewing a DHCP Lease

There really isn't a command to force a DHCP lease renew; instead, you can just release with one command, then obtain a new address with a second command. For example, to renew the lease on my second Ethernet card, I'd type:

```
dhcpcd -d -k eth1
dhcpcd -d -D -B eth1
```

Passing Parameters to *dhcpcd* at Boot Time

Knowing neat parameters like -R isn't much good from the command line, as `dhcpcd` is activated automatically—a script activates it at boot time. How, then, to tell `dhcpcd` to leave your `resolv.conf` alone? By modifying a file. Edit `/etc/sysconfig/network-scripts/ifcfg-eth0` and add this line:

```
DHCPCDARGS=-R
```

You can, of course, add any other parameters that you like to this line.

Finding Out Where You Got a Lease

What if you wanted to know which DHCP server you got your lease from, what IP address you got, and how long you had the lease? Find out by looking in the file `/etc/dhcpc/dhcpcd-eth0.info`:

```
cat /etc/dhcpc/dhcpcd-eth0.info
```

Changing from Static to DHCP

This is incredibly easy compared to how we're used to doing it in Microsoft operating systems. If you currently have your Ethernet card configured with a static IP address and want to go to DHCP, just issue a `dhcpcd` command to get an IP lease. For example, suppose I'd first assigned eth1 a static IP address of 200.200.200.100 with this command:

```
ifconfig eth1 200.200.200.100
```

Doing an ifconfig will show that eth1 is operating and with that IP address. To tell eth1 to forget 200.200.200.100 and use a DHCP-assigned address, I just do this:

```
dhcpcd -d -D -B eth1
```

An ifconfig will show that eth1 now has an IP address obtained from a DHCP server. To switch back, I'd first release the IP address from the DHCP server, then assign another static address:

```
dhcpcd -d -k eth1

ifconfig eth1 200.200.200.100
```

And I did all of this without a single reboot! But now let's move on to building a DHCP server.

Checking the Server Installation

Before we configure the DNS server, we need to be sure that it is installed correctly. Again, use the which command when you are logged in as root:

```
# which dhcpd
/usr/sbin/dhcpd
#
```

If that produces no output, systems with the rpm command can also try:

```
# rpm -q dhcp
dhcp-2.0p15-8
#
```

Note that you are querying for dhcp and not dhcpd. (Hey, that's the way they named the packages!) If that came back empty, you might just see if the file /usr/sbin/dhcpd exists. On Linux systems, dhcpd is almost always located in /usr/sbin.

Installing the DHCP Server

If you conclude that your system does not have the DHCP server installed, on RPM-based systems, you'll need to locate the rpm file (from your installation media or the Internet) and then issue a command such as:

```
rpm -ivh dhcp-2.0-71.i386.rpm
```

Your distribution may also provide its own tools, such as YaST (SuSE), that will help you locate and install packages.

> **NOTE**   As Red Hat automatically installs DHCP, you shouldn't have to do anything, but if necessary, you can install the DHCP server by inserting the CD-ROM and typing this command: `rpm -ivh /misc/cdrom/RedHat/RPMS/dhcp-2.0p15-8.i386.rpm`.

As I write this, DHCP is changing rapidly, so you may, therefore, want to either look around on the Internet for a newer RPM, or go to www.isc.org and download the source for a newer version of the DHCP server.

In any case, let's get started putting the DHCP server together. Before you start the DHCP server, you *must* set up two configuration files, dhcpd.conf and dhcpd.leases. Without those two files, the DHCP server will not start.

Configuring the DHCP Server

As mentioned above, the main configuration file for the DHCP server is /etc/dhcpd.conf. The server is extremely flexible and can be configured to perform a wide variety of services, but in its most basic form, it might look like:

```
subnet 192.168.0.0 netmask 255.255.255.0 {
  range 192.168.0.100 192.168.0.150;
  }
```

From your experience with NT, you should be able to figure out that this will define a range of IP addresses from 192.168.0.100 to 192.168.0.150. (In Windows NT/2000, we referred to this as the DHCP *scope*.) That's really all there is to it. Note that you had to create this file and there may or may not have been a sample provided.

You can include comments in dhcpd.conf using the standard # sign.

Lease Expiration Times

Okay, the next step is to configure the expiration times of the leases. This involves merely adding one or two lines to the dhcpd.conf file, as in:

```
subnet 192.168.0.0 netmask 255.255.255.0 {
  range 192.168.0.100 192.168.0.150;
  default-lease-time 604800;
  max-lease-time 604800;
  }
```

Now here the `default-lease-time` is what you may be used to in the NT DHCP Manager. It's simply the default expiration time for the DHCP leases, given in seconds. So in this example, the lease is 604,800 seconds or 7 days. Here's something a little tricky, though: it is possible for a DHCP client to request a longer expiration time, and if it does, it will get the amount of time requested rather than the `default-lease-time`. However, the `max-lease-time` takes care of this by specifying the maximum lease duration for a client that requests a specific time.

Configuring DHCP Options

If you recall from the Windows NT/2000 DHCP Manager, you can use DHCP to provide options such as the IP addresses of the router (default gateway), DNS servers, WINS servers, etc. The DHCP Manager even gave you a nice, little dialog box from which you could choose the options you wanted to configure. Well, all those options, and many more, are available to the Linux DHCP server, but you have to add them manually, and you'll need to do a `man dhcp-options` in order to see all the options you have. A typical `dhcpd.conf` with options might look like:

```
#
# set global options
#
option domain-name "birdeaters.com";
option domain-name-servers 199.125.85.1, 199.125.85.2;
option netbios-name-servers 192.168.0.1;
option netbios-node-type 8;
option nis-domain "mincomp";
#
# set up a subnet
#
subnet 192.168.0.0 netmask 255.255.255.0 {
  range 192.168.0.100 192.168.0.150;
  default-lease-time 604800;
  max-lease-time 604800;
  option subnet-mask 255.255.255.0;
  option broadcast-address 192.168.0.255;
  option routers 192.168.0.1;
  }
```

As you can see here, just as in NT/2000, you have the ability to create either global options or subnet-specific options. We're showing a simple file here serving only one subnet, but configuring the server to provide addresses to multiple subnets is as simple as copying and pasting the subnet {} block of text and defining a new subnet. The global options are simply those located outside of any subnet {} block.

Notice in the global options that we're also passing out WINS information for NT 4 (and other pre–Windows 2000 networks). Of course, it's called netbios-name-servers here because, after all, WINS is simply Microsoft's implementation of a NetBIOS name server. Samba can also function perfectly fine in this capacity.

In the local subnet-specific options, you can see we're passing out the subnet mask, the broadcast address, and the default gateway for that subnet. All of these options should be familiar to you if you worked at all with the NT DHCP Manager.

In our example, with only one subnet, it really doesn't matter whether you configure the options as global or local to a subnet, but obviously in a larger environment with multiple subnets, this *would* matter.

If your DHCP server is in a different subnet, then you have to add a subnet definition for that subnet, even if you're not going to hand out addresses for it. For example, if my DHCP server had IP address 192.168.50.11, then dhcpd would refuse to start until I added this line to dhcpd.conf:

```
subnet 192.168.50.0 netmask 255.255.255.0 {}
```

The *dhcpd.leases* File: A Note

If you're running Red Hat 7.3, then your DHCP server is ready to go. But on the off-chance that you're using a different distro, let me tell you about something that might trip you up.

The DHCP server needs a place to keep the database of leases that it has given out. Unlike NT, the Linux DHCP server stores this database as an ASCII text file. That file's name and location is /var/lib/dhcp/dhcp.leases.

Here's where the problem comes in: before the DHCP server will start, that file has to exist, even if the file is completely empty. And for some reason, the DHCP server software isn't smart enough to look in /var/lib/dhcp and say, "Oh golly, there isn't a dhcp.leases file; I ought to create one." Instead, it just refuses to start. Now, thankfully, Red Hat 7.3 includes an already-created blank file named dhcp.leases, so you needn't worry about this. The occasional DHCP server might not even want the file in /var/lib/ dhcp; look in man dhcpd.leases to find out for sure. (Won't it be neat when Linux really *is* "United"?)

In any event, should you ever have to make some distro happy by creating a place for its leases, creating an empty file is simple using the touch command:

```
# touch dhcpd.leases
# ls -l dhcpd.leases
-rw-r--r-- 1 root root  0  Jul 6 06:52 dhcpd.leases
#
```

You'll now see a file with a size of zero bytes.

That's it. Now the DHCP server should be able to start without any problem:

```
/etc/rc.d/init.d/dhcpcd start
```

Once the server is in operation, this dhcpd.leases file will be updated with information about what IP addresses are leased out. For your information, the file will look something like:

```
lease 192.168.0.100 {
    starts 4 2000/07/06 06:19:13;
    ends 4 2000/07/06 12:19:13;
    hardware ethernet 00:80:c8:84:36:3a;
}
lease 192.168.0.149 {
    starts 2 2000/06/27 01:52:10;
    ends 2 2000/07/04 01:52:10;
    hardware ethernet 00:e0:98:06:6f:e8;
    uid 01:00:e0:98:06:6f:e8;
    client-hostname "Eagle";
}
```

You can look at it at any time and see the information there. Note that the second entry above has information such as the client-hostname merely because the DHCP client on that machine provided that information.

DHCP Reservations

To ensure that DHCP always gives the same IP address to a given system, you can create a DHCP reservation by adding a host command to dhcpd.conf. The host command looks like:

```
host hostname {
```

```
hardware ethernet mac-address;

fixed-address IP-address;

}
```

For example, if I wanted a machine whose Ethernet card had MAC address 0080C71648A6 to have IP address 192.168.0.115, I would modify the dhcpd.conf that you saw a page or two back to look like this:

```
#

# set global options

#

option domain-name "birdeaters.com";

option domain-name-servers 199.125.85.1, 199.125.85.2;

option netbios-name-servers 192.168.0.1;

option netbios-node-type 8;

option nis-domain "mincomp";

#

# set up a subnet

#

subnet 192.168.0.0 netmask 255.255.255.0 {

    range 192.168.0.100 192.168.0.150;

    default-lease-time 604800;

    max-lease-time 604800;

    option subnet-mask 255.255.255.0;

    option broadcast-address 192.168.0.255;

    option routers 192.168.0.1;

    }

host mypc {

hardware ethernet 00:80:C7:16:48:A6;

fixed-address 192.168.0.115;

}
```

Starting and Stopping the DHCP Server

Alright, now that you have dhcpd installed and configured, you need to start it up. Like the other services, the start and stop of the DHCP server is controlled by the init scripts found out in /etc/rc.d/init.d (on most distributions). If you want to manually issue the command, you can do something like:

```
# cd /etc/rc.d/init.d
# ./dhcpd start
Starting dhcp server. done
# ./dhcpd stop
Shutting down dhcp server. done
#
```

Alternatively, you can use ./dhcpd restart to perform both actions at once. If the stop command does not work, you'll need to use ps to identify the process ID and then kill off the process.

Unlike Windows NT/2000, there is nothing particular you need to do here to "activate" a DHCP scope. If you modify the dhcpd.conf file to add another subnet, you simply restart the DHCP server and the new scope will be active.

When you installed the DHCP server package, it should have automatically created the appropriate scripts in the different runlevel directories (found in /etc/rc.d/rc*n*.d on most distributions, where *n* is the runlevel number). If you go into the higher-level directories, such as rc5.d, and do not see a S*xx*dhcpd start script, you will need to create one using a command such as:

```
# ln -s ../init.d/dhcpd S65named
```

Alternatively, in Red Hat 7.2, you can use the System services section of the setup command, as mentioned previously. With that you should be all set to keep on giving out IP addresses to all the clients that request them.

TIP The DHCP server writes information messages into /var/log/messages; it's the dhcpd version of the Event Viewer. You can see them by typing cat /var/log/messages|grep dhcpd.

Cookbook Summary: DHCP Server

This cookbook will set up a DHCP server on Red Hat 7.3 that does the following things:

- Gives away IP addresses between 192.168.0.100 and 192.168.0.150

- Assigns subnet masks of 255.255.255.0, broadcast addresses of 192.168.0.255, default gateway addresses of 192.168.0.1, DNS servers of 199.125.85.1 and 199.125.85.2, default domain name of foobirds.org, and WINS servers at 192.168.0.1

- Assigns leases for a week

- Preassigns the machine whose Ethernet card has MAC address 0080C71648A6 to IP address 192.168.0.115

Clearly that last item won't work on your system, as I own that particular Ethernet card—but if you like, substitute that value for the MAC address of an Ethernet in your example network. I did this on wren.foobirds.org, but you can actually do this on any Linux machine on the 192.168.0.0 subnet.

Install the Server

There should be nothing to do here; Red Hat's Setup installs a relatively recent DHCP server when you install Red Hat "with all the trimmings." Double-check by typing which dhcpd, and if it's not there, install the RPM from the CD-ROM with this command:

```
rpm -ivh /mnt/cdrom/RedHat/RPMS/dhcp-2.0p15.i386.rpm
```

Create */etc/dhcpd.conf*

Create /etc/dhcpd.conf to look like this:

```
#
# set global options
#
option domain-name "foobirds.org";
option domain-name-servers 192.168.0.10; # wren
option netbios-name-servers 192.168.0.1;
➥# delete if no WINS server there!
option netbios-node-type 8;
option nis-domain "mincomp";
#
# set up a subnet
#
subnet 192.168.0.0 netmask 255.255.255.0 {
  range 192.168.0.100 192.168.0.150;
  default-lease-time 604800;
```

```
max-lease-time 604800;

option subnet-mask 255.255.255.0;

option broadcast-address 192.168.0.255;

option routers 192.168.0.1;

}

host mypc {

hardware ethernet 00:80:C7:16:48:A6;

fixed-address 192.168.0.115;

}
```

Notice that I've included an `option routers 192.168.0.1` parameter. That only makes sense if your 192.168.0.1 system is an ICS or `ipchains`-type system that connects you to the Internet. If you don't have a system like that hooked up, then just delete that line, and the clients will not get a default gateway value. You should not need to do this, as the file should already exist, but if you need to, then you can create an empty leases file with this command:

```
touch /var/lib/dhcp/dhcpd.leases
```

Start the DHCP Server

Start the DHCP server like so:

```
/etc/rc.d/init.d/dhcpd start
```

You should see:

```
Starting dhcpd: [OK]
```

If you see nothing, then either you haven't created the two configuration files or you haven't installed the DHCP server correctly. If you got the [OK], then your server should now be handing out IP addresses. Check the `/var/log/messages` file for information on the addresses that `dhcpd` has assigned, or look in `/var/lib/dhcp/dhcpd.leases`. You can also ask the Microsoft DHCP clients where they got their IP addresses from—in Windows 95, type `winipcfg`; in Windows 98, NT, and 2000, just type `ipconfig /all`, and you'll see the IP address of the DHCP server that gave the client its address, so you can verify that it came from the Linux box. I've tested this exact configuration on Windows 95, 98, and 2000 clients.

Make the DHCP Server Start Automatically

To make the `dhcpd` process start automatically at any given runlevel, you'll need to create a link in `/etc/rc.d/rcn.d`, where *n* is the runlevel. We'll be doing most of our work in runlevel 3, so here's the command for runlevel 3:

```
ln -s /etc/rc.d/init.d/dhcpd /etc/rc.d/rc3.d/S65named
```

Linux As a Web Server: Apache

With DNS and DHCP under our belt, let's progress next to web—arguably Linux's most popular usage. Well, Dan tells me that there are actually *several* different web servers available for Linux systems, but the one included with pretty much all Linux distributions is the Apache web server. The Apache server is not specific to Linux and in fact is available for Windows and most versions of Unix. It's a true open source project maintained by a nonprofit organization. You can find more information about it at www.apache.org.

Checking the Server Installation

First, check to see if you have Apache installed. Fire up a web browser, point it at http://localhost/, and see what happens. If it's installed, you should see a welcome screen, typically customized by the company behind whatever distribution you've installed.

If that doesn't work, we're back to using good old tools like which again. Try this as root:

```
# which httpd
/usr/sbin/httpd
#
```

If that doesn't work, try:

```
# rpm -q apache
apache-1.3.23-11
#
```

Lastly, just use ls to see if the file /usr/sbin/httpd exists. If none of these tests work, you have to go install it.

Installing Apache

To install the Apache server on RPM systems, you'll need to mount the Red Hat Installation CD 2 and install two RPMs. Mount the CD as /misc/cd, change the directory to /misc/cd/RedHat/RPMS, and then issue these commands:

```
rpm -ivh mm-1.1.3-4.i386.rpm
rpm -ivh apache-1.3.23-11.i386.rpm
```

And if you'd like the Apache documents as well (a good idea), issue this command:

```
rpm -ivh apache-manual-1.3.23-11.i386.rpm
```

If, on the other hand, you're looking for the full Apache experience, you can go to www.apache.org, download the source tarball, and compile it as we talked about in Chapter 5.

Starting/Stopping the Apache Server

Once you have it installed, typically the start and stop of the DNS server is controlled by the init scripts found out in /etc/rc.d/init.d (on most distributions). If you want to manually issue the command, you can do something like:

```
# /etc/rc.d/init.d/httpd stop
Shutting down service httpd. done
# /etc/rc.d/init.d/httpd start
Starting service httpd. done
#
```

You're now ready to go!

After you have installed the Apache package, it should automatically create the appropriate scripts in the different runlevel directories (found in /etc/rc.d/rcn.d on most distributions). If you go into the higher-level directories, such as rc5.d, and do not see a S*xx*httpd start script, you will need to create one using a command such as:

```
# ln -s ../init.d/httpd S85httpd
```

> **WARNING** Again, if you don't see a start script with httpd, check to see if there is a similarly named script in the runlevel directory before creating one.

Configuring Apache

When you configure IIS on a Windows NT machine, typically all of the configuration is done through the various screens of the Internet Service Manager. In Linux, it's done through a series of configuration files.

Apache's configuration files are in the directory /etc/httpd/conf on Red Hat 7.3. (I say "on Red Hat 7.3" because where Apache configuration files go seems to vary from distro to distro.) You do most of your Apache configuration by modifying the file httpd.conf or, to use its full path, /etc/httpd/conf/httpd.conf.

The HTML documents—your web pages—go in /var/www/html. And, of course, you can change that if you like—take a peek, and you'll see this line:

```
DocumentRoot "/var/www/html"
```

So you can change this, if you care to.

Modifying the Apache Configuration with *httpd.conf*

httpd.conf contains zillions of commands that control various aspects of Apache's behavior. Configuring Apache could really be (and is) the subject of entire books, so I'm not going to cover everything here—just enough to make you dangerous!

> **TIP**   Usually when you install Apache, the Apache User's Guide is automatically installed on your server. To get to it, go to your web browser and type in the URL http://localhost/manual/. If this manual was installed, it will give you all sorts of information about all of the various directives that can be included in httpd. If you do not have this installed, you can find it out at the main Apache website of www.apache.org.

Let's take a look at httpd.conf. Note that comments in the file begin with the # sign, and blank lines and extra white space are allowed. Of the things that we'll care about, the major ones include:

```
Port 80
ServerRoot /etc/httpd
ServerName www.foobirds.org
User apache
Group apache
```

They'll all probably already exist in httpd.conf except ServerName www.foobirds.org.

As you might imagine, the Port directive specifies the TCP port number to which the httpd server will bind. The usual port is 80, but if you had some reason to run it on a different port, you would configure it here.

The ServerRoot is the directory containing the configuration files. Apache considers all other pathnames for configuration and log files relative to this directory.

ServerName is interesting because you can use it to tell a web browser that your machine has a different name from its "real" name. For instance, given our earlier DNS example, someone connecting to www.foobirds.com would in fact connect to wren.foobirds.com. Without the ServerName directive, the URL that the clients would see in their web browser would include http://wren.foobirds.com/ as the first part of the URL. By using ServerName we can tell the clients that they are connecting to www.foobirds.com.

> **WARNING**   Do realize that you cannot just invent a name to use with ServerName. Whatever name you use *must* resolve correctly to an IP address using DNS.

The last two directives shown in this example, User and Group, are important from a security point of view. You are probably going to be having people execute CGI scripts through your web server. There is always the potential that someone trying to break into your system could attack one of these scripts. Running the httpd server as the user nobody minimizes the damage that could be caused by a break-in.

I want to mention two other directives that might be of interest:

```
StartServers 8
MaxClients 150
```

You may change these according to how busy you think the server will be. StartServers denotes how many individual processes will be started when you launch httpd. If you start httpd with StartServers 10 and then do the command:

```
ps aux | grep httpd
```

you should indeed see 10 httpd processes running. Normally you probably won't need to tweak this, because Apache will just spawn more processes if it needs to in order to handle an increased load. However, if you know in advance that your site will receive heavy traffic, you can increase this number.

MaxClients is another case, though. As the name implies, this is the maximum number of simultaneous connections your server can handle. If your site is extremely busy, you may need to increase this number.

Two more directives that you should not need to change, but are good to understand, relate to log files:

```
ErrorLog logs/error_log
CustomLog logs/access_log common
```

Essentially, these tell you that your log files are located in the /logs subdirectory (relative to ServerRoot). The more interesting of these is access_log, which logs all the connections to your server. You may also see other entries for referer and agent logs, such as:

```
CustomLog /var/log/httpd/referer_log referer
CustomLog /var/log/httpd/agent_log agent
```

The referer (yes, that is the spelling. I know that in correct English it should be referrer, but they didn't do it that way) log keeps track of where people are coming to your site from. The agent log tracks which browsers (*user agents* in HTTP lingo) are connecting to your site. Both can provide very interesting statistics.

All the information in `access_log`, `referer_log`, and `agent_log` can be combined in a single log file (usually called `access_log`) by using:

```
CustomLog /var/log/httpd/access_log combined
```

Whether or not you will want to do this will depend on the program you are using to analyze your log files. This being the world of open source, there are literally *hundreds* of web log analysis programs available. Some of them use the combined log file while others use the separate files.

TIP If you don't believe me about the number of programs available, visit www.`freshmeat.net` and do a search on "web log analysis." A recent search found 2,153 matching entries! Not all of which were appropriate, of course, but many were.

Finally, there are two directives you may find in `httpd.conf` that tell Apache where the other two configuration files are:

```
ResourceConfig conf/srm.conf

AccessConfig conf/access.conf
```

Many times these directives are left out because the defaults (relative to `ServerRoot`) are built into the `httpd` program itself. If you see them there, they will point you to where those configuration files are located. However, on newer Apache systems—the ones that are slowly stamping out `access.conf` and `srm.conf`—you'll see these lines:

```
ResourceConfig /dev/null

AccessConfig /dev/null

DocumentRoot "/var/www/html"

DirectoryIndex index.html index.htm index.shtml index.php index.cgi
```

The `DocumentRoot` is the directory where you will store all the files you will publish through the web server. On a Windows machine, this would typically be `C:\InetPub\wwwroot`. All pathnames after the server name in a URL are relative to this directory location (unless an alias is used, but I'll talk about that below).

The next line, `DirectoryIndex`, is the critical line that tells us the name of the default file sent back to the web browser if the client does not specify a filename. In Windows, this is usually `default.htm`; in Linux and Unix, it is usually `index.html`. Note that you can have multiple entries on the line. The server will send back the first that it finds of those names listed. If you want to move over existing Windows documents, you can even list `default.htm` on this line.

> **_WARNING_** As you work with a Linux web server, you will notice one huge difference from a Windows web server. Filenames are case-sensitive. I've mentioned that before, but this is one place where it can really be an issue.

> **_NOTE_** RED HAT NOTE: The Apache web server in Red Hat accepts `index.html`, `index.htm`, `index.shtml`, `index.cgi`, `index.phtml`, `index.php`, `index.php3`, and `index.php4`. A pretty liberal list!

There's another line in `httpd.conf` that merits attention. Have you seen the URLs that are out there in the form `http://www.minasi.com/~mark/foo.html`? Have you ever wondered what the deal was with the tilde? Here's what's happening. In `srm.conf`, there is a `UserDir` directive:

```
UserDir public_html
```

What this says is that if a user creates a directory called `public_html` in their home *directory*, documents can be served out of there by adding *~user* to the server URL.

Here's how it works. There's a server called `www.foobirds.org`. I have a user account there under the name of mark. From my desktop system, I telnet to the server, log in, and am placed into my home directory, `/home/mark`. I create a directory called `public_html`, cd into that directory, and create a basic HTML document named `index.html`.

Back on my desktop system, I open my browser and enter in the location of `http://www.foobirds.org/~mark/`—ta da... I'm looking at the same page I just created in my Telnet session.

The great thing about this is that I can easily delegate out sections of the web server "space" to individuals. Since it's all in their home directories, I don't have to worry about permissions issues or about other people modifying someone else's files. (It also saves me as the system administrator from having to either open up permissions to the main `DocumentRoot` directory or constantly be copying files into that directory because regular users don't have permission to do so.)

Of course, this does introduce a potential security issue in that all the HTML documents for your site aren't in one location, and you do need to be careful not to give users the ability to execute CGI scripts out of their directories (unless you want them to do so).

Speaking of file locations and scripts, let's cover one last part of `httpd.conf`. If you look farther down in the file, you should see lines that resemble:

```
Alias /icons/           /home/httpd/icons/
Alias /manual/          /usr/doc/packages/apache/manual/
ScriptAlias /cgi-bin/ /home/httpd/cgi-bin/
```

These essentially redirect URLs sent to the `httpd` server to other locations on the disk. For instance, without the /manual/ alias, if I entered `http://localhost/manual/ install.html` into my browser, the `httpd` server would look for the file in the path:

```
/home/httpd/html/manual/install.html
```

assuming my `DocumentRoot` is /home/httpd/html. However, with the alias, `httpd` looks for the file:

```
/usr/doc/packages/apache/manual/install.html
```

You can use this to redirect requests to directories outside of the normal `DocumentRoot` directory.

The `ScriptAlias` is similar except that it indicates that the target directory contains executable CGI scripts.

Okay, we're almost done with the configuration; just a few more items that define what actions can be done inside of a directory and who can actually have access to the directory. A typical file may look like:

```
<Directory /home/httpd/html>
Options Indexes Includes
AllowOverride None
order allow,deny
allow from all
</Directory>
<Directory /home/httpd/cgi-bin>
AllowOverride None
Options ExecCGI
</Directory>
Alias /doc /usr/doc
```

```
<Directory /usr/doc>
order deny,allow
deny from all
allow from localhost
Options Indexes FollowSymLinks
</Directory>
```

I'll take this apart and discuss each entry separately. In the first entry, I'm defining access rules for the directory /home/httpd/html. I am allowing optional features such as "directory index" (the list of files you see if there is no index.html file in the directory) and also the use of "server-side includes" (another topic in and of itself, but essentially the ability to reference another HTML file from within an HTML file).

With the AllowOverride directive set to None, I am not allowing the /home/httpd/html directory *or any of its subdirectories* to override the security settings I am establishing here. If this were set to All, I could place a file typically called .htaccess into a directory and set the directory-specific security settings there.

Then we get to this allow,deny part, which confused me at first because it seemed backwards. Take a look at it:

```
order allow,deny
allow from all
```

What this says is that I will allow anyone to connect and see these documents. Let's make it a bit more interesting:

```
order allow,deny
allow from all
deny from minasi.com
```

Now this says that anyone can get to the pages *except* someone coming in from a host that resolves (via reverse DNS) to a hostname ending in minasi.com. It can match on hostnames, IP addresses, partial IP addresses, and more.

The order statement simply indicates which line is executed first. For instance, consider the statement later in the example file for /usr/doc:

```
order deny,allow
allow from localhost
deny from all
```

This will first evaluate the deny statement refusing connections from anyone except those listed on the allow line. (The order of the allow and deny lines does not matter. Execution is controlled by the order statement.)

Using these statements, I can achieve a high degree of control over exactly who can see what in each of the directories. I can also drive myself crazy thinking about all the overlapping possibilities, but that's another subject.

Moving on in the file, let's look at the next entry:

```
<Directory /home/httpd/cgi-bin>
AllowOverride None
Options ExecCGI
</Directory>
```

Notice here that the CGI scripts are located in a directory *outside* of the DocumentRoot directory (/home/httpd/html in this case). Usually, you do this so that someone experimenting with URL pathnames in their browser cannot somehow inadvertently enter into your CGI script directory and start viewing your scripts. Notice the ExecCGI option that allows me to execute scripts out of this directory.

In the final entry for /usr/doc, I've already talked about the security issues, but notice the FollowSymLinks option. What this means is that if I'm using my browser to go through /usr/doc and I encounter a symbolic link to a directory outside of the /usr/doc directory tree, I will, in fact, be able to follow it. This can be quite dangerous if allowed in general document directories. (Imagine if some unethical user put a symbolic link in their web directory pointing to /etc/passwd!) In this case, access is restricted to localhost, so it should be safe.

Those are the basics; to add more directories, just enter a <Directory> </Directory> section. Each entry will cover a directory and all of its subdirectories, unless those subdirectories are covered by a separate entry.

Publishing Information

Now let's talk about publishing information with our web server. In truth, there is not much to it. I already told you earlier how to find your DocumentRoot. All you do is put the files you want to publish into that directory (creating subdirectories if you wish to do so).

The only "gotcha" is to make sure that your home page for each directory and subdirectory is called index.html or one of the other filenames you provided on the DirectoryIndex line in httpd.conf. If you are moving files over from a Windows platform, you need to make sure you either change your home pages from Default.htm to index.html, or you put `Default.htm` on the `DirectoryIndex` line—Red Hat's Apache implementation will not, by default, use a `default.htm`. (Again, it'd be simple to add it to the `DirectoryIndex` line in `httpd.conf`; it's just not there by default.)

Beyond that, just put your files in the directory, and they will immediately be available. No need to restart the server or anything. That's it. Hey, *some* things in Linux are easy!

Virtual Hosts

Before we leave Apache, I want to talk about one more cool aspect of using Apache as your web server. Say you have two (or more) websites that you want to host on the same machine. You want each one to be separate and to appear to be its own server. In our example here, I want to set up `www.foobirds.com` and `www.birdeaters.com`. In the language of web servers, you want to establish a *virtual* host for one of your domains.

It used to be that in order to do this, you had two options. In one approach, you could set up a separate IP address for each virtual host (binding multiple IP addresses to the same NIC). Alternatively, you had to run a separate instance of `httpd` using a different TCP/IP port and play tricks with mapping ports.

However, there's an easier way to do it today. Version 1.1 of the HTTP protocol enables the server to identify what *name* the browser was using when it sent its request to the server. Given that most browsers (and all recent versions of Apache) today support HTTP/1.1, you can easily set up a virtual host using the server name. In NT and 2000-ese, we call it identifying a virtual site via *host header records*.

I'll demonstrate this using the info I set up earlier. First, let's take a look at some key lines in `httpd.conf` related to the primary website `www.foobirds.org` hosted on our website:

```
ServerName www.foobirds.org

ErrorLog logs/error_log

CustomLog logs/access_log common
```

and the following line in `httpd.conf`:

```
DocumentRoot /var/www/html
```

So we know what the name of the server is, where the log files go, and where the web documents go. We also need to know the IP address of the server, which in our example is 172.16.5.1.

Essentially, I am going to replicate all of this information for my virtual website, `www.birdeaters.com`, inside of a `<VirtualHost>` directive. Here's what I add to httpd.conf:

```
NameVirtualHost 172.16.5.1
```

```
<VirtualHost 172.16.5.1>

ServerName www.birdeaters.com

DocumentRoot //var/www/html/birdeaters

ErrorLog logs/birdeaters.com-error_log

CustomLog logs/birdeaters.com-access_log common

</VirtualHost>
```

Notice the first line with `NameVirtualHost`. This tells Apache that I am going to have virtual hosts on my server. I only need to include this directive once in the file. After that, I have the `<VirtualHost>` block that defines specific settings for my new host.

Note that I have put my web documents for the new site as a subdirectory in /home/httpd/html. I didn't have to do this. It was more for the convenience of having all of my HTML documents under one directory tree. By the way, as a side effect of doing this, both of these URLs:

```
http://www.birdeaters.com/

http://www.foobirds.org/birdeaters/
```

will now go to the same pages. Kind of cool, eh?

One other comment: In my virtual host, I added directives for the log files so that all connections to `www.birdeaters.com` would be logged separately from connections to the main server of `www.foobirds.org`. Again, this is just something I wanted to do. Had I left those directives out, all log entries for `www.birdeaters.com` would have been merged in with those of `www.foobirds.org`, which may or may not be what you want. It all depends again on how (or if) you intend to analyze your log files.

After doing all of this configuration, I do need to go create /home/httpd/html/birdeaters and put some documents in it. Next, I just restart Apache:

```
# /etc/rc.d/init.d/httpd restart
```

and my new host is in business.

There's one more little "gotcha" I should mention. What if someone tries to connect to your server as home.birdeaters.com or just birdeaters.com? Where will they go? Assuming that both of those addresses map to the IP address of the server, odds are that the visitor will find themselves looking at the main site of `www.foobirds.org`. To prevent this, I'll add one more line to my virtual host entry:

```
<VirtualHost 172.16.5.1>

ServerName www.birdeaters.com
```

```
ServerAlias *.birdeaters.com birdeaters.com

DocumentRoot /var/www/html/birdeaters

ErrorLog logs/birdeaters.com-error_log

CustomLog logs/birdeaters.com-access_log common

</VirtualHost>
```

Now anyone connecting to my web server using any variation of birdeaters.com will be shown the correct website.

That's really all there is to virtual hosting with Apache. To add an additional virtual host, you just add another <VirtualHost> section to httpd.conf and restart Apache.

Cookbook Summary: Web Server with Two Sites

This section has been a bit more wide-ranging than the others in this chapter simply because you'll probably find that in order to get Apache running on your Linux system, you needn't do *anything*. On every distribution that I've played with, simply pointing a web browser to http://localhost will bring up a default home page that is just some advertising for Apache. If all you want to do is move an existing website to a Linux box, then just take the HTML documents and copy them to /home/httpd/html. If you like, change any files named default.htm to index.html and even if you have an old copy of Apache, your content will display perfectly well. (Note that your Active Server Pages won't run without a third-party solution like Chilisoft's, but standard HTML and Perl CGI scripts should run without a hitch.)

In a few words, then, there's not much to do in this cookbook if we stick with the simple one-web-server, one-website scenario. So let's make it a bit more interesting. In this cookbook, I'll assume that you have a copy of Apache 1.3 (which Red Hat 7.3 includes) running on your system. I'll also assume that you're doing this on wren, the machine with IP address 192.168.0.10, and that you want to host two websites on that system which have no content in common: www.foobirds.org and www.birdeaters.com.

Create the Content

First, we'll need some *really* simple HTML content so that you'll know when you've reached foobirds.org or birdeaters.com. Create directories to store the content:

```
mkdir /var/www/html/birdeaters

mkdir /var/www/html/foobirds
```

Next, create this ASCII file—vi works fine to create it:

```
<html>
```

```
<p>Hello, you've found foobirds.org!</p>
</html>
```

Save the file as /var/www/html/foobirds/index.htm. Next, create this very similar file:

```
<html>
<p>Hello, you've found birdeaters.com!</p>
</html>
```

Save *that* as /var/www/html/birdeaters/index.htm. We now have two of the least-elaborate websites in history, sitting on one computer.

Configure Apache to Use the Sites

Apache ignores these sites until we tell it to use them. Do that by editing /etc/httpd/conf/httpd.conf. Add these lines anywhere in the file:

```
NameVirtualHost 192.168.0.10
<VirtualHost 192.168.0.10>
ServerName www.birdeaters.com
DocumentRoot /var/www/html/birdeaters
ErrorLog logs/birdeaters.com-error.log
</VirtualHost>
<VirtualHost 192.168.0.10>
Servername www.foobirds.org
DocumentRoot /var/www/html/foobirds
ErrorLog logs/foobirds.org-error.log
</VirtualHost>
```

Restart Apache

Tell Apache to reread the configuration file with this command:

```
/etc/rc.d/init.d/httpd restart
```

You should get:

```
Shutting down http: [ OK ]
Starting httpd:  [ OK ]
```

Test the Sites

At this point, you *should* be able to start up a browser on a different computer on your 192.168.0.0/24 network, point it at http://www.birdeaters.com/, and see the page that says "Hello, you've found birdeaters.com!", or point the browser to `http://www.foobirds.org` and see the page that says "Hello, you've found foobirds.org!" You've now successfully built a two-site web server.

Linux As a Mail Server: Sendmail

Next, let's set this network up to send and receive e-mail. In this cookbook, I want to show you how to set up your Linux box to act as an e-mail server for a small- to medium-sized office. While I'll build the example on our 192.168.0.0/24 network, you may want at some point to build a Sendmail server on a system that's live and connected to the Internet. If you do, then it's important that:

- The Linux box is connected to the Internet full time, either through a frame-relay, DSL, or cable-modem connection.
- The Linux box has a routable IP address visible on the Internet.
- You have the ability to put an MX record on some domain so as to point people to that Linux box when they send you mail.

What I'm saying is that you're not going to be able to host your own mail server if you have to dial in to the Internet to get connected (you need a persistent connection), or if your ISP randomly changes your IP address (you must publish the mail server's IP address in DNS in order for people to find your mail server).

In this section, you'll learn how to get Sendmail, the major Internet mail server, on your system, and how to use it to serve more than one domain—it'll be prepared to receive and send mail for both the foobirds.org and birdeaters.com domains. You'll also learn how to do some snazzy tricks with usernames, but I'm getting ahead of myself...

What Sendmail Does

The mail server included with pretty much all Linux distributions is the standard Unix/Linux workhorse Sendmail. Now, given that the standard reference book for Sendmail is literally three inches thick (there's even a bat on the cover, which I've always assumed symbolized the fact that trying to understand Sendmail drains your time the way a vampire would drain your blood), all I want to do here is to give you a taste of what this puppy can do. Along the way I'll introduce you to one of the most arcane-looking configuration files that exists in the world of Linux/Unix. It's not the only one in town by any means; another tool called qmail is very popular, as is a sort of a simplified version of Sendmail called Postfix. But we're going to use Sendmail despite its complexity because (1) I know for *sure* that you have a copy, and (2) we're not going to ask it anything terribly hard, so the actual configuration won't be that rough.

But first, let's talk about what Sendmail is and is not. In mail lingo, Sendmail is a mail transfer agent (MTA). It works entirely with the Simple Mail Transport Protocol (SMTP) to deliver mail to local and remote users. What that means in English is this: suppose you want to send a piece of mail to your friend `martin@thoseguys.com`. You're sitting at a Windows box running Outlook, and you compose this piece of mail to `martin@thoseguys.com`. Outlook knows (because you told it when you configured it) to communicate with your Linux box running Sendmail to send that message. The communication from Outlook on your desktop to Sendmail on the Linux server uses the SMTP protocol; Sendmail is ready, willing, and able to accept that kind of communication from e-mail client programs such as Outlook, Netscape Messenger, or Eudora. Sendmail then finds the e-mail server for the thoseguys.com domain by asking DNS for the MX record at the thoseguys.com domain. The DNS server for thoseguys.com might respond that there is indeed an MX record for thoseguys.com, and that the record says to send mail to a machine named exchange01.thoseguys.com.

> **NOTE** If you're fuzzy on how mail uses DNS and MX records to find a mail server, look in Chapter 14 of *Mastering Windows NT Server 4* or Chapters 6 and 7 of *Mastering Windows 2000 Server*.

Sendmail then transfers your e-mail to exchange01.thoseguys.com, again using the SMTP protocol. The message is now sitting on Martin's local mail server, waiting for him to start up his mail client (Outlook, Messenger, Eudora, or whatever) and retrieve the message from exchange01.thoseguys.com. Most of its journey is over.

What Sendmail *Doesn't* Do

Now, you might *think* that Sendmail sounds like an all-in-one e-mail system—but it's not. That last little part, about how Martin receives the message from his local mail server, *doesn't* use SMTP, and therefore *doesn't* involve Sendmail at all! In most of the Internet world, that leg of a mail message's journey typically uses one of three protocols:

- POP2 (Post Office Protocol, version 2)
- POP3 (Post Office Protocol, version 3)
- IMAP4 (Internet Messaging Application Protocol, version 4)

And those aren't the *only* possibilities, either. If Martin's company uses Exchange as its mail server (which certainly looks likely from the name of the mail server), then an Outlook client would talk to the Exchange server using a Microsoft protocol called the Messaging Application Program Interface (MAPI). Exchange can, however, also let you access your mail via POP3, so you needn't use Outlook on the desktop if you use Exchange on the server.

What does this mean to you? That in order to get a fully functional e-mail server running, you need not only SMTP software—that is, Sendmail—but also POP3 software.

Verifying Sendmail Installation

Because Sendmail is so basic to all Linux servers, it is pretty much always part of the standard installation. You will probably find that it is currently running on your system. Try using ps to see if it is there:

```
# ps aux | grep sendmail
root 504 0.0 0.2 1860 312 ? S Jun28 0:01 sendmail
#
```

If it's not already running, you can verify that it is on your system using the which command when you are logged in as root:

```
# which sendmail
/usr/sbin/sendmail
```

You should find it located in /usr/sbin.

If your system doesn't have Sendmail installed, then you can (if your system uses RPM) try:

```
# rpm -q sendmail
sendmail-8.11.6-15
```

If somehow it is not installed, I guess you're going to have to install it.

Installing Sendmail

At this point you're probably familiar with this installation routine. On RPM-based systems, you'll need to locate the rpm file (from your installation media or the Internet) and then issue a command such as:

```
rpm -ivh sendmail-8.11.6-15.i386.rpm
```

Verifying That POP3 Is Installed

We could use IMAP4, POP2, or POP3 for a delivery protocol, but let's set up POP3. The program that I've seen implement POP3 on Linux is named ipop3d, so do a which to see if it's installed:

```
which ipop3d
```

You'll probably find it in /usr/sbin. If not, however, then you'll have to install it with an RPM from the Red Hat CD-ROM with this command:

```
rpm -ivh /misc/cdrom/RedHat/RPMS/imap*
```

That RPM will automatically install the fragments necessary for xinetd. Red Hat 7.3 disables ipop3 by default, so you'll need to modify the file /etc/xinetd.d/ipop3 and change the line that says disable=yes to disable=no. Then restart xinetd to register your changes:

```
/etc/rc.d/init.d/xinetd restart
```

Starting and Stopping Sendmail

Regardless of whether or not you had to install Sendmail, you control it, like most other server services, by running the init scripts found in /etc/rc.d/init.d (on most distributions). If you want to manually issue the command to start Sendmail, you can do something like:

```
# /etc/rc.d/init.d/sendmail start
Starting sendmail:        [ OK ]
# /etc/rc.d/init.d/sendmail stop
Shutting down sendmail:   [ OK ]
#
```

Or use sendmail restart to perform both actions at once. If the stop command does not work, you'll need to use ps to identify the process ID and then kill off the process.

WARNING Don't just try to start up Sendmail by simply issuing the command /usr/sbin/sendmail. It needs a series of command-line options in order to start. Use the init scripts.

Now, you'll notice that I didn't configure anything yet. I just started the server up after it was installed. I did this because the default configuration files provided with Sendmail will allow it to start up perfectly fine. It won't really do much, although it *will* deliver mail between local users on the system. Our journey into Sendmail configuration is about to begin.

Setting Up MX Records

This is a bit redundant, but it can't hurt to reiterate that you could set up the finest Sendmail server on the planet, but it's no good if no one can find it, so be sure that you have an MX record pointing to your Sendmail server for every domain that server supports.

As I said, we're going to demonstrate using a single Sendmail server to serve both foobirds.org and birdeaters.com. In order for that to work, the foobirds.org zone must contain an MX record pointing to wren.foobirds.org, *and* the birdeaters.com zone must contain an MX record pointing to wren.foobirds.org—and if you look back to the DNS section, you'll see that we've already put those MX records in place.

Configuring Sendmail

In the world of Unix/Linux, there are many configuration files that look cryptic. There are many commands that have obscure and bizarre syntax. But there is nothing out there really that compares to the cryptic and strange text you will find in /etc/sendmail.cf. To get a taste of it, open the file in an editor and scroll down through the file. The top of the file looks fairly normal (as far as Linux configuration files go), but then you start seeing rulesets with text that looks like this:

```
R$* < @ $=w > $*        $: $1 < @ $2 . > $3
R$* < @ $=V > $*        $: $1 < @ $2 . > $3
R$* < @ $j > $*         $: $1 < @ $j . > $2
R$* < @ $=M > $*        $: $1 < @ $2 . > $3
```

Clear and easy to understand, right? Sure... in truth, there is a pattern to it. It's really just an incredibly long list of if-then rules that dictate how an e-mail address is rewritten and ultimately how it is delivered. Dan says the notation is so cryptic because they wanted Sendmail to operate extremely fast and parse the rules as quickly as possible, and I'm sure that was a really good idea back in the days when *One! Whole! MEGAHERTZ!* was pretty exciting. Nowadays, I'd be happy with a slightly less CPU-efficient language that was a bit more readable by humans. I particularly like the line written by the guy who designed Sendmail, Eric Allman. He explains that while Sendmail configuration looks complex *now*, the reader should remember how difficult programs written in C looked before the reader learned to program in C. Eric, baby—when you're writing a book for us network administrator types, I hate to say it, but many of us *can't write C programs*.

But here is the good news: you can safely ignore most of sendmail.cf. You can go through all your life working on Linux systems and *never* have to touch most of sendmail.cf! Twenty-something years of Sendmail evolution has brought about a pretty solid set of address rewrite rules. The basic sendmail.cf that you get with Red Hat will only require a minimum of modification to do the job.

But nowadays you're not supposed to mess with sendmail.cf; instead, there is a file /etc/mail/sendmail.mc that you work with and then run through the "m4" processor, which spits out a new sendmail.cf. It's kind of necessary because of some changes to Sendmail's default behavior.

You see, as of Sendmail 8.9, you can pretty much just about turn on a Sendmail server and start sending mail... as long as you're sitting at it. But *nothing*—and I mean nothing!—else in the world can talk to it. If you try to send mail to a server from another computer, you get "Connection actively refused."

The reason is that spammers—the evildoers who fill up your mailbox with junk offering to enlarge your manly parts, see celebrities naked with barnyard animals, start a home-based Internet business to make big bucks, turn back the clock with human growth hormone, and get a cheaper home mortgage—dare not use their own mail servers to send you this junk. (Do you ever wonder how these jerks stay in business? Who actually *buys* this garbage anyway?) They dare not because then you'd figure out who they were and perhaps get them shut down. Also, they'd have to use their own bandwidth, and the first rule of spamming is, "As long as I'm going to be the kind of person whom people compare to toads when they wish to insult toads, then I may as well steal someone else's bandwidth."

As you've seen, Linux by default runs Sendmail on just about every computer whether you asked for it or not. And, as Sendmail's old default settings caused the server to agree to send mail for anyone, well, there were plenty of places for spammers to exploit. Hence the new defaults for Sendmail 8.9 and later. (You're using 8.11 on Red Hat.) The only problem with this is that it frustrates the heck out of people trying to make Sendmail work the first time. You can make your Sendmail work to accept mail from other computers like so:

- First, edit `/etc/mail/sendmail.mc`.
- Find the line that includes the phrase `DAEMON_OPTIONS`...
- Put a "`dnl `" on the front of the line to comment it out—move your cursor to the beginning of the line that includes `DAEMON_OPTIONS` and type `dnl`, followed by a space. This `dnl` stuff is Sendmail-ese for "comment."

But we're not done with `sendmail.mc` yet....

Define the Domains

We want this mail server to accept mail for both foobirds.org and birdeaters.com. Sendmail is by nature paranoid, and so it'll ignore any mail that it's not been explicitly told to accept. Edit `/etc/mail/sendmail.mc` and look for the line that says `Cwlocalhost.localdomain`. Delete it, and tell Sendmail to accept mail for these two domains by adding these lines:

```
Cwfoobirds.org
Cwbirdeaters.com
```

Or, alternatively, you can combine them into a single line:

```
Cw foobirds.org birdeaters.com
```

It's less important, but you can then also add this line:

```
DMfoobirds.org
```

This tells Sendmail that for outbound mail, all local users will have @foobirds.org appended to their user ID. Without this, the full DNS domain name would be added. In my example, the user ID might wind up being mark@wren.foobirds.org. This is only relevant, however, if I'm sending mail while sitting at wren, and only with a very basic mail client. If I were sending mail from Outlook, Messenger, Eudora, or any other modern e-mail client, then that client would automatically specify the Reply To address.

Building a New *sendmail.cf*

Now go ahead and save sendmail.mc. Run m4 to create the new sendmail.cf like so:

```
m4 /etc/mail/sendmail.mc > /etc/sendmail.cf
```

After a quick restart of the Sendmail daemon (/etc/rc.d/init.d/sendmail restart), the changes will take effect.

As I suggested earlier, part of the magic here is that I earlier set up an MX record for foobirds.org as part of my DNS configuration. So when a remote SMTP server wants to deliver mail to user@foobirds.com, it will use DNS to find the MX record for foobirds.org, and then connect to that IP address using SMTP. On my end, Sendmail will wait for those inbound connections, accept them, and then deliver the mail appropriately.

Want to try it? If you've followed the examples so far and have a valid DNS zone configured for foobirds.org, you can test it out. I'll show you a test using the Linux mail command with a -v option for verbose output. As root, type:

```
# mail -v root@foobirds.org
Subject: Test
This is a test.
.<enter>
CC:<enter>
```

As soon as you type that period and hit the Enter key, you should see:

```
root@foobirds.org... Connecting to local...
root@foobirds.org... Sent
You have new mail in /var/spool/mail/root
#
```

The last line shows up because, well, you *are* sending mail to yourself. If this didn't work, check to make sure you have an MX record set up in your DNS zone for foobirds.org. If not, add one in and restart the DNS server.

Once this works, congratulate yourself because you've just configured Sendmail. Okay, so this was a really simple example. Don't worry, I'll show you some tougher stuff coming right up.

Setting Up Aliases

One of the first things you might want to do is set things up so that mail for several different e-mail addresses will wind up going to the same inbox. For instance, to take into account how people might address messages to me, I might want to receive mail at all of the following addresses:

```
mark@foobirds.org

markm@foobirds.org

mminasi@foobirds.org

mark.minasi@foobirds.org

info@foobirds.org
```

To do this, I need to modify the *aliases* file, /etc/aliases. Open this file; you'll see that the format is pretty straightforward, and you should see some aliases already defined for you.

To set up the situation above, let's assume my user ID is mark. Given this, I will already be set to receive mail at mark@foobirds.org. Setting up the remainder of the addresses is easy. I just add the following lines to the file:

```
markm:        mark

mminasi:      mark

mark.minasi:  mark

info:         mark
```

There's one more step. I have to tell Sendmail that the aliases file has changed. Because this is something frequently done, there is actually a special command for it:

```
# newaliases
/etc/aliases:37 aliases,longest 10 bytes,411 bytes total
#
```

Now all those aliases I added should work perfectly fine.

By the way, one interesting thing I can do with the aliases file is to create mailing lists. For instance, I'll add an entry:

```
authors:  mark, dan, craig
```

With this, any mail sent to authors@foobirds.org, or simply authors on the local machine, will be distributed to the three of us. You wouldn't want to run a large mailing list this way, but you certainly can use it for small lists.

Another interesting use of /etc/aliases is to redirect e-mail for a user to another e-mail address. For instance, let's say user dan isn't going to be connecting to our system to get e-mail, but I'd like him to have an e-mail address here. I can redirect this to his regular e-mail account by putting a line into /etc/aliases in the format:

    dan: dyork@lodestar2.com

Now e-mail to dan@foobirds.org will be redirected to dan@lodestar2.com. You get the idea.

Of course, after any of these changes are made you need to run the newaliases command.

Handling Multiple Domains

But I said that we're set up to handle more than one domain. What does that imply for usernames? Well, all those aliases I set up previously for foobirds.org now work for all users at birdeaters.com, too!

The truth of the matter is that the aliases file works for all users that Sendmail determines to be local users. Since I've now told Sendmail to treat both foobirds.org and birdeaters.com users as local, the aliases file will work fine for both domains.

Sounds good, but there's a "gotcha": What if I wanted mark@birdeaters.com to go to one user and mark@foobirds.org to go to another user? By default, that won't happen— mark@*anything* will go to the local mark account, so mail for both marks will end up in the same place. You can get around this also, but it involves a few more steps.

For starters, we need two separate user accounts for our two users. One of them could certainly be the user mark, but the other one needs a different user ID. In my example, I'll use the user IDs mark and markstwin. So you have two separate accounts.

The next step is to configure the *virtual user table* found in a file in the /etc/mail directory called virtusertable. The format is similar to /etc/aliases, except that addresses on the left side do not end in a colon. In my example, the file will look like:

    mark@foobirds.org   markstwin

Wait a minute. What about mark@birdeaters.com? Well, if I really wanted to, I could enter it here for the sake of clarity. But since Sendmail will treat birdeaters.com as local, and since a local user account exists for mark, mail to mark@birdeaters.com will be correctly routed to the inbox for the user mark.

Now if I had chosen a different user ID—say markm instead of simply mark—I *would* have to enter the lines in virtusertable as:

```
mark@foobirds.org     markstwin

mark@birdeaters.com   markm
```

In any event, I set up this table to map virtual users to local user accounts. It should just work, right? Wrong. Remember the newaliases command for /etc/aliases? We have to perform a similar action, but there's not a simple command to do it. If you list the files in /etc/mail, you'll see that there is virtusertable and virtusertable.db. I edited the text file and now need to generate the database file that Sendmail uses. The commands to do this are:

```
cd /etc/mail

make
```

As soon as that command is finished, I should have mail to those addresses routing correctly to the appropriate inboxes.

Tell the Server Who May Use It to Send Mail

Thus far, you've only sent mail by sitting at the mail server itself and sending mail. But if you were to go to another machine, perhaps a Windows box running Outlook, and you told Outlook to use this server as your SMTP server, then you'd get an error the first time that you tried to send mail out. For example, from Outlook Express, the error would look something like:

```
The message could not be sent because one of the recipients was
rejected by the server. The rejected e-mail address was
'joe@acme.com'. Subject 'test mail to the Internet', Account: 'My
account', Server: 'wren.foobirds.org', Protocol: SMTP, Server
Response: '550 5.7.1 <joe@acme.com>... Relaying denied. IP name
lookup failed [192.168.0.10]', Port: 25, Secure(SSL): No, Server
Error: 550, Error Number: 0x800CCC79
```

Believe me, if you do any Sendmail work at all, that'll become a well-known and hated error message. To understand the error, let's look more closely at what's happening.

The Sendmail server is sitting on some IP address, let's say 192.168.0.10. Your Windows box is on some other IP address, 192.168.0.50. You want to send to someone for a domain that the server at 192.168.0.10 *doesn't* handle—let's say, for example, Bill Gates. So you're sitting at Outlook, and you compose a message to billg@microsoft.com. You click the Send/Receive icon in Outlook, and Outlook says, "Hmm, I've got to get this message to someone named billg@microsoft.com. How do I do that? Oh, I see, I've been instructed to use this server at 192.168.0.10 to handle my outgoing mail," and starts an SMTP transaction to wren.foobirds.org.

Now, wren says to itself, "So this guy on some other system wants me to send some mail; well, that'd be all right if he's mailing someone on one of my domains, foobirds.org or bird-eaters.com. But he wants me to mail someone at some *other* domain. I dunno about that."

In SMTP talk, Outlook is asking wren to *relay* some SMTP mail for it. That wasn't a big deal until a few years ago, when the spammers arrived. Until about 1995, virtually every SMTP server on the planet was ready, willing, and able to relay mail from anywhere to anywhere. That's how the spammers send out so much junk but are hard to track down; by relaying, they "bounce" their mail off a bunch of servers.

It's considered good practice to *never* put an SMTP server on the Internet that acts in that old-fashioned sure-I'll-relay-your-stuff-no-problem way; such a server is called an *open relay*. But it's easy to get lazy and leave open relays around, particularly when e-mail servers are all installed by default as open relays. So the Sendmail guys decided for better or worse that as of Sendmail 8.9, they'd set up their servers to absolutely refuse to relay for anybody, forcing you to figure out how to relax their standards.

Suppose you have a network with a range of IP addresses from 192.168.0.1 through 192.168.0.254. You want to set up one mail server that any system in your network can use. Clearly, then, you have to say to this mail server somehow, "Go ahead and accept relays from anyone in the 192.168.0.0 network." You do that by modifying an ASCII file /etc/mail/access. You can enter domain names, hostnames, and network names, followed by the word RELAY. Here are a few examples:

- 192.168.0.50 RELAY tells the mail server to accept relays, but only from the machine at 192.168.0.50.

- 192.168 RELAY tells the mail server to accept relays from anyone in the range of 192.168.0.0 through 192.168.255.255.

- 192.168.0 RELAY says to accept relays from any IP address in the range of 192.168.0.0 through 192.168.0.255.

- minasi.com RELAY says to let anyone in the minasi.com DNS domain relay through this server.

I probably want my whole 192.168.0.*x* network to be able to use this e-mail server, so I enter 192.168.0 RELAY and save /etc/mail/access. Then I've got to type:

```
make
```

to have Sendmail create another database, and I restart Sendmail to have the changes take effect.

It's a bigger topic, but I'd mention that it's also possible to enter values other than RELAY. You can use numeric error codes, like the common 550:

```
junkmailers.com    550 we don't like your kind around here
```

Anyone e-mailing you with an e-mail name of *something*@junkmailers.com would, then, get a bounce message saying something like:

```
ERROR:  550 we don't like your kind around here
```

And while that might make you feel good, the fact is that spammers usually don't bother keeping their e-mail lists cleaned up, and responding *does* waste your outgoing bandwidth, so you could use the DISCARD command:

```
junkmailers.com  DISCARD
```

There is another command, OK, that says to accept mail that you might reject otherwise. For example, suppose you had these commands:

```
junkmailers.com    DISCARD

goodguy@junkmailers.com  OK
```

In this case, because goodguy@junkmailers.com is part of junkmailers.com, then any e-mail from him would be discarded—but the extra OK command overrides it. (More specific rules apply.)

Testing Your Sendmail Configuration

Now perhaps you'd like to test your configuration file to see if it all works. You could obviously actually send e-mail and check to see whether it gets to the appropriate person (by using Linux mail clients to read the mail). But Sendmail does have a command-line option -bt that allows you to test your configuration. If I issue this command, I'll get:

```
# sendmail -bt

ADDRESS TEST MODE (ruleset 3 NOT automatically invoked)

Enter <ruleset> <address>

>
```

My first reaction was, "Okay, now what?" Dan gave me a quick explanation that, basically, this allows me to run an address through all those rewriting rules that I mentioned were in /etc/sendmail.cf. He said to see the results I'm looking for, I need to run the address through rulesets 3 and 0. So armed with that cryptic information, my first attempt is a local user named mark:

```
# sendmail -bt

ADDRESS TEST MODE (ruleset 3 NOT automatically invoked)
```

```
Enter <ruleset> <address>
> 3,0 mark
rewrite: ruleset  3  input: mark
rewrite: ruleset 96  input: mark
rewrite: ruleset 96 returns: mark
rewrite: ruleset  3  returns: mark
rewrite: ruleset  0  input:   mark
rewrite: ruleset 199  input:   mark
rewrite: ruleset 199  returns: mark
rewrite: ruleset  98  input:   mark
rewrite: ruleset  98  returns: mark
rewrite: ruleset 198  input:   mark
rewrite: ruleset 198  returns: $# local $: mark
rewrite: ruleset  0  returns: $# local $: mark
>
```

Okay, I can interpret the output enough to know that this means mail is delivered to a local user. Now I'll try a full domain name of a user I know is local:

```
> 3,0 dyork@foobirds.org
rewrite: ruleset  3  input:   dyork @ foobirds . org
rewrite: ruleset 96  input:   dyork < @ foobirds . org >
rewrite: ruleset 96  returns: dyork < @ foobirds . org . >
rewrite: ruleset  3  returns: dyork < @ foobirds . org . >
rewrite: ruleset  0  input:   dyork < @ foobirds . org . >
rewrite: ruleset 199  input:   dyork < @ foobirds . org . >
rewrite: ruleset 199  returns: dyork < @ foobirds . org . >
rewrite: ruleset  98  input:   dyork < @ foobirds . org . >
rewrite: ruleset  98  returns: dyork < @ foobirds . org . >
rewrite: ruleset 198  input:   dyork < @ foobirds . org . >
rewrite: ruleset 198  returns: $# local $: dyork
rewrite: ruleset  0  returns: $# local $: dyork
>
```

Again, the results are fairly easy to figure out. One more test before I try my virtual user. This time I'll try a nonlocal user:

```
> 3,0 dyork@lodestar2.com
rewrite: ruleset   3  input:   dyork @ lodestar2 . com
rewrite: ruleset  96  input:   dyork < @ lodestar2 . com >
rewrite: ruleset  96  returns: dyork < @ lodestar2 . com . >
rewrite: ruleset   3  returns: dyork < @ lodestar2 . com . >
rewrite: ruleset   0  input:   dyork < @ lodestar2 . com . >
rewrite: ruleset 196  input:   dyork < @ lodestar2 . com . >
rewrite: ruleset 196  returns: dyork < @ lodestar2 . com . >
rewrite: ruleset  98  input:   dyork < @ lodestar2 . com . >
rewrite: ruleset  98  returns: dyork < @ lodestar2 . com . >
rewrite: ruleset 195  input:   dyork < @ lodestar2 . com . >
rewrite: ruleset  95  input:   < > dyork < @ lodestar2 . com . >
rewrite: ruleset  95 returns:  dyork < @ lodestar2 . com . >
rewrite: ruleset 195 returns:  $# esmtp $@ lodestar2 . com . $: dyork
➥ < @ lodestar2 . com . >
rewrite: ruleset   0 returns:  $# esmtp $@ lodestar2 . com . $: dyork
➥ < @ lodestar2 . com . >
>
```

This one looks a little stranger, but at the end, I see that instead of local, I see esmtp. According to Dan, this is the method that Sendmail will use to deliver the message. Essentially, it's going to use SMTP. (Note that on your system you may see a slightly different delivery method, but the key thing is that it will not be local.)

Now, finally, I'll show you the virtual user:

```
> 3,0 mark@foobirds.org
rewrite: ruleset   3  input:   mark @ foobirds . org
rewrite: ruleset  96  input:   mark < @ foobirds . org >
rewrite: ruleset  96  returns: mark < @ foobirds . org . >
rewrite: ruleset   3  returns: mark < @ foobirds . org . >
rewrite: ruleset   0  input:   mark < @ foobirds . org . >
rewrite: ruleset 199  input:   mark < @ foobirds . org . >
rewrite: ruleset 199  returns: mark < @ foobirds . org . >
```

```
rewrite: ruleset  98 input:   mark < @ foobirds . org . >
rewrite: ruleset  98 returns: mark < @ foobirds . org . >
rewrite: ruleset 198 input:   mark < @ foobirds . org . >
rewrite: ruleset  97 input:   markstwin
rewrite: ruleset   3 input:   markstwin
rewrite: ruleset  96 input:   markstwin
rewrite: ruleset  96 returns: markstwin
rewrite: ruleset   3 returns: markstwin
rewrite: ruleset   0 input:   markstwin
rewrite: ruleset 199 input:   markstwin
rewrite: ruleset 199 returns: markstwin
rewrite: ruleset  98 input:   markstwin
rewrite: ruleset  98 returns: markstwin
rewrite: ruleset 198 input:   markstwin
rewrite: ruleset 198 returns: $# local $: markstwin
rewrite: ruleset   0 returns: $# local $: markstwin
rewrite: ruleset  97 returns: $# local $: markstwin
rewrite: ruleset 198 returns: $# local $: markstwin
rewrite: ruleset   0 returns: $# local $: markstwin
>
```

It's a bit longer, but notice that in the end it did correctly indicate that the mail will be delivered to the local user markstwin. There are many more ways you can test addresses, but this should give you just about enough to make you dangerous.

Oh, yeah, one more thing. You're probably wondering how to get out of this Sendmail test mode and get back to the prompt. If you're like me, you tried various commands:

```
> exit
No address!
> quit
No address!
> end
No address!
>
```

I also tried Ctrl+C. The trick is to use Ctrl+D. There is actually a bit of sense here, believe it or not. You may know that in the Microsoft world, we indicate the end of a text file with a Ctrl+Z. In the Unix world it's been Ctrl+D; so Sendmail is just interpreting our input as a file, and it stops when there's no more file.

With that, I'll wrap up this little tour of Sendmail. Your server should now be functioning, and all of your aliases and virtual users functioning.

Cookbook Summary: Sendmail

This cookbook will set up a Sendmail server on Red Hat 7.3 that receives Internet mail for *anyname@foobirds.org* and *anyname@birdeaters.com*. Do this on the 192.168.0.10 machine, wren.foobirds.org.

Install the Server

```
rpm -ivh /mnt/cdrom/RedHat/RPMS/sendmail-8*
```

This is on the Red Hat Installation CD 1, so you'll have to eject CD 2 if you've still got it in your drive.

Check the MX Records   Make sure that both the /var/named/foobirds.org.zone and /var/named/birdeaters.com.zone files contain this MX record:

```
birdeaters.org.  IN  MX 10 wren.foobirds.org.
```

Modify */etc/mail/sendmail.mc*

Edit /etc/mail/sendmail.mc and locate the line Cwlocalhost. Replace it with these lines:

```
Cwfoobirds.org
```

```
Cwbirdeaters.com
```

Find the line that includes the phrase DAEMON_OPTIONS and put "dnl " in front of it.

Generate a new /etc/sendmail.cf:

```
mt /etc/mail/sendmail.mc > /etc/sendmail.cf
```

Restart Sendmail:

```
/etc/rc.d/init.d/sendmail restart
```

Create User Accounts

Demonstrate that both domains can have a mark account and still get mail delivered correctly. Create an account named markfoo and another named markeater.

Create the *virtusertable*

In /etc/mail/virtusertable, type the following lines:

```
mark@foobirds.org    markfoo
mark@birdeaters.com markeater
```

Save the file.

Define Who Can Relay

In /etc/mail/access, add this line:

```
192.168.0  RELAY
```

Then type these two lines to translate that information to Sendmail:

```
cd /etc/mail
make
```

Start the Sendmail Server

Restart the Sendmail server like so:

```
/etc/rc.d/init.d/sendmail restart
```

You should see:

```
Stopping sendmail: [OK]
Starting sendmail: [OK]
```

Try It Out

Put a Windows machine on the 192.168.0.0/24 network and configure Outlook or Outlook Express to use wren as its POP and SMTP servers, then try sending mail to mark@foobirds.org or mark@birdeaters.com. Then sit at wren, log on as either markfoo or markeater, and type mail to receive and view your mail.

Linux As an FTP Server

The final "server" service I'll take a look at on Linux is using it as an FTP (File Transfer Protocol) server. It works a little bit differently than some of the others.

Why do we care about FTP? Well, it's still the major protocol used on the Internet for transferring files. It can also be an extremely useful tool for moving files within an intranet or the Internet. And, well, it can also be a security hole—but oh, by the way, it's usually configured to be active in most normal installations, so at the very least we might want to understand how to shut it down.

Checking the Server Installation

Let's first check to see if FTP is installed already. Here's the simplest test:

```
# ftp localhost
ftp: connect: Connection refused
ftp>
```

At this point, just type bye and press Enter and get back to a prompt.

If you do *not* have it installed, then pop the Red Hat Installation CD 2 into your CD-ROM drive, mount the drive, change to the RPM directory, and type:

```
rpm -ivh wu-ftpd-2.6.2-5.i386.rpm
```

Red Hat uses Washington University's version of FTP.; it's called wu-ftp because it's from Washington University. It's pretty standard on Linux servers. Once it is installed, the actual binary will be /usr/sbin/in.ftpd.

Just on a tangent, if FTP is already installed, and you'd like to find out what the package name is (for future reference), you can use one of those RPM tricks we learned earlier:

```
# rpm -qf /usr/sbin/in.ftpd
wu-ftpd-2.6.2-5
#
```

So if you *had* had to install it, you'd have used wu-ftpd-2.6.2-5.i386.rpm, as we saw in the rpm -ivh example.

Making FTP Function

So now you've got an FTP server... but it doesn't work. Why? Look in /etc/xinetd.d/wu-ftpd—it's an ASCII text file—and you'll see the line:

```
disable = yes
```

Another example, I suppose, of "Setup knows best!" You see, you might have explicitly *told* Red Hat Setup that you wanted an FTP server, but Red Hat Setup knows that FTP is inherently insecure—all those clear text passwords, don't you know—and so it craftily said, "Well, I suppose I have to install the thing, but I'll disable it in the process." Don't you just love patronizing Setup programs? I guess Red Hat's taken a few lessons from our friends in Redmond. Here's how to tell Red Hat that you mean business and really *want* the silly thing running:

```
vi /etc/xinetd.d/wu-ftpd
```

Once in the editor, change the disable=yes to disable=no and save the file.

Restart the xinetd "super server":

```
/etc/rc.d/initd.d/xinetd restart
```

Starting and Stopping FTP

Why'd we restart FTP with xinetd? Isn't there an ftpd or something like that? Yes, there is, but you don't use it to start FTP.

Here's what's happening. Remember xinetd, the "super server"? Almost all Linux systems configure FTP to be started by xinetd rather than having it be started as a stand-alone daemon. I can see this with a quick test:

```
wren# grep ftp /etc/xinetd.d/*

/etc/xinetd.d/rsync:# description: The rsync server is a good
addition to am ftp

 server, as it \

/etc/xinetd.d/wu-ftpd:# description: The wu-ftpd FTP server serves
FTP connections. It uses \

/etc/xinetd.d/wu-ftpd:service ftp

/etc/xinetd.d/wu-ftpd:  server                    = /usr/sbin/in.ftpd

wren#
```

(You may have more output, depending on what you've got loaded on your system.) There it is. We now know that there is a file /etc/xinetd.d/wu-ftpd that gives instructions to xinetd about how to launch in.ftpd.

So the truth of the matter is that to start FTP, I don't need to do anything; xinetd will take care of it for me automatically.

So, how do I shut down FTP? If I want to completely disable FTP, all I do is remove the wu-ftpd file from the /etc/xinetd.d directory.

Well, okay, that's not all I have to do. I have to tell xinetd to reread its configuration file. Rather than start and stop it, since it might be rather busy dealing with other network requests, I'm going to send it the HUP signal to tell it to reread the file. Also, rather than use ps to find out its process ID and then use kill to send the signal, I'm going to use the killall command, which lets me provide the process *name*:

```
killall -HUP xinetd
```

Now FTP should be disabled.

Configuring the FTP Server

With the exception of anonymous access, which I'll discuss below, there really isn't a whole lot to configure with FTP. When I use the `ftp` command (or some GUI tool) to connect to the `ftpd` server, I supply a username and password. Assuming they are correct for a local user account, I will be placed into the home directory for the user ID. So if I connect with `ftp` as user mark, odds are that I'll wind up in /home/mark.

> **NOTE** I should mention that when you log on to FTP using your username and password, that name and password are sent in clear text over the network; anyone could then see your password. In contrast, you probably know that you can log on to FTP servers using the magic name "anonymous"—we'll talk about that in a bit—which does not require passwords. From a security point of view, then, I would only use FTP for anonymous access to data that I didn't mind the whole world seeing.

It's very much like using Telnet to log in remotely. I can `cd` to different directories. I have the same permissions restrictions I would if I were logged in. The difference is that essentially I just have two commands to download and upload files: `get` and `put`.

There are, however, three files worth mentioning: `ftpusers`, `ftphosts`, and `ftpaccess`. If they are on your system, you should find them in /etc. Most systems include an `ftpusers` file by default, but the other two may or may not be there.

/etc/ftpusers has the basic purpose of listing which user accounts are *not* allowed to log in using FTP. When I open mine, I find a long list in the format:

```
root
bin
daemon
adm
lp
...
```

My file goes on at some length, but you get the idea: just one user ID per line. So if I want to restrict someone from connecting in with FTP, I simply add their user ID to /etc/ftpusers. No need to restart `ftpd` or anything, since all of that is handled by `xinetd`. The next time someone tries to connect with FTP, `xinetd` will start up `in.ftpd`, which will read the `ftpusers` file and respond accordingly.

`/etc/ftphosts` allows a finer level of control. What if I want to allow fred to connect with FTP, but only when he is connecting in from his desktop machine called sparrow? Or perhaps I have a contractor called sally whom I want to be able to connect using FTP from anywhere on the internal network, but not from the Internet?

I solve these scenarios by adding either `allow` or `deny` lines to `ftphosts`. The format is:

```
allow fred sparrow

allow sally 172.16.0.0/16

allow mark *.minasi.com

allow craig sparrow osprey wren

deny dan

deny craig puffin.foobirds.org
```

Notice the variations I have used for matching the address. I can use a single hostname, a space-separated list, a full domain name, or a partial domain name with a wildcard match. In the case of `deny dan`, I am denying him access from *any* host, which amounts to being the same thing as if I had put him in the `/etc/ftpusers` file.

NOTE   The format I used for the IP address, 172.16.0.0/16, says to evaluate only the first 16 bits of the (32-bit) address. If you are not familiar with this notation, it is the same thing as saying that I want to use a subnet mask of 255.255.0.0. In fact, I *could* have used that notation here, but the format would be `172.16.0.0:255.255.0.0`.

I find these three files interesting, because it seems like `ftpd` started off with just a very basic access control mechanism in `ftpusers`, then developed to have a bit finer control with `ftphosts`, and then finally evolved into a large amount of access control with `ftpaccess`.

Yes, with `/etc/ftpaccess`, there are many different types of settings you can configure for `ftpd`. There's a catch, however. The default setting of `ftpd` is *not* to use the file. Why not? My guess is that since `ftpd` has been around since the very early days of the Internet, the program's developers did not want to roll out a new version and break the access control systems everyone already had in place. So they made the use of `ftpaccess` an option that sites could enable if they want to. That's my guess, anyway. I can check this by looking in the `/etc/xinetd.d/wu-ftpd` file:

```
# default: on
```

```
# description: The wu-ftpd FTP server serves FTP connections. It uses
➥#          normal,unencrypted usernames and passwords for authentication.
service ftp
{
        socket_type            = stream
        wait                   = no
        user                   = root
        server                 = /usr/sbin/in.ftpd
        server_args            = -l -a
        log_on_success        += DURATION
        nice                   = 10
        disable                = yes

}
```

If the line for server args contains -a at the end, my system will look for /etc/ftpaccess. If not, it won't. If I want it to, all I have to do is edit /etc/xinetd.d/wu-ftpd and add -a to the end of the line.

The contents of ftpaccess control several different aspects of ftpd. Here's a look at my file:

```
class  all   real,guest,anonymous  *
email root@localhost
loginfails 5
readme README*   login
message /welcome.msg        login
compress        yes         all
tar             yes         all
chmod           no          guest,anonymous
delete          no          guest,anonymous
overwrite       no          guest,anonymous
rename          no          guest,anonymous
log transfers anonymous,real inbound,outbound
shutdown /etc/shutmsg
```

And guess what? The man page for ftpaccess will show another dozen or so options I can put in here. Yes, it's a bit of a step up from the plain, old ftpusers file.

Forgetting about the first line for a moment, the rest of the file really just describes what messages users see, what capabilities they have, and what information gets logged. There's also a line in there (loginfails) that will close the FTP connection after five failed login attempts. And there's the e-mail address of the FTP server maintainer (this appears in some messages from the FTP server to the user).

But the interesting line for the access restrictions I am concerned with is the very first line:

```
class  all  real,guest,anonymous  *
```

Right now, this establishes a "class" called all that allows all types of access from anywhere on my internal or external networks. Note that ftpaccess defines three types of access to the FTP server:

real   Users provide a valid user ID and password.

guest   Users provide a guest user ID and password.

anonymous   Standard anonymous FTP.

A guest user is like a "real" user, except they are restricted to certain areas of the FTP site and have other restricted permissions. Note that a guest user *does* have to provide a valid password. I'm not going to cover it here, but there are additional directives for the ftpaccess file that allow you to designate certain user IDs as "guest" IDs.

I want to show you a better example:

```
class internal real,guest,anonymous 172.16.0.0/16
class all real *
```

In this example, I will allow any type of FTP access from within my internal network, but someone coming in from another network (such as the Internet) will have to provide a real username and password. As in the ftphosts file, I can use IP addresses, hostnames, and full or partial domain names (with wildcards) in my matching statements.

WARNING The order of the class statements is very important. If multiple statements could apply to a given connection, the *first* one listed in the file will take effect. Essentially, ftpd just goes down the class statements until it finds one that can match the incoming connection.

If there is no class statement that will apply for a given inbound connection, access will be denied. As in ftphosts, I also have a deny statement:

```
deny *.foocats.org
```

but notice that this is denying users based on *hostname* (or IP address) rather than denying access based on the *username*.

That's a quick trip through ftpaccess. As I mentioned earlier, this file has a great number of other options available, but this should get you going.

Configuring Anonymous FTP Access

I went through all of this discussion about access control to be able to talk about how to restrict "anonymous" FTP access on your server.

Doing an Anonymous Logon

First, let's talk about what anonymous FTP access is really all about. When I use my web browser to connect to an FTP server to retrieve software, I am using *anonymous* FTP. Essentially, my web browser is connecting in to the server and literally logging in as the user anonymous. No joke. If you have never used command-line ftp, try this out:

```
# ftp localhost
Connected to localhost.
220 localhost FTP server (Version wu-2.5.0(1)
504 AUTH GSSAPI not supported.
504 AUTH KERBEROS_V4 not supported.
KERBEROS_V4 rejected as an authentication type
Name (localhost:mark): anonymous
331 Guest login ok, send your complete e-mail address as password.
Password:
230 Guest login ok, access restrictions apply.
Remote system type is Unix.
Using binary mode to transfer files.
ftp>
```

You can see that for the username, I actually typed the word anonymous. Trust me, after you do this for a while you get very good at spelling *anonymous*. For a password, I followed the convention of entering my e-mail address, which the server will enter into a log file.

Okay, so now I'm in. I can type ls and see a very basic directory structure:

```
ftp> ls
227 Entering Passive Mode (127,0,0,1,41,136)
```

```
150 Opening ASCII mode data connection for /bin/ls.

total 6

d--x--x--x  2 root root 1024 May 26 1999 bin

d--x--x--x  2 root root 1024 May 26 1999 etc

drwxr-xr-x  2 root root 1024 May 26 1999 lib

drwxr-xr-x  2 root 50    1024 Mar 21 1999 pub

226 Transfer complete.

ftp>
```

It looks kind of like my regular system, but it's not.

Where Anonymous Users' Data Resides

Here's what's happening. In my /etc/passwd file, I have defined a user called ftp as
follows:

```
ftp:x:14:50:FTP User:/var/ftp:/sbin/nologin
```

> **NOTE** I found that if I installed ftp with the rpm, then the system did not create
> the /var/ftp directory, so you might have to with mkdir /var/ftp.

The important thing is the home directory, in my case /var/ftp. If I look at the contents
there:

```
# ls -l /var/ftp

total 4

d--x--x--x  2 root   root 1024 May 25 1999 bin/

d--x--x--x  2 root   root 1024 May 25 1999 etc/

drwxr-xr-x  2 root   root 1024 May 25 1999 lib/

drwxr-sr-x  2 root   ftp  1024 Mar 21 1999 pub/
```

Gee, look familiar? This is the directory tree into which the anonymous FTP user is
placed. They can't cd anywhere else on your system. As far as they are concerned, they
are seeing the top-level root of your system.

> **NOTE** Summarizing, then, anonymous FTP users see only whatever's in the
> /var/ftp directory. People who log in with recognized user accounts, however,
> don't see /var/ftp; rather, they see their home directories.

By convention, if I am going to make files available through anonymous FTP, I place them in subdirectories underneath the /pub (as in "public") directory. I don't have to. I can create directories here in /var/ftp if I want. But the convention is that everything goes underneath /pub.

Disabling and Enabling Anonymous Access

So this is all great, but what if I don't want to allow anonymous FTP access? How do I disable it? (Or conversely, if it is disabled on my system and I *want* it, how do I enable it?)

It turns out that there are really four different ways (and places) to disable anonymous access. I only need to use *one* of the methods. I'm telling you all of them because there may be a time when you are trying to *enable* anonymous FTP access, and you'll need to check all four of these items.

- First off, I can simply delete the FTP user from /etc/passwd. No user. No access. Simple. Easy.

- As a second approach, I just add the name anonymous to the /etc/ftpusers file. Again, simple.

- My third approach would be to go into /etc/ftphosts and add the line:

      deny anonymous

  Again, not terribly difficult.

- Finally, I could go into /etc/ftpaccess and change the line:

      class all real,guest,anonymous *

  to:

      class all real,guest *

  (If I'm feeling really paranoid, I could remove guest access as well.)

After doing any of these four steps, I will have disabled anonymous access to my FTP server.

By the way, with some FTP servers, the inbound user might not know immediately that anonymous access was disabled. On my Red Hat system, after doing one of the above, it looks at first like I can still get in:

ftp localhost
Connected to localhost…
Name (localhost:mark): **anonymous**
331 Guest login ok, send your complete e-mail address as password.

```
Password:
530 Login incorrect.
Login failed.
ftp>
```

Notice the message that says "Guest login ok...". Guess again: it's not!

Anonymous FTP can be a great way to make information available to other users and also to the general public. But some people do consider it a security risk, and therefore you can disable it. It's your call, but at this point I distribute important files via HTTP pages.

Cookbook: FTP

There's not really much to do here. Tell xinetd to enable the FTP service and tell DNS that you've got an FTP server available. To make sure that wren.foobirds.org acts both as ftp.foobirds.org and ftp.birdeaters.com, just create CNAME records to that effect.

In the /var/named/foobirds.org.zone file, include this line:

```
ftp        IN    CNAME  wren.foobirds.org.
```

Then, in /var/named/birdeaters.com.zone, include this line:

```
ftp        IN    CNAME  wren.foobirds.org.
```

There is not, to my knowledge, a way to create multiple "virtual" FTP sites—I don't think there's a way for the ftp.foobirds.org people to see different files than the ftp.birdeaters.com people.

Creating a Larger Network

Up until now, I've been describing services that you could run on a Linux server to publish information or communicate with people on the Internet. DNS, Apache, Sendmail, and FTP are all useful services, but what if you don't have an Internet connection in the first place?

In this next part of the chapter, I'm going to look at several different ways to set up a Linux server to be part of a larger network. First I'm going to talk about setting up a system with multiple Ethernet cards, as this is the method of connection I can use with either a cable modem or a DSL connection. Then I'll take a look at dial-out modem connections. And then I'll show you a great Linux feature called IP masquerading and talk about some basic security functions.

Multiple NICs and Routing

Obviously the first thing I have to do to set my Linux server up with a second NIC is, well, shut down the machine and install the second NIC!

There's nothing different about it in Linux than in NT, 2000, or any other operating system that runs on Intel-based hardware. Shut it down, open the box, plug in the card... and oh, yeah, I may still have to worry about IRQs and I/O ports. Sorry, but that's an Intel issue. If I have newer PCI cards, I may be all set, but with older ISA cards, I may need to know (and configure) the specific parameters.

WARNING In all honesty, I (Mark) just plain don't even *own* that many ISA Ethernet cards anymore, as I write this in mid-2002. Because of the increased ease of configuration of PCI cards over ISA cards, I want to stress that I really recommend using only PCI Ethernet cards on desktops. Of course, on laptops it's a different story, as PC Card is about it; Linux doesn't support Cardbus all that well yet. The following example, however, includes an ISA Ethernet card just to make it as "rich" (to borrow some Microsoft-speak) as possible.

Now, before I shut my Linux server down, I *can* take a look at what interrupts and I/O ports are currently in use. The files I want to look at are /proc/interrupts and /proc/ioports. (Remember that things in /proc look like files although they are actually maintained by the system.) Here's what my /proc/interrupts looks like:

```
wren# cat /proc/interrupts
          CPU0
   0:  43490505    XT-PIC  timer
   1:     23446    XT-PIC  keyboard
   2:         0    XT-PIC  cascade
   5:         0    XT-PIC  Sound Blaster 16
   8:         2    XT-PIC  rtc
  10:         0    XT-PIC  usb-uhci
  11:    310943    XT-PIC  eth0
  12:     92962    XT-PIC  PS/2 Mouse
  13:         1    XT-PIC  fpu
  14:   1668767    XT-PIC  ide0
  15:         5    XT-PIC  ide1
```

Pretty straightforward. I can see my first Ethernet card there at IRQ11. It looks like right now IRQ3 or 7 would be available. Alternatively, you might see the device name listed (eth0), but you might also see the name of the card (3c509).

WARNING   Note that you *won't* see information for an Ethernet card that's not working yet. If, in the previous example, you typed ifconfig eth0 down and then tried a cat /proc/interrupts again, you would not see eth0 listed. Just as with the Windows NT Diagnostics, you can't display interrupts of hardware that's installed—only hardware that's installed and *functioning*. Furthermore, the truth is that in an all-PCI system this kind of information tends to be "read-only"—you usually can't tell a PCI card to use a different IRQ unless your BIOS supports that notion. (Which, by the way, is a pretty good thing to look for when buying computers.)

Due to its length, I'll spare you the printout of /proc/ioports, but a quick glance should tell you which I/O ports are available for your use.

Installing the Second NIC

Time to install the second NIC. When you open up the PC to install it, make a note about the brand and model of both the second NIC and, now that you have the cover off, the first NIC. That way, if Linux emits some error message about (for example) an "NE2000," then you'll have a clue about which NIC is giving it fits.

Now, if I happened to install the identical type of NIC as the first NIC already in my box, then chances are that during the boot process I'll see a message indicating that Linux automatically found my second NIC. It might look something like:

```
3c90x.c:v0.99L 5/28/99 Donald Becker
eth0: 3Com 3c905B Cyclone 100baseTx at 0xc000, 00:10:5a:25:e7:d8, IRQ 11
   8K byte-wide RAM 5:3 Rx:Tx split, autoselect/Autonegotiate interface.
   MII transceiver found at address 24, status 786d.
   MII transceiver found at address 0, status 786d.
   Enabling bus-master transmits and whole-frame receives.
eth1: 3Com 3c905B Cyclone 100baseTx at 0xc100, 00:10:5a:53:a5:10, IRQ 3
   8K byte-wide RAM 5:3 Rx:Tx split, autoselect/Autonegotiate interface.
   MII transceiver found at address 24, status 786d.
   MII transceiver found at address 0, status 786d.
   Enabling bus-master transmits and whole-frame receives.
```

TIP   If this scrolled by too quickly during boot, you can always get it later by using the dmesg | less command. The later messages, once Linux enters interactive mode, appear in /var/logs/messages.

If this worked, I should be able to type ifconfig and see information now for both eth0 and eth1. Now, eth1 will not yet have any IP information, but it should at least show up.

Even if the NICs are different, there's a good chance that the second one may have been detected. If so, I'm all set and can go on to assign the IP address information to the second NIC.

If I don't see eth1 with ifconfig, a couple things could be wrong. Try this first:

```
ifconfig eth1 up
```

Or try configuring eth1 via DHCP, if you have eth1 on a network with a DHCP server:

```
dhcpcd -d -B eth1
```

If that doesn't work, and if you're sure that there's a DHCP server on eth1's segment, then look in /var/logs/syslog to see why the lease process failed.

If eth1 still doesn't show up on an ifconfig, though, I'll use ping to test that my first NIC is still working. There could be IRQ conflicts that could have disabled both NICs, although truthfully that's pretty unlikely if your NICs are all PCI cards. Assuming that works, I've got to dig a little deeper to see what the problem is.

One issue, especially common with ISA NICs, is that the kernel may not be autodetecting the cards. To configure the second NIC to be detected, I will need to modify /etc/modules.conf. In my file, the only network-related line I have is:

```
alias eth0 3c90x
```

Your file may have numerous other lines in there as well. Let's say that my other NIC is a garden-variety ISA NE2000–compatible card. All I need to do is change the text to read:

```
alias eth0 3c90x
alias eth1 ne
```

Now, how did I know that the driver for an NE2000 is ne? What I did was go over to the directory /lib/modules/*kernelversion*/kernel/drivers/net (such as /lib/modules/2.4.18-3/kernel/drivers/net—yours will be for whatever version of the kernel you have installed) and look at the available NIC drivers. Quite frankly, I guessed at it.

I'm almost ready. One other issue is that because this is an ISA card, I need to supply the driver at least the I/O port of where the card is. So I'll add another line here:

```
alias eth0 3c90x
alias eth1 ne
options ne io=0x330
```

At this point, I will simply issue the command:

```
wren# modprobe eth1
```

I should now see the eth1 interface with ifconfig. If this doesn't work, I might try adding the IRQ onto the line:

```
options ne io=0x330 irq=3
```

By the way, if you're really having trouble here, rather than constantly modifying /etc/modules.conf, you might just try using the driver and options directly with modprobe until you figure out what you need. Then you can put the information into /etc/modules.conf. The sequence is:

```
wren# modprobe ne io=0x330, irq=7
wren# ifconfig eth1
```

And then repeat until you either see eth1 or give up in frustration and decide to try using a different NIC card.

WARNING   If this still isn't working, you need to consider whether or not the NIC is correctly configured. Some older NICs need to have a software program run in order to configure their settings. Oh, and by the way, most of those are *DOS*-based programs. Hopefully you can find a bootable DOS floppy that has the appropriate configuration programs on it.

One final note on all of this: What if I had two NIC cards that used the same drivers, but I needed to hand-enter the information to get those NICs jump-started? For instance, what if I had two NE2000 cards? The entries in /etc/modules.conf are only slightly different:

```
alias eth0 ne
alias eth1 ne
options ne io=0x300,0x330 irq=3,11
```

The first of each pair of numbers refers to eth0 (I/O address 0x300 and IRQ 3); the second refers to eth1 (I/O address 0x330 and IRQ 11). With that, I should be all set.

Assigning IP Information to the Second NIC

At this point, I have the second NIC installed and operational. When I type `ifconfig eth1`, I see:

```
eth1 Link encap:Ethernet HWaddr 00:80:C8:84:36:3A
    UP BROADCAST RUNNING MTU:1500 Metric:1
    RX packets:136706 errors:0 dropped:0 overruns:0 frame:0
    TX packets:147459 errors:0 dropped:0 overruns:0 carrier:0
    collisions:16 txqueuelen:100
    Interrupt:11 Base address:0x330
```

Now all I need to do is assign IP address information. Let's assume that my internal network is using IP addresses in the Class C network of 192.168.1.0/24, and the external network I am connecting to uses network number 172.20.20.0/24. My internal NIC, eth0, has an IP address of 192.168.1.10. My external NIC, eth1, is going to have 172.20.20.32. Both networks use a subnet mask of 255.255.255.0.

To configure eth1 with this information, all I need to do is use the `ifconfig` command string I talked about back in Chapter 4. Here it is:

```
ifconfig eth1 172.20.20.32 netmask 255.255.255.0
➥broadcast 172.20.20.255 up
```

Now, before I celebrate, I'm just going to check the routing table (I'm using -n with `route` to get the "numbers;" i.e., I don't want it to try to go off and resolve hostnames using reverse DNS):

```
route -n
Kernel IP routing table
Destination  Gateway  Genmask        Flags  Metric  Ref  Use  Iface
192.168.1.0  0.0.0.0  255.255.255.0  U      0       0    0    eth0
172.20.20.0  0.0.0.0  255.255.255.0  U      0       0    0    eth1
127.0.0.0    0.0.0.0  255.0.0.0      U      0       0    0    lo
```

If it looks like this, I'm all set. In theory, when a new NIC is configured and brought up, the new route should be added automatically.

If the route did not appear, I would need to issue the following command:

```
route add -n 172.20.20.0 netmask 255.255.255.0 dev eth1
```

A quick check with `route -n` should show the route in place. I should also now be able to `ping` hosts on both networks.

NOTE   An alternative command that many people will use, especially those coming from Unix, is `netstat -rn`. It produces essentially the same information as `route -n`.

Routing between the Networks

So now that I have my system connected to two networks and the routes are all set, I'd like to have it function as a router between the two networks. All the pieces are in place. There's just one more thing.

You know how to do Ethernet-to-Ethernet routing in Windows NT: as explained in Chapter 14 of *Mastering Windows NT Server 4*, you have to turn on IP forwarding by going into the Network Control Panel, then TCP/IP, and then the Advanced tab, where there is one annoying little check box. (As you might have learned in Chapter 7 of *Mastering Windows 2000 Server*, it's a bit more complex, requiring you to install Routing and Remote Access Services.) Well, there's the same sort of thing here in Linux. I need to see the value of a file in /proc:

```
cat /proc/sys/net/ipv4/ip_forward

0
```

Oops, it's zero. That means IP forwarding is turned off. Here's how I turn it on:

```
echo 1 > /proc/sys/net/ipv4/ip_forward
```

That's it. Now my box will route packets between the subnets.

But wait a minute, you say; I thought you said those "files" out in /proc weren't really files and that you couldn't edit them? Well, that's mostly true. But there are exceptions and this is one of them.

Oh, and by the way, that change to /proc/sys/net/ipv4/ip_forward won't survive a reboot. In order to make sure that my machine recovers from a reboot and starts routing correctly, I'll add the line:

```
echo 1 > /proc/sys/net/ipv4/ip_forward
```

to my `/etc/rc.d/rc.local` or another similar startup file. (Or you can edit /etc/ `sysctl.conf`, and change "net.ipv4.ip_forward = 0" to "net.ipv4.ip_forward = 1". This works on Red Hat but not most other distributions.)

Now for my system to truly work as a router between the networks, I will need to inform the systems on both sides of the network that I am now available as a router. On my internal network, I might point the default gateway of my other systems to 192.168.1.10 (my eth0). If I have control of the other network, I could point their default gateway to 172.20.20.32 (my eth1). If I don't change their default gateways, I will need to somehow clue them in to the fact that the route is available.

Now maybe you're not going to route between two networks, but the basic concepts I discussed here will come into play a little bit later in the chapter when I talk about cable modems and DSL, because cable modem and DSL connections are just Ethernet connections. To let a bunch of computers in your house share a cable modem or DSL connection, then, you must have two Ethernet cards in the computer attached to the Internet—one Ethernet card connected to the cable modem or DSL and another connected to your home network. But you can't just turn on routing and have the computers on your home network immediately gain access to the Internet; you'll have to use something called *IP masquerading*—and we'll get to all of that, later in this chapter.

Connecting to the Internet

You have a bunch of server services running, but so far it looks like you're missing one pretty important piece: you're not connected to the Internet. Doing that is, according to Dan, "Quite simple: install a modem, set up PPP, and get connected." But he has an evasive grin as he says that. Sounds like there's a catch, Dan, hmmm? "Well, yes," he admits. "There's this, oh, minor issue with internal modems…" Seems that if you want to get Linux to dial up, you *really* want an external modem. And having followed his instructions on dialing up to the Internet from Linux, I've *got* to agree: if you want a good challenge, then go square the circle, or unravel the Gordian knot without any sharp objects. But if you want to get on the Internet, get an external modem.

Once you have your modem squared away, you then create a PPP connection, which is the technical term for something you've probably done dozens of times with Windows, NT, and 2000—that is, create an entry in your Dial-Up Networking phone book. That part can be a bit of work, but it's far easier than getting an internal modem to work, and as time goes on, it gets easier.

Installing a Modem

Here's how to be sure that your modem works with Linux: get an external modem and put it on either COM1 or COM2. If you care at all about your sanity, run, don't walk, down to your local computer store and buy yourself an external modem. That's the secret.

> ***TIP*** I'm not kidding. I spent a couple of days trying to get an internal modem (and not a *winmodem*; you can just about totally forget about those babies) to work on Linux and never *did* get it to work. Then I plugged in a no-name 56K modem that I had on another system, and things got a *lot* easier. Please, save yourself the trouble, go get an external model. You see, that way you don't really need to "introduce" the modem to Linux, as Linux only has to interact with the serial port, and serial ports are extremely well-understood and supported devices. Additionally, I've always preferred externals (even though they do take up more space) because they have lights and a separate power switch—when they lock up on you, you just cycle the power switch. With an internal, the only way to cycle the power switch is to turn the whole *PC* off. Not optimal. Sorry to beat this drum as much as I have, but I *really* want to get the point across.

Oh, yes, many internal modems will work fine with Linux. Typically, the older ISA plug-in card modems will work fine. Believe it or not, PCMCIA modems will work, too. But Linux currently has problems with many of the PCI-based modems.

And then there are these peculiar animals referred to generically as *winmodems*. Modems historically have had all the necessary pieces built into them to take your digital data, process it, buffer it, and convert it to analog signals to go out over a phone line. If you look at a modem card, there's all sorts of chips and things all over the card. Well, sometime in the late 1990s, some genius took a look a modem card and said, "Hey, why can't we do some of the digital processing in software? We could make use of the faster computers and save ourselves some money on the cost of manufacturing our hardware!"

Thus was born a modem that is a hybrid of hardware and software. The hardware part of the modem still converts a signal from digital to analog and vice versa. But now a piece of software handles much of the other processing that was typically done in hardware chips. This type of modem was, of course, quickly embraced by hardware manufacturers who are already living on razor-thin profit margins. Laptop vendors, too, always looking for ways to save on weight (and heat requirements), started using these types of modems.

There's only one slight problem with all of this. The vast majority of the software *only runs on Windows!* Hence the nickname of a winmodem—most won't even run on NT or 2000! So yes, if you have one of these puppies in your system, stop beating your head against a wall and just go buy an external modem. Your chances of having the thing actually work with Linux are pretty slim. How will you know? Odds are that if you can't remove a card—i.e., it's built onto the motherboard somehow—then you've got yourself a winmodem.

> **NOTE** Having said all this, there is an ever-intrepid crew of Linux developers hard at work attempting to develop drivers that will work with this type of modem. If you are stuck with one, visit www.linmodems.org to see if they have found a way to have Linux work with your system. Some work pretty well; for example, my Toshiba 4260 laptop's winmodem works with a set of drivers, built by Lucent Technologies, that I found at www.linmodems.org.

Warnings aside, you *can* make modems work with Linux. I'll take the easy case first (externals), then offer some advice about trying to make internals work.

Using an External Modem

To start using an external modem, I need to connect it to a serial port, and I need to figure out what the device is called in Linux. Here's how they are mapped:

```
COM1 = /dev/ttyS0
COM2 = /dev/ttyS1
COM3 = /dev/ttyS2
```

and so on.

> **NOTE** You may find some documentation referencing /dev/cua*n* instead of /dev/ttyS*n*. Prior to the Linux 2.0 kernel, there was one device for calling out (for instance, /dev/cua0) and a separate device for dialing in (/dev/ttyS0). However, the ttyS*n* devices now perform both roles, and the use of the cua*n* devices is strongly discouraged. It is expected that they will be removed from the Linux kernel at some future point. Red Hat 7.3, for example, calls them /dev/ttyS0, /dev/ttyS1, etc.

The next step is to make sure that there is no IRQ conflict with using the modem on that serial port. If my machine just has the two basic serial ports, I'm all set, as it's fairly uncommon for devices to use IRQs 3 or 4. If I'm going to use COM3, COM4, or beyond, I'll run into a problem because COM1 and COM3 share an IRQ, as do COM2 and COM4.

The answer is that if I need to use a different IRQ with the serial port, first I have to configure the hardware, and then in one of my startup scripts (such as `rc.local`), I need to include a line like:

```
setserial /dev/ttyS2 irq 7
```

In my case, I have your basic system, and my modem is plugged into what Windows calls COM1. So I'll use /dev/ttyS0.

Want to check the modem out? When working with a new modem under Windows, NT, or 2000, I like to start up a basic terminal program like Windows Terminal or Hyper-Terminal and just type ATT, followed by an Enter. A functioning modem should respond, "OK." Linux has a program like that, called minicom. Just start minicom and type ATT, then press Enter, and you ought to get "OK" back from the modem. (In my experience, I have to first get into minicom, tell it to talk to the correct serial port and at the right speed, and then save that as the default configuration. Next I exit minicom, turn off the modem, and turn it back on. Then I reenter minicom. It's all menu-driven and you won't find it hard; it just may require some experimentation.)

That's pretty much all you have to do at the basic hardware level. After I talk about internal modems, I'll explain the dial-out configuration.

Using Internal Modems

So maybe you don't really feel like shelling out the extra money for an external modem. Maybe you have no extra serial ports. Maybe you just don't like the thought of not being able to use a device that you paid for and that came with your system. The truth is, I can't guarantee that we can help you make it work, and it'd probably take another chapter to go into all of the details, so what follows is an outline of how you'd go about making (or trying to make) an internal modem work. Internal modems fall into five basic categories:

- Winmodems
- PCMCIA modems
- ISA modems
- PCI modems
- ISA plug and play modems

Winmodems and PCMCIA Modems   As mentioned previously, if you have a built-in winmodem, you're probably out of luck. But it never hurts to try. Yours just might work. Dan tells me that the built-in modem on his little Sony VAIO laptop worked like a charm, but it fails on newer models of the same laptop. But the guys at www.linmodems.org keep improving their stuff, so you might try downloading and compiling their linmodem support programs.

In Dan's case, here's how he got his internal laptop modem to work: Since his laptop came with Windows 98, he looked into the configuration there and found out that his modem was set up to be on COM2. Once he booted into Linux, he simply configured chat—which you'll learn about a bit later in this chapter—to work with /dev/ttyS1, which, as I mentioned above, is the Linux equivalent of COM2. It worked.

PCI Modems   Now, if you have a PCI modem card, there is an issue with support for some PCI modems not yet being available in the Linux kernel. To see if your card is one of the lucky ones that will work, you should visit:

> http://www.o2.net/~gromitkc/winmodem.html

Non–Plug and Play ISA Modems   If your modem card is an older ISA card, you may be able to get it to work by manually providing parameters with setserial, as in:

> setserial /dev/ttyS1 irq 7

You will need to put this in a file such as rc.local for it to start up at boot time.

ISA Plug and Play Modems   Lastly, if the modem card is an ISA card that supports Plug and Play, there is a program for Linux called isapnp that will attempt to load in your card. Essentially, I would run the command:

> wren# isapnp /etc/isapnp.conf

The configuration file must exist prior to executing the command. This command string must also be put into a startup file in order to survive a reboot.

One Final Modem Note

Just one last comment about modems. If you use the graphical tools that come with many of the distributions to install your modem, you will find that typically, they make a symbolic link from /dev/modem to whichever serial port your modem is connected to. Essentially, the programs have done this:

> wren# ln -s /dev/ttyS0 /dev/modem

This is fine, and you can do it if you want a handy reminder of which serial port you are connected to, but most programs should be able to work fine without the link.

Dialing Out to an ISP

So you finally have your modem installed and you're ready to connect. Now you need the Linux equivalent of Windows Dial-Up Networking. As usual in the Linux world, there are many options. If you spend a lot of time in a GUI environment, there are some excellent tools such as kppp, tkppp, and Kwvdialbut just to name a few. All of these will make it quite easy to configure your connection to an ISP, initiate the connection, monitor the status, and hang up the connection.

As I've spent most of the book talking about ways to do things without the GUI, I'm going to continue that and talk about a couple of options that you have. And no, there's no dishonor in ducking out to the GUI and firing up kppp (it's pretty self-explanatory) if all else fails. But you can probably imagine cases where being able to attach a fairly low-power machine to the Internet might be useful, and while it's true that Linux runs well on low-power machines, it's *not* true that it runs GUIs very well on low-power machines. For example, I have an old Pentium 133 that I want to make into a generic dial-up Internet gateway. The idea is that I want to connect it to my house network; then I'll be able to get to the Internet from any room in the house by just plugging a computer into the house Ethernet and trying to access the Internet—that'll trigger the Pentium 133 to dial out and connect to the Net. But it ain't gonna work very well if I have to run KDE or GNOME to make it happen!

I should note that all of these methods I'm mentioning, including the GUI tools, are really scripts that ultimately launch the PPP daemon, pppd, in the background to handle the connection. Once the connection is established by any of the tools, I can get to a shell prompt and type:

```
wren# ifconfig ppp0
```

to see the status of my connection.

wvdial

Red Hat includes a program called wvdial (pronounced, for some reason, as "Weave-Dial," according to their website). It makes setting up a connection to an ISP very easy. All you do is type wvdialconf at the command line and then edit the resulting file. Here's what happened when I did it on my machine:

```
wren# wvdialconf /etc/wvdial.conf
Scanning your serial ports for a modem.
Port Scan<*1>: Scanning ttyS0 first, /dev/modem is a link to it.
ttyS0<*1>: ATQ0 V1 E1 -- OK
ttyS0<*1>: ATQ0 V1 E1 Z -- OK
ttyS0<*1>: ATQ0 V1 E1 S0=0 -- OK
ttyS0<*1>: ATQ0 V1 E1 S0=0 &C1 -- OK
ttyS0<*1>: ATQ0 V1 E1 S0=0 &C1 &D2 -- OK
ttyS0<*1>: ATQ0 V1 E1 S0=0 &C1 &D2 +FCLASS=0 -- OK
ttyS0<*1>: Modem Identifier: ATI -- Zoom V.90 Serial s052099g -I Z207
ttyS0<*1>: Speed 4800: AT -- OK
```

```
ttyS0<*1>: Speed 9600: AT -- OK

ttyS0<*1>: Speed 19200: AT -- OK

ttyS0<*1>: Speed 38400: AT -- OK

ttyS0<*1>: Speed 57600: AT -- OK

ttyS0<*1>: Speed 115200: AT -- OK

ttyS0<*1>: Max speed is 115200; that should be safe.

ttyS0<*1>: ATQ0 V1 E1 S0=0 &C1 &D2 +FCLASS=0 -- OK

Found a modem on /dev/ttyS0, using link /dev/modem in config.

Modem configuration written to /etc/wvdial.conf.

ttyS0<Info>: Speed 115200; init "ATQ0 V1 E1 S0=0 &C1 &D2 +FCLASS=0"

wren#
```

As you can see, it scanned my serial ports and figured out various settings for my modem.
Here's my /etc/wvdial.conf file:

```
[Dialer Defaults]

Modem = /dev/modem

Baud = 115200

Init1 = ATZ

Init2 = ATQ0 V1 E1 S0=0 &C1 &D2 +FCLASS=0

ISDN = 0

Modem Type = Analog Modem

; Phone = <Target Phone Number>

; Username = <Your Login Name>

; Password = <Your Password>
```

The format should look familiar to anyone who's been around the Windows world for a
while; it's pretty much an INI file. But it's not going to work until I fill in my particulars—
phone, account name, and password. Once I've done that, it might look like:

```
[Dialer Defaults]

Modem = /dev/modem

Baud = 115200

Init1 = ATZ

Init2 = ATQ0 V1 E1 S0=0 &C1 &D2 +FCLASS=0

ISDN = 0
```

```
Modem Type = Analog Modem
Phone = 555-1234
Username = marktminasi
Password = f00bird
```

Notice one slight issue here in that my password is here in plain text. Now, only the root user can view this file, but you should still be aware that your password is here out in the open.

Now all I do is literally type wvdial at the prompt. It will go read /etc/wvdial.conf and connect out to my ISP. There is an issue here, though: it will take over the console and not give you your prompt back. If I hit Ctrl+C, this will cause wvdial to terminate the connection. This, incidentally, is how I cause wvdial to hang up when I am done using the connection.

This isn't a big deal if I'm in a GUI and I've issued the command in an xterm window (just bring up another xterm). But if I'm in a console window, it can be a headache. I have a couple of options. For one thing, I could switch to another virtual console (using Alt+F2, Alt+F3, etc.) and work there. Alternatively, I could use the shell background functions, as shown in this sequence:

```
wren# wvdial > /var/log/wvdial.log &
[1] 6354
wren#
```

When you want to bring the connection down, you have two choices. Either:

```
wren# kill %1
```

which will kill off your background job 1 (assuming that was the number given when you put wvdial into the background in the previous step); or you can more simply do:

```
wren# killall wvdial
```

Both of these commands will cause wvdial to close the connection and hang up the modem.

Anyway, wvdial is one option. The key strength it has is that it will autodetect your modem, and it has a very simple configuration file.

chat

Other than wvdial, one of the main command-line programs used for connections is a program called chat. Like wvdial, it needs a configuration file, but unlike wvdial, it's one you have to create yourself.

Now, chat is also different in that it is usually run as *part* of another script. Often Linux systems may have a script called ifup-ppp or ppp-on that reads some configuration information and then executes chat to make the connection.

Let me walk you through how it is installed on a Red Hat system. All the magic happens down in a directory called /etc/sysconfig/network-scripts. Inside of here, there are several scripts that I have to pay attention to. I'm going to set up the interface ppp0 (my first and only PPP connection), so I need to create a script called chat-ppp0. It has the contents:

```
'ABORT' 'BUSY'
'ABORT' 'ERROR'
'ABORT' 'NO CARRIER'
'ABORT' 'NO DIALTONE'
'ABORT' 'Invalid Login'
'ABORT' 'Login incorrect'
'' 'ATZ'
'OK' 'ATDT5554444'
'CONNECT' ''
'ogin:--ogin:' 'markm'
'ord:--ord:' 'f00birds'
'TIMEOUT' '5'
'~--' ''
```

As in wvdial.conf, I'm supplying the phone number, user ID, and password. Again, the password is stored here in plain text.

One thing you'll notice is that I didn't configure the serial port here. Well, I'm not done editing yet. I need to open up the file ifcfg-ppp0. Here's what it looks like on my system:

```
DEVICE="ppp0"
ONBOOT="no"
USERCTL="no"
MODEMPORT="/dev/ttyS1"
LINESPEED="57600"
PERSIST="yes"
DEFABORT="yes"
```

```
DEBUG="yes"
INITSTRING="ATZ"
DEFROUTE="yes"
HARDFLOWCTL="yes"
ESCAPECHARS="no"
PPPOPTIONS=""
PAPNAME=""
REMIP=""
NETMASK=""
IPADDR=""
MRU=""
MTU=""
DISCONNECTTIMEOUT=""
RETRYTIMEOUT="5"
BOOTPROTO="none"
```

Here you can see that I set the serial port and connection speed.

Now, you'll notice in this directory a script called ifup-ppp. That script is what uses these files and ultimately executes chat. However, I do *not* call this script directly. Instead, I use the standard ifup (interface up) command. It actually doesn't matter what directory I am in when I do the command, but I type:

```
wren# ifup ppp0
wren#
```

In the background, the ifup command will in turn activate ifup-ppp, which will execute the appropriate scripts. I won't see any feedback, but I should hear the modem if the speaker is turned on.

When I want to disconnect, all I do is type:

```
wren# ifdown ppp0
wren#
```

which will instruct pppd to close the connection and hang up the modem.

The good news with chat is that there are usually sample chat scripts lurking around somewhere on your system that can help you get up and running. Once configured, it's pretty basic to use.

Automating the Connection

Now I can bring up or down the connection any time I want, but what if I want to make it so that the connection automatically starts up any time there is outbound Internet traffic?

The good news is that developers out there in the open source world have come up with a couple of different approaches. The bad news is that they are currently in such a state of development that I can't really write about them here.

Probably the best-known of these programs is one called dialid. Essentially, it sets up a fake network interface on your system and points all outbound traffic to that interface. Whenever packets go to that interface, dialid automatically brings up the PPP connection and transfers those packets out via PPP. It also includes some access control so that you can monitor and control which packets bring up the connection.

dialid was under heavy development for quite some time, but then went into a state of suspension for actually a couple of years. Just shortly before I started writing this book, though, a new developer stepped forward, and it looks like development is once again underway. Check out the website for more information: dialid.sourceforge.net.

Dan tells me that he used to use dialid all the time and found it quite effective for his home office network. However, when he recently upgraded his main server to SuSE 6.4, the installation included both wvdial and also a script called wvdial.dod, which provides dial-on-demand connections using wvdial. In his own words, Dan said, "wvdial.dod totally rocks!" I guess you can tell he's quite happy with it. Unfortunately, at the moment it seems to be a SuSE-specific program, but keep your eye out, and you may find it available for other distributions.

Using Cable Modems and DSL

These days many of you may be able to access the Internet using so-called "cable modems" or through DSL (digital subscriber line) connections. Linux works fine with either of these connection types, and there's not really a whole lot to say.

Usually when you get one of these connections, it terminates in your house with a piece of hardware that ultimately has an RJ-45 jack for an Ethernet cable. With a cable-TV connection, that device is your "cable modem" (in truth, it's more like a bridge, but we won't quibble... the cable marketing folks thought that "cable modem" sounded better). With DSL, or at least the ADSL flavor of DSL (the most popular one), the device is an ADSL Network Termination (ANT). (And yes, the marketing people are now calling these "DSL modems." Sigh; makes me as mad as when people call V.90 modems "56,000 *baud*" modems, when any fool knows they're 56,000 *bits per second*.)

Essentially, then, this is how you connect via most cable modems and all DSLs: First, get the connection installed in your house. Second, put an Ethernet card in your system. (In my experience, the cable and DSL providers sometimes sell you an Ethernet card as part of your setup package.) Third, hook up a Cat5 patch cable between them (which, by the way, may have to be a *crossover* cable, a variation on the standard Cat5 patch cable, so it can't hurt to have a crossover cable in your box of communications stuff). Turn the computer on and convince Linux to see that Ethernet card, configuring the card for DHCP—the cable or DSL folks will probably give you an IP address via DHCP. Do *not*, however, hook up that RJ-45 connection on the cable modem/ANT to a hub so that you can hang a bunch of computers on the cable/DSL connection—that's not going to work. To connect your computer both to the cable/DSL outside connection and to some other computers in your house, you'll need to put a second Ethernet card in your computer. One segment attaches to the cable/DSL, and the other to the extra computers.

You're immediately going to wonder, "Can I turn the PC connected to the cable/DSL into a router so that my other computers can surf at high speed?" Not immediately, as the cable/DSL provider only gave you one routable IP address. But there's a way around that, something that we Microsoft types would call Network Address Translation but that the Linux world calls *IP masquerading*. Stay tuned: I'm going to show you how to do that in the next section, and it's actually quite simple. The *hard* part is getting Linux to recognize the stupid Ethernet cards, but then that's not news to you if you've gotten this far in the book.

That *ought* to be everything you need to know to connect to cable/DSL. But if you are interested in learning more about cable modems and/or DSL connections, your best bet is to occasionally browse through the appropriate HOWTOs to see if there is anything new to report:

```
http://www.tldp.org/HOWTO/DSL-HOWTO/
```

```
http://www.linuxdoc.org/HOWTO/Cable-Modem/index.html
```

Otherwise, just enjoy your fast connection and try not to think of all the folks out there slugging away at 56K or less.

Sharing the Internet: IP Masquerading

Okay, so I have my modem (or second NIC in the case of cable and DSL) configured correctly, and my connection to my ISP all set. Now I'd like to share that connection with the other systems on my internal network.

To do this I need to use IP masquerading. This is a form of what's called Network Address Translation (NAT). Essentially, all of the systems on your internal network hide behind the single IP address that your Linux server uses to connect to the Internet. As far as the outside world knows, all the packets coming from your network are coming from a single machine, when in reality they may be coming from any number of systems located behind the Linux server. As I mentioned earlier in this chapter, this does about the same thing as the Internet Connection Sharing feature of Windows 98 SE, Me, and Windows 2000.

Let me give you an example. I have my foobirds.org network, and wren.foobirds.org is my main server. It has a NIC connected to my internal network with an IP address of 192.168.1.10. It also has a modem that dials out to an ISP and gets a dynamically assigned IP address each time it connects. The wren server, then, is my in-between machine, the one connected both to the external Internet and to my internal network. I want to share this connection with all the other systems on my internal network.

To do this, I'm first going to configure some software on wren (I'll explain soon) to support IP masquerading. Then I'll simply point the default gateways for all the other internal machines to wren's internal IP (192.168.1.10). Somewhere in here I'll bring up the PPP connection on wren. And that's really it. All the internal users can connect to the live Internet. From the perspective of all the external web (and other type) servers, all they see is requests coming to them from `wren.foobirds.org`. The actual clients that are making the requests are invisible to the external servers.

The beautiful thing about this is that I don't have to do anything to the clients other than change their default gateway. There's no additional software or anything. This is all happening on the packet level.

Steps to making this work include:

1. Set up the internal, nonroutable network (our 192.168.0.0 network).

2. Set up the connection to the Internet, whether via modem, cable modem, DSL, or whatever, on a system that's also attached to the internal network. That's the in-between machine, as it has one foot in the internal network and the other one in the Internet.

3. Configure the routing piece `ipchains` on the in-between machine.

Configuring the Internal Network

The first thing I need to do is to make sure that the IP addresses I am using on my internal network do not conflict with those used on the live Internet. If my network has not been connected to the Internet yet, it hasn't mattered what I've used for IP addresses. Now it does. If I am using addresses that are, in fact, allocated to someone else, my local systems may not be able to get to those "real" systems, and what if one of those was a major website that I needed to access? Well, I'm out of luck.

So I need some bogus IP addresses. As it happens, the folks involved with creating the Internet thought about this and defined in RFC 1918 three blocks of addresses that will be *permanently unassigned* on the live Internet. They referred to these as for "private internets." The three ranges are:

- 10.0.0.0: An entire Class A range
- 172.16.0.0–172.31.255.254: A range of Class B addresses
- 192.168.0.0: An entire Class B range

I can choose any range in here and use an appropriate subnet mask.

For the purpose of my examples, I'm going to use the network of 192.168.1.0, and since I only have a few systems, I'm going to treat it as a Class C address block and use a subnet mask of 255.255.255.0.

If you've followed along with my examples, you'll notice that all my systems are already set up with appropriate addresses. The key address I need here is the one for wren.foo-birds.org: 192.168.1.10.

Configuring the External Network

I've already done this earlier in the chapter by getting wren set up to use an external modem and PPP to connect to an ISP. I just wanted to point out here that you *do* need this connection to be operational before you can do IP masquerading. In the case of PPP, it doesn't need to be online while we're doing this configuration, but it needs to have at least been configured.

Note, too, that IP masquerading can work not only with dial-up modem connections, but also with cable modems, DSL connections, and full-time leased-line connections. It will work with most types of Internet connection.

Configuring the Server

Now let's teach the in-between machine to route. From a command prompt, type these three lines:

```
modprobe ipchains
ipchains -P forward DENY
ipchains -A forward -j MASQ
echo 1 > /proc/sys/net/ipv4/ip_forward
```

As a matter of fact, you don't even have to remember to type the third line, as the second ipchains command warns you to! Go over to a machine on the internal network and ping some distant IP address, and you'll get a response!

That at-the-command-line stuff was great for instant gratification, but let's make this all survive a reboot. Log on to the server as root and create a file in /etc/rc.d called rc.firewall. (It's not a magic name; you can actually call it anything that you like.) Change its attributes to make it a script that the root can execute:

```
chmod 700 /etc/rc.d/rc.firewall
```

Then just reenter the three commands that you just executed:

```
ipchains -P forward DENY
ipchains -A forward -j MASQ
echo 1 > /proc/sys/net/ipv4/ip_forward
```

That's essentially it. Execute the script (make sure the Internet connection is up before you do so), pop open a web browser on an internal machine, and you should be able to view external websites.

> **NOTE** For masquerading to work, the Internet connection needs to be operational. However, if the connection goes down (as in the case of a PPP modem), you do *not* need to reexecute the script when the link comes back up. Once the ipchains rules are in effect, they will remain so until either they are modified or the system is rebooted.

Now, in order for this to survive a reboot, you need to add the execution of the rc.firewall script to rc.local. Just find it (it's probably in /etc/rc.d; that's where it is on Red Hat) and add this line anywhere in the rc.local file:

```
/etc/rc.d/rc.firewall
```

Save rc.local, and you're ready for the next reboot.

Let's just take a quick look at what this script does. It is using a tool that came into existence with the Linux 2.2 kernel called ipchains. Essentially, it creates a "chain" of rules about what to do with TCP/IP packets that are received by the kernel. I'll talk more about ipchains later, but for right now I'll tell you that this script is modifying the rules for the "forward" chain. Whenever a packet is to be forwarded, the kernel checks the forward chain to see if there are any rules that apply to this particular outbound packet. If there are, the kernel applies those rules. If it gets to the bottom of the chain and has not yet found a rule that matches, the kernel uses the chain's policy to guide what it does with the packet.

Clear as mud, eh? Well, I'll explain the example above. In the first line, I'm setting (-P) a default policy for the forward chain. The policy tells the kernel that if it cannot find a rule that matches the outbound packet, it should *deny* forwarding the packet. Just don't do it.

Now in the second line, I am adding (-A) a rule to the forward chain that says that any packets that are forwarded should automatically be masqueraded. Essentially, I'm overriding the policy. So why set the policy in the first place? Well, I don't want any nonmasqueraded packets to be forwarded. But would they get by that rule? No... but I guess you might just say it's a good policy (har, har) to set the default policy at the beginning of an ipchains ruleset.

The third and final line is what we did before in the section on routing to simply enable IP forwarding in the first place. Without this, the rules won't matter.

Now this was an *extremely* simple version of an IP masquerading script. In truth, it won't solve all our problems because there are some protocols that need some additional kernel modules loaded in order for them to work properly with IP masquerading.

Here's an example of a better IP masquerading file (again, save this as rc.firewall, make it executable, and then reference it in rc.local or one of the init scripts):

```
#!/bin/sh
# Load some kernel modules (there are more
# you can load)
depmod -a
modprobe ip_masq_ftp
modprobe ip_masq_raudio
# Enable IP forwarding
echo "1" > /proc/sys/net/ipv4/ip_forward
# If I'm connecting and getting a dynamic IP
# address (such as via DHCP on a PPP link), set this:
echo "1" > /proc/sys/net/ipv4/ip_dynaddr
# Enable IP fragmenting
echo "1" > /proc/sys/net/ipv4/ip_ip_always_defrag
# Set up IP forwarding rules
ipchains -P forward DENY
ipchains -A forward -s 192.168.1.0/24 -j MASQ
```

Notice in the last line that I have added -s 192.168.1.0/24. All this does is say that the packet should only be forwarded if the source address is from my internal network. In the scenario of my small network that I described earlier, I could have left it out. But this is just a small hint of what lies ahead with security.

Those are the basics of IP masquerading; there's obviously a whole lot more to it. If you want to know more and see other examples, I'd recommend that you view the IP Masquerading HOWTO at:

```
http://www.linuxdoc.org/HOWTO/IP-Masquerade-HOWTO.html
```

> **NOTE** Red Hat 7.3 also includes a replacement for ipchains called iptables that does much of the same thing as ipchains, with a lot more added. I've left it out of this edition because ipchains still works fine, but in case you run across references to iptables, then I want you to know what iptables is. Red Hat's set up so that if you give it both ipchains and iptables commands, it must run either ipchains or iptables, and for whatever reason Red Hat decided to set it up so that whenever there's a conflict, ipchains wins—which was another reason for staying with ipchains for the moment.

Creating a Dial-In Server

Now that I have my modem working for dial-out capabilities, I'd like to also add the ability for someone to dial in and connect (using PPP) to my system. I *might* want this because I'm looking to reproduce what NT provides with Remote Access Service, or I might just want to become a little one-line ISP.

Assuming that I already have a modem and PPP working, all I really need to do now is activate some type of program that will monitor the modem to see if someone has dialed in. Within the world of Linux and Unix, such a program is called a getty program. (Dan thinks it is "get tty", where tty is the historical name for a terminal.) There are, of course, several of them, but the one provided with almost all distributions of Linux seems to be mgetty.

One of the interesting things about mgetty is that it lets you use a single phone line for both dialing in and dialing out. Additionally, mgetty can differentiate between inbound data and fax calls and either connect the user (if data) or save the fax (if fax). I'll take a look here at how to configure it.

Checking the Installation

Here's some good news. All of the distributions I worked with put the configuration files for mgetty in the same place! Yes, as strange as it may seem in Linux, every distribution puts the mgetty setup files in a directory called /etc/mgetty+sendfax.

If for some reason I don't have that directory, I need to do the standard commands I've been using to verify that programs are installed:

```
# which mgetty
/sbin/mgetty
#
```

For your info, the exact location of the mgetty binary does seem to vary. Sometimes it is in /sbin and other times in /usr/sbin. If the file wasn't found, I can query with rpm, which *should* return something like:

```
# rpm -q mgetty
mgetty-1.1.28-3
#
```

If I conclude that it's not there, I'll have to find my installation media and install the RPM with:

```
# rpm -ivh mgetty-1.1.28-3.i386.rpm
```

As I mentioned, though, almost all of the distributions should have installed this by default. There are several steps I need to go through now.

Configuring *mgetty*

In order for this to work, I need to do a couple of things. First, I have to set up mgetty to monitor the modem, then I need to set up PPP to act as a server. I'll take you through the steps. I'm going to assume in these examples that my modem is on /dev/ttyS0 (the port formerly known as COM1).

Modifying */etc/inittab*

My first step is to modify /etc/inittab so that at startup it will launch mgetty. You may find that you already have an appropriate line in the file, but it has been commented out. In my file, I found a line and uncommented it, and then made sure it read:

```
S0:2345:respawn:/sbin/mgetty ttyS0 -D /dev/ttyS0
```

Let me explain this line. The first part, S0, is just an abbreviation for the serial port we are using. The next, 2345, indicates the runlevels at which we want to have mgetty operational.

respawn essentially tells `init` that we want `mgetty` to be active (the other entry you could see there is `off`, which does what it says). And then there is the command string.

The `mgetty` command really could just be `/sbin/mgetty ttyS0` (which tells it to start up `mgetty` on serial port `/dev/ttyS0`). But I added the `-D /dev/ttyS0` option, because that tells `mgetty` to receive only data on that serial port. I'm not going to use this system for inbound faxes.

I now have one more step to do. I have to tell `init` to reread its configuration file and launch `mgetty`. To do so, I use the `telinit` command:

```
wren# telinit q
wren#
```

I should now be able to see an `mgetty` process running with the `ps` command.

Configuring *pppd*

Next I'm going to configure `pppd` to be set up to receive connections as a server. Up until now it has been running as a PPP client. My first task is to create an options file for PPP. Since `pppd` may already have a valid options file for *dialout* in the standard location `/etc/ppp/options`, I am going to create my new file as `/etc/ppp/options.server`. Here are the contents:

```
auth -chap +pap
modem
crtscts
login
proxyarp
lock
-detach
ms-dns 192.168.1.10
```

Briefly, the first line says to use some type of authentication, but do not use CHAP and do use PAP. Next it says I'm using a modem. `crtscts` says to use hardware flow control. `login` says to use the `/etc/passwd` file. `proxyarp` makes your system pretend to be the remote system as far as ARP is concerned. `lock` just uses lock files to ensure that no other process can use the modem. Finally, `-detach` tells `pppd` to *not* fork off a separate background process. It turns out that some systems may have a problem if this is not here and will not hang up the modem when a session is finished.

The last line is interesting: ms-dns specifies a DNS server that is passed down to the Windows clients connecting to my box. I could pass along multiple DNS servers simply by having multiple ms-dns lines. What about Linux clients? It turns out that they will still need to have their own valid /etc/resolv.conf file.

Modifying */etc/ppp/pap-secrets*

Since I said to use PAP as my authentication protocol, there's another file to be concerned with: /etc/ppp/pap-secrets. Now this file *can* contain usernames and passwords, but since those passwords are stored in plain text, I want pppd to authenticate using the passwords in /etc/passwd. I did this by adding login to the pppd options.server file I built above.

So all I really have to do is check /etc/ppp/pap-secrets to make sure there are no lines in here that will conflict. Really, I want there to be a single line with the format:

```
*  *  " "  *
```

Now there are no passwords stored here.

Assigning an IP Address

Somewhere in here I have to give the serial port a valid IP address that the PPP user will use to communicate on our network. To do that, I will create a file called /etc/ppp/options.ttyS0 (change the name if you're using a different serial port). Its contents are simply:

```
192.168.1.10:192.168.1.50
```

The first IP address is that of my server. The second is the address that I am going to assign to the serial port. Notice that I am statically assigning the address to this port. There may be a way somewhere out there to assign this dynamically from a DHCP server, but I couldn't find it.

If you think back to Windows NT, RAS configuration gave you the same option of assigning an IP address to the serial port.

Modifying *login.config*

There's one more thing. I have to tell mgetty to automatically start up PPP when there is an inbound data connection, and also to use my new options.server file I created. To do all this, I cd over to /etc/mgetty+sendfax and open the file login.config. There's probably already a line in there for what I want to do. I need to find it and make it read as follows:

```
/AutoPPP/ - - /usr/sbin/pppd file /etc/ppp/options.server
```

Believe it or not, with that, I'm done. Since I've already told `init` to reread its configuration file, `mgetty` should just be out there listening.

Configuring PPP Clients

Our server is now fully operational. On the client side, there's not really much to say. If it's a Linux system, you will need to follow the instructions earlier in the chapter about how to set up a connection to the Internet (only in this case it is your own server). If it's a Windows system, you'll typically go into Dial-Up Networking and create a new connection.

Basic Server Security

The subject of security on Linux/Unix servers is one that could and does consume many entire books, documents, and online websites. I'm not going to turn you into an expert overnight, but I want to give you just some very basic things that you can do to make your system more secure. You can choose to implement some of my suggestions or to explore the topics I raise further and implement even stronger security. It all depends upon your level of paranoia and what level of risk you are willing to tolerate.

Passwords

I hope it would go without saying that you need to use good passwords for all of your user accounts. By "good" I mean ones that are not dictionary words, pet names, birth dates, home towns, etc. Yes, you want your passwords to be easy to remember, but you don't want to make them easy to guess.

Some distributions include security commands such as `crack`, `saint`, and `cops` that will check your `/etc/passwd` file and attempt to break the passwords. These tools can be quite useful in seeing how secure your servers are. They are, of course, available on the Internet.

Many of the distributions also use something called Pluggable Authentication Modules (PAMs), and you have some configuration options there. Look on your system to see if you have a directory called `/etc/pam.d`. The files in this directory control the authentication that takes place through various commands.

To provide some checking of passwords, I'm going to go into `/etc/pam.d` and open the file `passwd`. I want to verify that there is a line here that reads:

```
password  required  /lib/security/pam_cracklib.so
```

What this will do is check new passwords when a user is changing their passwords with the passwd command. If the new password is based on a dictionary word, the user will be warned. They actually will still be able to use the password, but they will be warned.

While in this file, I will also remove the words nullok if I see them there. This will allow a user to have an empty password. I don't want that.

There's a whole lot more that PAM can do. Take a look at some of the other files here and the man pages for more information.

Disable Unneeded Services

A basic thing to do is to stop running services that I don't need. There are two ways to do this, because I really have two different types of services. Some are started by their own startup script and others are launched through xinetd.

I'll take care of the xinetd services first. To disable an xinetd-based service, I just find its file in /etc/xinetd.d and ensure that the file contains the line "disable = yes".

After I've gone through and disabled all unnecessary services, I have to tell xinetd to reread its configuration file. The easiest way is to do this:

```
killall -HUP xinetd
```

Now I have to go deal with my startup scripts. I need to cd over to /etc/rc.d (on most distributions) and look at the rc.n directories. Inside there are various scripts of the format Sxxdaemon. But if I look at them with ls -l, I find that they are actually just symbolic links to the scripts over in the init.d directory. I'll show you. Here's one that is running on my system for which there is no reason for it to run: S20rwhod. (There's a command called rwho that let's you see who's logged in on a remote system.) If I list its information, I find:

```
ls -l S20rwhod
lrwxrwxrwx 1 root root 8 Jun 9 16:20 S20rwhod -> ../init.d/rwhod
```

Now I have two options. One is to just simply remove the symbolic link. Just do:

```
rm S20rwhod
```

and the problem is solved. But what happens if later I *want* this service to run? What is the appropriate number to use in the init sequence? A more subtle approach is to simply change the beginning of the filename from a capital *S* to a lowercase *s*. This will cause it not to be started, but the file will still be there for the future. I just do:

```
mv S20rwhod s20rwhod
```

As an added bonus, these disabled services will now show up on the bottom of my standard ls directory listing.

Note that you will need to go into *each* of the /etc/rc.d/rc.*n* directories and disable services that would start up at that runlevel.

There's no need to modify the K kill scripts because, well, they stop services from running and that's what we're trying to do.

A final note. The procedure here stops a service from starting up in the future. However, that service may be running right now. To be sure that it is stopped, I need to use ps and kill to stop the current instance of the process:

```
wren# rm S20rwhod
wren# ps aux | grep rwhod
root   9314 0.0 0.4 1056 544 ? S Jun 03 0:00 rwhod
root 21317 0.0 0.3 1132 416 pts/6 S 08:03 0:00 grep rwhod
wren# kill 9314
wren# ps aux | grep rwhod
root 21325 0.0 0.3 1132 416 pts/6 S 08:05 0:00 grep rwhod
```

Note that if it was still alive in the second ps, I would need to use kill -9 with the process ID.

Disabling Unneeded Apache Modules

While I'm on the subject of disabling unnecessary things, the Apache web server comes by default loading all sorts of modules for various services that they thought I just might need at some future point. But who knows if sometime there will be a vulnerability found in one of those modules? By the time I might find out about it, someone may have exploited the hole and penetrated my system.

To disable these modules, I need to find my httpd.conf file. Remember our discussion of web servers? You have to find that file. Mine is in /etc/httpd/conf/httpd.conf. Inside I find a whole string of lines with the format:

```
LoadModule php3_module modules/mod_php.so
```

Now, some of these I need, but others I don't. The one I show here will let me use PHP (an open source scripting language similar to Active Server Pages) in my web pages, but if I'm not, why do I need it? All I do is comment it out:

```
#LoadModule php3_module /usr/lib/apache/libphp3.so
```

and then restart Apache. The Apache online manual should give you a good idea of what all these modules do. You should be able to find it at:

```
http://localhost/manual/mod/index.html
```

Disabling Unneeded CGI Scripts

Continuing on the theme, you should look in the directory where your Apache server keeps its CGI scripts. On my Red Hat system, this is /var/www/cgi-bin, but it may vary on your system. If you don't know why the script is there, get rid of it! Move it somewhere else. Delete it. Whatever.

Sometimes, distributions include sample scripts to give you an idea of how to write CGI scripts. It's nice of them to help, but if you don't know what these are for, you don't know if they are opening up security holes.

Using TCP Wrappers

If you have used Linux distributions other than Red Hat (or even older versions of Red Hat), they used inetd instead of xinetd, and there was an inetd.conf file. If you were to look in that file, you would see this text on each line that says /usr/sbin/tcpd. Here's an example:

```
telnet stream tcp wait root /usr/sbin/tcpd in.telnetd
```

This actually implements a feature called *TCP wrappers* that checks an access control file (actually two) before actually launching the service. The two files it checks are /etc/hosts.allow and /etc/hosts.deny. With xinetd, you are no longer explicitly calling the tcpd command, but the files are still used by xinetd.

Here's how it works. When inetd calls tcpd, tcpd does the following steps:

1. Checks in /etc/hosts.allow to see whether there is a rule that specifically allows the connection.

2. If there is no match, it checks in /etc/hosts.deny to see if there is a rule that denies the connection.

3. If there is still no match, access is granted and the service is launched.

So what's in the two files? A series of rules in the format:

```
servicename: (hosts that can connect)
```

There are also special keywords such as ALL and LOCAL.

Let me show this through an example. Here's how I could set my system up to be very restrictive:

```
wren# cat /etc/hosts.allow
ALL: LOCAL
ALL: .birdeaters.com
wren# cat /etc/hosts.deny
ALL:ALL
wren#
```

> **NOTE** In this context, LOCAL means all hosts that connect to your machine using simply a single "hostname" and not an FQDN. This *should* be all the machines on my local network. Assuming I am in the foobirds.org domain, I don't need to also put .foobirds.org specifically in the file for *local* machines. Now if I have remote machines in the foobirds.org domain and I want them to access my system, I will need to adjust the line appropriately: ALL: .birdeaters.com, .foobirds.org.

Let's look at this script. In hosts.allow, I am allowing any connections from local machines or from those in birdeaters.com. Because of the ALL:ALL in hosts.deny, all other connections are refused.

Okay, that was a wee bit harsh set of rules. Basically, nobody from the outside can get in. Let's say that I want to let everyone in, except for specific hosts. In this case, I don't really need hosts.allow, because if a service is not denied in hosts.deny, it is by default granted. So here are my rules:

```
wren# cat /etc/hosts.allow
wren# cat /etc/hosts.deny
ALL: .crackers.com
in.telnetd: badguy.birdeaters.com, fred.foobirds.org
in.ftpd: fred.foobirds.org, .usomewhere.edu
ALL EXCEPT in.ftpd: contractor.foobirds.org
wren#
```

Here you can see that anyone coming in from a host at crackers.com will be denied. I am then restricting a couple of specific machines and entire domains from connecting using Telnet and FTP. Finally, I am restricting all connections from contractor.foobirds.org except for FTP.

In the end, I just have to come up with the combination of rule sets that will only allow the specific people I want to connect to my machine. There are, of course, many more things you can do with TCP wrappers, but this should get you started. Do a man on hosts.allow for more information.

Examine Your NFS Exports

One other hole to look at is how open your exported NFS filesystems are. Remember from our discussion of NFS that exported filesystems are found in /etc/exports. (Of course, if you're not doing NFS, then there's nothing to worry about.) If I set a filesystem up with essentially no security, such as this:

```
/tmp        (rw,insecure)
```

then anyone on my network, or conceivably on the Internet if I have no firewall, can connect to my machines using the command:

```
mount -t nfs wren.foobirds.org:/tmp /mnt/tmp
```

They can then mess around with whatever is there.

One obvious way to check this is to examine the actual /etc/exports file. Another way is to use a command called showmount, which is installed by most distributions. On my local system I can just type:

```
wren# showmount -e

Export list for wren:

/tmp (everyone)

wren#
```

From a remote system, I would just add the domain name:

```
puffin# showmount -e wren.foobirds.org

Export list for wren.foobirds.org:

/tmp (everyone)

puffin#
```

This should clue you in to the fact that you need to modify the /etc/exports file and restrict this to your local network.

> **WARNING**   Remember that after you modify /etc/exports, you need to run
> exportfs -a to have the NFS server reread the exports file.

If you don't have showmount installed, unfortunately I can't really tell you which package
it's in, because that varies widely. On a Red Hat system, it was in the package named nfs-
utils, while on a SuSE system it was in a package named nfsserv. Hopefully you'll just
have it installed.

Modifying */etc/issue*

Whenever I log in to my system, either on the console or through Telnet, the system greets
me with a nice little login message:

```
Red Hat Linux release 7.3 (Valhalla)
Kernel 2.4.18-3 on an i386
wren login:
```

What's wrong with this? Well, I've just given a potential intruder a good bit of information. He or she now knows what type of operating system I'm running (indeed, even the
type of machine I'm running it on) as well as the level of my current Linux kernel. Armed
with this information, the intruder now has a better idea of where there might be vulner-
abilities with my system.

Why give away this information? Let's be a little more protective. This login message is
stored in a file called /etc/issue. To change it all you have to is change the file. How's
this for an edit?

```
------------------------------------------------

Unauthorized Access Prohibited.

Intruders will be strung up by their toenails.

------------------------------------------------
```

Okay, perhaps a little melodramatic and an invitation to be attacked, but you get the
point. Now this will be seen every time someone goes to log in.

Firewalling with *ipchains*

Finally, the big topic. Remember the bare-bones ipchains file we created earlier in the
chapter to configure masquerading? Well, it only represented one small part of what
ipchains does. In truth, ipchains is primarily a TCP/IP packet filter. It's designed to be

used as a firewall. It just happens that along the way it also does IP masquerading. So now let's talk about packet filtering.

> **NOTE** As I explained earlier, Red Hat 7.3 (and in fact any Linux distro using the 2.4 kernel) has iptables, which provides even more capabilities (such as stateful packet inspection) and flexibility. However, as Red Hat 7.2 uses ipchains by default, we're going to cover that here and leave iptables for your own exploration. To learn more about iptables, visit www.netfilter.org.

As I said earlier, ipchains works with "chains" of packet-filtering rules. Earlier we worked with the forward chain, but in truth there are three predefined chains:

- input: for all packets coming into the server
- output: for all packets leaving the kernel
- forward: for all packets being forwarded to another machine

Let me describe how this works. Let's say I have an inbound HTTP packet coming into my server on my Ethernet card eth0. The kernel sees the packet and checks the input chain to see what it should do with it. There are three choices: ACCEPT, DENY, or REJECT. (The difference between DENY and REJECT is that REJECT sends back an error message. DENY just drops the packet.)

If it accepts the packet, the kernel then consults its routing table to see where to route the packet. The packet destination is going to be either local or remote. If it is for the local machine, the kernel then consults the output chain to see if there are any rules there. If not, it passes the packet to the appropriate local server service.

If the packet is destined for a remote machine, the kernel consults the forward chain to see what to do. Here, the kernel has the same three choices, but also a fourth choice of MASQ. Assuming the result is either ACCEPT or MASQ, the kernel then does an additional check of the output chain to see if there are any rules that apply there. If not, it hands the packet to the networking software to forward to the appropriate destination.

The rules are essentially just if-then tests. Let's take a look at a sample. It's going to first set up the standard masquerading information, and then it is going to set up rules for *forwarding*. Instead of just blindly forwarding *all* packets I get, I'm going to be a bit more selective about what I forward:

```
# make sure that forwarding is set
echo 1 > /proc/sys/net/ipv4/ip_forward
#
```

```
# If I'm connecting and getting a dynamic IP
# address (such as via DHCP on a PPP link), set this:
#
echo "1" > /proc/sys/net/ipv4/ip_dynaddr
#
# Enable IP fragmenting
#
echo "1" > /proc/sys/net/ipv4/ip_ip_always_defrag
#
# load kernel modules needed
#
depmod -a
modprobe ip_masq_ftp
modprobe ip_masq_raudio
#
# "flush" all the ipchains rules so that they are empty
ipchains -F
#
# set a forward policy of DENY so that only masq'd
# packets get through
#
ipchains -P forward DENY
#
# add forwarding rules. Packet will only be forwarded
# if TCP port matches '-p' and destination port matches
# '-d'
#
ipchains -A forward -p tcp --dport www -j MASQ
ipchains -A forward -p tcp --dport 443 -j MASQ
ipchains -A forward -p tcp --dport ssh -j MASQ
ipchains -A forward -p tcp --dport smtp -j MASQ
```

```
ipchains -A forward -p tcp --dport telnet -j MASQ

ipchains -A forward -p udp --dport domain -j MASQ

ipchains -A forward -p tcp --dport domain -j MASQ

ipchains -A forward -p tcp --dport ftp -j MASQ

ipchains -A forward -p tcp --dport ftp-data -j MASQ

ipchains -A forward -p tcp --dport pop3 -j MASQ

ipchains -A forward -p icmp -j MASQ

#

# if it hasn't been forwarded, DENY it and log it

#

ipchains -A forward -j DENY -l
```

Looking through all of that, essentially I am specifying a series of rules. If the protocol type and destination port match, masquerade the packet. If not, deny it.

Now, this is fine for forwarding packets, but if our machine is live on the Internet, this has done nothing to protect us from inbound intruders. So I'm going to add a piece onto the file that will protect my ppp0 interface:

```
#

# Accept masqueraded packets (which use port numbers

# between 61000 and 65096)

#

ipchains -A input -i ppp0 -p tcp --dport 61000:65096 -j ACCEPT

ipchains -A input -i ppp0 -p udp --dport 61000:65096 -j ACCEPT

#

# Accept all TCP or UDP inbound or outbound DNS packets

#

ipchains -A input -i ppp0 -p tcp --dport domain -j ACCEPT

ipchains -A input -i ppp0 -p udp --dport domain -j ACCEPT

ipchains -A input -i ppp0 -p tcp --sport domain -j ACCEPT

ipchains -A input -i ppp0 -p udp --sport domain -j ACCEPT

#

# Accept all inbound HTTP packets to our web server

#
```

```
ipchains -A input -i ppp0 -p tcp --dport http -j ACCEPT
#
# Accept all inbound SMTP packets
#
ipchains -A input -i ppp0 -p tcp --dport SMTP -j ACCEPT
#
# Only accept certain type of inbound ICMP packets not just
# blindly accepting all (and leaving one open to certain
# type of "ping of death" attacks)
#
ipchains -A input -i ppp0 -p icmp --icmp-type pong -j ACCEPT
ipchains -A input -i ppp0 -p icmp --icmp-type time-exceeded -j ACCEPT
ipchains -A input -i ppp0 -p icmp --icmp-type
➥destination-unreachable -j ACCEPT
ipchains -A input -i ppp0 -p icmp --icmp-type source-quench -j ACCEPT
ipchains -A input -i ppp0 -p icmp --icmp-type
➥parameter-problem -j ACCEPT
#
# If it fails to match any of these rules, DENY and log
# the packet
#
ipchains -A input -i ppp0 -j DENY -l
```

I think my comments in the code should guide you through it. Notice that I didn't modify the output chain at all. The other two chains take care of what I need to do. And notice that I'm not letting in some services such as FTP.

This is one example of how ipchains can be established, and in truth there's a whole lot more I could do with it. I would point you to the IP masquerading and ipchains HOWTO documents for a more thorough discussion of the topic, but you should know enough now to provide some basic filtering.

Well, that's our basic "how to set up Linux services" chapter. It's either one of the world's longest chapters or one of the world's shortest books on Linux server administration. That does it for the basic server services—but what about making Linux work well with those Microsoft systems that we've spent so much time with? That's the topic for the next chapter.

9

Linux/Microsoft OS Interoperability

Perhaps, after reading this book, you decide to incorporate a Linux box or two into your existing Microsoft network. How hard would it be to make the Microsoft NT, Windows 9*x*, 2000, and XP systems interoperate with the Linux computers? In particular:

- Can the Linux and Microsoft computers share data?
- Can the Linux and Microsoft computers share programs?
- Are there network services that will allow Linux and Microsoft systems to work smoothly together?

It's surprising how often the answers to those questions are "Yes."

Microsoft and Linux computers both offer file sharing services. While there is no single preferred file server tool for Linux, I'd guess that Sun's Network File System is the closest thing to that, as NFS is the most commonly used file server in the Unix world. But Microsoft computers can't read or write NFS servers unless those Microsoft computers are equipped with NFS client software—and they aren't, by default. But we can work data sharing the other way, from a Microsoft-centric approach. Linux has a set of tools called Samba that let a Linux box exploit a Microsoft file server, and that let a Linux box appear to *be* a Microsoft file server. Once installed and configured, the Samba tools make moving data between

Microsoft and Linux boxes as simple as moving data between NT machines. You'll read about Samba in this chapter. (Samba is so popular in the Linux world, in fact, that it might be a *more* popular file server than NFS amongst the Penguinites, largely due to the fact that many Linux-using networks also have Windows boxes on them, and NFS clients for Windows cost money, where Samba clients for Linux are free.)

NT and 2000 *can* actually employ some Linux applications, to a limited extent. Both NT and 2000 include a POSIX subsystem that will run a subset of standard Unix programs. (XP does not have the POSIX subsystem, unfortunately, although Microsoft will sell it to you as Services for Unix 3.0. Not cheap.) The Resource Kits for NT and 2000 include a POSIX-compliant C compiler, so with the Resource Kit installed, you should be able to download, compile, and use some Linux programs. Don't get your hopes up—most stuff won't work— but some tools will work fine under NT and 2000, like grep for example. NT, Windows 9*x*, and 2000 can also "use" Linux applications in another sense, in that you can run the built-in Microsoft Telnet clients to run text-based programs on a Linux box remotely from any network-capable Microsoft OS. Additionally, as you've already seen in Chapter 7, the X Window emulators available for Windows let you run graphical Linux programs remotely.

Linux can run *some* Windows programs with a tool called Wine, which you'll read about in this chapter. It's still an early project, but it's a promising (and, of course, free) avenue for running your favorite Windows programs on a Linux computer. And if you have older DOS programs, there is a more mature Linux tool called dosemu ("DOS emulator") that lets your Linux computer directly run DOS programs. It's extremely complex to get working and, given that DOS programs are pretty sparse these days, I didn't cover it in this chapter in any detail. But if you're interested, you can find source code, RPMs, and documentation at www.dosemu.org.

Finally, Microsoft and Linux machines can interoperate very nicely when using standard protocols: Linux boxes can happily work as clients to Microsoft web, FTP, Telnet, e-mail, DHCP, DNS, or (with Samba) WINS servers. Similarly, Microsoft systems can work as effective clients with Linux servers in those same roles.

In the rest of this chapter, I'll look in more detail at the two interoperability tools that I've not covered yet: Wine and Samba. But first, two quick Microsoft-to-Linux tips...

Converting Microsoft Text Files to Linux Text Files

You may have tried, at some point, to cook up a Linux .conf file of some kind with some version of the Windows Notepad. Presumably text is text no matter what OS you're using, right? So all you should have to do is to create the file in Notepad, copy it to a floppy, stick the floppy into the floppy drive on a Linux box, and then copy the file from the floppy to /etc or wherever the .conf file is supposed to go.

As you know if you've tried it, it doesn't always work. You see, in the Microsoft world, text files end each line with a hexadecimal 0x0D or "carriage return," followed by a hexadecimal 0x0A or "line feed." In Linux however, each line ends simply with 0x0A, a line feed. Some Linux programs see Microsoft text files and can't figure out why there's that spurious 0x0D at the end of each line, so they disregard the whole line. Other Linux programs show you the text, but show a "^M" at the end of every line. Not a big deal, but just visually annoying. To get around this issue, you can use a great little Linux tool named dos2unix to take a DOS text file and create a Linux text file with the carriage returns stripped out:

```
dos2unix -n dosfile linuxfile
```

For example, if I've worked up the XF86Config file to end all such files in Notepad, I'll save it to a floppy as XF86Config.txt. I get it onto a Linux system and then make it Linux-ready with this command:

```
dos2unix -n XF86Config.txt XF86Config
```

Or the mcopy program in mtools has a cool -t option to "translate" between Linux text format and DOS text format:

```
mcopy -t a: /myfiles
```

Controlling Dual Boots: LILO

The idea of interoperability includes being able to use a particular computer either as an NT, Windows, 2000, or Linux workstation as needed. As you've seen, Linux will set itself up to coexist with other operating systems using a tool called LILO, the LInux LOader. Once your distribution's setup program has gotten Linux on your system successfully, here's how to control what LILO does.

A Typical *lilo.conf*

LILO is controlled by an ASCII configuration file called lilo.conf, which is (as far as I can see) always located in /etc. (You saw this back in Chapter 5, when we talked about reconfiguring the kernel.) A typical lilo.conf follows.

```
prompt
timeout=50
default=linux
```

```
boot=/dev/hda
map=/boot/map
install=/boot/boot.b
message=/boot/message
linear

image=/boot/vmlinuz-2.4.18-3
    label=linux
    initrd=/boot/initrd-2.4.18-3.img
    read-only
    root=/dev/hda3
    append="hdc=ide-scsi"

other=/dev/hda1
    optional
    label=DOS
```

Notice that lilo.conf is broken into several sections. The first part is the "global" portion, although it's not set off with a header like [global] or anything like that. The last two sections are called *image sections*. An image section either starts with image=, which means it's describing a Linux kernel, or other=, which means it's pointing to some other bootable item, most likely DOS, Windows, NT, 2000, XP, or some other operating system. This lilo.conf has two image sections. The first boots a file named /boot/vmlinuz-2.4.18-3, which is of course Red Hat 7.3's kernel; the second boots a copy of DOS (Windows 98 without the GUI, actually). The line label= obviously gives the image a name; LILO uses that to let you choose which image to load.

When LILO boots, it shows a low-resolution graphic image of the Red Hat logo and offers the two labels. You can alternatively press Ctrl+X to get the text LILO startup screen, where you see boot:, and either press Enter for the default or press Tab to see your boot options.

The image= or other= statement tells LILO exactly *what* to load. For example, in this lilo.conf file, I have a line that says image=/boot/vmlinuz-2.4.18-3. If I choose that image (the one labeled simply linux), then LILO goes to the /boot directory and looks for a file named vmlinuz-2.4.18-3 to load. That file is the basic kernel program.

In the case of a non-Linux image, the other= points to a partition, like /dev/hda1 (recall that hda1 is the first partition—that's the "1"—of the first EIDE drive—that's the "a."). So when you choose the option labeled windows, then LILO just goes and gets the first sector of that partition, and then executes it. If you had yet another non-Linux image, you'd really just need to add another other= line and give it a label.

Suppose you want to put Windows 95, 2000, *and* Linux on the same computer. How would you do it? Your best strategy would be to first make the Microsoft operating systems work together, *then* add Linux. As Windows 95 doesn't know anything about Windows 2000, first put 95 on the computer, *then* install 2000. In the process, 2000 would install NT's operating system chooser, and as a result, when you turn your computer on, you'd get a boot menu from 2000 offering to either run 95 or 2000. Then install Linux, and the Linux setup routine will put LILO on your system. LILO will respect the 2000 boot information, which in turn will protect the 95 boot information. When you start Linux, LILO gives you two options, linux or other. To run Windows 95, choose other, which starts up the 2000 boot process, and *that* displays the operating system chooser. Then you can choose Windows 95.

Is there a way to *first* install Linux on the computer, and then Windows, NT, and/or 2000, and get everything to boot nicely? I don't know of such a way. The Windows, NT, or 2000 setup programs will blow away the old LILO, so editing lilo.conf at that point isn't very valid. You *could*, however, create a Linux boot diskette when the setup program offers; then you can always get to your Linux image by booting from that floppy.

Choosing a Default Image

You may have several images on your system—say, perhaps, a Linux image and a copy of 2000—and LILO will usually start one or the other after some period of time, even if you don't press any keys. (I'll tell you how to configure that in a moment.) But which image does it load? It depends.

lilo.conf contains a line default=. You can just name an image with this command, and after LILO times out, it'll load that image. For example, my sample lilo.conf has a line default=linux, which is the image that this Red Hat system will load if I just turn the computer on and wait.

Controlling Timeouts

You control what LILO does in the absence of a keystroke with the prompt and timeout= values. Just specify a timeout value as a number in tenths of seconds; for example, timeout=50 tells LILO to wait five seconds before loading the default image.

The `prompt` command tells LILO not to load an image unless it gets some kind of keystroke. Press Enter and the default loads immediately; press Tab and LILO will show you the image names; type in an image name and press Enter and LILO will load that one. But `timeout=` beats `prompt`; if you have a `prompt` command *and* a `timeout` command (as is usually the case), then once the timeout period has elapsed, LILO starts anyway. Using `prompt` all by itself without a timeout guarantees that LILO just sits and waits forever for your command. With no `prompt` command at all, LILO starts loading the default image—probably the best option on a server with just one image, unless you want the `boot:` prompt to let you type in a VGA mode setting or the like.

Offering Boot Messages

The global section includes a `message=` command. It points to a simple ASCII text file that offers an informative boot message. It's an optional command but might be helpful if you've included a sort of simple "emergency boot kernel" as a boot option; you can use `message=` to essentially document your images.

Making *lilo.conf* Changes Take Effect

LILO doesn't read `lilo.conf` every time it boots. Instead, it loads and executes a boot image file, typically a binary file named `/boot/boot.b`. But you needn't worry about that, as LILO creates `boot.b` every time you modify `lilo.conf`—*as long as* you remember to tell LILO about it.

When you make a change to `lilo.conf`, save it; when you're back at the command prompt, type:

```
lilo
```

and you'll see LILO rebuilding the boot image.

Run Your Windows Programs with Wine

Linux has many fine features (as I hope I've convinced you by now), but a wide availability of polished, commercial-quality applications *isn't* one of them. Suppose you have a Windows program that does a particular job for you, a program that you know and love, but that lacks a Linux version—what then? Wine to the rescue—as long as you don't mind running some pretty early-release, pre-beta-stage software. Wine is an emulator for the Win32 programming subsystem, the foundation of Windows 9*x*, NT, and 2000 applications. One day it'll run just about anything, but right now you'll find that more complex applications probably won't run. Nevertheless, it's worth a try, given the following note.

NOTE Wine may run, provided that you have a copy of Windows 98 or Me on your system; Wine will not run with any kind of reliability on a system installed on an NTFS directory, nor will it run very well in tandem with Windows 2000 or Windows XP. That will probably change in time, but for now your best bet is to start from a computer that has Windows 95, 98, or Me on it and load Linux alongside that Windows 9x/Me install.

Red Hat 7.3 ships with Wine's version 20020327, so if you installed "with everything," then you've already got it on your system. That said, given how young Wine is (I am steadfastly avoiding "vintage" puns, but it's a struggle), you might seriously consider getting a newer copy before embarking on a serious Wine project. You can find Wine and links to its download sites at www.winehq.org. At that site, you'll find:

- Links to places where people store the source code and where many have prebuilt RPM files for the latest Wine build
- Wine documentation
- A database of Windows applications, listing how well (or badly) more than 2,000 Windows applications have run on Wine

NOTE Unfortunately there's a bit of bad news with Wine: it's actually much harder to get to work, and it will refuse to work altogether in far more cases than it did back in 2000. My guess is that Corel, who was very committed to making Windows apps work on their Linux, took control of a big part of Wine. That would have been a really good thing, except Corel bailed out of Linux in 2001 for various reasons, money being the biggest. I suspect that they left a lot of things half-done, putting the Wine volunteers in a tough spot. I'd recommend holding off on Wine until early 2003—hit their website and see what they've got now. That's not to say that you *can't* make Wine work, but your chances of succeeding are unfortunately lower than they would have been in 2000.

Getting Your System Ready for Wine

Wine runs best on a system that includes both Windows and Linux on the same computer, because a system like that already has some Windows applications loaded and ready to try out.

Wine will work better if it has read/write access to your Windows drivers, suggesting that systems on NTFS won't work well—recall that the NTFS filesystem mounter is read-only.

Examine Wine's *config* file

You configure Wine through its configuration file `config`.

Unlike other Linux programs you've met, Wine doesn't have a single configuration file in `/etc`; it did once, but now it creates a separate configuration file for every user. It puts that in a hidden directory that it creates in the user's home directory called `.wine`; the file is called `config`. So, as I'm logged in as root, Wine creates a file named `/root/.wine/config`. If Jane were logged in as jane and ran Wine, then Wine would create its configuration file for Jane in `/home/jane/.wine/config`.

Wine creates the `config` file the first time that a user runs Wine. You can announce your presence, so to speak, to Wine by asking for its version with the –v option:

```
# wine -v
Wine version 20020310
```

I ran this on a computer running Windows 98 on `/dev/hda1` formatted as FAT32. Now I have a file in `/root/.wine/config`. It's an ASCII text file that looks like a Windows INI file. The first few lines look like this:

```
[Drive C]
"Path" = "/usr/share/wine-c"
"Type" = "hd"
"Label" = "MS-DOS"
"Filesystem" = "win95"

[Drive D]
"Path" = "/mnt/cdrom"
"Type" = "cdrom"
"Label" = "CD-Rom"
"Filesystem" = "win95"
"Device" = "/dev/cdrom"
```

This maps out the available drives in a style that Windows programs understand—C, D, etc. Each lettered drive has a section named [Drive *letter*], followed by some descriptive information about that drive.

Notice that it's mapped the C drive as `/usr/share/wine-c`. I didn't do that... Wine did. If I do a "mount," then I'll see that /dev/hda1–C in Windows—is indeed mapped to /usr/share-wine-c.

The `Path=` statement is self-explanatory: it points to the Linux path corresponding to the drive. So defining C for Wine is a two-step procedure: First, mount the device on a directory that serves as a mount point, then tell Wine about it via the Path= statement in a section of `wine.conf`. The `Type=` tells Wine how the drive should *look* to Windows. Legal values are `floppy`, `hd`, `cdrom`, and `network`. Understand that these labels have nothing to do with the actual storage devices; instead, this describes how Windows will see it. So, for example, I could replace `hd` with `network` and Windows would still see the device as drive C, but Windows would think that my underlying network software was providing this drive, instead of it being a partition of a locally attached physical hard disk. (It might be useful for troubleshooting an application's behavior when working with a mapped drive versus a partition on a local physical hard disk.) The `cdrom` value is also self-explanatory. The `Filesystem=` piece takes one of two values: `win95` and `msdos`. `win95` work for FAT32 or EXT2 drives; `msdos` is for older FAT16 drives.

If I look a bit further down, I see a section labeled `[wine]`, containing these lines:

```
[wine]
"Windows" = "c:\\windows"
"System" = "c:\\windows\\system"
"Temp" = "e:\\"
"Path" = "c:\\windows;c:\\windows\\system;e:\\;e:\\test;f:\\"
"Profile" = "c:\\windows\\Profiles\\Administrator"
"GraphicsDriver" = "x11drv"
"ShellLinker" = "wineshelllink"
```

Let me take a minute and explain why the lines look so odd.

In Linux-ese, you use a backslash to warn Linux that you're about to use a "strange" character. For example, if you had a Linux directory with the name "My Pictures," then doing something like:

```
cd My Pictures
```

wouldn't work; cd would think that you'd passed it the parameter "My" because Linux, like Windows, sees spaces as separators. `cd My Pictures` looks like "Run the command cd and feed it two parameters, `My` and `Pictures`," instead of what you want, which is to run the program cd and feed it one parameter, `My Pictures`. One way to tell a Linux command line that you're feeding it a parameter with a space in it is to prefix the space with a backslash, as in:

```
cd My\ Pictures
```

Similarly, the backslash itself is one of those "strange" characters. Expressing `c:\windows`, then would require `c:\\windows`–as the backslash is intended to prefix "strange" characters, you express an *intended* backslash with two backslashes.

Once you understand backslash-ese, you're ready to look into modifying `config`.

Set the `Windows=` line to point to the top-level directory of your copy of Windows. `System=` should point to the system directory, and `Temp=` should point to some directory where Wine can store temporary files. The `Profile=` line is very important, as it tells Wine where to find a `user.dat` Registry file. You see, many applications simply won't run if they can't find a Registry key that contains the information that they need to get started. For example, Word 2000 will refuse to run if it can't find a Registry, saying that you must run Setup.

The Wine default value:

```
Profile=c:\windows\Profiles\Administrator
```

only works if you've enabled profiles on your copy of Windows. If you haven't, then Wine won't be able to find `user.dat` in the `c:\windows\Profiles\Administrator` directory, as there won't *be* a directory by that name. If you're not using profiles, just change the value to:

```
Profile=c:\windows
```

If you're running Wine on a Linux box that shares disk space with Windows 2000 or XP—which, as I said, may or may not work—then of course the profiles are in the directory `\Documents and Settings`. In backslash-ese, the Administrator's profile on a 2000 or XP system would look like:

```
"Profile" = "c:\\Documents\ and\ Settings\\Administrator"
```

If you're going to run Wine in tandem with 2000 and XP, you should also add `system32` to the path, inserting `c:\\windows\\system32`.

Finding Out If Wine Runs

By now, Wine should be ready to go. Try it out with this command:

```
wine -v
```

Wine should report a version number and stop. Now try it out on a real, live Windows application:

```
cd /c/windows
wine calc
```

You don't *need* to be in the program's directory, but it helps some Windows programs. The Windows Calculator should start up and run now.

Finding Out If Wine Runs Your App

You're now ready to run your Windows applications. There's no nice Start ˃ Programs menu, so you'll have to find the actual name and location of the EXE file to start up an app; for example, on my system I must type this to start Word 2000:

```
wine "c:\Program Files\Microsoft Office\Office\winword.exe"
```

Handling a Wine Crash

It's not unusual at all for Wine to completely seize the screen. For example, I tried to run an Install program for a Windows application, but the application just maximized to fill the entire X desktop and then started flashing rectangles on the screen; nothing seemed to fix it. Now, this might look like a power-down situation, but it's not.

Recall that you can press the Ctrl+Alt+F2 keys to start up another text session. Log in as root and then find and kill the Wine processes:

```
ps -A|grep "wine"
```

You'll get a list of processes and, most important, their PIDs. Just kill them with `kill -9 pid` and then return to your X session with Ctrl+Alt+F7. If you have your X control back, great; if not, then return to Ctrl+Alt+F2 and kill another Wine process, and so on. You'll find a copy of Wine running for each Windows app that you run.

If you can't make a particular application run, don't be discouraged. Remember, this isn't even beta code yet—as I write this, the Wine people are calling their tool an "alpha-level release." Wait for the next build and try it again. Or search the Usenet message traffic on `comp.emulators.ms-windows.wine`. Or you could spend a little money, as the next section suggests.

Use VMware

I've already mentioned this in Chapter 7, but it's worth mentioning again that VMware is an operating system that lets you run more than one OS on the same computer.

At the same time.

Yes, you read that right. You load VMware on your system, and it lets you simultaneously run NT, Windows 2000, Windows 9*x*, or Windows 3.1 in one window and Linux in another. (Or NT in one window and 2000 in another, or whatever combination you'd like.) It's a pretty neat tool and reasonably priced. If you don't mind spending a little money, then this is a far easier answer than struggling with Wine to run a Windows app or two in conjunction with Linux. It is a little pricey—$300—but it can save you a ton on hardware and is an excellent answer. If you intend to use VMware, then you should of course have as much PC power as you can—a 2GHz system with 2GB of RAM will clearly run a lot more virtual machines than will a 266MHz with 64MB of RAM.

What about DOS Apps?

As I mentioned earlier, a Linux tool called dosemu allows you to build virtual DOS machines and then run DOS programs in those virtual machines. It's very similar to the approach that Windows 3.*x*, 9*x*, NT, and OS/2 2.*x* use to support DOS programs. If you have a DOS application that you absolutely *must* get running, this may be the way to go.

The basic idea behind dosemu is that you supply it a bootable DOS image, from either a hard disk (it can read a Windows 9*x* boot image from your hard disk if the system is Windows/Linux dual-booting) or a bootable floppy. (You can use a bootable floppy from Windows 95 or 98; they count as "bootable DOS images.") dosemu then takes all of the files in this bootable image—io.sys, msdos.sys, command.com, and whatever other files you give it—and makes them all one, big Linux executable. You then configure it with a file called dosemu.conf and run the program by typing either dos (which can only do command-line DOS programs) or xdos (which can run graphical programs as well, and which you must run under X Window).

The trouble with dosemu is its documentation. There's plenty of it—READMEs, ViewDoc files, man pages, a Quickstart manual—but none of it is very clear. It's obvious that the people who wrote this worked very hard at it, but without clearer documentation, it's just not possible to debug dosemu's behavior. In my experience, dosemu works fine if your DOS application is a text-mode app that uses expanded memory. But none of the applications that I've seen that require graphics or extended/DPMI memory seem to work under dosemu. Perhaps in the near future, some new documentation will appear that more clearly walks the prospective dosemu administrator through setting it up for graphical and extended-memory programs—but until then, VMware might not be a bad investment.

Linux As Print Server for Windows, NT, and 2000

You read in Chapter 5 how to install a printer on a Linux box. You also read that Linux uses a client/server model for printing, even local printing, where the print server piece is called lpd and the print client piece is called lpr. But how can a Windows, NT, or 2000 exploit a Linux box as a print server?

Microsoft has actually included support for printing on Unix print servers since NT 3.5. NT includes a tool called Microsoft TCP/IP Printing that you can load from the Control Panel: choose Network, then Services, then Add. (You can read more about it in *Mastering Windows NT Server*, Chapter 14.) But don't worry about having to learn a new skill—I'll bet you've already done this before. Do you have any Hewlett-Packard laser printers directly attached to your network with some kind of HP JetDirect hardware? (Again, if not, consult Chapter 14 in *Mastering Windows NT Server*.) NT lets you connect any server to a JetDirect printer by just specifying its IP address. Once you do that, you then just share the printer over the network as if the printer were attached to the server with a parallel cable. So to use a Linux printer as a shared NT printer, just add the Microsoft TCP/IP Printing module to an NT server, then tell the NT server that you have a new printer. When the server asks which port it's on—parallel, serial, or whatever—tell it that it's attached via a TCP/IP port and fill in the IP address of the Linux print server. Any Microsoft network client can then share the printer.

Additionally, when you install Microsoft TCP/IP Printing, you *also* install a service called TCP/IP Print Server—not started by default—which is basically an NT implementation of lpd.

Samba: Microsoft Networking for Linux

Of all of the server software that I use, the one that gets the most use is undoubtedly the file server (although e-mail and web protocols are contenders as well). Linux has a file server system of its own, but having a great file server protocol is of no value if there's no one to talk to; as someone has observed, "You know what salesman I admire most? The guy who sold the *first* telephone!"

If Linux is to live with the rest of the world, file server-wise, then it needs to be able to talk to the Big Names in file serving. Of course, the biggest name is Microsoft—and Linux has met that challenge. By running a tool called Samba, you can drop your Linux box right into the middle of a Microsoft network, and all of the other systems will think that the Linux box is just another Microsoft file server. Additionally, Linux includes software that lets your Linux box not only act as a file *server*, but as a file *client* as well: Linux includes *two* tools that let your Linux workstations behave like Windows boxes as far as Microsoft file servers are concerned, letting those boxes read and write files from and to Microsoft file servers.

File (and print) servers each use a protocol all their own, a protocol intended to run quickly but at the same time run with sufficient security. The Novell world has for years used NetWare Core Protocol (NCP) and, as you've already read, much of the Unix/Linux world uses the Network File System (NFS). Ever since the earliest days of Microsoft peer-to-peer networking in mid-1985, Microsoft networks have used a protocol called Server Message Block (SMB). While it has changed a bit over the years, each version is very backward-compatible, so you can pretty much use the same language as a file server client to talk to all of these Microsoft networking products:

- Windows XP and .NET Server
- Windows 2000 Server and Professional
- Windows NT Server and Workstation
- Windows 9*x*
- Windows for Workgroups 3.11 and 3.1
- The Microsoft Workgroup Add-On for DOS 6.*x*
- Lantastic
- OS/2 LAN Server
- Microsoft LAN Manager

As you can see, a lot of server products are or were built around SMB. So it was logical that somebody in the Linux community would put something together that could act as a server and/or client for SMB. That's not as easy as it sounds, largely because SMB isn't really a documented protocol—oh, yes, there are written documentation and specifications, but the actual client and server programs from Microsoft don't follow that documentation and specification.

An Australian named Andrew Tridgell needed an SMB compatibility tool for Unix and began figuring out how SMB worked by looking at a similar tool named PathWorks (which was built not for Unix but for Digital's VMS operating system). PathWorks didn't tell Tridgell all that he needed to know, so he put a sniffer on his network and watched the packets go by as Windows boxes talked to NT servers. With that information, he built an early version of what would become Samba. Not long after, Jeremy Allison, working at Sun, had a similar need, and so Tridgell and Allison started working together. Since then, several others have joined with them to constitute the Samba open source project. While you can find the latest source code for Samba at www.samba.org, every Linux distribution that I've seen includes with it *some* version of Samba.

I mention the fact that you can get the latest Samba from www.samba.org for a specific reason. The Samba folks are trying to stay compatible with Microsoft's SMB protocol, and that protocol changes regularly, even in service packs and hot fixes. Every time that Microsoft plugs a security hole, they will potentially "break" Samba. Sometimes you can fix that "breakage" with a new version of Samba, which means (here's the bad news) that it's probably in your best interests to learn how to compile and install the latest version of Samba. That's in contrast to most Linux subsystems, which (I'd argue) offer *nice* new features but not so new that I can't wait for my favorite distribution to offer a new version, complete with the new Linux subsystem.

> **NOTE** Red Hat 7.3 includes a pretty up-to-date version of Samba, version 2.2.3a. But you can always get the latest RPMs from Red Hat at `http://www.redhat.com/apps/download/`. Scroll down to the bottom of the page, where you can search for RPMs.

Even *with* the latest version, however, you'll sometimes find that you just can't make a connection that you ought to be able to make. For example, as I'm writing this, I'm testing the Linux SMB client software against two Windows 2000 machines (a Pro box and an Active Directory domain controller), an NT 4 domain controller, and two NT 4 servers. I can access shares on both 2000 machines fine, and on the domain controller, but for some reason every attempt to log on to the NT 4 member server fails. So I strongly suggest having a few NT or 2000 machines around when trying this all out.

Samba and related software let your Linux box mimic either a Microsoft filesystem client (so the Linux box can access an NT or 2000 share) or a Microsoft file server (so a Microsoft machine would see your Linux box as just another file server). With no special software, then, your Windows, NT, or 2000 machine could access files on the Linux box.

In this section, we'll take up both of those issues. First, you'll see how to make your Linux box a Microsoft file server's client; then you'll see how to make your Linux box act like a Microsoft file server; and finally, I'll take you through the steps that you'll need to know in order to download and install the latest Samba.

One more point before I continue: Let me warn you that Samba is a very large and comprehensive package. I'd need a book or two to cover it in its entirety, so all I'm going to do here is to give you the overview of how to set it up and how to build a few common configurations—a few useful "cookbooks." If you have a special need that you don't see answered in this one section of one chapter of a book, then don't give up on Samba—look further at its online documentation, and you'll probably be pleasantly surprised at what it can do.

SMB Clients

First, let's look at SMB *clients*—that is, the software that you'd use to connect your Linux machines to NT- or 2000-based file servers. There are actually two different tools that come in the box with most Linux distributions that will let you attach to Microsoft network file shares:

- Assuming that you have Samba installed, you can use the `mount` command to attach to SMB file shares.

- `smbclient` is an older SMB client that only offers a fairly primitive FTP-like command-line interface, *and* does a couple of things that `smbmount` can't, including browsing a workgroup and sending messages.

If you read the book's first version, back in the Samba 2.0 days, then you'll recall that the Samba clients were a bit flaky. In my experience that's (thankfully!) no longer the case, and connecting Linux boxes to NT, 2000, XP, or .NET file shares is simple.

mounting with smbfs

As you read in Chapter 5, the Linux world likes to organize all of its mass storage so that it appears that every drive connects via a single tree structure off the / root. With Samba versions 2.0.6 and later (recall that you have 2.2.3a), you can use the `mount` command, as Linux now includes support for the SMB filesystem—hence the name `smbfs`. Mount a Microsoft network share like so:

```
mount -t smbfs -o username=username/domainname%password
➥//servername/sharename /mountpoint
```

As with the other commands in this book, let me remind you that this should just be one line, even *if* the publisher ended up having to break it on the page because of space constraints. Notice that Linux uses forward slashes, even when referring to Microsoft server names, rather than the backslashes that we normally see.

So, for example, if I want to attach to a share named GOODIES on a Windows 2000 server named OURSERVER, I'd first need a directory on my Linux box to act as the mount point, as you saw in Chapter 5 when mounting CD-ROMs or floppies. Suppose I create a directory for that purpose called /ntshare. Remember that even though this is a directory, I won't really store files on it. It just gives Linux a sort of "reference point" for accessing the file share. So I'll create the directory:

```
mkdir /ntshare
```

I could have called it anything. And I'll only have to create that directory once; now that I've created it, I can reuse it the next time I need to attach to this share.

Next, I'll need a username and password that the Win2K server recognizes. Suppose I have a user account named mminasi on the OURSERVER server, with password swordfish. I can construct a `mount` command like so (again, all on one line):

```
mount -t smbfs -o username=mminasi%swordfish
➥//ourserver/goodies /ntshare
```

Once properly typed, I'll probably just get a Linux prompt in return; mount doesn't offer a lot of chatter. Instead of using a % sign to indicate the password, I can also use the password= parameter, as in this alternate command formulation:

```
mount -t smbfs -o username=mminasi,password=swordfish
➥ //ourserver/goodies /ntshare
```

Now, in both of those cases, the mminasi account that I am using is a local account for \\OURSERVER–the mminasi account lives in \\OURSERVER's local SAM file. But if I want to authenticate using a domain account, then I need only add a forward slash and the domain's name—either the newer DNS-like Active Directory name or the old-style NetBIOS name—and smbfs will know how to find my account. Assuming that mminasi has an account on an Active Directory domain named acme.com that has a NetBIOS name of acme, any of these variations on the command will work:

```
mount -t smbfs -o username=mminasi/acme,password=swordfish
➥//ourserver/goodies /ntshare
```

```
mount -t smbfs -o username=mminasi/acme.com,password=swordfish
➥ //ourserver/goodies /ntshare
```

```
mount -t smbfs -o username=mminasi/acme%swordfish //ourserver/goodies
➥ /ntshare
```

```
mount -t smbfs -o username=mminasi/acme.com%swordfish
➥ //ourserver/goodies /ntshare
```

Note that you can *not*, at least as far as I can see, use a UPN-type logon name like mark@acme.com—smbfs seems unable to parse that at the moment.

Notice that you mustn't put any spaces after commas (like the one between username=mminasi and password=swordfish), or the command won't work and you'll get an error message telling you that you're clearly an idiot who doesn't know how to use mount. Once you have the mount command working, then typing ls /ntshare shows the contents of the share. Notice that, unlike most Linux commands, the server and share names are *case-insensitive*. The -o refers to the comma-separated *options*, and Table 9.1 lists the ones you'll care about.

Of those options, one is particularly important: ip. Unlike the pre-February 2000 version of smbfs, this filesystem mounter seems completely unaware of WINS, lmhosts, and the other tools that we use to help systems resolve NetBIOS names. smbfs just broadcasts to find the server, so when I did the mount command earlier for a server named \\ourserver, my Linux box just shouted out over the network, "Anybody here named 'ourserver'?" Of course, those shouts don't make it across routers, so if \\ourserver were on the next subnet over (or perhaps in Venezuela), then the command would fail. In that case, you have to help smbfs out a bit. Suppose, then that \\ourserver is at IP

Table 9.1 smbfs Options

Option	Function
username=username	Tells smbfs what user account name to present to the SMB server. You can't use 2000-style logon names like mark@acme.com, so stick with your shorter, NT-style name. If necessary, include the domain's name as username/ domainname, as in mark/acme.
password=password	The password for the user account.
ip=a.b.c.d	A very useful option. If you specify this, then smbfs doesn't even try to resolve the NT/2000 server's NetBIOS name—it just goes to that IP address. Particularly useful when accessing a server across the Internet or just on another subnet, or when you suspect that it's name resolution that's getting in the way.
guest	Don't bother prompting for a password and/or user account, and instead log on to the SMB server as a guest. Usually more relevant when the SMB server is a Windows 9x or LAN Manager system, but if you have the guest account enabled on an NT or 2000 system, then it's useful.
ro	Mounts the share as read-only.
rw	Mounts the share as read-write (default).

address 110.58.20.19. And, just to make the example a bit richer, let's say that I only want to open the \\ourserver\goodies share as a read-only share. The mount command would look like this one long line:

```
mount -t smbfs -o username=mminasi,password=swordfish,
➥ip=110.58.20.19,ro //ourserver/goodies /ntshare
```

If you connect to an SMB share from a Linux workstation and don't access that share for a while, SMB does a kind of "soft disconnect." It happens with NT and 2000 all the time, but you don't notice it because most SMB client software just automatically reconnects you. Linux SMB software has in the past shown an inability to handle the soft disconnect/reconnect, but this post–February 2000 code handles it. However, you *may* see a message when the reconnect occurs, like this:

```
smb_trans2_request, result=-32, setting invalid

smb_retry: newpid=895, generation=2
```

If you see a message like that, don't be alarmed; it's just Linux being informative. To disconnect, use umount, as in Chapter 5:

```
umount /ntshare
```

What's that you say? You don't much relish putting your password out for all to see? Then create a text file that looks like this:

```
username = joe

password = swordfish
```

and point smbfs to it with the credentials= parameter. Supposing you called your file /home/joe/cred.txt, the mount command would look like:

```
mount -t smbfs -o credentials=/home/joe/cred.txt
➡ //server1/someshare /mynetshare
```

But are you ready for the weird part? If you wanted to specify a domain account, then you write it as domain/username, rather the other way around; if Joe's account were not on the //server1 SAM but instead on the domain BIGFIRM, then the cred.txt file would look like:

```
username = bigfirm/joe

password = swordfish
```

And if you want these shares connected automatically at startup, then add them to the file /etc/fstab like so:

```
//server1/someshare /mynetshare smbfs
➡credentials=/home/joe/cred.txt 0 0
```

How *smbfs* Does NetBIOS Name Resolution

This works well if connecting to a server on the same subnet as your workstation, but how would you make an SMB connection across subnets? If you know the IP address of the file server, then you can use the ip= parameter, as we've seen. For example, to talk to a share called data on a server called \\bigserver that's at IP address 10.10.10.20, you could type:

```
mount -t smbfs -o username=joe,password=swordfish,
➡ip=10.10.10.20 //bigserver/data /mymountpoint
```

Notice that the parameters after the –o have no spaces between them!

Using *lmhosts* But if you didn't want to have to hard-wire an IP address every time, then you could help `smbfs` out by modifying the file `/etc/samba/lmhosts` to include this line:

```
10.10.10.10 bigserver
```

You could then issue the command:

```
mount -t smbfs -o username=joe,password=swordfish
➥ //bigserver/data /mymountpoint
```

Or, if Joe had a credentials file in `/home/joe/cred.txt`:

```
mount -t smbfs -o cred=/home/joe/cred.txt
➥ //bigserver/data /mymountpoint
```

Using a WINS server But, as we all know, that `lmhosts` stuff is massively passé, a kind of '80s thing in networking; let's move into the '90s and use a WINS server. You don't tell `smbfs` about the WINS server with an option; rather, you must edit an ASCII file called `smb.conf`, which Red Hat 7.3 stores in `/etc/samba/smb.conf`.

Edit `/etc/samba/smb.conf` and look for the line that says:

```
wins server = w.x.y.z
```

And change `w.x.y.z` to whatever your WINS server's IP address is. *Do not* change the line above it, which says `wins support=no`, to `yes`–Samba won't be able to talk to your WINS server if you do.

Save `/etc/samba/smb.conf`, and then your `mount` commands will work... but Samba may complain about not being able to open `/var/cache/samba/unexpected.tdb`. (What more should it expect from a file named "unexpected?") Samba's just complaining because it wants to write to the file but can't find one, so create one for it:

```
touch /var/cache/samba/unexpected.tdb
```

`smbmount` rereads the `smb.conf` file every time you invoke the command, so there are no services to restart or to make rebooting necessary.

A More General-Purpose SMB Client Tool: *smbclient*

Either the best thing about Linux or the worst thing about Linux are the choices that it offers. Sometimes you find yourself looking at man pages for two different programs that seem to do the same thing, leading you to scratch your head and say, "Why do we have two tools?"

Well, get set for some more scratching, because we've got yet another SMB client tool, with the somewhat obvious name of `smbclient`. Why did someone come up with `smbclient`? I'm honestly not sure, but from what I can piece together in the documentation for Samba in general, I gather that someone outside of the Samba team originally put `smbmount` together; `smbclient` was the "official" Samba client tool. Now that Tridgell has taken over development on `smbclient` and `smbfs`, however, I'm not sure how much longer `smbclient` will be relevant. (Or I could easily have all of this wrong; it's not like there's a central archive of historical information on the various open source tools for Linux.) And it seems to ship with the Samba files, so the Samba guys may have just assimilated `smbclient`.

But `smbclient` should still have a place in your Linux tool belt, as it can do things that `smbfs` *can't* do. In particular, `smbclient` will let you send messages to NT, 2000, and Windows workstations, and display browse lists. It'll also duplicate `smbmount`'s functions in that it lets you connect to SMB file shares, although in a somewhat less user-friendly manner than `smbfs`.

Sending Pop-up Messages with *smbclient* You may know the `net send` command, which allows you to send real-time, pop-up messages to machines on a Microsoft network, like this:

```
net send johnsmith Can you come over? I need some help.
```

That would cause a box to pop up on John's machine requesting help. The `net send` command can be directed to machine names as well as usernames, so if John's machine was named \\JPC01, then the message could as easily be `net send jpc01 hi there!` and the same action would result. `smbclient` can accomplish this with the `-M` command:

```
smbclient -M jpc01
```

The program will establish contact with \\JPC01 and wait for you to type in your message. You end the message by pressing Ctrl+D; `smbclient` then sends the message. As with many Unix/Linux commands, the option's case is essential—you must invoke `smbclient` with the `-M` option, *not* `-m`.

One way in which `smbclient` differs from `net send`, however, is that `smbclient` does not allow wildcards. You can annoy your whole network with a command like `net send * Hey, anyone want to get a beer after work?`, as the message would end up appearing on every screen on your local subnet. But `smbclient -M *` wouldn't work.

Browsing a Workgroup with *smbclient* Sometimes you want to connect to a share on a server but cannot remember the name of the share; in that case, you can either examine its list of shares via Network Neighborhood or My Network Places, or you can use the command-line command `net view \\servername`. `smbclient` can furnish those same capabilities with its `-L` command. But servers won't tell just *anybody* what shares they have—you'll have to prove that you're a recognized user. That's where `-U` (again, an uppercase option) comes in. Most Samba tools let you pass a user account name and, optionally, a password to Samba. You specify a username as just -U `username`, or a user-name and password as -U `username%password`. The command looks like this:

```
smbclient -L servername -U username%password
```

So, for example, if I wanted to see the shares on an NT server named \\OURSERVER and I had an account on that system named mminasi with a password of swordfish, I could type:

```
smbclient -L ourserver -U mminasi
```

or:

```
smbclient -L //ourserver -U mminasi%swordfish
```

In the first case, `smbclient` would prompt me for a password. If the system that you query is a domain controller, then it'll also display the list of servers in the workgroup. Notice a couple of things here: for one, it doesn't matter whether you use upper- or lowercase on user account and server names. For another, notice that the -L and -M options don't require slashes in front of the name.

I found that `smbclient -L` seems not to work on Windows 2000 Professional and Server systems unless you specify the name of a *local* user. For example, if I have a workstation named W2KWS that is a member of a domain named us.com, and I have a domain administrator account named mminasi, then there's no point in typing:

```
smbclient -L w2kws -U us\mminasi
```

I'll get an error indicating that `smbclient` couldn't connect. But if I have an account created on W2KWS's local SAM (remember that Windows 2000 workstations and member servers still have SAMs), then `smbclient` will work. To query a machine that happens to be a domain controller, *then* you can use a domain account.

Connecting to File Shares with *smbclient*   `smbclient` lets you access NT, Windows, and 2000 shares from a Linux box, but it doesn't let you access them in the way that `smbmount` does. Instead, you use `smbclient` to attach to a share, and then you copy files to and from Microsoft network shares using FTP-like commands. Again, not as convenient, but more reliable.

You connect to a share with this command:

```
smbclient //servername/sharename -U username
```

This command *does* work with Windows 2000 systems, thankfully. So, for example, if \\OURSERVER contains a share named goodies and my mminasi account with password swordfish has access to that share, I could connect with this line:

```
smbclient //ourserver/goodies -U mminasi%swordfish
```

It'll prompt you for a password or, as before, you can add a percent sign and a password to the end of the username and then it needn't prompt you. You'll then get a prompt that looks like smb>, and you issue commands from that prompt.

The first group of commands that you'll find useful are cd and lcd. These should look familiar if you're an old hand with FTP. lcd specifies the default directory on your workstation, the place that smbclient looks to find files that you want to send and where it puts received files by default. cd specifies the default directory on the server. So, if you're connected to a share, that share contains a directory named /mail, and you want to copy some files from that directory to a directory named /mymailfiles on your local Linux box, you could set those as default directories by typing:

    cd /mail

    lcd /mymailfiles

But don't try a cp command; we'll get to the commands to copy files to and from the SMB server in a minute.

You can now list the files and directories on the SMB server with the ls or dir commands. But what about if you want to ls the local directory on the Linux box? In my experience, if you ls a local directory, then you get your requested ls, *but* then the smb session is terminated. So you need to remember to do one thing when issuing commands intended for the *local* filesystem rather than the remote SMB filesystem: prefix your command with an exclamation point.

Thus, this command in smbclient:

    smb>ls

will show you the contents of the directory on the remote SMB server, but *this* command:

    smb>!ls

will show you the contents of your current directory on the Linux machines. (Notice in both examples that the smb> is the prompt that the system presents to you, not something that you should type.)

Next, you'll want to copy files. You do that with the get and put commands: get filename tells smbclient to get a file named *filename* from the Microsoft network server and copy it to your local Linux box's disk. put does the reverse, moving files from the local workstation to the server. Again, these are just the same commands that you'd use in FTP. Unfortunately, however, put and get don't take wildcards—you can't put *.* or the like. To do wildcard transfers, use mget and mput, "multiple" get/put.

This all sounds pretty good until you try it: Hook up to a share and try to suck down its files with a mget *, and you'll find that the silly thing *pauses* between each file to ask you if you really want it to get the file! But you can keep that from happening with the prompt command. Use prompt to toggle on and off whether you want a confirmation message for each file.

By the way, seasoned FTP users are probably nodding their heads but waiting for me to introduce a binary command, another toggle that tells FTP whether the incoming files are ASCII or binary. There isn't a command like that in smbclient, however; it just treats every file as if it were binary.

As with FTP, the rd and rmdir commands let you remove directories on the remote system. There's a DOS attrib-like command called setmode that lets you make files read-only (the option +r) or read-write (-r), hidden (+h) or visible (-h), system or not, with similar syntax to the DOS, NT, and 2000 attrib command; for example:

```
setmode myfile.txt -h
```

would unhide the file myfile.txt.

smbfs sometimes needs some help finding your prospective target SMB server, and smbclient has the same name resolution needs. If your system has an smb.conf file with a wins= command, as explained in the previous section, then you're in good shape, as smbclient knows to look for an smb.conf file. But you needn't have an smb.conf file to make smbclient work, because of the -I option. -I lets you fill in the IP address of the desired SMB server. So, if in the earlier example I knew that \\OURSERVER had an IP address of 110.58.20.19, then I could pretty well guarantee that my connection would be successful with the following smbclient invocation:

```
smbclient //ourserver/plans -I 110.58.20.19 -U mminasi%swordfish
```

The -I option must be uppercase.

Configuring an SMB Server

Attaching to NT and 2000 servers (and, for that matter, Windows boxes doing file sharing) as a mere *client* is all well and good, but what would be *really* cool would be convincing all of the Microsoft boxes on your network that your Linux machine was a Microsoft file server! So let's do it.

The Basic, No-Security Server

We'll start off with possibly the simplest Samba file server configuration. Make sure the Linux box running Samba is on the network and the network software is working—do a ping or something to make sure that it's connected.

Then let's prepare a directory that we can share. On the Linux box running Samba, type:

```
mkdir /samtest
```

Put a few files—anything will do—into the new /samtest directory. And just to keep things easy, set the file permissions on it to be wide open:

```
chmod 777 /samtest
chmod 777 /samtest/*
```

Next, you'll create a basic Samba configuration file. You've actually already got one that we don't want to lose, so let's back that up:

```
mv /etc/samba/smb.conf /etc/samba/smb.conf.original
```

Then create a new one:

```
vi /etc/samba/smb.conf
```

Type this in, as it's a pretty basic smb.conf, and save it:

```
[global]
wins server = fill in
workgroup = fill in
server string = Test Samba Server
netbios name = Linuxbox
security = share
[firstshare]
comment = Our first Samba share
path = /samtest
writeable = yes
guest ok = yes
```

Where I've typed *fill in*, enter the values for your WINS server's IP address and the name of your workgroup (which is really the name of your domain here).

Next, restart Samba:

```
/etc/rc.d/init.d smb restart
```

Now let's see Samba in action. You *should* be able to sit down at a Windows *9x*, NT, or 2000 machine and type nbtstat -A *ipaddress* (but don't type *ipaddress*; instead type the Samba server's IP address) and get a standard `nbtstat` output. `nbtstat`'s output varies from Microsoft OS to Microsoft OS, but it'll look something like this:

```
E:\>nbtstat -A 192.168.0.2
Node IpAddress: [192.168.0.170] Scope Id: []


         NetBIOS Remote Machine Name Table

     Name               Type       Status
   ---------------------------------------------
     LINUXBOX      <00>  UNIQUE     Registered
     LINUXBOX      <03>  UNIQUE     Registered
     LINUXBOX      <20>  UNIQUE     Registered
     ..__MSBROWSE__.<01> GROUP      Registered
     WIN2KTEST     <00>  GROUP      Registered
     WIN2KTEST     <1D>  UNIQUE     Registered
     WIN2KTEST     <1E>  GROUP      Registered


     MAC Address = 00-00-00-00-00-00
```

In that example machine, I'd set up my Samba server to have machine name or NetBIOS name of Linuxbox, in a workgroup/domain named WIN2KTEST. The important thing is this: we fooled the Microsoft box—it thinks it's talking to some kind of NT, 2000, or .NET server, or perhaps a Windows for Workgroups, XP, or Windows *9x* machine!

This Samba server should respond to other NetBIOS commands as well. From a Windows, NT, or 2000 machine, try `net view \\linuxbox` (or the alternative format, `net view \\192.168.0.2`), and you'll see something like this output:

```
C:\>net view \\linuxbox
Shared resources at \\linuxbox


Test Samba Server


Share name  Type  Used as  Comment


---------------------------------------------
firstshare  Disk           Our first Samba share
The command completed successfully.
```

You can even type `dir \\linuxbox\firstshare` from your Microsoft machine, and you should see the contents of `/samtest` on the Linux box. And yes, those directories can be on an EXT3 partition—when viewed through the "filter" of a network, Microsoft OSs have no idea that they're accessing an EXT3 partition.

A Note on Changing *smb.conf*

If you start trying this stuff out, then you'll logically wonder how long it'll take to see the effects of any changes that you make in `smb.conf`. In general, Samba rereads `smb.conf` every 60 seconds, so you could wait that long. If you don't feel like waiting that long, however, you can just find and kill the two Samba processes, `smbd` and `nmbd`.

While the Samba documentation says that all you need do is the above—wait a minute or restart the daemons—it goes on to explain you may need more than a minute to see changes, and I've seen that in my experience as well. Once I'm logged on to a Samba share with a particular set of permissions, then I keep those permissions no matter how recently Samba has reread my `smb.conf`. In order to see all of the changes to a set of Samba permissions, I have to log my Windows, NT, or 2000 clients off and then log them back on. The easiest way to do this, of course, is from the command line, typing:

```
/etc/rc.d/init.d/smb restart
```

Examining the Basic *smb.conf* Options

Go back and look at that `smb.conf` and look at the section that starts with the word `[global]`. It contains some basic commands that you'll see in just about any `smb.conf`. The commands are mainly self-explanatory, but there are a few wrinkles worth being aware of.

- `wins server` just contains the IP address or DNS name of a WINS server. The Samba server then becomes a client of that WINS server.

- `workgroup` tells the Samba server which workgroup/domain it is a member of. If you *don't* name a workgroup, then the value of the `workgroup` setting is just WORK-GROUP, as in Microsoft network software. But be sure to set it—we can tell in my network who the dodos are by just browsing the workgroup named WORKGROUP.

- `server string` is just a comment about the server. The comment shows up when you browse the workgroup. It's completely optional.

- `netbios name` is, as its name suggests, the NetBIOS name that the Samba server should assume. If you set this to `starbuck`, for example, then you can view this server's shares by typing `net view \\starbuck`. If you do *not* set this, then Samba just sets the NetBIOS name equal to the hostname of the computer. If your computer is named mypc.acme.com, then you'll end up with a NetBIOS name of \\mypc.

Security Options for Servers: Overview

If you're still with me, then congratulations, you've made your Linux box into a very basic SMB server! I say "basic" because I had you set up a wide-open share—*anybody* can get to this data. *Clearly* we need to do a better job than that.

File server security requires two things:

- Authentication: a list of known users and a way for users to prove that they are indeed who they claim to be
- Permissions: a description of what each of those users is permitted to do with each directory and file

Here's another way of saying that. The whole point of security on file servers is to allow us to say, "Frank can access anything in the \\server1\files share, both reading and writing files, but he can't even look in the \\server2\otherfiles share; Darcee, in contrast, can read files from either share, but can't write to either share." But how does a computer know that the person tapping on the keys is Frank, Darcee, or someone else? Through authentication: the server has a list of usernames that it knows, as well as the secret passwords associated with those usernames.

NT stores those usernames in a file called \winnt\config\SAM, and, as you know, a group of NT systems called a *domain* can share a SAM (thus avoiding having to manage a Darcee account for every single system in the company) by keeping that SAM on a special NT box called a domain controller. Windows 2000 domains are more complex and the filename's different (NTDS.DIT), but the basic idea is the same—machines share a central list of username/password combinations, and the network requires people to produce a username and password so that the system knows who it's talking to.

Once the system recognizes you, however, a file server isn't done with its work. It might well be that you are indeed Ignatz Semmelweiss, but that the system has been instructed not to let Ignatz see anything—merely being authenticated doesn't guarantee that you can do anything. Somewhere the system must have a list that describes—for every directory and file—which users can and can't access those directories and files, and what level of access those users can have. In the NT and 2000 world, we call that list the access control list (ACL).

If a Samba server is to truly behave like a Microsoft file server, then it'll need to somehow authenticate users and then, once it's done that, it'll need something like an ACL for each share. I'll consider authentication options, then show you how to "fake an ACL" for a Samba-based share.

Authentication Options for Samba

Samba offers four different options for authentication, and you control which one your Samba server uses with a command in the [global] section called security =. Possible legal values are share, user, server, or domain. Once I describe these, you'll probably decide that you want security = domain.

security = share   This simplest Samba authentication level is really a *non*authentication level: it doesn't authenticate users at all. In that sense, it mimics the behavior of Windows for Workgroups shares and Windows 9*x* shares when 9*x* is configured to do "share-level" rather than "user-level" shares. The beauty of security = share is that it's simple and nearly foolproof.

With security = share, you can only secure the files in a share two ways. First, you can make the share read-only, so that no network user can modify files in the share, nor add files to the share. Second, you can put a password on the share. But it's just one password for everyone, so that password isn't likely to be a big secret, and there's no way to say that Janet and Bill can read and write the share but Laura can only read it. (I'm simplifying a bit, but that's basically right.)

As with NT, however, there are two levels of permissions to deal with: the share permissions and the file and directory permissions. From the point of view of the Samba system, anyone's welcome to access files on a server with security = share, but the Linux file permissions may have a different opinion. Once you've seen that you can freely read and write the \firstshare share on \\LINUXBOX from any Microsoft client, walk back over to the Linux box that is acting as "\\LINUXBOX" and try this:

```
chmod 770 /samtest/*
```

(If you want to change permissions on any subdirectories *inside* that directory, don't forget the -R option: chmod -R 770 /samtest/*.) Here, we're setting the permissions in the test share wide open for the file owner and group, but "no access" for the world. Try to copy a file from \\LINUXBOX, and you'll get "access denied." The Samba program was perfectly happy to give you the file, but the Linux filesystem refused.

security = user   This second option is a step up. Here, Samba *does* require you to authenticate. Recall that Linux boxes have a SAM-like thing of their own, a file named /etc/passwd, a list of known users and their encrypted passwords. So with security = user, the Samba server authenticates you *against the local Linux /etc/password*. In other words, if Tom, Amy, and Sue want to access the NT-like file shares on a Samba box, they'd better each have user accounts on that Samba box.

Sounds like *another* set of passwords to change every month or so—or does it? Well, yes and no. Samba has a cool feature that will automatically keep the passwords for the NT account and the Linux account in sync; that's the good news. The not-so-good news is that it's a bit complex to make work but, once set up, it'll handle everyone's passwords; you needn't reconfigure it for every user.

Despite the password-synchronization feature, though, I'd give this one a miss, unless of course for some reason you wanted authentication *and* an available Microsoft file server but didn't have an NT or 2000 box available.

This is actually the option that many Samba books and documents talk the most about, as it's the one that you essentially end up using when you make your Samba box into a primary domain controller for a bunch of Win9x boxes. It's a perfectly good alternative for many Samba users, as there's a large class of folks who have Windows boxes on the desktop and who want centralized authentication but don't want to have to shell out big bucks to Microsoft for server software and client licenses. In this scenario, they just run Samba on a Linux box and use a Samba feature that lets the Samba box mimic a primary domain controller on an NT 4.0-style domain.

As I'm assuming that most folks reading *this* book already have an NT/2000/.NET server infrastructure, though, I assume that you would be more interested in learning to make a Samba box into a *member server* integrated into an existing NT domain. So I've focused most of this discussion on the `security = domain` option, as you'll read later.

security = server With the `security = server` option, you "borrow" an NT box's SAM for authentication. That's very much like what machines do in a regular NT or 2000 domain—they all use the SAM or `NTDS.DIT` on a small group of systems acting as domain controllers in order to authenticate. But here, Samba goes NT and 2000 one better and basically lets you use *any* machine as a source of authentication information.

Here's an example. Suppose Tom, Amy, and Sue want to access Samba file shares on the Linux box calling itself \\LINUXBOX. (Again, they probably haven't got a clue that it's a Linux box and not a Windows 2000 file server.) You can't afford a copy of NT Server, so you haven't been able to build a domain controller—recall that NT Workstation and Windows 2000 Professional cannot assume the role of domain controller. But you, the network administrator, have created user accounts for Tom, Amy, and Sue on an NT workstation named \\ASTRO. Perhaps you did that because you've been using \\ASTRO as an inexpensive file server; after all, the file server software in NT workstation is the same software as in Server, with the one exception that it limits you to 10 concurrent users. But it's about maxed out and you want a second file server—and you're looking for an economical solution.

You *could* put up another NT workstation, but then you'd have to rebuild the Tom, Amy, and Sue accounts on that second workstation. Hmmm, more duplicate accounts—nope, let's skip that, and, besides, Workstation costs a couple of hundred bucks. So you get a copy of Linux for two bucks and set up a Samba server. You'd like to have some kind of security and don't want to have to rebuild accounts on the second server, the Linux box. In this case, security = server is perfect. As the Linux Samba box authenticates from the user accounts on the NT Workstation, you needn't keep track of duplicate accounts (almost—I'll explain in the next paragraph that you do have to do a minimal amount of duplication), and the price is right.

That's almost how it works, with one difference: you *do* have to create user accounts for Tom, Amy, and Sue on the Linux box. But it's really not a big deal; all you have to do is just create the accounts. You needn't set passwords on them, nor do you have to worry about keeping passwords for those Linux accounts in sync with the NT passwords; you just create Amy's account once on the Linux box and never think about it again until she leaves the company and it's time to delete the account.

You configure a Samba server to authenticate from a server, or even a *set* of servers, with the following lines in [global]:

```
[global]
security = server
password server = SERVERNAME1 SERVERNAME2 ...
```

Those names are regular old 15-character NetBIOS names or, if the servers are Windows 2000 machines, they should be the "downlevel" names that Windows 2000 maintains for backward-compatibility with NT. Don't use IP addresses or DNS names.

You'll need to do one more thing. NT 4 Service Pack 3 introduced a more secure logon system intended to plug a few security holes. Any NT 4 system with Service Pack 3 or higher, Windows 98 system, or Windows 2000 system uses that more secure logon method. Samba accommodates that with a global setting encrypt passwords = yes; assuming that you have those newer operating systems in your network, you'll need to include that command. So in the Tom/Sue/Amy case, you'd have these lines in the smb.conf file:

```
[global]
security = server
password server = ASTRO
encrypt passwords = yes
```

I'll discuss how you'd restrict a particular user's access to a share later, in the permissions section.

security = domain   This is the option that most of us will want to use. If you have an already-functioning NT or 2000 domain, then you can tell your Samba server to go to a domain controller to authenticate. Here are the high points of how to make a Samba server authenticate from an NT or 2000 domain controller, then I'll show you a couple of examples.

- You put the `security = domain` and `encrypt passwords = yes` commands into `[global]`.

- You name the domain controllers in your domain with the `password server =` command, or, if you're running Samba 2.0.6 or above, you can just say `password server = *` and Samba will find the domain controllers via WINS, as NT machines do.

- You must create an account on the Linux box for every one of your domain users. You'll never do anything with these accounts—you needn't even set passwords for them—but they've got be there as a sort of "placeholder" for Samba.

- You then add the Samba computer to the NT or 2000 domain with Server Manager or Active Directory Users and Computers, and then join the Samba computer with the domain using the `smbpasswd` command, whose syntax looks like:

```
smbpasswd -j domainname -r NetBIOS-name-of-PDC
```

That's a bunch of steps, so let's take a look at a couple of examples. For the first, suppose we had a domain named LAWYERS with a primary domain controller in our network named YOURHONOR and backup domain controllers named DEWEY, CHEATEM, and HOWE. A server at 10.10.17.5 is the WINS server. There are only three user accounts in the domain, or rather, only three user accounts in the domain that will ever want to access the Samba server: usernames tom, amy, and sue. Let's also assume that they want to call this Samba server by the NetBIOS name linuxbox. Here's what you'd do:

1. If you haven't done it yet:

   ```
   touch /var/cache/samba/unexpected.tdb
   ```

2. Create a local user account for each user, on the Linux box running Samba. You don't have to do anything fancy—just a simple `useradd` command will do the trick. If Tom, Amy, and Sue are domain members and you want them to be able to access items on the Samba box, then walk over to the Samba box (or log in remotely, of course) and type:

   ```
   useradd tom
   useradd sue
   useradd amy
   ```

Again, this assumes that their NT or 2000 usernames are tom, sue, and amy; if NT knew them as tsmith01, sjones04, and along01, then you'd use those names in the useradd. Yes, this is a bit of a pain, but it's a necessary evil in Samba.

3. Samba has an annoying way of making itself the local master browser, the domain master browser, the emperor of the Universe, and whatever other titles it can get that aren't nailed down. Suppress that behavior with these commands in [global]:

```
domain master = no
local master = no
os level = 0
preferred master = no
```

Now, if this were the *only* SMB-running server on a given subnet, then it'd be fine to set local master = yes.

4. Tell the Samba server to use domains with these commands in the [global] section of smb.conf:

```
[global]
security = domain
password server = *
encrypt passwords = yes
smb passwd file = /etc/samba/smbpasswd
netbios name = linuxbox
```

The password server = * tells Samba to use the normal NT methods to find a domain controller. You can, if you like, just give Samba a list of DCs, as in password server = yourhonor dewey cheatem howe.

5. Create the password file /etc/samba/smbpasswd.

6. Handle the names and name resolution methods with these commands, also in [global]:

```
workgroup = lawyers
netbios name = linuxbox
name resolve order = wins lmhosts bcast
wins server = 10.10.17.5
wins support = no
```

7. Finally, you have to get your Samba server to join the NT or 2000 domain. You do that by first creating a machine account for it with Server Manager or Active Directory Users and Computers, as you've been doing for years with NT (and for less time with 2000). Use the NetBIOS name that the Samba box is assuming—LINUXBOX in my example. Then go to the Linux box and introduce it to the domain with this command:

```
smbpasswd -j lawyers -r yourhonor
```

The `password server =` command doesn't care whether you point it to a BDC or a PDC or a combination of those, but it *does* need to be directed to the PDC here—BDCs can't join computers to a domain in NT 4! By the way, you can avoid having to precreate an account in Server Manager/Active Directory Users and Computers by adding the parameter `–U` to `smbpasswd`, followed by the name and password of a user empowered to create and destroy machine accounts on the domain.

8. Finally, restart the Samba daemons (find and kill the `nmbd` and `smbd` processes or use `/etc/rc.d/init.d/smb restart` to restart) and you're in business. Any domain member can be authenticated for this server by any of the domain controllers that you named in the `password servers =` list.

I'll wrap this up with a more complete top-to-bottom example, but first let me finish this section with a review of when you'd use each of the four `security =` options (Table 9.2).

Table 9.2 Samba Security Options

Option	How It's Useful	*smb.conf* Commands	What Else You Must Do To Make It Work
share	Very simple, not a bad way to offer a public read-only share.	security = share	Nothing.
user	Allows user-specific permissions and does not require any Microsoft servers to make it work.	security = user	Create a user account for every user, on that Linux box, and, if those users also use NT elsewhere, somehow keep the passwords in sync.

Table 9.2   Samba Security Options *(continued)*

Option	How It's Useful	*smb.conf* Commands	What Else You Must Do To Make It Work
server	Lets cheaper NT workstations, 2000 Professional boxes act as central authentication devices for Samba servers; gives you domain controller-like functionality without having to buy Server.	security = server password server = *server NetBIOS name* encrypt passwords = yes	Have an NT or 2000 box of any kind around, and build your user accounts on it so that the Samba boxes can authenticate from them.
domain	Makes a Samba box integrate more traditionally into an NT domain; participates in domain authentication like other Microsoft servers.	security = domain password server = pdcname bdcname1 bdcname2... encrypt passwords = yes	Create user accounts on the domain controller (which you've probably already done if you have a domain); create user accounts on the Samba box; create a machine account for the Samba box using either Server Manager or Active Directory Users and Computers, then use smbpasswd to allow the Samba box to join the NT or 2000 domain.

A Step-by-Step Samba-to-NT-Domain Example

Before moving on to permissions, let's do one more example of setting up a Samba server and add it to an NT 4 domain. This time, I'll cover the example in a more complete fashion, with enough information that you could, if you wanted to, replicate what I'm discussing here. (You don't *have* to do that, I'm just offering a very complete example that can act as a model if you find yourself having no luck with Samba.) We'll assume that:

- The Samba server will use a NetBIOS name of myserver.

- The Samba server will have one share on its /samtest directory, which is advertised as \\linuxbox\firstshare.

- The server will be part of a domain named REALM, which has an existing NT Server acting as primary domain controller named BIGBOSS and a backup domain controller named NUMBERTWO.
- There are three users in this domain with usernames paula, gina, and bob.
- The domain has a WINS server at 130.10.20.5.

I'll assume that you have a computer running Linux with Samba installed.

Create the files */var/cache/samba/unexpected.tdb* As before, `touch /var/cache/samba/unexpected.tdb`. Also, `touch /etc/samba/smbpasswd`.

Create the Basic *smb.conf* In /etc/samba, create a file named `smb.conf` with these contents:

```
[global]
name resolve order = wins lmhosts bcast
wins server = 130.10.20.5
wins support = no
domain master = no
local master = no
os level = 20
preferred master = no
workgroup = REALM
server string = Test Samba Server
netbios name = MYSERVER
security = domain
password server = *
encrypt passwords = yes
smb passwd file = /etc/samba/smbpasswd

[firstshare]
comment = Sample Samba Share
path = /samtest
writeable = yes
guest ok = no
```

Check Connectivity   Next, ensure that the Linux computer can connect to the PDC; name resolution accounts for a lot of Samba hassles, just as it does in the Microsoft networking world. `ping` the IP address of the PDC, and be sure to use the IP address, not the DNS or NetBIOS name; we're just checking the underlying IP routing structure first.

Second, try out a neat Samba tool called `nmblookup` to check that Samba can resolve the NetBIOS name of the PDC. Just type `nmblookup pdcname` or, in this example, `nmblookup bigboss`. You can also use `nmblookup` to find the master browser for any workgroup/domain with the –M option:

    nmblookup -M realm

That command would find the master browser for the workgroup or domain named "realm." Simply typing:

    nmblookup -M -

(that's `nmblookup` with a –M and a dash by itself) returns the identity of the master browser (or browsers). Doing an `nmblookup` with the –S option says to not only resolve the name but to fetch *all* NetBIOS names registered to that IP address, both group and unique names. If you did this on a domain controller, for example, you'd get a dozen more names returned.

You should get a positive acknowledgement from `nmblookup`. If it *doesn't* work, that means your Linux box can't resolve the PDC's NetBIOS name—so here are a few troubleshooting alternatives:

- First, double-check the WINS address that you included in the `smb.conf`.

- Second, look on your Linux computer for `/var/log/samba/log.nmb`. It's cryptic, but sometimes there's a clue in there.

- Samba accomplishes NetBIOS name resolution by first looking in `/etc/hosts`, then `/etc/lmhosts` (which you probably don't have), then by looking in WINS, then broadcasting. You control that with a command in `[global]` called `name resolve order`. You can rearrange its order to match how NT and 2000 do it, using the keywords `lmhosts`, `wins`, `hosts`, and `bcast` to refer to their obvious options:

      name resolve order = lmhosts wins bcast hosts

You might even try creating an `lmhosts` file—they have the exact same layout as in Microsoft OSs—and putting it in `/etc`. Remember that when you make a change to `smb.conf`, it's best to restart Samba with `/etc/rc.d/init.d/smb restart`. In theory, Samba reexamines `smb.conf` for changes every 60 seconds, but the restart seems to be the best bet.

> **NOTE** If you're unclear on the details of NetBIOS name resolution, read Chapter 14 of *Mastering Windows NT Server* or Chapter 7 of *Mastering Windows 2000 Server*.

Create the Share and the User Accounts Now we'll set up a place to put the shared files: create a directory named /samtest (mkdir /samtest) and copy a few files in there (cp /etc/p* /samtest).

Once finished with that, create "dummy" user accounts for each of your users on the Linux Samba box:

```
useradd paula
useradd gina
useradd bob
```

Remember that these are essentially placeholder accounts; you'll never have to worry about them again.

Check Connectivity Again This time, see if the PDC can ping the Samba box. From the PDC this time, type:

```
ping myserver
```

Also, by now the server should be able to resolve its own name in WINS, so from the Samba box, type:

```
nmblookup -R -U ip-address-of-WINS-server myserver
```

The extra parameters are there to force nmblookup to query the WINS server; for some strange reason, it *always* broadcasts first, no matter how the name resolve order command is set. -R and -U followed by the IP address of the WINS server are what force nmblookup to use the WINS server.

Join the Samba Computer to the Domain On an NT computer in the REALM domain, run Server Manager and create a new computer account (Computer ⟩ Add to Domain...), and for Computer Type, choose Windows NT Workstation or Server. Fill in "myserver" where it asks for a computer name, then click the Add button and the Done button.

Back at the Linux Samba computer, log on as root and type:

```
smbpasswd -j realm -r bigboss
```

You'll see a response like:

```
2002/08/09 12:17:41 change_trust_account_password:
  Changed password for domain REALM
Joined domain REALM.
```

Restart Samba:

```
/etc/rc.d/init.d/smb restart.
```

Test It Now log on to an NT machine on the REALM domain using the paula, gina, or bob account. Open up a command line; type `net view` and press Enter; you should see a server named LINUXBOX among the other servers in the domain. Type `net view` `\\linuxbox`, and you should see the \firstshare file share. Finally, type `dir \\linuxbox\` `firstshare`, and you should see the contents of the share. If it worked, then congratulations, you've attached a Samba server to an NT domain!

Now let's take it a step further and demonstrate that paula, gina, or bob did indeed have to authenticate with a domain controller in order for Samba to permit them access to the share. Create an NT user named larry in the REALM domain. Log on to an NT machine as larry and type `dir \\linuxbox\firstshare`; the Samba server will deny the request:

```
1326: Logon failure: unknown user name or bad password.
```

In other words, "Domain members only, please!"

Controlling Share Permissions in Samba

You create other shares in Samba as you did the first share; each gets its own section in brackets. The name in brackets is the share name, and the basic settings look like the following:

```
[sharename]
comment = descriptive comment
path = /full path of the directory on the Linux box
writeable = yes|no
guest ok = yes|no
```

Simple Permissions without User Accounts Take a look at the following example share section, perhaps the simplest possible:

```
[pubshare]
path = /publicfiles
guest ok = no
```

With this setting, any domain user can *read* the information in this file, but not write to it. You could let people write to the share as well by adding a `writeable = yes` line:

```
[pubshare]
path = /publicfiles
guest ok = no
writeable = yes
```

Valid and Invalid Users   `writeable` is a nice command if you're not going to specify particular users who can and can't access a share, but it's unnecessary if you name particular users. So now let's take it a step further and start getting user-specific about who can read or write a share. You do that with the `read list`, `write list`, `valid user`, and `invalid user` settings.

`valid user` looks like a list of usernames separated by blanks, as in this example:

```
[pubshare]
path = /publicfiles
guest ok = no
writeable = yes
valid user = jane jim sue
```

Adding that one line to the share changes things quite a bit. Previously, anyone in the domain could access this share—but *now*, only jane, jim, and sue can access it. Once you have a `valid user` list in a share, then you'd better be on that list, or you simply don't get access.

Again, if you *don't* include a `valid user` command, then every domain user is valid. The setting in the example in the last section, with `writeable = yes` without any `valid user` setting, is basically the same as "Everyone/Full Control" in NT lingo. But once you use a `valid user` statement, then you're saying implicitly that anyone who *isn't* on that statement should have no access to the share.

If you want to *really* make sure that some specific person does not get access to your share, then you can use a command that the Samba team calls a "paranoid" command, the `invalid user` command:

```
invalid user = john paul
```

This is the Samba equivalent of the NT `deny access` command—no matter what other permissions someone might get in Samba, being on the `invalid user` list means no access, period. You can also put the `invalid user` and `valid user` commands into the `[global]` section of a `smb.conf` file; every share on that server then handles the valid and invalid users accordingly. So if you want to be sure that you've locked a given user out of a server, put him or her on an `invalid users` list and put that list in [`global`].

Specifying Who Can Read or Write a Share   So far, all we've done is to specify who can read and write a share with a combination of the `writeable` and `valid users` commands. That's all that you need if you only need to give several people access to a share *and* you want to give them all read-only or read-write permissions. But let's get more specific about who can read and write a share. Two commands, `read list` and `write list`, let you list users who have read-only or read-write access. For example:

```
[pubshare]
path = /publicfiles
guest ok = no
writeable = yes
read list = sam mary phyllis
write list = dawn jane joe bill
```

On this share, sam, mary, and phyllis have access but just read-only, and dawn, jane, joe, and bill have read-write access. Giving someone `write list` access overrides a `writeable = no` setting. (And no, the lack of a `valid users` line wasn't an error—read on.)

invalid users* Beats *write list   So being on the `write list` trumps a `writeable = no` setting; does being on the `write list` overcome being on the `invalid users` list? In other words, consider this share section:

```
[pubshare]
path = /publicfiles
guest ok = no
writeable = yes
invalid users = sam dawn bill
read list = sam mary phyllis
write list = dawn jane joe bill
```

The user named dawn has write access, but she's also on the `invalid users` list—does she get access or not? She does not. Simplified, Samba *first* checks to see if you're a valid user, *then* determines your read or write permissions. So, for example, consider this `smb.conf`:

```
[pubshare]
path = /publicfiles
```

```
guest ok = no
writeable = yes
valid users = mary
read list = sam mary phyllis
write list = dawn jane joe bill
```

Which users can read this share? Write this share? Here's Samba's thought pattern:

- First, are there any `valid users` or `invalid users` lists? (If not, then every domain member is a candidate to read or write the share, at least before it encounters any read list or write list commands.) There *is* such a command—`valid users = mary`. Result: no one but mary can access this share in any way. The presence of a list of names in a `valid users` statement implicitly denies access to everyone not named on the list.

- Second, are there any read or write restrictions? `writeable = yes` says that by default people can write to the share. But mary is on the `read list`, so she's restricted to read access.

How *write list* and *read list* Interact with *writeable* Consider the following set of permissions:

```
valid users = andy bobbi carol
write list = andy
read list = bobbi
writeable = yes
```

Here, we have a share that is in general read-write, because of the `writeable` command. But there's a `read list` and a `write list`, which leads to two questions:

- carol is a valid user, but not mentioned on the `read list` or `write list`. If there were no read or write list at all, then there's no question that she could write to the share, but given that there's an explicit `write list` *and* she's not on it, what access level will she get? The answer: carol has read-write access.

- bobbi is a valid user of this read-write share, but she's mentioned on the `read list`. Does that imply that Samba should simply take her initial permissions (read-write) and add "read" to them, leaving her with read-write or read-only permission? The answer: bobbi has read-only access.

As it turns out, `read list` and `write list` aren't like `valid users`–the fact of a `write list` doesn't deny write access to anyone who's otherwise valid. But being on the `read list` restricts an account to read-only, unless that account is *also* on the `write list`.

Specifying Administrators in Samba

You may want your administrators to have unfettered access to the shares on your Samba file servers. (I mean, hey, what else are administrators for?) You can do that with the Samba command admin users, which can either go into a share's section or in [global]. So if I wanted to give a user named pete admin control of my server's shares, I'd just add this line to the [global] section of my smb.conf:

```
admin users = pete
```

Again, you'll need a pete account both on the domain and on the Samba server to make this work.

Using Groups in Samba

That's all very good, but who wants to list a pile of users, one by one? In the NT and 2000 world, we're used to handing out permissions using groups. Samba lets you name groups in its permission lists also, but it's a two-step process: You see, Samba will let you name groups, but they're *Linux* groups, not NT groups. I know—you wanted to use *NT* or *2000* user groups, not Linux groups. The second step solves that, as Samba includes a usermap feature.

You've seen already that a user with username bob must have a corresponding account named bob on the Linux box. But the names don't *have* to match—it just makes things easier for the administrator that way. If your users' NT/2000 usernames don't match, then you use a usermap command in smb.conf and a text file that matches the Linux names to the NT/2000 names.

Adding a group to a valid users, write list, read list, or invalid users command is easy—just use the group's name and prefix it with an @ sign. To give a group named engineers write access to a share, you'd put this command in that share's section of smb.conf:

```
write list = @engineers
```

Again, that will refer to a Linux group named engineers, so be sure to create a group with that name (groupadd engineers). Next, let's hook that up with an actual NT or 2000 group named engineers. Put this command into the [global] section:

```
username map = /etc/linuxtont
```

/etc/linuxtont (you can name it anything, by the way) is a simple text file with entries that look like this:

```
Linux name = NT/2000 name
```

We'd then enter this line into /etc/linuxtont to connect the NT engineers group to the Linux engineers group:

```
engineers = @engineers
```

Setting Up a Few Shares: An Example

Suppose you have a Samba server with two directories that you want to share: /publicstuff and /privatestuff. You want everyone to be able to read /publicstuff with the share name public, but no one to be able to write it except the gerry user account. Then suppose you have a share /privatestuff that you only want members of the managers group to be able to access (read and write), using the share name private.

For simplicity's sake, let's assume that we're still working in my old example of the REALM domain. Here's what an smb.conf for that might look like:

```
[global]
wins server = 130.10.20.5
workgroup = REALM
server string = Test Samba Server
netbios name = LINUXBOX
security = domain
password server = *
encrypt passwords = yes
username map = /etc/linuxtont
[public]
path = /publicstuff
guest ok = yes
writeable = no
write list = gerry
[private]
path = /privatestuff
guest ok = no
valid users = @managers
write list = @managers
```

The /etc/linuxtont file would have one entry:

```
managers = @managers
```

In the first share, I used guest ok and didn't use a valid users statement because I don't much care who accesses it, but then writeable = no ensures that no one modifies it—except for gerry. In the second share, disabling guests and explicitly only making members of the managers group into valid users locks everyone else out.

Linux File and Directory Permissions and Samba

As with NT and 2000, accessing some data on a share can't be done solely with the permission of the file sharing software; on NT and 2000, you need the agreement of the NTFS file and directory security system and, in Linux and Samba, it's the same story.

As you learned in Chapter 6, you can use the chmod command to set permissions on files or directories in Linux. If you do this, then anyone trying to access data on a Samba share must both satisfy the Samba permissions (write list or read list) *and* the file and directory permissions. But recall that Linux doesn't offer as rich a set of file and directory permission possibilities, so be careful how you set those permissions. This extra layer of security is great, but realize that if you spend a lot of time fine-tuning your security with both share and file/directory permissions, then you run the risk of creating a support problem later—if you exclude someone via a directory permission and then forget that you did, it'll drive you crazy when you give that person write list permission and he still can't access the share!

A Note about Windows 2000

My examples have involved NT 4 domains so far. You can do the same things with Windows 2000 domains as well; your Samba servers can easily authenticate on a Windows 2000 domain, just as any NT 4.0 system can join an Active Directory. But there are few special things to be aware of when attaching your Samba server to Windows 2000.

First, if you were to set Active Directory's "Do not accept NTLM logins" setting, then of course both your NT 4.0 boxes and your Samba boxes couldn't be a part of the domain. NT 4.0 cannot use Kerberos, and if Active Directory only understands Kerberos logins then you're out of luck. Samba runs atop Linux, and Linux *does* understand Kerberos, but not in a way that Active Directory likes. You can, however, read an interesting article on the Internet about how someone got pretty far in getting his Linux box to log on to an Active Directory at http://acd.ucar.edu/~fredrick/linux/ad.html.

Second, when you create the machine account for the Samba server with Active Directory Users and Computers, you'll see a check box that says Allow Pre-Windows 2000 Computers to Use This Account. Check it. If you're new to Windows 2000 and aren't quite sure how to create a computer account in the first place, follow these instructions:

1. Log on to a W2K domain controller.
2. Click Start ➤ Programs ➤ Administrative Tools ➤ Active Directory Users and Computers.
3. On the icon in the left panel representing the domain, right-click and choose New ➤ Computer.
4. On the resulting panel, check the box labeled Allow Pre-Windows 2000 Computers to Use This Account and click OK.

Third, when you refer to the Windows 2000 domain or domain controller, refer to it by its old-style NetBIOS name. For example, if your Windows 2000 domain is named acme.com, then there's probably a "downlevel" name of ACME for the domain. If the domain controller is named bigdog.acme.com, then its downlevel name is probably \\BIGDOG.

Authenticating Linux Users with an NT/2000 Domain: *winbind*

With Samba 2.2 came a potentially quite useful feature: the ability to log users on to a Linux box using an NT 4.0 or Active Directory domain account. You've already read in Chapter 6 that it's possible to make a Linux box an NIS server, where you can store a set of centralized user and group accounts, freeing you from having to rebuild user accounts for each user on each Linux box. But that would mean you'd still have to maintain two centralized sets of user accounts: the NIS accounts and the Microsoft domain. winbind lets you tell Linux, "When someone wants to log in, go ask the Microsoft NT or AD domain controllers in such-and-such domain to authenticate this user."

winbind requires a number of pieces:

- Of course, the Samba programs (smbd and nmbd) have to be running.
- A new daemon, winbindd, has to be running.
- You must join each Linux box that will allow Microsoft-based authentication to the domain using the smbpasswd -j command.
- You must tell Linux to accept Microsoft authentication by modifying a set of files that control something called *PAM*, the *Pluggable Authentication Modules*.

Let's see how to set up this system, a piece at a time. I'll assume that you're starting from a new Linux system that you have just now installed Samba on, and I'll go through the configuration steps. Then I'll present a concrete step-by-step example of making a Linux box accept logins from a domain named BIGFIRM.

Set up *smb.conf*

As we'll need Samba working, we'll need an /etc/samba/smb.conf file. The parts that are relevant for winbind all go in the [global] section. The settings that I've found work well for winbind look like this:

```
[global]
name resolve order = wins lmhosts bcast
```

```
wins server = <your WINS server IP address>
wins support = no
domain master = no
local master = no
os level = 10
preferred master = no
workgroup = <your domain name>
server string = Test Samba Server
netbios name = <some NetBIOS name for this PC>
security = domain
password server = *
encrypt passwords = yes
smb passwd file = /etc/samba/smbpasswd
winbind separator = +
winbind gid = 10000-20000
winbind uid = 10000-20000
template shell = /bin/bash
template homedir = /home/%D/%U
winbind enum groups = yes
winbind enum users = yes
```

The first part, from `name resolve order` through `smb passwd file`, are no different from what we've already discussed. Here's what the other commands do.

winbind separator = +

Linux, and `winbind` in particular, needs to know, when you're referring to a user, whether that user's account lives in the system's local `/etc/passwd` file, or on a Microsoft domain controller. There are a number of ways that the Samba folks could have set it up, but they decided to mimic the standard Microsoft approach of referring to a user as *domain name\username*, as in using bigfirm\mark to say, "There's a user account named 'mark' in an NT or AD domain whose NetBIOS name is 'bigfirm.'"

There is a problem with doing that. Recall that Linux uses \ to mean, "Get ready; I'm about to use an unusual character" in command lines. So if you *really* wanted to use names like bigfirm\mark, you'd have to write them as bigfirm\\mark—not terrible, but the chances are good that if you told your users they had to type in their domain name, *two* backslashes, and their username at the Linux login prompt, you'd get a lot of help desk calls.

Samba lets you decide which character to use as a domain name/username separator with the command "template separator." Here, I've followed an emerging winbind convention and used a plus sign. Thus, if my user account is named mark, and I'm a member of a domain whose NetBIOS name is bigfirm, then I'll log on to Linux as bigfirm+mark.

winbind gid = 10000-20000 and winbind uid = 10000-20000

Recall that Linux gives every user account and group account a *gid* (group ID) or *uid* (user ID) very much like a Microsoft SID. Where SIDs are over 120 bits long (meaning that if a SID were ever written out as a number, it'd be over 40 digits in length), Linux tends to hand out uids and gids in the range of 100 or so.

When dealing with a user whose account lives not locally in /etc/passwd but instead on a domain, Linux still needs to hand out a uid to any domain-based user and a gid to any domain-based group. The idea with these two commands is to tell Linux to give a uid or gid to a domain-based object not down amongst the locally-maintained accounts, but instead in a different range.

template shell = /bin/bash

This is probably self-explanatory. As you saw in Chapter 6, when a user logs in, Linux assigns him or her a command processor like the CMD.EXE file that gives C:\> in an NT command-line session. bash is most popular in the Linux world, so we'll stay with it.

template homedir = /home/%D/%U

This finds the home directories. Recall that in the Linux world, home directories are far more significant than in the Microsoft world; users pretty much get dropped in their home directories when they log on, and that's usually the *only* place where they can write or modify files. %D means, "Substitute the name of the domain here," and %U means, "Substitute the name of the user here." So if a user named bigfirm+mark logged on, Linux would drop him in a directory named /home/BIGFIRM/mark. (For some reason, %D always returns names in uppercase.)

winbind enum groups = yes and winbind enum users = yes

This tells winbind to go out and prefetch the entire list of users and groups from the domain as soon as the Linux box is up. That information is then cached on the Linux box, to speed up logins. If you set these to no, then winbind will take a little more time when logging a domain user on, as it's got to go out to the Microsoft domain controller. I usually set it to yes, but on very large enterprises, you might set these to no; if you had a domain with several thousand users, then it might take quite a bit of time for the Linux box to suck the entire user list off the domain, which would tax the domain controller.

Make Samba Start Automatically

We've done this before, but to keep the example self-contained, let's see how to tell Linux to make Samba start automatically in runlevel 3. You do it by creating a symbolic link in the /etc/rc.d/rc3.d directory to the script in /etc/rc.d/init.d/smb:

```
ln -s /etc/rc.d/init.d/smb /etc/rc.d/rc3.d/S91smb
```

Create *unexpected.tdb*

As before, Samba needs to see a file named /var/cache/samba/unexpected.tdb:

```
touch /var/cache/samba/unexpected.tdb
```

Start Samba

The next time that you reboot, Samba will come up, but hey, this is Linux; it might be years before you next reboot—so let's start Samba:

```
/etc/rc.d/init.d/smb start
```

You should see a response like:

```
Starting SMB services:    [  OK  ]
Starting NMB services:    [  OK  ]
```

Check NetBIOS Name Resolution

Whether we're talking about Windows clients or Linux clients, one of the most common and vexing causes of logon failures is a simple inability to resolve computer names. NT, 2000, XP, and .NET lack a simple tool to check this, but Samba has a very useful one in nmblookup. nmblookup will let you find a NetBIOS name both by broadcasting and by querying a WINS server; we will try both. The commands look like:

```
nmblookup netbiosname
```

which will try to resolve a NetBIOS name via broadcasts, and:

```
nmblookup -R -U wins-server-address netbiosname
```

In order for a lot of the upcoming code to work, the Samba service on your Linux box *must* be able to resolve your domain's PDC. Let's say, then, that your NT or Active Directory domain's PDC (or, in the case of Active Directory, its PDC emulator) has the NetBIOS name DC1 with IP address 10.10.10.70. Let's also say that the IP address of your WINS server is 10.10.10.50. You'd tell Samba to broadcast to try to find DC1 with this command:

```
nmblookup dc1
```

And, if successful, you'll see some output that looks like:

```
querying dc1 on 10.10.10.0
10.10.10.70 dc1<00>
```

Then tell it to query the WINS server like so:

```
nmblookup -R -U 10.10.10.50 dc1
```

And you'll get a response like:

```
querying dc1 on 10.10.10.50
10.10.10.70 dc1<00>
```

Join the Linux PC to the Domain

Once you know that the Linux box can find at least one DC, you're ready to join the domain. Use this command (the same one that you saw earlier):

```
smbpasswd -j <domain name> -r <pdc name>
↪-U <domain admin name%password>
```

If I had a domain administrator named Susan whose password was blueSky on a domain named bigfirm with a PDC named DC1, I'd type:

```
smbpasswd -j bigfirm -r dc1 -U susan%blueSky
```

If Susan does indeed have domain admin powers on the domain bigfirm and a password of blueSky, and if bigfirm's PDC is named DC1, then you'll see output like:

```
Joined domain BIGFIRM.
```

Edit *nsswitch.conf*

You may recall from our discussion of NIS that Linux uses a file named nsswitch.conf to determine what order to search for passwd and group information—local files, NIS servers, etc. That counts here as well: we're going to tell this Linux box to expect to find both passwd and group information not just on a local file but also from the winbind service.

Open up /etc/nsswitch.conf in a text editor. Once you get past the opening comment lines (recall that an octothorpe # in the first column indicates a comment), you'll see three lines like so:

```
passwd:    files nisplus
shadow:    files nisplus
group:     files nisplus
```

Change the nisplus to winbind for passwd and group, so that the lines look like:

```
passwd:    files winbind
shadow:    files nisplus
group:     files winbind
```

Make *winbind* Start Automatically

Like Samba, we want winbind to start automatically. As winbind needs Samba and Samba starts as service 91, we'll start winbind as service 92:

```
ln -s /etc/rc.d/init.d/winbind /etc/rc.d/rc3.d/S92winbind
```

Lend *winbind* a Domain Account

If you've ever created an Active Directory with dcpromo, then you may have noticed a question that goes something like, "Do you want to retain compatibility with pre-Windows 2000 systems?" That refers to the fact that under NT 4.0, anyone could inspect the list of users on a domain without even logging in. Of course, you couldn't extract passwords, but even seeing the list of users is, in the eyes of many, a security hole. So Microsoft plugged that hole with Active Directory—it's no longer possible to inspect a user account without being authenticated first. You needn't be an administrator to do this, just anyone with a domain account.

But many older NT programs still assumed that they could anonymously inspect the user list. So running a program like that on an Active Directory that has been configured to *not* maintain compatibility with pre-Windows 2000 networks would fail. In this case, you could solve the problem in one of two ways: either replace the NT 4 program with something that knows to at least log on to the domain before querying the user list, or relax the security on the Active Directory.

You can relax the security on an Active Directory by adding the Everyone group to the group in Builtin called "Pre-Windows 2000 Compatible." Until recently, winbind required you to do that if it was to communicate with an Active Directory. But winbind has a nice workaround whereby you simply say to it, "Whenever you need to inspect the list of users, use this account to log in." You tell winbind to use a particular account when looking over the list of users with this command:

```
wbinfo -A username%password
```

You need only do this once, and you need only give it a normal user-level account. So, for example, I could create a user account on bigfirm called normaluser with password nothingspecial and let winbind use it like so:

```
wbinfo -A normaluser%nothingspecial
```

You needn't prefix the name with a domain, as wbinfo *expects* to be fed a domain account.

Start winbind

By now, winbind should be ready to run. Start it up:

```
/etc/rc.d/init.d/winbind start
```

You should get the [OK] message as usual.

Test the Domain Connectivity

winbind should now be able to read lists of users and groups and authenticate users. You test it with wbinfo, a useful troubleshooting tool, and getent. Try these commands:

- wbinfo -u should produce a list of domain users.
- wbinfo -g should produce a list of domain groups.
- getent passwd should produce a passwd file augmented by the domain users.
- getent group should produce a list of groups, augmented by the domain groups.

Create the Home Directory

We've set things up so that Linux will give a user named Jane in a domain named ACME a home directory named /home/ACME/jane. But in order for the processes that automatically create those home directories to work, we need to first create /home/ACME. Do that like so:

```
mkdir /home/<domainname in caps>
chmod 755 /home/<domainname in caps>
```

For example, if our domain were indeed named ACME, then we'd type:

```
mkdir /home/ACME
chmod 755 /home/ACME
```

Modify the PAM Configuration

I haven't talked about PAM much in this book, but it's basically an attempt on the part of the Linux world to centralize and "regularize" authentication. PAM stands for Pluggable Authentication Modules, and the idea is that there are many ways to prove that Jane is indeed Jane—that is, to authenticate her. In most cases, we use passwords—PAM can, I'm told, talk to things like fingerprint readers, so there are alternatives to passwords—but there are many types of account/password combinations. We've already met the simple shadow password model, where Linux stores user account information in a couple of ASCII files in /etc. There's NIS, which networks that information, and there's winbind, which looks up names and passwords on an NT or Active Directory domain. There are pam modules for each.

Red Hat Linux has a directory /etc/pam.d that contains ASCII files with names like login and samba that are just lists of pam modules to use when trying to authenticate. For example the file named login tells the login process how to go about authenticating users. A look inside login, though, shows this line:

```
auth required /lib/security/pam_stack.so service=system-auth
```

What that means in English is that /etc/pam.d/loginpam's instructions to log in—basically says, "Ummm, don't ask me; ask the file system-auth." So we'll modify the file /etc/pam.d/system-auth to tell Linux to employ winbind. Bring up /etc/pam.d/system-auth in a text editor, and you will see three lines that start with auth:

```
auth required /lib/security/pam_env.so
auth sufficient /lib/security/pam_unix.so likeauth nullok
auth required /lib/security/pam_deny.so
```

These three lines tell Linux how to authenticate you. First, pam_env sets the basic environment variables. Then pam_unix does the usual stuff to try to actually authenticate you—checks the password that you punched in to the one in /etc/shadow, etc. Third, pam_deny says, "Set the authentication to failed; deny access." So, on a normal day, these three work like this:

- First, pam_env sets the environment variables.
- Then, pam_unix tries to authenticate you, using the password that you gave. The fact that it has sufficient on its line means, "If pam_unix was successful, don't look at any of the other auth modules." Thus, if pam_unix was successful, then pam never gets to pam_deny.
- On the other hand, if you *do* get to pam_deny, then you're denied access and the login fails.

We're going to add a whole new pam module, one that uses winbind. The line will look like:

```
auth sufficient /lib/security/pam_winbind.so
```

But where to put it? Well, clearly it goes after the pam_env module. And clearly it must come before pam_deny–once you hit that, it's all over. So it either goes before pam_unix or after pam_unix. If we put it before, the auth section looks like:

```
auth required /lib/security/pam_env.so
auth sufficient /lib/security/pam_winbind.so
```

```
auth sufficient /lib/security/pam_unix.so likeauth nullok

auth required /lib/security/pam_deny.so
```

This will work, but it'll produce an unpleasant side effect. Whenever a local account tries to log on, that local name and password will be tested first by pam_winbind, and of course it will fail, as winbind looks up names in a domain, not in /etc/shadow. Control then passes to the pam_unix module, which says to itself, "Hey, we need a password from this guy," and puts a second:

```
Password:
```

prompt on the screen. The net effect is that when root signs in, she has to type her password twice—ugh.

There is a workaround; pam_unix will take a parameter use_first_pass that says, "Reuse the password that the last module tried." We add that to the end of the pam_unix line, and our auth section looks like:

```
auth required /lib/security/pam_env.so

auth sufficient /lib/security/pam_winbind.so

auth sufficient /lib/security/pam_unix.so
➥ likeauth nullok use_first_pass

auth required /lib/security/pam_deny.so
```

Now this will work fine. Summarized, change /etc/pam.d/system-auth in this way:

1. Find the line that starts with auth and includes pam_unix.

2. At the end of the pam_unix line, add the parameter use_first_pass.

3. Above the pam_unix line, add the line:

   ```
   auth sufficient /lib/security/pam_winbind.so
   ```

4. Save the file.

Next we have to tell login that if someone logs in who's never been here before, we need to create a home directory for her. There is a pam module to do that as well. Edit /etc/pam.d/login and add this as the last line (type it as all one line):

```
session required /lib/security/pam_mkhomedir.so
➥ skel=/etc/skel umask=0022
```

Reboot, and you'll be able to log in as *domainname+username*.

Oh, and one more thing: the file /etc/pam.d/system-auth gets rewritten by the operating system whenever you run authconfig. I don't know why you would run it, but if you do, then you'll have to edit /etc/pam.d/system-auth to add the pam_winbind.so line again.

Setting Up Linux to Authenticate from a Domain: An Example

If you're like me, then something as complex-looking as this is tough to grasp without a fully worked-out example. So let's go through one in close detail.

My goal is to create a Linux PC that can accept logons from a domain named BIG-FIRM. My tests used an Active Directory domain named bigfirm.biz that had a Net-BIOS name of BIGFIRM, but this should work just as well with an NT 4.0 domain named BIGFIRM.

BIGFIRM has a PDC named w2ksv at IP address 192.168.0.154. BIGFIRM's WINS server is on the same computer, at that same IP address. The administrator for the domain has the password swordfish. There is a normal user account wally with password wally.

When testing this example, I started from a fresh Red Hat install. I chose the Custom option and then deselected all packages. (This example worked just as well for an "install everything" option, but my Custom option installs with just Installation CD 1 and takes only about 20 minutes instead of three hours!)

1. Of course, verify that basic IP networking works on the Linux PC—you should be able to acquire an IP address either by setting one statically or via DHCP, and you should be able to `ping` 192.168.0.154.

2. Get Samba on the system. (If you installed everything, then you've already got it.) Mount Installation CD 1 and first install a few `rpms` that Samba needs:

    ```
    mount /dev/cdrom /mnt/cdrom
    cd /mnt/cdrom/RedHat/RPMS
    rpm -ivh libjpeg*
    rpm -ivh libtiff*
    rpm -ivh libpng*
    rpm -ivh cups-libs-1.1.14-15.i386.rpm
    rpm -ivh perl-5.6.1-34.99.6.i386.rpm
    cd \
    ```

    Unmount the CD by typing `eject`. Insert the second CD and mount it:

    ```
    mount /dev/cdrom /mnt/cdrom
    cd /mnt/cdrom/RedHat/RPMS
    rpm -ivh samb*
    ```

3. Now create an `smb.conf`. This is the shortest one that I could come up with that will do everything we want `winbind` to do:

```
[global]
name resolve order = wins lmhosts bcast
wins server = 192.168.0.154
wins support = no
domain master = no
local master = no
os level = 10
preferred master = no
workgroup = bigfirm
server string = Test Samba Server
netbios name = linuxbox
security = domain
password server = *
encrypt passwords = yes
smb passwd file = /etc/samba/smbpasswd
winbind separator = +
winbind gid = 10000-20000
winbind uid = 10000-20000
template shell = /bin/bash
template homedir = /home/%D/%U
```

4. Make Samba autostart: all on one line, type:

```
ln -s /etc/rc.d/init.d/smb /etc/rc.d/rc3.d/S91smb
```

5. Create `unexpected.tdb`: type:

```
touch /var/cache/samba/unexpected.tdb
```

6. Start Samba: type:

```
/etc/rc.d/init.d/smb start
```

7. Verify NetBIOS name resolution:

```
nmblookup w2ksv
nmblookup -R -U 192.168.0.154 w2ksv
```

8. Join the domain:

```
smbpasswd -j bigfirm -r w2ksv -U administrator%swordfish
```

9. Edit /etc/nsswitch.conf and change the lines:

```
passwd:    files nisplus
shadow:    files nisplus
group:     files nisplus
```

to look like:

```
passwd:    files winbind
shadow:    files nisplus
group:     files winbind
```

Save the file.

10. Make winbind autostart: again, all on one line type:

```
ln -s /etc/rc.d/init.d/winbind /etc/rc.d/rc3.d/S92winbind
```

11. Give winbind a user's name so it can access the user list:

```
wbinfo -A wally%wally
```

12. Start the winbind service:

```
/etc/rc.d/init.d/winbind start
```

13. Try wbinfo: type:

```
wbinfo -u
```

and you should see an output like:

```
BIGFIRM+Administrator
BIGFIRM+wally
BIGFIRM+guest...
```

14. Create a place for the home directories with two commands:

```
mkdir /home/BIGFIRM
chmod 755 /home/BIGFIRM
```

15. Edit /etc/pam.d/system-auth so that it looks like this (changes are in boldface):

```
#%PAM-1.0
# This file is auto-generated.
# User changes will be destroyed the next time authconfig is run.
auth          required        /lib/security/pam_env.so
➥
```

auth sufficient /lib/security/pam_winbind.so

```
auth          sufficient      /lib/security/pam_unix.so
➥ likeauth nullok use_first_pass
auth          required        /lib/security/pam_deny.so


account       required        /lib/security/pam_unix.so


password      required        /lib/security/pam_cracklib.so
➥ retry=3 type=
password      sufficient      /lib/security/pam_unix.so nullok
➥ use_authtok md5 shadow
password      required        /lib/security/pam_deny.so


session       required        /lib/security/pam_limits.so
session       required        /lib/security/pam_unix.so
```

NOTE Note that if you ever run the Red Hat configuration program authconfig, it will overwrite this file, and you'll have to reapply the above changes.

16. Edit /etc/pam.d/login so that it looks like this (changes are in boldface).

```
#%PAM-1.0
auth       required    /lib/security/pam_securetty.so
auth       required    /lib/security/pam_stack.so service=system-auth
auth       required    /lib/security/pam_nologin.so
account    required    /lib/security/pam_stack.so service=system-auth
password   required    /lib/security/pam_stack.so service=system-auth
```

```
session    required    /lib/security/pam_stack.so service=system-auth
session    optional    /lib/security/pam_console.so
session required /lib/security/pam_mkhomedir.so
➥ skel=/etc/skel umask=0022
```

17. After saving the files, reboot. You should now be able to log on as bigfirm+administrator with password swordfish, or as bigfirm+wally with password wally, or similarly with any other domain account.

And Just a Couple More Features...

I haven't got time to cover more of Samba; then again, I only intended to give you some of the basics. But if you find that Samba's interesting, here are a couple more things that you might want to look into.

Disk Quotas   NT admins wished for disk quotas for a long time and finally got them in Windows 2000, but they turned out to be pretty lame. Well, Samba has a great set of disk quota software. Actually, this is a side benefit not so much of Samba but of Linux.

Multiple Virtual Servers   This is pretty neat. You can make one single Samba machine look like multiple servers. You could create one virtual server that was a member of the ENGINEERING domain and another that was a member of the MARKETING domain. Even better, each virtual server would display a different set of shares, so someone browsing the ENGINEERING and MARKETING domains wouldn't have a clue that these two servers were the same machine.

10

Conclusions: Linux versus Microsoft, Linux *and* Microsoft

Let's wrap up with a bit of summary about what we've seen as Linux's strengths compared to Microsoft operating systems, Linux's weaknesses compared to Microsoft operating systems, and a few thoughts about how to use the two together most effectively.

Linux's Strengths Relative to NT/2000/XP/.NET

It should surprise no one that Linux has been growing in popularity. It draws from both a wealth of time-tested Unix code and a highly motivated group of programmers dedicated to proving that they've got the best operating system solution around.

Linux's Greatest Strength Is Open Source

You've read in this book and elsewhere, or perhaps you know from experience, that much of Linux's code is very reliable and rock-solid. That's the most compelling argument for uprooting some already-existing server application and replacing it with Linux: reliability. But where did that reliability come from? Are Linux programmers just somehow smarter than NT and 2000 programmers, and so therefore turn out better code?

No, not at all. But most Linux programs are open source, meaning that anyone can see the program code, the "blueprints" of any application. Exposing a program's code offers the possibility that an unscrupulous competitor could read that code and steal your original idea, which is why many companies don't expose their code. But keeping code secret has its costs, as well. For one thing, any programmer who knows that her code is open and available for any other programmer to examine will work a bit harder to produce cleaner, higher-quality code. For another, software vendors lose out on the potential help that customers can provide. As I argued in Chapter 3, the "big name" OSs that the world relies upon now became reliable largely because IBM, DEC, and Unix customers received not only the executable files but the source code for their software. Those customers could then fix bugs in those vendors' products and send the bug fixes to the vendors. It wasn't "open source" in the sense that, if I fixed an MVS bug, I was allowed to distribute it myself—that was up to IBM—but the net effect was the same: many eyeballs looking for a bug.

Years ago we'd decide between two or more competing software products by looking at their capabilities and perhaps speed—for example, NetWare 286 was simply more full-featured and faster as a network server than Microsoft's MS-NET product in 1987. Nowadays, however, both Novell and Microsoft's network operating systems are roughly equivalent in their capabilities, so companies make the Novell-versus-Microsoft decision on other criteria. But what happens as time goes on and the differences between competing OS options get smaller, except for one thing—reliability? At some point, the software-buying public will grow tired of having to cope with products whose defect lists are in the tens of thousands. At that point, the "killer app" might be the one with the shortest list of bugs.

Linux Is Inherently Multi-Vendor

As of mid-2000, it was official: Microsoft *is* a monopoly, at least in terms of desktop software, according to the court. (They clearly aren't a monopoly in the server market, with a little more than 40 percent of that business. Interestingly enough, an IDC survey in 2001 suggested that Linux had almost as large a server market share as NT/2000.) They got to be a monopoly by a combination of good marketing and good technology, and my hat's off to them for that accomplishment.

Monopolies can be good in the sense that they promote—or, rather, *create* and *enforce*—standards. That doesn't mean that you need a monopoly to have standards, but it helps establish them in the first place. Standards are great in that they make buying and supporting things easier: If there were three major desktop PC operating systems, each with about a third of the market share, then it's possible that we'd *also* have a different market-leading office suite for each of those, and that those suites might not interchange documents. Businesses would have trouble interchanging information without a lot of document conversion work. It was like that in the PC world in the mid-'80s, believe me—I was there, it wasn't any fun. Standards *are* good.

But monopolies can do scary things also. Like increase the prices of their products without fear. I paid $40 for Microsoft's PC operating system (DOS) in 1981. Now their PC OS (Windows 2000 Professional) costs $319, an eight-fold increase in 19 years, an 11 percent annual price increase, in a time period when inflation only ran about 3 percent annually. Yes, no question, 2000 Professional offers far more than DOS did, but how much of the difference is due to market control? Or, to offer another example, compare the 1996 price of NT Workstation 4.0 ($200) to the current price of 2000 Professional. This time, a 12 percent annual increase in price, in a time period when OS/2, another product with a rich and growing set of capabilities (even if it *doesn't* have any market share to speak of) hasn't increased in price at all.

Or what if Microsoft decides to stop selling software that you install and use for as long as you like, and instead sells you software that stops working after a year, forcing you to rebuy it every year? They could do that; it would be perfectly legal, and they'd be within their rights. Heck, it might even be a good move for Microsoft shareholders. Could you go to the competitive operating system, the one that's as easy to cross over to as it is to switch from Honda to Ford? No. There isn't any such OS and there never will be.

In mid-2002, Microsoft angered many customers by announcing "Licensing 6.0," which is somewhat complex but can be boiled down to a few basic ideas. First, they will no longer sell upgrade versions of their software. For example, suppose you buy a laptop in late 2003 that comes with XP, and then in 2004 Microsoft ships the replacement to XP—call it Windows YQ. If you want YQ on your system, you'll have to buy a brand-new, complete copy of the OS, rather than the "Upgrade your system to YQ from a previous version of Windows" version. (The upgrade version has typically been half the price of the full version.) Second, you can choose to enroll any copy of Microsoft software in their "Software Assurance" program. When you do this, you agree to pay Microsoft some amount of money every year as a kind of upgrade insurance policy; it buys you the right to use any future new version of the software. Thus, when you buy that new laptop in 2003, you'll have some number of days to enroll your new copy of XP in Licensing 6.0. You pay your fee every year whether Microsoft releases a new version of their desktop OS or not. When Microsoft *does* come up with Windows YQ, then you're entitled to a copy of it, and to put that copy on your laptop.

A lot of folks have said that Licensing 6.0 has annoyed a lot of customers, and it has. Others have said that it'll drive people into the arms of Linux, and perhaps it will. On the other hand, as a guy who's purchased Red Hat versions 6.0, 6.1, 6.2, 7.1, 7.2, and 7.3, I've got to say that Red Hat has never offered me an "upgrade" cost on any of those copies. On the other *other* hand, Red Hat's pretty cheap—even at $60 list, Red Hat Personal 7.3 is cheaper than any Windows upgrade package I've ever purchased.

Now let's consider Linux. Linux has standards, without requiring a monopoly to create them. Additionally, as I observed in Chapter 3, what if Linus decides that he'd like to be the first Finnish hecto-billionaire and so starts turning the screws on Linux users, charging a license fee and putting timers on the Linux kernel to shut it down after a year's work. What can Linuxers do then? Simple: the existing Linux code was released under the GPL. Anybody who wants to could find and rip out the time-bomb code, then compile and use the resulting operating system. She could even sell it if she liked, so long as she gave away the source code.

For years, people used to ask me why I used PCs and not Macintoshes. Part of the reason was, as I've explained earlier, that I'd spent too many years working with minority-market computer systems and I wanted to remain in the largest desktop computer market, so that I would have a wide range of compatible hardware and software available. Part was simple inertia—I'd invested a lot of time in PCs. But I was also troubled by the fact that Apple worked so hard to keep others from creating Mac clones. Macs have always been more expensive than PCs and still are, even if you take into account all of the goodies that come with them. I avoided Macs partially because they were a monopoly—the PC hardware business is a ragtag industry in some ways, but when I'm buying hardware, I'm in the driver's seat, and as a consumer, I like that. Perhaps I should be thinking the same thing about my operating systems.

Still, the reality for corporate Linux users is that Red Hat has the mindshare for business users, and they're just as good at reneging on promises as is Microsoft. Red Hat used to offer a service for $240 where they'd help you set up a particular server service, such as walking you through building a Samba or Sendmail box. That's not true anymore; now your only option is to pay $1,500 for Advanced Server support. Kind of expensive for a few answered questions. *But* it entitles you to get basically any Linux question answered *for a whole year*—Sendmail, DHCP, DNS, Apache, Samba, etc. included. Not a bad deal. But what if I were to move my business over to Linux in the anticipation that this service would be available every year, only to have Red Hat pull the rug out from under me in a year or two? Since the stock market Tech Wreck in 2000, the fact is that Linux businesses have disappeared like water off a sidewalk on a hot summer day. I do *not* want to have depend on the kindness of newsgroups to keep my network running!

Linux Benefits from Tons of Free Software

Ages ago, people wrote and gave away software for early Unix. A bit later, the BSD people started building and giving away even more software. The GNU people build and give away software. The Linux people build and give away software.

And just about all of it runs on Linux.

Very often in the Linux world, the question is not, "Is there a program that can do this in Linux?" Instead, the questions are, "*Where* is the program that can do this in Linux?" and, "How hard will it be to get this free program working the way that I need it to?" Some of it's very well documented, some isn't, but there's a wealth of free, often high-quality software for Linux.

Linux Licensing Is Free…and Thus Simpler

No, I'm not going to say to buy Linux because it's free and so you'll save money on software. Instead, I'm going to say to buy Linux because it'll save you money on legal bills.

Quick now—suppose you have a computer on your desk at work, a laptop, and a computer at home. You use each of these machines to run Word for your company's work, although you never use more than one machine at a time. How many copies of Word must you buy?

The answer: two. The Word license lets you put Word on your corporate desktop and a laptop. The home machine needs a license as well. Word's license is machine-specific, not person-specific, so even though there's only one of you, you'll need two copies of Word. Ah, but now suppose you use your machine at home to attach to a Windows 2000 Terminal Server, and you then run Word in a Terminal Server window—do you need another license? Is Word "running" on the Terminal Server (a new piece of hardware, so you'd need another license) or on your home machine (so you might not need another license, as you already have a Word license for home). The answer is the latter: you need not have a license for an already licensed system to run Word over a Terminal Server connection to another machine. Confused yet? Well, then let's consider the same questions vis-à-vis the Microsoft Exchange Client, which uses an 80 percent/20 percent model of usage…

Software licensing in this day and age is a nightmare. My experience talking to corporate IT managers tells me that the only people who are actually in compliance with the licensing terms for their applications are people who deliberately over-buy licenses "just in case." The paperwork and administrative support required to keep track of software licenses is quickly approaching the amount of support required to keep track of income taxes. One vendor admitted to me that he believed that most customers were not in compliance, but that their noncompliance was merely honest misunderstanding of the intricacies of software licenses. But what keeps a big software company from showing up at a firm's door with a federal marshal, auditing a firm's computers, and collecting six- or seven-figure fines for this unintended noncompliance? Well, nothing, and as a matter of fact, a couple of organizations (the Business Software Alliance and the Software & Information Industry Association) make their living finding noncompliant firms and receiving bounties on fines collected from flagrant license violators—but who draws the line between flagrant and inadvertent? In short, software license accounting is a new avenue of risk for enterprises, an avenue that did not exist a few decades ago.

What's one way to avoid this risk? Use software whose license does not require stringent per-person or per-workstation accounting, like Linux.

Linux Provides Remote Control

Remotely administering NT was a royal pain until recently, with 2000 and .NET Server's Terminal Services. That's important for administrators who must control worldwide enterprises—or even just for the administrator of a small office who'd rather log in over a phone line at 3 A.M. than drive 30 miles to work to troubleshoot a problem late at night.

2000, .NET, and XP have largely solved that problem, with a graphical remote desktop tool (RDP, Remote Desktop Protocol) that runs well even on bandwidth as slow as the 33Kbps range. But Linux has *always* been a remote champ.

Linux, however, doesn't require any scripting to get basic admin jobs done—the commands already exist. Where 2000 is just learning to let administrators do their work from the command line, that's always been the first place that Linux admins go—GUI admin tools are available, but they're usually incomplete compared to Linux's rich Unix legacy of powerful command-line tools. Because of this, Linux is a natural for Telnet-based administration. Of course, if you really want to, you can run a remote GUI session, but you'll find that X is much more bandwidth-hungry than RDP, at least 10 times more so. In the year 2000, I said that Linux won this category hands down. But I'd have to say it's now a tie—Windows has the better graphical remote control solution, but Linux's strong command-line orientation makes it the low-bandwidth champ.

Linux Is Robust

Much of Linux's foundation code and structure is wonderfully stable and robust. Once a Linux server system is running, you can often just forget about it until a hardware failure brings it down. (Understand that here I'm talking about the server pieces like Apache, BIND, Samba, Sendmail, and the like—don't assume that the newer pieces like the GUIs can be trusted implicitly.) Along the same lines, you have to like Linux's ability to reconfigure itself on the fly without reboots. Where NT seems to need rebooting whenever you do anything more complex than changing the background color, most Linux configuration takes effect without a reboot. Yes, this is lessened in 2000, but only lessened; Linux can do many things without reboots that 2000 can't touch without a reboot.

While I have not seen that same robustness in GUI-based products—Linux's strength continues to be more in the server realm than in the workstation realm, in my opinion—the operating system's intrinsic reliability shows through on the GUI side as well on those occasions when the GUI locks up. In the Microsoft world, such an event requires a hard power-down to fix. In the Linux world, a few keystrokes and a `kill` command zaps the GUI without affecting any of the non-GUI applications that were running in the first place. In contrast, shutting down the GUI on NT or 2000 crashes the system.

Linux Admin Tasks Can Be Scripted

I mentioned this earlier in my discussion of remote control, but I didn't want to miss highlighting it in its own section. Since its inception, NT has had very nice GUI-based administration tools—User Manager, Server Manager, Control Panel—and then 2000 continued the trend with Active Directory Users and Computers, the Manage Computer snap-in, and the like. GUI tools are terrific for beginners and occasional users; if I don't create a user account more often than every six months, then the simple point-and-click ease of User Manager, which exploits your existing knowledge of the Windows GUI, is perfect—"If you know Solitaire, then you're halfway to being an NT or 2000 administrator."

But when faced with pointing and clicking two thousand times to create the user accounts for this semester's crop of Computer Science students, the average college IT administrator might just wish for something a bit more terse in its user interaction needs—something scriptable. Linux's `useradd` command is perfectly suited to the job—give me a file containing the list of desired usernames, and in a few seconds I can convert it into a list of `useradd` commands, execute it as a script, and the accounts and home directories are built.

Of course, that's not to suggest that NT and 2000 tasks *can't* be scripted. As a matter of fact, the 2000 Server beta included a sample script to create user accounts from a list of users. But a look at the script shows that it took some pretty scary-looking Active Directory Scripting Interface (ADSI) coding to make it work. Instead of `useradd name`, the 2000 script required this:

```
Call CreateUsers(strDomain, strFile, strCurrentUser,
➡strPassword, strPropertyArray, strPropertyValueArray)
```

You see, someone who had a lot of experience creating user accounts with Active Directory Users and Computers (ADUC) would have no experience whatsoever that would help him in building a script to automate ADUC's tasks. In contrast, someone who'd built a few user accounts in Linux with `useradd` would immediately see how to script the process. Yes, there are scripting tools in NT and 2000, but many are unsupported Resource Kit tools, or require learning a whole new set of programming commands. The fact that Linux admins face a somewhat steeper *initial* learning curve than NT/2000 admins means that learning to script later down the road is easier for the Linux folks than it'll be for the NT/2000 people.

Linux wins here, but as I write this, the .NET Server beta shows that Microsoft has seen the light and has included a bunch of command-line tools to let you do just about everything. Once we all become facile with them, building "scripts"—batch files, really—will be a snap. Check back in 2004.

LILO and/or GRUB Greatly Simplifies Dual-Booting

Anyone who's struggled with putting multiple operating systems on a single computer has to like Linux's LILO loader. It's fairly flexible and can live in a partition, or the Master Boot Record, or a floppy. It's a nice, free, multiple-OS chooser. Granted, this is a relatively small matter for administrators—very few of us will care whether or not we can put two operating systems on our production servers—but a great convenience for developers and power users.

NT/2000 Strengths Relative to Linux

Sounds like The Penguin's got the edge, eh? Well, you know, there *is* a reason (or two) why NT and 2000 are collectively the most-used server software in the world. Let's shift directions here and look at NT's and 2000's advantages over Linux.

Actually though, before I do, let me make a comment about this comparison. Sometimes you'll see a Product A versus Product B comparison, and it's clear that Product A is better, but the writer felt the need to make the comparison look balanced somehow. I want to stress that I'm *not* doing that here. Consider that NT/2000 and Linux both have large market shares in the server world, and in fact, according to some statistics, they hold the number one and number two spots, respectively. In a world with as many choices as we enjoy today, there's really no way that either of the top two best-selling products wouldn't both be at least good to very good. So let me stress again: you could be perfectly happy with either OS, or with both OSs.

Linux Installation Routines Are Better But Still Troublesome

Without doubt, the single worst thing about using Linux—or *trying* to use Linux— is the initial installation. But Linux's setup routines in the year 2002 are miles ahead of what I saw in 2000. I put Red Hat 7.3 on a variety of systems, but I did most of the work on three computers:

- A Compaq 333MHz Pentium II Presario with 144MB RAM and an 8GB hard disk, a video capture card (built-in), a 3Com 10/100 Ethernet card, a Philips CD-RW burner, an integrated sound system, and a Zip 250 USB drive. Red Hat handled the NIC, the video card, the Zip drive, and the CD-RW burner without prompting. It got the sound running after I ran the command-line `setup` routine, but it never made the video capture work.

- A Toshiba Satellite 4260, a Pentium III system with a 450MHz processor, 196MB RAM, an 8GB hard disk, integrated winmodem, and a PCMCIA Ethernet NIC. Everything worked without a problem except for the sound, the winmodem, and the NIC. The sound worked after I ran `setup`. I was able to make the NIC work by doing a `dhcpcd` command from the command line, so I knew that all I needed to do was to cook up an `ifcfg-eth0` script. I never did get the winmodem to work.

- An IBM T21 ThinkPad with an 850MHz Pentium III processor, a DVD-CDRW drive, mini-PCI Ethernet, winmodem, Orinoco wireless card, DataStor FireWire PC Card, and integrated sound. The video, Ethernet, sound, and burner all worked; again, I needed to run `setup` to wake the sound up. Winmodem never worked. The wireless card and FireWire cards never worked, and Red Hat's for-pay support's perspective was that FireWire and wireless networking were both in the "We'll do it one day soon, but for now you're on your own, pal" areas.

In every case, these installs (and others on other systems) were *much* better than my 2000 experience. While Red Hat's installation routines were among the worst of a set of uniformly frustrating Linux setup routines, they're much better now.

But Red Hat's perspective on wireless and FireWire are troubling in 2002—neither are unusual from a Windows perspective. Yes, I know, if I'm willing to take the knife between my teeth and free-dive into a pool of code that's inadequately documented and that no one's going to support, then I'm sure I could get both working… but that's not an answer, in my opinion. Telling people that the answer to a problem is merely to compile some unsupported code just isn't how we do it in a modern IT shop. That's fine ror hobbyists and researchers, and thank goodness those folks are busy cooking up that code—but it's not a production IT answer. (Having said that, the pace of change in the Linux world is such that by the time you're reading this book, there may well be a Red Hat 7.10 with fully automatic 802.11b and 1394 support.)

Winmodems may not be utterly essential to life on Earth, but they're still useful, particularly for traveling users. The prospect of having to drag an external modem with me because Linux doesn't like internal modems would be troubling, were Linux my only OS.

Is it reasonable that I should have to cook up a script to get my Ethernet card to work? Recall from Chapter 4 that doing something as simple as choosing the DNS server requires knowing that a file called `resolv.conf` controls that, and that setting your system's hostname involves spelunking your `/etc/sysconfig` directory. Ditto sound—the `config` program is great if you know to run it; why doesn't it run automatically?

Having said all that, I should repeat my comment earlier in the book that Red Hat's Professional help in Setup was well worth the $150 I spent for 60 days of help. Microsoft has nothing like that at all, and should seriously consider something on the order of Red Hat's Professional Server offering.

In response to what I've said here, some Linux advocates retreat to a position wherein they say, "Well, just as Microsoft doesn't support every piece of hardware, neither does Linux." (Microsoft won't support systems not on their Hardware Compatibility List, or HCL.) It's a bogus argument for two reasons. First, the fact is that Microsoft OSs *will* run on most non-HCL hardware; go buy a generic clone and it'll run 2000, XP, 98, .NET, or whatever version of Windows you like. Second, the Linux "HCLs" are tiny compared to the hardware world in general—get on Red Hat's site and look at their HCL, then compare it to XP's. If Linux advocates *truly* want to say that Linux can only be expected to run on HCL hardware with such a short HCL, then they must face the fact that they are saying that Linux will only run on a small minority of PCs and that, in effect, it is nothing more than a niche operating system. I imagine that's not what they intend to say, nor am I suggesting it: with enough work, you can make Linux run on many non-HCL systems. (And let's not forget that, in some parts of the market, Linux supports *more* hardware than NT or 2000—you wouldn't run NT or 2000 on an 8MB, 25MHz 486, but you *could* run Linux on that hardware.) Instead, I think that the Linux world should be more forthcoming in setting people's expectations about the difficulty of getting Linux on many systems. The bottom line is that Linux is far easier to install than it used to be, but it's still no picnic.

Getting and Installing Applications Is Cumbersome

An operating system is no good without applications. But the Linux world is hampered by several factors there.

At one point, I wanted to run the absolutely latest version of Samba. So, using the same procedure that I outlined in Chapter 5, I downloaded, unzipped, untarred, and compiled it... that wasn't too bad. But then I found that the Samba folks arrange their files in a nice, intelligent directory structure under /usr/local/samba/*. Unfortunately, however, no Linux distribution that I've found uses that directory structure, instead scattering the Samba files to the four winds—or, rather, to four or five directories. Getting the new copy of Samba to replace the one shipped with Red Hat 7.3 then, was a bit of a hassle.

The best answer seems to be to get applications not as source code that needs compiling and making, but rather to find an RPM that works on your system. Unfortunately, an RPM that works for one distribution might not work for another. One answer is to just buy Red Hat, because even if there's only one RPM available, then it'll be a Red Hat–compatible RPM. (Dan tells me that Linux is moving toward a standard RPM format that all distros will support. That's great news, and I look forward to watching its implementation in future distros.)

Linux advocates never want to hear this, but the fact of the matter is that there is a significantly smaller pool of available, commercial-quality, useful applications for Linux than there are for Windows, NT, or 2000. Yes, I know, Oracle, Sybase, PeopleSoft, and the other database vendors are coming to Linux slowly, but others aren't. Autodesk, the market leader in CAD, offers only a viewer and a renderer that run on Linux. The major desktop applications in the business world are Microsoft Office apps, and they don't run on Linux. Sure, Applixware, Sun, and Corel offer office suites, but the fact is that clients—publishers, in my case—want Word-compatible files, and I've lost too many hours and too much work to applications that produce "compatible" files to want to try another bunch. Yes, it's unfortunate, but it's a business reality. You won't find Quicken for Linux. And despite the fact that Linux is something of a hobbyist OS for many, the list of available games is pretty small. I said earlier in this chapter that there is a wealth of apps for Linux, but I also said that they're often not documented well, nor do they have the polish of commercial apps.

Will that change; will we see more commercial-quality apps for Linux? In the first version of the book, I said, "Possibly." Now my answer is, "Yes, definitely," although I don't know what the time frame for that will be. Even though the number of useful, polished apps available for Linux is tiny compared to the number available for Windows, the number has grown quite a bit since 2000.

People have to be able to make a living from the software business, and the strong religious aversion to paying for software in the Linux world really hurts the guy who'd like to put together a game or small app for $50 or so—he normally gets a cold shoulder from the Linux community. Products that have made a name for themselves outside the Linux world with their for-pay software—WordPerfect, Lotus Notes, Oracle—are, in contrast, welcomed as a sign of Linux's "maturation" or "legitimacy." In other words, the only way to create a successful commercial program that runs under Linux is to first create a success *outside* the Linux market. *Then* you'd be accepted as for-pay software in the Linux market. That doesn't make Linux a very fertile ground for building the initial versions of "killer apps"—anyone wanting to be successful at creating great, profitable new programs would do best establishing his or her market in the NT and 2000 world *first*, and port to Linux later.

Basic Setup Help Is Lacking

It is often quite difficult to figure out some of the most basic things about getting a new application (or aspect of basic Linux) to work. The man pages and other online help are notoriously lacking in examples. Further, stand-alone systems (BIND, Samba, Sendmail, and others) often lack basic walk-throughs that would help you set up at least a basically useful server. For example, when trying to learn Samba, I soon needed a way to incorporate NT groups into my permissions lists, to be able to not just say, "John is allowed on this share," but to say, "the Managers group is allowed on this share." (This is, let's face it, a far more realistic example; very few real-world NT and 2000 permission work happens with specific user accounts rather than groups.) Despite the fact that the current Samba distribution even includes the full text of a book on Samba, there is not a single completely worked-out example of using an NT group in a Samba permissions list.

It's almost *too* easy to point to Sendmail as an example of an inadequately documented server subsystem, so I won't belabor that point. But consider the simple "cookbooks" that we have in this book. In my opinion, they shouldn't have been necessary. Yes, if someone wants to build some nonstandard configuration of some server product, then certainly she should expect to pay a consultant some money. But not if she just wants a mail server for a department, or a file server.

There's plenty of rumored help out there on the newsgroups and mailing lists; legend has it that all you have to do is ask and you get helpful people. In my experience, politely worded requests for help, backed up by proof that I *have* taken the time to first read the FAQs, READMEs, HOWTOs, and man pages, gets me either no assistance or an unhelpful suggestion to go back and read the HOWTO again.

That's not to say that there's no help out there: many sympathetic souls have posted web pages describing how they solved some Linux problem, and a search of altavista.com, ask.com, or google.com has answered more questions than any other source. And professional help is available—Linuxcare and Red Hat offer for-pay help, but the help isn't cheap. (It's sure cheaper than Microsoft's help, though!) Nor is that to imply that the help's not worth it—but, to compare Linux again with my Microsoft NT and 2000 experience, I have been able, using Microsoft documentation and online assistance, to set up basic systems that do what I need without having to engage consulting support.

Linux GUIs Lack "Fit and Finish"

I've written elsewhere in this book about this, so I'll recapitulate it briefly. The Linux GUIs, KDE and GNOME, are certainly more professional-looking than their window-manager predecessors fvwm2 and the like. But they seem clumsy compared to the components of the Windows 9*x*, NT, and 2000 UI. As with other parts of Linux, they are getting better, but they've still got a long way to go.

For example, try opening Netscape for the first time: three or four introductory and licensing agreement dialog boxes all appear, demanding an OK before they'll go away. No matter what resolution you run Linux in, it seems that every dialog box fills an inconvenient part of the screen. (In their favor, however, I should point out that most of the dialogs can be resized to be smaller, and they seem to recall from run to run the size that you set—something that Windows can't do.)

Uniformities that we take for granted in Windows, like Ctrl+X, +C, and +V for cut, copy, and paste, appear sporadically in X applications. Windows-like functions such as context menus (the menus that you get when you right-click instead of left-click) aren't implemented in a standard manner either: for example, when trying to bring up a context menu in Netscape, you right-click as in Windows, but then you have to hold the mouse button down as you make your choice. For those of us afflicted with carpal tunnel syndrome, having to hold a mouse button down *hurts*!

Perhaps Linux's greatest GUI weakness is its font model. Take two computers. Put Windows XP and Internet Explorer on one, and put Linux with the latest KDE or GNOME and Netscape/Mozilla/Konqueror on the other. Point the web browsers to the same site and look at them side by side. The text on the XP box will look far more readable, 99 percent of the time. Even if you were to copy the Windows TrueType fonts into Linux, the difference in the way the GUIs look is still striking.

NT/2000/.NET's File Permissions Model Is More Powerful

In NT and 2000, we have a powerful file and directory permissions model. If I want group A to have full control, group B to have read-only access, deny all access to group C, and give guest-level access to group D, I can do that with a few clicks. I can then extend that control down to the file level—it's simple to say that the franksmith user account has full control, the Managers group has read access, and the Marketing group has no access to a particular file.

As you read in Chapter 6, Linux has a fairly simple file permissions model. You can set user-specific permissions for a file or directory, but only for one user, the owner. It is simply impossible in Linux to say that Al and Dave have full control, Betty and Shirley have no access, and Carol and Jane have read-only access on a file. Similarly, you can set group permissions for a file or directory, but only for one group.

Linux's NIS Domain Model Is Insecure

NT and 2000 let us centralize user accounts in a single computer called a domain controller, so that we needn't rebuild user accounts for every user on every machine. Linux lets us do that also, using NIS. NIS is an old Sun system that Sun has since replaced with NIS+ and now, under Solaris 8, with an LDAP-based system.

As a first try, NIS is pretty good and not too hard to set up. But it was developed in a day of lower concern for network security, so it's not built to be as security-oriented as modern networks require. In particular, NIS sends passwords across a network in clear text, a real no-no for network security. NIS+ fixed that, but for some reason NIS+ doesn't have much currency in the Linux world, as simple NIS is what gets shipped with most distributions.

This is not impossible to get around, as there is apparently an NIS+ implementation for Linux, but, as the HOWTO on NIS and NIS+ says, "Support for NIS+ under Linux is still under development." NT and 2000 domain logons, in contrast, happen over an encrypted link, and passwords aren't transmitted in clear text.

Of all of the things that I'm commenting on in this chapter, this is probably the one that I'd bet was most likely to change in the next couple of years. The Unix world has seen an explosion of interest and work in the field of LDAP-based authentication systems. My guess is that by 2004, Linux will have something nifty that runs off Kerberos and LDAP and that NIS will be nothing but a bad memory. *Or*, even better (from my point of view), Samba will continue to develop, and it'll just make the most sense to use Samba's "authenticate to a domain controller" feature.

It's Easier to Learn Basic NT/2000 Administration

This is the flip side of my earlier observation that Linux administrators will find scripting simpler than NT and 2000 administrators. If you will never *need* to learn scripting or scripting skills, if you'll never build a large network, then you might not care that your administrators will never "graduate" to a command line from a GUI.

In some ways, the Linux versus NT/2000 support tradeoff goes like this: Linux is more complex to get set up but, once set up, it's easy to keep running. NT and 2000 are simpler to set up with their GUI and wizard interfaces, but they're also prone to problems, so they're harder to *keep* working once they're in place.

NT/2000 Has Better Hardware Support

NT and 2000 are better fixed for hardware and driver support. If you're configuring a system with new hardware, you'll probably have trouble finding drivers for Linux, and far less so for NT or 2000. If you're configuring a system with expensive hardware, perhaps a high-end SCSI host adapter, then you're more likely to find an NT or 2000 driver for it, as the Linux volunteer programming force just may not *own* that expensive SCSI host adapter. I've already commented on FireWire and IEEE 802.11b problems, so I'll leave the subject at that.

In general, Linux needs the support of hardware vendors, and surprisingly that support still doesn't exist. I'm accustomed, under Windows 9*x*, NT, XP, or 2000, to going to a vendor site whenever I acquire a new piece of hardware to get the latest drivers before I try to install the hardware. I'd do that for Linux as well but unfortunately, hardware vendors seem not to *put* Linux drivers on their websites. Given Linux's increasing market popularity, you'd think that would change—but apparently some vendors still don't want to show the world the source code to their device drivers, which is a shame. After all, they're not selling the drivers, they're selling the hardware, and the drivers are no good without the hardware. And think of the potential open source benefits to both users and vendors of hardware!

Linux Doesn't Support All Microsoft Proprietary Protocols and Interfaces

This isn't the fault of the Linux community, but it's a special concern that anyone planning to integrate Linux and NT/2000 should be aware of. As we all know from painful experience, Microsoft doesn't build their products strictly along the lines of standard protocols and interfaces. Sometimes they come up with a protocol all their own, such as when they use the Messaging Application Programming Interface (MAPI) for mail transport rather than the standard SMTP and POP3 protocols. Other times, they take standards like HTML and expand them with tools like Active Server Pages. ASPs are great—I've built my website around them, and it was a great convenience being able to use my existing VBScript knowledge to be able to avoid having to learn a new programming language—but they're also proprietary to Microsoft's Internet Information Server unless you're willing to spend more money for a third-party add-on that runs some, but not all, ASP scripts—and none of them run VBScripts.

We see another example in Windows 2000's DNS server. It implements all of the latest RFCs about dynamic DNS and incremental zone transfer, which is great. If you try to create a Linux-based DNS server to incorporate it as a secondary DNS server, you'll run into two problems. First, by default BIND doesn't enable dynamic DNS.

The second problem you'll run into concerns the way that 2000 has solved the security problem. As there is no RFC about how to secure dynamic DNS (or rather, there wasn't one as of 1999, when Windows 2000's final development happened), Microsoft offered the option to secure their DDNS servers via Active Directory. Using that feature, you solve the security problem and improve upon the way that DNS servers replicate their data. Unfortunately, that feature—"Active Directory DNS integration"—isn't standard, so Linux DDNS servers can't be part of it. Again, that's not Linux's fault by any means, as no one can be expected to have to follow and mimic all of Microsoft's proprietary protocols. But, on the other hand, it's hard to ascribe evil intent to Microsoft's actions, as Windows 2000 really *needed* DDNS, but it *also* really needed some kind of security, or it's likely that many Microsoft customers might well have decided to give Active Directory a miss altogether, so Microsoft did the right thing by adding security to DDNS. (BIND 9 now has a pretty sophisticated security system; perhaps with time we'll see Microsoft's DNS support it.)

Summing Up the Differences

In short, then, on the plus side for Linux, it often offers higher-quality software and the promise of freedom from a single vendor's control, both through open source. It includes some extremely reliable infrastructure server tools for mail, web, FTP, and other basic, essential services. Ironically, one of those services is a system, Samba, that mimics Microsoft's own file server system, and does a better job of it than Microsoft did!

Linux has accumulated many programs, built by volunteers both for Linux and its predecessor Unixes over the years, and some of that code is quite good. In addition, all of this excellent code is free or very cheap to buy, and its nearly nonexistent licensing requirements could easily translate into huge savings and reduce the need for administrative staff to handle licensing.

Once administrators learn how to administer Linux servers from the command line, they will be almost immediately able to start using the power of scripting to automate tasks. Some firms are beginning to offer quite good support for Linux, both the basic services and more complex parts. Finally, that fact that Linux offers a no-cost network server and client is making it increasingly popular at colleges and universities, meaning that as time goes on, more and more Computer Science and Information Technology graduates will have a better footing in Linux than in NT, so one day soon it might be easier to find a competent Linux administrator than a Windows 2000 administrator!

On the minus side for Linux, it has a somewhat steeper learning curve than NT and 2000, despite the hard work of many volunteer documentation authors; current NT and 2000 administrators, as well as Windows desktop support specialists, would require a nontrivial amount of retraining. Linux is also more difficult to get set up in the first place, due not only to the need for new skill sets for administrators and support staff but also because of complex, opaque, and sometimes unreliable setup programs. Setup is further complicated by a relative paucity of hardware driver support when compared to the Microsoft offerings.

Linux has only a fraction of the amount of commercial server software available that NT and 2000 have, an even tinier fraction of desktop productivity software, and that software is not as user-friendly as Windows users are accustomed to. The same developer community that is avidly dedicated to producing fast, low-defect code does not yet seem dedicated to spending CPU power on the niceties of leading users by the nose through difficult tasks or ones only occasionally executed. And while enterprises not currently using Microsoft technology would care about this, Linux systems do not, in general, support Microsoft's proprietary protocols and services.

Using Linux in a Microsoft Environment: Some Ideas

Let's finish off with some ideas for where you can use Linux and NT, 2000, and Windows 9*x* together.

Set Up a Mail Server

When I moved to Windows 2000, I found that my free, NT-based SMTP/POP3 mail server would not work on my Windows 2000 Server. I've never been a fan of Exchange, and in any case I wasn't too keen on the idea of spending several thousand dollars for a Microsoft mail server just to support my handful of e-mail accounts. I was also annoyed that Microsoft had orphaned my Digital Alpha server by stopping work on 2000 for the Alpha. And I'd always heard that when Microsoft bought Hotmail, they tried to move it over to Exchange, but Exchange couldn't handle it… so they stayed with qmail on a Unix platform.

I had no proprietary needs, so I looked to Linux. For $70, I got the Red Hat 6.1 Standard Edition version of Linux for the Alpha and set up Sendmail on the system. It's a 64-bit version of the operating system, so ever since early 2000, I've been exploiting the power of my Alpha in a way that NT 4 Terminal Server (the Alpha's previous job) never could. I knew almost nothing about setting up Sendmail, so I called Red Hat to purchase a support call for $240. The technician was completely helpful and walked me through the procedure, refusing to get off the phone until we had sent mail back and forth. (As I said, unfortunately Red Hat no longer offers this $240-per-problem support.) Even though I spent $310 total for my mail software, I now have a fast, robust mail server that I have quite literally not rebooted in two years, that's not going to become obsolete any time soon, and that cost less than just about any other mail server on the market. (But you can do it even more cheaply—just get Red Hat and follow the instructions in Chapter 8.)

Use a Linux DNS Server

If you're not yet using Active Directory, then you might consider either moving your DNS infrastructure over to Linux, or using a Linux server as secondary DNS server. I find the NT and 2000 GUI tools easier to work with than Linux's need to edit zone files, but then building zone files by hand isn't all that challenging in a small- to medium-sized network.

If you *are* using Active Directory, then you might choose not to integrate your DDNS with Active Directory, if you have a firewall in place that would keep outsiders from registering on your domain. In that case, you could install DNS on Linux with DDNS enabled and have a reliable secondary DNS system—it might be a great use for a Pentium 100 that's too slow to run Windows 2000!

Create Web Terminals

I have a computer in my kitchen, which is attached to my home network, which is in turn constantly connected to the Internet. That computer only needs to do one thing: get to the Web. I use it to look things up without having to go off to my office. For this simple task, I've experimented with different options, and one of those options was Linux on an old Pentium 133, with 32MB RAM and a 1GB hard disk, that was paid for long ago.

Obviously this system runs Netscape, so any websites that require client-side VBScripts simply can't work. And many websites require Microsoft fonts to look decent, but as you've seen you can convince XFree86 to use the basic Windows TrueType fonts, solves some of the "This was clearly made for Internet Explorer" problems so common when using Netscape.

But a firm wanting to experiment with Linux workstations can easily take this further than just Web access with a very small expenditure. For about $100 per desktop, you can purchase Applixware, a desktop office suite product that is apparently quite file-level compatible with Office—in fact, Dan used it to read the Word files that I sent him as we worked on the book together.

Build Cheap Firewalls and Routers

Need to create a separate subnet for the company's training lab, a network that you can isolate from the corporate network with a firewall? Use a Linux box with two Ethernet NICs in it and the `routed` and `ipchains` (and, now, `iptables`) programs that come with every Linux distribution. No, it probably won't be as fast as a Cisco router, but the link between a classroom network and the enterprise network really needn't be all that terribly fast—and most firms are sadly a bit stingy with their training budgets, so Linux's low cost can be a real lifesaver in that case.

Add an Inexpensive File Server or Web Server with Samba or Apache

Need a file server for that underfunded training lab? Or maybe just need an extra file server as a place to upload user data as you upgrade workstations from Windows 98 to Windows XP? You *could* put up another Microsoft server for the time being, but why pay the extra money for a Server license that you'll only use for a few weeks? Instead, use Samba, save the company a few hundred bucks, and see if they'll share some of the savings with you.

As Linux web servers can't serve your existing VBScript-based ASP pages, you might not be able to add Apache to your internal web farm as a backup server. But if all you need is a simple intranet web server to hold onto some static pages, then Apache can do the job and, again, the price is right. Or you might use it as a testbed to start learning how to do dynamic content using not Active Server Pages but, instead, Perl, a more transportable approach!

By now, I hope that we've convinced you that Linux is worth understanding and perhaps incorporating in your existing Microsoft network, and that with a bit of help (which I hope this book has provided), you can reuse many of your hard-won Microsoft desktop support and networking skills to become proficient in Linux.

In the first version of the book, I said that I didn't think Linux was merely a fad, and in 2002, it's clear that my belief was borne out. Some firms that were significant contributors to Linux's growth were sufficiently hurt by the Tech Wreck to leave some parts of Linux in the lurch (I'm thinking of Corel here and its effect on Wine, which seems actually *less* useful in 2002 than it did in 2000), but there's still a lot of work under way. In my experience, the thing that kills operating systems is a lack of software, and, while Linux doesn't have as many commercial applications available as Windows 9x, NT, and 2000, there are still an awful lot of apps out there, even if they are a bit uneven in terms of setup complexity. (Sometimes I wonder whether, in the long run, Linux might *not* turn out to be a short-term phenomenon, though not for the reason that its detractors cite. Here's why: What if Linux introduced people to the benefits of Unix, and so those same people then decided they definitely wanted Unix—but from a "big name" company with paid programmers? In other words, what if in the end Linux merely turns out to be an inadvertent but wildly successful marketing machine for Sun, or for Apple's Mac X OS, which is nothing more than BSD under the hood and an Apple GUI?)

The percentage of servers running NetWare, VINES, and several commercial Unix products has declined in recent years, and Linux and NT/2000 have been the OSs swallowing up the market share that the others have left behind. The well-rounded network professional needs some familiarity with both the Microsoft offerings *and* Linux. Consider, for example, the small- to medium-sized network market. This is a very price-sensitive market segment: a dentist needing a network of one or two servers and some desktops might well look at a potential payment to Microsoft of $10,000 for server software, versus about $50 for a Linux distribution, and decide that saving ten thousand bucks might pay for a bit of setup and configuration consulting. In that case, it wouldn't hurt if *you* were the nearest consultant *and* you happened to know Linux. Engineers, technicians, and all other sorts of problem solvers come to know as many tools as they can—take the time to add Linux to your tool belt, and I'll bet it'll save you a few bucks or a few hours.

I can't stress enough how much fun I have when working with Linux. Despite the bumps in the road, it never ceases to be fascinating to learn about open source, Unix/Linux, and the incredible treasure trove of tools and toys that come with Linux. If you haven't yet done so, make some space on a couple of computers, put Linux on them, and start playing around with it. I'd be very surprised if you didn't soon start seeing uses for it in your office, either for reasons of straightforward reliability or low cost. Best of luck!

Linux Resources

In the process of putting this book together, I've found several useful Linux resources—really too many to count—but this is a list of the most significant ones that I came across.

Linux Distributions

A few of the larger distributions' sites. If you have patience and a fast enough Internet link, you can get a complete copy of their distributions at these sites.

Red Hat	www.redhat.com
Debian	www.debian.org
Slackware	www.slackware.com
TurboLinux	www.turbolinux.com
Caldera OpenLinux	www.caldera.com
Mandrake Linux	www.linux-mandrake.com
SuSE	www.suse.com

If you have a great amount of time on your hands and want to see a wide range of Linux distributions, visit the Linux Weekly News' distribution page at: `http://www./lwn.net/ Distributions/`.

Linux Information Web Sites

As befits the Linux world, there's more information stored as bits that zing around the Web than as ink on pulp.

`www.slashdot.com`	Bills itself as "news for nerds," but there's a lot of Linux news here.
`www.linuxdoc.org`	The Linux Documentation Project site. Home of HOWTO documents, man pages, and several guides.
`www.lwn.net`	Linux Weekly News has been providing news about Linux for a good number of years. Does an excellent job at putting news into context.
`www.linuxtoday.com`	All Linux, all the time. Daily list of pointers to new info about Linux appearing on the Internet.
`www.linuxnewbie.org`	Nice site that publishes how-to articles aimed at beginners.
`www.linuxjournal.com`	Major Linux periodical; all print content seems available on their site.
`www.linuxworld.com`	IDG publication on Linux.
`www.redhat.com/apps/support`	Red Hat's knowledge base. Many problems and solutions.
`www.linuxcare.com/help-yourself`	Linuxcare's knowledge base, another great (free!) source of Linux problems and solutions.
`www.lintraining.com`	Database of sources of Linux training.

Sources of Linux Software

Most of these are places to find the more stable, well-tested Linux software; Sourceforge and Stormix are where you find the really new stuff. Just about all of it's free, too.

www.freshmeat.net	Looking for an open source answer to some problem? Look here.
www.sourceforge.net	Similar idea, a central distribution point for open source software.
www.linuxapps.com	The LinuxApp download site.
www.linuxberg.com	The TUCOWS Linux download affiliate.
www.linuxmall.com	Sales site.
www.cheapbytes.com	Sales site.
www.download.com.	Software download site.

Newsgroups

Sometimes you can find help at the newsgroups `linux.*` and `comp.os.linux.*`; I can't say that I've had any luck.

Organizations Offering For-Pay Support

In the long run, companies won't be able to make any money giving away software. But *support...* well, that's a demand that won't go away any time soon.

Red Hat	www.redhat.com
Linuxcare	www.linuxcare.com

Index

Note to the Reader: Throughout this index **boldfaced** page numbers indicate primary discussions of a topic. *Italicized* page numbers indicate illustrations.

A

-a option
   in gpasswd, 193, 198
   in ls, 94
   in rpm, 160
-A option
   in gpasswd, 198
   in ipchains, 395
   in ps, 153
   in top, 155
   in wbinfo, 463
a option in fdisk, 113
A (address) records, 310
ACCEPT option, 408
access file, 358
access_log file, 338–339
access time, sorting files by, 94
AccessConfig directive, 339
accounts. *See* groups; user accounts
acl command, 301
Active Directory, 487
Active Server Pages (ASPs), 13–14
Adapter tab, 46, 46
address (A) records, 310
admin users command, 455
administration, difficulty in, **486**
administrators in Samba, **455**
ADSL Network Termination (ANT), 391
afio command, 139
AFS (Andrew Filesystem), 12
Afterstep window manager, 264
aliases file, 355–356
aliases for Sendmail servers, **355–356**
all keyword, 128
Allison, Jeremy, 426
Allman, Eric, 352
allow directive, 342–343
allow file, 404–406

AllowOverride directive, 342
alnum character class, 111
alpha character class, 110–111
Alpha processors, 18–19
ampersands (&) for background programs, 239–240
Andrew Filesystem (AFS), 12
anonymous FTP access, **371–374**
AnotherLevel window manager, 264
ANT (ADSL Network Termination), 391
any keyword, 322
Apache servers, 13–14, **335**, **490–491**
   configuring, **336–344**, 347
   content for, **346–347**
   daemons in, 179
   disabling modules in, **403–404**
   installing, **335**
   publishing with, **343–344**
   starting, **336**, 347
   stopping, **336**
   testing, **347–348**
   virtual hosts in, **344–346**
apmd daemon, **188**
appliance computers, 18
applications
   compiling, **163–166**
   documentation for, **162–163**
   DOS, **424**
   for graphics and GUIs, **284–286**
   installing, **156–160**
   problems with, **482–483**
   uncompressing, **162**
   for X Window System, **254–255**
applications menu in KDE, 272
Applixware application, 285
aquarium program, 255
architecture-dependent RPMs, 161
Arla AFS, 12
ASPs (Active Server Pages), 13–14

asterisks (*) in searches, 95–96, 109
at symbol (@) for variables, 310
AT&T
 and BSD, **28**
 and Unix, **24**
attempts option, 293–294
authentication
 in NT/2000 domains. *See* winbind
 in Red Hat installation, **54**
 in SMB, **441–447**
auto.master file, 86
auto.misc file, 86
autofs service, 86
automatic partitions, 52
automating
 backups, **141–142**
 Internet connections, **391**
 startup
  DHCP servers, 334–335
  DNS servers, **321**
  NIS clients, **223**
  NIS servers, **218–219**
  Samba, **461**
  winbind, **463**
automounters, 86
autoraise feature, 242

B

-b option
 in mv, 102
 in useradd, 196
-B option in dhcpd, 324–326
background programs, **239–240**
backslashes (\) for metacharacters, 110
backups
 automating, **141–142**
 incremental and differential, **141**
 limitations of, **144–145**
 restoring, **140**
 to tape, **138–144**
 verifying, **140**
 viewing, **140**
 to Zip drives, **142–144**

batch files. *See* script files
-bd option, 248
Berkeley Internet Name Domain (BIND)
 program, 15
Berkeley Software Distribution (BSD), **27–28**
bg command, 240
-bg option, 248
/bin directory, 89
binary files, 156
 directories for, 89
 in smbclient, 436
BIND DNS server, 179
BIND (Berkeley Internet Name Domain)
 program, 15
-bitmap option, 248
bitmaps for backgrounds, 248
blank character class, 112
blanks in filenames, **93–94**
bonobo toolkit, 265
boot.b file, 418
/boot directory, 89
 boot.b file in, 418
 kernels in, 167–168
boot options, kernel as, **173–175**
boot partitions, **50–52**, 115
bootable DOS images, 424
bootable floppy disks, **47**, **55**, **118**, **121**
booting, dual boots, **58**, **415**
 default images for, **417**
 lilo.conf for, **415–417**
 LILO loader for, **480**
 messages for, **418**
 timeouts for, **417–418**
bootloaders in Red Hat installation, 53
braces ({})
 in regular expressions, 109
 in statements, 301
brackets ([]) in searches, 96, 98, **107–111**
browsing workgroups, **433–434**
BRU program, 138
BSD (Berkeley Software Distribution), **27–28**
bug fixes in open source code, **29–30**
bunzip2 command, 136
burning CD-R discs, **118–119**

business model, **5**
Business Software Alliance, 477
.bz files, **136–137**
bzImage file, 172
bzip2 command, **136–137**

C

-c option
   in grep, 105
   in tar, 138–139
   in useradd, 193, 195
cable modems, **391–392**
caching servers, 296, **304**
CAD applications, 285, 483
cal command, **188**
calculator, 237–238, 237
Caldera Linux, **36**
   printing in, 129
   site for, 493
calendars, **188**
canonical name (CNAME) records, 310
carets (^) in regular expressions, 107–111
carriage returns, 415
case sensitivity
   of commands, 91
   of filenames, 97, 340
   of passwords, 56
   in searches, 98
cat command, **102–103**
cd command
   in Linux, **92**
   in smbclient, 435
CD-R discs, burning, **118–119**
CD-ROMs, mounting, **85–86**
CDE (Common Desktop Environment), 266
cdrecord command, 118–119
cfdisk program, 113
CGI scripts, disabling, **404**
changing
   directories, **92**
   permissions for, **206–207**
character classes, 110–111
characters, counting, **188**
chat program, 254, **388–390**

check-names option, 302–303
chess game, 254
chgrp command, 209
chmod command, 145, **210–213**
chown command, 208
circumflexes (^) in regular expressions, 107–111
classes of characters with grep, **110–112**
clean command, 165–166
clear text passwords, 194, 485–486
click-to-type focus policy, 242
clients
   in DHCP, **324–326**
   in NFS, **228–230**
   in NIS, 214–215
      activating, **220–222**
      programs for, **219–220**
      setting up, **225**
      starting, **220, 223**
   in SMB, **427–428**
      smbclient, **432–436**
      smbfs, **428–432**
   in X Window System, **255–260, 281–282**
clock chips, 73
clustering concepts, 33
CNAME (canonical name) records, 310
cntrl character class, 112
coas program, 129
Coda file server, 12
code forks, 32
color in X Window System, **247–248**
COM1 ports, 383–384
COM3 ports, 383
command-line sessions, 236
command prompts, 56
commands, help for, **132–134**
commas (,) in regular expressions, 109
comments
   in Apache files, 337
   in user accounts, 193
   in zone files, 309
commercial distributions, **34–35**
   Caldera, **36**
   Debian, **36–37**
   Red Hat, **35–36**

selecting, 38
Slackware, 37
sources of, **493–494**
SuSE, 37
UnitedLinux, 37–38
Common Desktop Environment (CDE), 266
Common Object Requests Broker Architecture
    (CORBA) model, 265
compat option, 221
compatibility
    of file formats, 20
    with Microsoft. *See* Microsoft OS
        interoperability
compiling
    applications, **163–166**
    kernel, **171–172**
    modules, **172–173**
compressed files, **136–138**
concatenating files, 103
conf directory, 336
conf.modules file, 378
config command, 170
configuration files
    backing up, **144–145**
    directories for, 89
    for DNS, **299–308**
configure command, 163–164
configuring
    Apache servers, **336–344**, **347**
    DHCP servers, **327–330**
    FTP servers, **367–371**
    IP masquerading, **393–397**
    mgetty, **398–401**
    name servers, **296**
    networks. *See* network interface cards (NICs)
    PPP clients, **401**
    printers, **128–132**
    resolvers, **293–295**
    Sendmail servers, **352–357**
    SMB servers. *See* SMB (Server Message Block)
    video. *See* video adapters
connecting to file shares, **434–436**
connections, Internet, **381**
    cable modems and DSL for, **391–392**

dial-in servers for, **397–401**
dialing out to ISPs, **385–391**
IP masquerading in, **392–397**
modems for, **381–385**
console sessions, 236
converting text files, **414–415**
cops command, 401
copying
    files, **100–101**, 435
    kernels, 173
copyleft, 25
CORBA (Common Object Requests Broker
    Architecture) model, 265
costs, **25–26**
counting
    grep lines, 105
    words and characters, **188**
Cox, Alan, 176
cp command
    in Linux, **100–101**
    in smbclient, 435
cpio command, 139
crack command, 401
creating, permissions for, **206–207**
cron command, 141
crontab file, 141
crossover cables, 392
crtscts command, 399
curly braces ({})
    in regular expressions, 109
    in statements, 301
current directory
    for script files, **146–147**
    shorthand for, 92
cursor keys with Telnet, **151–152**
CustomLog directive, 338–339

D

-d option
    in dhcpd, 324–326
    in gpasswd, 193, 198
    in ls, 93
    in tar, 140
    in useradd, 193, 195–196

-D option
    in dhcpd, 324–326
    in useradd, 195–196
d option in fdisk, 113
daemons, 176, 179
dashes (-) in searches, 96
database servers, **17–18**
date command, 187
dates
    integers for, 201
    setting, **186–187**
dd command, 120
DDNS (Dynamic DNS), **321–323**
Debian distribution, **36–37**, 493
debug option, 293
default-lease-time option, 328
defaults
    dual boot images, **417**
    startup mode runlevel, 178
    user accounts, **195–196**
        settings, **195–196**
        shells, **191**
deleting
    directory trees, 103
    files, **103–104**
    groups, **198**
    Linux, **74–77**
    partitions, 52
    permissions for, 204, **206–207**
    user accounts, **196**
    users from groups, 198
deny directive, 342–343
deny file, 404–405
DENY option, 408
dependencies, 171–172
descriptions for user accounts, 191, 193
desktop, Linux on, **19–21**
/Desktop directory, 273–274
desktop environments, 234
    GNOME, 264, **267–269**
        basics of, **277–279**, *277–278*
        vs. KDE, **269–271**
    KDE. *See* KDE desktop environment
    window managers for, **264–265**

destroying partitions, **112–115**
-detach option, 399
/dev directory, 82–84, 89
development kernels, 176
development systems, **16–17**
Device Manager, **45–46**, *46*
devices
    directories for, 89
    names for, **82–84**
df command, **92**
DHCP. *See* Dynamic Host Configuration Protocol
    (DHCP)
dhcpcd command, 60, **324–326**
dhcpcd-eth0 file, 325
dhcpd.conf file, 322, 327, 330–331
dhcpd daemon, 322
dhcpd.leases file, 322, **329–330**, 334
dial-in servers, **397**
    installing, **398**
    mgetty for, **398–401**
diald program, **391**
dialing out to ISPs, **385–391**
dictionary hacks, 190, 402
differential backups, **141**
digit character class, 110–111
digital subscriber line (DSL) connections, **391–392**
directories
    changing, **92**
    in copying files, 100–101
    creating, 82, 85, **99**
    listing, 56–57, *56*, 211
    permissions for. *See* permissions
    for script files, **146–147**
    standard, **88–91**
    viewing, **91–96**
DirectoryIndex directive, 339, 343–344
Disable days field, 201
disabling
    CGI scripts, **404**
    FTP anonymous access, **373–374**
    modules, **403–404**
    network interface cards, 68
    services, **402–403**
    user accounts, **196–197**

Disk Druid tool, 48
disk quotas, 471
disk structure, 80–81
    CD-ROMs, 85–86
    FAT/FAT32 drives, 86–87, 88
    floppies, 81–85
    hard disks, 81, 81
    navigating, 92
    NTFS drives, 88
    standard directories in, 88–91
-DISPLAY option in export, 260, 263
-display option in X Window, 249
DISPLAY variable, 148
displaying files, 102–103
distributions. See commercial distributions
dmesg command, 187
DNS. See Domain Name Service (DNS)
dns option, 221
doc file, 134
documentation
    for applications, 162–163
    HOWTOs for, 135–136
    info for, 134
    man for, 132–134
    for monitors, 45
    for Red Hat installation, 40
DocumentRoot option, 339
dollar signs ($)
    for parameters, 148
    in regular expressions, 108
domain command, 293
domain model, limitations of, 485–486
Domain Name Service (DNS), 291–292
    configuration files for, 299–308
    dynamic, 321–323
    name server configurations in, 296
    resolvers in, 292–296
    reverse zone files in, 314–315
    search lists in, 295–296
    servers for, 14–15, 489–490
        installing, 297–298, 316–320
        for NICs, 66
        starting and stopping, 299, 320–321
    testing, 298–299
    zone files in, 308–313

domain option, 447
domains
    authentication with. See winbind
    joining, 462
    for NIS, 214, 217
    for Samba, 447
    for Sendmail servers, 353–354
DOS applications, 424
dos2unix tool, 415
dosemu tool, 424
dosutils directory, 47, 121
downloading kernel, 175–176
drive letters, 81
drivers
    lack of, 486–487
    for printers, 123–124
    with Xconfigurator, 72
DSL (digital subscriber line) connections,
        391–392
du command, 92
dual boots, 58, 415
    default images for, 417
    lilo.conf for, 415–417
    LILO loader for, 480
    messages for, 418
    timeouts for, 417–418
dump command, 139
Dynamic DNS (DDNS), 321–323
Dynamic Host Configuration Protocol (DHCP),
        322–323
    clients in, 324–326
    servers for
        configuring, 327–330
        installing, 326–327, 333
        reservations from, 330–331
        starting and stopping, 332
        summary, 332–334
dynamic zones, 322

E

-e option
    in rpm, 160
    in useradd, 194–195
-E option in grep, 107–111

echo command, **147–148**
edit mode in vi, 63–64
editing
    nsswitch.conf, **462–463**
    smb.conf, **439**
    with vi, **62–64**
    XF86Config-4, 71
educational institutions, 32
educational systems, **16–17**
egrep command, **107**
-eject option, 118
emacs application, 254
emulators, 418
encryption
    in NIS, 214–215
    for passwords, 190
    in ssh, **152–153**
Enlightenment window manager, 264
environment variables, **147–148**
erase command, 141
erasing
    files, **103–104**
    tapes, 141
ErrorLog directive, 338
escaping metacharacters, **110**
ESSID line in wireless.opts, 69
/etc/aliases file, 355–356
/etc/auto.master file, 86
/etc/auto.misc file, 86
/etc/conf.modules file, 378
/etc/dhcpd.conf file, 322, 327, **333–334**
/etc directory, 89, 144
/etc/exports file, **226–228**, 406–407
/etc/ftpaccess file, 368–371
/etc/ftphosts file, 368
/etc/ftpusers file, 367
/etc/group file, **193, 202**
/etc/gshadow file, **202**
/etc/hosts file, 65, 449
/etc/hosts.allow file, 404–406
/etc/hosts.deny file, 404–405
/etc/httpd directory, 336
/etc/inittab file, 177, **398–399**
/etc/issue file, **407**

/etc/lilo.conf file, 174
/etc/lmhosts file, 449
/etc/mail/access file, 358
/etc/mail/sendmail.mc file, 352–353
/etc/mail/virtusertable directory, 356–357
/etc/mgetty+sendfax directory, 398
/etc/named.conf file, 320
/etc/nsswitch.conf file, 221–222
/etc/pam.d directory, 401, 465
/etc/passwd file, 190, **200**, 221
/etc/ppp/pap-secrets file, **400**
/etc/printcap file, 129
/etc/rc.d directory, 332
/etc/rc.d/init.d directory, 290–291
/etc/rc.d/rc.firewall file, 395
/etc/rc.d/rc.local file, **185**
/etc/resolv.conf file, 66, 292–296, 325
/etc/securetty file, 150
/etc/sendmail.cf file, 352, 354–355
/etc/shadow file, **201–202**
/etc/sysconfig/network file, 66
/etc/sysconfig/network-scripts directory, 389
/etc/wvdial.conf file, 386–388
/etc/xinetd.d/wu-ftpd file, 365
/etc/yp.conf file, 218, 220
eth0 interface, 60
Ettrich, Matthias, 266
Exceed server, 261
exclamation points (!) in SMB, 435
excluding lists in grep command, **109–110**
EXE files, 156
ExecCGI option, 343
execute permissions, **204–205**, 210–212
expiration times
    for DHCP leases, **327–328**
    for zones, 312
Expire date field, 201
expiring user accounts, **194**
export command, **147–148**, 260, 263
exportfs command, 228
exports file, **226–228**, 406–407
EXT3 format, 42
external modems, 381, **383–384**

F

-f option
  in cp, 101
  in mv, 102
  in rpm, 160
  in tar, 137–142
FAT/FAT32 drives, 42, **86–87**, *88*, 116
fdformat command, 117
fdisk tool, 48, **112–115**
features
  for kernel, **170–171**
  in open source code, **29**
fg command, 240
-fg option, 248
FHS (File Hierarchy System), 89
file command, **188**
file extensions, sorting files by, 94
file format compatibility, 20
File Hierarchy System (FHS), 89
file servers, **11–12**, **490–491**
file shares, **434–436**
files
  compressed, **136–138**
  concatenating, 103
  copying, **100–101**, 435
  deleting, **103–104**
  displaying, **102–103**
  editing, **62–64**
  finding, **95–99**
  listing, *56–57*, *56*, **91–96**
  moving, **101–102**
  permissions for. *See* permissions
  renaming, **101–102**
  sharing. *See* Network File System (NFS)
  type of, **188**
  users of, **188**
files option, 221
filters
  grep for, 106
  in printing, 124, 131
find command, **97–98**, 291
finding
  files, **95–99**
  with grep. *See* grep command
finger command, 197

fips utility, **43**
firewall file, 395
firewalls, **16**, **53**, **407–411**, **490**
fixed-focus focus policy, 242
fixed-space fonts, 251
floppy disks
  bootable, **47**, **55**, 118, **121**
  formatting, **117–118**
  mounting, **81–85**
-fn option, **249–250**
Focus command, 242
focus follows mouse focus policy, 242
focus policies, 239, **241–242**
FollowSymLinks option, 343
fonts, **250–252**
forking, 32
formatting
  floppy disks, **117–118**
  partitions, **116–117**
forward chains, 408
forward slashes (/), 81
forwarding, **408–410**
FQDNs (fully qualified domain names), 295
free command, **155–156**
free disk space, **92**
free software, **254–255**, **476–477**
frequencies, video, 44, 73
Friendly Virtual Window Manager (fvwm),
      245–247, *246*
FTP servers, **364**
  anonymous access to, **371–374**
  configuring, **367–371**
  installing, **365–366**
  starting and stopping, **366**
  summary, **374**
ftpaccess file, **368–371**
ftphosts file, 368
ftpusers file, 367
fully qualified domain names (FQDNs), 295
fuser command, **188**
fvwm window manager, **245–247**, *246*

G

-g option
  in groupmod, 198

in useradd, 192–193
in wbinfo, 464
in X Window system, 249–250
-G option
in groupmod, 198
in usermod, 192
games, 254, 483
Games menu, 272
GDI printer, 123
gedit program, 279
-geometry option, **249–250**
get command, 435
getent command, 464
GhostScript program, 124
gids (group ids), 460
Gimp program, 261–263
GNOME (GNU Network Object Model
  Environment), 264, **267–269**
  basics of, **277–279**, *277–278*
  vs. KDE, **269–271**
GNOME panel, 276, 278
gnome-session command, 276–277
gnome-terminal program, 279
GNU (GNU's Not Unix), **26–27**
GNU Network Object Model Environment
  (GNOME), 264, **267–269**
  basics of, **277–279**, *277–278*
  vs. KDE, **269–271**
GNU Public License (GPL), **26–27**
gnumeric program, 279
gpasswd command, **193**, 198
GPL (GNU Public License), **26–27**
graph character class, 111
graphics and GUIs, **233–235**. *See also* window
  managers; X Window System
  applications for, **284–286**
  limitations of, **484–485**
  in Red Hat installation, 55
  in remote sessions, **152**
  startx for, **279–280**, **282–283**
  unfreezing, **283–284**
  xinit for, **280–282**
Graphics menu in KDE, 272

grep command, **104–106**
  for classes of characters, **110–112**
  excluding lists in, **109–110**
  for filters, **106**
  metacharacters with, **107–108**, **110**
  with regular expressions, **106–112**
  repeating patterns in, **108–109**
Group directive, 338
group file, **193**, **202**
group ids (gids), 460
groupadd command, 197
groupdel command, 198
groupmod command, 197–198
groups
  adding users to, **192**
  creating, **197**
  deleting, **198**
  in directory listings, 57
  joining, **198–199**
  managing, **198–199**
  memberships in, **191–193**, **198**
  permissions for, **208–209**
  in Samba, **455**
  in smb.conf, 460
growth of Linux, **33–34**
GRUB bootloader, 53, **480**
gs program, 124
gshadow file, **202**
guest access in FTP, 369–370
guest option in smbfs, 430
GUIs. *See* graphics and GUIs; window managers;
  X Window System
gunzip program, 136–137
.gz files, **136–137**

H

-h option
  for command help, 132
  in top, 155
  in useradd, 196
-H option in dhcpd, 324–325
hard disks, structure of, **81**, *81*
hard mounts, 230

hardware
    in Red Hat installation, **40–41**
    requirements for, **6–7**
    support for, **486–487**
hardware compatibility list (HCL), 482
--hctosys option, 187
hdparam command, 116
header pages, 131
height of windows, 250
help
    HOWTOs, **135–136**
    info, **134**
    man, **132–134**
    for script files, **149**
    setup, lack of, **483–484**
--help option, **132–133**
hidden files
    for configurations, 144
    listing, **94**
high-level formatting, **117**
hints file, 300, **305**
home directories
    in FTP, 372
    setting, 196
    in smb.conf, 460
    for user accounts, 191, 193
    for winbind, **464**
/home directory, 89, 191
horizontal video frequencies, 44, 73
host command, 330–331
host header records, 344
host names for NICs, **65–66**
hostname command, 66
HOSTS entry for NICs, **65**
hosts file, 66, 449
hosts in Apache servers, **344–346**
HOWTOs, **135–136**
httpd file, 179, 336
httpd.conf file, **336–343**
hwclock command, 186–187
Hyperterminal program, 152
hyphens (-) in searches, 96

I

-i option
    in hdparm, 116
    in locate, 98
    in mv, 102
    in rpm, 158–159, 161–162
-I option in smbclient, 436
ICE Window Manager, 264
-iconic option, 249
ICS (Internet Connection Sharing), 16, 289
ifcfg-eth0 file, 61, 68
ifconfig command, 59–61, *59*, 66–67
ifup command, 390
ifup-ppp script, 389–390
images
    for dual boots, **417**
    kernel, 172
    in lilo.conf, 416
IMAP4 (Internet Messaging Application
    Protocol), 349
imm module, 143
-iname option, 96
include command, 301
incremental backups, **141**
inet6 option, 294
inetd daemon, 402
info routine, **134**
init.d directory, 290–291
init script, **177–179**
initial groups, 191
initrd image, **173**
inittab file, 177, 398–399
input chains, 408
input filters in printing, 131
insert mode in vi, 62–63
insmod command, 168
installing
    Apache servers, **335**
    applications, **156–160**
    DHCP servers, **326–327**, 333
    dial-in servers, **398**
    DNS servers, **297–298**, **316–320**

FTP servers, 365–366

Linux. *See* Red Hat Linux

modems, **381–385**

multiple NICs, **376–378**

POP3, **350–351**

Sendmail servers, **350**

interactive mode in lpc, 128

Intermezzo network system, 12

internal modems, 381–382, **384**

international language support, 268

Internet Connection Sharing (ICS), 16, 289

Internet connections, **381**

cable modems and DSL for, **391–392**

dial-in servers for, **397–401**

dialing out to ISPs, **385–391**

IP masquerading in, **392–397**

modems for, **381–385**

Internet menu in KDE, 273

Internet Messaging Application Protocol
(IMAP4), 349

interoperability, Microsoft OS. *See* Microsoft OS
interoperability

interrupts file, 375–376

invalid users command, 455

invalid users in Samba, **452–455**

ioports file, 375

IP addresses, 392–393

for dial-in servers, **400**

for NICs, 60–61, **379–380**

with smbfs, **431–432**

IP masquerading, 16, 381, **392–397**

ip option, 430

IP routing, **16**

ipchains program, 16, 290, 394–395, **407–411**

ipconfig command, 322

iptables program, 16

IRQs for external modems, 383

ISA modems, **385**

isapnp program, 385

ISO files, 118, **120–121**

ISPs, dialing out to, **385–391**

issue file, **407**

iwconfig command, 69

J

joining

domains, **462**

files, 103

groups, **198–199**

K

-k option

in dhcpd, **324–326**

in man, 134

in top, 155

KDE desktop environment, 264, **266–267**, 272

vs. GNOME, **269–271**

in-the-box programs, **272–273**

navigation in, **271–272**

as remote desktop, **275–276**

session-to-session memory in, **273–274**

tricks in, **274–275**

.kdelnk file, 274

KEA! X server, 261

kedit program, 279

Kerberos system, 235

kernel

as boot option, **173–175**

compiling, **171–172**

downloading, **175–176**

features for, **170–171**

initrd image for, **173**

linking, **171–172**

modules for, **168–169**

recompiling, **166–176**

source code for, **169**

storage of, **167–168**

upgrades to, **30–31**

key command, 301

KEY line in wireless.opts, 69

keyboard in Red Hat installation, **48**

keyword searches, 134

kill command, 153–154

killall command, 402

killing processes, 153–154, 181

KOffice tools, 273

Kppp program, 386
ksysv program, 182

L

-l option
  in ls, 93
  in rpm, 159
  in ssh, 153
-L option
  in smbclient, 433–434
  in usermod, 196
l option in fdisk, 113
languages in Red Hat installation, **48**
Last Change field, 201
LaStrange, Tom, 238
lcd command, 435
leases in DHCP
  dhcpd.leases file, 329–330
  expiration times for, **327–328**
  file for, 322
  obtaining, **324–325**
  releasing, **324**
  renewing, **325**
less command, **96–97**, 103
/lib directory, 89
/lib/modules directory, 168
libraries
  directories for, 89
  purpose of, 157
licenses, **2–3**, **25–26**, **477–478**
Licensing 6.0, **475**
lilo command, 173–174
lilo.conf file, 174, **415–417**
LILO loader, **480**
  for dual boots, **415–418**
  in Red Hat installation, 53
line counts in grep, 105
line feeds, 415
line numbers with cat, 103
linking
  kernel, **171–172**
  modules, **172–173**
  programs, 163

links, symbolic
  creating, **104**
  for kernel, 168
linux directory, 169
Linux native partitions, 50
LinuxCAD, 285
Linuxcare, support from, 495
linuxconf program, 129, 199
listing
  files and directories, 56–57, 56, **91–96**
  permissions, **209–210**
  permissions for, **205–206**
lmhosts file, **432**, 449
ln command, **104**
lo section, 60
load modules, 156
local file, **185**
local host files, 300, **305–306**
localhost file, 305
localnets keyword, 322
locate command, **98**
locked programs, **153–155**
log files
  for DNS, 301
  for printers, 131
logging command, 301
logging in, first time, 55–57
login file, 465
login.config file, **400–401**
long file listings, 93
loopback domains, 305
lost clusters, 89
/lost+found directory, 89
low-level formatting, **117**
lower character class, 111–112
lpc command, 124, 127–128
lpd command, 12, 121–122, 125, 129
lpq command, 126
lpr command, 12–13, 121–122, 124–126
lprm command, 124, 126–127
ls command, 56–57, 56, **91–96**
lsmod command, 168

M

-m option
    in free, 156
    in useradd, 195
-M option
    in gpasswd, 193
    in smbclient, 433–434
    in tar, 139
    in top, 155
    in useradd, 195
m option in fdisk, 113
Macintosh computers, 8–9
mail command, 354
mail exchanger (MX) records, 310, 312–313, **351**
mail servers, **15**, **489**
    defining, **312–313**
    Sendmail. See Sendmail servers
mail transfer agent (MTA), 349
make command, 163–165
make bzImage command, 172
make clean command, 165–166
make config command, 170
make dep command, 171–172
make install command, 164–165
make menuconfig command, 170
make modules command, 172
make mrproper command, 166, 169
make xconfig command, 170
Makefile file, 216
makewhatis command, 134
man online help system, **132–134**
Mandrake distribution
    kernel in, 168
    NICs in, 66
    printing in, 129
    site for, 493
MAPI (Messaging Application Program
        Interface), 349
maps, NIS, 214, 217
mars_nwe project, 12
MASQ option, 408
master servers
    in DNS, 296, 302
    in NIS, 214

max-lease-time option, 328
MaxClients directive, 338
May Change field, 201
mbrwipe.com program, **75–77**
mcopy program, 85, 415
mdel program, 85
mdeltree program, 85
mdir program, 85
meminfo file, 155
memory
    in KDE, **273–274**
    for swap partitions, 49–50
    system use of, **155–156**
    for video, 44, 73
menuconfig command, 170
menus for twm, **242–245**
MERGE_GROUP option, 216
MERGE_PASSWD option, 216
messages
    for dual boots, **418**
    with smbclient, **433**
Messaging Application Program Interface
        (MAPI), 349
metacharacters, **107–108**, **110**
metaphors, desktop, 265
mformat program, 85, 117
mgetty program, **398–401**
mgetty+sendfax directory, 398
MI/X program, 260–261
mice in Red Hat installation, **48**
Microsoft OS interoperability, **413–414**
    DOS applications, **424**
    dual boots, **415–418**
    networking. See Samba program
    NT/2000 domain authentication. See winbind
    printer servers, **424–425**
    text files, **414–415**
    VMware for, **423–424**
    WINE for, **418–423**
Microsoft TCP/IP Printing tool, 425
minicom program, 384
Minix operating system, **24–25**
MINUID option, 216
minus signs (-) in searches, 96
/misc directory, 90

mkbootdisk program, 118
mkdir command, 82, 85, **99**
mkfs.msdos command, 116
mkinitrd command, 173
mkisofs command, 118
-mmin option, 98
mmove program, 85
/mnt directory, 83, 90
MODE line in wireless.opts, 69
modems
   cable, **391–392**
   installing, **381–385**
modified files in searches, 98
modprobe command, 119, 142, 169
modules
   compiling and linking, **172–173**
   disabling, **403–404**
   for kernel, **168–169**
modules command, 172
modules directory, 169
monitors
   documentation for, 45
   in installation, **45**
   Xconfigurator for, **72–73**
monopolies, 474–475
monospaced fonts, 251
more command, 97
Motif Window Manager (mwm), 264
mount command, 81–82, 85, 87–88, 228–230
mountd daemon, 227–228
mounting
   CD-ROMs, **85–86**
   floppy drives, **81–85**
   in NFS, 229–230
   with smbfs, **428–432**
mouse in Red Hat installation, **48**
moving files, **101–102**
mren program, 85
mrproper command, 166, 169
msdos type, 82
mt command, 141
MTA (mail transfer agent), 349
-mtime option, 98
mtools programs, 85

mtype program, 85
multi-user systems, runlevel for, 178
multi-vendor nature of Linux, **474–476**
Multimedia menu in KDE, 273
multiple domains for Sendmail servers, **356–357**
multiple NICs, **375–376**
   installing, **376–378**
   IP information for, **379–380**
   routing with, **380–381**
multiple tapes in tar, 139
multiple virtual servers, 471
multiple X Window System sessions, **263**
multiprocessor systems, 33–34
multitasking, **237–238**
Murdock, Deb and Ian, 37
mv command, **101–102**
mwm (Motif Window Manager), 264
MX (mail exchanger) records, 310, 312–313, **351**
MySAP product, 285
MySQL database, 17

N

-n option
   in cat, 103
   in groupmod, 197
   in top, 155
n option in fdisk, 113
-N option in top, 155
-name option, 98
name resolution
   in Samba, 449
   with smbfs, **431–432**
   with winbind, **461–462**
name resolve command, 449
name servers, configuring, **296**
named.conf file, **301**, 306
   creating, 320
   options statement in, **301–302**
   sample, **303–304, 307–308**
   zone statement in, **302–303**
named daemon, 179, 291–292, 300
named.local domain, 305
names for devices, **82–84**

nameserver command, 293

nameserver (NS) records, 310

NameVirtualHost directive, 344–345

NASA version, 32–33

NAT (Network Address Translation), 289–290, 392

native partitions, 50

navigating

  disk structure, **92**

  KDE, **271–272**

nbtstat program, 437–438

Nero Burning ROM, 120

net send command, 433

netatalk, 12

netbios name command, 439

netbios-name-servers option, 329

netconfig command, **61–62**

netstat program, 315, 380

Network Address Translation (NAT), 289–290, 392

network file, 66

Network File System (NFS), 12

  clients in, **228–230**

  example, **230–231**

  servers in

    /etc/exports file for, **228**

    security for, **406–407**

    shares for, **225–227**

    starting, **227–228**

Network Information Service (NIS), **213–215**

  clients in

    activating, **220–222**

    programs for, **219–220**

    setting up, **225**

    starting, **220, 223**

  example, **230–231**

  servers in, **215**

    automatic starting of, **218–219**

    domains for, **217**

    files for, **216–217**

    passwords in, **224**

    portmap service in, **215–216**

    setting up, **224–225**

    updating, **223–224**

    ypbind tool for, **217–218**

  for user accounts, 194

network interface cards (NICs), 58

  activating, **60–61**

  disabling, **68**

  DNS servers for, 66

  host names for, **65–66**

  HOSTS entry for, **65**

  multiple, **375–381**

  in Red Hat installation, 41

  routing information for, **64–65, 380–381**

  static IP addresses for, **60–61**

  testing, **59–60,** *59*

  wireless, **66–69**

network-scripts folder, 61, 68

networks

  configuring for IP masquerading, **393–397**

  Microsoft. *See* Samba program

  in Red Hat installation, 53

newaliases command, 356

newgrp command, **198–199**

newsgroups, 495

NFS. *See* Network File System (NFS)

nfsd daemon, 228

NICs. *See* network interface cards (NICs)

NIS. *See* Network Information Service (NIS)

NIS+, 215

nis option, 221

nisplus option, 221

nmbd command, 179, 439

nmblookup tool, 449, 461–462

no-check-names option, 294

non-intel hardware, **15–17**

non-routable addresses, 289

nroff language, 124

NS (nameserver) records, 310

nslookup command, 322

nsswitch.conf file, 221–222, **462–463**

NT/2000 domains, authentication with. *See* winbind

NT/2000/XP interoperability, **3–4**

NT Diagnostics program, 45

ntds.dit file, 199

NTFS drives, 88

number signs (#)

  for comments, 337

  for prompts, 56

O

.o extension, 165, 170

-o option
in free, 156
in mkisofs, 118

object models, 265

octothorps (#)
for comments, 337
for prompts, 56

office suites, 483

Omni-X server, 261

online documentation
HOWTOs for, **135–136**
info for, **134**
man for, **132–134**

open relays, 358

open source
benefits of, **29–30, 473–474**
costs of, **25–26**

OpenAFS AFS, 12

operating systems
creating, **5–6**
interoperability between. *See* Microsoft OS
interoperability
VMware, **284, 423–424**

/opt directory, 90

options command, 293–294

options statement, **301–302**

Orinoco Gold NICs, **66–69**

Outlook application, 349

output chains, 408

overwriting
in copying files, 100–101
in renaming files, 102
in tar, 139

owners, permissions for, **207–208**

P

-p option
in rpm, 158–162
in tar, 140

-P option
in ipchains, 395

in lpr, 125
in lprm, 126–127
in top, 155

p option in fdisk, 113–114

packages
installing, **156–160**
in Red Hat installation, **54**

pagers, 278

pam.d directory, 401

pam_deny module, 465

pam_env module, 465

pam_unix module, 465–466

PAMs (Pluggable Authentication Modules)
for passwords, 401–402
for winbind, **464–466**

panels in GNOME, 276, 278

parallel port version for Zip drives, 142–143

parameters in scripts, 148

Partition Magic program, **43–44**

partition tables, 114

partitions
creating, **112–115**
deleting, **74–77, 112–115**
formatting, **116–117**
in Red Hat installation, **41–44, 48–52**

passwd file, 190, **200, 221**

password option, 402, 430

passwords, 190
in /etc/gshadow, 202
in /etc/shadow, **201–202**
in NIS, 194, **214, 216, 218, 224, 485–486**
in Red Hat installation, **53–54**
in server security, **401–402**
in SMB servers, 441–447
for user accounts, 190–191, **195–196**

PATH variable, 148

paths
for scripts, 146–148
for shell programs, 193
in wine, 420

PathWorks tool, 426

pattern searches, **95–96, 108–109**

PC-Xware server, 261

PCI modems, **385**

PCMCIA modems, **385**
PCMCIA service, 67
periods (.)
    for current directory, 92, 146
    in filenames, 94
    in regular expressions, 108
permissions
    in backups, 140
    example, **205–207**
    execute, **204–205**
    for groups, **208–209**
    limitations of, **485**
    listing, **209–210**
    for owners, **207–208**
    read, **203**
    in Samba, **451–455**, 457
    setting, **210–213**
    in SMB servers, 440
    world, **209**
    write, **203–204**
Personal edition of Red Hat, 40
PgUp and PgDn keys with Telnet, 151–152
pids (process IDs), 153–154
ping command, 59
pipe symbols (|) in searches, 96–97
plain text passwords, 194, 485–486
plug-and-play modems, **385**
Pluggable Authentication Modules (PAMs)
    for passwords, 401–402
    for winbind, **464–466**
point size, 251
pointer (PTR) records, 310, 315
points, 251
POP (Post Office Protocol), **349–351**
pop-up messages, **433**
Port directive, 337
portmap daemon, **215–216**, 219
position of windows, **249–250**
POSIX interface, 25
Post Office Protocol (POP), **349–351**
PostScript language, 124
pound signs (#)
    for comments, 337
    for prompts, 56

PowerPC processors, 18–19
ppa module, 143
PPP clients, **401**
ppp-on script, 389
pppd, **399–400**
primary servers, 296
print character class, 111
print servers, **12–13**, **424–425**
printcap file, 129
printers
    configuring, **128–132**
    controlling, **122–123**
    drivers for, **124**
printing
    commands for, **124–126**
    queues for, **126–128**
    text, **121–122**
printtool tool, 129
private internets, 394
/proc directory, 90
/proc/interrupts file, 375–376
/proc/ioports file, 375
/proc/meminfo file, 155
process IDs (pids), 153–154
processes, killing, 153–154, 181
Professional edition of Red Hat, 40
programs, background, **239–240**
prompt command
    for dual boots, 418
    in smbclient, 436
proprietary protocol support, **487**
proxyarp command, 399
ps command, 153–155
PTR (pointer) records, 310, 315
public-key encryption in ssh, **152–153**
publishing with Apache servers, **343–344**
puns in Linux names, 14
put command, 435
PuTTY program, 153
pwd command, 92

Q

q option in fdisk, 114

-q option in rpm, 159–162
QPL license, 267
Qt programs, 267
queues, print, **126–128**
Quicklaunch bar, 278–279
quotas, disk, 471
quotes (' ")
    in grep, 107
    for search patterns, 97

R

-r option
    in cp, 100–101
    in exportfs, 228
    in grep, 112
    in ls, 94
-R option
    in dhcpd, 325
    in ls, 94
    in nmblookup, 461–462
    in rm, 103
r permission, 210
Raise command, 241
raising windows, **241–242**
ranges in searches, 96, 109
rawrite utility, 47, 121
rc.d file, 178
rc script, 178–179, 181
rd command, 436
rdate command, 187
read list command, **453–455**
read permission, **203**, 210–211
README files, 162–163
real access in FTP, 369–370
real time clock (RTC), 186–187
reboots
    need for, 478
    runlevel for, 178
recompiling kernel, **166–176**
recording scripts, 149
recursion
    in grep, 112
    in names, **14**

Red Hat Linux, **35–36**
    installation
        authentication configuration in, 54
        boot floppies for, **47**, 55
        without CD-ROMs, **119–121**
        GUI setup in, **55**
        hardware detection in, **40–41**
        improvements in, **39–40**
        installation type in, **48**
        language, keyboard, and mouse in, **48**
        LILO loader in, **53**
        networks and firewalls in, **53**
        NICs in, 41
        package selection in, **54**
        partitions in, 41–44, 48–52
        problem areas in, **41–42**, 480–482
        root passwords in, **53–54**
        video adapter detection in, **54**
        video strategies in, 44–46, *46*
        X Window configuration in, 42
    kernel storage in, 168
    lease location of, 329
    NTFS support in, 88
    printing in, 129
    rc in, 178–179
    runlevel scripts in, 181
    script location in, 291
    site for, 493
    support from, 495
Red Hat Package Manager (RPM), **156–160**
referers, 338
Reflection X server, 261
refresh cycles for zones, 312
/registerdns option, 322
registers, 76
regular expressions, 95–96, **105–112**
REJECT option, 408
relays with Sendmail servers, **357–359**
releasing DHCP leases, **324**
reliability, 20, 473–474
reload option for scripts, 180
remote control, **478**
remote desktop, KDE as, **275–276**
remote procedure calls (RPCs), 215

remote sessions, **261–263**

remote systems, **149–153**

renaming

    files, **101–102**

    groups, 197

    kernel, 173

renewing DHCP leases, **325**

repeating patterns in grep, **108–109**

research institutions, 32

reservations in DHCP, **330–331**

resizing partitions, **43–44**

resolution, video, 73–74

resolv.conf file, 66, 292–296, 325

resolver code, 291

resolvers in DNS, **292**

    configuring, **293–295**

    search lists for, **295–296**

ResourceConfig directive, 339

resources in X Window System, **249–254**

restart command, 128

restart option, 180

restore command

    for dump, 139

    for tar, 141

restoring backups, **140**

retension command, 141

retry cycle for zones, 312

reverse zone files, 300, **314–315**

rewind command, 141

Ritchie, Dennis, 24

rm command, **103–104**

rmdir command, 436

rmmod command, 169

ro option, 430

robustness, **478–479**

root directories, 81, 90

root partitions, 50

root passwords in Red Hat installation, **53–54**

root_squash option, 227

rotate option, 294

routable IP addresses, 289

route command, 65

route add command, 64–65, 379–380

routers, **490**

routing information for NICs, **64–65, 380–381**

rpc.mountd daemon, 227–228

rpc.nfsd daemon, 227–228

RPC portmapper daemon, 215

RPCs (remote procedure calls), 215

RPM (Red Hat Package Manager), **156–160**

rpmfind.net site, 158

RTC (real time clock), 186–187

runaway programs, **153–155**

runlevel scripts

    finding and running, **177–179**

    starting services with, **179–185**

-rv option, 248

rw option, 430

rwho command, 402

S

-s option

    in ln, 104

    in useradd, 193, 195

-S option

    in ls, 94

    in man, 133–134

saint command, 401

Salary Survey, 8

Samba program, 12, **425–427**

    administrators in, **455**

    automatic startup, **461**

    daemons in, 179

    for file servers, **490–491**

    groups in, **455**

    permissions in, **451–455**, 457

    shares in, **450–456**

    and SMB clients, **427–428**

        smbclient, **432–436**

        smbfs, **428–432**

    and SMB servers

        authentication options for, **441–447**

        basic, **436–439**

        example setup, **447–451**

        security options for, **440–447**

        testing, **451**

    with Windows 2000, **457–458**

saving vi files, 63

sawfish window manager, 264

/sbin directory, 90–91

-scanbus option, 118–119

Schliefler, Robert, 235

scope in DHCP, 327

screens, displaying output by, **96–97**

script files, **145**

    benefits of, **479–809**

    directories for, **146–147**

    disabling, **404**

    executable, **145–146**

    help for, **149**

    variables in, **147–148**

script tool, **149**

scroll bars in GNOME, 279

SCSI support

    for disks, 171

    for Zip drives, 142

search command, 293

search lists in DNS, **295–296**

search-pattern syntax, 95–96

searches

    for files, **95–99**

    with grep. *See* grep command

searching in vi, 64

secondary servers, 296, **306–307**

securetty file, 150

security

    Active Directory for, 487

    in NIS, 214

    server. *See* server security

    ssh for, **152–153**

security option, **441**

security = domain option, **444**

security = server option, **442–443**

security = share option, **441**

security = user option, **441–442**

semicolons (;)

    for comments, 309

    in statements, 302

sendmail.cf file, 352, 354–355

sendmail.mc file, 352–353

Sendmail servers, 15, 348

    aliases for, 355–356

configuring, 352–357

domains for, 353–354

installing, **350**

limitations of, 349–350

MX records for, **351**

operation of, 348–349

relays with, 357–359

starting and stopping, **351**

summary, 363–364

testing, 359–363

serial numbers in SOA records, 311

serial ports for modems, 383–384

server command, 301

server configuration files, **281**

Server Message Block. *See* SMB

    (Server Message Block)

server option, 447

server security, **401**

    disabling items for

        CGI scripts, **404**

        modules, 403–404

        services, 402–403

    /etc/issue in, **407**

    firewalls for, **407–411**

    NFS exports in, 406–407

    passwords for, 401–402

    SMB servers, 440–447

    TCP wrappers for, 404–406

server string command, 439

ServerName directive, 337

ServerRoot directive, 337

servers

    database, **17–18**

    DHCP

        configuring, 327–330

        installing, 326–327, 333

        reservations from, 330–331

        starting and stopping, **332**

        summary, 332–334

    DNS, 14–15, 489–490

        installing, 316–320

        for NICs, **66**

        starting and stopping, 320–321

    file, **11–12**, 490–491

    FTP, **364**

anonymous access to, 371–374
configuring, 367–371
installing, 365–366
starting and stopping, **366**
summary, **374**
Internet connections with. *See* Internet connections
mail, **15**, **489**
defining, 312–313
Sendmail. *See* Sendmail servers
NFS
/etc/exports file for, **228**
security for, 406–407
shares for, **225–227**
starting, **227–228**
NICs for, 375–381
NIS. *See* Network Information Service (NIS)
print, **12–13**, **424–425**
prototype networks for, **289**
requirements for, **288–290**
security for. *See* server security
services with, **290–291**
SMB
authentication options for, **441–447**
basic, **436–439**
example setup, **447–451**
security options for, **440–447**
testing, **451**
types of, **288–289**
Web. *See* Apache servers
in X Window System, 255–260, 281
services, **176–177**, **290–291**
disabling, 402–403
DNS. *See* Domain Name Service (DNS)
init, **177–179**
starting, **179–186**
stopping, **186**
sysinit, **177**
session-to-session memory in KDE, 273–274
setmode command, 436
Settings menu in KDE, 273
setup
without CD-ROMs, **119–121**
help for, **483–484**
shadow file, **201–202**
shadow password program, 190

shadow passwords, 190, 201–202, **214**
share option, 446
shares and sharing
in NFS. *See* Network File System (NFS)
in Samba, **450–456**
shells for user accounts, **191**
shortcuts, 104
showmount command, 228, 406–407
showrgb command, 247
shutdown command, **57–58**
shutting down, **57–58**
Simple Mail Transport Protocol (SMTP), 349
single-user maintenance mode, runlevel for, 178
size
of partitions, **43–44**
of windows, **249–250**
Slackware distribution, 37, 493
slashes (/) for root partition, 50
slave servers, 214, 296, 302, **306–307**
SMB (Server Message Block), **426–427**
clients, **427–428**
smbclient, **432–436**
smbfs, **428–432**
servers
authentication options for, **441–447**
basic, **436–439**
example setup, **447–451**
security options for, **440–447**
testing, **451**
smb.conf file, 437, 439
creating, **448**
editing, **439**
for winbind, **458–460**
smbclient program, **432–433**
browsing workgroups with, **433–434**
connecting to file shares with, **434–436**
pop-up messages with, **433**
smbd daemon, 179, 439
smbfs program, **428–432**
smbpasswd command, 462
SMTP (Simple Mail Transport Protocol), 349
SOA (start of authority) records, **310–312**
soft mounts, 230
software
free, **476–477**

licenses for, **2–3**, 25–26, **477–478**
sources of, **495**
Software Assurance program, **475**
Software & Information Industry Association, 477
-solid option, 247–248
sorting
    file listings, **94**
    processes, 155
sound, setting up, **74**
source code, 5, 19, **169**
sourceforge.net site, 495
space character class, 112
spam, 353, 358
-speed option in cdrecord, 118
spool directory, 131
spreadsheets, 279
square brackets ([]) in searches, 96, 98, 107–111
ssh program, **152–153**
sshd service, 153
stable kernels, 176
Stallman, Richard, 26–27
standard directories, **88–91**
standards, 474, 476
standby mode, **188**
StarOffice application, 285
start of authority (SOA) records, **310–312**
start option, 180
starting
    Apache servers, **336**, 347
    DHCP servers, **332**, **334**
    DNS servers, **299**, 320–321
    FTP servers, **366**
    NIS clients, **220**, **223**
    NIS servers, **217–219**
    processes, 182
    Samba, **461**
    Sendmail servers, **351**
    services, **179–186**
    winbind, **463–464**
startkde command, 276
StartServers directive, 338
startx command, 279–280, 282–283
static IP addresses, **60–61**
status option, 180

stop option, 180
stopping
    Apache servers, **336**, 347
    DHCP servers, **332**
    DNS servers, **299**
    FTP servers, **366**
    locked programs, **153–155**
    Sendmail servers, **351**
    services, **186**
storing resource information, **253–254**
su program, 151, **187**
supplementary groups, 191
support, sources of, **495**
SuSE distribution, 37
    printing in, 129
    site for, 493
suspend mode, **188**
swap partitions, **48–50**
symbolic links
    creating, **104**
    for kernel, 168
sysinit script, **177**
system-auth file, 465–466
system clock, 186–187
system halted runlevel, 178
system messages, **187**
system partitions, **50**
system.twmrc file, 243
System V approach to runlevel scripts, 181
--systohc option, 187

T

-t option
    in ls, 94
    in mount, 82, 87
    in tar, 140
t option in fdisk, 114
-T option in top, 155
tab window manager (twm), 238, *238*, **240–241**, *240*
    focus in, **241–242**
    menus for, **242–245**
    raising windows in, **241–242**
Tanenbaum, Andrew, 24

tapes
    backups to, **138–144**
    caring for, **141**
.tar files, **136–138**
tar program, **137–142**
Tara Term Pro, 152–153
TCP wrappers, **404–406**
tcpd file, 404
telnet, **149–152**, 262
template homedir command, **460**
template shell command, **460**
temporary files, directories for, 91
terminal sessions, 236
terminal windows, 237
testing
    Apache servers, **347–348**
    DNS, **298–299**
    NICs, **59–60**, *59*
    Sendmail servers, **359–363**
    SMB servers, **451**
    WINE, **422–423**
    X configuration, 70
TeX formatter, 124
text files
    OS interoperability with, **414–415**
    printing, **121–122**
Thompson, Ken, 24
three-button support, 48
tildes (~) in URLs, 340
time
    in searches, 98
    setting, **186–187**
    sorting files by, 94
time to live (TTL) in zone files, 310–312
time zone setting, 53
timeout command, 417–418
timeout option, 293
timeouts
    for dual boots, **417–418**
    for resolver, 293
title bars, 241
-title option, 249
tksysv program, 182
/tmp directory, 91
toasters, 18

top utility, **155**
Torvalds, Linus, 24, 26, 176
Tridgell, Andrew, 426
troff language, 124
TrueType fonts, **251–252**
TTL (time to live) in zone files, 310–312
TTSSH program, 153
TurboLinux, site for, 493
twm (tab window manager), 238, *238*, **240–241**, *240*
    focus in, **241–242**
    menus for, **242–245**
    raising windows in, **241–242**
type of files, **188**

U

-u option
    in cp, 101
    in ls, 94
    in top, 155
    in useradd, 195
    in wbinfo, 464
-U option
    in nmblookup, 461–462
    in smbclient, 433–434
u option in fdisk, 114
uids (user ids), **194–195**, 460
umount command, **84–85**
uncompressing applications, **162**
unexpected.tdb file, 461
unfreezing GUIs, **283–284**
uninstalling packages, 160
UnitedLinux distribution, 37–38
Unix operating system, **4–5**, 24
updating NIS server information, **223–224**
upper character class, 111–112
URLs, 340–341
used disk space, 92
user accounts, **189**. *See also* groups
    adding users to groups, **192**
    centralizing, **213**
    creating, **190–192**
    default settings for, **195–196**
    deleting, **196**
    disabling, **196–197**

expiring, **194**
location of, **199–202**
NIS for. *See* Network Information Service (NIS)
options for, **193**
passwords for, 190–191, **195–196**
for SMB servers, **450**
user ID numbers for, **194–195**
user agents, 338
user.dat file, 422
User directive, 338
user ids (uids), **194–195**, 460
user option, 446
useradd command, **190–193**
userdel command, 190, 196
UserDir directive, 340
usermod command, 190, **192**, 196–198
username option, 430
USERNAME variable, 147–148
usernames
    in /etc/shadow, 201
    in Samba, 430
    for user accounts, 191
users command, 198
users in Samba, **452–455**
/usr directory, 91
/usr/sbin/tcpd file, 404
/usr/share/doc file, 134
/usr/src/linux directory, 169
Utilities menu in KDE, 273

V

-v option
    in cat, 103
    in cdrecord, 118
    in mail, 354
    in mkbootdisk, 118
    in tar, 137–140
v option in fdisk, 114
-V option in rpm, 160
valid users command, 453, 455
valid users in Samba, **452–455**
/var directory, 91
/var/ftp directory, 372
/var/log/samba directory, 449

/var/named directory, **317–320**
/var/yp directory, 216–217
variables
    in script files, **147–148**
    in zone files, 310
VariCAD, 285
Varimetrix CAD, 285
VBScript language, 13–14
vendor support, 486–487
verifying backups, **140**
versions, kernel, **31–33**, 173, 176
vertical bars (|) in searches, 96–97
vertical video frequencies, 44, 73
vfat type, 82, 87
vi editor, **62–64**
video adapters
    in Red Hat installation, **44–46**, *46*, *54*
    Xconfigurator for, **72–74**
video chips, 44–45
viewing directories, **91–96**
virtual hosts, **344–346**
virtual memory, report on, 156
virtual servers, 471
virtual user tables, 356–357
virtusertable directory, 356–357
vmlinuz file, 167–168, 173–174
VMware operating system, **284**, **423–424**

W

w command, 198
w option in fdisk, 114
w permission, 210
Warning days field, 201
wbinfo command, 463–464
wc program, **188**
Web servers. *See* Apache servers
Web sites, list of, **494**
Web terminals, **490**
webmin tool, 308
WEP (Wireless Encryption Protocol), 69
which command, **98–99**, 297
white box support, **29–30**
who command, 198
width of windows, 250

wildcard characters
in copying, 101
in deleting, 103
in searches, 96
winbind, **458**
for domain accounts, **463–464**
example, **467–471**
home directories for, **464**
name resolution for, **461–462**
nsswitch.conf for, **462–463**
PAM configuration for, **464–466**
for Samba startup, **461**
smb.conf setup for, **458–460**
startup of, **463–464**
winbind enum groups command, **460**
winbind gid command, **460**
winbind separator command, **459–460**
window managers, 234, **238**, *238*
for desktop environment, **264–265**
fvwm, **245–247**, *246*
GNOME, 265, **267–269**
basics of, **277–279**, *277–278*
vs. KDE, **269–271**
KDE. *See* KDE desktop environment
list of, **264**
operation of, **239**
twm, **240–245**, *240*
windows
position and size of, **249–250**
raising, **241–242**
Wine (Wine Is Not an Emulator) project, 414,
418–419
crashes in, **423**
for GUI applications, **284**
preparing for, **419–422**
testing, **422–423**
/.wine/conf file, **420–422**
winmodems, 383–385
WINS server, **432**, 439
winsock, 152
Wireless Encryption Protocol (WEP), 69
wireless NICs, **66–69**
wireless.opts file, **68–69**
wmaker window manager, 264

words, counting, **188**
workgroup command, 439
workgroups, browsing, **433–434**
world permissions, **209**
wrappers, TCP, **404–406**
write list command, **453–455**
write permissions, **203–204**, 210–211
writeable command, **452–454**
wu-ftp program, 365
/wu-ftpd file, 365
wvdial.conf file, 386–388
wvdial program, **386–388**
www.cheapbytes.com site, 495
www.download.com site, 495
www.freshmeat.net site, 495
www.lintraining.com site, 494
www.linuxapps.com site, 495
www.linuxberg.com site, 495
www.linuxcare.com/help-yourself page, 494
www.linuxdoc.org site, 494
www.linuxjournal.com site, 494
www.linuxmall.com site, 495
www.linuxnewbie.org site, 494
www.linuxtoday.com site, 494
www.linuxworld.com site, 494
www.lwn.net site, 494
www.redhat.com/apps/support page, 494
www.slashdot.com site, 494

X

X command, **235–236**
X-Deep/32 server, 261
-X option in ls, 94
-x option in tar, 137–138, 140
x permission, 210
X Window System, **69–70**
clients in, **255–260**, 281–282
color in, **247–248**
fonts in, **250–252**
free applications for, **254–255**
history of, **235**, 255–256
multitasking in, **237–238**
in Red Hat installation, 42

remote sessions with, **261–263**
resources in, **249–254**
servers in, **255–260**, 281
settings for, **70–71**
with Windows NT, **260–261**
X command for, **235–236**
Xconfigurator for, **72–74**
xinit and xterm, **236–237**, 236
X Window terminal, runlevel for, 178
X-WinPro server, 261
xbill application, 254
xboard application, 254
xcalc program, 237–238, 237, 241, 255
xchat application, 254
xclock program, 241, 255
xconfig command, 170
Xconfigurator program, **72–74**
.Xdefaults file, 253
xdigit character class, 112
xearth application, 255
xedit command, **250–251**
xemacs application, 254
xeyes program, 258–260
XF86_FBDev system, 72
XF86_SVGA system, 72
XF86_VGA16 program, 72
XF86Config-4 file, **70–71**
xfd program, 251
xfishtank application, 255
xfontsel program, 252, 254
xhost client, **259**
xhost command, 262
xinetd daemon, **183–185**
xinit, **236–237**, 258
   for GUIs, **280–282**
   for terminals, 262
xinitrc file, 281–282
.xinitrc file, 281–282
xkill application, 254
xload application, 254
xlsclients application, 255, 260
xlsfonts command, 250

xmag application, 254
xman application, 254
xpdf application, 254
.Xresources file, 253
xserverrc file, 283
xset application, 254
xsetroot command, 247–248
xterm program, **236–237**, 236, 253, 255
-xvpf, 140
xwininfo application, 255

Y

YaST program, 129
Year 2038 problem, 201
Yellow Pages, 213–214
yp.conf file, 218, 220
yp directory, 216–217
ypbind command, **217–218**, 223
ypcat command, 218, 220
ypmatch command, 218
yppasswdd daemon, 224–225
ypserv command, 217, 219
YPSRCDIR option, 216
ypwhich command, 218

Z

z flag, 139
z option, 138
Zip drives, **142–144**
.zip extension, 135–136
zip-like functions, **136**
zip program, 136
zone command, 301
zone statement, **302–303**
zones and zone files, 300, **308–311**
   of authority, 301
   dynamic, 322
   mail servers, **312–313**
   reverse, **314–315**
   SOA records, **310–312**

The *Craig Hunt* Linux Library

- Series content provides in-depth advanced coverage of key Linux topics that Linux professionals need to know

- Written or meticulously reviewed by Craig Hunt—best-selling author, renowned speaker, and Linux guru—along with top Linux authors

- Specifically written for networking professionals and systems administrators

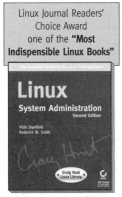

Linux Journal Readers' Choice Award one of the **"Most Indispensible Linux Books"**

Linux System Administration Second Edition

0-7821-4138-2 • $49.99

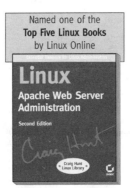

Named one of the **Top Five Linux Books** by Linux Online

Linux Apache Web Server Administration Second Edition

0-7821-4137-4 • $49.99

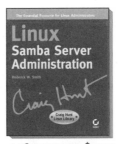

Linux Samba Server Administration

0-7821-2740-1 • $39.99

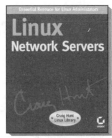

Linux Network Servers

0-7821-4123-4 • $49.99

Linux Sendmail Administration

0-7821-2737-1 • $39.99

Linux DNS Server Administration

0-7821-2736-3 • $39.99

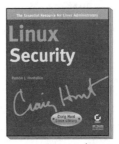

Linux Security

0-7821-2741-X • $49.99

Linux NFS and Automounter Administration

0-7821-2739-8 • $39.99

Written for Professionals, by Professionals

SYBEX®
www.sybex.com

TELL US WHAT YOU THINK!

Your feedback is critical to our efforts to provide you with the best books and software on the market. Tell us what you think about the products you've purchased. It's simple:

1. Go to the Sybex website.
2. Find your book by typing the ISBN number or title into the Search field.
3. Click on the book title when it appears.
4. Click **Submit a Review.**
5. Fill out the questionnaire and comments.
6. Click **Submit.**

With your feedback, we can continue to publish the highest quality computer books and software products that today's busy IT professionals deserve.

www.sybex.com

SYBEX Inc. • 1151 Marina Village Parkway, Alameda, CA 94501 • 510-523-8233